FRANCIS ALŸS

RUSSELL FERGUSON
CUAUHTÉMOC MEDINA
JEAN FISHER
MICHAEL TAUSSIG

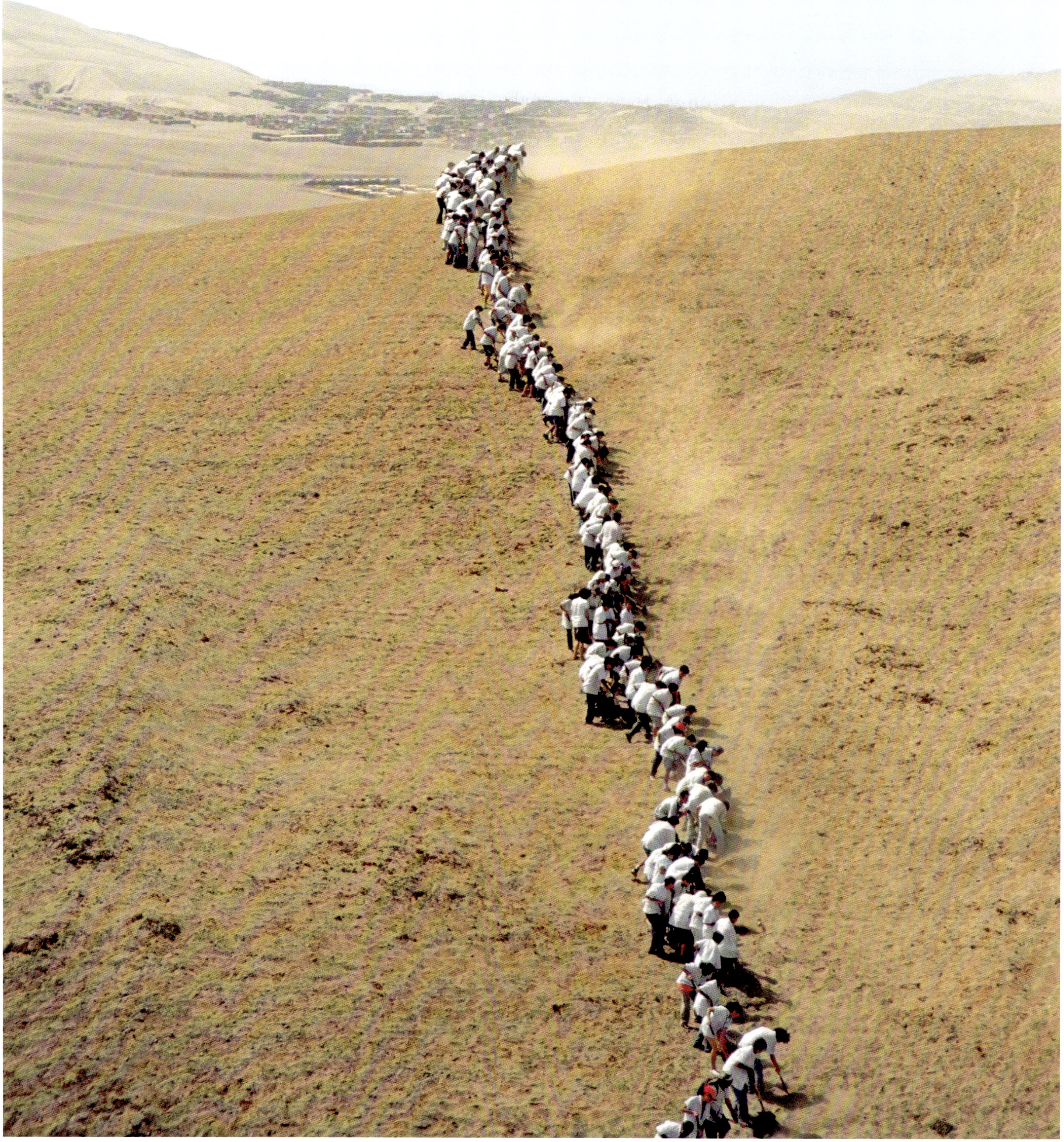

WHEN FAITH MOVES MOUNTAINS, 2002
IN COLLABORATION WITH CUAUHTÉMOC
MEDINA AND RAFAEL ORTEGA
PHOTO DOCUMENTATION OF AN EVENT,
LIMA, PERU

CONTENTS

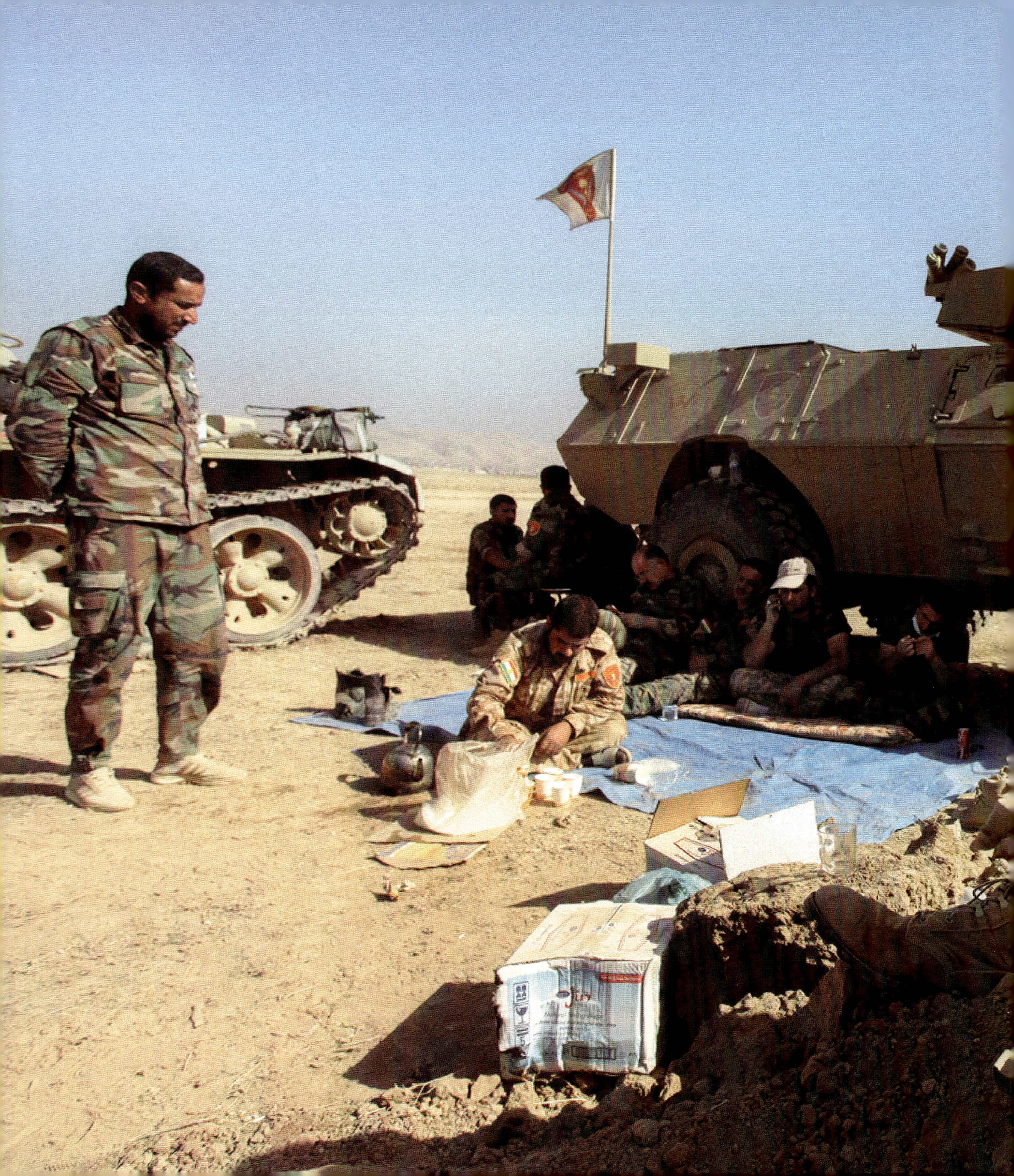

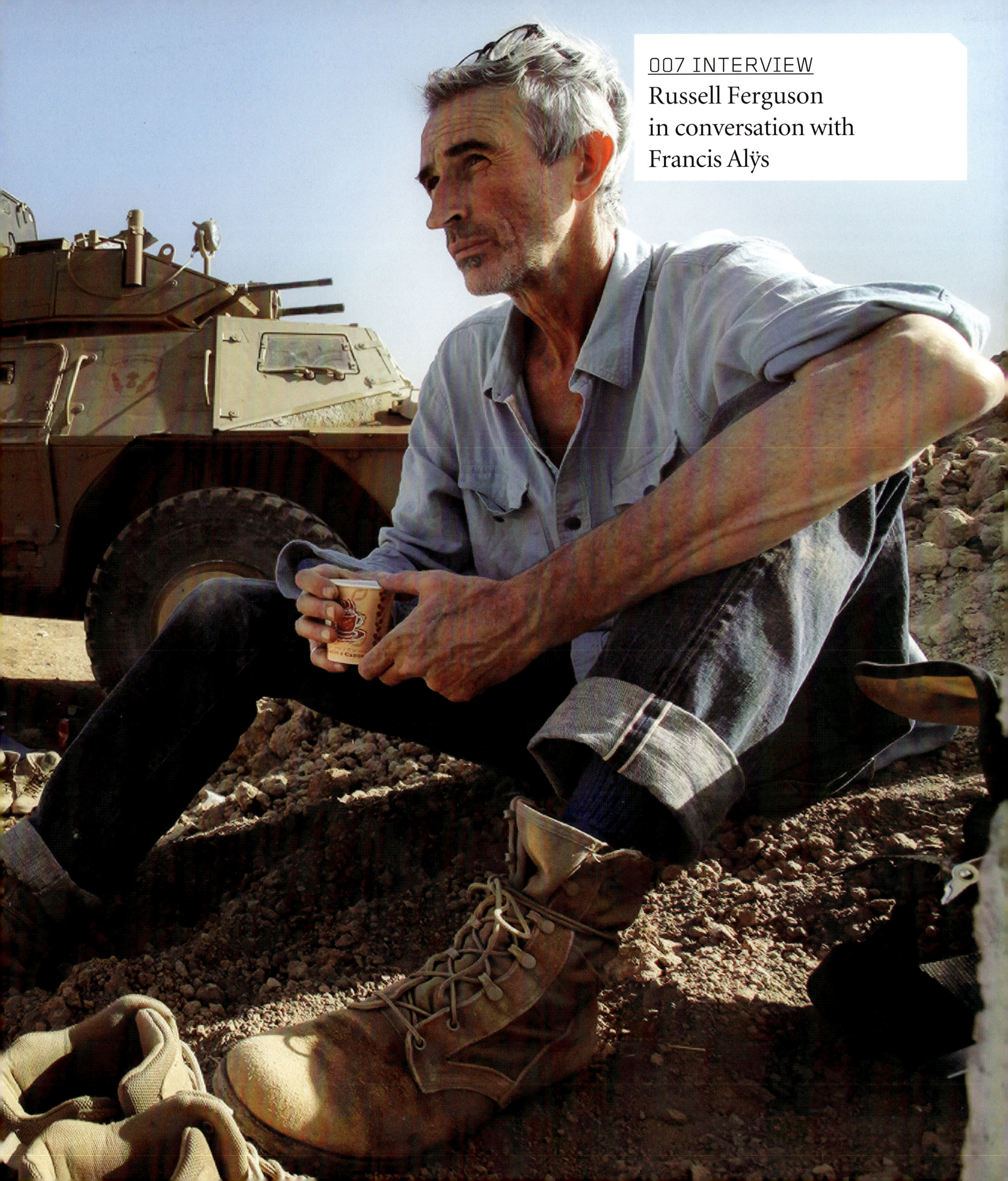

007 INTERVIEW

Russell Ferguson in conversation with Francis Alÿs

previous pages,
FRANCIS ALŸS, MOSUL, IRAQ,
2016

RUSSELL FERGUSON: *When did you first come to Mexico?*

FRANCIS ALŸS: In February 1986, in the aftermath of the earthquake. Before that I had been studying and working as an architect in Venice. I was drafted by the Belgian army, and to fulfill that commitment I went to the south of Mexico to work as an architect for non-governmental organizations. In the summer of 1989, because of a number of personal and legal matters, I found myself stuck in Mexico City. My contract had ended and I couldn't go back to Europe. Nor did I really want to. In front of me I suddenly had this enormous amount of free time, like an imposed sabbatical, and I decided to give a chance to something that had always interested me from an outsider's point of view: art practice. Although by then I had been in Mexico for over three years, I had never really considered living here, and I found it quite difficult to accept the move. The first works – I wouldn't call them works – my first images or interventions were very much a reaction to Mexico City itself, a means to situate myself in this colossal urban entity.

FERGUSON: *What was it about the city that was difficult for you compared to other cities?*

ALŸS: The immensity of it, also the culture shock, I suppose, and how dysfunctional the whole thing seemed. I could not decipher the city's codes. I had no entry point. In short, I could not understand how the whole society functioned. I had never lived in a megalopolis. Mexico City was also going through a series of major changes after the earthquake – in its urban shape, obviously, but also in its perception of itself.

Mexico City has a very crude and raw side, very much in your face, and it can easily beat you. When you are confronted with the dizzying complexity of a city whose nature is to overwhelm you, you have to react to that complexity somehow. I think the first stage was a period of observation, to see how other people managed to function within this urban chaos. I was living in the old Centro Histórico, where there were all these characters, for lack of a better word. I saw how they felt the need to make up an identity, to invent a role for themselves, a ritual that would justify their presence on the urban chessboard – like this guy in his mid-forties I would see every morning walking up and down the Zócalo with a metal wire bent into a hook with a circle at the end of it, kind of like a bicycle wheel without spokes. Starting from the top left corner of the plaza he would follow all the little cracks between the stones of the pavement, methodically pacing the entire plaza. That was the role he had invented for himself. That was his way of being there, of being part of the life of the city. Encountering such people has often been the entry point to my walks or interventions, the crude and poetic entry point.

FERGUSON: *What did Mexico offer you that Europe didn't?*

ALŸS: Retrospectively, I think I was very lucky in my timing with Mexico. They say that certain people can only find their place within a specific historical or geopolitical context. There was something in the chemistry between my Belgo-European upbringing and the Mexican culture that triggered a whole field of investigation. I think also that my status as an immigrant freed me from my own cultural heritage – or my debt to it, if you like. It provided me with a kind of permanent disjunction, a filter between myself and my being. Maybe what I have been looking for since then is this moment of coincidence between the experience of living and the consciousness of existence. The city turned into an open laboratory for testing and playing and

LA MALINCHE, 1997
PHOTO DOCUMENTATION
OF AN ACTION, MEXICO CITY

'La Malinche' is the popular nickname given to Marina, the lover and translator of Hernán Cortés during the time of the Spanish conquest.

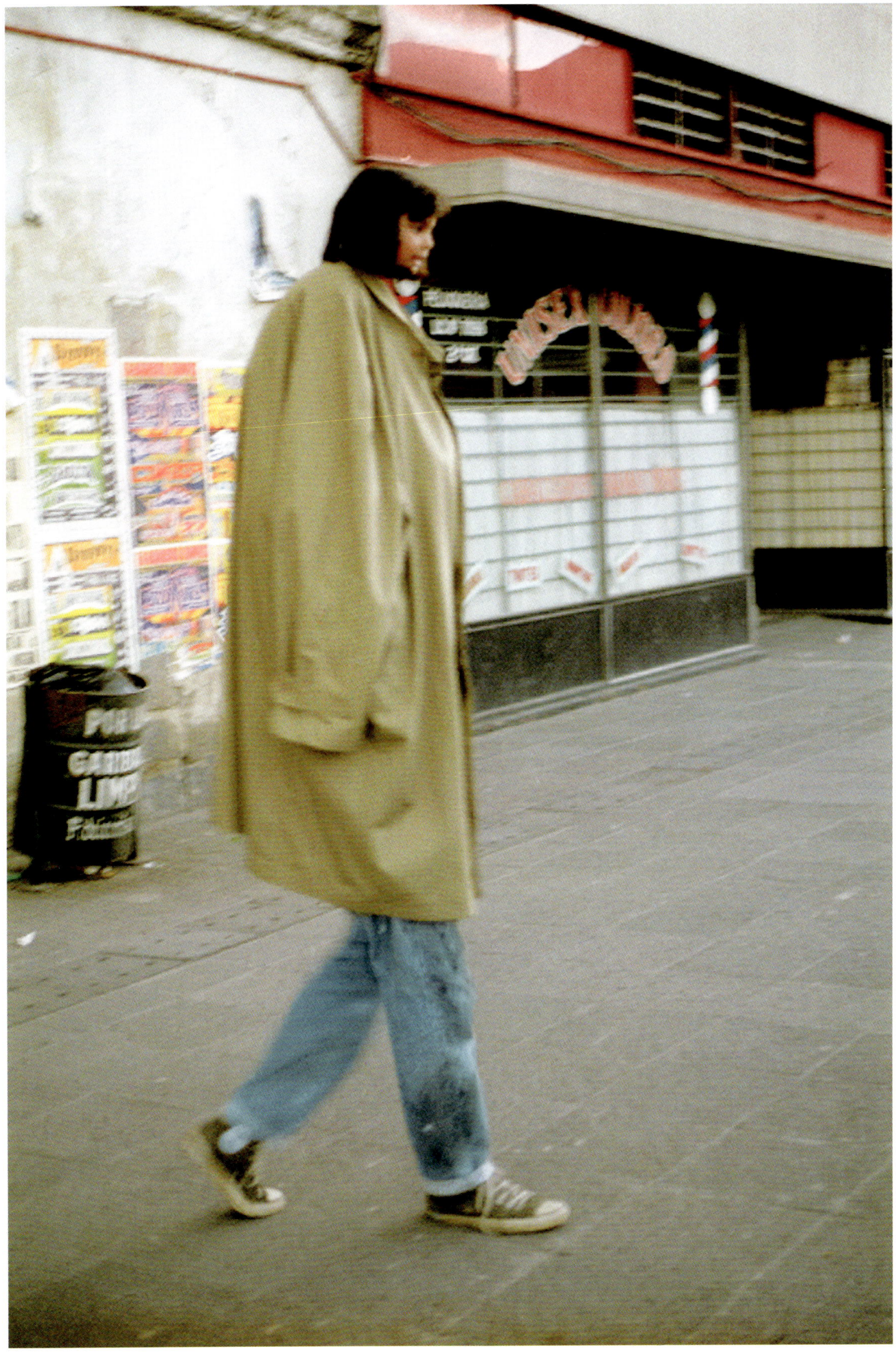

TURISTA, 1994
PHOTO DOCUMENTATION OF AN ACTION, METROPOLITAN CATHEDRAL, MEXICO CITY

On 10 March 1994 I went to the Zócalo and stood in the middle of a line of carpenters, plumbers and house painters, offering my services as a tourist.

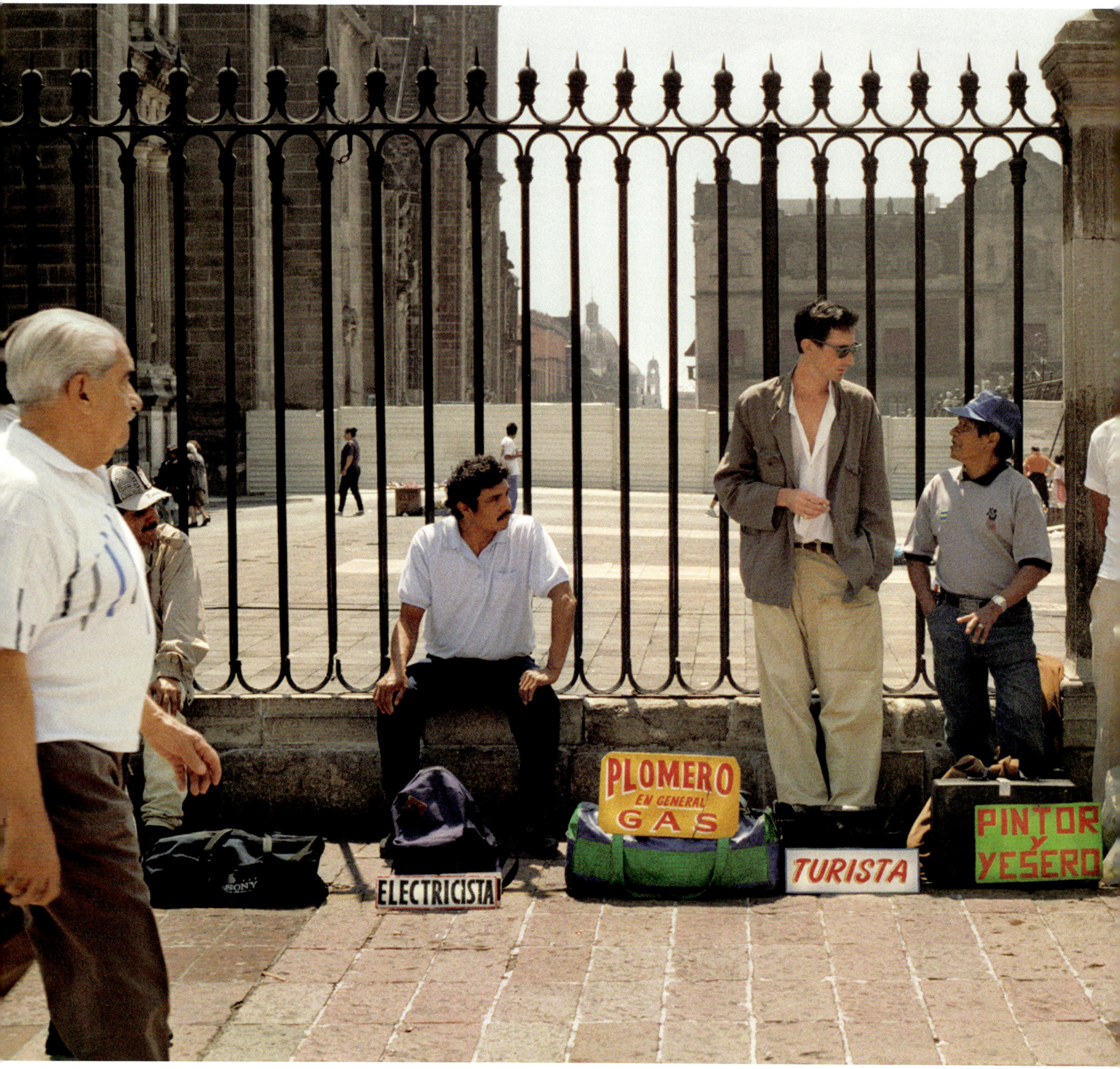

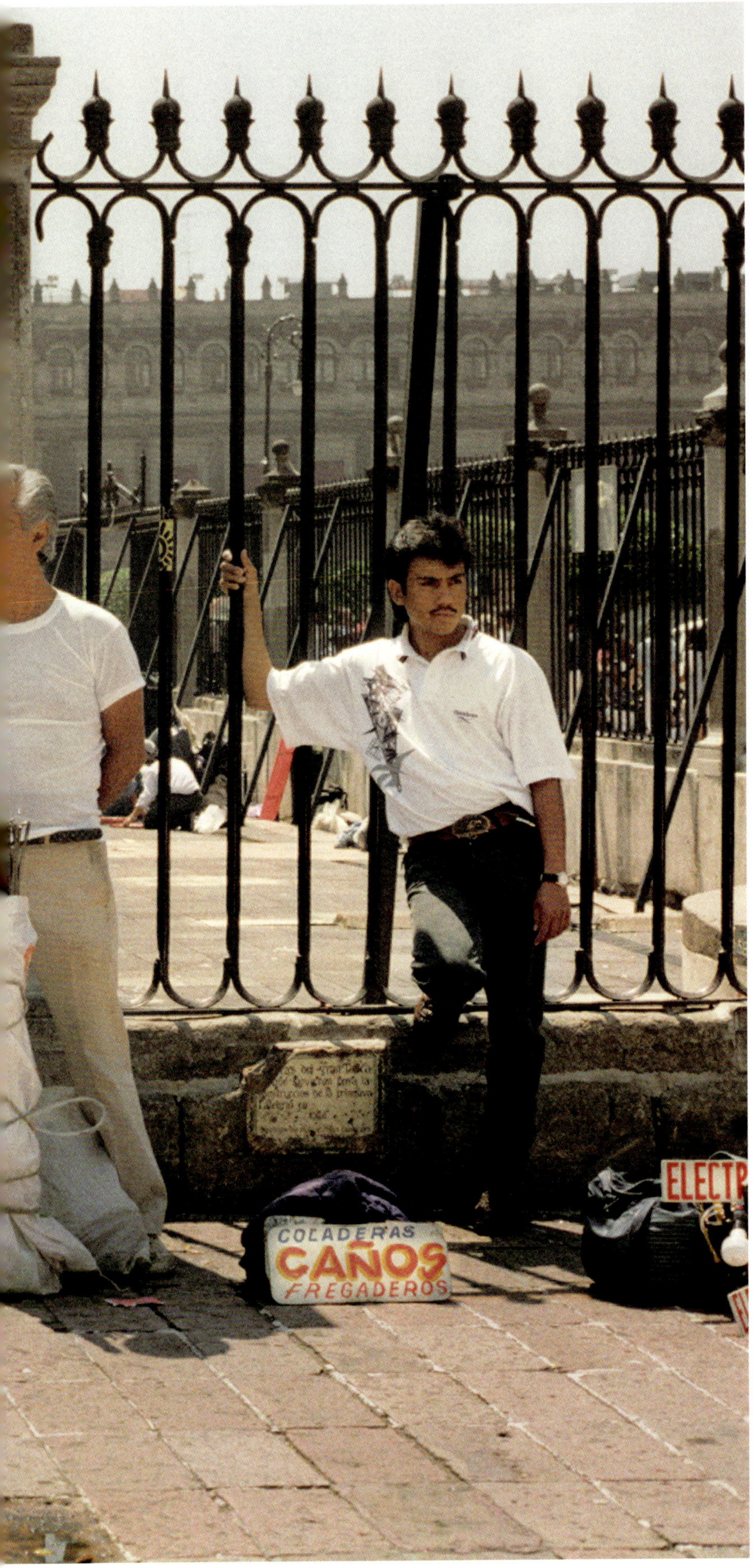

experimenting in all kinds of contradictory directions. I was new in town. Nobody cared. I had nothing to prove to anyone but myself. It gave me an enormous sense of freedom and an open-ended time frame to build a language, an attitude, away from a world and culture that I saw as saturated with information. I think Europe has an extraordinarily rich culture, but I see it more as a place of consumption – of arts, food, architecture and so on. Here there were things to do, things to say, and urgently. Eventually I lost the distance, but at first it was what helped me make the jump.

FERGUSON: *At what point did you realize that you were not going back to being an architect?*

ALŸS: I worked in parallel as an architect and artist for a couple of years, but I dropped architecture altogether around 1993. I got hooked very quickly by the new game, the art game, and early on I met people like Rubén Bautista, Guillermo Santamarina, Cuauhtémoc Medina, Gabriel Orozco, Abraham Cruzvillegas, Melanie Smith and many others. The contemporary art scene was very open at the time. There was a lot of collaboration and discussion going on. But then again, I was younger. Now I think the rules are different.

FERGUSON: *Do you think that individuals work in more isolation from each other now?*

ALŸS: Well, there was no real market at the time. Artists were making art to show to their artist friends, and things were moving faster. You would not wait for a curator to come. You had to show it immediately.

FERGUSON: *There is a lot more infrastructure now.*

ALŸS: The infrastructure is better, yes, and there is much more curiosity from abroad about the emerging scene, the younger generation, which is good. But it can also lead to some generational gaps, to the point that sometimes production can be aimed towards export rather than trying to function first in its context of fabrication, whether its local or national context. The link with the older generations is somewhat broken.

FERGUSON: *So now, after almost thirty years, to what extent are you a Mexican artist?*

ALŸS: It's clear that the place has imprinted itself on the making of my work and probably on the perception of my work abroad. Retrospectively I can see that there have been different steps in my relationship to Mexico.

When in 1994 I went and stood outside the cathedral next to the Zócalo with a sign at my feet saying 'turista', I was denouncing but also testing my own status, that of a foreigner, a *gringo*. 'How far can I belong to this place? How much can I judge it? Am I a participant or just an observer?' By offering my services as a tourist in the middle of a line of carpenters and plumbers, I was oscillating between leisure and work, between contemplation and interference.

FERGUSON: *People do think of you as an artist from Mexico. How do you feel about representing the country?*

ALŸS: I think I am quite local but I'm not. Or I'm not but I am. It's a trap. It's funny, you have to leave the place you come from to be asked if you belong to it. In 1998 when Rina Carvajal invited me to participate in the São Paulo Biennial, she asked a straightforward question: 'How do you position yourself – as a European or Westerner

CUENTOS PATRIÓTICOS (PATRIOTIC TALES), 1997
IN COLLABORATION WITH RAFAEL ORTEGA, MEXICO CITY
VIDEO DOCUMENTATION OF AN ACTION
24 MIN. 40 SEC.

In the midst of the social upheaval of 1968, thousands of bureaucrats were herded into the Plaza de la Constitución (Zócalo) to demonstrate in favour of the government. Showing their frustration in an act that was both rebellious and ridiculous, they turned their backs on the official tribune and began to bleat like a vast flock of sheep.

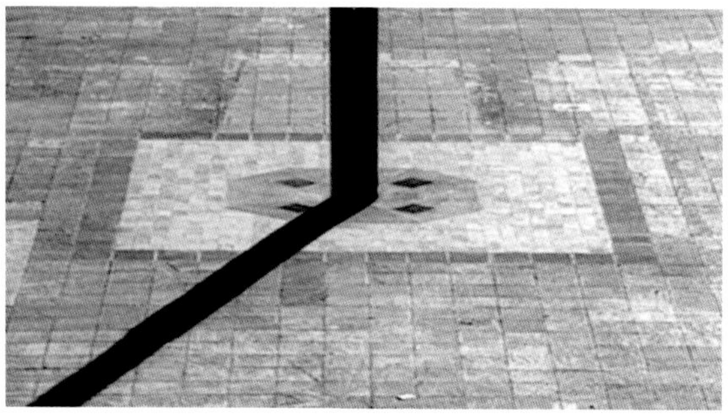
00:00:30

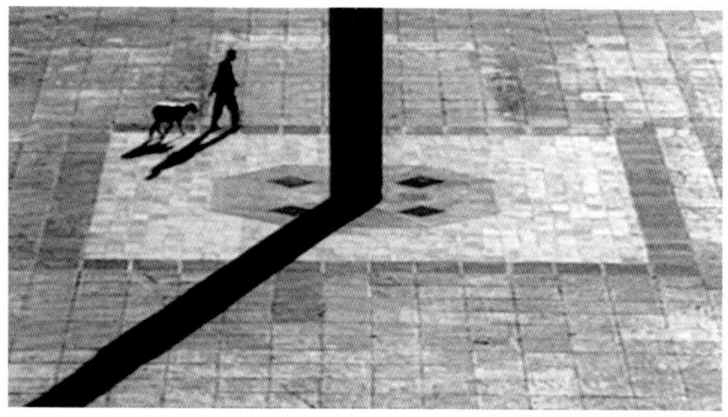
00:00:45

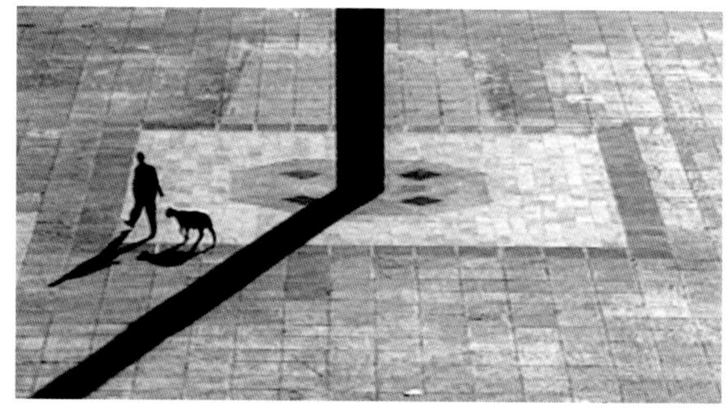
00:00:52

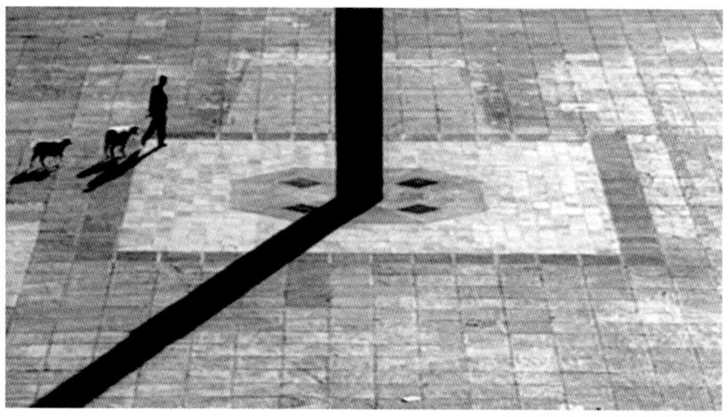
00:01:00

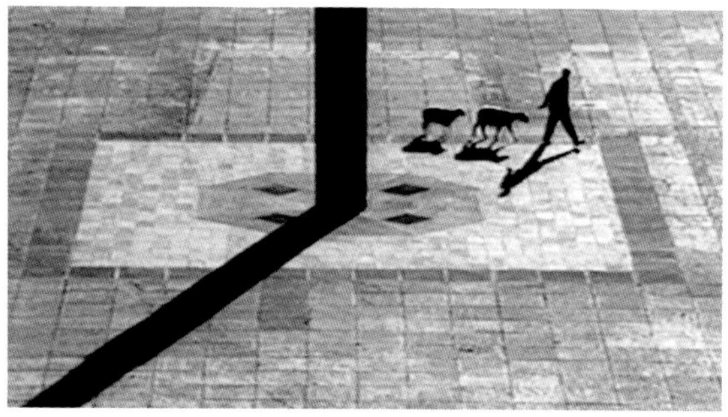
00:01:07

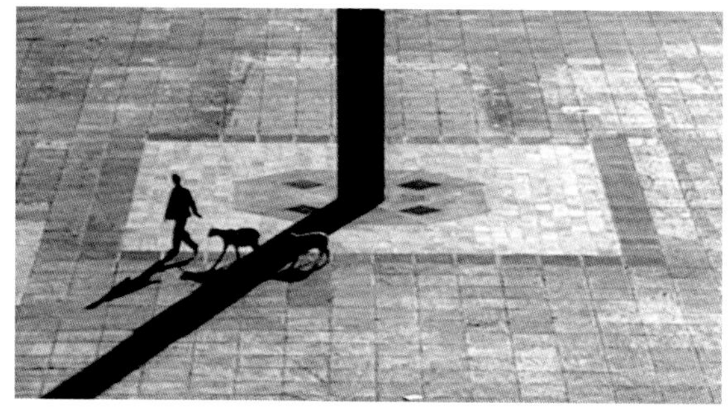
00:01:18

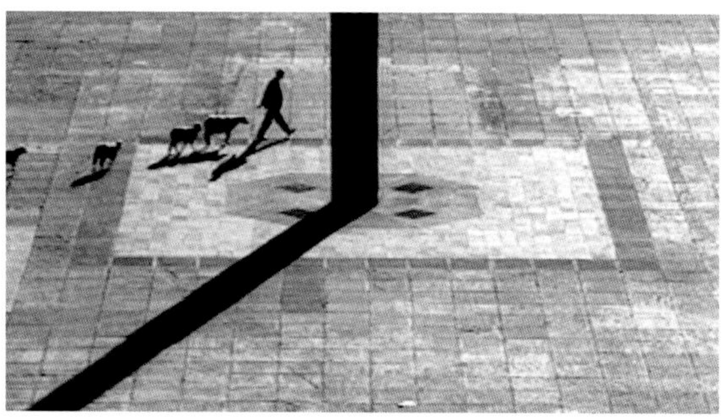
00:01:25

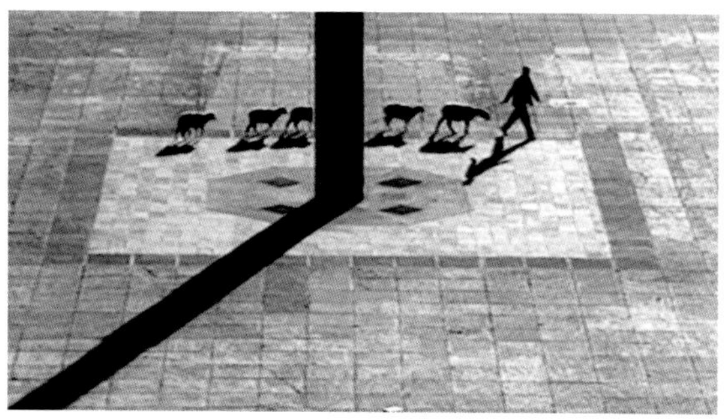
00:03:38

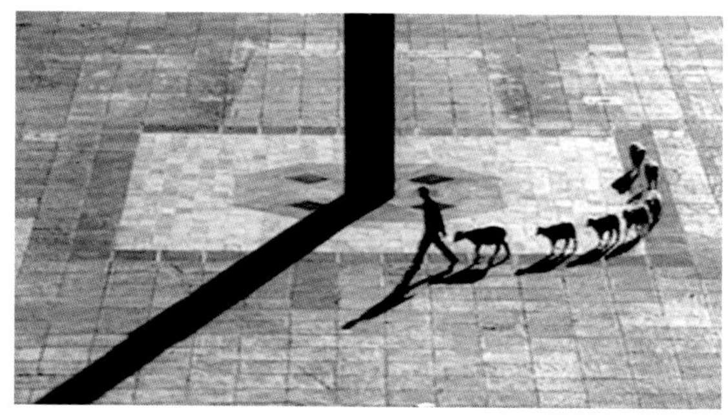
00:05:05

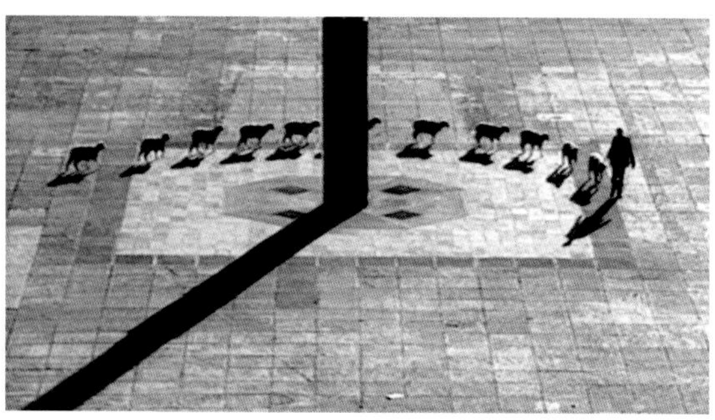
00:08:34

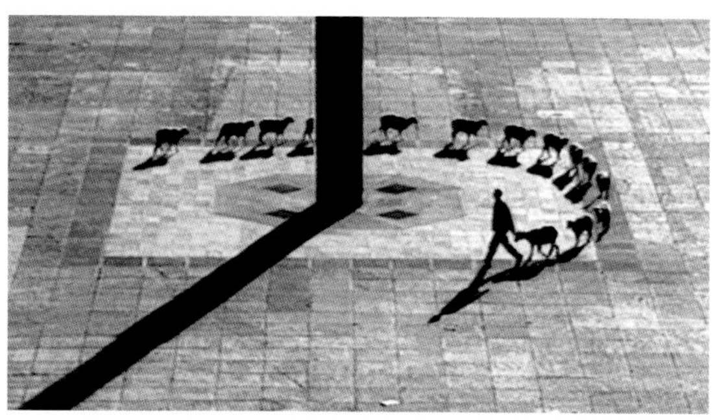
00:10:19

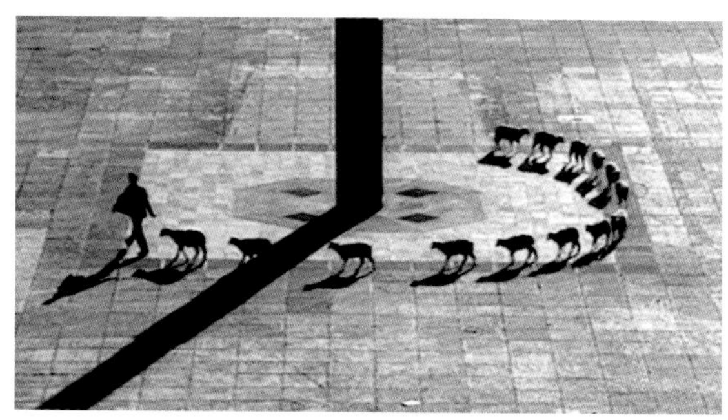
00:10:25

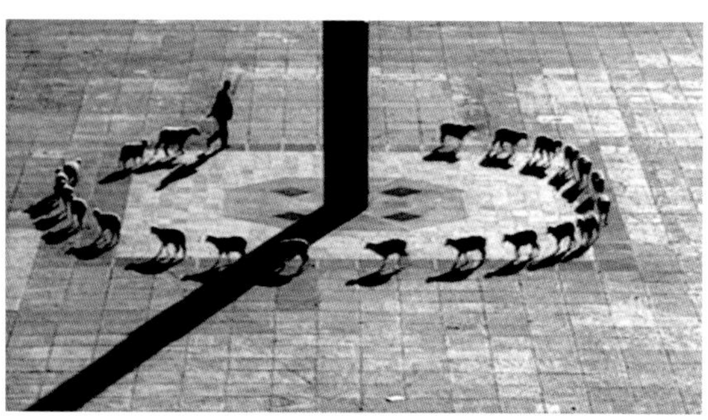
00:12:30

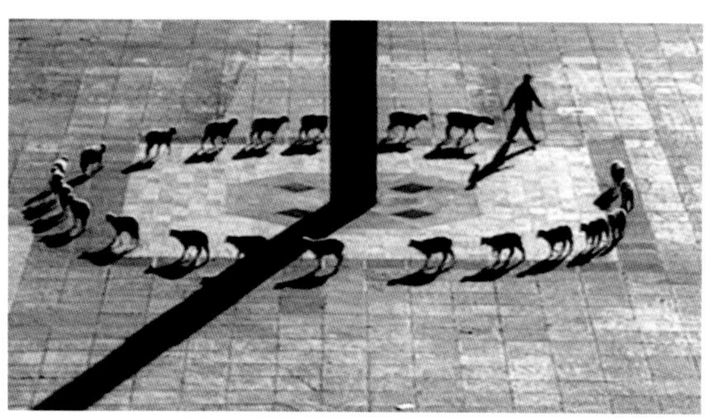
00:13:10

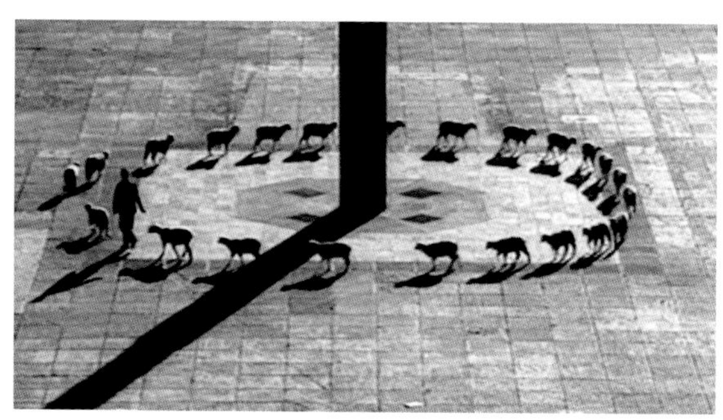
00:13:50

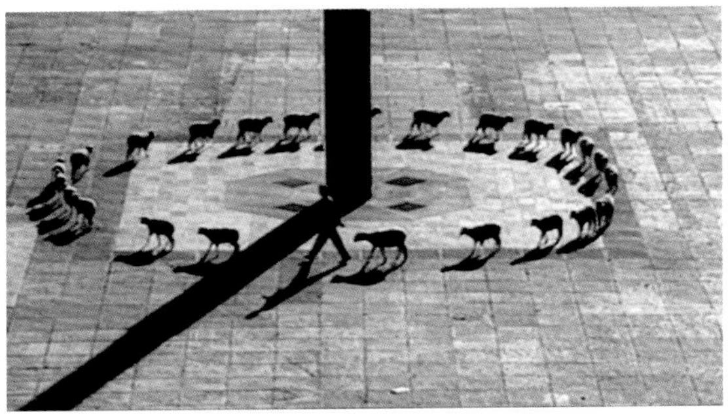

00:14:10

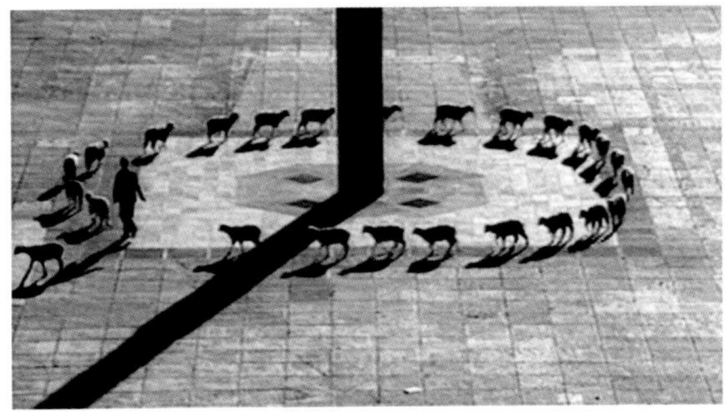

00:14:15

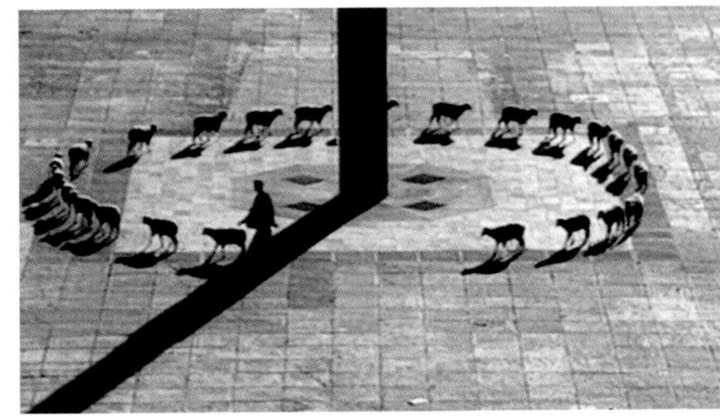

00:15:05

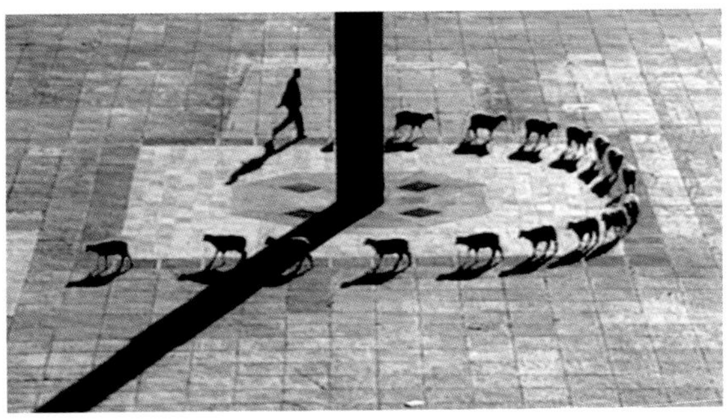

00:16:30

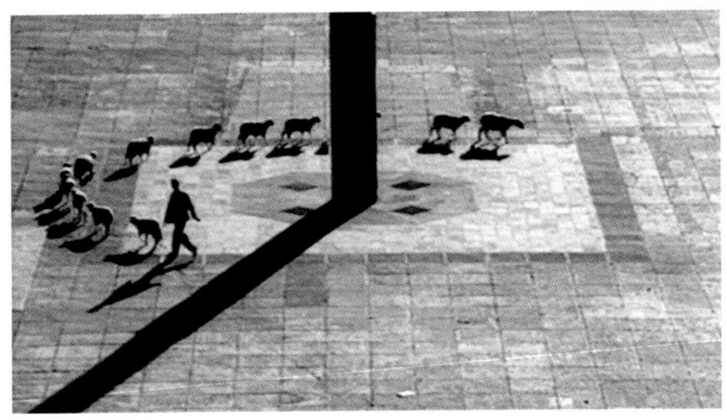

00:17:05

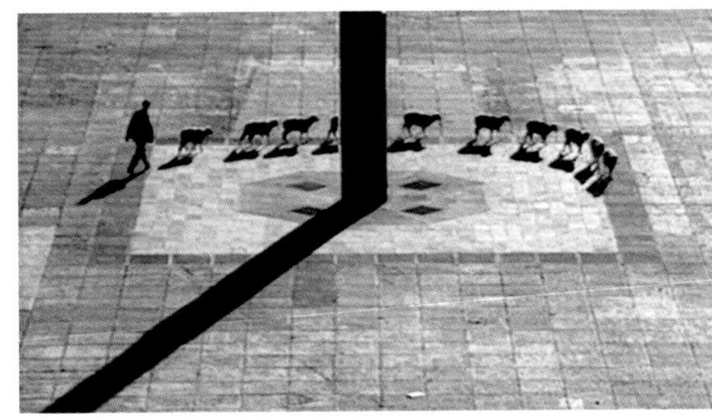

00:17:54

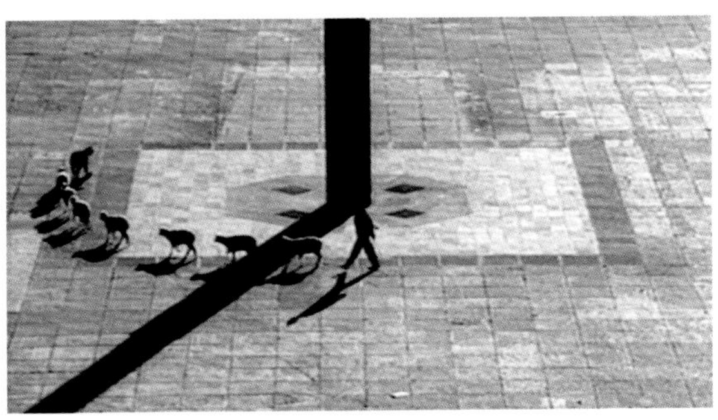

00:18:05

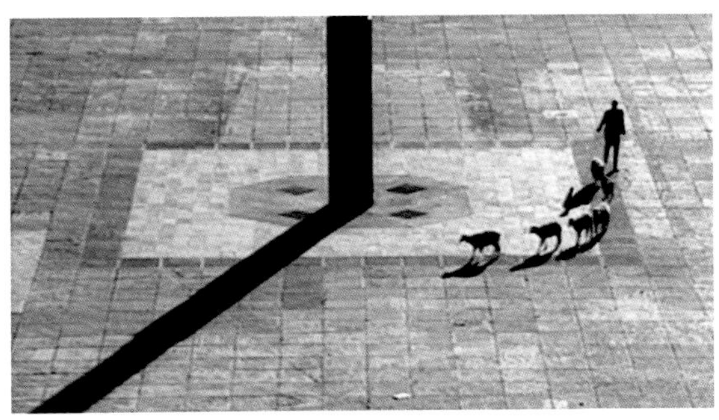

00:19:59

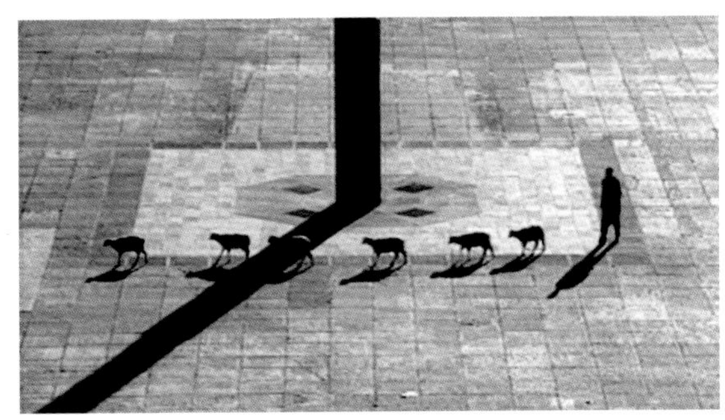

00:20:05

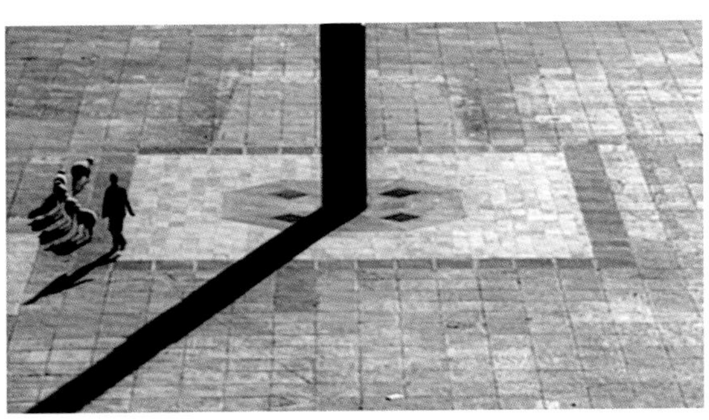

00:21:50

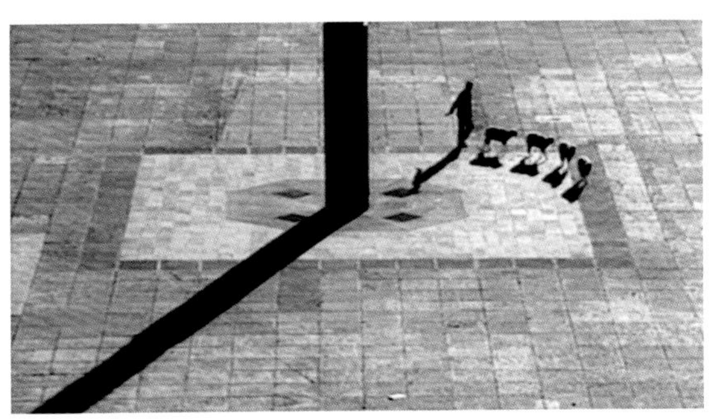

00:22:05

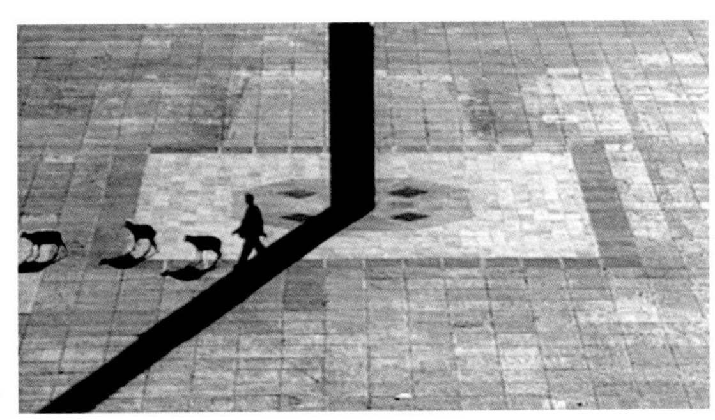

00:22:50

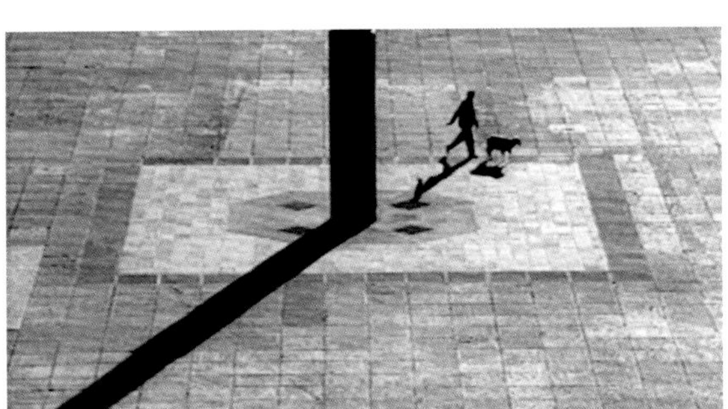

00:22:30

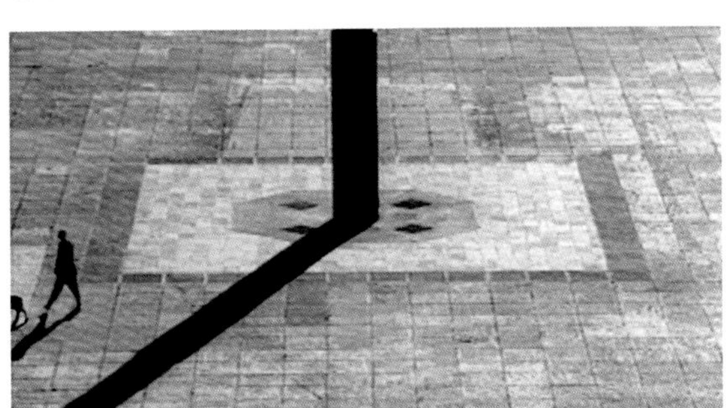

00:23:40

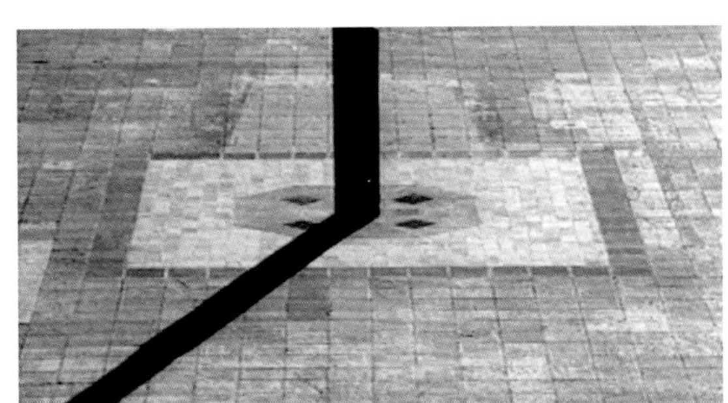

00:23:54

If you are a typical spectator, what you are really doing is waiting for the accident to happen, 1996
Zócalo, Mexico City
Video
10 min.

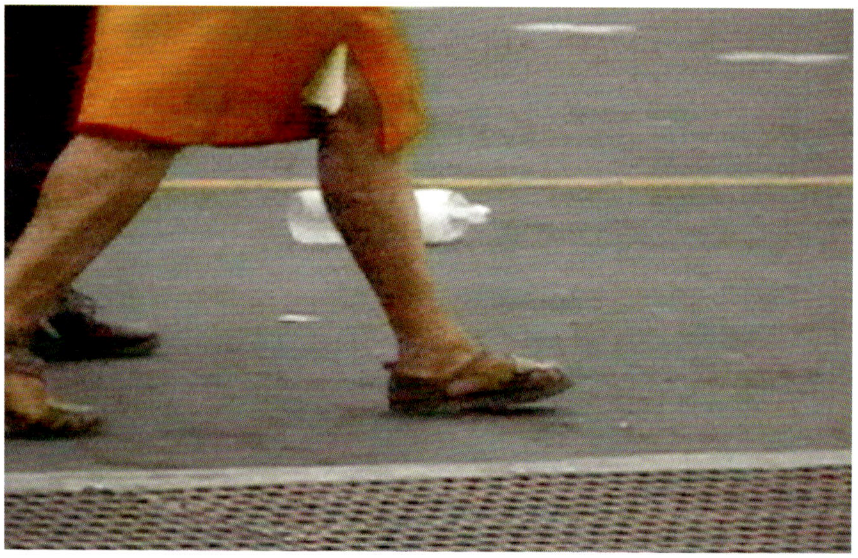

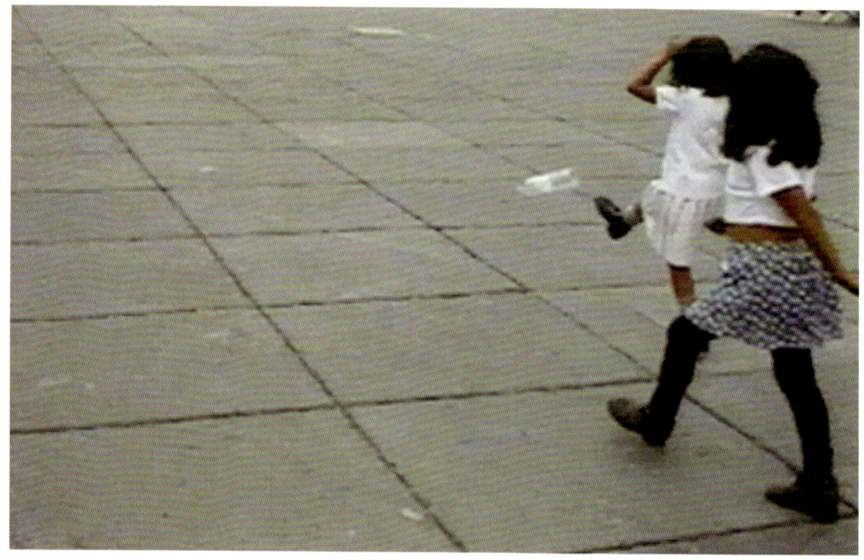

– in relation to your host country, with the place and culture where you choose to live and develop your practice?' To address that issue I looked into one of the West's most controversial exports, the model of modernization (as moving away from tradition), in order to analyse Mexico's complex relationship to that imported ideology, and to investigate in particular how the syndrome of progress and the dogma of productivity are lived and understood south of the U.S. border.

FERGUSON: *You referred once to your 'disguise' as a foreigner. Did you feel you dropped the disguise at some point?*

ALŸS: I wish I could, but I can't. I am a misfit. I am too tall, too pale and too *gringo* looking. But things are not always that schematic. In the building where I live in the city centre the population is very young. I have been around for much longer than most of them, so in a way, for them, beyond my foreignness I have become a sort of local reference. I suppose I may be even a character for some of them. When – very occasionally – a big-shot collector comes to visit the studio, he shows up in a limo with black smoked windows and two carloads of bodyguards. So, as everyone in the building deals some kind of shit, they must think I'm doing big-time deals for these big-time mafiosos to come here and visit me. So it gives me some kind of status in the hood after all.

FERGUSON: *And what came after* Turista*? You continued to work around the Zócalo, I know.*

ALŸS: A couple of years later I put together a short film called *If you are a typical spectator, what you are really doing is waiting for the accident to happen* (nicknamed *Bottle*). I say 'put together' because I went back to some discarded video footage, stuff I had kind of absentmindedly filmed on the Zócalo in early 1996, while I was waiting for the flag-raising ceremony to take place. It turned out that the material perfectly illustrated a preoccupation I had in mind. The camera was following an empty plastic bottle being blown around by the wind. There was to be no interaction between the camera (that is, me) and the protagonist (the bottle). The camera would just follow the bottle, record its *dérive* and wait for an accident to happen to it. Ultimately what happened turned out to be quite different. First, passers-by felt provoked or stimulated by the camera, and they started interacting with my subject, kicking the bottle around and jumping over it and so forth, and later on, as I was filming with my eye glued to

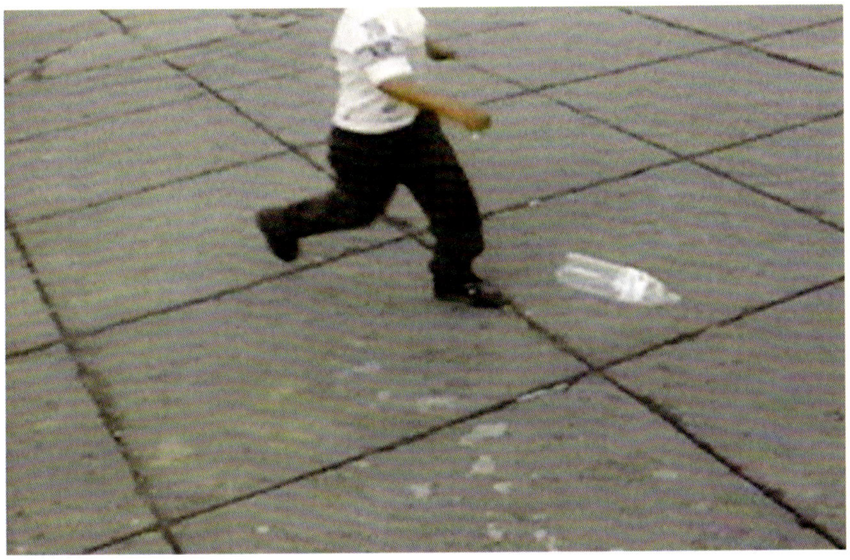

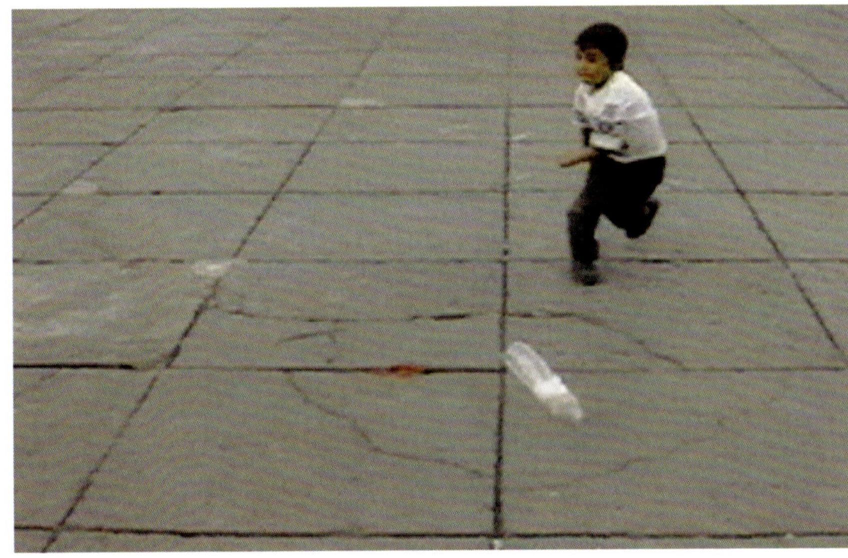

the viewfinder, the bottle left the main square and crossed a busy street. As I followed it hastily, I was hit by a car – nothing dramatic, but hard enough to send the camera flying into the air and crashing on to the ground. End of the take. I went back to that footage because I loved the fact that whereas one expects something to happen to the subject – the bottle – the accident actually happens to the observer of the bottle. The fact is that the act of observing had interfered with the course of things. My contemplative, non-interference contract was coming to an end.

FERGUSON: *So the bottle piece really marked a change in your status as an observer, from an outsider to someone a bit more directly involved.*

ALŸS: Something new was triggered. On the one hand, as there had been a shift in my relationship to the place, I started to produce a series of works reflecting on the state of local politics. *Cuentos Patrióticos (Patriotic Tales)* (1997) was directly inspired by a political episode that had happened on the Zócalo in 1968, and its disguised re-enactment on the same location nearly thirty years later was a direct comment on the current state of politics, the way history was repeating itself, and how the whole political scene was frozen by a corrupted and dysfunctional political apparatus. On the other hand I continued questioning the mechanics of artistic production and the status of production itself with a piece called *Paradox of Praxis 1* (1997). It was composed of two symmetrical, though opposing, principles: 'sometimes making something leads to nothing' and 'sometimes making nothing leads to something'.

In parallel I started working on my first animated movie, *Song for Lupita* (1998), in which a woman endlessly pours water from one glass into another and back. I wanted to demonstrate the Mexican saying 'el hacerlo sin hacerlo, el no hacerlo pero haciendolo' – literally 'the doing but without doing, the not doing but doing'. It staged a kind of resignation to the immediate present by inducing a complete hypnosis in the act itself, an act which was pure flux, without beginning or end. Animation is all about timing, and I think it was around this moment that I realized that Latin America's relationship to modernity and the dogma of efficiency could be explored from that angle. I understood that through films, events or performances the *mise en scéne* of certain time schemes could render the time structure I had encountered here in Mexico. From then on I started developing what would become over the following years a discursive argument composed of episodes, allegories or parables that staged that experience of time.

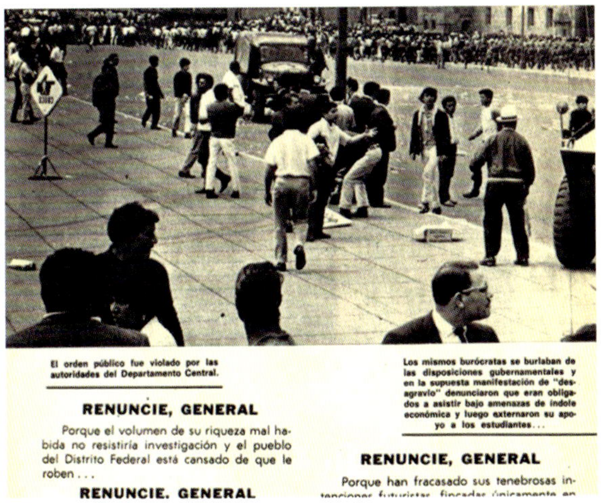

El orden público fue violado por las autoridades del Departamento Central.

RENUNCIE, GENERAL

Porque el volumen de su riqueza mal habida no resistiría investigación y el pueblo del Distrito Federal está cansado de que le roben . . .

RENUNCIE, GENERAL

Los mismos burócratas se burlaban de las disposiciones gubernamentales y en la supuesta manifestación de "desagravio" denunciaron que eran obligados a asistir bajo amenazas de índole económica y luego externaron su apoyo a los estudiantes...

RENUNCIE, GENERAL

Porque han fracasado sus tenebrosas in-

NEWSPAPER CLIPPING ABOUT THE 'CEREMONIA DE DESAGRAVIO', 28 AUGUST 1968, ZÓCALO, MEXICO CITY
FROM THE ARTIST'S ARCHIVE

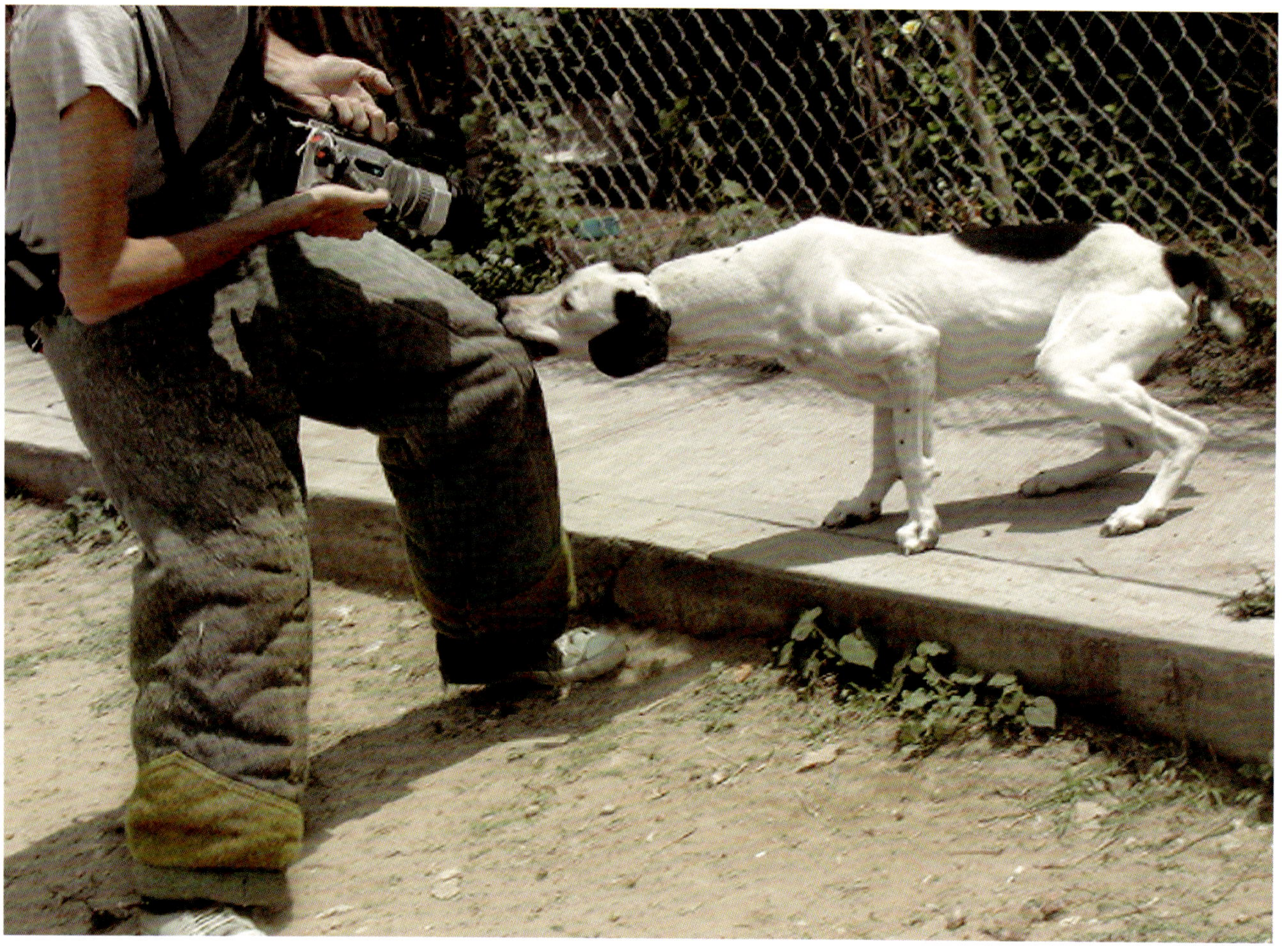

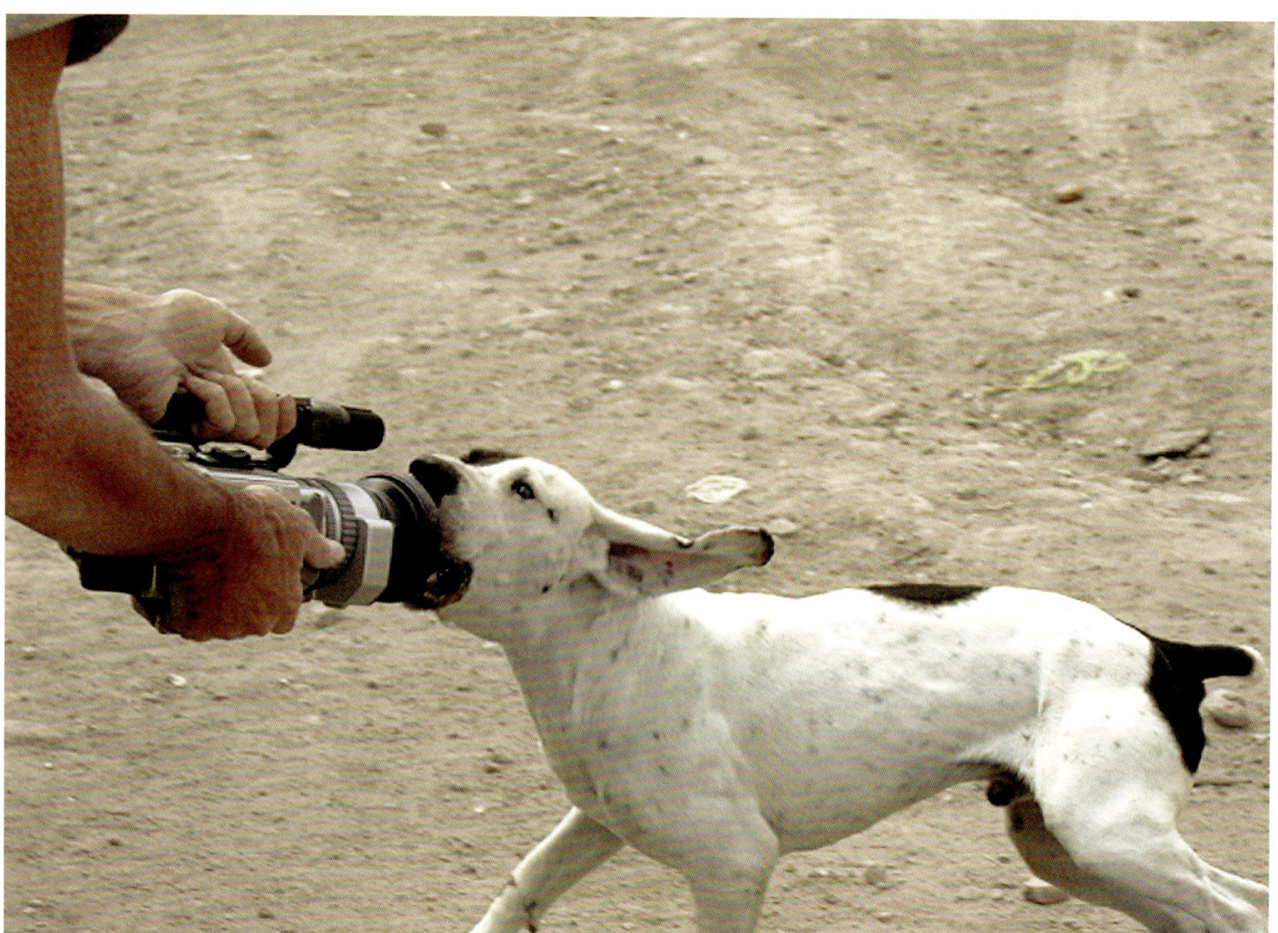

EL GRINGO, 2003
IN COLLABORATION WITH
RAFAEL ORTEGA,
HIDALGO, MEXICO
VIDEO
5 MIN

Protagonist: the camera

Object of conflict: a narrow passageway at the entry to a village

Agents of the conflict: the dogs

Plot: the camera tries to break its way through a pack of dogs blocking the passageway.

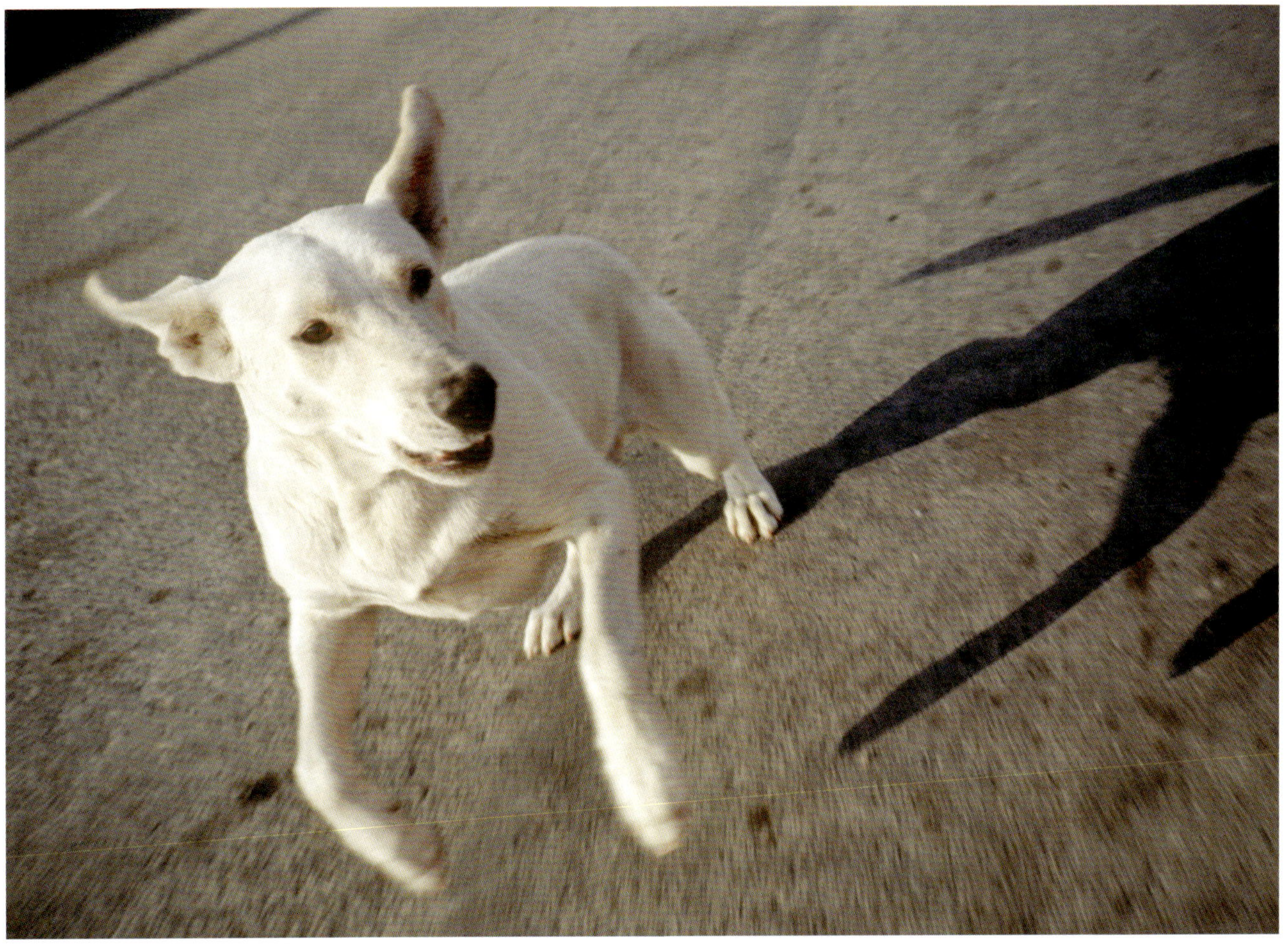

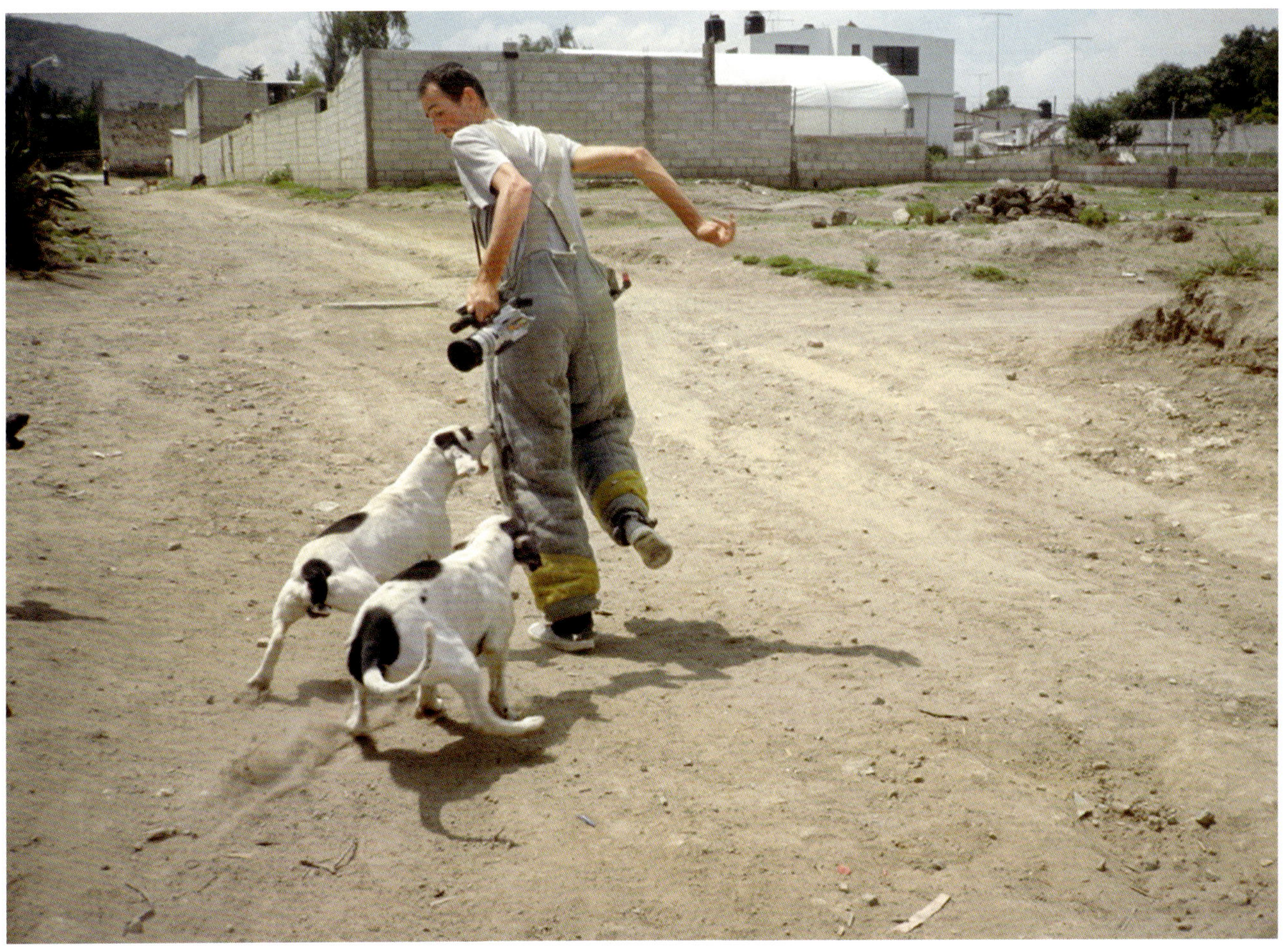

SONG FOR LUPITA, 1998
ANIMATION DRAWINGS
PENCIL ON TRACING PAPER
EACH 35 X 29 CM

Mañana, mañana
Is soon enough for me.

FERGUSON : *What was the first attempt?*

ALŸS: My first trial was a video installation called *Cantos Patrióticos (Patriotic Songs)* (1998–99). It was based on a story I had heard of a ferryman who, while transporting people from one side of a river to the other, gets blinded by the sun in the middle and loses his sense of orientation. No longer knowing which side to row to, he gets lost – as they say here, 'entre dos aguas' (between two waters) – and rows around in circles. The story is interpreted by several singers, with the narration in a mirror construction – the last verse is the first, the penultimate is the second, and so on – and the singing is chopped up by a series of stops that also rule a game of musical chairs on the opposite screen. The interruptions of the lyrics produce a progressive disarticulation of the narrative, and soon any understanding of the story becomes lost in the assemblage of words and syllables, notes and bars, and the attempt to tell the story takes the lead over the story itself. I was looking at Latin America as a kind of broken mirror, a single reality constituted by a multiplicity of dispersed fragments.

Something quite ironic happened during the long making of *Cantos*. Over time, like my ferryman lost his orientation, I lost what I was trying to say, and the more the piece progressed, the less I could remember why I was doing it. The only thing that brought the piece to completion was the energy of all the people involved in the film and my responsibility to them as its instigator. The experience taught me a lot about collaboration, how it is about letting the original scenario go, letting it be translated by others and bounced back and forth. If the story is good enough, it will get back to you or achieve its shape by itself. If it isn't, then it's better for it to die away.

FERGUSON: *One of the things that seems very characteristic about Mexico City – at least from the outside – is a constant pushing back and forth between the embrace of modernity and a resistance to it.*

ALŸS: It probably happens in other places too, but this is the one I know the best. It seems particularly palpable in this part of town, the old city centre with all its anachronisms. Its three layers – pre-Hispanic, colonial and modern – co-exist more than overlap. I think you could say that all the ingredients are present for Mexico to enter modernity, but there is this inner resistance. Somehow it's a society that wants

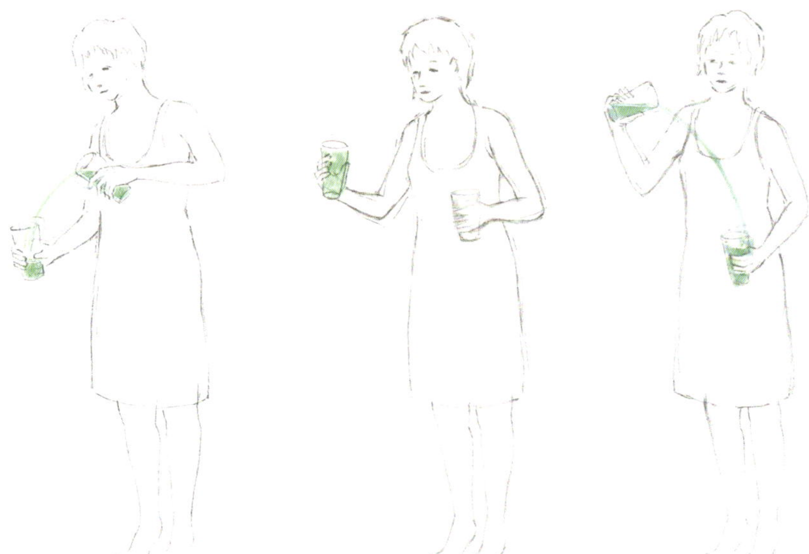

CANTOS PATRIÓTICOS (PATRIOTIC SONGS), 1998–99
IN COLLABORATION WITH RAFAEL ORTEGA,
MEXICO CITY
THREE-CHANNEL VIDEO
28 MIN. 30 SEC.

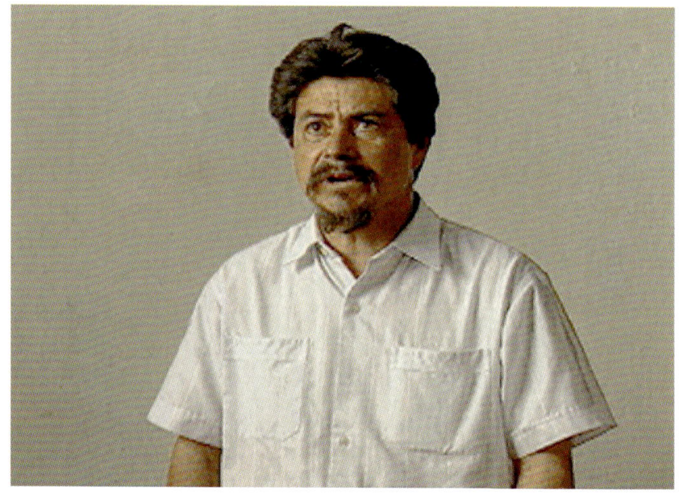

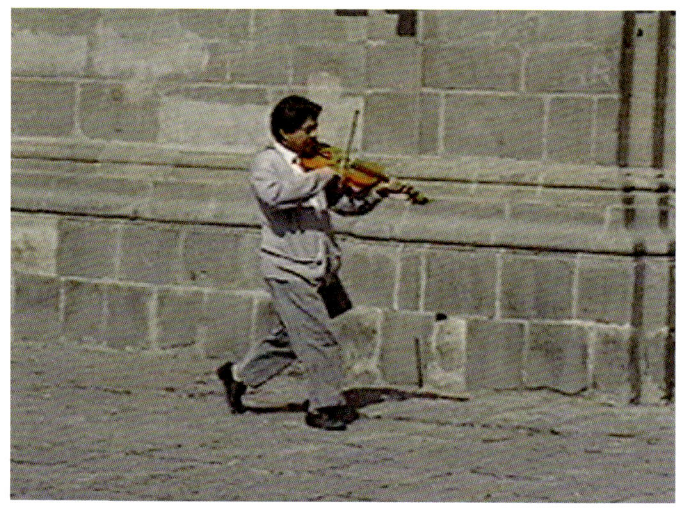

(REFRAIN)
With the current and against it
Don't know where you're rowing to
Is it backwards is it forwards
Is it forwards is it back

(VERSES)
It's the serpent of the story
Who is swallowing his tail
Listen well and do not hurry
So you'll understand my tale
Where the end is the beginning
And the start is the finish is

Over the Rio Grande waters
Luis the boatman ferried folk
On his craft and with the current
From one shore to that in front
And then the other way about
South to north day in day out

Right in the middle of the river
Listen to what happened next
As his course he tried to set
He sighed and gazed ... up at the sun
Lost was Luis he knew no whither
By the sun he started at ... dazed.
There in the middle of the river

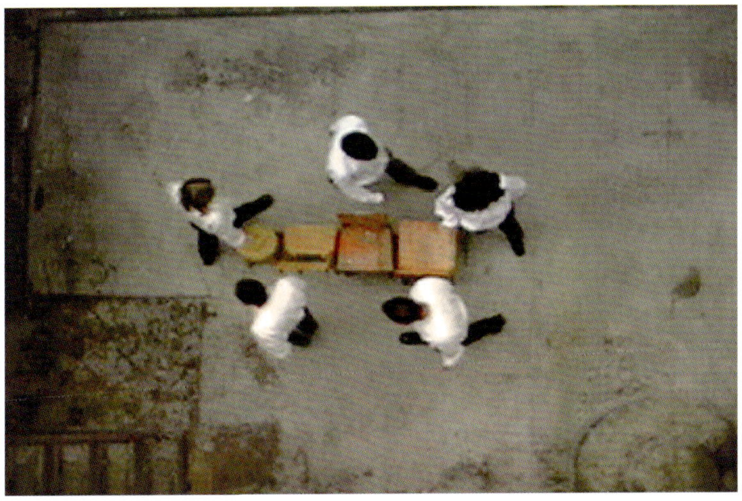

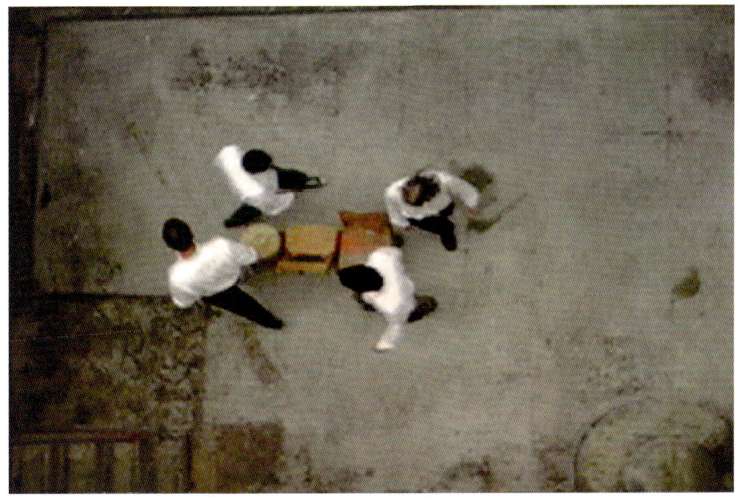

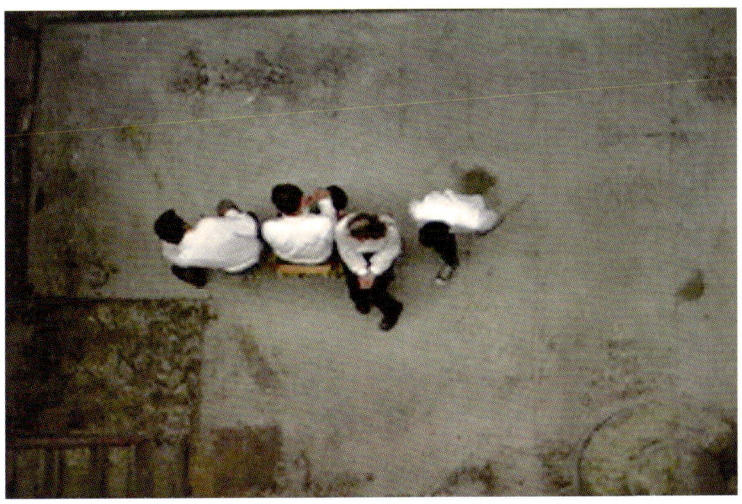

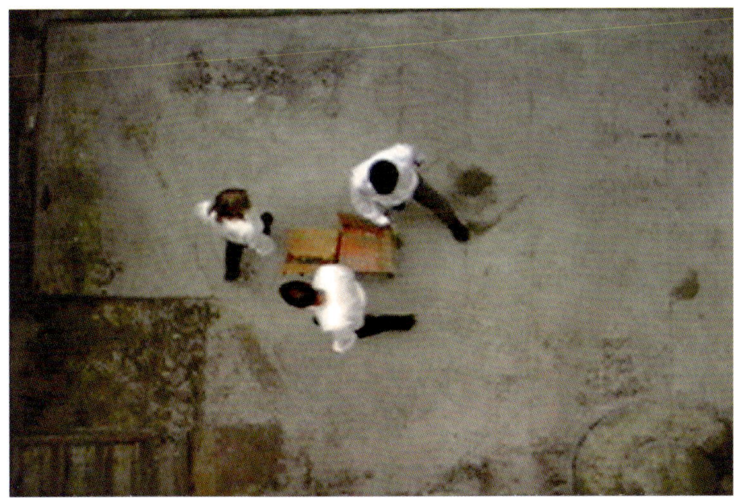

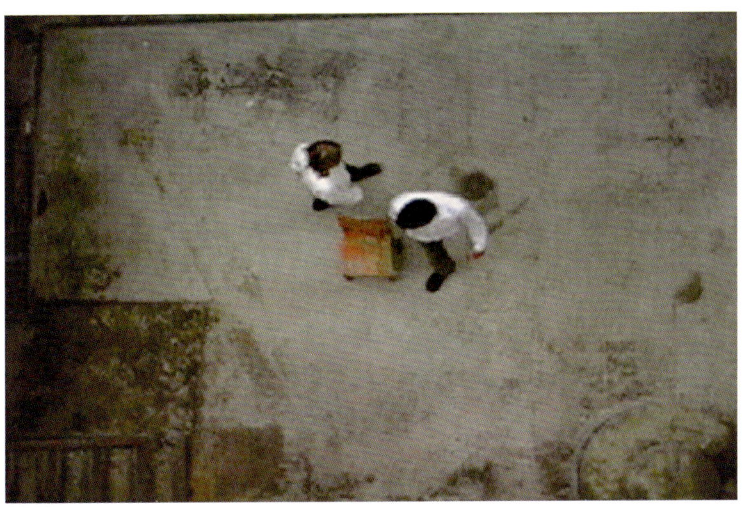

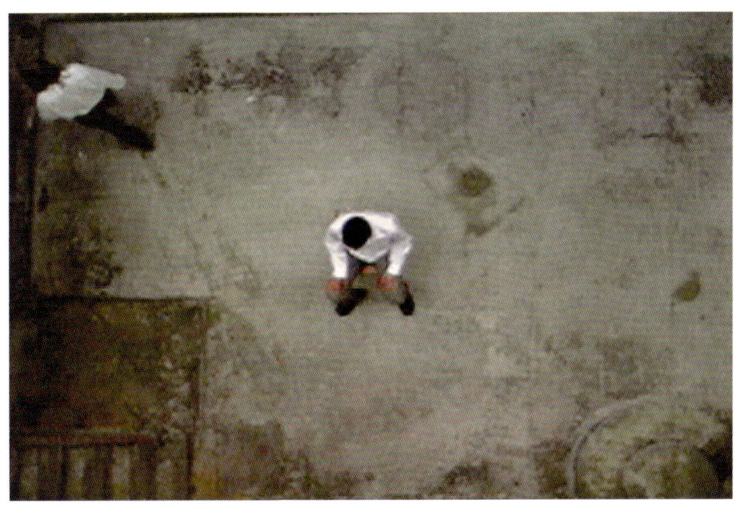

Listen to what happened next
Trying once more to set his course
Sighing at the sun he gazed
His orientation was restored
Though by the sun's light he
was dazed

By the sun he stares at ... dazed
Lost was Luis he knew no whither
He sighed and gazed ... up at the sun
As his course he tried to set
Listen to what happened next
Right in the middle of the river

South to north day in day out
Then the other way about
From one shore to that in front
On his craft and with the current
Luis the boatman ferried folk
Over Rio Grande waters

And the start the finish is
Where the end is the beginning
So you'll understand my tale
Listen well and do not hurry
Who is swallowing his tail?
It's the serpent of the story.

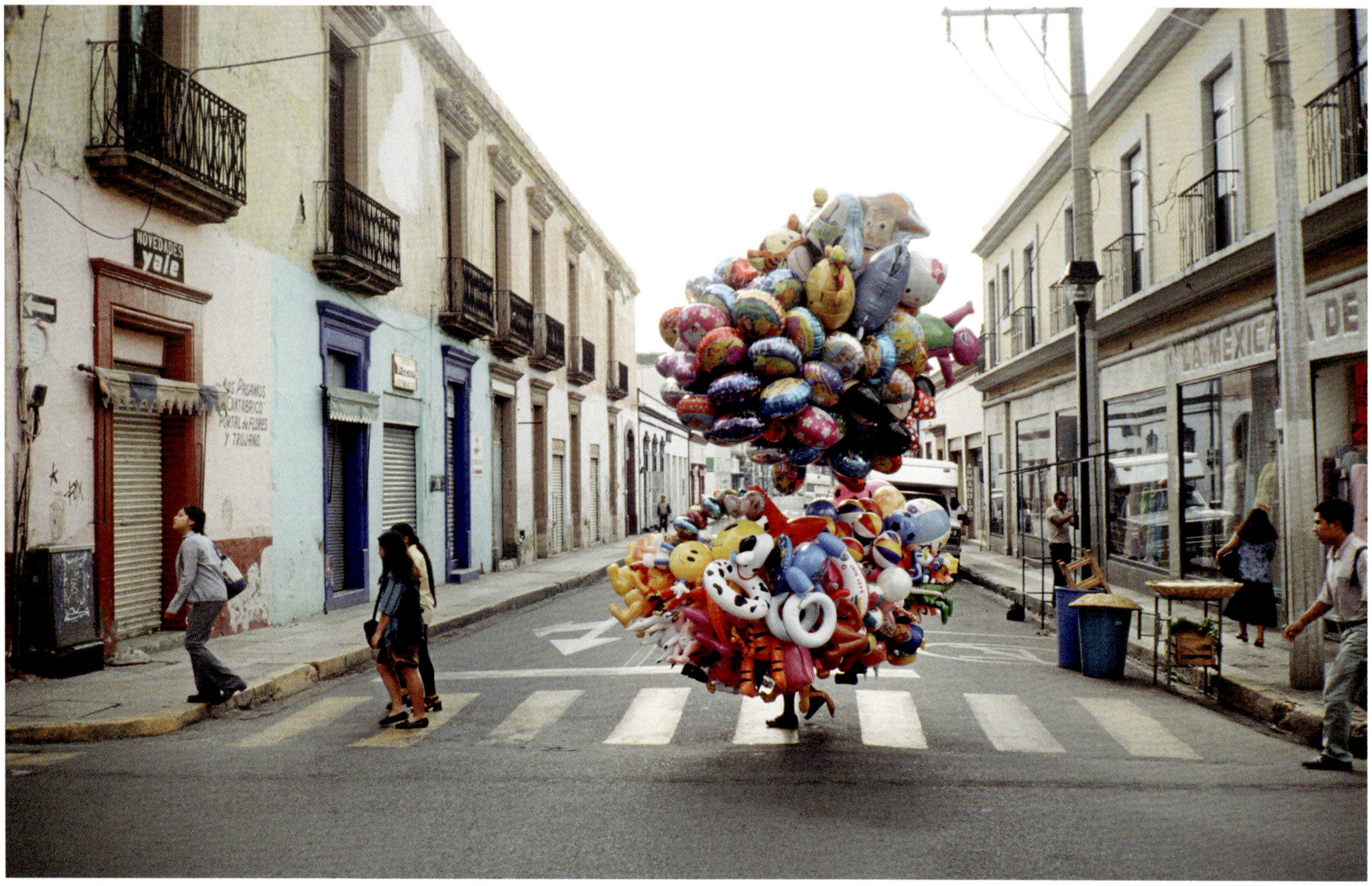

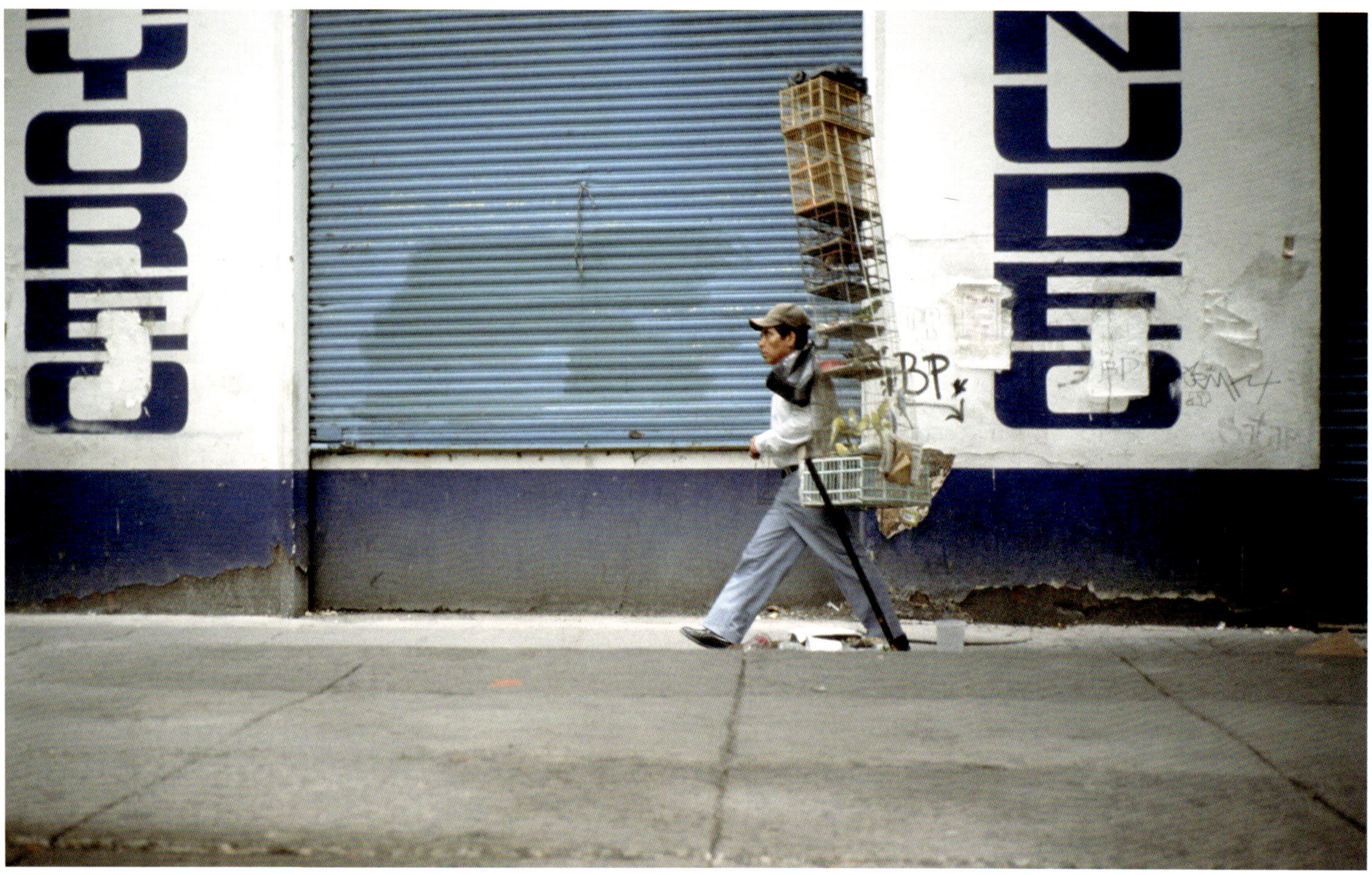

AMBULANTES, 1992–PRESENT
MEXICO CITY
2 OF 80 35 MM SLIDES

to stay in an indeterminate sphere of action as a way of defining itself against the imposition of modernity.

It's this capacity of flirting with modernity without giving in that fascinates me. I suppose that in our age of the global market economy you could argue about whether that modernity was ever even achieved. But what matters now is the memory of it, whether it was a reality or a fiction. You can have a nostalgia for something that never really happened.

FERGUSON: *I noticed a cartoon pinned to your studio wall with an old man saying, 'Of course, it was a long time ago, but at the time it seemed like the present.'* [laughs]

ALŸS: I think there is a whole aspect of my practice that just tries to deal with all these anachronisms, to represent and to document them. I have seen some urban activities disappear from one day to another because of a radical change in city policies. When I first went to Lima, the Old Centre was very much like the Centre here, with street sellers everywhere. A year later there was not one street seller to be found. From one visit to another a whole culture had been wiped out. What I am saying, simply, is that to have witnessed those kinds of drastic evolutions in the life of a city makes you want to document more systematically the manifestations of these parallel, informal economies that are the obligatory components of the Latin American megalopolis.

The style of the documentation series is influenced by August Sander's *People of the Twentieth Century* or the eighteenth-century prints *Cries of London*. My method of shooting is always systematic and tries to respond technically to the encountered situations. *Sleepers* (1999–present) will always have the camera at ground level. *Beggars* (2002–04) takes a quasi-hypocritical high viewpoint. *Ambulantes* (1992–present) is always shot perpendicularly to the passing subject at a distance of five metres or so. In that sense it is as neutral a register as can be, and it is that which might give it its archival value over time.

FERGUSON: *You once referred to yourself as 'a former European'. Earlier I asked you if you were a Mexican artist. Are you a Belgian artist in any sense?*

ALŸS: As you know, since you are Scottish, Belgium has certain imprints that you can't wash away. And being a Flemish-born French speaker doesn't help.

FERGUSON: *Do you see a continuation of your work as an architect in your art?*

ALŸS: Beyond the obvious fascination with urban phenomena, there's the fact that methods and practice of architecture are based on collaboration. It's a team product.

FERGUSON: *There is a stereotype of the architect as an egomaniac who collaborates out of necessity but at the same time attempts to exert total control. In a lot of your projects you*

GIOVANNI VENDRAMINI
(AFTER FRANCIS WHEATLY)
HOT GINGERBREAD FROM
CRIES OF LONDON, C. 1772
ENGRAVING
43 X 33 CM

AUGUST SANDER
BRICKLAYER'S MATE, 1928
GELATIN SILVER PRINT
29 X 23 CM

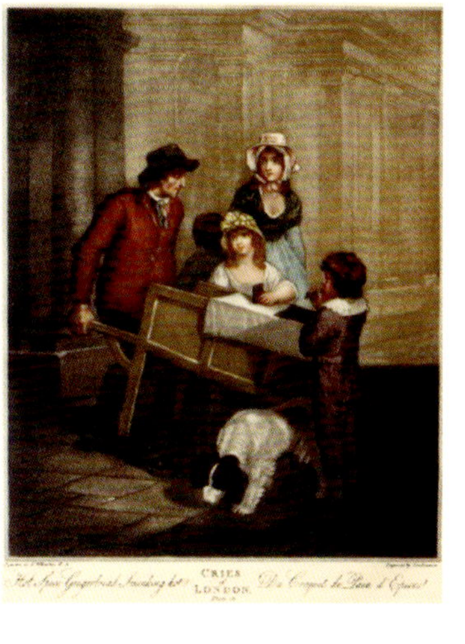

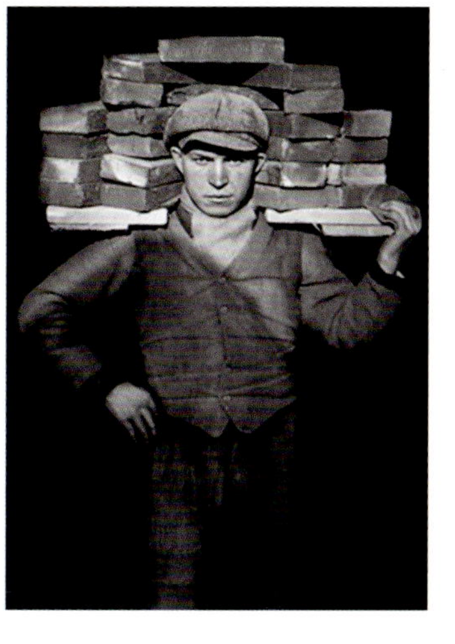

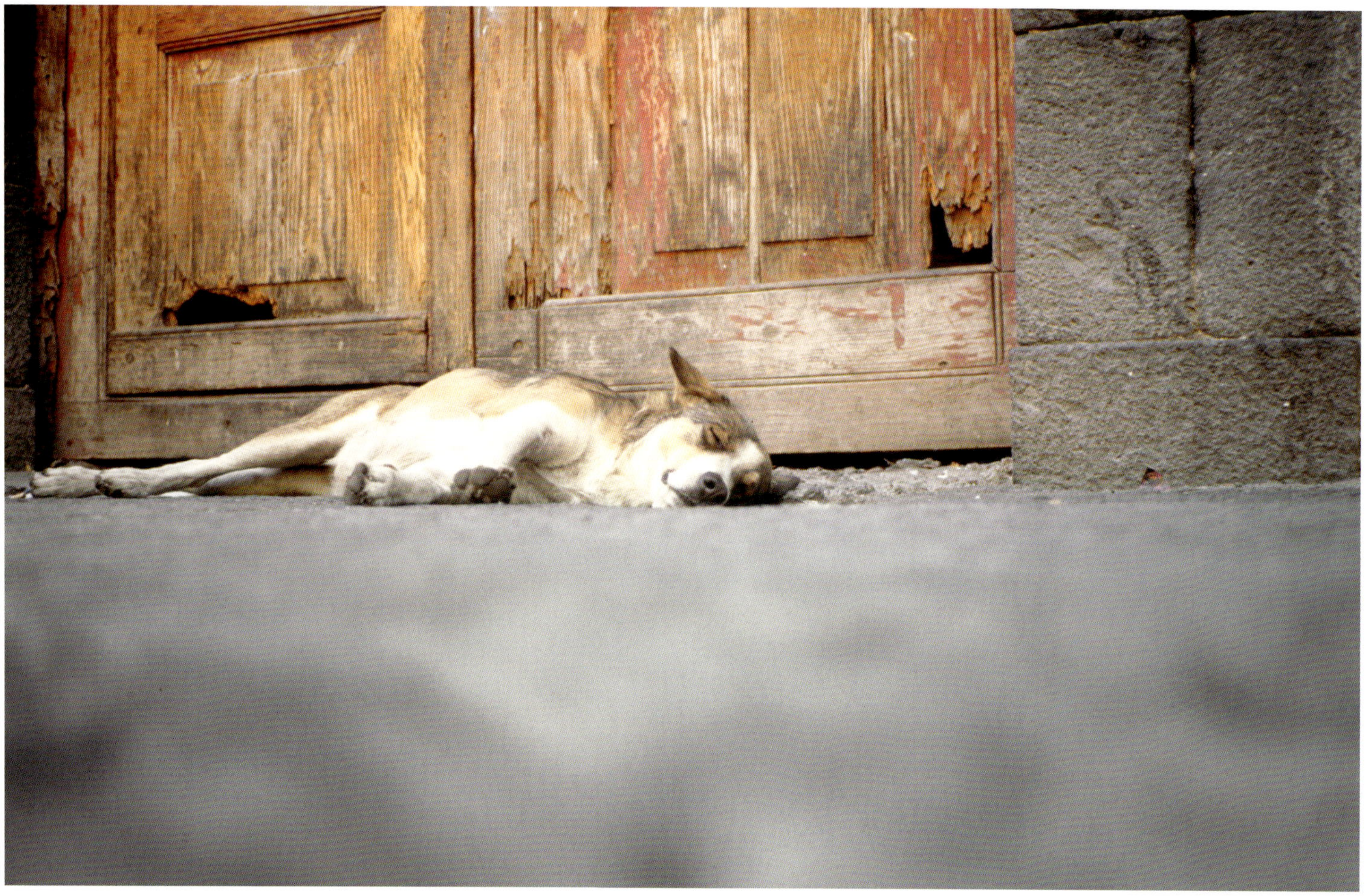

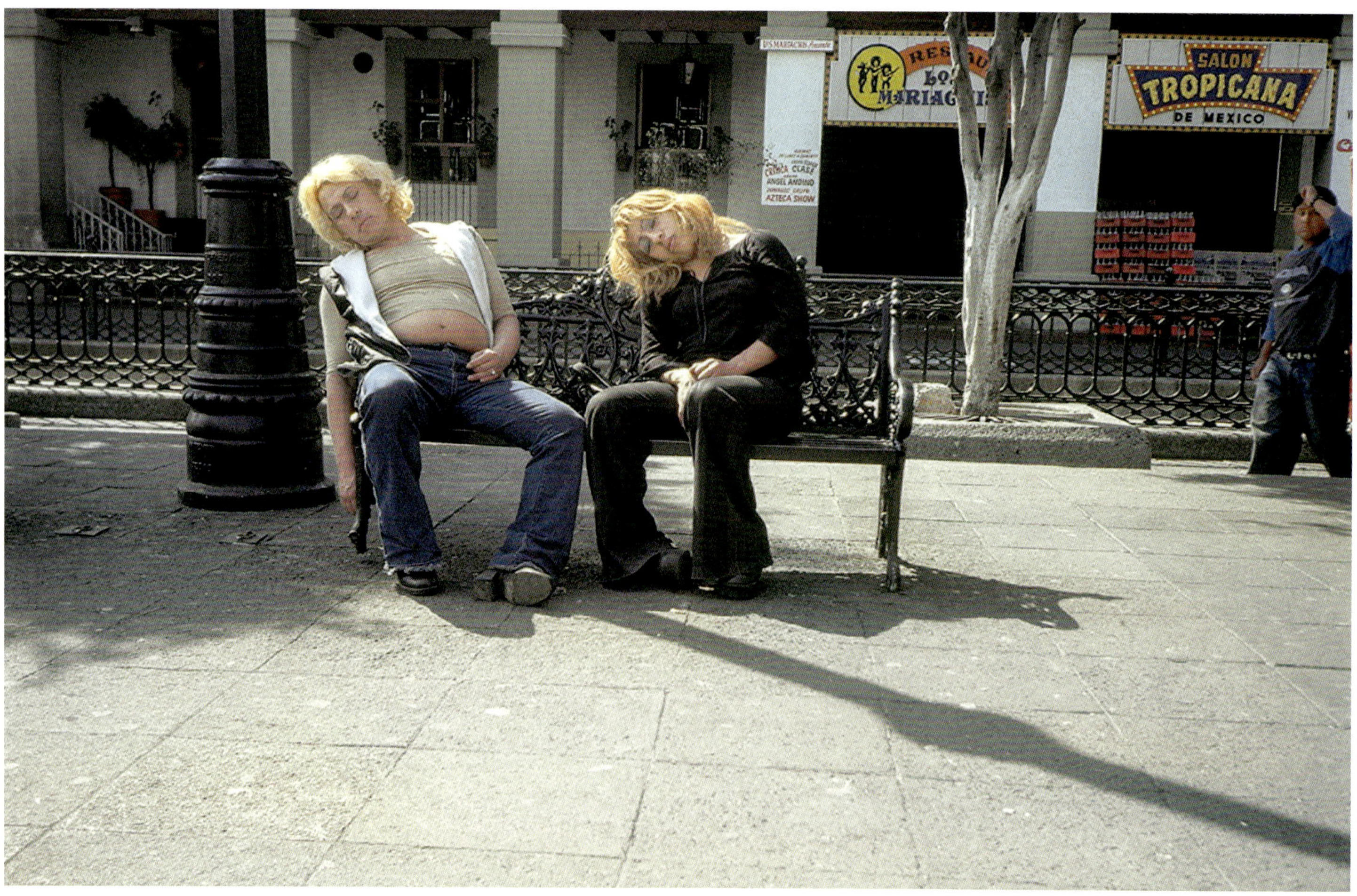
SALON
TROPICANA
DE MEXICO

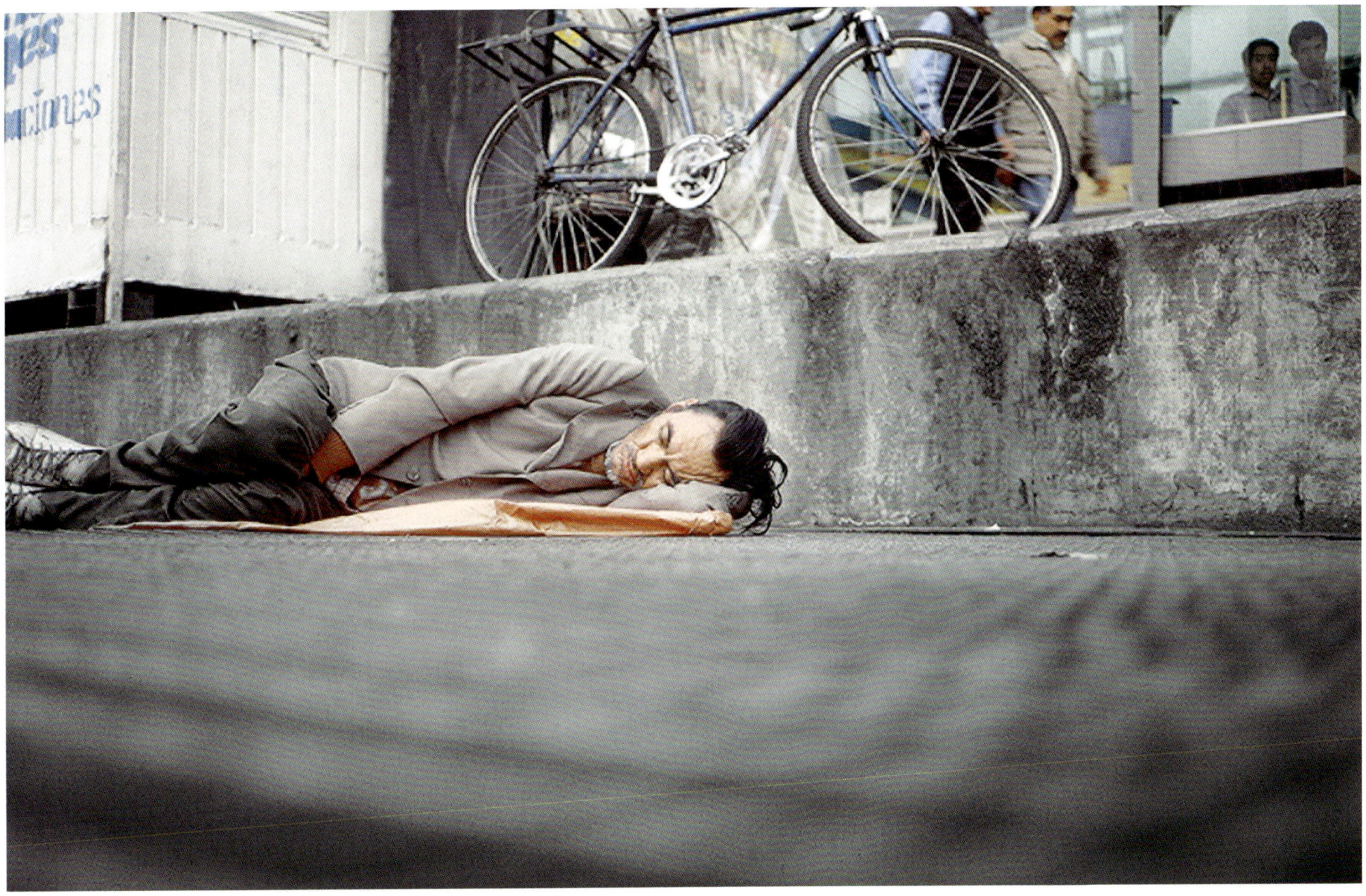

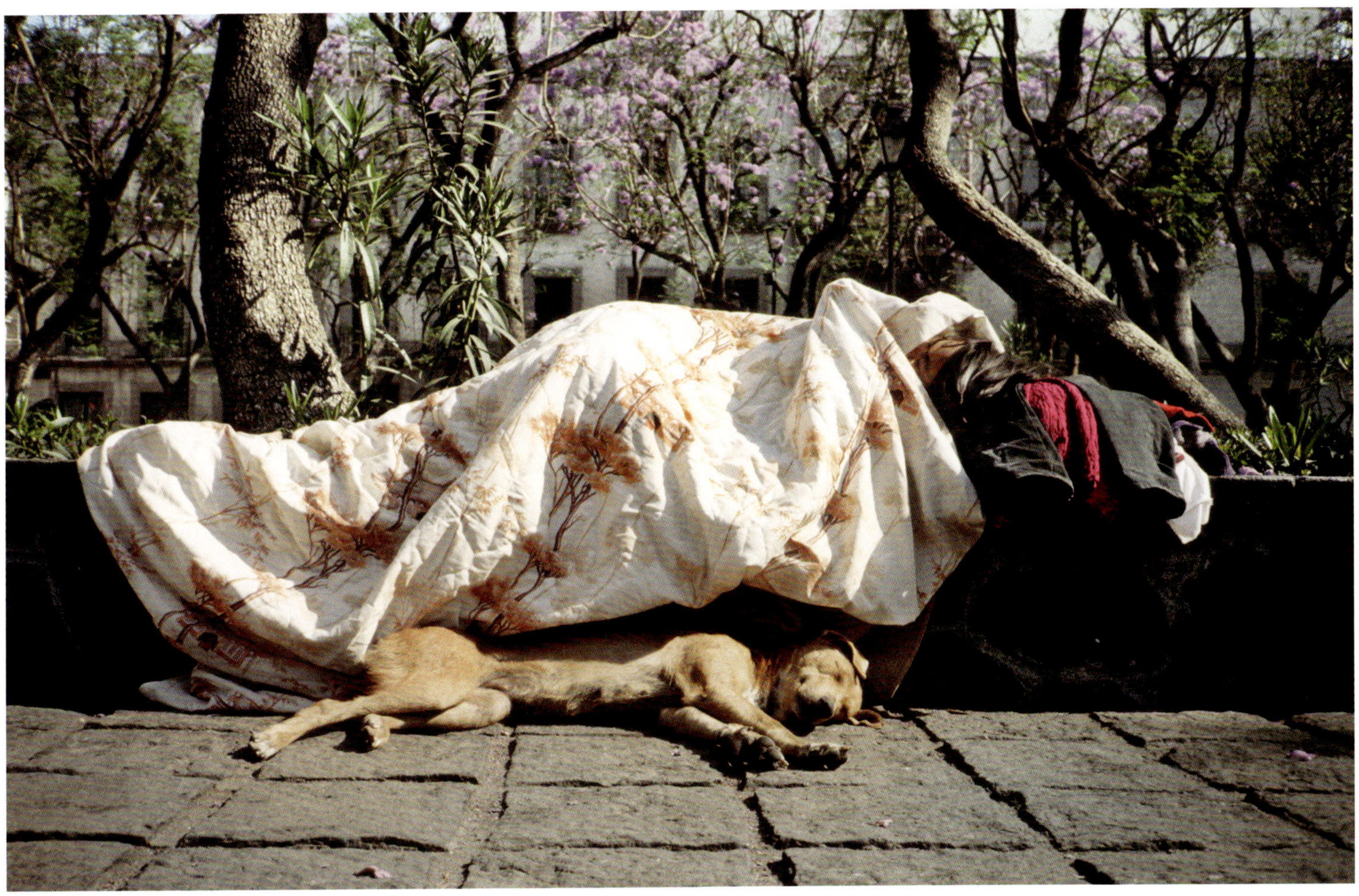

SLEEPERS, 1999–PRESENT
MEXICO CITY
4 OF 80 35 MM SLIDES

SLEEPERS, 1999–PRESENT
MEXICO CITY
2 OF 80 35 MM SLIDES

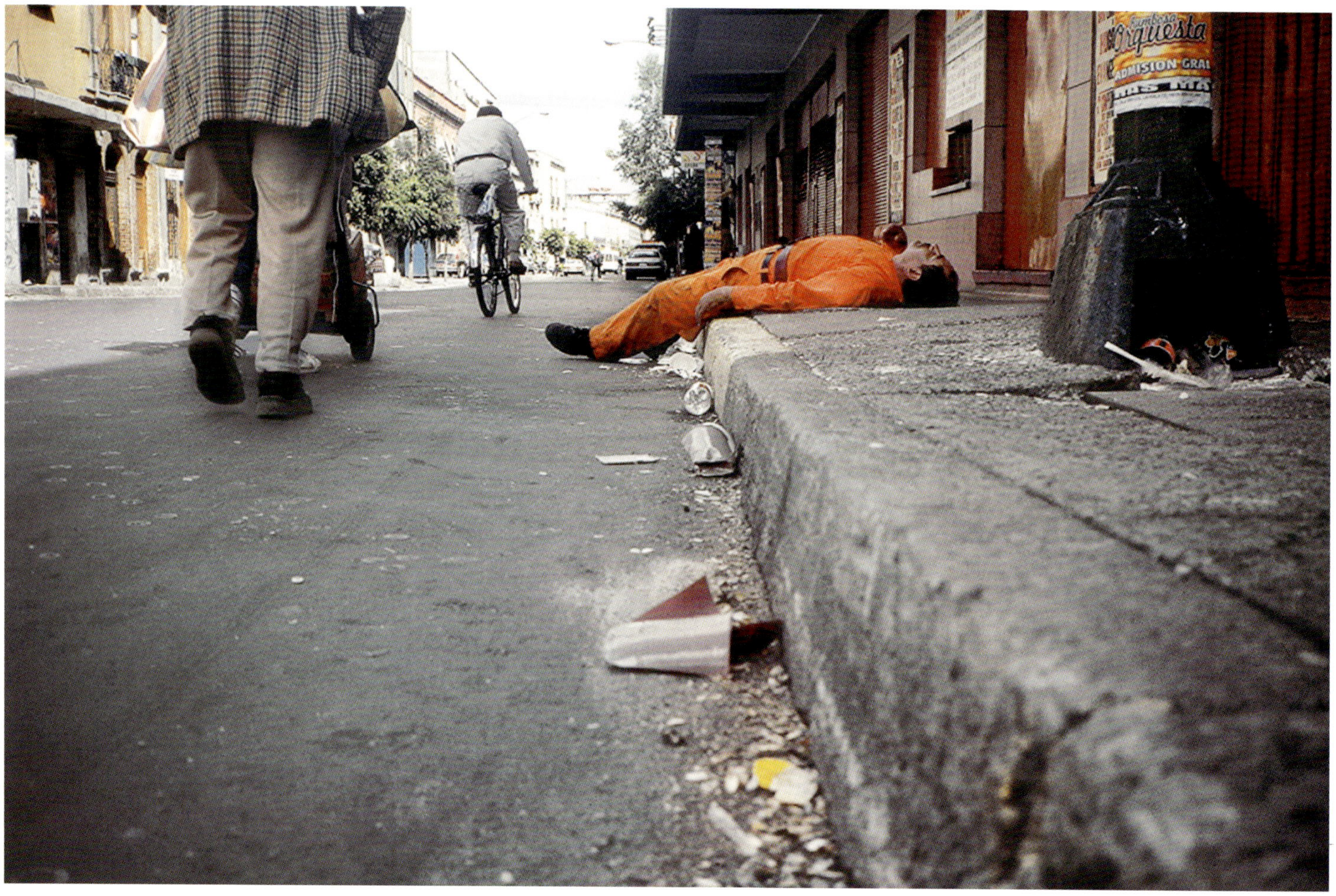

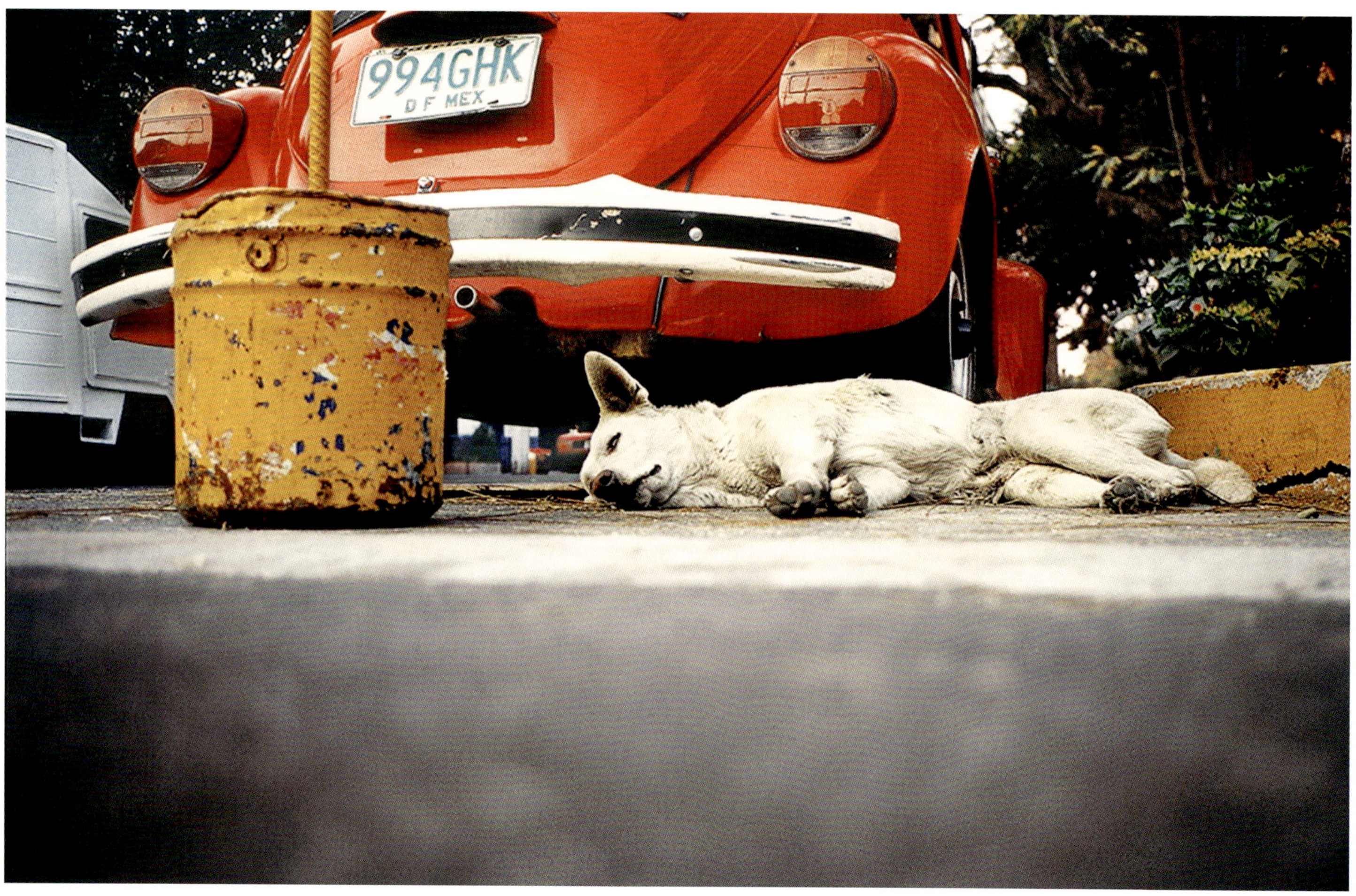

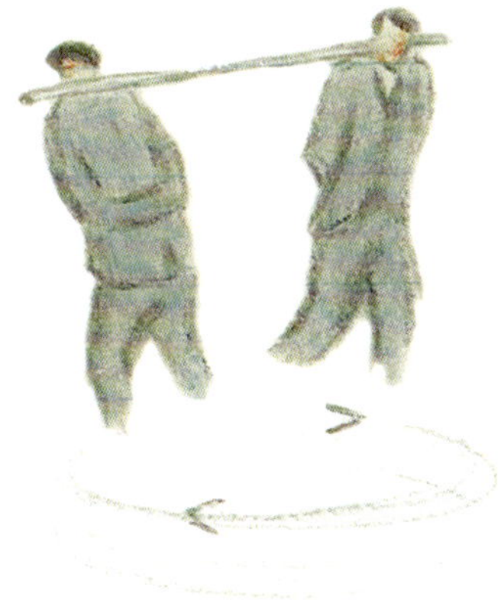

UNTITLED, 1997
COLOUR PENCIL ON PAPER
5 X 4 CM

Given:
A generic situation – for example, a small town where many people cross paths.

If somebody were to say something to someone, and that someone were to repeat it to someone else, and that someone were to repeat it to someone else ... then, at the end of the day, something is talked about, but the source has been lost along the way.

Premise:
- The rumour is instigated and spread verbally by one or several agents.
- The rumour is fed until any physical evidence appears as a direct consequence of the rumour.
- The rumour attempts to infiltrate a given situation without adding or subtracting any physical element to it.

have worked collaboratively with a variety of other people. I'm wondering to what extent you are attracted by the possibility of surrendering some control, and to what extent you need to retain control personally over what you produce.

ALŸS: Perhaps you should ask my collaborators. [*laughs*] The collaboration process is to watch an idea bounce back and forth, and eventually develop its own course in that bouncing (*el rebote*). The project starts with a mess of notes and drawings, incidental quotes and documents, and usually out of that process the medium defines itself spontaneously. At that stage I start looking for specialists in that specific medium to enter the project, and their translation of the plot automatically reshapes the original concept. The more the project evolves, the more this bouncing back and forth between myself and the collaborators intensifies, and it can lead to a final shape sometimes quite far from the original intention. It's in that process that the project takes on its own life and develops. The more ambitious the logistics of the project, the more I will turn into a producer or a coordinator of the project and, when it happens, a spectator of my own fantasy.

And then there are all the other ingredients of the live event. Once the axiom has been posed and the location set, the development and outcome of the piece happen within an open field of possibilities, in the sense that any outcome of the event becomes a valid answer to the premises of the piece. Once the action is launched, there is no longer any strict or unilateral plan to be followed. Only the actual course of the action itself will provide a response to the preliminary axiom.

The only constant rule I have witnessed is that if the storyline – the plot proposal – is clear and strong enough, it will resist all these mutations. The situation will unfold in a way not unlike what your intuitive expectations were. It is the test of the scenario. If the scenario does not hold, the action will deviate and become something else.

FERGUSON: *Despite the inevitable collaborative element in architecture, it is also about making something that is very fixed and with very clear boundaries. It seems that perhaps one of the things that led you away from architecture is an interest in where those boundaries are more permeable, or where there are spaces between fixed entities.*

ALŸS: You mean the cracks in the system?

FERGUSON: *Yes. I'm also thinking about the man in the Zócalo who spends his time scraping the gaps between the flagstones with a wire hook. I thought of that figure as in a way a self-portrait of you, in the sense of this interest in exploring the spaces in between.*

ALŸS: When I stepped out of the field of architecture, my first impulse was not to add to the city, but to absorb what was already there, to work with the residues, or with the negative spaces, the holes, the spaces in between. Because of the immense amount of material produced on a daily basis by a huge city like Mexico City, it is very difficult to justify the act of adding another piece of matter to that already saturated environment. My reaction was to insert a story into the city rather than an object. It was my way of affecting a place at a very precise moment of its history, even just for an instant. If the story is right, if it hits a nerve, it can propagate like a rumour. Stories can pass through a place without the need to settle. They have a life of their own. If the script meets the expectations and addresses the anxieties of that society at the right time and place, it may become a story that survives the event itself. At that moment, it has the potential to become a fable or an urban myth.

I'll try to always keep the plot simple enough so that these actions can be imagined without an obligatory reference or access to visuals – the story of the mouse that was freed in the storage space of the largest collection of contemporary art in Mexico (*The Mouse*, 2001), or of the guy who pushed an ice block until it melted down completely (*Paradox of Praxis 1*) – something short, so round and simple that it can be repeated as an anecdote, something that can be stolen and, in the best-case scenario, enter that land of minor urban myths or fables I mentioned.

FERGUSON: *You're making it clear that the source of a lot of your work lies in things observed in the real environment, and yet, at the same time, I feel that there is a strong element in your work of the dreamlike.*

ALŸS: What do you see as dreamlike?

FERGUSON: *There are certain elements singled out that defy conventional rationality, and for me that has something of a dreamlike quality in the sense that everything seems very real and convincing yet at the same time somehow irrational. This is perhaps especially true of the paintings.*

ALŸS: I think a lot of what is happening in this world is way more irrational than what I am illustrating. But it's true, when it comes to images, painted images in particular, the rules are different. What justifies my recourse to painting is that it's the shortest way – or the only way – to translate certain scenarios or situations that cannot be said, that cannot be filmed or performed. It's about entering a situation that could not exist elsewhere, only on the paper or canvas. They are images, and I want for them to live as such – like in a children's book.

Also, painting allows me to retreat from the sometimes hectic rhythm of the performances and film productions, and to distance myself from them without losing contact with them. Painting functions as a sort of therapeutic space in the middle of the rat race. When I am translating an ongoing film plot into an image, I'll try to create an image that reflects the intention behind the plot rather than illustrating the facts of the film. It functions more like a correspondence.

And of course, last but not least, painting has freed me from some economic pressure by allowing me to finance numerous projects that proved not to be very lucrative. Now I remain my own master, and up to the last moment I can change, postpone or cancel any ongoing production.

FERGUSON: *I guess I see what I'm calling the dreamlike aspect of your work also in some of your performative works, not just your paintings – for example, the loose thread on the sweater that unravels further and further and further (*Fairy Tales*, 1995–98). It is a real thing that takes place in the world, yet it also –*

ALŸS: Yes, but it can also travel as an anecdote or fable.

FERGUSON: *So you see them as fables or parables rather than as dreams, or even daydreams. Like the man whose sweater catches on something and who doesn't notice for a mile.*

ALŸS: Until someone else notices. In Stockholm, once the walk was done and the sweater unravelled I retraced my steps to document the journey, following the long blue thread on the street and in the park. Midway back I ran into this old lady who was patiently rolling a ball of blue yarn under her arm, carefully gathering up the wool of my unravelled sweater – maybe to knit a similar one at home.

FERGUSON: *Is the passing on of the story where humour comes in? In some of your projects there is a pungent humour that contributes to its persistence as a story.*

ALŸS: Humour helps to catch the spectator's attention. It's a way of trapping him in the narrative. You make me think of something else. My iconography has often been described as naïve, flatly figurative, two-dimensional, but that simplicity can sometimes

THE MOUSE, 2001
PHOTO DOCUMENTATION OF AN ACTION, MEXICO CITY

On Saturday 3 March 2001 at 5 p.m. I entered the Jumex Collection with a mouse in my pocket. At 5:10 p.m. I freed the mouse.

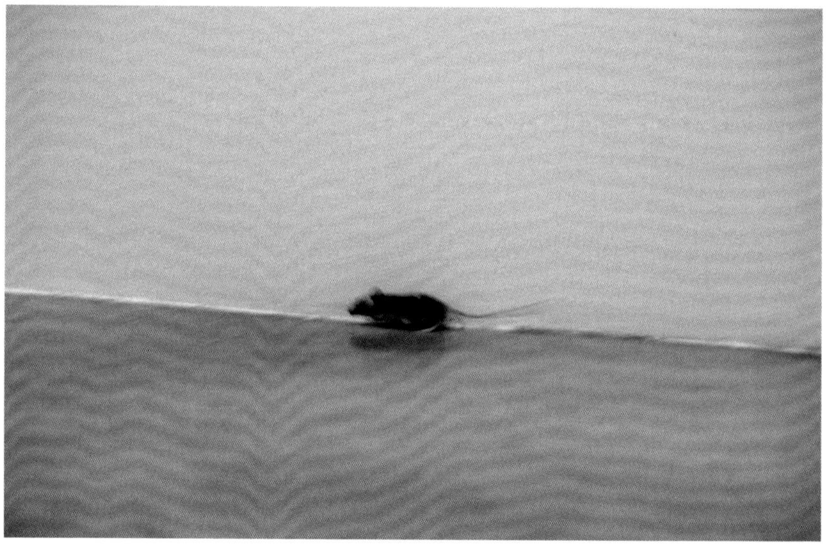

FAIRY TALES, 1995–98
PHOTO DOCUMENTATION OF AN ACTION, STOCKHOLM

Whereas the highly rational societies of the Renaissance felt the need to create utopias, we, of our times, must create fables.

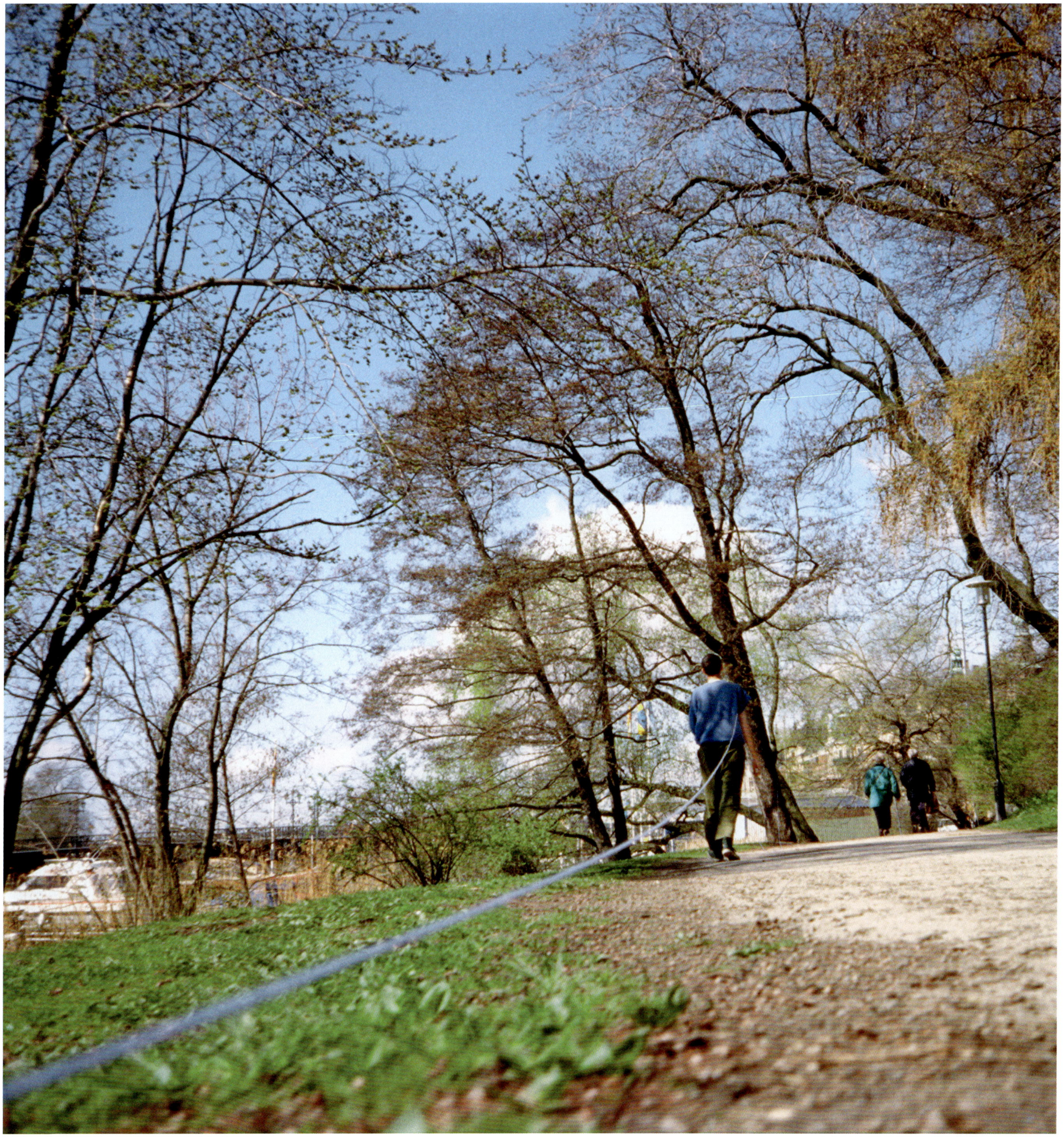

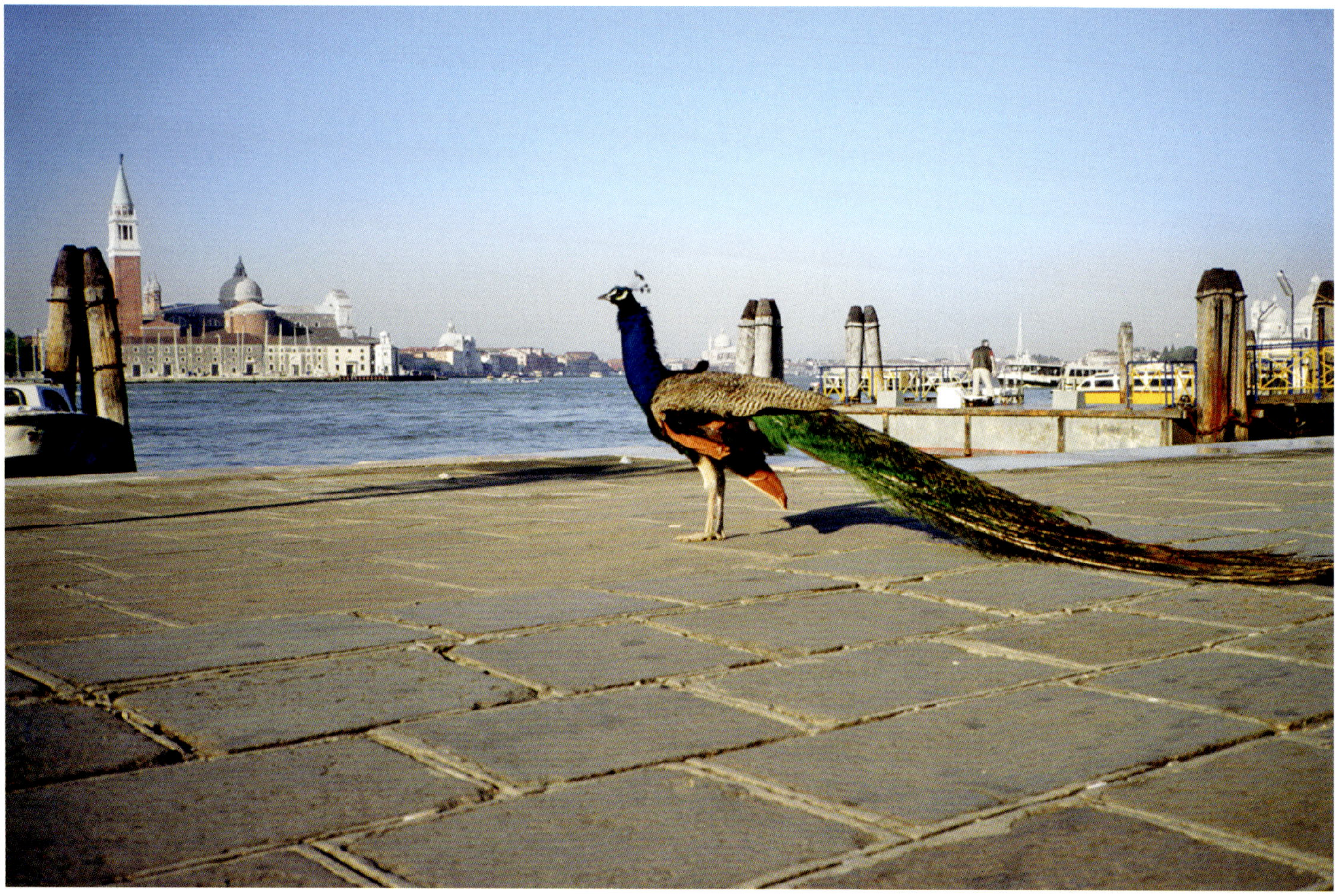

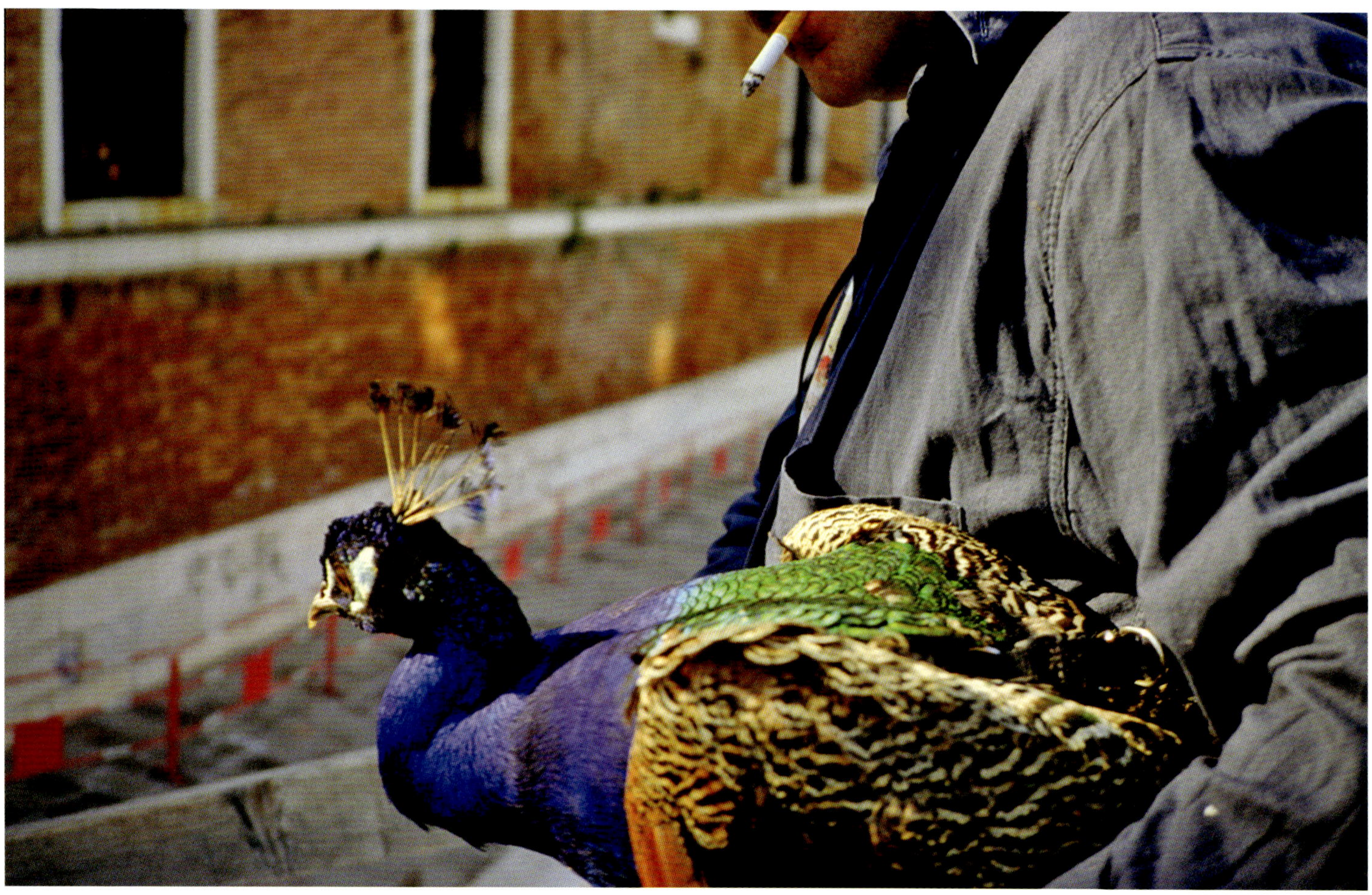

THE AMBASSADOR, 2001
PHOTO DOCUMENTATION
OF AN ACTION, VENICE

Mr Peacock represented Mr Alÿs at the 49th Venice Biennale.

help seduce the viewer's eye. It's the direct language of the sign painters, where communication for any audience comes first. That's what fascinates me about Magritte. His painting is so flat and somehow physically disappointing, yet it is so performative and communicative. Magritte himself was coming from the world of advertising. There are billions of images around us, and they move fast and are extremely persuasive and efficient. Painting works against that speed effect. It is slow, very poor in a way, so if you can make that little contact, provoke that little spark in someone's head, it is a small miracle amid the speed of our digital age.

FERGUSON: *Sending a peacock to the opening of the Venice Biennale (*The Ambassador*, 2001) is very funny, but it also has an element underneath that is critical. People who are there see the peacock and think it is funny, but the peacock is also functioning as a critique of all the preening people who are attending the opening.*

ALŸS: Humour has a critical dimension. To laugh can be a way of abstracting yourself from a situation, a way of negating its reality. When the public first saw Manet's *Olympia* their reaction was to laugh, because they could not understand it and maybe they did not want to understand it, and laughter was the only answer they could give to its physical presence. Humour is a double-edged weapon.

FERGUSON: *It can be attack and defence. It can be both the sword and the shield.*

ALŸS: *The Last Clown* (2000) was trying to illustrate that situation, with the artist and the curator in their ultimate roles: the great entertainers, the acrobats, the ones expected to fall.

FERGUSON: *I guess the other side of my suggestion that there is a kind of dream element in the work is that there is also a lot of work in the work. Just looking around the studio it seems that there is a lot of work going on here, a lot of production.*

ALŸS: The studio is a bizarre place. Some of the things you see lying around have been here for years.

FERGUSON: *It gives the impression there's a lot of work.*

ALŸS: There is and there isn't. The images build themselves in layers over a long period of time, with all the moods and accidents that can happen in between. It's the great receptacle of all complaints and illusions, the purgatory space for all projects.
My studio has become something in between a sentimental refuge, a logistical base and a storage space. It is a place I need to go back to on a regular basis, but only to recharge batteries and leave again.

FERGUSON: *So the work is not really generated primarily in the studio?*

ALŸS: Not so much any more. In the days of the sign paintings project, yes, because we were all working here. But now the mechanics are more complex. The studio is where the raw material is processed and passed on to others. It's the relay point. I think most of the creative process happens in the spaces in between – in between home and the studio, the studio and the lab, in between conversations with collaborators, and also, as I am always working on several projects in parallel, in between different states of mind over the course of a day. And bouncing back and forth between these different scenarios is the only way for me to have a critical distance with any of them and for me to progress. I am never exclusively in one narrative at the time. Rather, I am always linking data from different sources. Recently this aspect has exploded geographically, but it could easily

THE LAST CLOWN, 2000
ANIMATION DRAWINGS
OIL AND PENCIL ON TRACING PAPER
EACH 29 X 38 CM

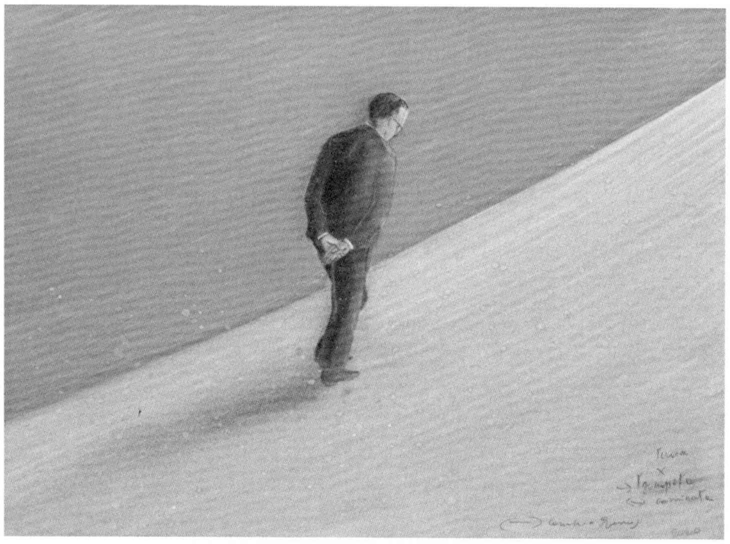

0:00:12

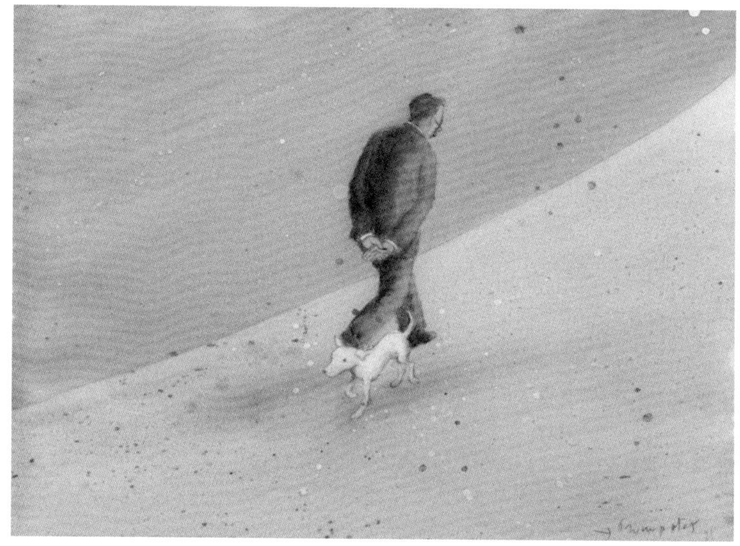

0:01:09

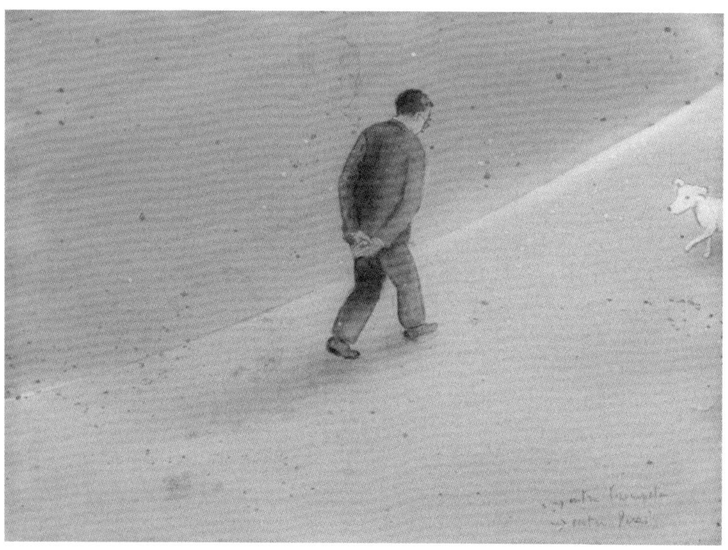

0:01:05

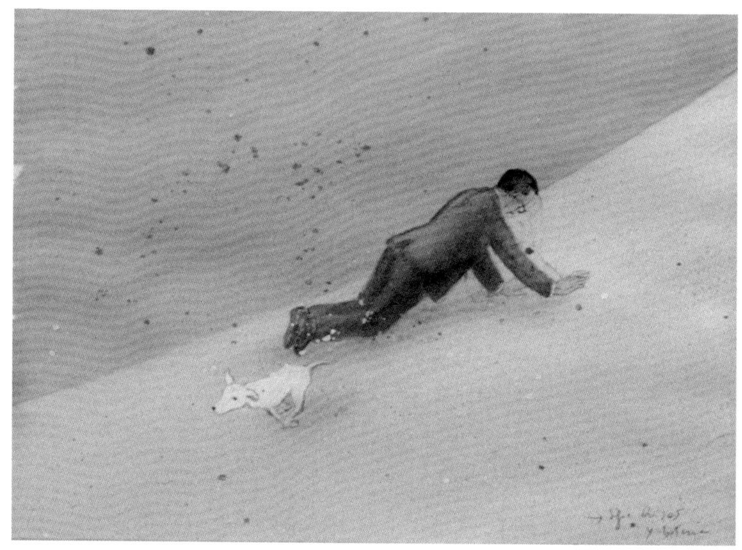

0:01:10

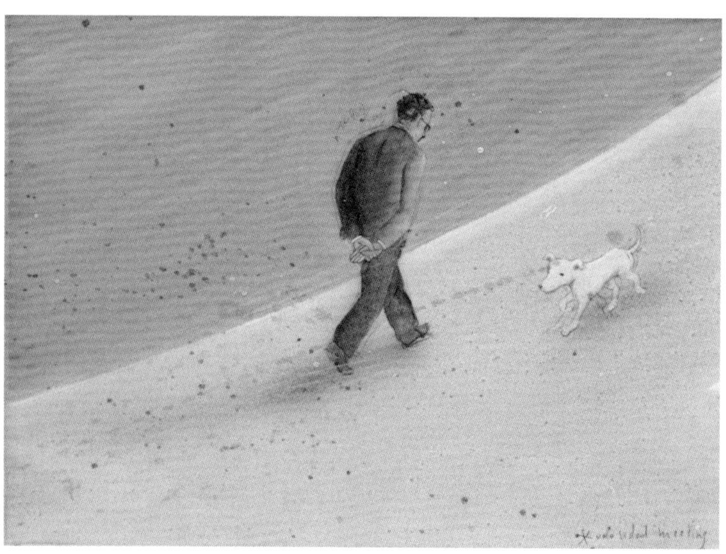

0:01:07

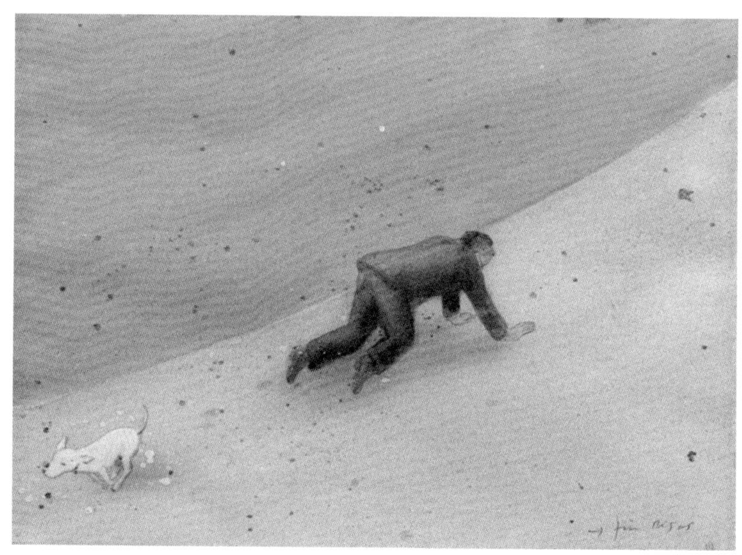

0:01:11

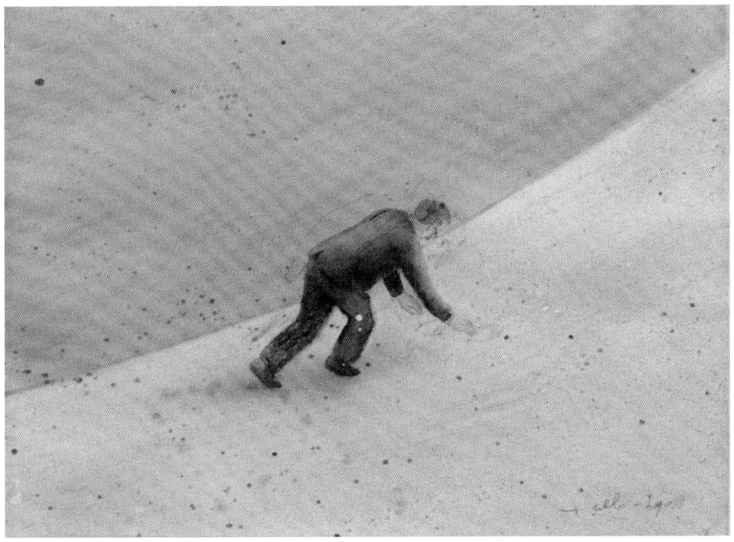

0:01:12

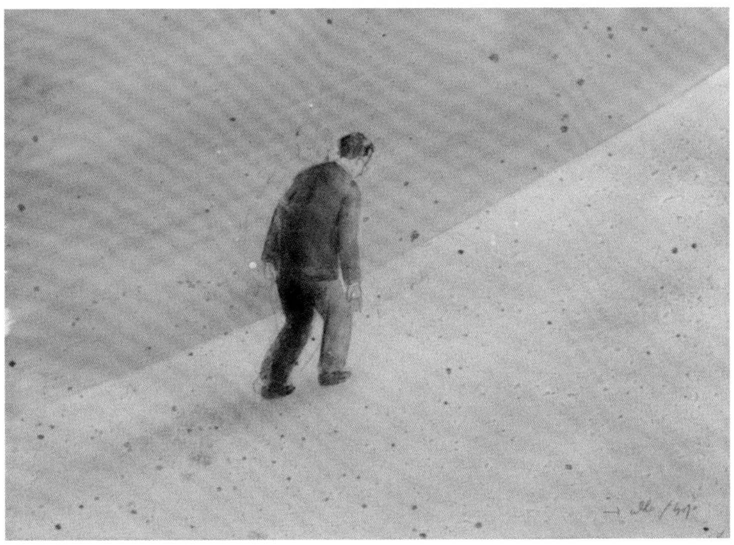

0:01:13

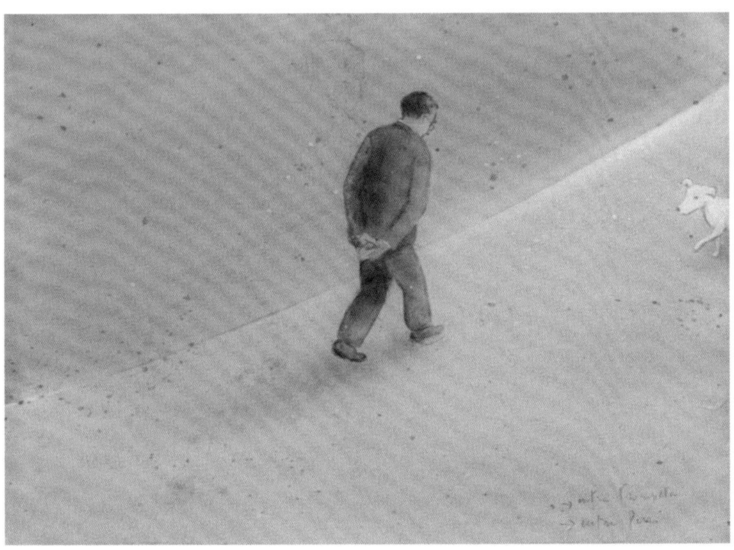

0:02:10

go back to just one location when the time comes. Again, all these parallel stories try to be part of a single narrative. It's like when you walk in the city. Walking here from the Zócalo there have been fifty different situations happening, with fifty incidental noises, smells and images. They've all just been furtive glimpses, bits of incidental information, but while walking lost in your thoughts you have somehow integrated them all, and they have shaped your thoughts at the arrival point.

FERGUSON: *But you're a fast walker.*

ALŸS: Because, unlike a few years ago, I wouldn't want to be confused with a tourist. [*laughs*] In Mexico City only innocent tourists go slowly.

FERGUSON: *I wanted to ask you about the importance of walking in your work, starting with walking around your neighbourhood here, but also more generally about walking as a generator of projects and ideas and stories.*

ALŸS: Walking, in particular drifting, or strolling, is already – within the speed culture of our time – a kind of resistance. Paradoxically it's also the last private space, safe from the phone or e-mail. But it also happens to be a very immediate method for unfolding stories. It's an easy, cheap act to perform or to invite others to perform. The walk is simultaneously the material out of which to produce art and the modus operandi of the artistic transaction. And the city always offers the perfect setting for accidents to happen.

There is no theory of walking, just a consciousness. But there can be a certain wisdom involved in the act of walking. It's more an attitude, and it is one that fits me all right. It's a state where you can be both alert to all that happens in your peripheral vision and hearing, and yet totally lost in your thought process. I see the slide carousels series as an attempt to reproduce those furtive meetings, those side glimpses I mentioned earlier, when you look at someone or something for two seconds while walking on the street and yet it is enough time to fully capture the tragic dimension of the situation.

FERGUSON: *In* Ambulantes *all of the people shown have a very defined purpose to their pushing and pulling. They are walking in the city because they need to move something from one place to another. There seem to be two kinds of walking in your work. There are pieces that have a set script or set of thngs that will happen during the course of the walk, and there are others that are aimless or drifting. Maybe* Narcotourism *(1996) is the most aimless of all your walks.*

ALŸS: *Narcotourism* responded to a very specific invitation. For the first time, after having been in Mexico for nearly ten years, I was asked to do a work in Europe, in Denmark. Copenhagen is for me a real archetype of the bourgeois European city. I realized I had no desire to be there, so my response was to be physically present but mentally absent. The drugs became a means of escaping the reality of a return I was not ready to face.

FERGUSON: *Does the model of the* flâneur *interest you?*

ALŸS: The *flâneur* is a very nineteenth-century European figure. It goes with a kind of romanticism that does not have much space in a city like Mexico. The city is too crude and too raw, and everything seems to happen in an immediate present. There is no space for nostalgia.

SHADY/SUNNY, 2004
LONDON
PENCIL AND OIL ON TRACING PAPER
25 X 32 CM

A walk in South East London on the shady side of the street always.
A walk in South East London on the sunny side of the street always.

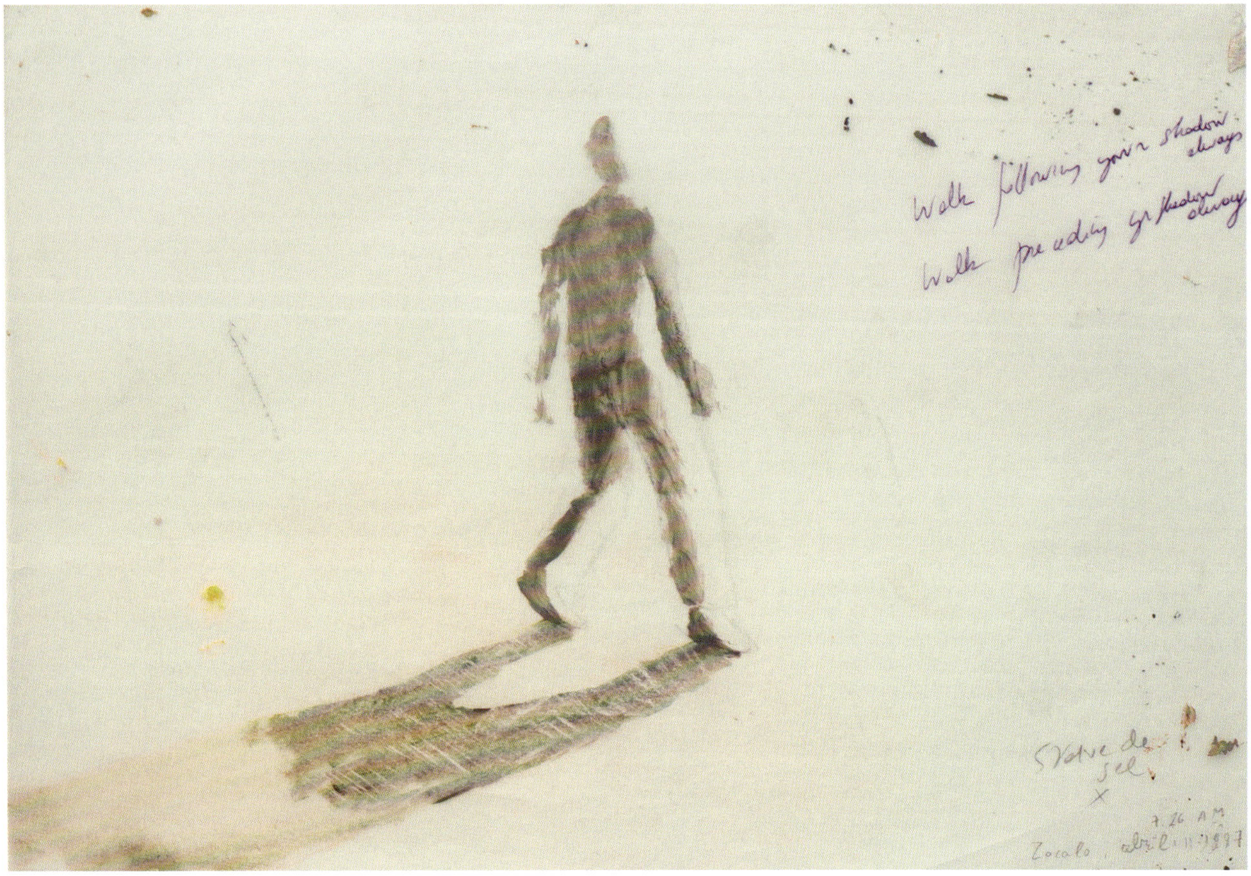

FERGUSON: *Certainly to attempt to re-enact that model is to participate in a kind of nostalgia or romanticism. Of course, at the time of Baudelaire the* flâneur *was the essence of modernity. 'It was a long time ago, but at the time it seemed like the present.'*

There is, even in the earliest conception of the flâneur, *a detachment from the city as well. The* flâneur, *modern or passé, is someone who observes the city but is never a participant in the action of the city. I think your walks, wherever they are, at least hold out the possibility of participant action that will have an effect – or, as you say, an echo – that will persist afterwards. Perhaps the true* flâneur *in your work is* The Ambassador, *Mr Peacock. He conducts a kind of* flânerie *around the gardens of Venice and is admired but does not participate in events. So perhaps Mr Peacock is your surrogate* flâneur.

ALŸS: Yes, absolutely. He could be a real nineteenth-century gentleman. [*laughs*] He should be doing this interview.

FERGUSON: *You have made other works in Venice.*

ALŸS: In June 1999 I did this sort of homage to Fluxus with a musical piece, a walk titled *Duett*. It was inspired by Plato's speech of Aristophanes, which in short is that it is in our nature to be incomplete, to be bisexual. I entered Venice by the train station, while a friend of mine, the Belgian artist Honoré d'O, arrived on the same day via Marco Polo Airport. We started wandering, looking for one another in the labyrinth of Venice, each of us carrying one half of a tuba, hoping that we would be led to one another. There was a simple dramatic construction to the piece, with A and B needing to find each other. Eventually, there was a happy ending, maybe even a moral to the story, with the physical reunion of the two halves and the resulting production of a sound.

RAILINGS, 2004
IN COLLABORATION WITH RAFAEL ORTEGA
AND ARTANGEL, LONDON
VIDEO DOCUMENTATION OF AN ACTION
6 MIN. 57 SEC.

Upon arriving in London, pick up a stick, run it along the architecture and listen to the music of the city.

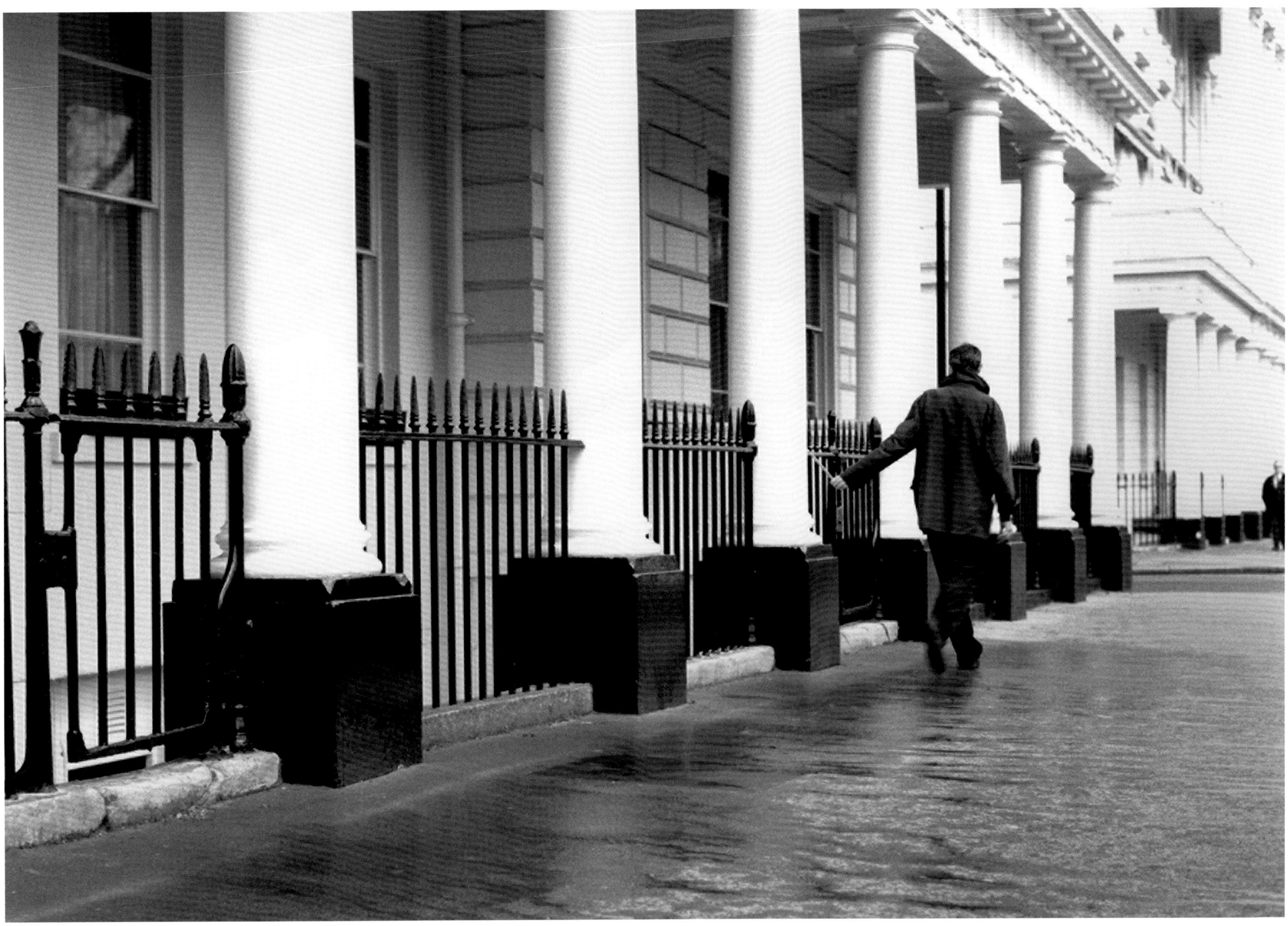

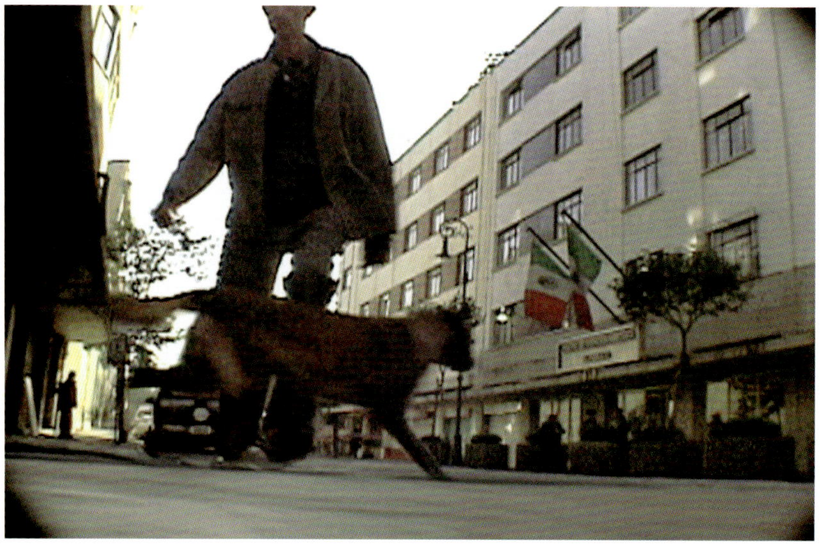

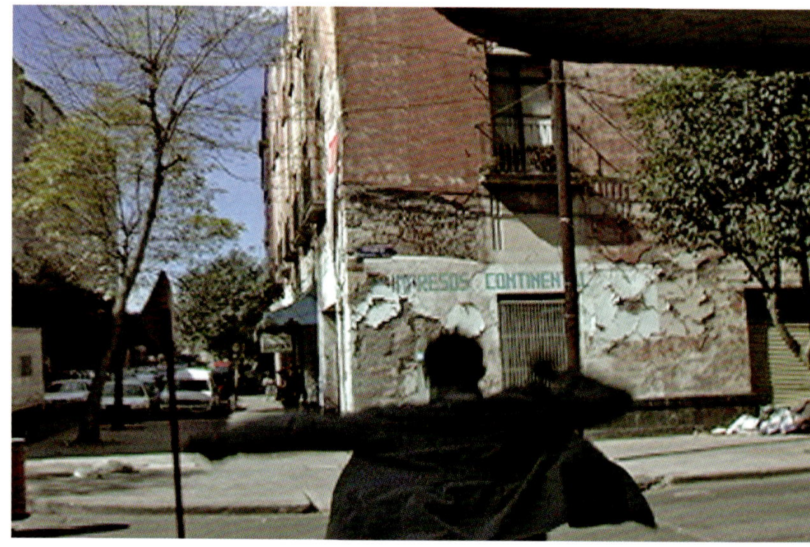

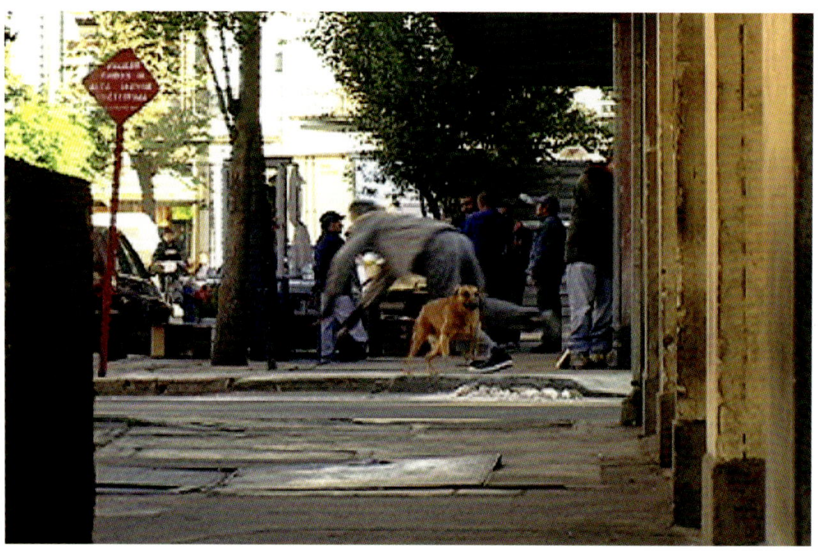

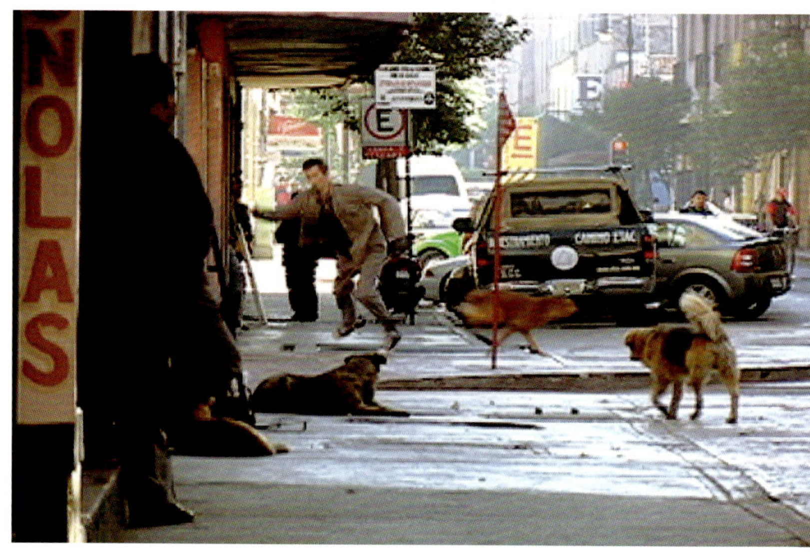
NOLAS

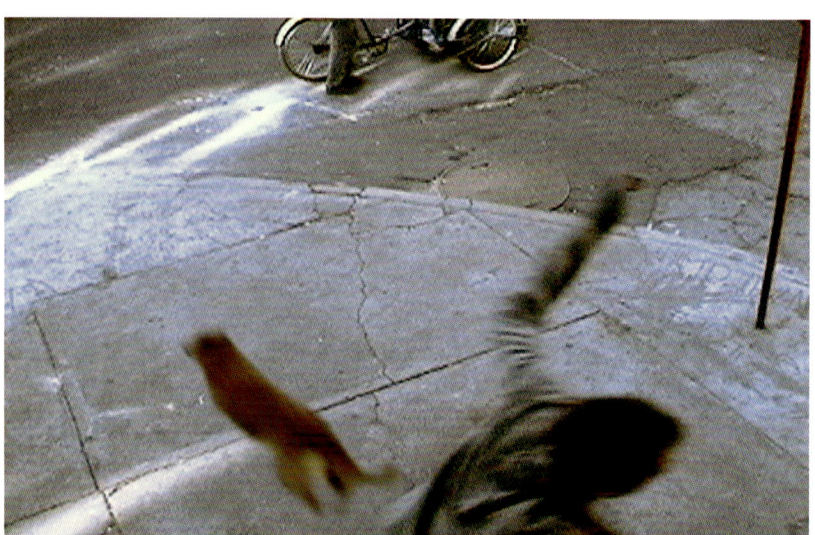

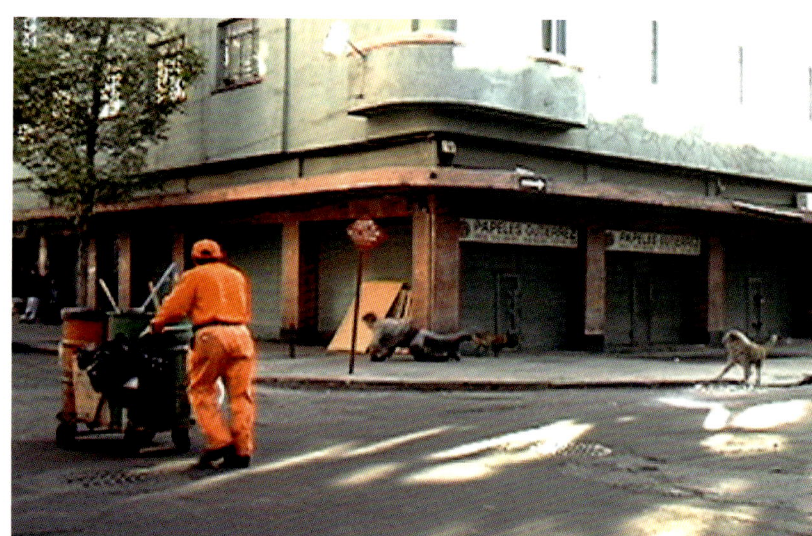

CHOQUES, 2005
MEXICO CITY
9-CHANNEL VIDEO

Nine hidden cameras record nine points of view of an accident on the corner of Calle del cincuenta y siete and Calle república de Cuba.

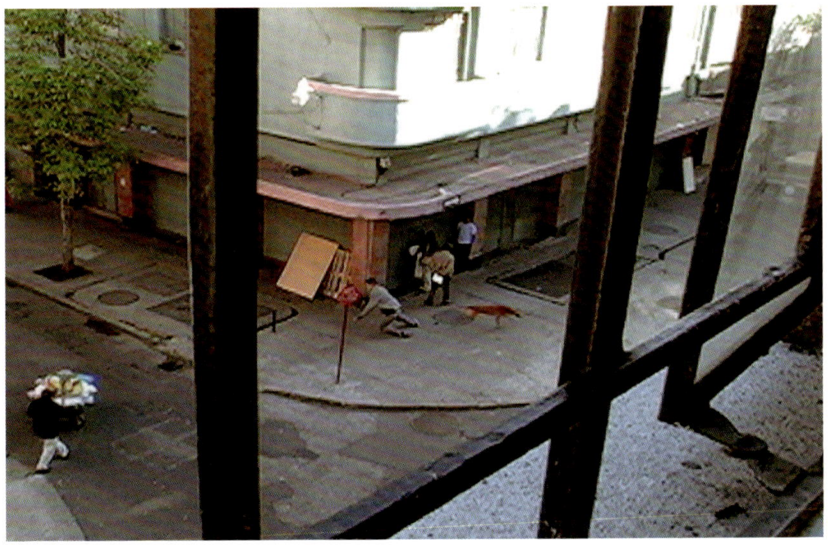

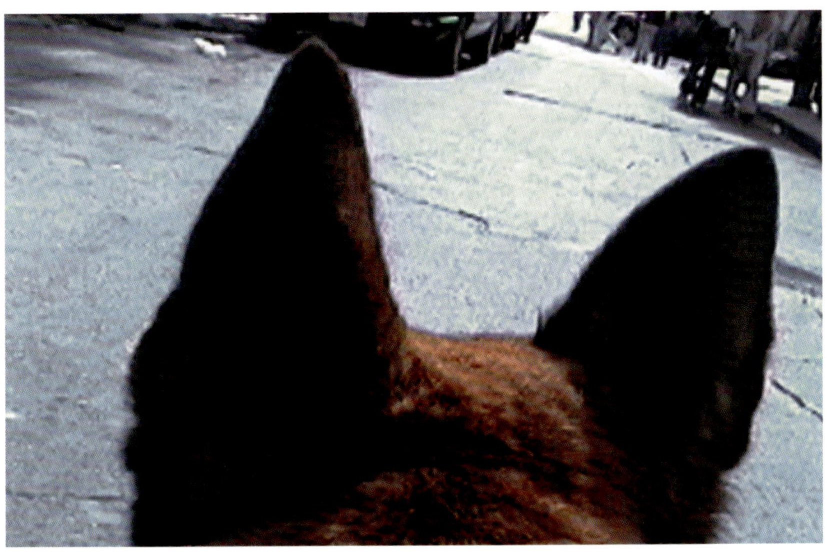

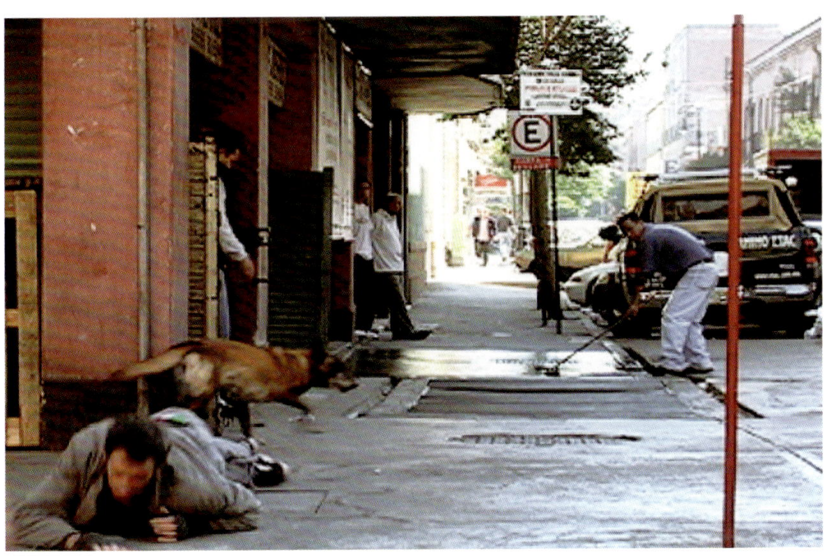

DUETT, 1999
IN COLLABORATION WITH
HONORÉ D'O
PHOTO DOCUMENTATION OF AN
ACTION, VENICE

(moderato)
A and B arrive at opposite ends of Venice. A is carrying the upper part of a tuba helicon. B is carrying the lower part.

(andante)
A and B wander through the city looking for each other.

(crescendo)
Upon meeting, A helps B re-assemble the tuba.

(vibrato)
With one breath B plays a note for as long as he can. A claps for as long as he can hold his breath.

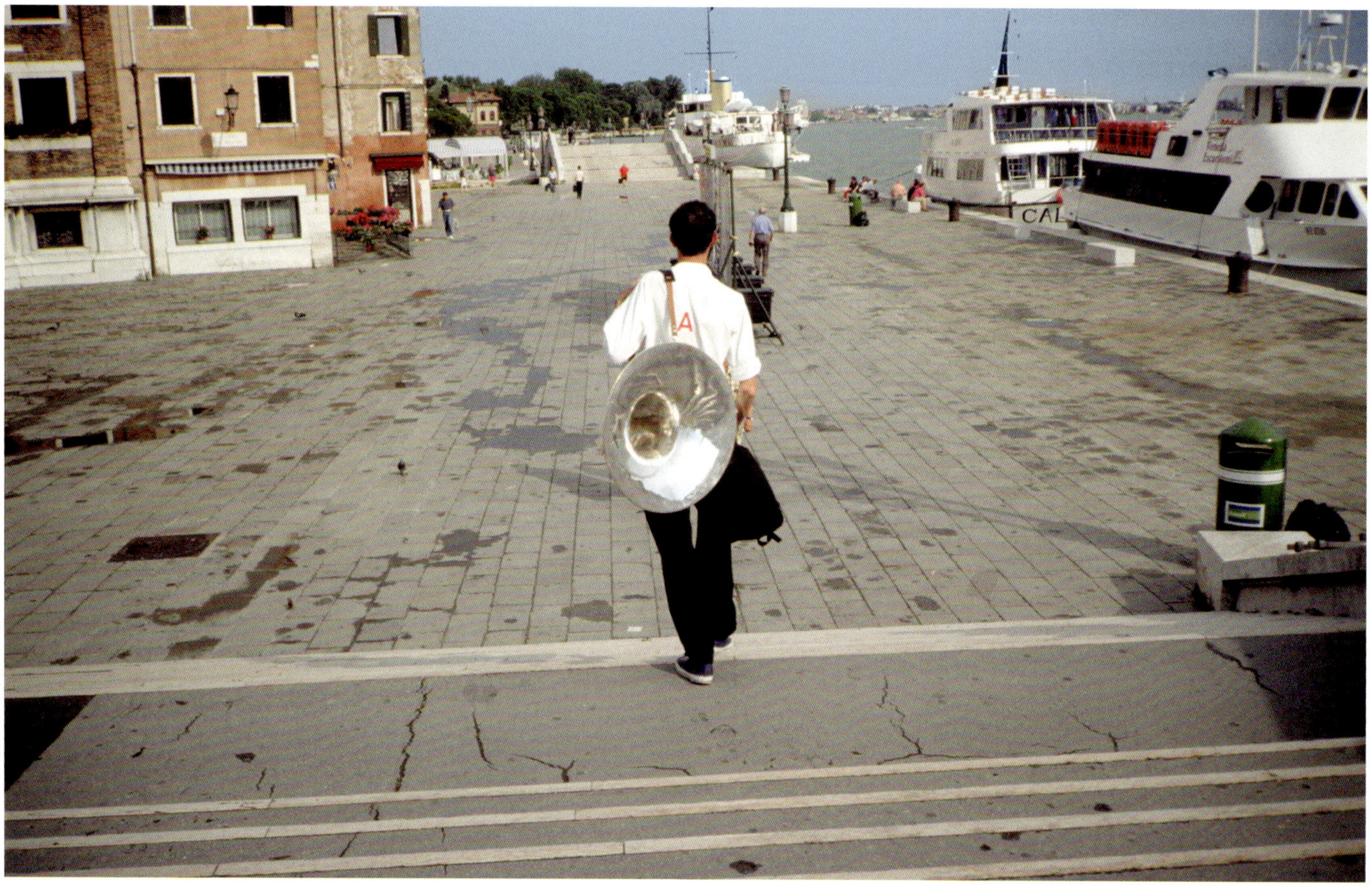

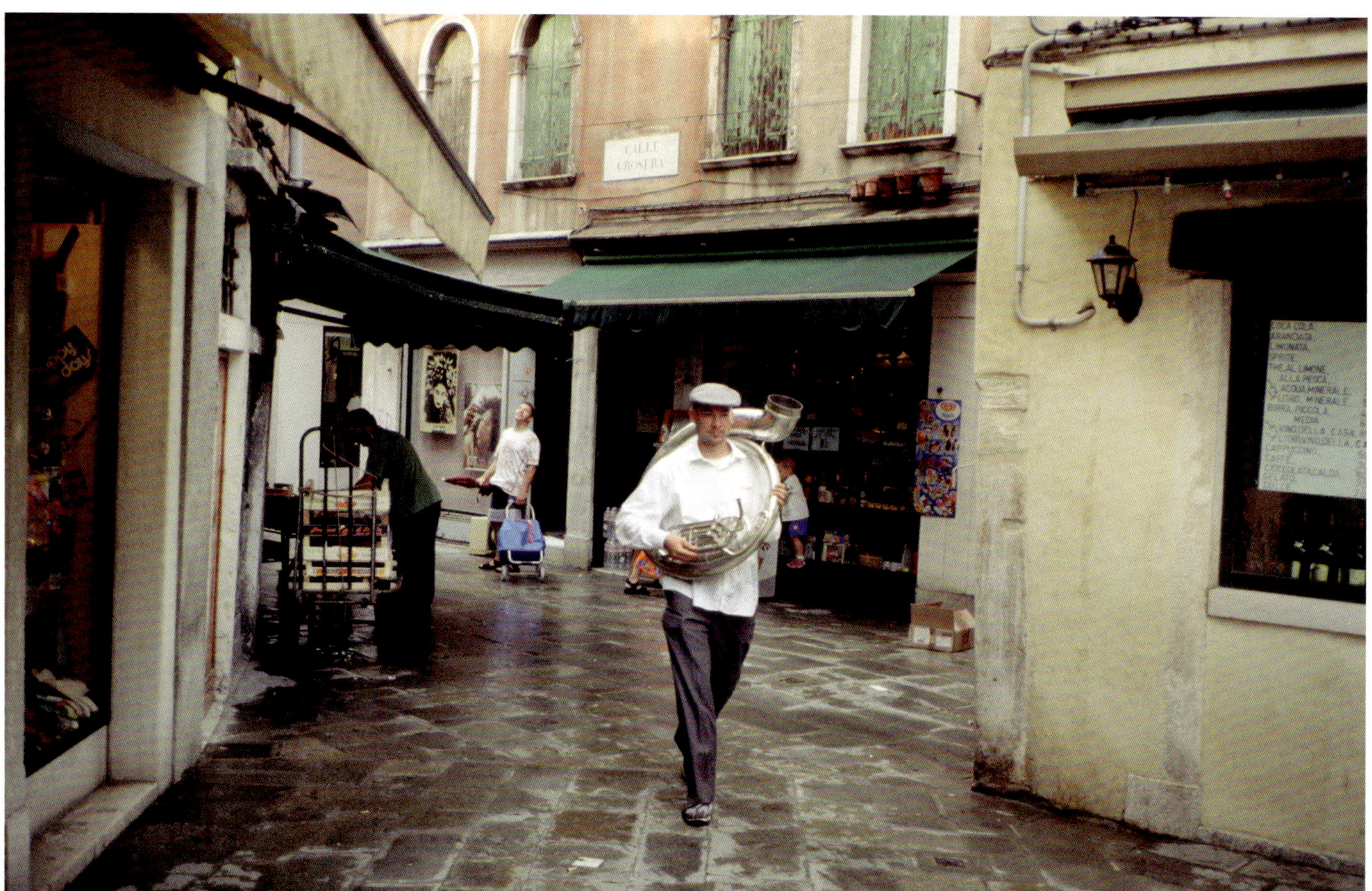

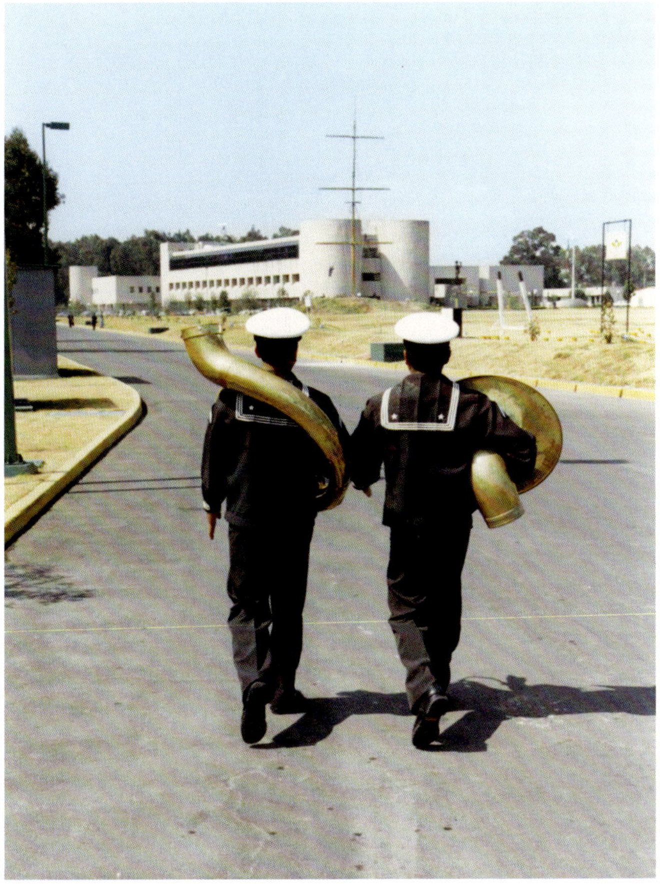

MEXICO CITY, 1992
COLOUR PHOTOGRAPH

In 2004 with the help of Artangel and Rafael Ortega I orchestrated an event in London based on similar mechanics but introducing a different dimension (*Guards*, 2004–05). I re-staged the plot with a regiment of sixty-four Coldstream Guards. Each soldier entered the City of London walking normally. When he heard the steps of another soldier he would join in, fall into step, and the two would start marching together. They would eventually meet another soldier or group of soldiers and repeat the same protocol, continuing until the full formation was complete. It was like the spreading of a rumour, but also the progressive building of a square, as the final figure to be formed by the full company was an eight-by-eight soldier square. You have to imagine the whole thing performed by this perfect machine of synchronization of a British regiment. In *Duett* when two people were looking for one another it had a kind of sexual dimension, but when the number of participants grew to sixty-four what had been a love story turned into a social allegory.

FERGUSON: *If we extrapolate from there, to what extent do you see your work playing an instrumental role in the political sphere? Do you think your art, or art in general, can produce change in the world?*

ALŸS: I wish. [*laughs*] Political could be read in the Greek sense of 'polis', the city as a site of sensations and conflicts from which the materials to create fictions or urban myths are extracted. I think being based in Mexico City, and functioning in Latin America, the political component is an obligatory ingredient to address the situation. But it would be very hard to say to what extent your act can have a real echo, and even more to what extent there is any relevance for a poetical act to take place in a location going through a political, military, religious, social or economic crisis.

Back in the summer of 1995 in São Paulo I performed a walk with a leaking can of paint (*The Leak*) that was described as a poetic gesture, a *beau-geste*. More recently, on the fourth and fifth of June 2004, I re-enacted that same performance by tracing a line through the city of Jerusalem (*The Green Line*). Whereas the original walk belonged more to what you called the drifting category, the second walk strictly followed the section of the Green Line that runs through the municipality of Jerusalem. By re-enacting the same action but now performing it in a completely different context, I was questioning the pertinence of an artistic intervention in a context of political, religious and military crisis.

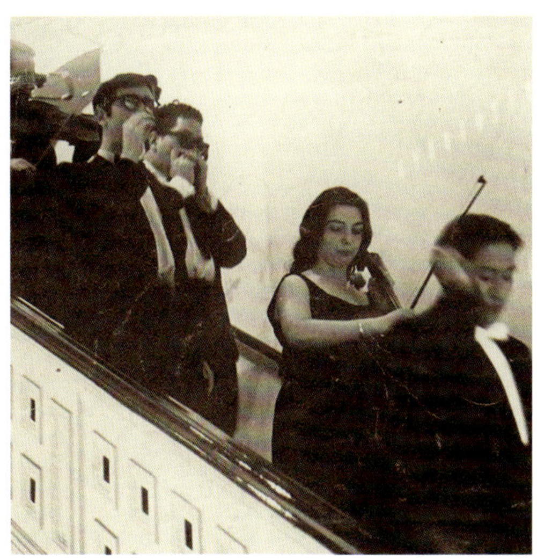

FLUXUS SYMPHONY ORCHESTRA PERFORMS PHILIP CORNER'S 4TH FINALE, CARNEGIE RECITAL HALL, NEW YORK, 27 JUNE 1964

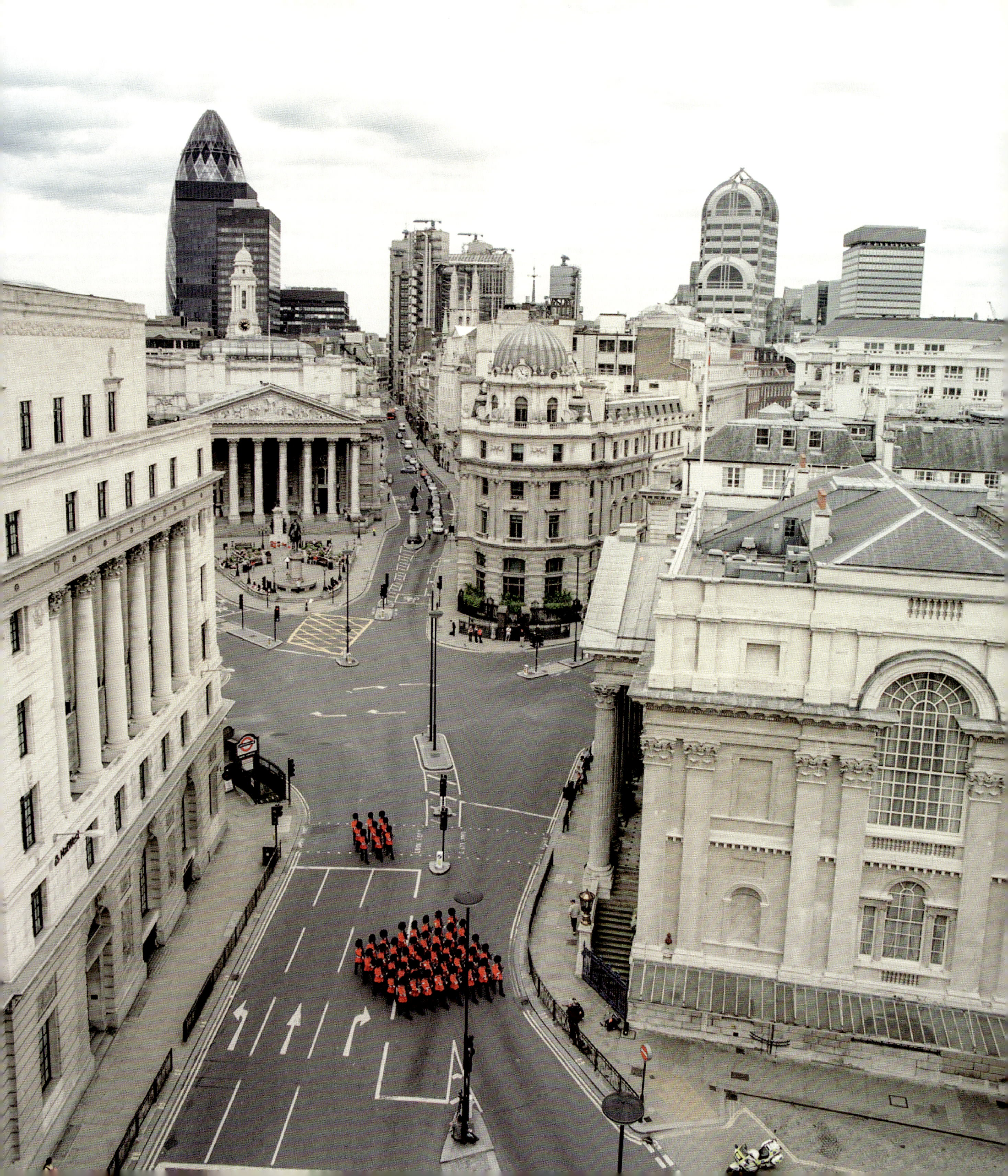

KNOTS, 2005
GRAPHITE AND INK ON PAPER
EACH 30 X 24 CM

previous page,
GUARDS, 2004–05
IN COLLABORATION WITH RAFAEL ORTEGA
AND ARTANGEL, LONDON
VIDEO DOCUMENTATION OF AN ACTION
30 MIN

Sixty-four Coldstream Guards walk separately in the City of London, entering through different streets and unaware of one another's route.

The guards wander through the City looking for one another.

Upon meeting, they fall into step and march together, looking for more guards to join up with.

When a square measuring eight by eight guards is built, the complete formation marches towards the closest bridge.

As they step on to the bridge, the guards break step and disperse.

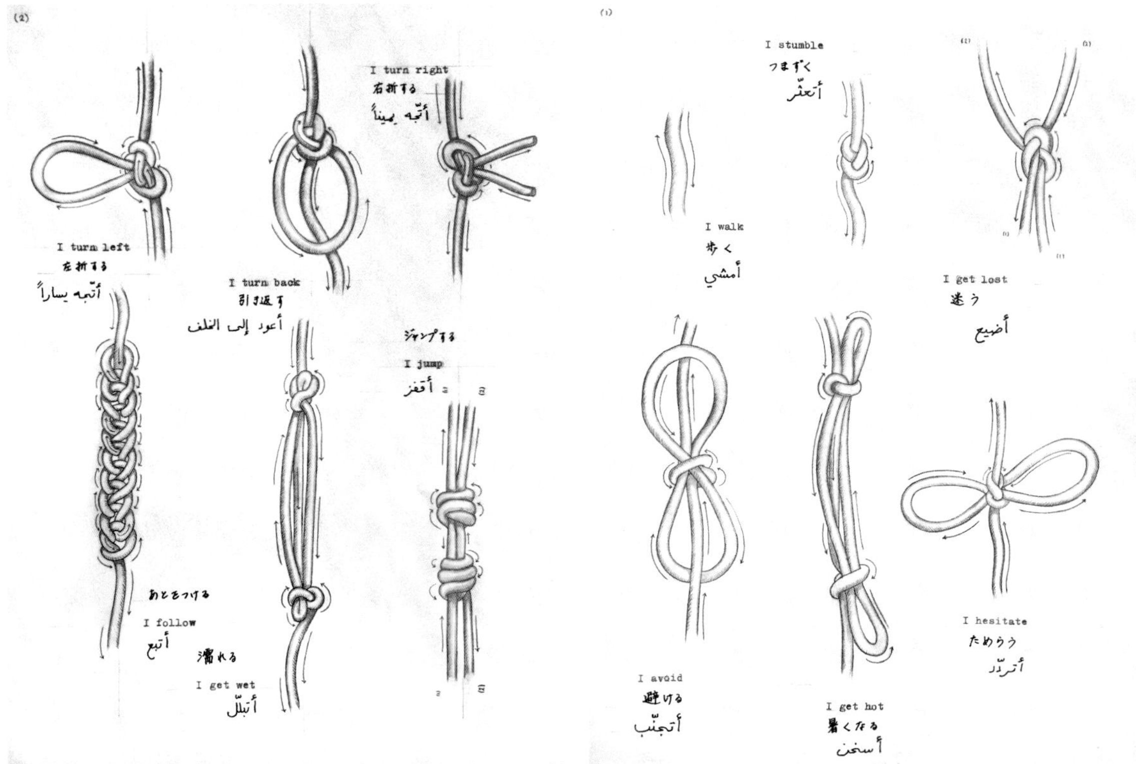

FERGUSON: *This question of what art can achieve in a politically charged context is a very complex question.*

ALŸS: Society allows, and maybe even expects, the artist – unlike, say, the journalist, the scientist, the scholar or the activist – to issue a statement without any demonstration. This is what we call 'poetic licence'. Fine. But this condition leads to a series of questions. Can an artistic intervention truly bring about an unforeseen way of thinking, or is it more a matter of creating a sensation of 'meaninglessness', one that shows the absurdity of the situation? And can an absurd act provoke a transgression that makes you abandon the standard assumptions about the sources of conflict? Can an artistic intervention translate social tensions into narratives that in turn intervene in the imaginary landscape of a place? And finally, can those kinds of artistic acts bring about the possibility of change? In any case, how can art remain politically significant without assuming a doctrinal standpoint or aspiring to become social activism?

FERGUSON: *In general with your work, even if it is an echo rather than a statement, do you see it in a broader sense as a kind of resistance to political power as it is currently constituted?*

ALŸS: Considering the present state of politics in a good part of the planet, yes absolutely.

FERGUSON: *A straight answer.* [laughs] *Are you aspiring to make something that is both poetical and political?*

ALŸS: In Jerusalem the axiom behind the walk was, 'Sometimes doing something poetic can become political and sometimes doing something political can become poetic.' I tried to confront a situation that I might have dealt with more obliquely in the past, like in Lima for example. I had reached a stage where I could no longer hide behind the ambiguity of metaphors or poetic licence. What I try to do really is to spread stories, to generate situations that can provoke through their experience a sudden unexpected distancing from the immediate situation and can shake up your assumptions about the way things are, that can destabilize and open up, for just an instant – in a flash – a different vision of the situation, as if from the inside.

THE GREEN LINE, 2004
VIDEO DOCUMENTATION
OF AN ACTION, JERUSALEM
17 MIN. 45 SEC.

Sometimes doing something poetic can become political, and sometimes doing something political can become poetic.

'During the months from December 1947 through June 1948, there was heavy fighting in Jerusalem and its immediate vicinity. The city was divided in two by the front lines. The statutory basis on which the partition of Jerusalem rested was the cease-fire agreement signed on 30 November 1948 between Moshe Dayan, "commander of all the Israeli forces in the Jerusalem region", and Abdullah al-Tal, "Representing the Arab Legion and all the other forces in the Jerusalem area". The lines were sketched on a mandatory 1:20,000 scale map. Moshe Dayan drew the Israeli line with a green grease pencil, while Abdullah al-Tal marked his front line with a red one.'

(Meron Benvenisti, City of Stone, University of California Press, Berkeley, 1996)

Poetic licence functions like a hiatus in the atrophy of a social, political, military or economic crisis. Through the gratuity or the absurdity of the poetic act, art provokes a moment of suspension of meaning, a brief sensation of senselessness that reveals the absurd of the situation and, through this act of transgression, makes you step back or step out and revise your prior assumptions about this reality. And when the poetic operation manages to provoke that sudden loss of self that itself allows a distancing from the immediate situation, then poetics might have the potential to open up a political thought.

FERGUSON: *There is a certain amount of repetition that is integral to your work. Certain motifs are repeated, and the whole idea of repetition itself is quite present. Is that a way of tying different storylines together or just of letting a particular storyline develop through time?*

ALŸS: I think that there is only so much one has to say.

FERGUSON: *What about* Re-enactments *(2000), in which a certain sequence of events are repeated?*

ALŸS: *Re-enactments* belongs more to the drifting category, although the scenario is very linear, following the seven steps of a classical dramatic construction. I think I was looking for a 'round' scenario, and the one in which I buy a gun and start walking down the street waiting for something to happen was likely to have all these steps: a context (the city), a protagonist (me), a cause for the conflict(I buy a gun), a conflict (I walk with the gun on the street), a response to the conflict (the reaction on the street), a climax (the arrest scene), and a moral (I am taken away by the police).

Retrospectively I think I made a fundamental mistake. Whereas I could have chosen a number of other scenarios, I got entangled in one that responded too well to the general expectation, the image of Mexico City that was exported at the time, with its ingredient of urban violence. And that last aspect seems to be the one that prevailed in the public's memory. I forgot a basic rule. When a work is produced within a very local context, it can easily acquire a totally different reading later, so the parameters for the piece need to take into account its possible life as an export. I had a similar problem with the sign-painting project. It was often reduced to an exotic exercise of style, conveniently bypassing the market proposal I had projected.

More than anything I was looking for an action whose dramatic construction could be easily re-enacted, which is what occurred, since the next day the exact same action was filmed again, but this time with everything pre-arranged. The people on the street were warned. The police were accomplices and even played themselves. Everything was staged. The idea was to juxtapose two films, each presenting an identical action, except that

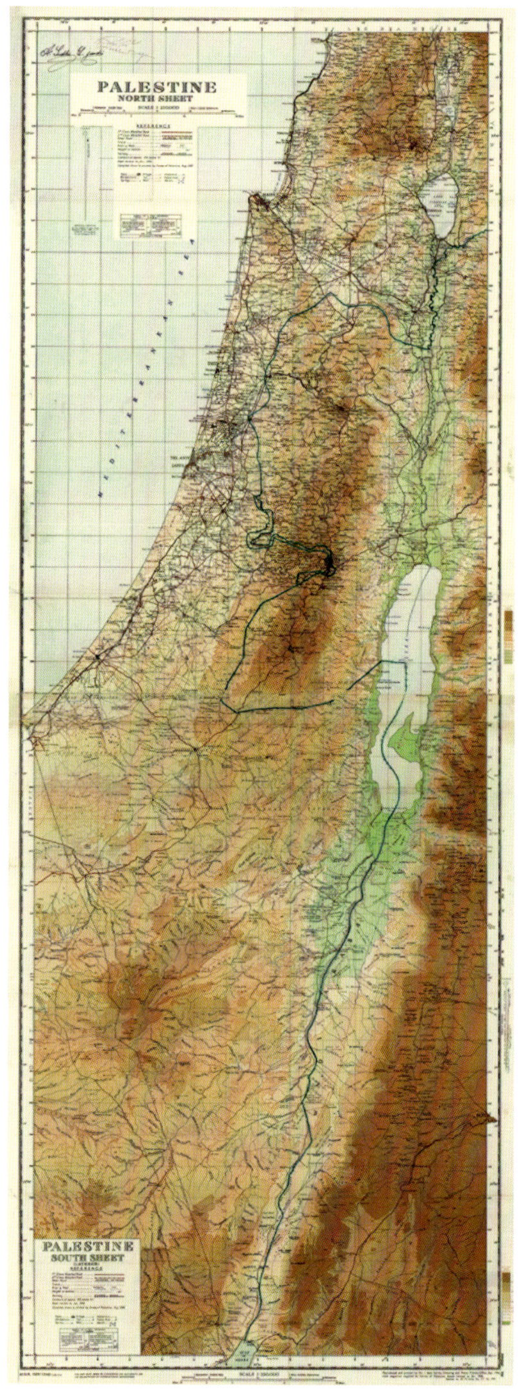

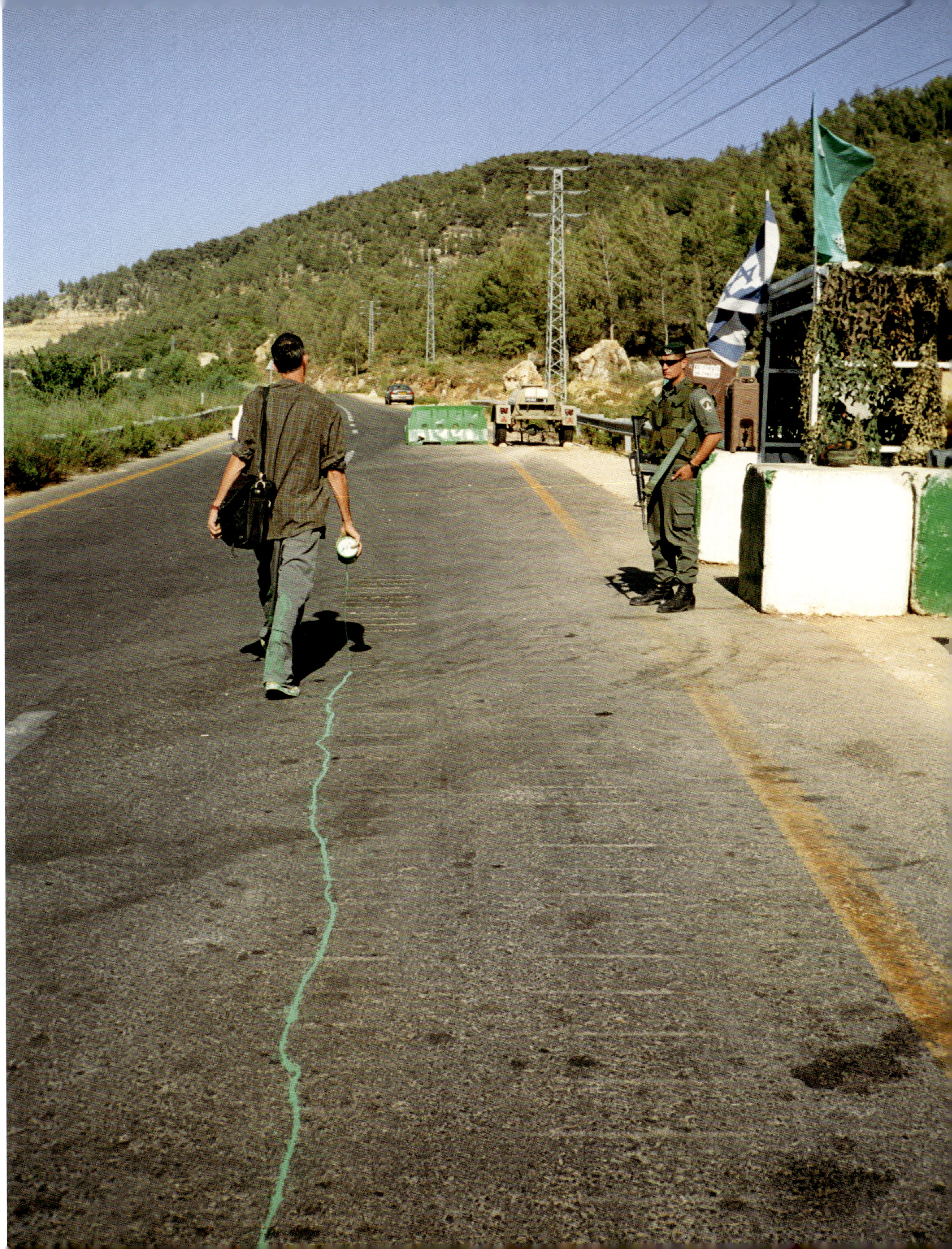

one would be the documentary of a real event, of 'the way it happened', and the other would be a scrupulous re-creation of the course of events as they appeared in the first film, thereby fictionalizing the reality of those events. I wanted to question the rapport we have today with performance and the ways in which it has become so mediated, particularly by film and photo, and how media can distort and dramatize the immediate reality of the moment, how they can affect both the planning and the subsequent reading of a performance. What is supposed to be so unique about performance is its underlying condition of immediacy, the imminent sense of risk and failure. At the time I needed to re-address my relationship to that medium.

FERGUSON: *That was echoed in an institutional way with* The Modern Procession *(2002), to mark the Museum of Modern Art's temporary move to Queens. In the end the Public Art Fund commissioned the procession, and the Museum of Modern Art commissioned the film of the procession, insisting on the distinction between the event and the record of it in a way that, to outsiders, might seem arbitrary.*

ALŸS: Yes. It was the necessary legal trick to make it all happen.

FERGUSON: *Do you see the possibility of a further move into the realm of the cinematic, where you could pursue a more complete story, rather than a fragment or an iconic image that functions as an echo. Is that a possibility for you in the future?*

ALŸS: It is tempting, of course, although I rarely deal with more than one idea per work, one situation at a time. In that sense, paradoxically, I am not a storyteller. Except if you look at a story as a succession of episodes. But if I were to make what you call a 'more complete story', a feature film, I would not start at the beginning or the end. I would need to work from some middle, because the middle point, the in between, is the space where I function best.

FERGUSON: *My understanding of the initial development of the* rotulista *work was that the cycle back and forth between you and the sign painters could potentially have continued endlessly with changes introduced by you or by them in each round.*

ALŸS: Like a visual version of Chinese whispers. But I think we were also trying to propose an alternative system to the market, one where we could impose our own rules.

FERGUSON: *Was there an element of making each one different so that it could carry a higher price, as a unique object?*

ALŸS: Yes and no. Yes, each of them was unique. Yet they all belonged to various series, as they were all referring to a similar model, so they depended on one another. It was their grouping or proximity that made them exist. As for their price, the fact that we were – and still are, for sure – maintaining copyrights on each image, allowed us to maintain a low market value, one that went against the idea of the unique and the rare – hence expensive – 'original' product. Retrospectively it was a naïve attempt to challenge the rules of the market, as recent resale prices in auction houses of some of these paintings have demonstrated, but for a moment it functioned. In the space of three years we produced a massive number of paintings, invading the market if you will, saturating the demand, which allowed us of course to maintain low prices but also to make a decent living out of it. Incidentally, the project acquired an unexpected documentary dimension. Over the last decade the sign-painting tradition has nearly disappeared. It has been driven out by computer-generated signage.

FERGUSON: *To me Mexico City still seems to have an enormous amount of hand-painted signage everywhere, compared to the United States at least.*

RE-ENACTMENTS, 2000
IN COLLABORATION WITH RAFAEL ORTEGA, MEXICO CITY
TWO-CHANNEL VIDEO
5 MIN. 20 SEC.

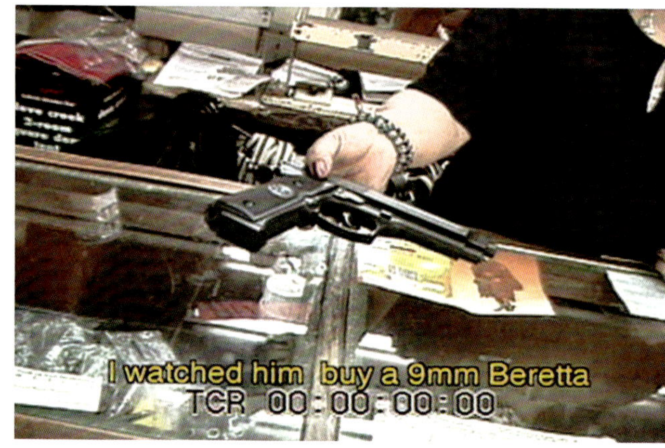

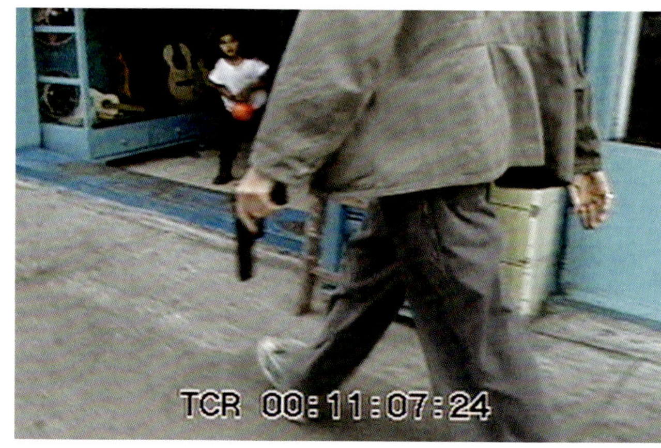

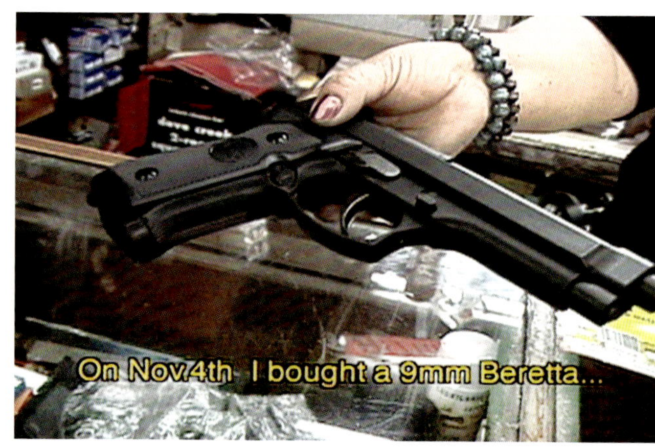

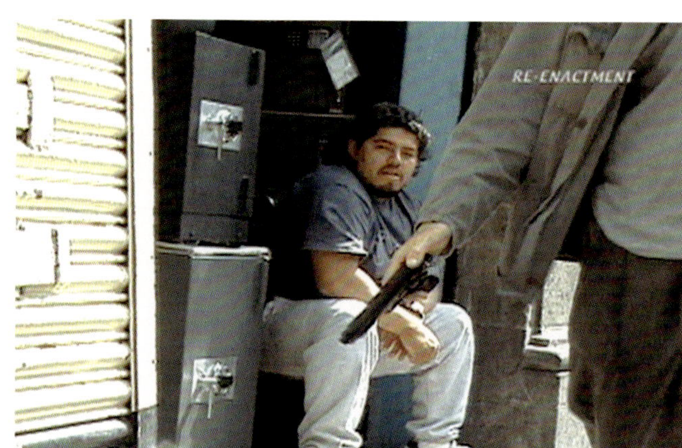

Real (left projection):
On 4 November Francis asked me to meet him downtown in a gun shop on Calle de Palma. I watched him buy a 9 mm Beretta, load it and leave the shop holding the gun in his right hand. I trailed him with my Sony Handycam and filmed the following scenes. (Rafael Ortega)

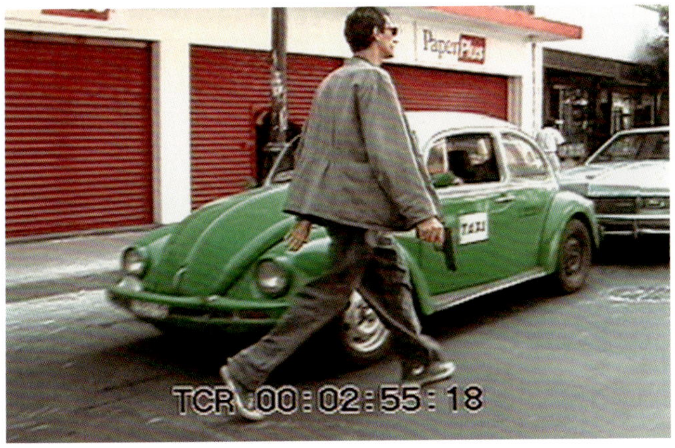

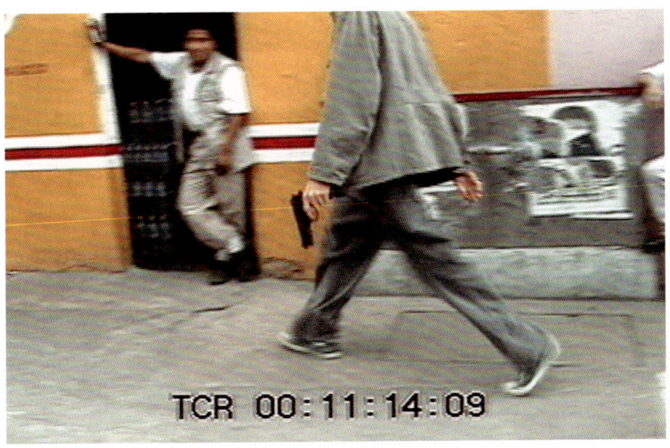

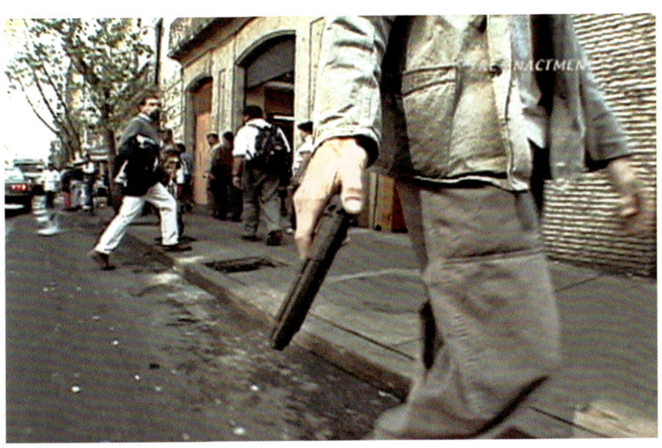

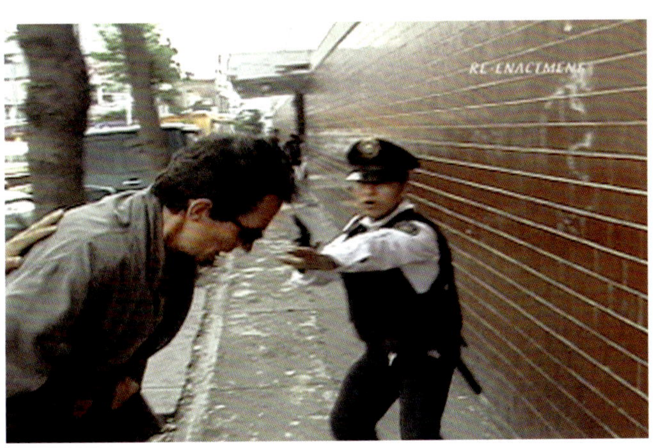

Re-enactment (right projection):
On 4 November I bought a 9 mm Beretta in a gun shop on Calle de Palma. At ten past one I left the shop holding the loaded gun in my right hand and started wandering downtown waiting for something to happen.

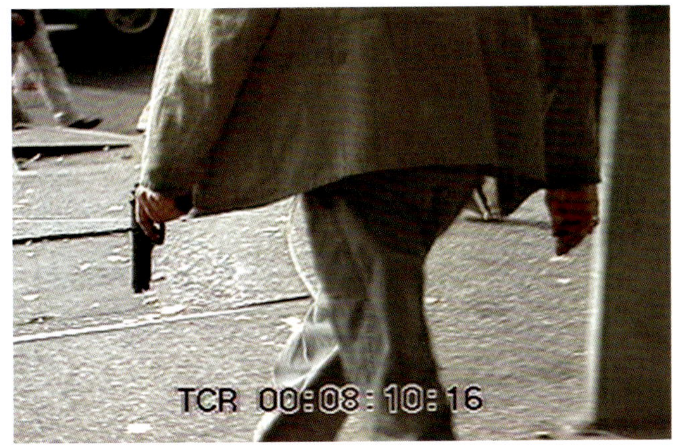

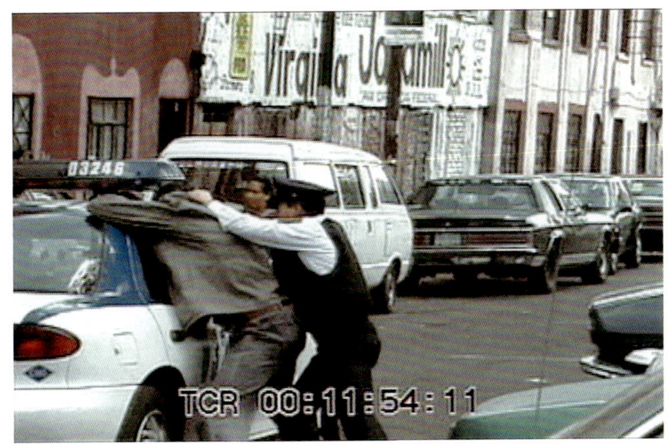

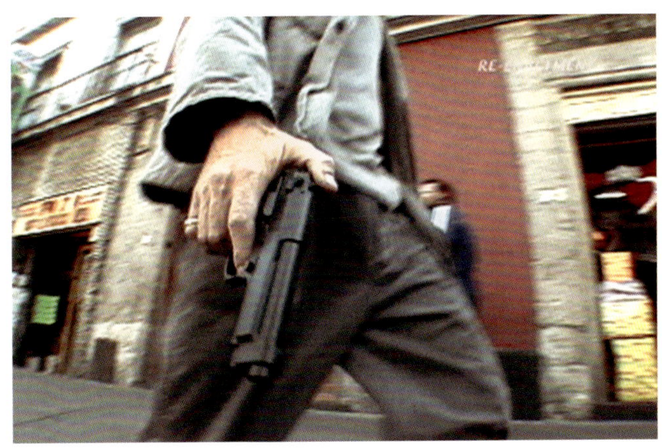

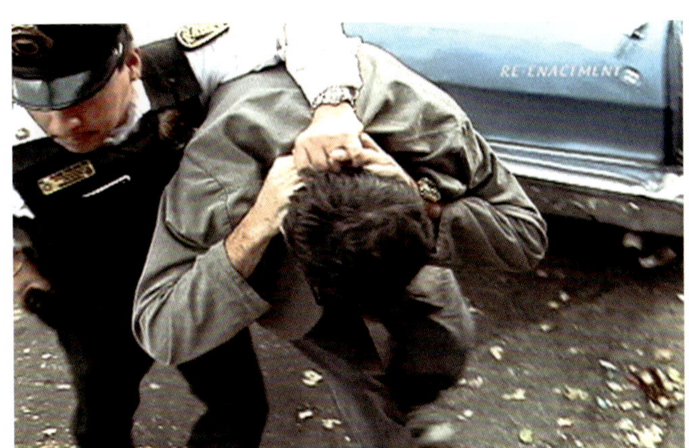

THE MODERN PROCESSION, 2002
IN COLLABORATION WITH RAFAEL ORTEGA, THE PUBLIC ART FUND AND THE MUSEUM OF MODERN ART, NEW YORK
VIDEO DOCUMENTATION OF AN EVENT
7 MIN. 22 SEC.

The Modern Procession announced the temporary move of the Museum of Modern Art from Manhattan to Queens, and celebrated the entry of its permanent collection into the periphery. The pilgrimage took the guise of a traditional procession. A selection of MoMA's masterpieces were carried on palanquins, a Peruvian brass band set the pace of the journey, and rose petals were strewn along the way while fireworks rose at street corners.

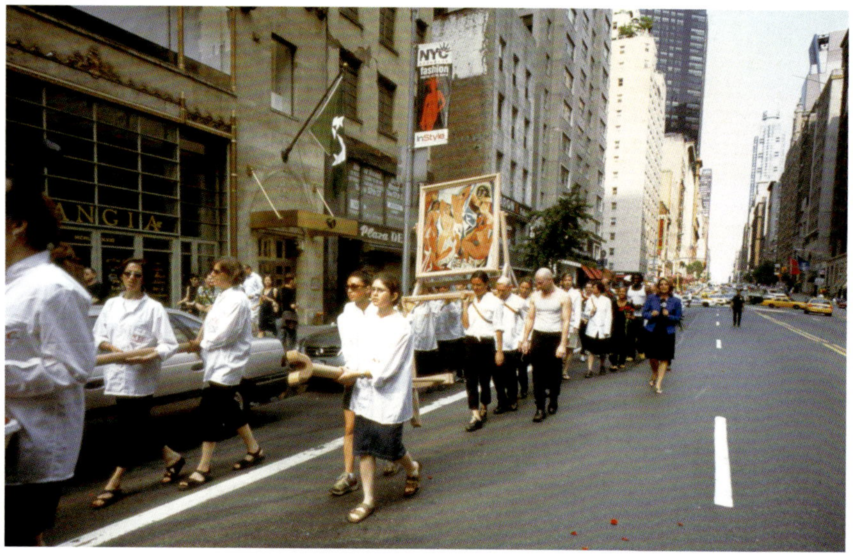

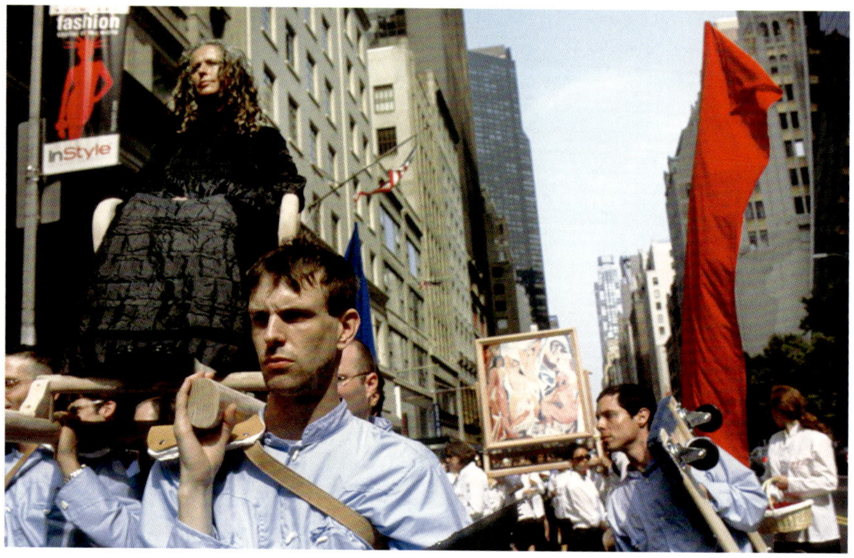

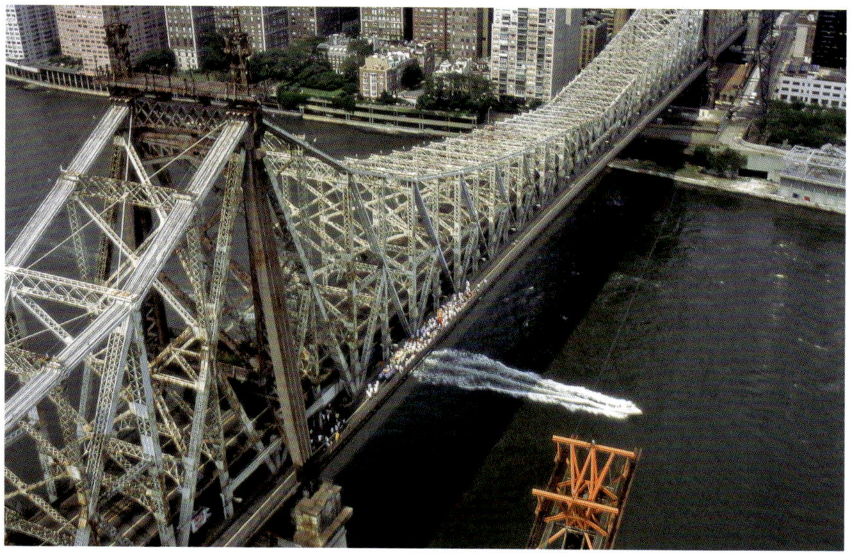

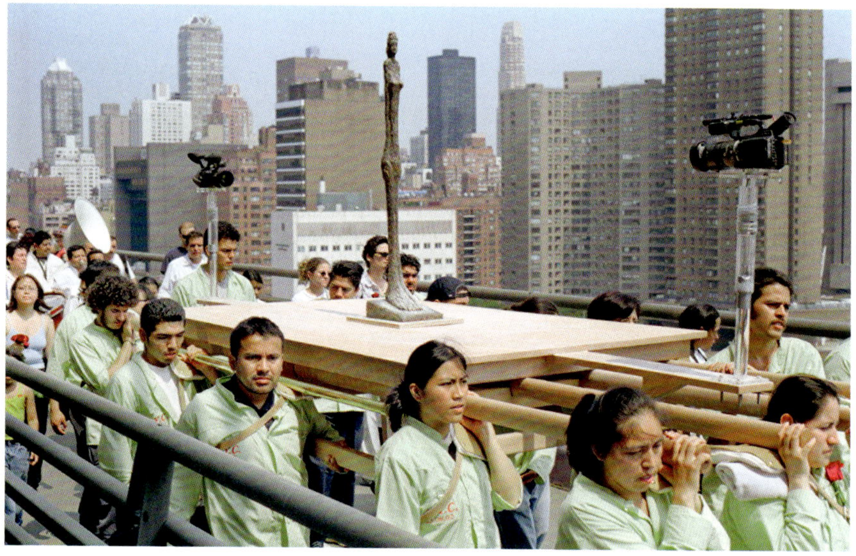

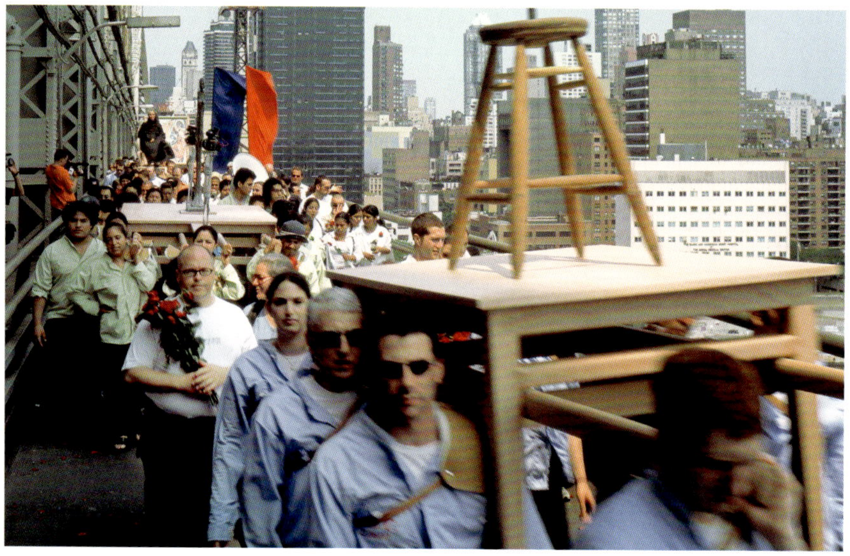

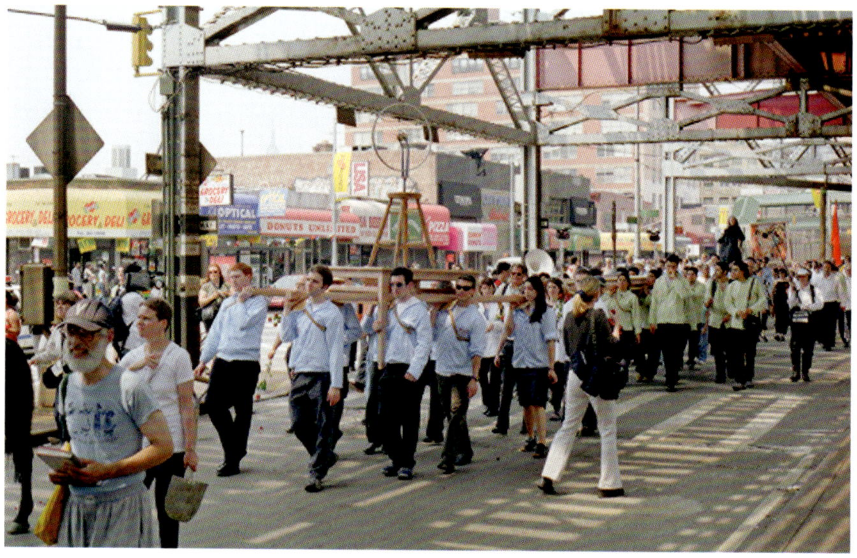

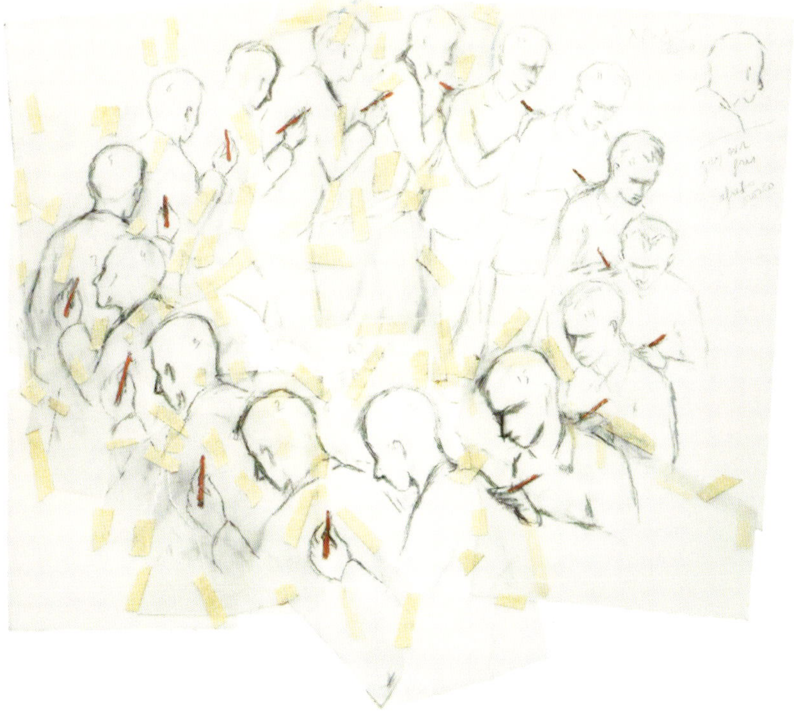

UNTITLED (STUDY FOR LA RONDE), 2002
PENCIL ON TRACING PAPER
42 X 46 CM

ALŸS: What really disappeared are its figurative elements. The signs are more text-based now. But then that could have a positive reading. It could mean that in the last couple of decades the literacy rate has increased enough that the figurative ingredients are no longer indispensable.

FERGUSON: *But in terms of repetition more broadly, not just vis-à-vis the sign painters, you have an ongoing interest in the idea of rehearsal. One of the key elements in a rehearsal is repeating something until you can do it properly. So there is a strong repetitive element in the idea of rehearsal as well.*

ALŸS: Yes, but it was another dimension that interested me, the way in which through repetition the narration could be indefinitely delayed, recalling the Latin American scenario in which modernity is always delayed. The recourse to the mechanics of rehearsal was more a method to physically render this constant postponement, the avoidance of the conclusion.

Sound and rhythm also have been key tools in that process, as a means to destabilize the perception of time, a way of diluting time. In animation you learn that true synchronization of sound and image is virtually impossible. An audio accent takes four frames, whereas a visual accent happens in just one frame. So in film you can only suggest the illusion of synchrony.

Again, the *Rehearsal* films are part of a more extended narrative, Latin America's ambiguous relationship to the concept of production and the dogma of efficiency. That investigation really started in the mid-1990s with the piece in which I pushed a block of ice during an entire day through the streets of Mexico City until it melted completely. It framed the debate by questioning the imminent contract of production: sometimes making something leads to nothing.

In the *Rehearsals* series there is a progression in the argument. In *Rehearsal 1* (1999–2001) the action is quite hypnotic, with the little VW going up and down the hill like a pendulum. After a while, the attention shifts form the finality of the action to the act itself, something I had played with already in the animation *Song for Lupita*.

RELIGIOUS PROCESSION
IN TEPOZTLÁN, MORELOS,
MEXICO, 2000

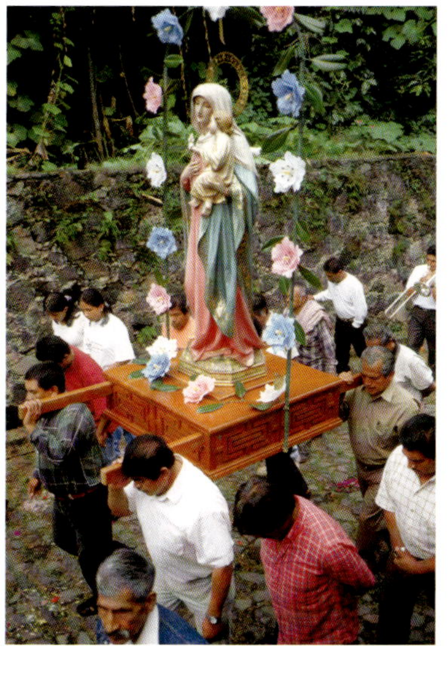

In *Rehearsal 2* (2001–06) we have a scenario in which the development of a mechanics – such as two steps forward, three steps back, four steps forward, three steps back – and in which, although the progression is not linear and occurs in a different temporality, there is some kind of progress at the end of the day. It's just a different pace. Postponement or delaying does not mean stagnation. There is always a progression, but through a different mode.

FERGUSON: *Because it is something that nominally has a beginning and an end, if you keep starting it and stopping it again, the beginning and the end become part of a bigger process or story.*

ALŸS: Yes. You end up within this middle sphere. This aspiration to something that cannot be defined can also become a sphere for a society to function, a way of resisting an imported concept of progress. It's a story of struggle more than one of achievement, an allegory of process more than of synthesis.

FERGUSON: *I wonder how much repeating something prevents its resolution or its conclusion. How does that relate to a project such as* When Faith Moves Mountains

PARADOX OF PRAXIS 1, 1997
PHOTO DOCUMENTATION OF AN ACTION, MEXICO CITY
VIDEO
5 MIN.

Sometimes doing something leads to nothing.

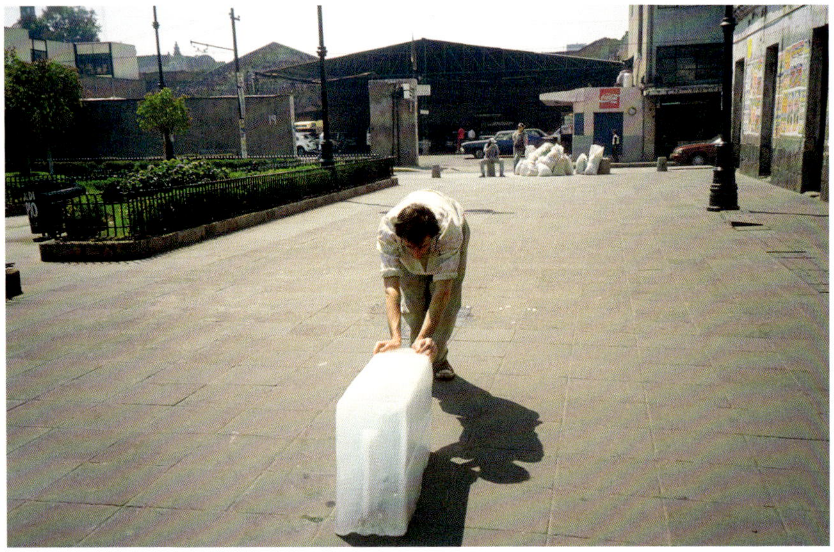

9:15 A.M.

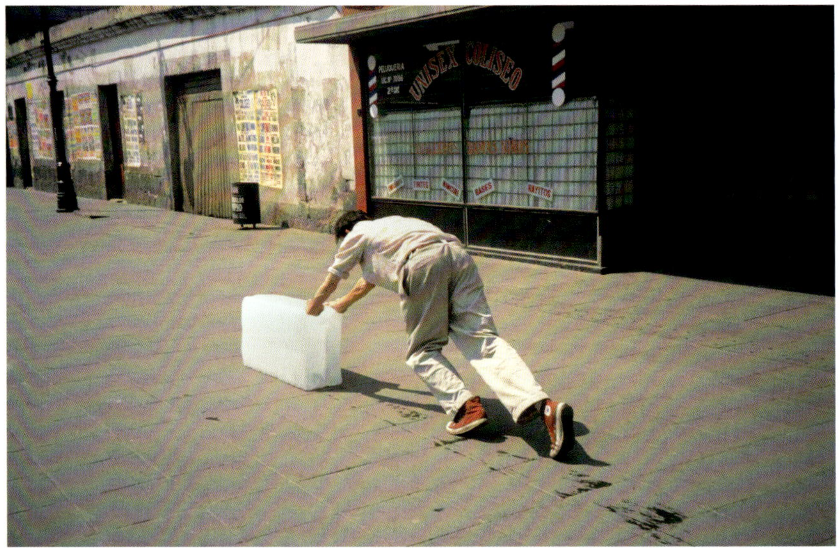

9:34 A.M.

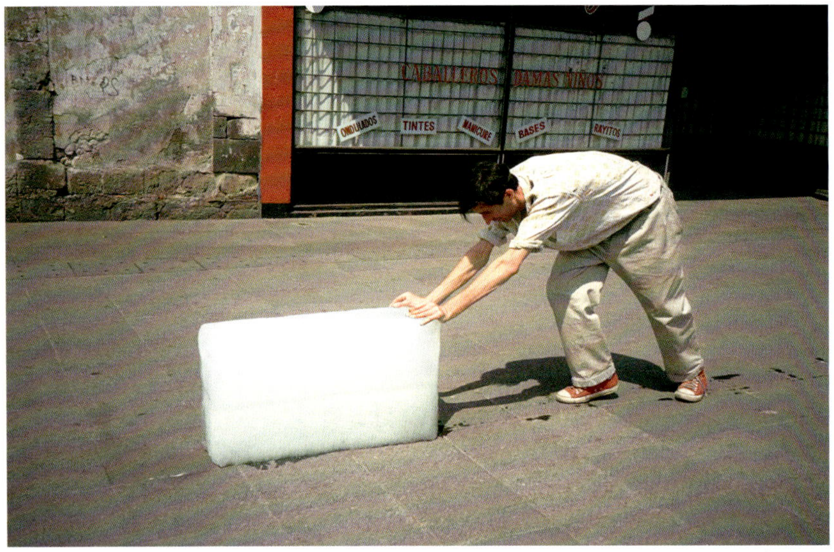

9:35 A.M.

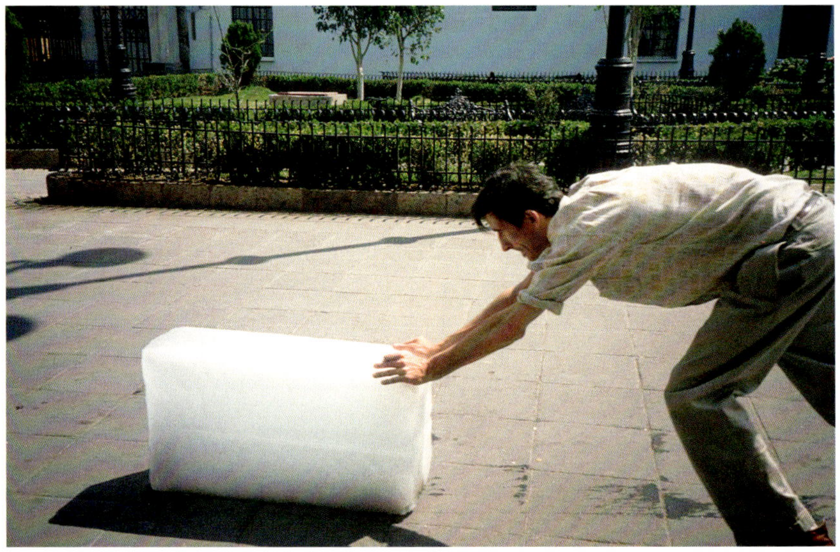

12:05 A.M.

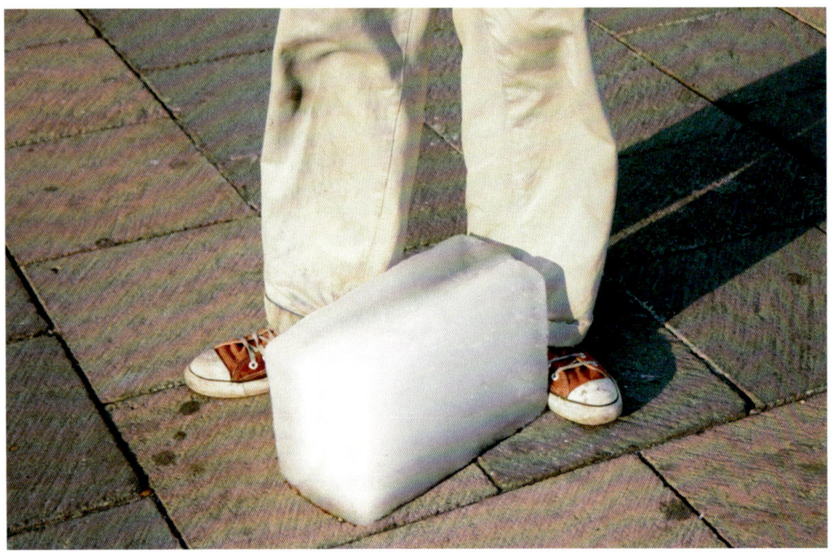

3:10 P.M.

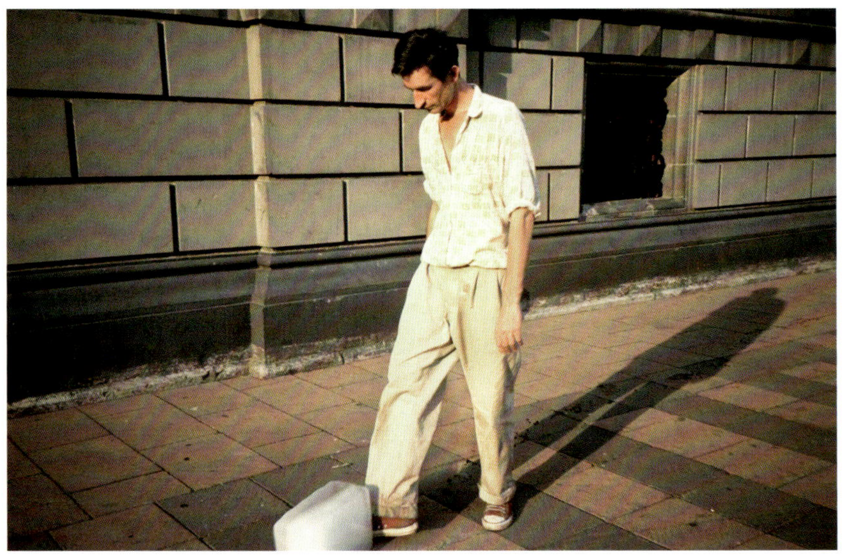

3:30 P.M.

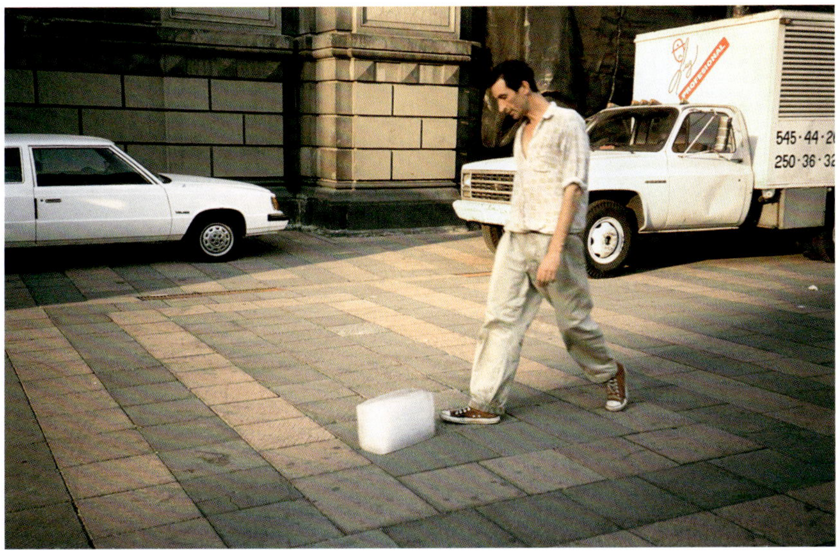

3:34 P.M.

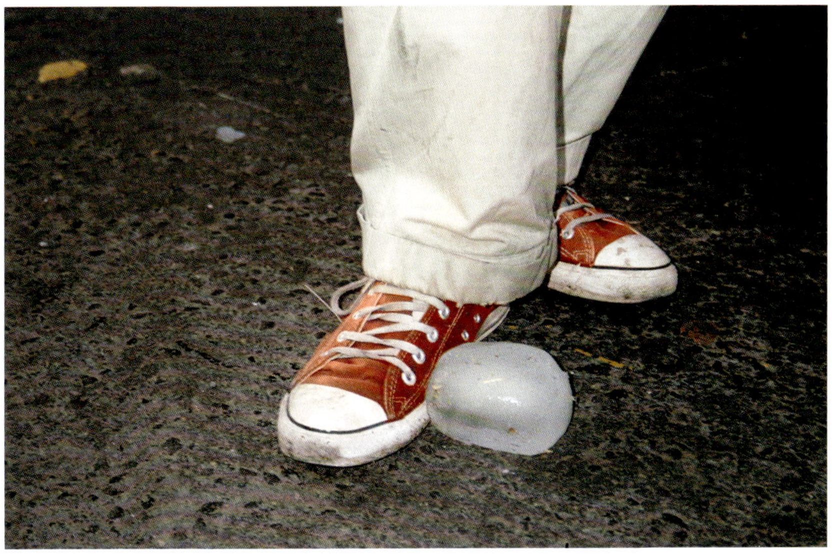

5:15 P.M.

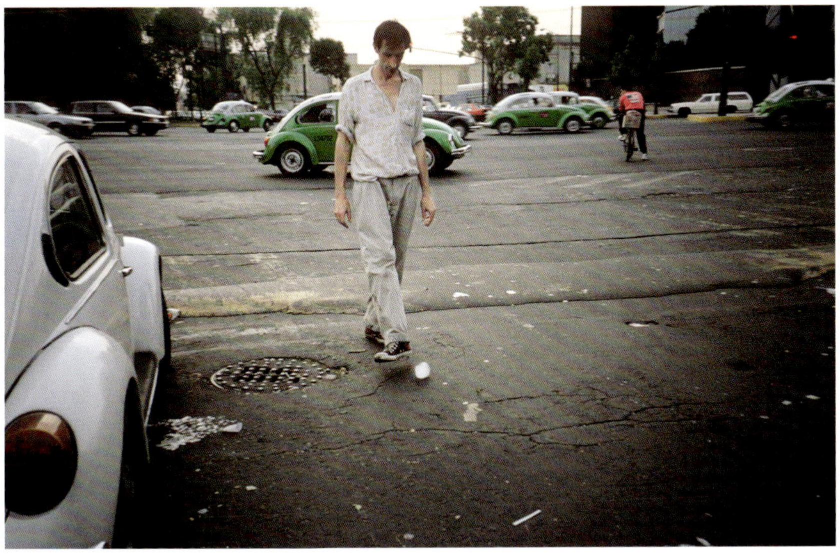

5:45 P.M.

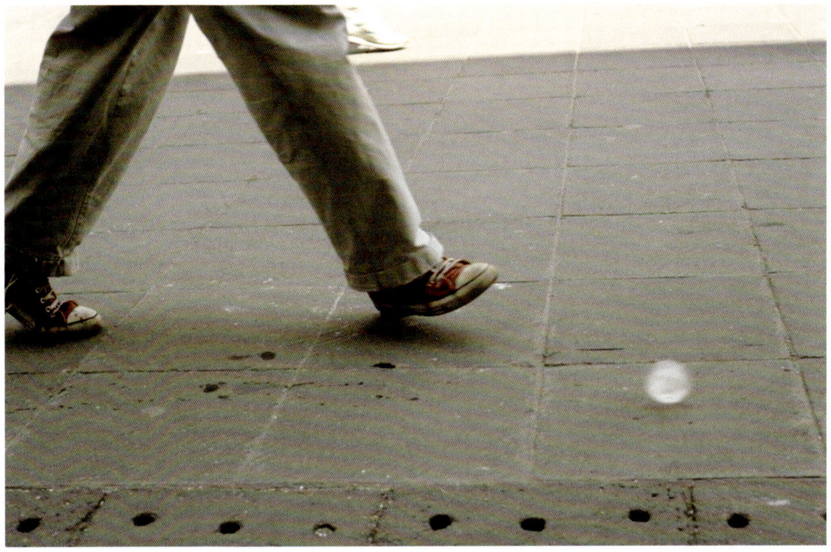

6:05 P.M.

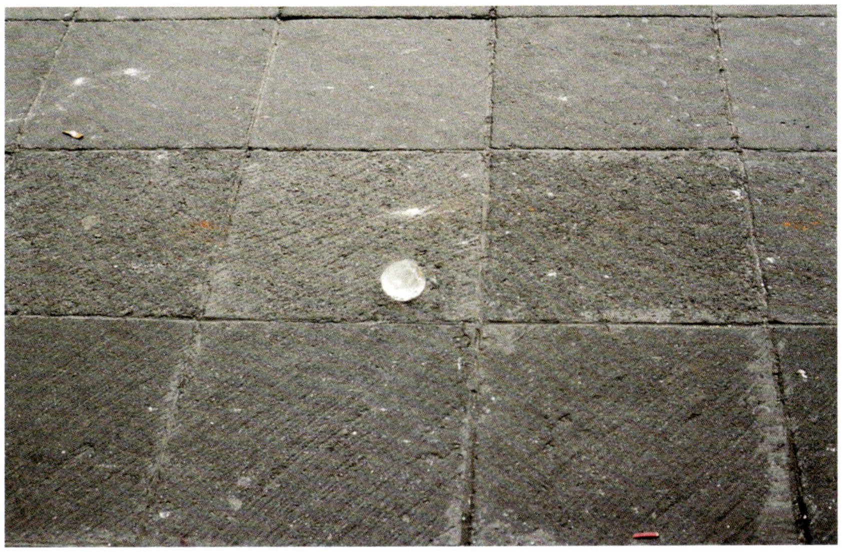

6:32 P.M.

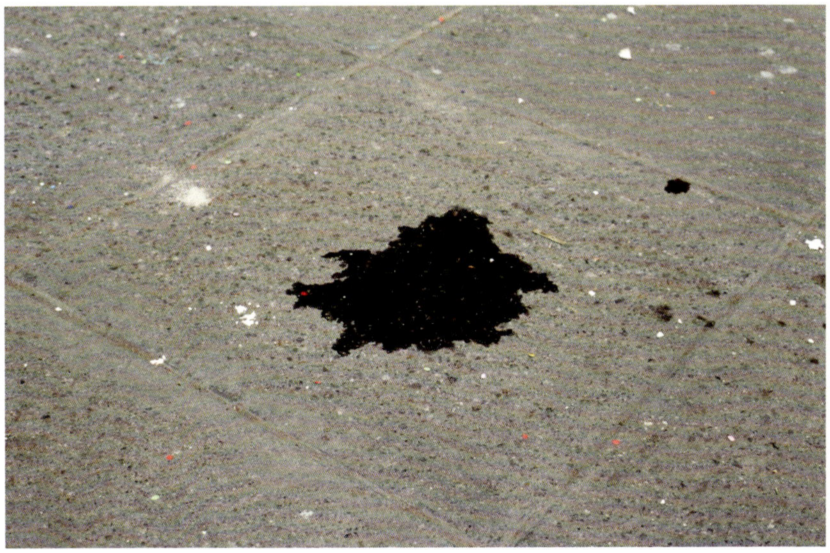

6:47 P.M.

(2002), where there is an almost ridiculous, endless amount of work, but something was actually achieved, in that this giant sand dune mountain really was moved a few inches in one direction. On the other hand there is an inherent futility in the gigantic amount of labour it took to achieve that result. Do you see a connection between that piece and the idea of rehearsal and repetition?

ALŸS: The motto of *When Faith Moves Mountains* is 'maximum effort, minimum result' – simultaneously stating the ridiculous disproportion between an effort and its effect, referring to a society in which minimal reforms are achieved through massive collective efforts. But the action also wants to suggest an alternative to imported models of development, to modernity's concept of linear progress.

Speaking of *When Faith Moves Mountains*, I always found it quite ironic that some people criticized the project for its gratuitousness, when voluntary collaboration was the *sine qua non* condition of the action. I suppose nowadays political correctness has moved on to economic correctness. But more to the point, I think today it's difficult to pass on an attitude that doesn't conform with the climate of scepticism or systematic criticism, an attitude that's more optimistic or even naïvely utopian. Words like 'change', 'faith', or 'bridge', when they are not coming out of the mouth of politicians or evangelical preachers, seem somehow out of place.

FERGUSON: *The idea of maximum effort and minimum result reminds me of* The Loop *(1997), in which you travelled from Tijuana to San Diego, basically by circumnavigating the globe, looping around the entire perimeter of the Pacific Ocean. You only had to go a few miles, maybe only a few metres, but you travelled tens of thousands of miles. The essence of a loop is that it can be repeated – you could go round again, even if in this case you probably would not want to. Equally, in Lima they could presumably move the sand dune another few inches, or even move it back.*

ALŸS: As the action of the wind constantly does to sand dunes.

FERGUSON: *In a way it is also like the myth of Sisyphus, this desire to keep pushing the boulder up the hill.*

ALŸS: Apparently, yes, but, unlike in the Sisyphus myth, which is utterly fatalistic and doomed to repeat itself, there is a element of redemption involved here, a progress of sorts – even if it is different from the Western linear understanding of progress – but also a blind faith in the need for the action to happen. Though its arithmetic may be dreadful, it still needs to be carried out.

The impossible condition in which the vanity of the action is paired with its absolute necessity is addressed – heroically and ridiculously – in the tornado chase (*Tornado*, 2000–present) or in a recent piece in which a 16 mm camera pursues mirages as they appear and vanish perpetually into the horizon (*A Story of Deception*, 2003–6). I found in that pursuit the perfect image of *fuite en avant*, of fleeing forwards. What immediately seduced me in the mirage's endless escaping was that it materialized the very Latin American scenario in which development programmes function in precisely the manner of a mirage, 'a historical goal that vanishes perpetually into thin air as soon as it looms into the horizon' (to quote my friend Cuauhtémoc). If you look into the larger cinematic or literary tradition, mirages have always been called upon in order to introduce scenes of apparition, like the one in *Lawrence of Arabia* in which Sherif Ali ibn El Kharish first appears. But I tend to see the mechanism of the mirage as exactly the opposite. While one approaches it, the mirage eternally escapes across the horizon line, always deceiving or eluding our progress, inevitably preceding our footsteps. It is

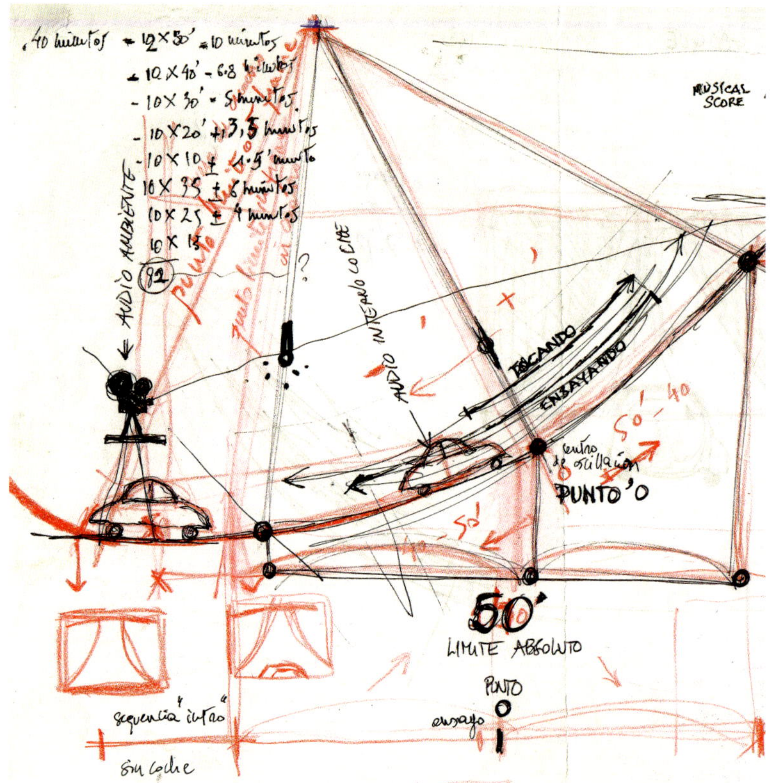

REHEARSAL I, 1999–2001
IN COLLABORATION WITH RAFAEL ORTEGA,
TIJUANA, MEXICO
PREPARATORY SKETCH

REHEARSAL I, 1999–2001
IN COLLABORATION WITH RAFAEL
ORTEGA, TIJUANA, MEXICO
VIDEO
29 MIN. 25 SEC.

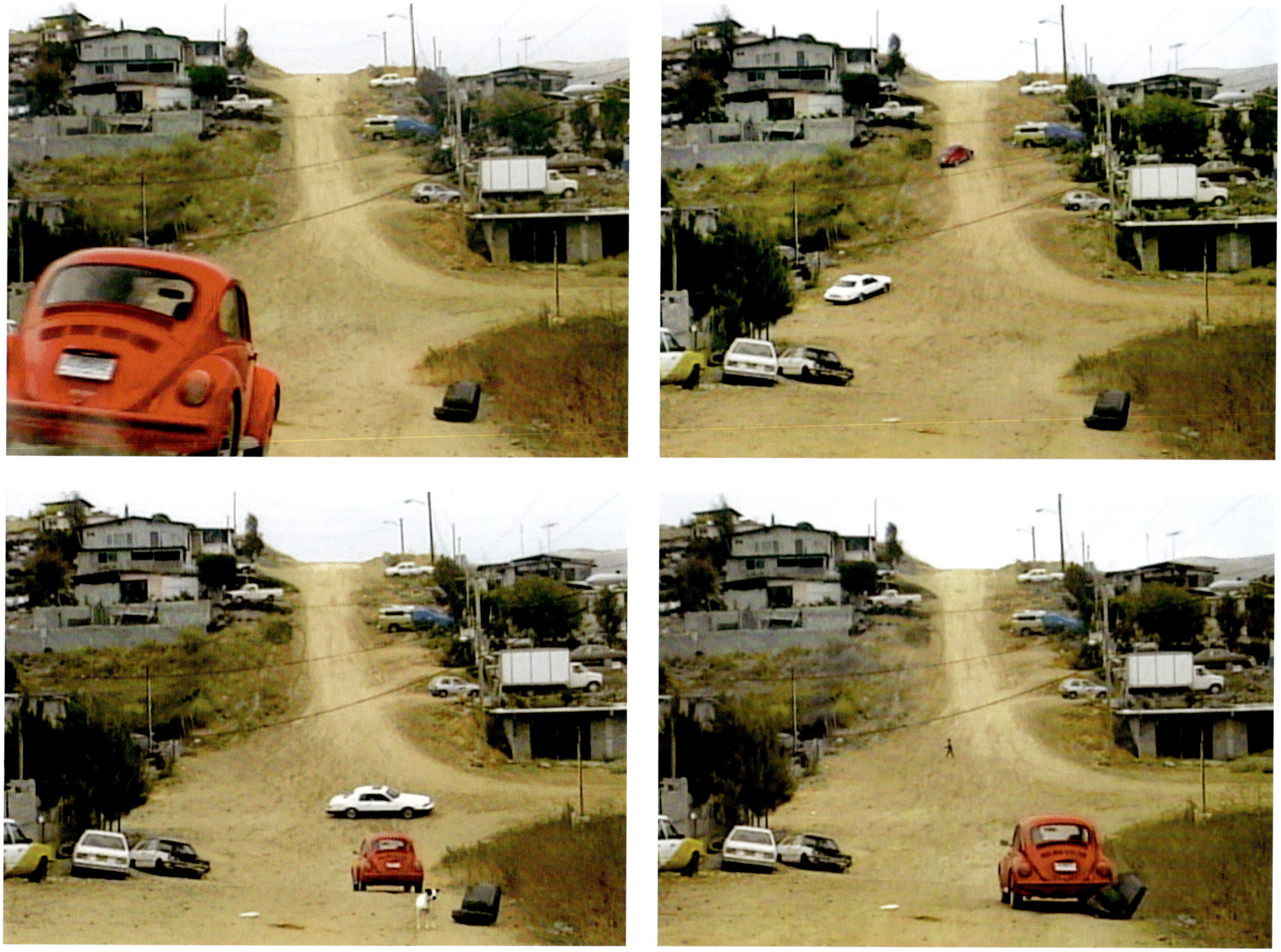

Soundtrack: the rehearsal of a Danzon by a brass band in Juchitan, Mexico.

Image: a Volkswagen Beetle repeatedly tries to ascend a hill without ever succeeding.

Mechanics: the driver of the VW listens to a tape recording of the rehearsal session.

While the musicians play, the car goes uphill.

When the musicians lose track and stop, the car stops.

While the musicians are tuning their instruments and are discussing, the car rolls downhill.

BARRENDEROS (SWEEPERS), 2004
IN COLLABORATION WITH JULIEN DEVAUX,
MEXICO CITY
VIDEO DOCUMENTATION OF AN ACTION
6 MIN. 36 SEC.

A line of street sweepers pushes garbage through the streets of Mexico City until they are stopped by the mass of trash.

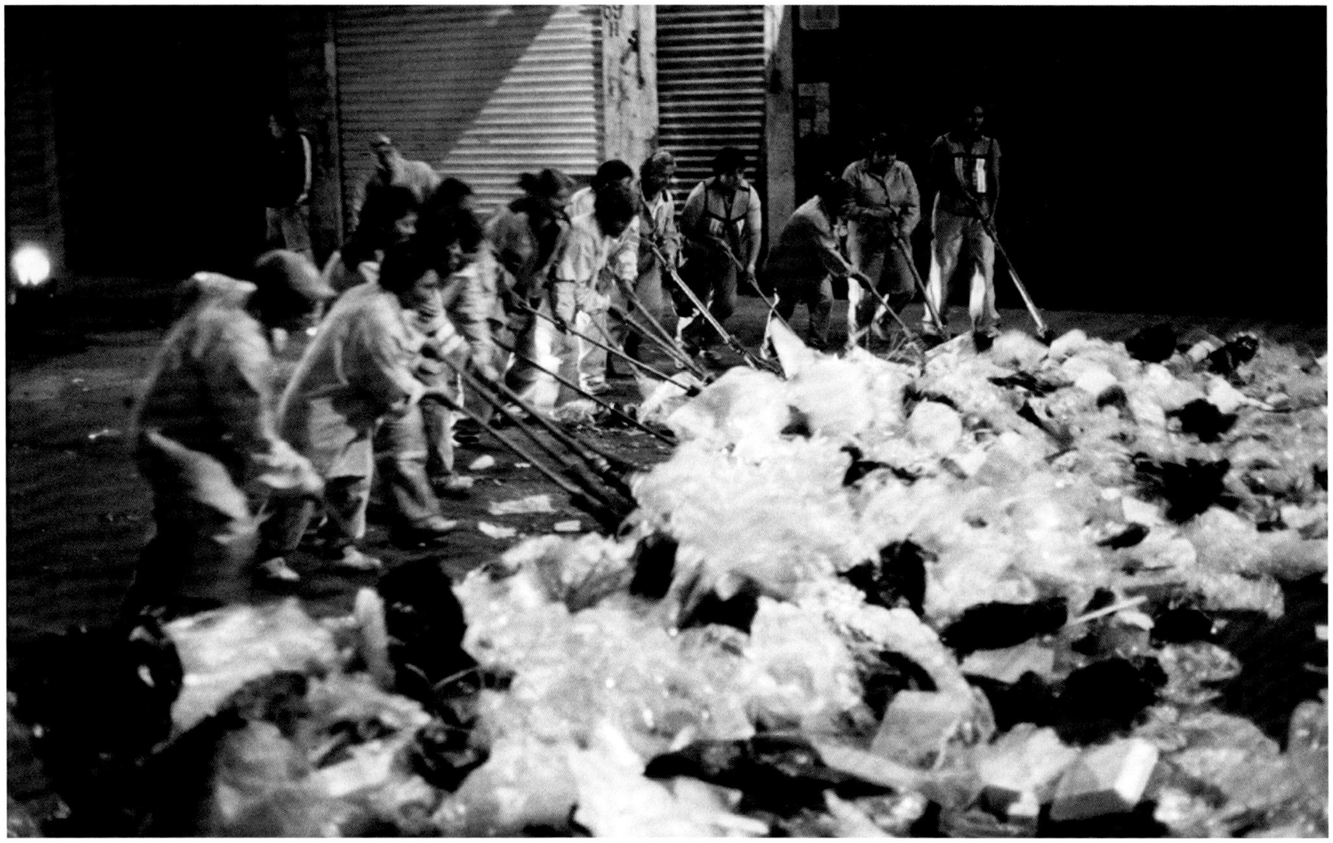

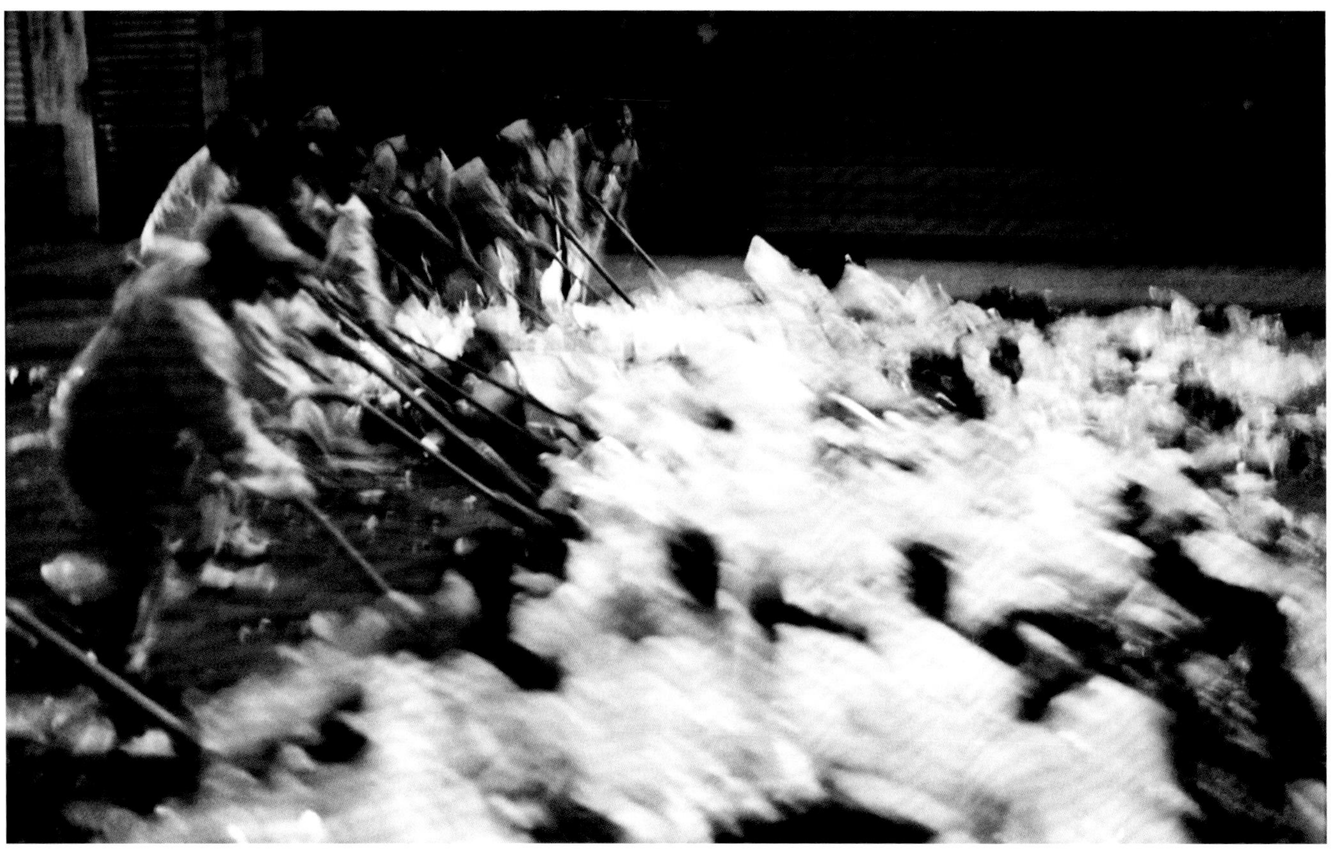

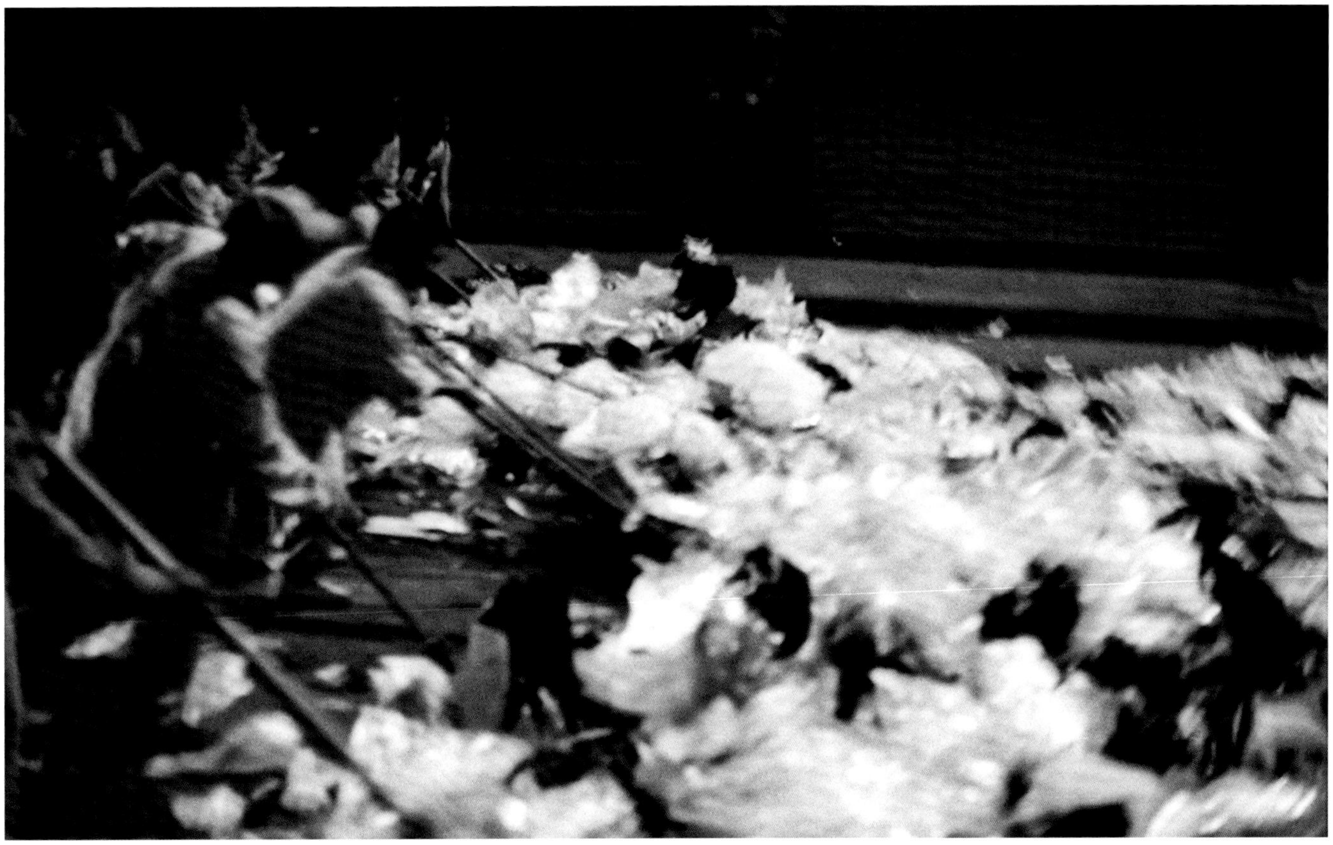

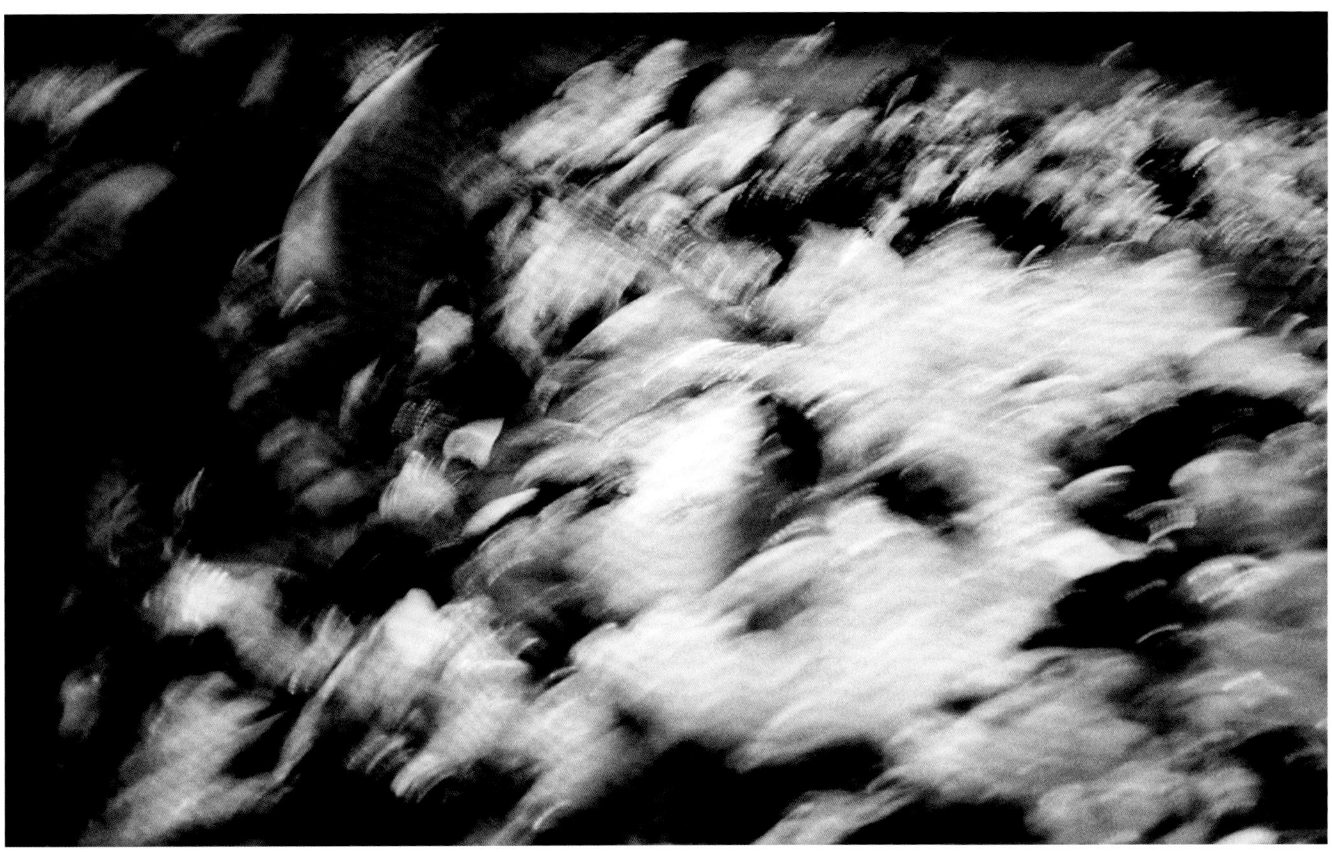

THE LOOP, 1997
GRAPHIC DOCUMENTATION
OF AN ACTION, TIJUANA
TO SAN DIEGO

In order to go from Tijuana to San Diego without crossing the Mexico/United States border, I followed a perpendicular route away from the fence to circumnavigate the globe heading 67° SE, NE and SE again until I reached my departure point. The project remained free and clear of all critical implications beyond the physical displacement of the artist.

a phenomenon of constant disappearance, a continuous experience of evasion. Without the movement of the observer, the mirage would be nothing more than an inert stain, an optical vibration in the landscape. It is our advance that awakens it, our progression towards it that triggers its life. It is in the obstinacy of our intent that the mirage comes to life, and that is the space that interests me. If there is disillusionment, it is because we want to catch it, to touch it.

When I refer, by way of the mirage metaphor, to the modernity that always seems to be within our reach but escapes us, I don't mean to say that modernity is the goal or what we should be pursuing. What interests me is the intent, the movement towards the mirage. For me, the emphasis is on the act of pursuing itself, in this escape forwards. I see the attempt as the real space of production, like the field of operations of a real or realistic development. Obviously you could reply that all this is purely a projection of mine, pure fantasy, that I've fallen into the mirage's trap.

FERGUSON: *We have come back over and over again in this conversation to the role of fiction and storytelling. Placing a story into circulation is very important in your work. But I am also interested in how the image relates to the story.*

ALŸS: I started making paintings because the street interventions and the three-dimensional objects I was making at the time were getting more and more hermetic. They were becoming art-world products, and I was losing contact with a wider audience, with the public. The images were a way of breaking that pattern.

The language that I used at the time was directly borrowed from sign painters and their characters. The man in the suit was the main protagonist of those street advertisements. A lot of the situations that the paintings illustrated were echoes of actions that happened on the street but which had no reason to exist as a photo document. I called the sign painters, who ended up being the co-authors of those images, because the language they were using was the most direct and communicative I could think of. I was not a painter. I had no interest in style, and their iconography fitted my needs. Also, I try to make a clear distinction between what will be addressing the street and what will be directed to the gallery wall.

The sign painters' main skill lies in the aesthetic resolution of a visual plot or a situation. In the beginning I would give them quite resolved and elaborate images, but over time I began giving them just sketches. They would really be the ones proposing the way of communicating that situation at its maximum power.

FERGUSON: *Either the story or the image can work in your mind, or your collaborator's mind, or the viewer's mind, and generate some other event or image.*

ALŸS: Yes, it is always kind of bouncing or ricocheting.

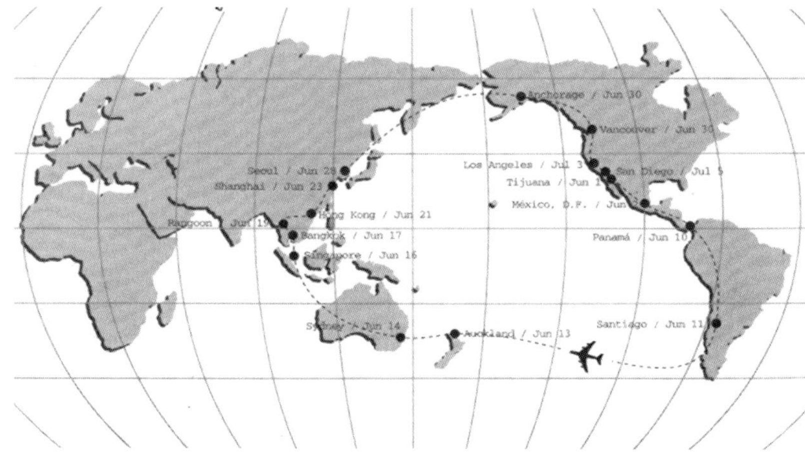

Subject: SHANGHAI /23 June 1997
Sent: 6/23/97 10:11 AM
Received: 6/23/97 11:15 PM
From: FRANCIS ALŸS, 110123.630@compuserve.com
To: Olivier Debroise, debroise@laneta.apc.org

Not much to do with the Tintinesque Shanghai of my childhood, but exoticism still flourishes.
Insignificant details transport me,
Is it just a matter of geography?
At this point, whether I travel east or west, it would take me a week to reach a homeland.
As I become progressively unable to read the local codes, I'm happily losing knowledge of my self.
At night I crash, emptied.
I don't even dare resist the vain romanticism which disguises the crude reality of a mutating Shanghai.
Pure present.

Hardly any dogs around.
The few I saw are discreetly being walked late at night.
Most have been killed during a cleansing of the city.
They are the advance victims befe a three year plan of "modernization" of the whole downtown area.

After a methodic packing ceremony, the morning's next ritual is the quest for coffee.

WHEN FAITH MOVES MOUNTAINS, 2002
IN COLLABORATION WITH CUAUHTÉMOC MEDINA AND RAFAEL ORTEGA
PHOTO DOCUMENTATION OF AN EVENT, LIMA, PERU

500 volunteers were equipped with shovels and asked to form a single line in order to displace by 10 cm a 500 m long sand dune from its original position.

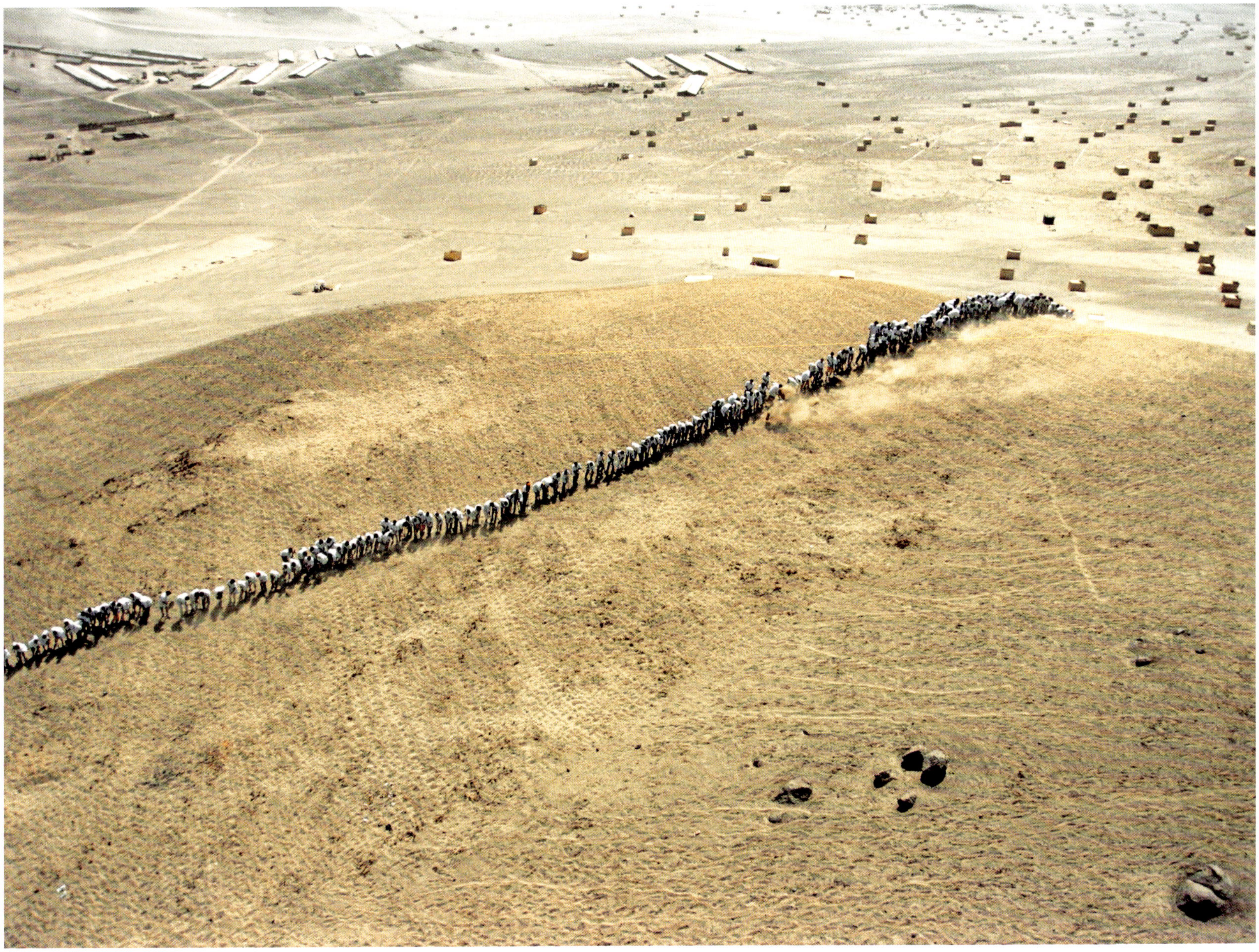

A STORY OF DECEPTION, 2005
IN COLLABORATION WITH RAFAEL ORTEGA AND
OLIVIER DEBROISE
16 MM FILM
4 MIN. 20 SEC.

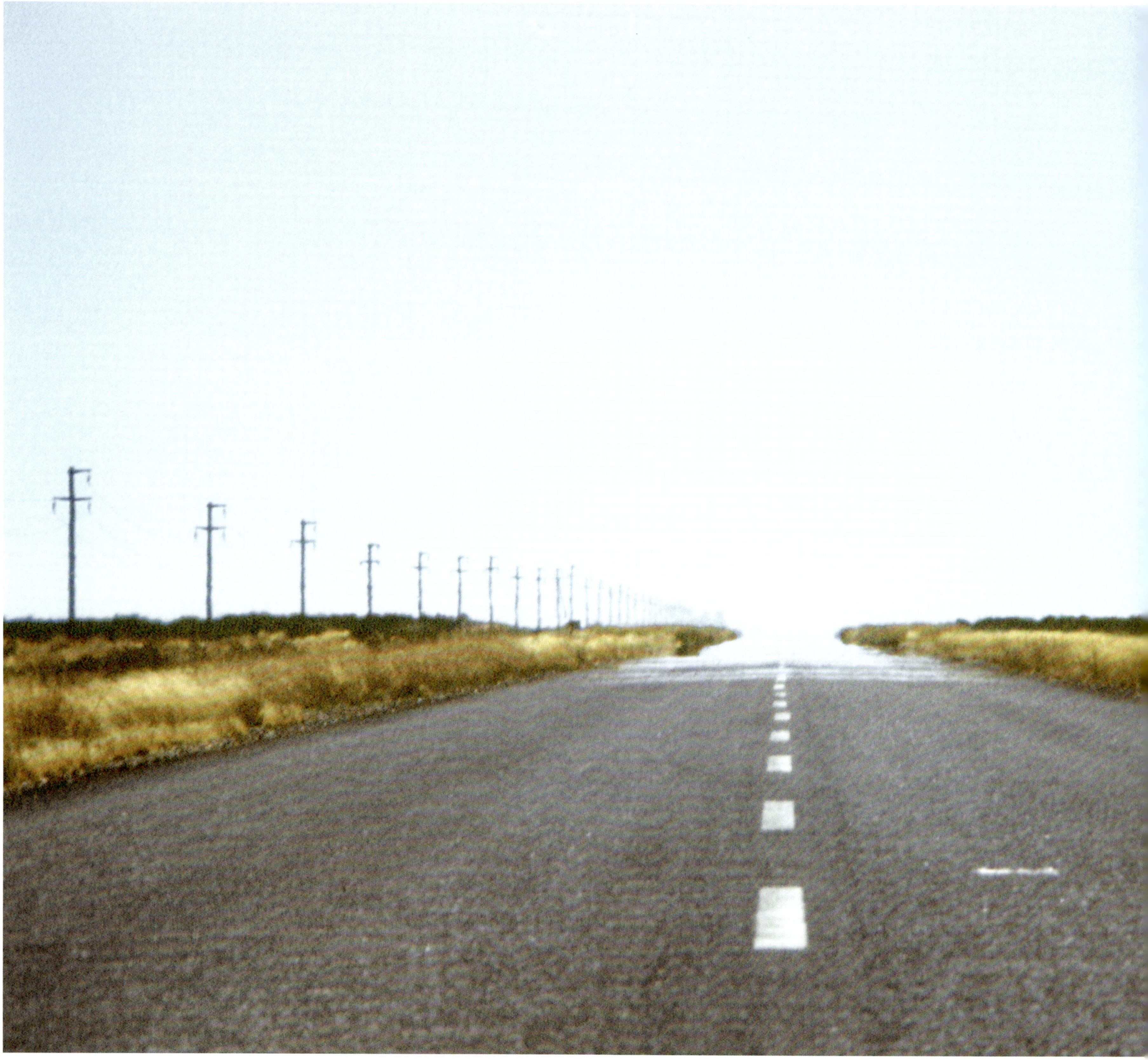

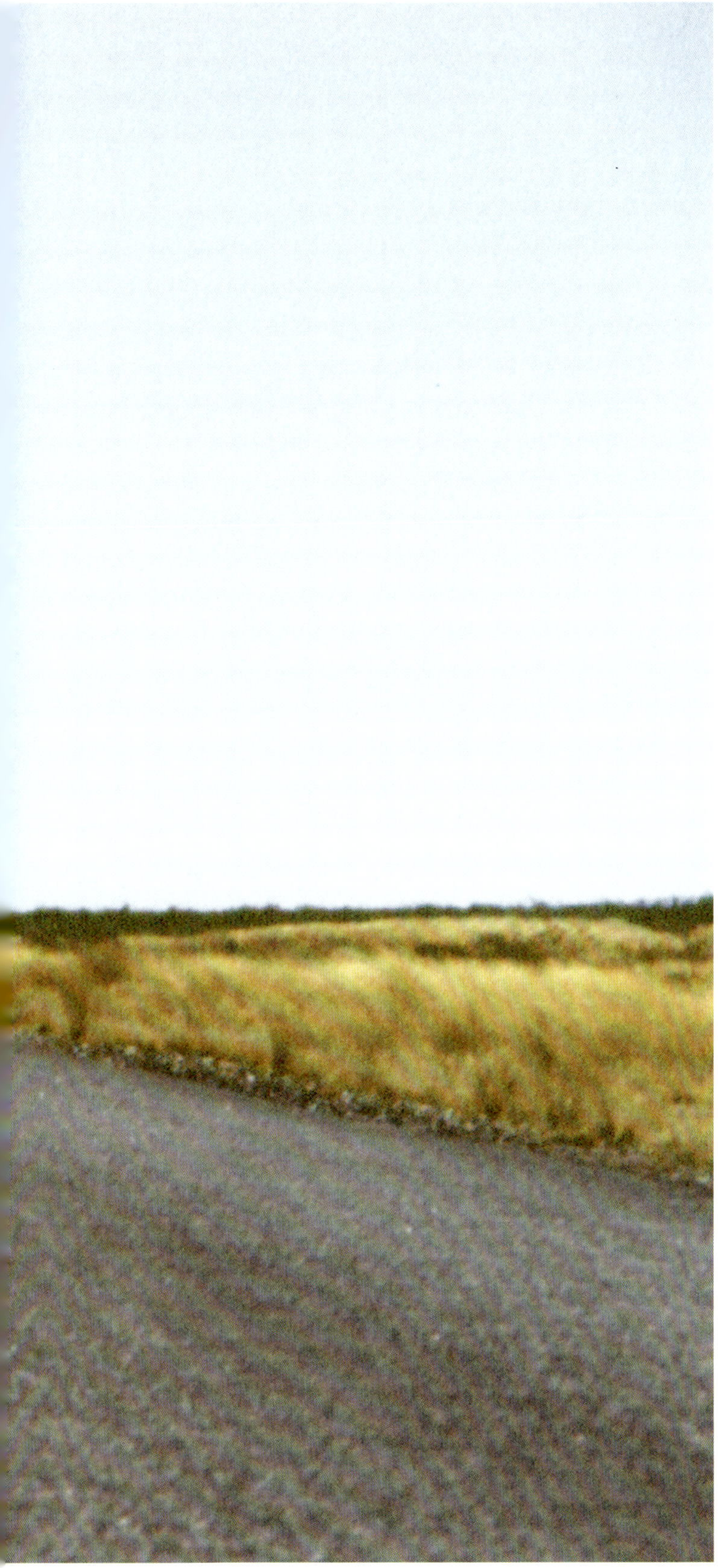

NOTEBOOK: A STORY OF DECEPTION, 2005
IN COLLABORATION WITH RAFAEL ORTEGA AND OLIVIER DEBROISE
15 X 22 CM

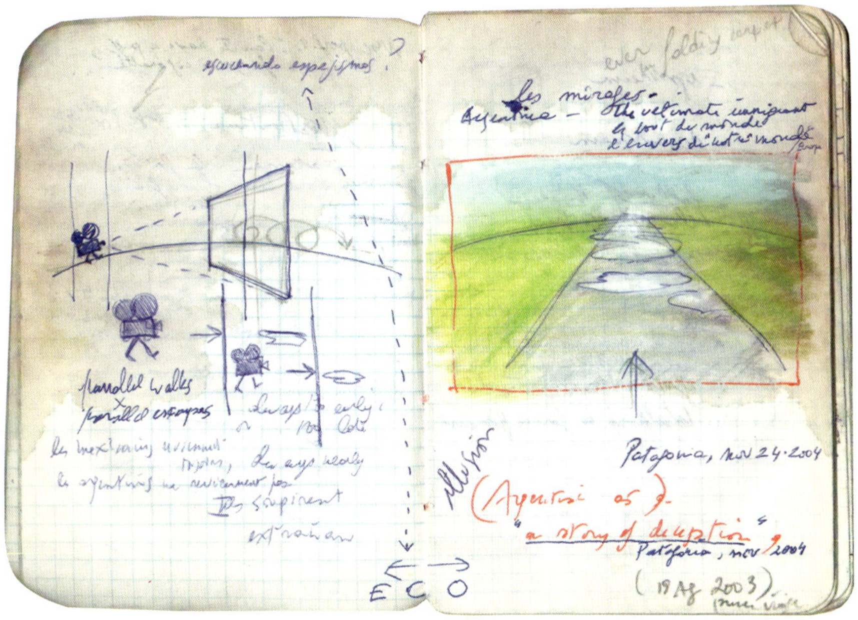

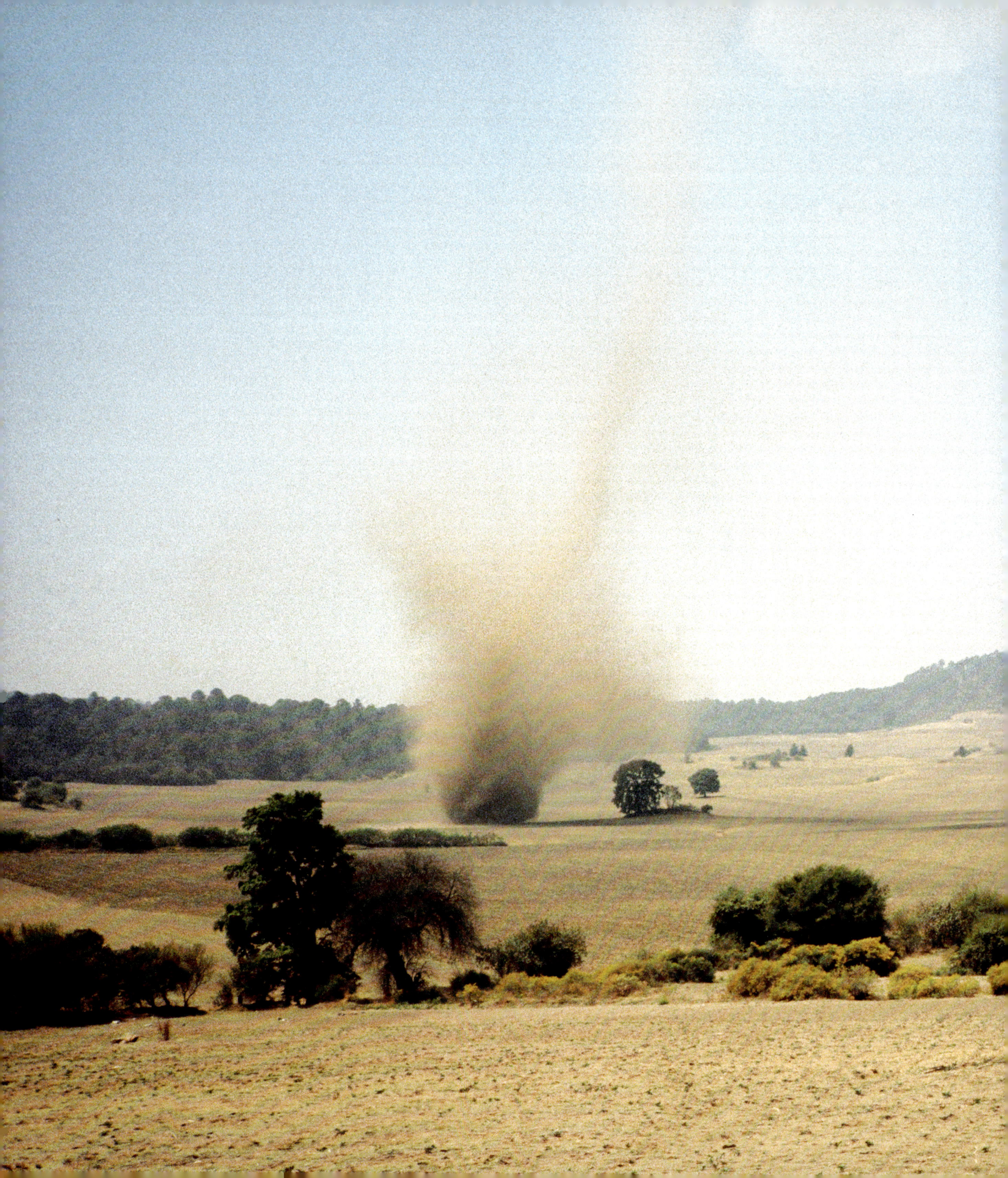

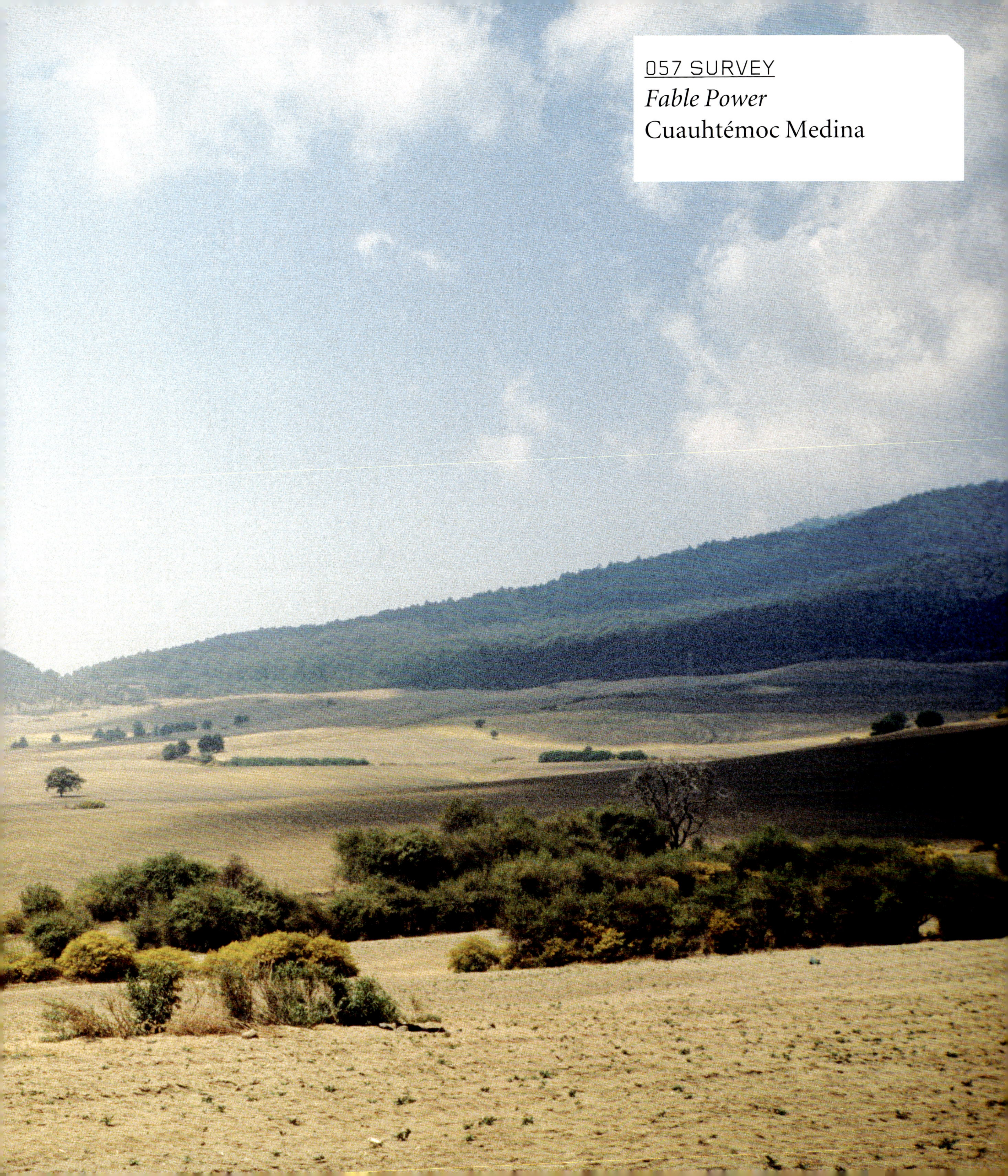

057 SURVEY

Fable Power

Cuauhtémoc Medina

previous pages and below,
TORNADO, 2000–10
IN COLLABORATION WITH JULIEN DEVAUX,
RAFAEL ORTEGA AND FELIX BLUME
VIDEO DOCUMENTATION OF AN ACTION
30 MIN.

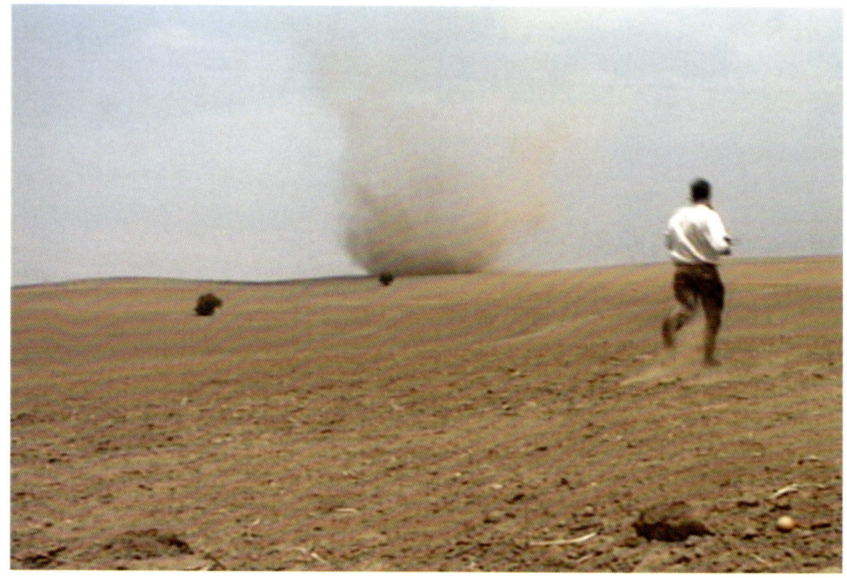

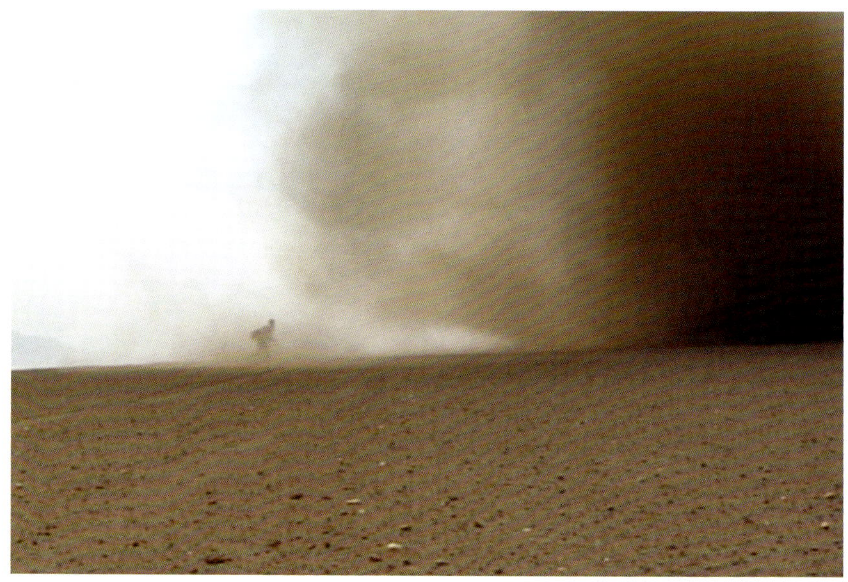

In the Eye of the Tempest

Every year since 2001, Francis Alÿs has eagerly awaited the month of March, the high point of the dry season, to drive his Volkswagen Beetle to the southeast edge of Mexico City, where smoky clouds rise from cornfields burning after harvest, and grey swirls of ash and sand loom against the horizon. Carrying his video camera, Alÿs runs towards these tornadoes, hoping to catch them as a surfer catches a wave. Upon reaching one, he penetrates its thick brown walls until he reaches the peaceful eye of the storm, intending to stay as long as possible inside the swirl. His nose and mouth protected by nothing more than a handkerchief, he films the monochromatic interior of the windy sanctuary, an indefinable colour field that ranges from violet to grey to yellow, before the aerodynamics of the whirl expel him back into the open. His sole purpose is to extract a few sublime instants from the entrails of this hostile metereological formation, to achieve a glimpse, as he puts it, of 'some kind of immediate, absolute present that reflects a society in which survival tactics elude any future further than the next rent to pay'.[1]

Alÿs's apparently absurd act forges a moment of bliss in the midst of chaos. As Don Quixote told Sancho Panza, 'Fortune doth address our affairs better than we ourselves could desire.'[2] What we usually see as an index of the growing ecological disaster around one of the biggest cities in the Third World – a form of pollution caused by a relatively archaic form of agriculture adding to the already greying skies of central Mexico – becomes an occasion for adventure. These are the things of which stories are made.

A Fable within a Fable

In the mid-1980s, Francis (Alÿs) de Smedt was living in Venice, writing a dissertation for a Doctorate in Urbanism at the Istituto di Architettura di Venezia. Reading historical accounts and documents, but above all closely studying the details of ancient paintings – from the famous *Allegory of Good Government* (1338–40) in the Palazzo Pubblico of Siena by Ambrogio Lorenzetti, to the Venetian city scenes painted by Gentile Bellini at the end of the fifteenth century – he intended to reconstruct the central processes involved in social control. One of these was the eradication of animals from early Renaissance cities – not only wild animals but also working ones – and their transformation into the 'leftovers of our society'.[3]

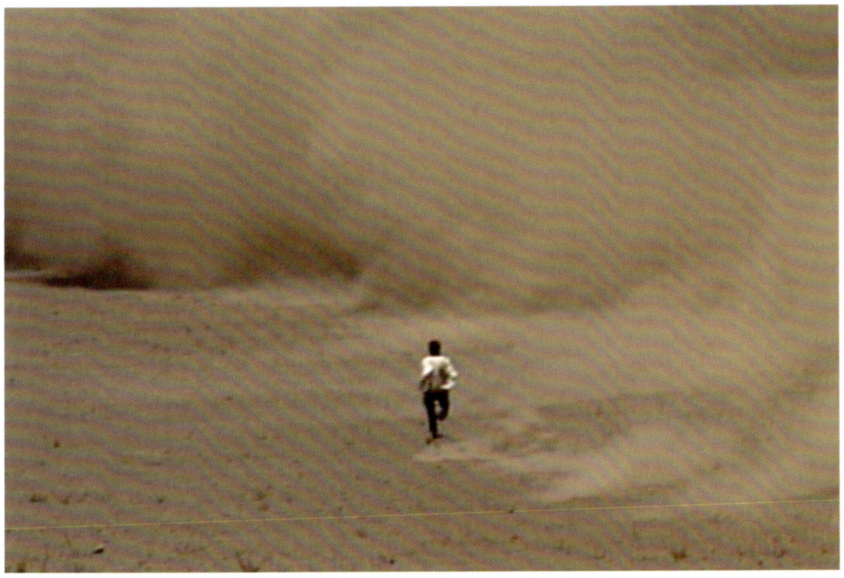

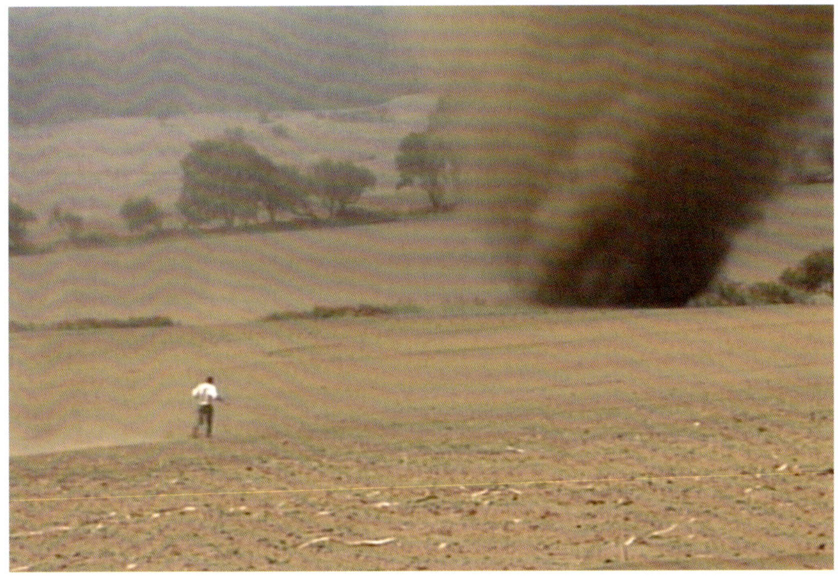

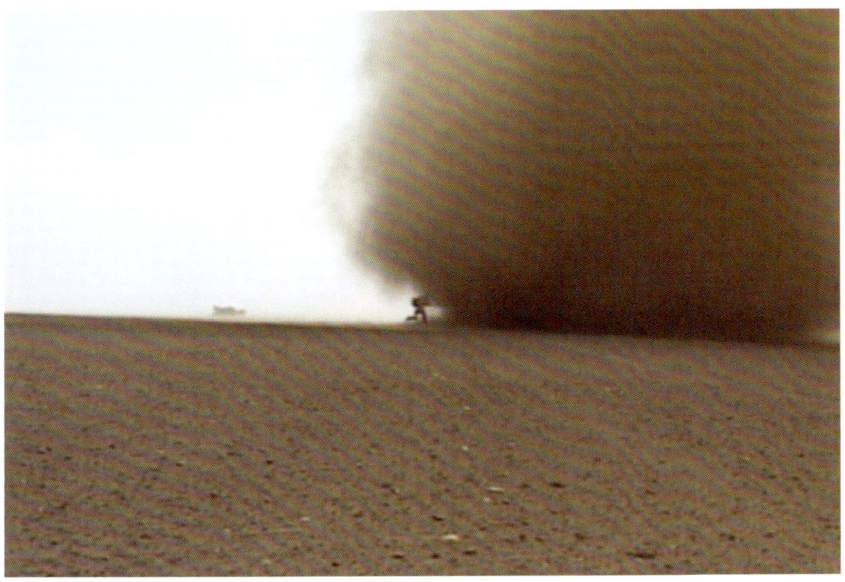

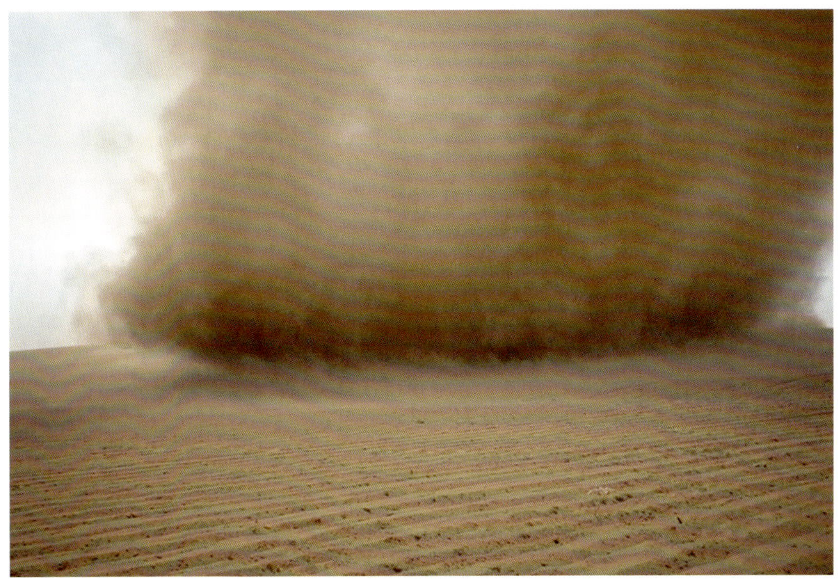

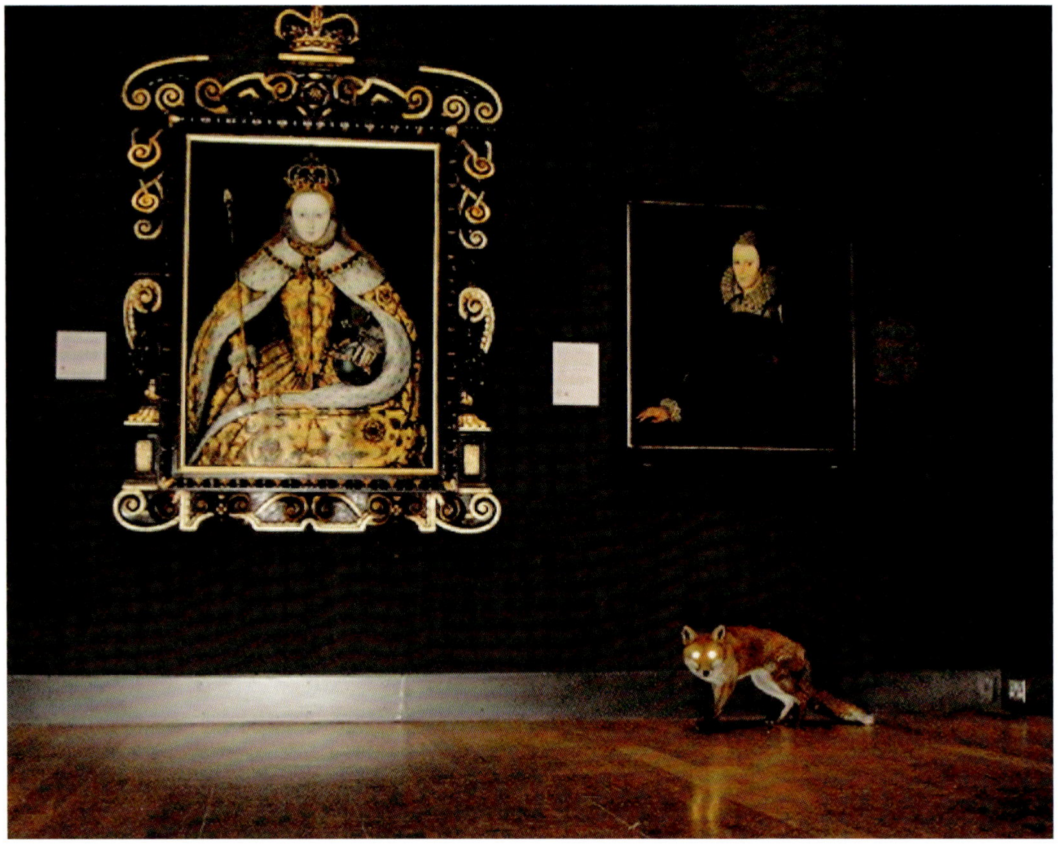

THE NIGHTWATCH, 2004
VIDEO DOCUMENTATION OF AN ACTION, NATIONAL PORTRAIT GALLERY, LONDON
20 VIDEOS ON 20 MONITORS
EACH 16 MIN.

On the night of 7 April 2004, a fox was freed in the National Portrait Gallery.
Its wanderings through the galleries were recorded by the institution's CCTV system.

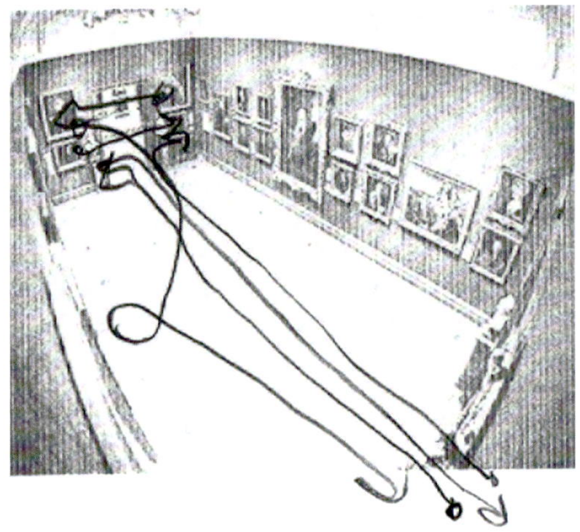

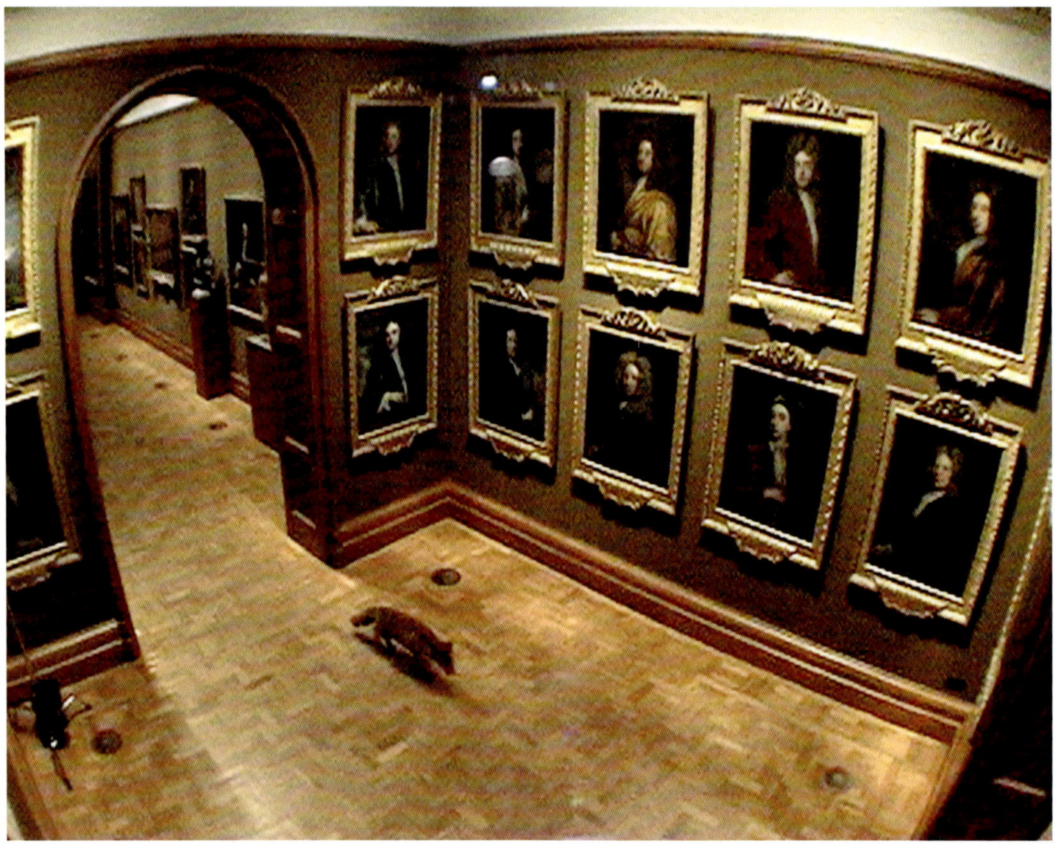

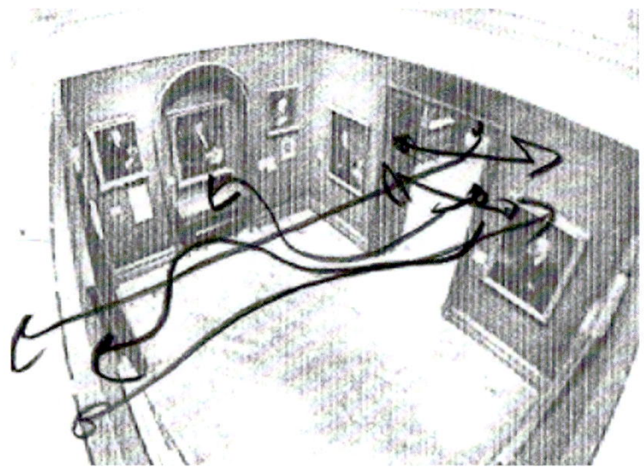

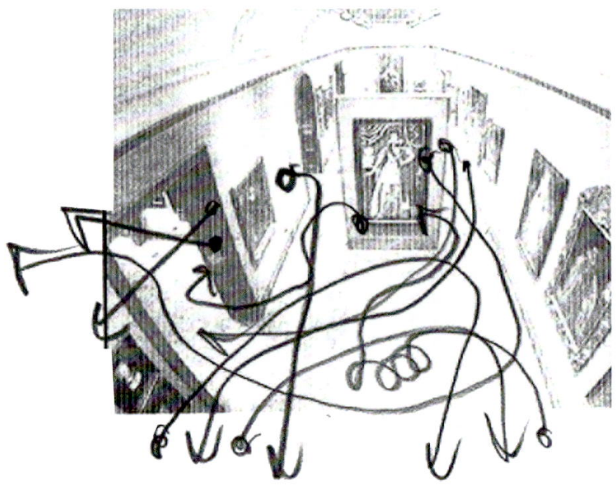

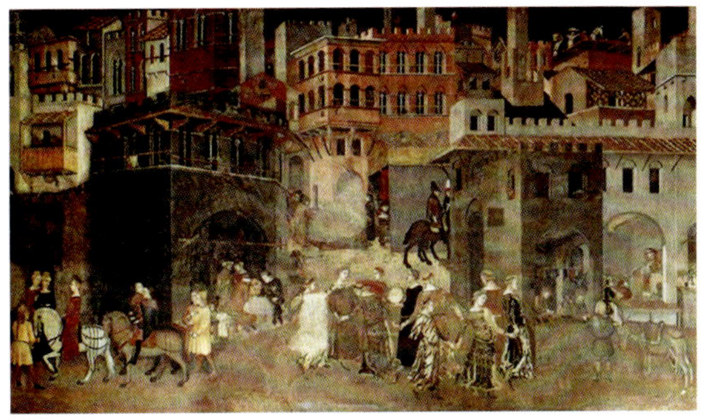

AMBROGIO LORENZETTI
GLI EFFETTI DEL BUONGOVERNO [DETAIL], C. 1348
FRESCO
SALA DEI NOVE, PALAZZO PUBBLICO, SIENA

This phenomenon had run in tandem with the first signs of the emergent modern era: the development of 'rational' scientific discourse, the colonization of the New World, the decay of medieval faith, the first notions of hygiene, and the development of perspective as a means to convey a mathematical and spatial world view.[4]

Alÿs came to conceive of animal life as a central index of the drive towards the transformation of the city from a concentration of historic practices to a space ruled by social administration and characterized by the pursuit of order and hygiene. For him, those misfits became a living metaphor for the forms of existence suppressed by the process of modernization. An important stage in the emergence of this way of thinking was a visit to the city of Palmanova around 1985, which offered him his first insight into how one might intervene in the imaginary of the city without assuming the role of the architect-master. Palmanova, the so-called 'star-shaped city', a town devised by the Republic of Venice in 1593 as an advanced military outpost against attacks by the Turks and the Austrians, is a remarkable example of an emergent baroque citadel that, from the sixteenth century onwards, was to become a prominent model of the new type of homogeneous and globally predetermined city with all its isolation and disenchantment.

Studying Palmanova, Alÿs was impressed by the desolation of this military and political utopia: 'When faced with this dysfunctional utopia, I could not think of any urbanistic, architectonic, nor artistic answer to shake off the apathy of the place. I could not convince myself that adding matter (an object, a sound or an architecture) to that site could in any sense alter its own inhabitants' perception or the outsider's. So my reaction was to try to affect its memory: I invented a fake episode that would have taken place at the heart of the place, hidden in the remote corners of its memory. Of course animals (as heroes of a recently negated era, the great misfits of the Renaissance imaginary and urbanism) became its protagonists. The format of the fable unfolded naturally as the only possible method of intervention.'[5]

With time, Alÿs turned this lesson into a leitmotiv that could be condensed into his succinct slogan: 'Whereas the highly rational societies of the Renaissance felt the need to create utopias, we of our modern times must create fables.'[6]

Lessons from the Rubble

In February 1986, after finishing his studies, De Smedt was drafted into national service. Disinclined to military life, he took the only possible escape: to join an aid project to regenerate Mixtec Indian towns in the southern Mexican state of Oaxaca. Although the enterprise was relatively successful, it confirmed Alÿs's scepticism

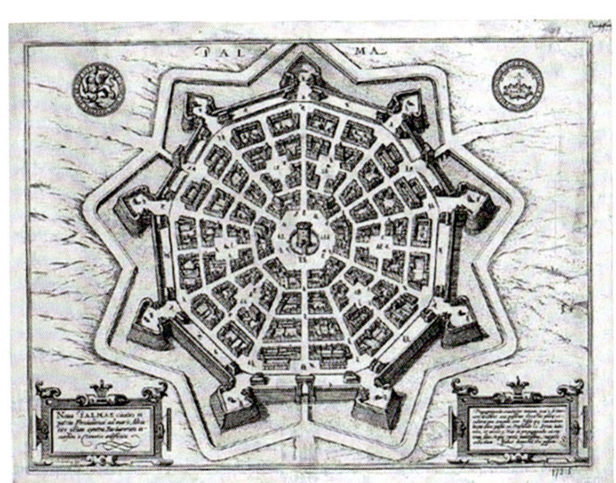

MAP OF PALMANOVA, ITALY, C. 1598

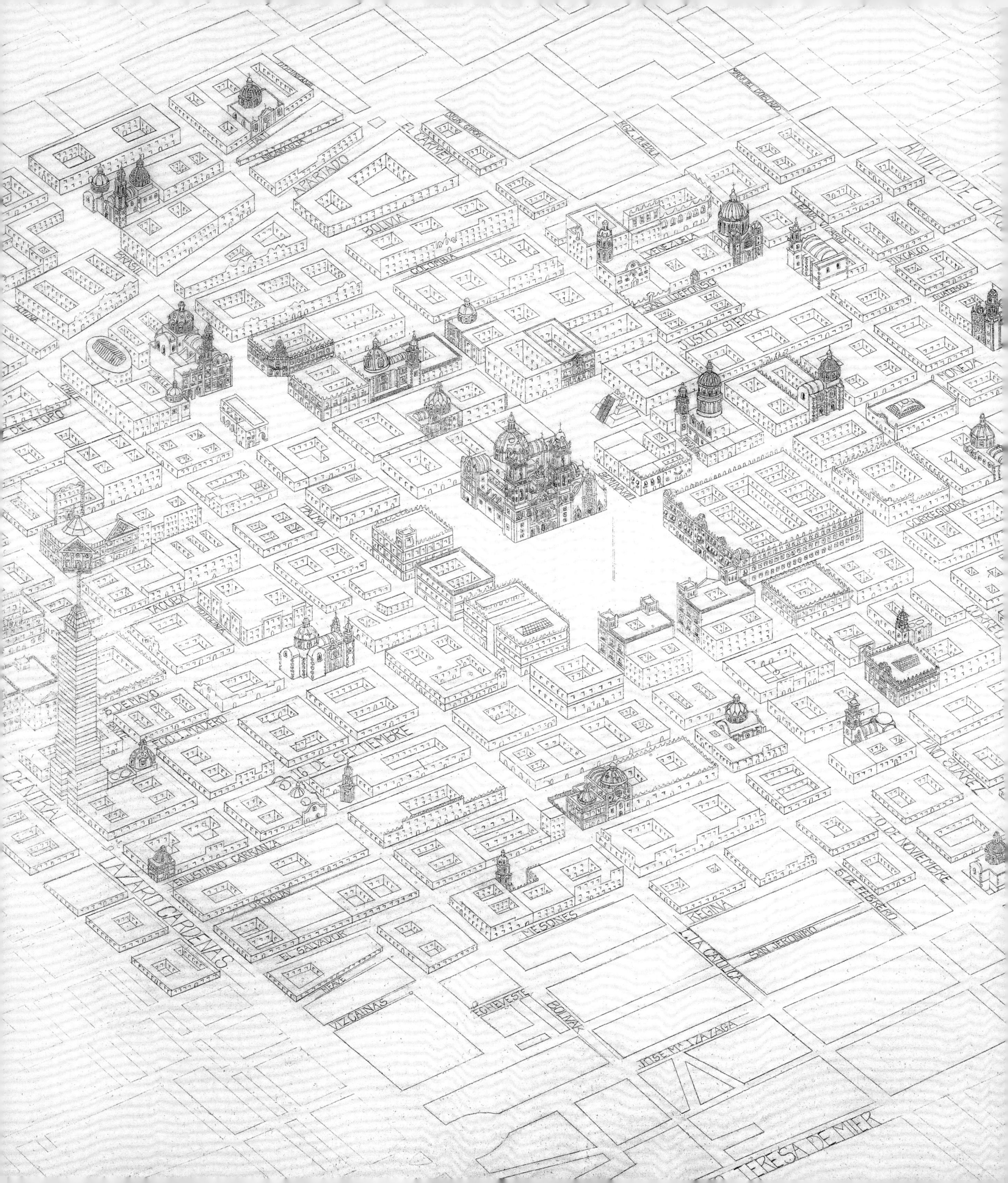

APARTADO
EL CARMEN
BOLIVIA
COLOMBIA
VENEZUELA
SAN ILDEFONSO
JUSTO SIERRA
GUATEMALA
MONEDA
CORREGIDORA
SEMINARIO
PALMA
TACUBA
5 DE MAYO
FCO. I. MADERO
16 DE SEPTIEMBRE
CENTRAL
LAZARO CARDENAS
VENUSTIANO CARRANZA
EL SALVADOR
MESONES
REGINA
SAN JERONIMO
LA CATOLICA
5 DE FEBRERO
20 DE NOVIEMBRE
PINO SUAREZ
VIZCAINAS
ECHEVESTE
BOLIVAR
JOSE Mª IZAZAGA
TERESA DE MIER

MAP OF THE CENTRO HISTÓRICO OF MEXICO CITY (DETAIL), 2004
PENCIL ON TRACING PAPER
70 X 90 CM

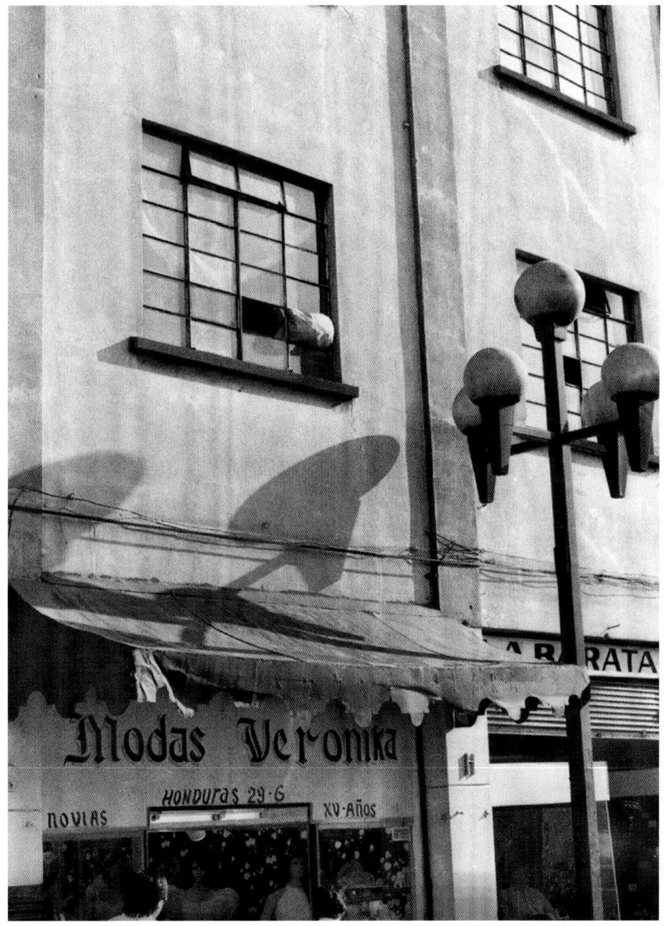

PLACING PILLOWS, 1990
PHOTO DOCUMENTATION
OF AN ACTION, MEXICO CITY

While walking around the centre of Mexico City I placed pillows in the frames of broken windows.

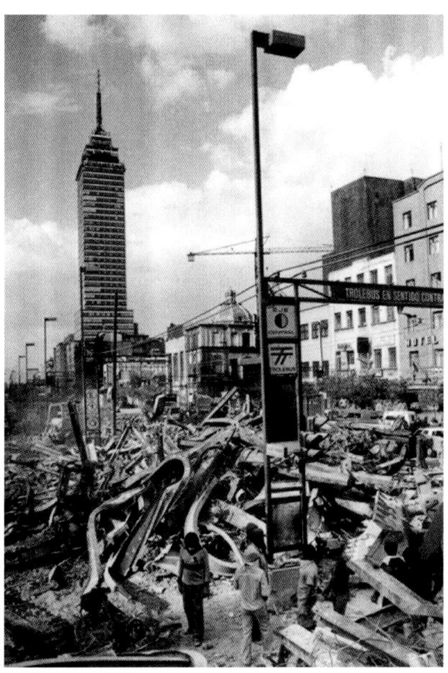

ANDRÉS GARAY NIETO
UNTITLED, 1985
BLACK AND WHITE PHOTOGRAPH

EARTHQUAKE DAMAGE ON THE EJE CENTRAL LÁZARO CÁRDENAS IN MEXICO CITY

about the politics of urbanism, the cultural differences he experienced there underlining his distrust of the presumption of transforming other people's ways of living.

When legal problems forced him to stay in Mexico City, what started out as a temporary visit led to a permanent residency. He was not the only one who was trapped in the country's spider web; during those years a number of artists from England, Argentina, the United States and Cuba (including Melanie Smith, Thomas Glassford, José Bedia, Jimmie Durham) also found themselves living in Mexico and unable to leave. De Smedt's migration was marked by a change of both name and profession. He was still nominally in military service, so in order to avoid conflict with the Belgian authorities, he created a pseudonym. Thus 'Francis Alÿs' was born.

Very quickly, Alÿs fell under the allure of Mexico City. His fascination had nothing to do with the reasons foreign artists and intellectuals had traditionally gravitated to Mexico in the twentieth century; he was neither called by the dream of the southern revolutionary nor of the Indian utopia, and although he had used the country as a means to escape the army, he was not a political refugee as such. His eye was caught by a certain urban texture that fulfilled his questioning of the modern notion of city life, and by the opportunity for creative experimentation that he found in the emerging artistic circles of the city. During the late 1980s and early 1990s, the improvisatory character of the local art world became a perfect setting in which to engage in his aesthetic self-training.

Even if Alÿs did not articulate it until years later, Mexico City stood as a sort of allegory for the failure of modernism. The city was undergoing a particularly critical moment in its history, but this crisis also opened up of a number of new possibilities. A year before Alÿs arrived, the megalopolis experienced a catastrophe. At 7:19 a.m. on 19 September 1985, Mexico City woke up to the worst earthquake of its history: a three-minute seismic event that registered 8.1 on the Richter scale. Like the student massacre of 1968, 1985 became a watershed in the history of the country. It symbolically toppled the last illusions of development, already seriously undermined by the 1976 and 1982 economic crises and the six-decade single-party rule of the Revolutionary Institutional Party (PRI). For a few weeks in September 1985, a spontaneous non-political revolution occurred in which ordinary people took control of the streets. Amid the ruins, thousands enjoyed a rare moment of collective autonomy. The ambivalence of those events (both murderous and liberatory) was to define the social and political climate of the following decades.

These forces made living in Mexico City, where the apocalyptic sight and rotten smell of the mountains of rubble combined with a widespread feeling of renewed social possibilities, a particularly intense experience. In the ensuing years any semblance of a central order in the

MILKY WAY, 1995
MEXICO CITY
COLOUR PHOTOGRAPH

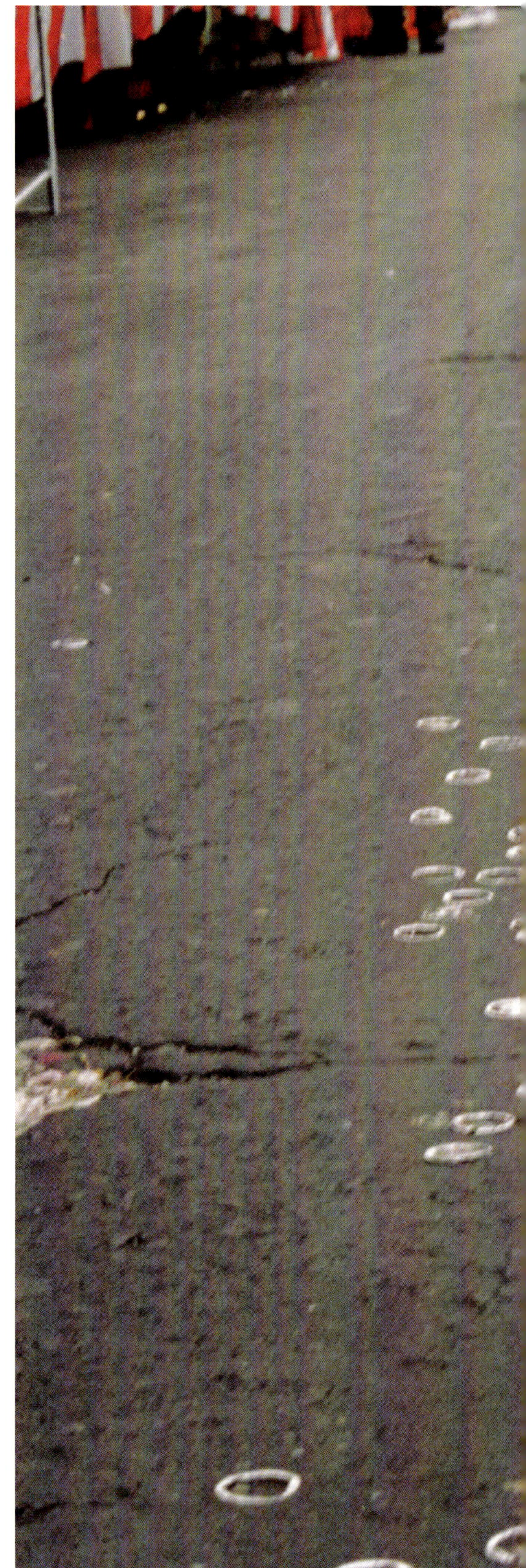

city disappeared, turning a significant number of people into illegal street vendors and creating a parallel capitalist economy. Mexico City is one of the main forefronts of the strife between the neo-liberal modernization projects of the West and the diffuse but effective social resistance of entire populations who have taken control of the former space of colonial and national power as an arena for labour and survival. The 'deconstruction' of the city by the earthquake provoked a reconstruction of the vernacular, pre-modern neighbourhood, and the emergence of a non-administrative usage of the street. Interestingly to Alÿs, the city was densely populated by street dogs, animals that, unlike in Europe, had never been banished.

To Be Picked Up

Alÿs's early walks through Mexico City constituted an attempt literally to find a position: both a physical space and a form of activity. As a 'passer-by constantly trying to situate' himself in a 'moving environment',[7] he had left Europe both physically and symbolically – putting into brackets its modernist ideology of social hygiene, visual order, economic stability, architectonic harmony and cultural purity – to immerse himself in an unknown territory where he was conspicuously acting under the uncomfortable but sometimes convenient mask of 'foreigner'. In fact, it was impossible not to notice this very tall, slender, white character strolling amidst the street markets in a densely populated, mixed-blood, Third-World city. With a camera Alÿs started recording what he saw in the streets – an array of pipes, old chairs, cord, bricks and buckets, for instance, used to reserve a parking space; an improvised plastic tent placed over an open sewage drain that functioned as street toilet; or the remarkable constructions that served as improvised canteens on the sidewalk. These structures and materials were examples of an endless bricolage, posed in direct confrontation with modern urban rationality, which spoke of parallel economies beneath the great ideological social systems. These 'street installations', as Alÿs called them, became his main visual referent. 'Street installations can be formal incidents – like a galaxy casually formed by hundreds of bottle taps stuck in the asphalt (*Milky Way*, 1995) – or more careful arrangements serving economical purposes – street-side commerce, storage, advertisements, etc. They can be directly connected to the urban structure – like the city drain converted into a toilet – or just be lying on sidewalks – displaced domestic items in search of a new function. What the street scene offers me is a whole range of situations and attitudes in which further developments are implied.'[8]

Sometime around 1989 Alÿs found his attention drawn to broken windows, many of them in houses abandoned after the earthquake. He placed pillows in these broken window frames, creating a place to dream fifteen metres above the street (*Placing Pillows*, 1990). This simple action was his first physical attempt to introduce a narrative dimension into the city fabric. With the utmost simplicity, he had both preserved and covered the gap left by the broken glass in order to turn it into a place where the street and the domestic space intersect, a space for rest and a space for circulation, a bridge between somewhere

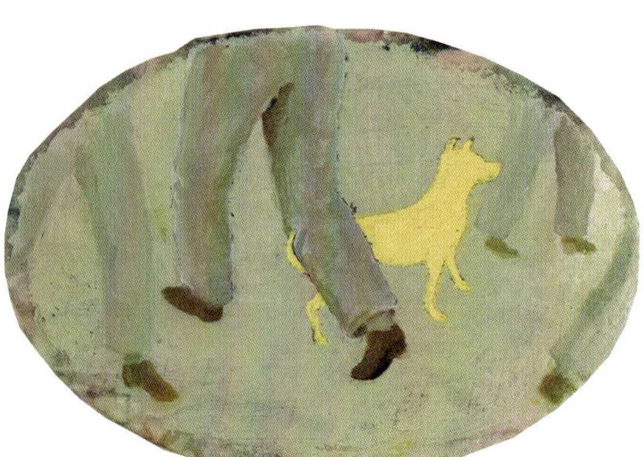

UNTITLED, 1996
FROM THE SERIES DÉJÀ VU
OIL ON CANVAS
DIPTYCH (PART 1)
17 X 23 CM

Each of the images in the Déjà vu series has an exact copy. The paintings in each pair are displayed in separate rooms along the visitor's journey through the exhibition space.

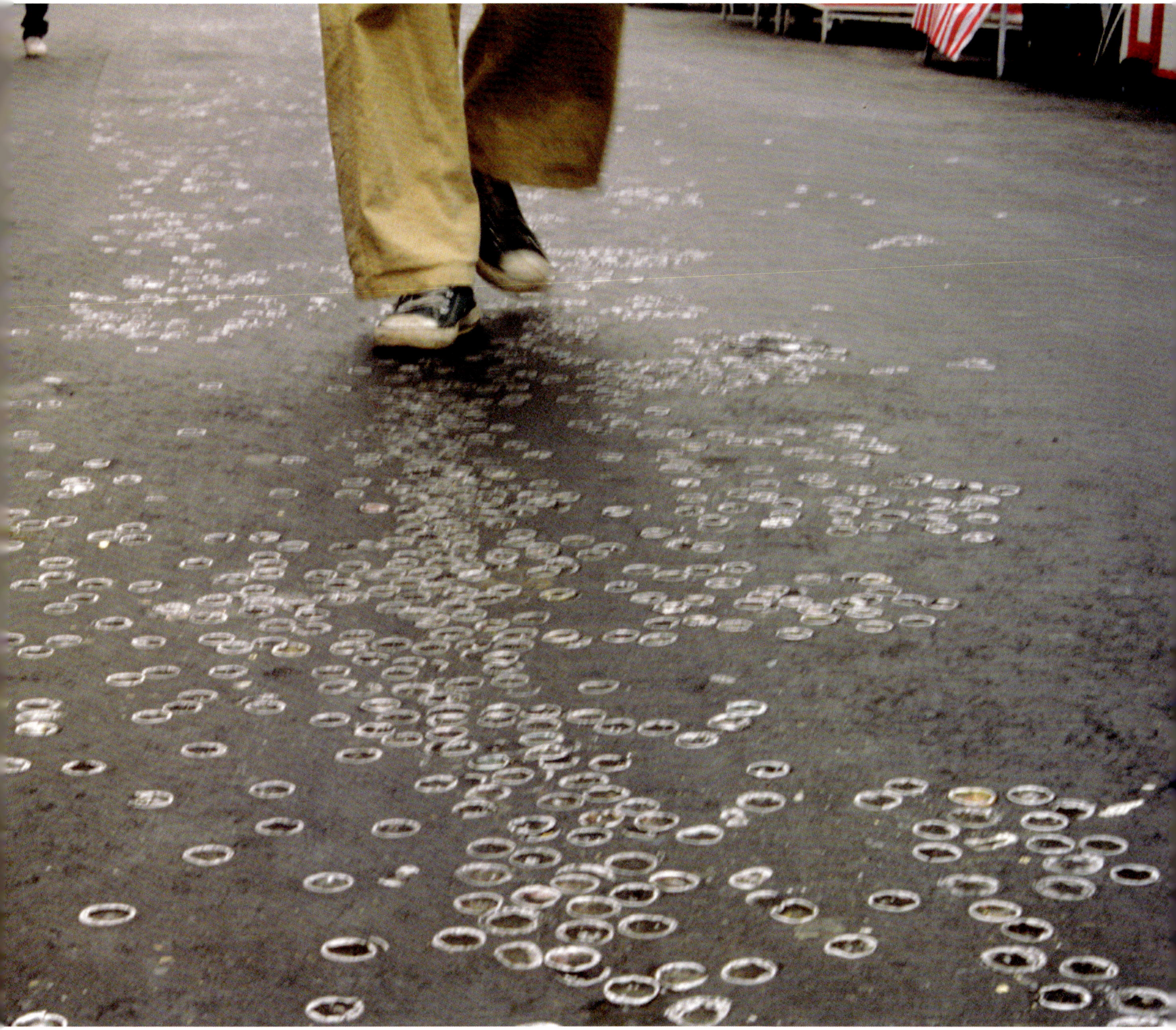

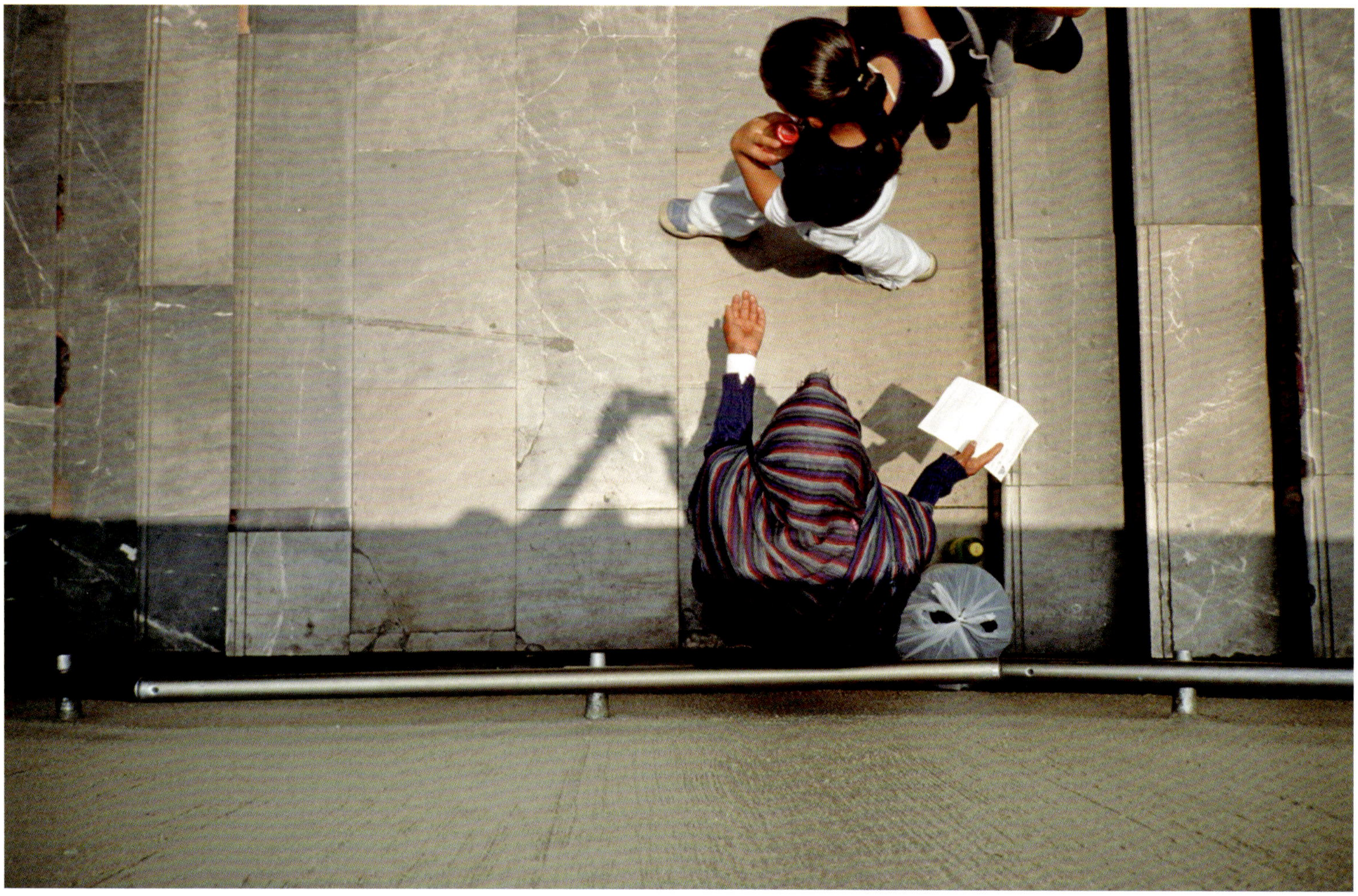

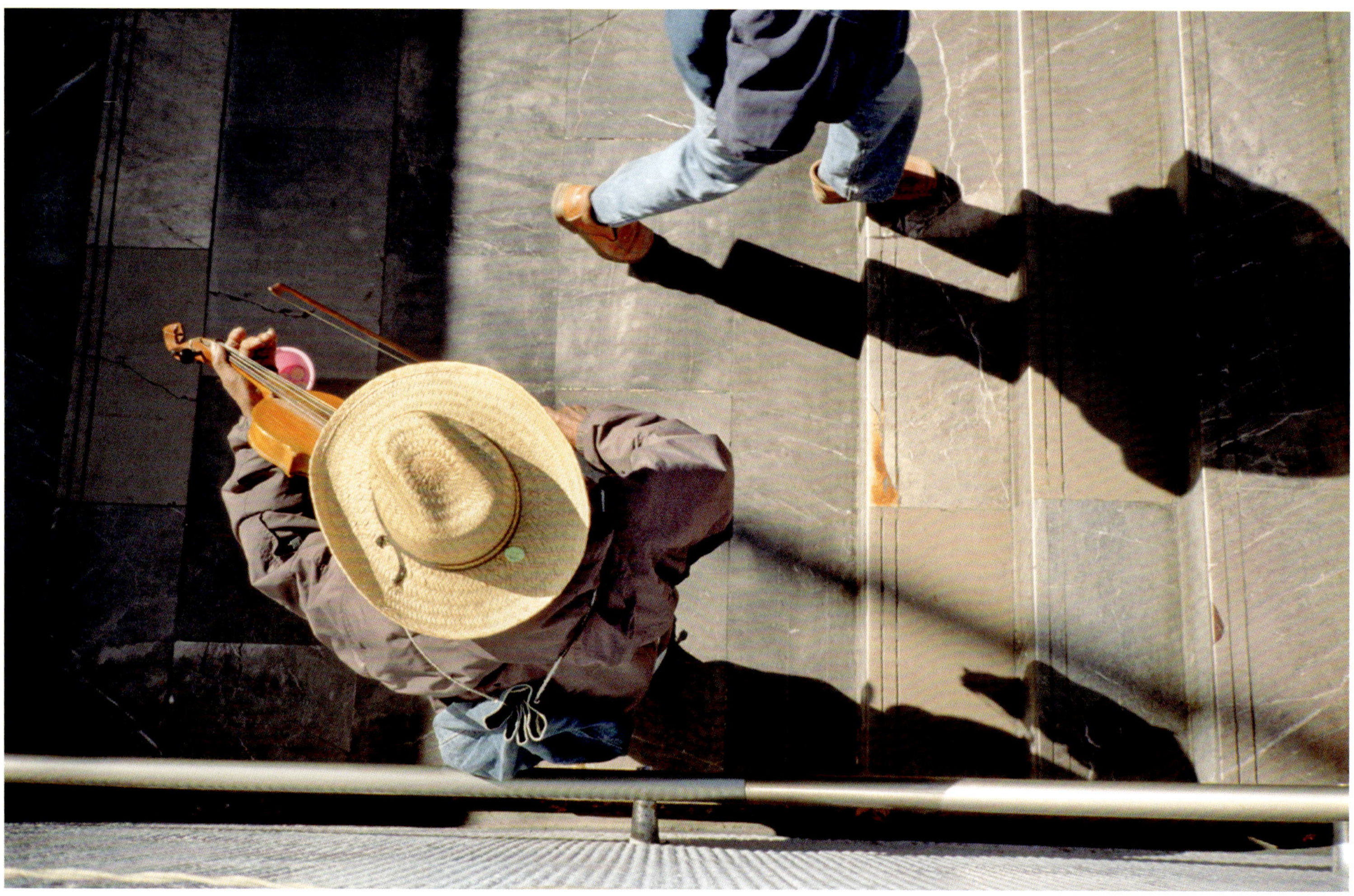

BEGGARS, 2002–04
MEXICO CITY
2 OF 80 35 MM SLIDES

UNTITLED (ZICTE/CHEWING GUM), 1994–97
MEXICO/UNITED STATES
1 OF 80 35 MM SLIDES

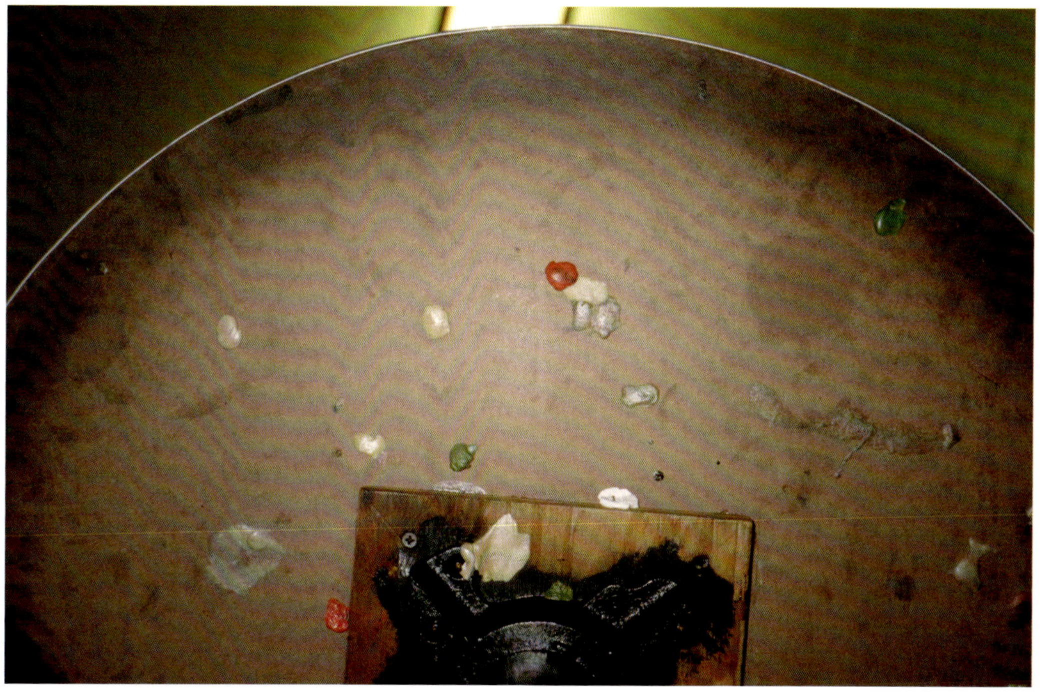

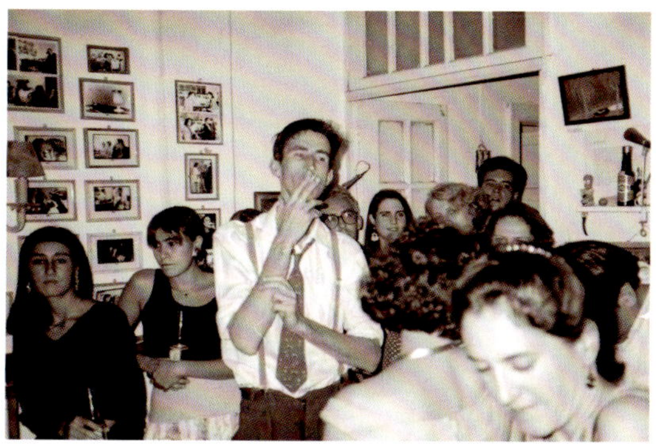

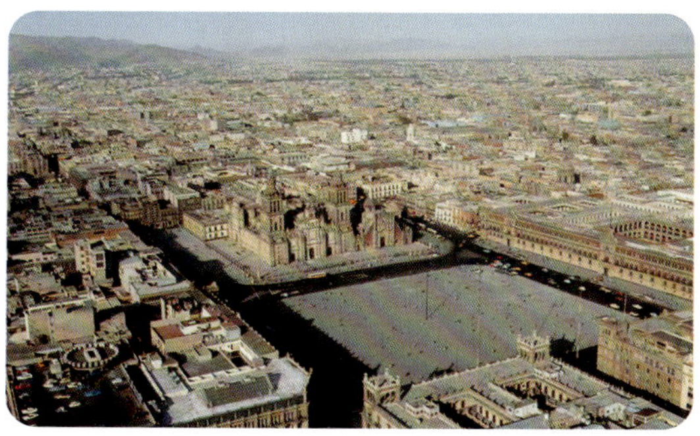

THE ARTIST AT MEL'S CAFÉ, MEXICO CITY, 1991

POSTCARD OF MEXICO CITY
FROM THE ARTIST'S ARCHIVE

and nowhere. In the meantime, *Placing Pillows* taught Alÿs how to turn his walks into sculptural operations.

The subtlety of those early street interventions was characteristic of a milieu born of a remarkably disenfranchized cultural practice. The main advantage that could be enjoyed by people like Alÿs in joining the emerging artistic network developing in Mexico City at the end of the 1980s was that it was as de-regulated as the activities of the illegal vendors on the streets. Venues like the Salón des Azteques (an independent art space run by artist and impresario Aldo Flores), Mel's Café (a Sunday restaurant started by Alÿs and artist Melanie Smith around 1990) and the impromptu curatorial projects of people like Guillermo Santamarina, Rubén Valencia or Maria Guerra were all defined by their belief in the polymorphic productivity of amateurism. No precondition of artistic stature, nationality, ideology or training was required; one could become an artist overnight. The lack of a market and the relatively low interest that audiences, journalists and academics showed in emergent artistic practices proved useful in the long term for nurturing forms of art directly linked with social critique and first-hand experience. For Alÿs, research and imagination, representation and intervention became part of his movement through the city.

Over the years, Alÿs was to develop an archive of images that lay between the nineteenth-century genre of Costumbrista works (the famous lithographs of Mexico City characters by Claudio Linati or the drawings of Lima types by self-taught Peruvian artist Pancho Fierro) and the Neue Sachlichkeit (New Objectivity) photographic project that included August Sander's visual census of the German population in the 1920s and 1930s. Along with his compilation of the periphery still lifes, spontaneous sculptures and street installations he had encountered in Mexico City, Alÿs began a record of the social situations and people who use the street as a temporary shelter. *Ambulantes* (1992–present) shows peddlers pushing their trolleys full of commodities or immense bundles of garbage through squares and avenues; *Sleepers* (1999–present) features people and dogs lying on the streets; and *Beggars* (2000–present) depicts the ever-present panhandlers who expose their misery on the steps of the subway. In these works Alÿs has focused on uses of the street that contradict the strict separation of public and private space. Over the years he was to add further photographic series documenting other symbols of transit: a catalogue of the images of the green 'walk' men used in traffic lights around the world – surprisingly diverse, despite their conventional nature – or the quasi-pictorial arrangements to be found in the patterns of chewing gum stuck under bar tables or on walls and trees (*Untitled [Zicte/Chewing Gum]*, 1994–97).

The pursuit of such chance encounters was bound to become a matrix for performance. Alÿs began to turn his walks into conceptual games. In one work, for example, he looked for another pedestrian who vaguely resembled

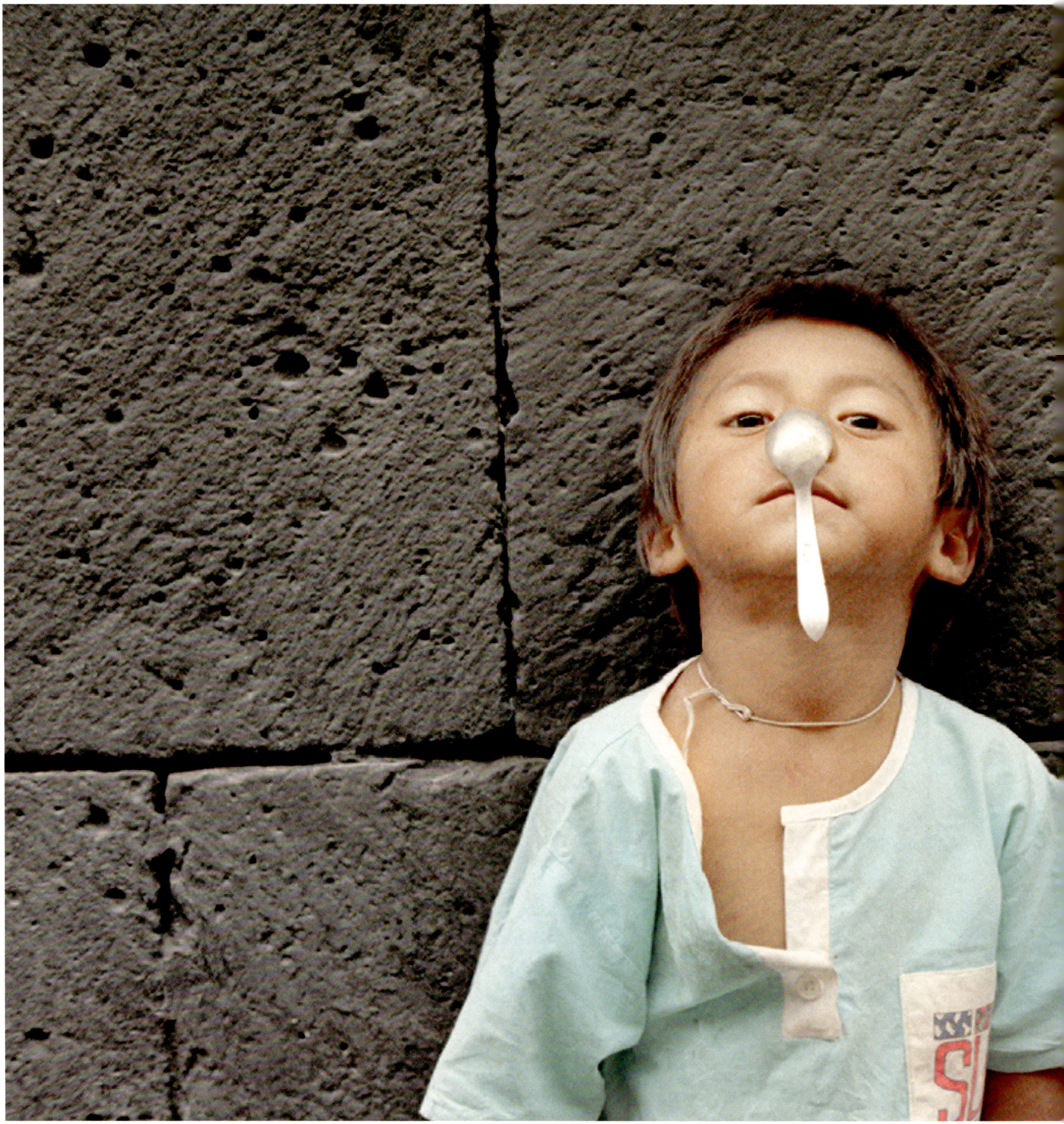

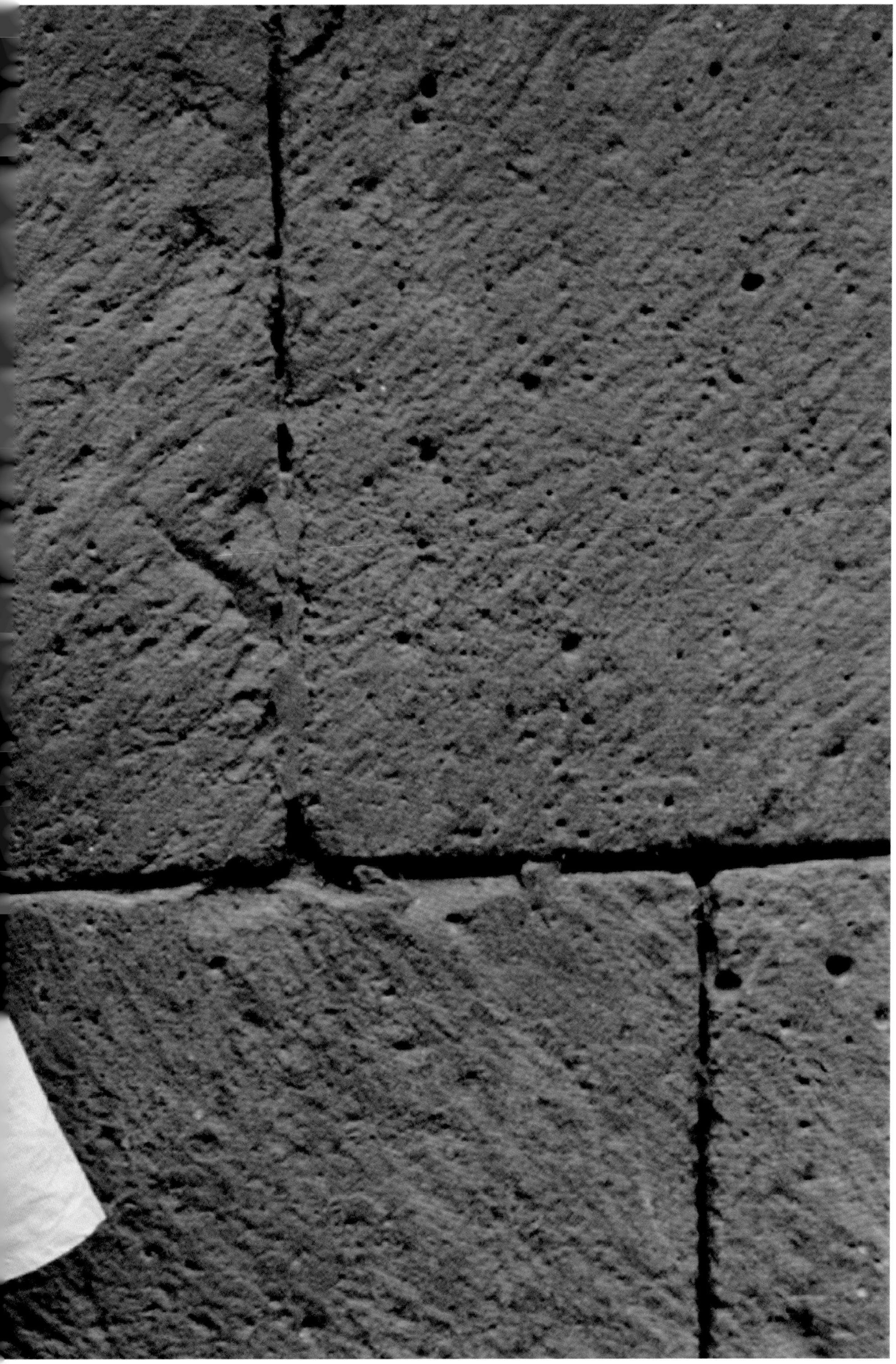

MEXICO CITY, 1991
COLOUR PHOTOGRAPH

him (and who could have thus been him) and followed him like a shadow. These works (*Doppelgänger*, 1999) have a quasi-paranoid edge, as if the artist wanted to become his own persecutor. There are similarities between these actions and Vito Acconci's *Following Piece* (1969, part of his *Street Works* series), in which for twenty-three days Acconci followed different people in the street until they disappeared inside a building. The *Doppelgänger* series, however, is less about accepting somebody else's lead than about trying to put oneself in the mental landscape of a foreign place through surrogate means. In the artist's own words: 'I am usually trying to assimilate cities, and because I never really belong to them, I try to invent myself a role. I attempt to insert myself as another character to gain some kind of identity in a new neighbourhood.'[9]

Yet at times foreignness can also become a form of integration. In the early 1990s, Alÿs photographed himself wearing green shades and reclining against the railings of Mexico City Cathedral, a place where plumbers, electricians, carpenters, locksmiths, housepainters and any number of other tradesmen tout for business. A hand-painted sign lies at his feet, inscribed with the word 'turista' (tourist). This portrait (*Turista*, 1994) stands as a marker of identity; Alÿs pretends to have been absorbed by the downtown area of Mexico City to the point of becoming just another of its workers. As will be seen later, this conflation of the worlds of leisure and work suggests the degree to which his own wanderings as a visitor had become a way of life.

Moving Tales

'In my city everything is temporary', Alÿs has stated, meaning that his sculptural ideas are based on fleeting social and material occurrences. Works derived from walks, such as *Placing Pillows*, activated the street as a stage of displaced objects, suggesting the way in which people and activities are loosely connected in social composites. Alÿs advanced a mode of sculpture that dwelt in the encounter and articulation of objects and bodies, producing images that depended on the faintest possible material relation between things.

For *Mexico City* (1991), he invited a child on the street to balance a spoon on the tip of his nose. The resulting

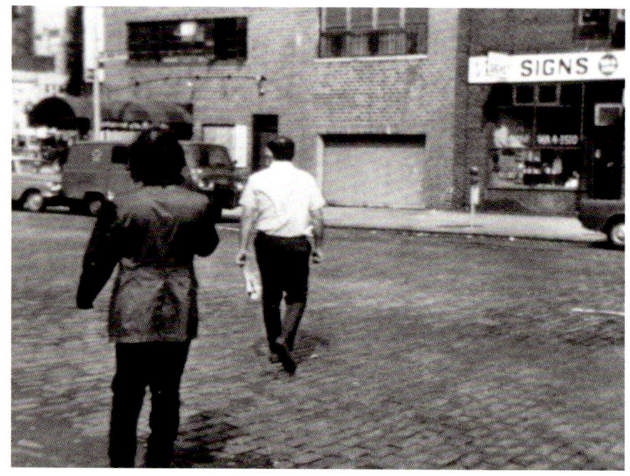

VITO ACCONCI
FOLLOWING PIECE, 1969
ACTIVITY, 23 DAYS; VARYING TIMES EACH DAY
VARIOUS LOCATIONS, NEW YORK

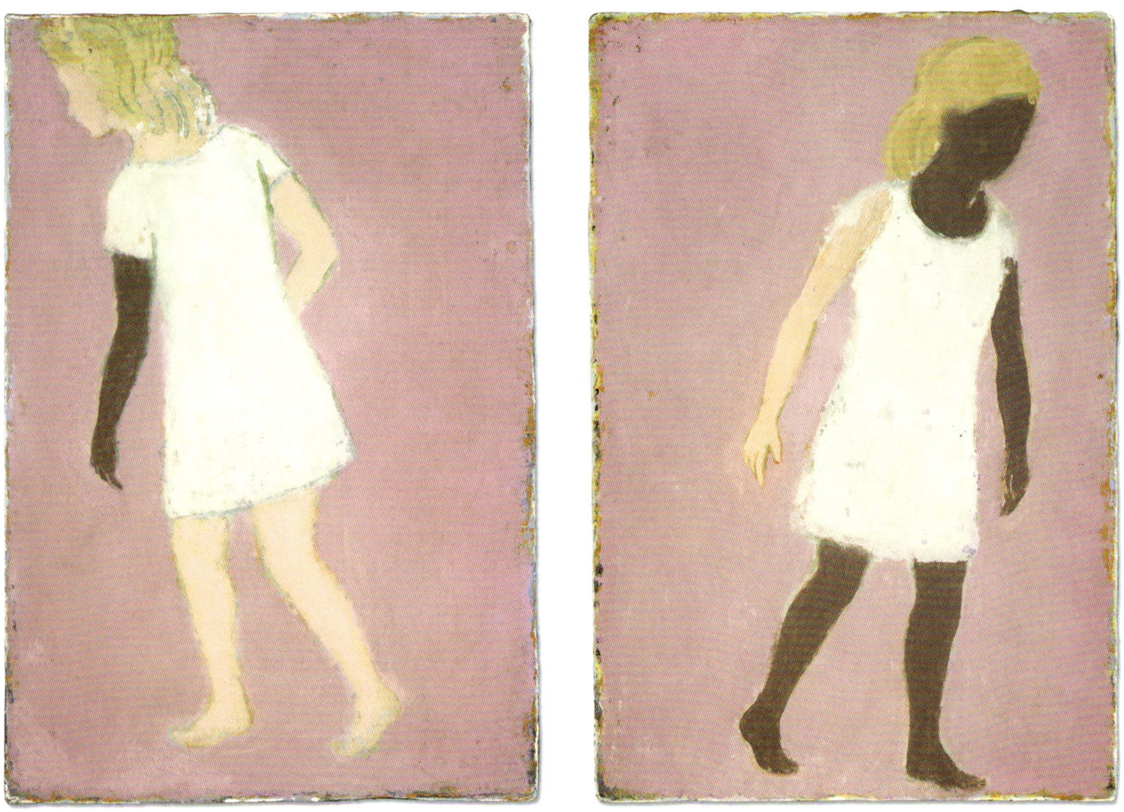

TWO SISTERS, 1999–2002
DIPTYCH
OIL AND ENCAUSTIC ON CANVAS
EACH 29 X 19 CM

<u>DOPPELGÄNGER</u>, 1999–PRESENT
2 OF 80 35 MM SLIDES

```
When arriving in a new city, wander,
looking for someone who could be you.
If the meeting happens, walk behind your
doppelgänger until your pace adjusts to
his/hers. If not, repeat the quest in
the next city.
```

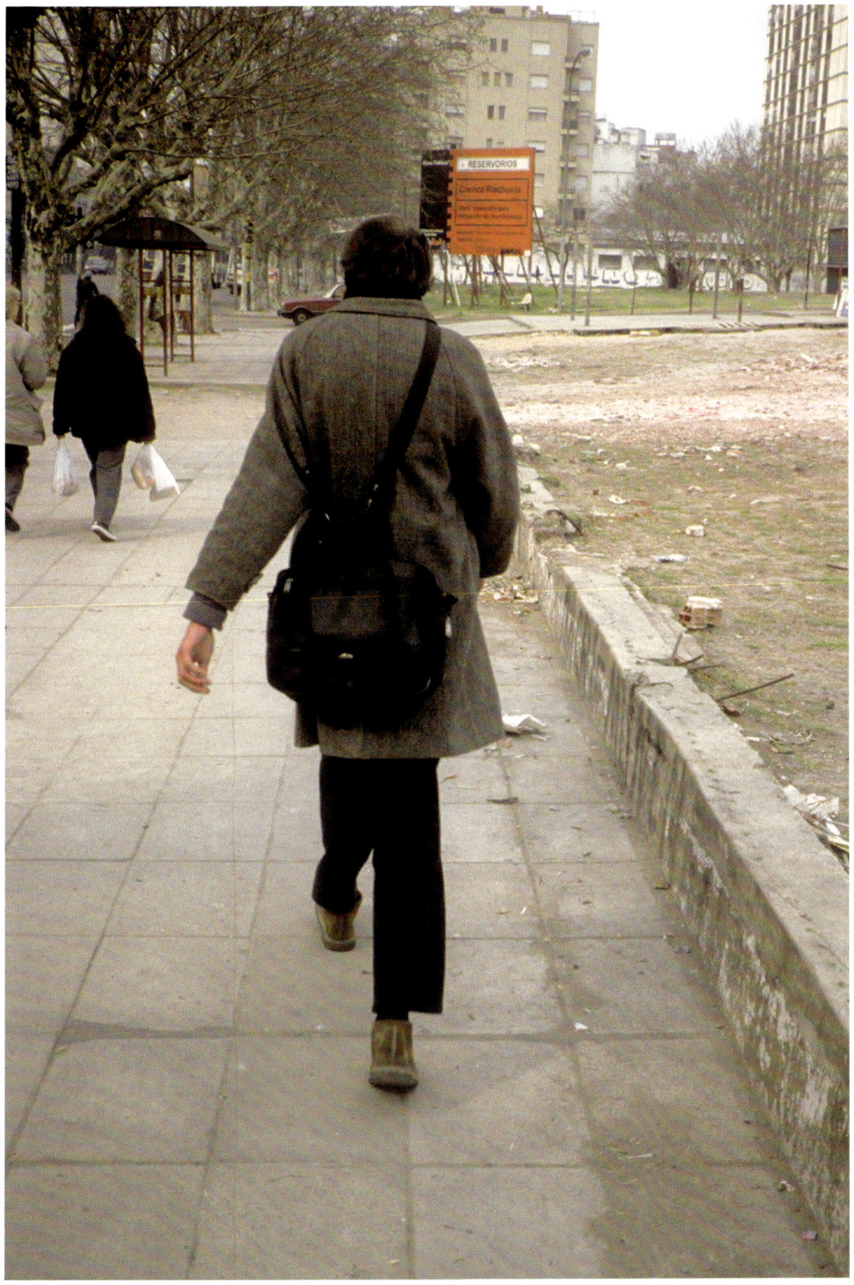

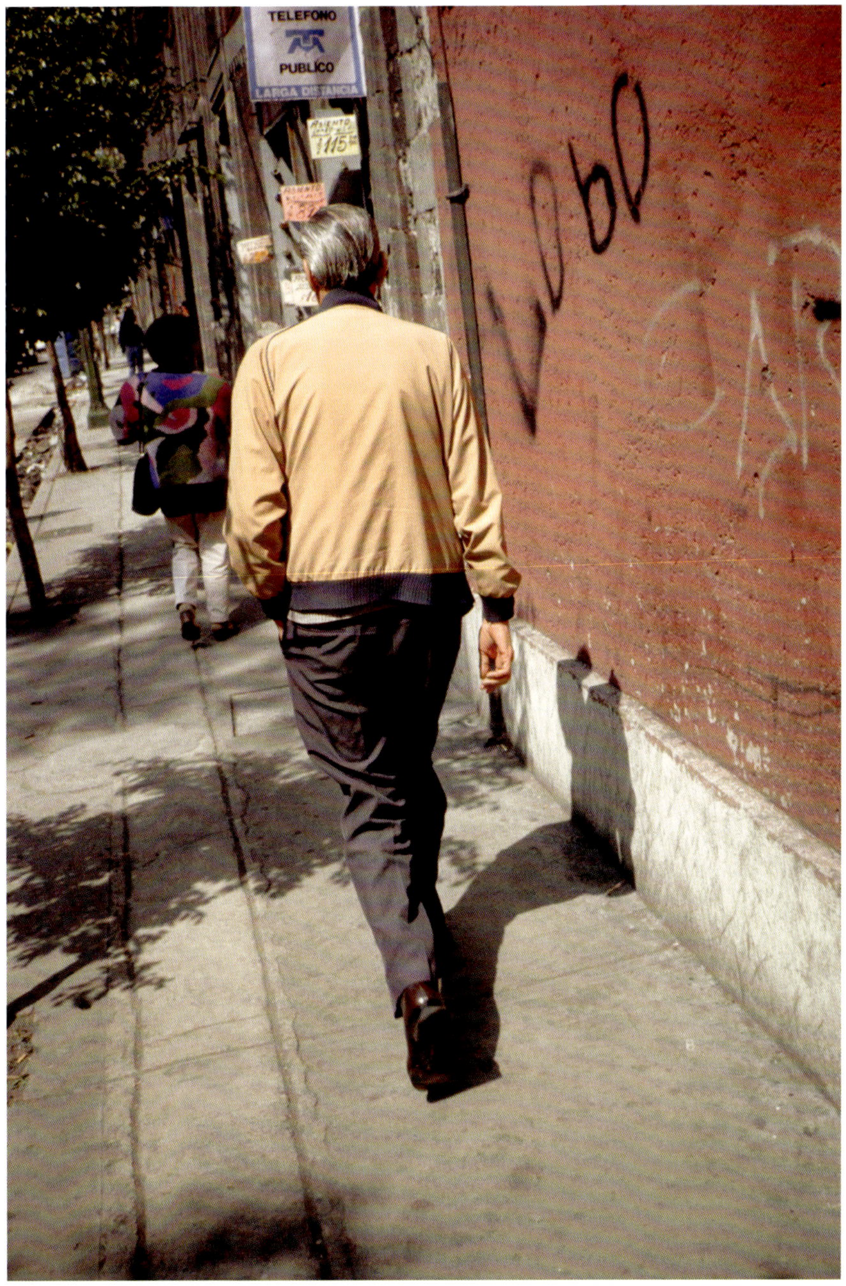

photograph clearly represents a conception of sculpture made of moments of contact, attraction, friction and collision between objects and social formations. Throughout these works, Alÿs rejected both the authority of the notion of social and industrial design and the symbolic weight of sculpture understood as a permanent material erection above the ground. Instead of the ideology of construction, he explored physical and social connections that glowed like a magnetic field. Rather than dwelling on social and mental structures, he was inclined to investigate the cracks in the urban narrative.

Between 1990 and 1991, Alÿs devised the idea of staging a walking fable. His proposal had a certain homeopathic character, the hope of applying 'the hair of the dog' to the urban malaise. He imagined the need for staging a return of the 'animal hero' (the urban parasite) to the centre of the polis. If the pursuit of modern utopias had banished animals, he felt the need to reinsert them metaphorically in the guise of an animated object able to gather leftovers, an animal collecting 'personal losses'.[10] This is how *The Collector* (1990–92) entered the scene.

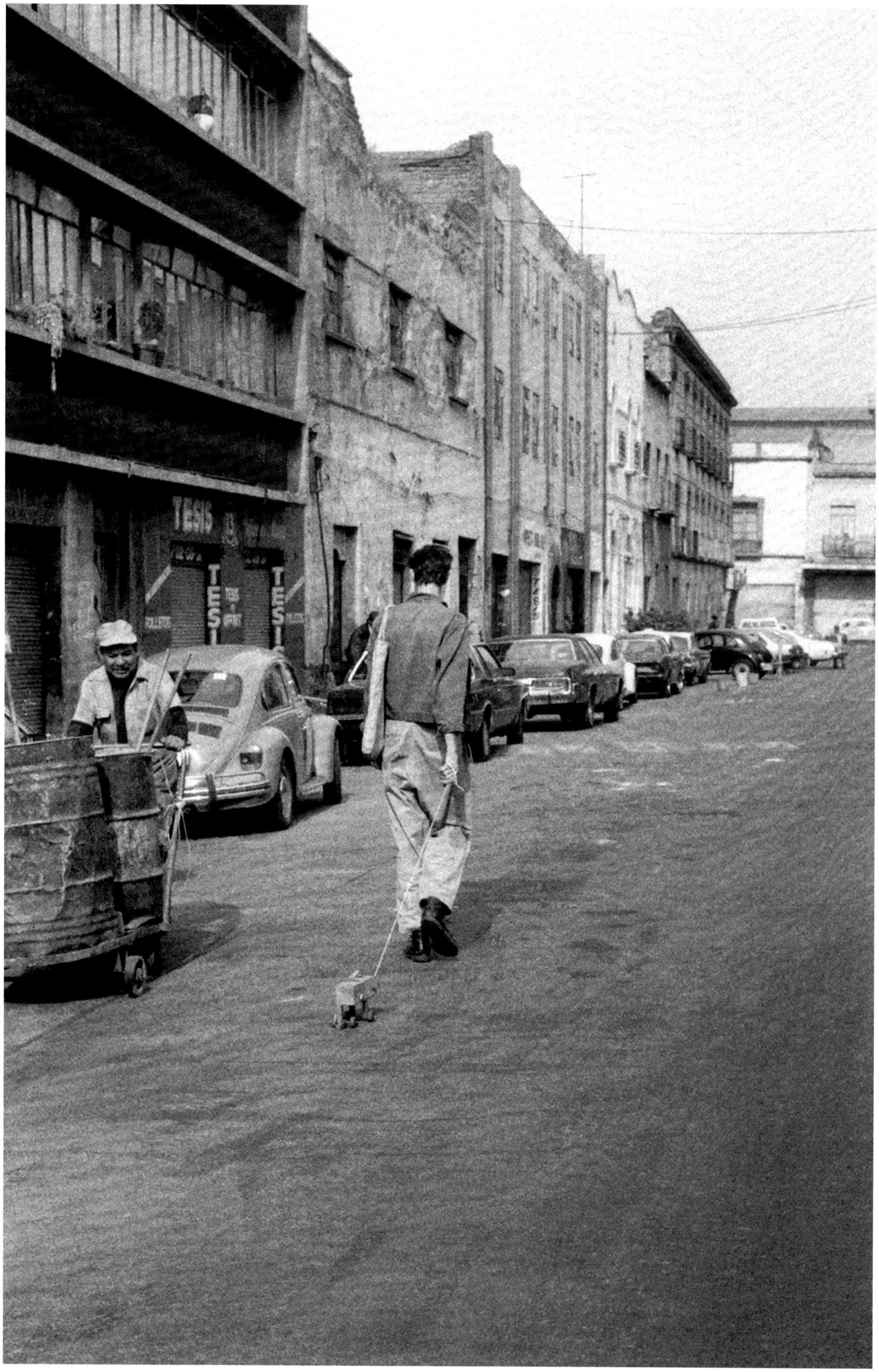

THE COLLECTOR, 1990–92
IN COLLABORATION WITH
FELIPE SANABRIA
PHOTO DOCUMENTATION
OF AN ACTION, MEXICO CITY

For an indeterminate period of time, the magnetized collector takes a daily walk through the streets and gradually builds up a coat made of any metallic residue lying in its path. This process goes on until the collector is completely covered by its trophies.

THE COLLECTOR, 1990–92
IN COLLABORATION WITH
FELIPE SANABRIA
PHOTO DOCUMENTATION
OF AN ACTION, MEXICO CITY

below,
THE COLLECTOR, 1990–92
IN COLLABORATION WITH
FELIPE SANABRIA
PENCIL ON PAPER
6 X 9 CM

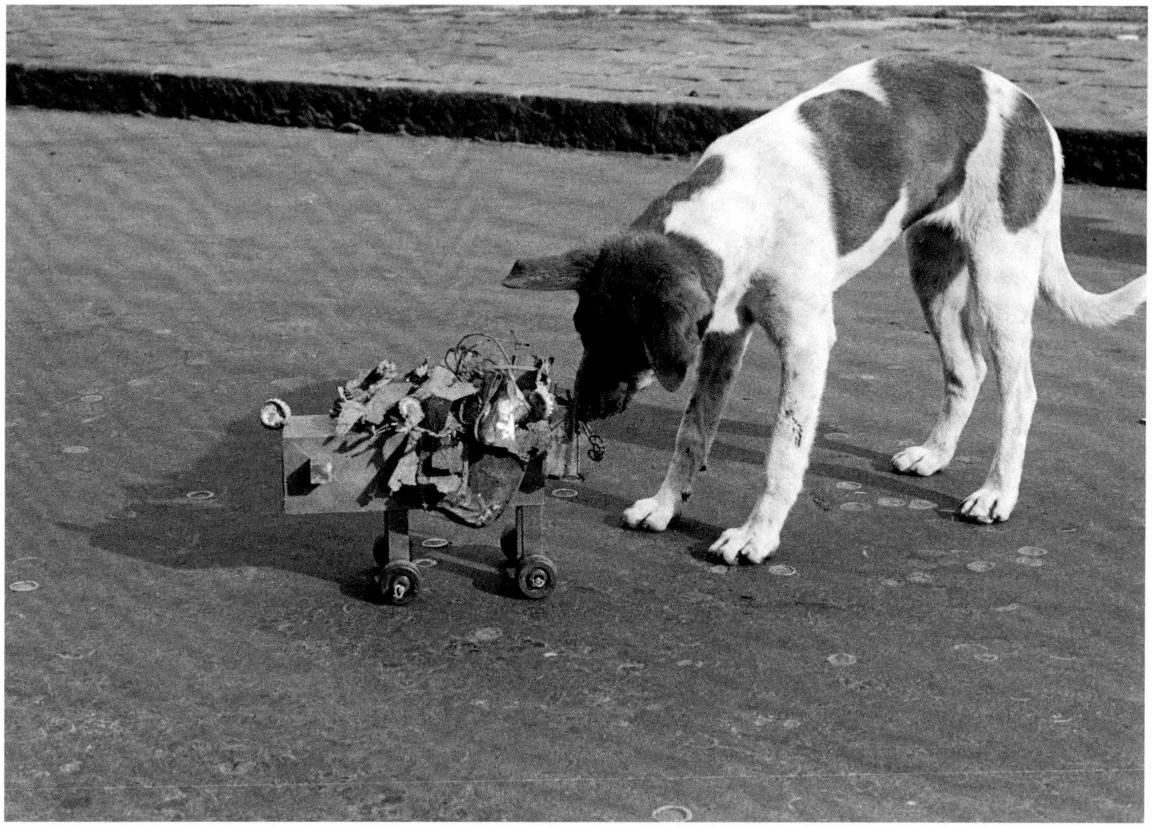

The story of this project is significant in that it shaped the methodology of collaboration that Alÿs was to develop in the following years. After producing a number of wooden and metal models in 1990, during the summer of 1991 he started working with the small industrial workshop of Felipe Sanabria to produce a magnetic animal to be pulled through the streets like a child's toy. The wheeled magnet would attract all the scraps of metal lying in its path until they formed a coat of residue. Despite its simplicity, the project underwent a series of mutations. In the beginning, this 'urban toy' was to be an experimental application of what Alÿs called 'visible science'. But after several failed attempts to infuse a 'magnetic memory' in the metal object by means of an electric current, he finally filled the object with lodestone to ensure a permanent magnetic field. Finally, in the winter of 1991–92 he took *The Collector* on to the streets and walked with it until the prototype was entirely covered with a thick, rusty skin of crooked nails, bits of wire, bottle caps and scraps of metal.[11]

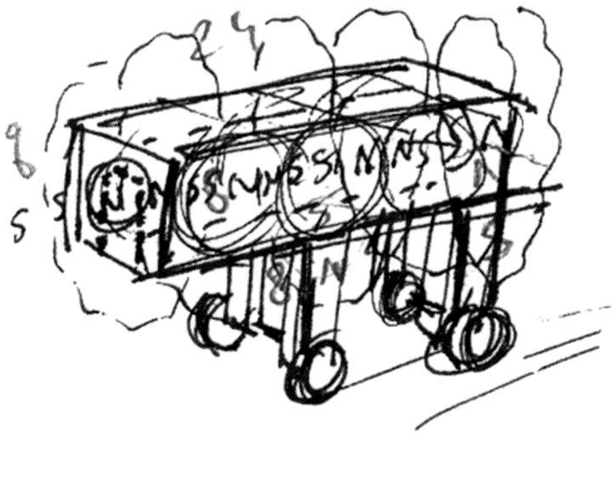

The Collector defined for Alÿs a whole new modus operandi. With this work he self-consciously confirmed walking as his main strategy of intervening in the urban space – exploring social narratives and institutions – and of settling accounts with the history of art. In understanding his actions as 'fables', Alÿs took the decision not to turn his strolls into performance art nor, indeed, any other established genre (painting, sculpture, architecture), instead inventing a creative matrix (and a new poetics) that, through a sense of affinity, develops into a self-evolving spiral of further interventions. His *dérives* were actions/fictions evolving into a series of variations and reverberations. For more than a decade since, Alÿs has lent his body and mind to the development of a new art of storytelling, an objective narrative that, whether recorded by a camera or disseminated through flyers or postcards, strove to remain in the viewer's mind as episodes of a new (though modest) brand of mythology.

One of the earliest and most poetic of those walks may be read as a reversal of the accumulation process employed in *The Collector* but also as an apt variation on the myth of Ariadne or the story of Hansel and Gretel. In *Fairy Tales* (1995) Alÿs perambulated the streets while unravelling the yarn of his sweater, leaving behind a thread that became both a trace and an urban drawing. In May 1994, he expanded the metaphor of his magnetic animal when he wore a pair of *Zapatos Magneticos (Magnetic Shoes)* to walk through the streets of Havana during its fifth Biennial. The magic of those shoes was a symbol of recycling and survival, as well as a meditation on the allure of objects and commodities during the so-called 'special period' of Cuba's socialism-of-one-island system, in which materials were scarce. On that occasion Alÿs took a step further away from the traditional exhibition venue by displaying and producing the documentation of the event during the walk itself. While strolling in his shoes he wore a sandwich board, on which he gathered evidence of the action, from Polaroid photographs to route maps and any number of souvenirs picked up along the way.

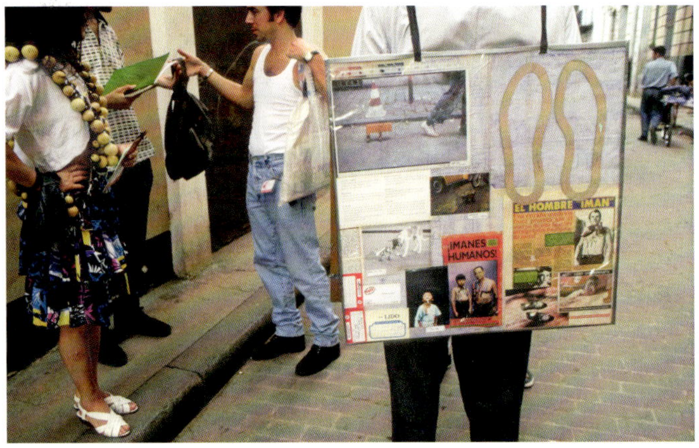

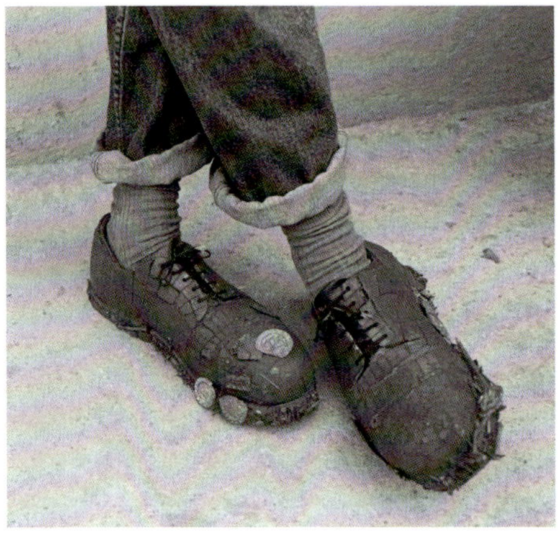

LOS ZAPATOS MAGNETICOS (MAGNETIC SHOES), 1994
PHOTO DOCUMENTATION
OF AN ACTION, HAVANA

During the 5th Havana Biennial, I put on my magnetic shoes and took daily walks through the streets, collecting scraps of metal lying in my path.

Like traditional fables, most of Alÿs's walks have a subtle but nonetheless seductive moral; they tend to assume an Aesopian role as social and political satire. In the several versions of *The Leak* (1995), for instance, he took painting for a walk. Carrying a can of paint from which the pigment trickled through a hole in its bottom, he set out from a gallery and wandered the meandering streets of the city, producing a kind of Jackson Pollock along the way, and finally returned to the exhibition space. If such a path symbolically indicates that his walks are not attempts to escape the artistic and commercial circuit as such, *The Leak* can also be seen as a variation on *Fairy Tales*. At the end of the day, it is a parable of the way in which artistic 'production' is made of loss.

Critique of the Flâneur

With his promenades Alÿs entered a long genealogy of practices that employ the artist's legs to intervene in the social and symbolic imaginary and to assert the right of the citizens to a social space devised for human beings, not for their machinery, traffic and policing systems. Whether because marching became the mode of mass politics in the twentieth century – the theme of Giuseppe Pellizza da Volpedo's *Quarto Stato* (1898–1901) and Joseph Beuys' *La Rivoluzione Siamo Noi* (1972) – or due to the search for new modes of visuality and mobility, walking has been one of the foremost catalysts of the modern imagination. Alÿs's political and poetical explorations of the city have frequently led to associations with two such strategies: the contemplative perambulations of the *flâneur*, as defined by Charles Baudelaire and Walter Benjamin, and the psychogeographic *dérive* practised by the members of the Situationist International.

If walking has become so central in art and politics, it is due to the way in which it goes against the grain of the social, physical and psychic development of modern capitalism. While industrial means of transport threaten to make our limbs and our senses obsolete – confining

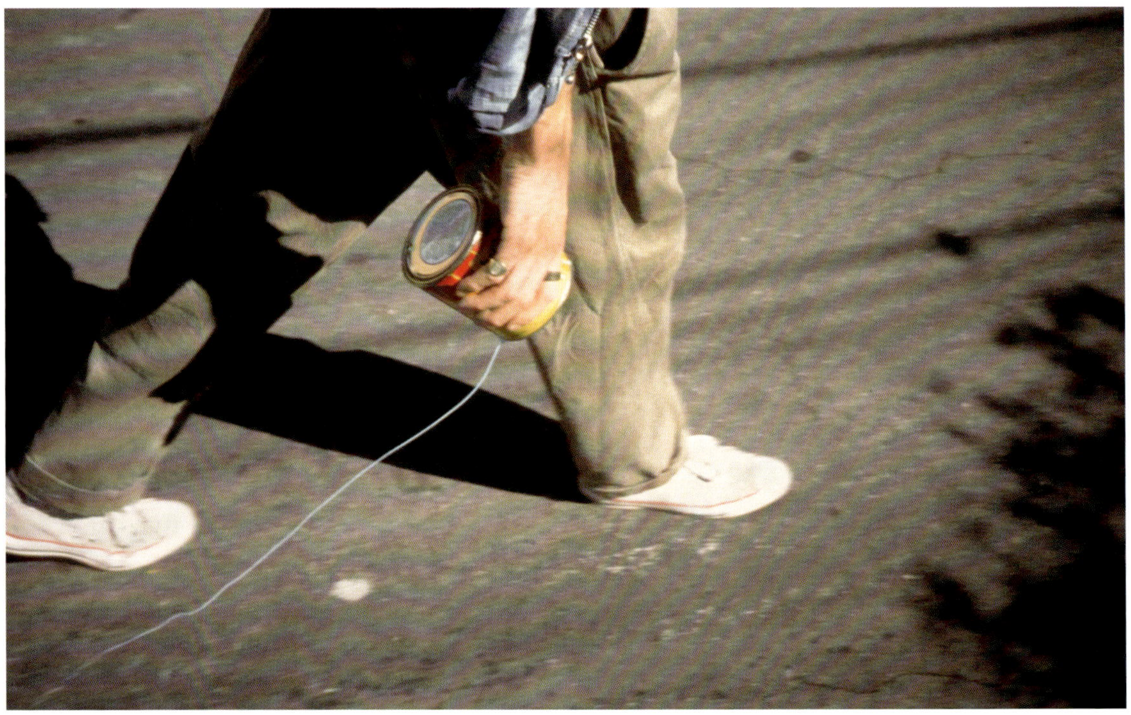

right and below,
THE LEAK, 1995
PHOTO DOCUMENTATION
OF AN ACTION, SÃO PAULO

Having left the gallery, the artist wanders through the neighbourhood carrying a leaking can of paint. His dripping action ends when, finding his way back to the gallery thanks to the paint marks, he hangs the empty can on the wall of the exhibition space.

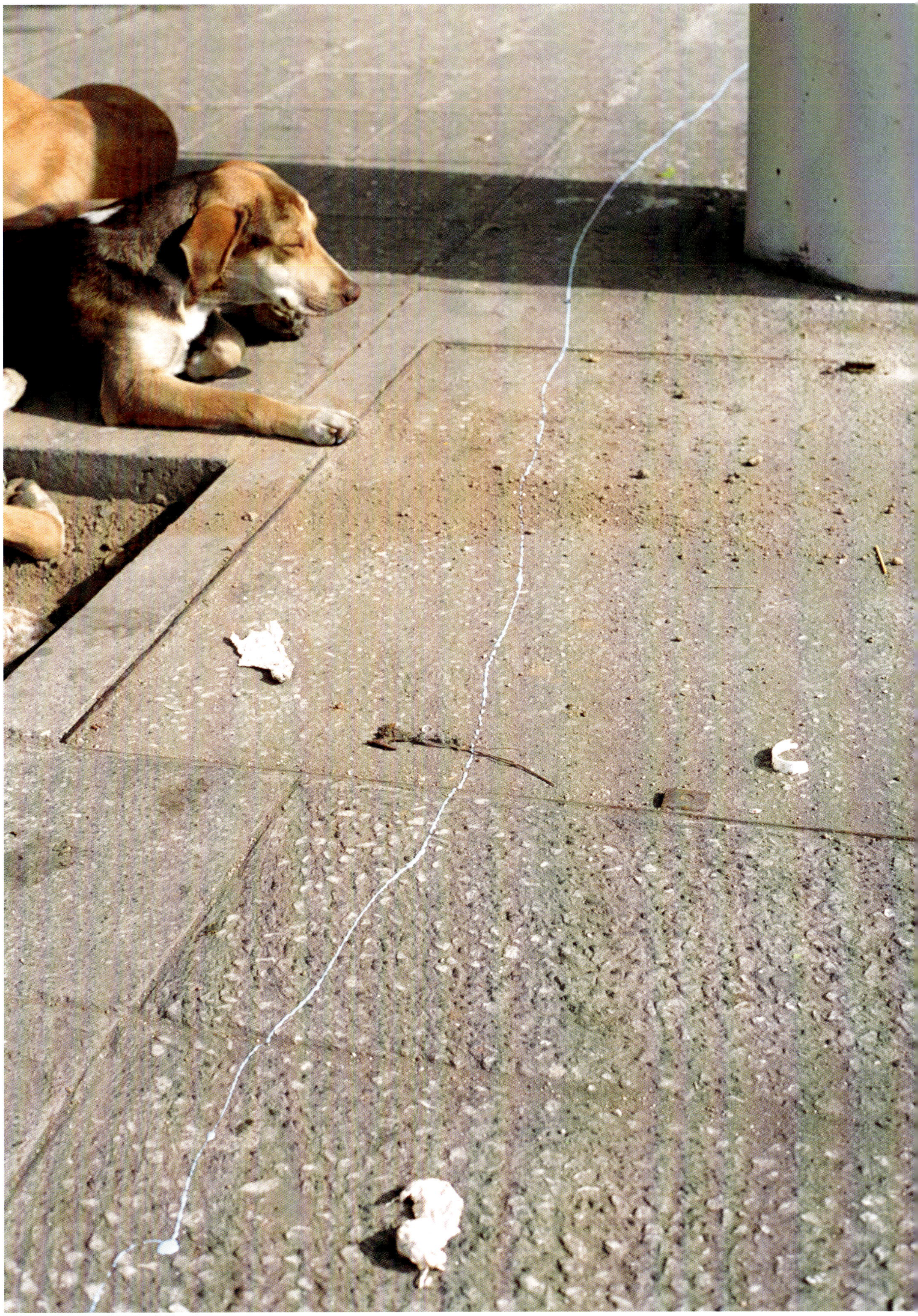

NARCOTOURISM, 1996
GRAPHIC DOCUMENTATION OF AN ACTION, COPENHAGEN
46 X 32 CM

Over the course of seven days I will walk in the city of Copenhagen under the influence of a different drug each day.

NARCOTOURISM / KBH 5-II MAY 1996

I will walk in the city* over the course of seven days,under the influence of a different drug** each day. My trip will be recorded through ~~photographs,~~ notes, and any other media that become relevant.

*the *project* is about being physically present in a place , while mentally elsewhere.

**dosage:drugs were consumed in order to maintain a continuous effect for 14 h.a day.

May 5 ....Spirits (I)
May 6 ....Hashish (2)
May 7 ....Speed (3)
May 8 ....Heroin (4)
May 9 ....Cocaine (5)
May 10 ....Valium (6)
May II ....Ecstasy (7)
(8)

(I) Spirits.(due to practical problems in finding the stuff,I decide to start with local liquors and alcohol).Difficulties in connecting mentally with my physical state. Inner resistance. Inability to trust my reflexes or sight. I walk clumsily among many strange occurences.

(2) Hashish. Slow motion. Awareness of every muscle in action. Everything is enormously funny. Soundless speech. Walking with my eyes closed. A pastrami sandwich tastes heavenly.

(3) Speed. Deambulatory paranoia. Cold feet. I fear the signs of my own presence, and avoid encounters on the street.As I walk, I always keep a familiar spot in sight.

(4) Heroin. Feeling of inner warmth which helps me break the ice and feel attuned to the place. A sequence of frozen images as I walk along the Danube. The effects fade fast, but they return at the end of the day. Difficulty breathing at night.

(5) Cocaine. Awareness of a change of state, but not followed by a visual echo. Auditory acuity enhanced. Appetite gone Smoking diminished. At night, nausea and thirst.

(6) Valium. Weariness. Aesthenia. Indifference to context. Regular smoking. Frequent pissing and occasional vomiting. While walking, bittersweet memories pop up at regular intervals.

(7) Ecstasy. Visual brightening and erotic impulses. My shoes move and I feel the urge to walk out. Everything I turn to moves, not physically but conceptually. I feel like the epicenter of the world.

(8)The journey was followed by a period of depression. I understood it but could not help sinking into it.

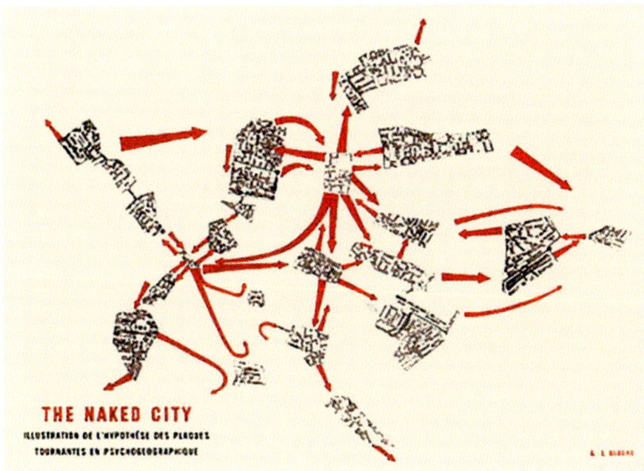

GUY DEBORD
THE NAKED CITY, 1957
COLOUR PSYCHOGEOGRAPHIC
MAP ON PAPER
33 X 48 CM

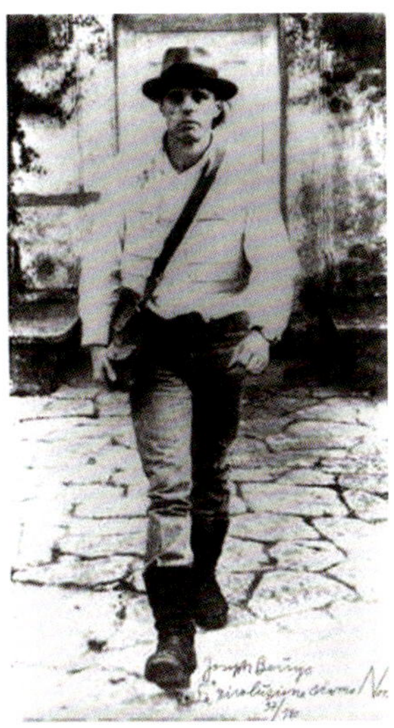

JOSEPH BEUYS
LA RIVOLUZIONE SIAMO NOI,
1972
DIAZOTYPE AND RUBBER STAMP
ON POLYESTER, COMPOSITION
AND SHEET
192 X 101 CM
COLLECTION, THE MUSEUM
OF MODERN ART, NEW YORK

daily life to an oscillation between jobs, media indulgence and shopping – walking persists in defining human life as a matter of territorial and political activity. However, it would be entirely mistaken to subsume this remaining space of freedom into a flat or homogeneous practice. The way in which walking interlocks with living and thinking actually opens up a polemical field of alternatives.

In many ways, and despite common assumptions, acts like Alÿs's walks can be discussed as a critique of the Baudelairean and Surrealist *flâneur*. Despite the fact that he opted to ramble in the midst of one of the largest urban concentrations on the planet, Alÿs's actions are not a form of social voyeurism because, among other reasons, they call attention both to the acts of the stroller and to his interference with his surroundings, rather than to the mere social scenery. In fact, one of his most significant walks was aimed at distracting his sensibility from the 'civilized' living conditions of Copenhagen, which he saw as a veritable caricature of European bourgeois values. Intending to be 'physically present in a place, while mentally elsewhere', in May 1996 Alÿs drifted through that city for seven days, each of them under the influence of a different psychotropic drug. Rather than a mere experiment in intoxication, *Narcotourism* (1996) allowed Alÿs to point out his distance from the expectations of regulation and self-control in the developed world.

On the other hand, according to Baudelaire the *flâneur* is above all a spectator of modern mores and actions, someone who plunges himself into the midst of the crowd to absorb the magnificence of modernity, while cherishing his anonymity as a means of perfecting his voyeurism. His pleasure lies in looking while avoiding the gaze of others for the sake of preserving the spectacle. He displaces his connoisseurship and eroticism – in a word, his fetishism – on to the beauty in the street. The views that the *flâneur* extracts from daily life are, of course, the fruits of his estrangement. 'His passion and profession is to marry the crowd. For the perfect wanderer, for the impassioned observer, it is an immense pleasure to find dwelling in the multitude, the shifting, in the movement, the fugitive and infinite. An observer is a prince who is everywhere in possession of his incognito. Life's lover makes his family of the world, the same way the fair sex lover composes it with all the beauties found, to be found or impossible to find, and the same way the art lover lives in the midst of an enchanted society of dreams painted on canvas.'[12]

As Benjamin argues, the *flâneur*'s task consists in 'botanizing on the asphalt',[13] gathering dead samples of life from the marketplace and the street, as if intending artistically to ameliorate the shock provoked by the brutal experience of living in the emerging metropolis. Small surprise that Benjamin compares the experiences recorded by the *flâneur* to 'the isolated "experiences" of the worker at his machine'.[14] The amusement of the *flâneur* is as fragmented as modern work, and above all it is to a great extent a means of adaptation to modernization rather than a questioning of its pace and direction.

Alÿs's rapport with the cityscape is not a compilation of typical characters but a research into (and an amplification of) those alternative moments that oppose the rationale of city planning and the understanding of modernization as social engineering. No doubt these concerns were not foreign to the Situationist International's critique of urbanism as the 'capitalist domestication of space'.[15] Since the mid-1950s a random and transient drifting (the *dérive*) that traverses the different psychogeographical ambiences of the city[16] was seen by the Situationists as the first step towards the development of a 'Unitary Urbanism'. This involved the construction of situations and 'participatory games' that would create a new social space in which to redress the increasing alienation of the inhabitants of the modern city.[17] The Situationists never thought of their *dérives* as specific artworks but as the founding experience of a new kind of architecture and urbanism that understood the city as a 'continuous *dérive* based on complete disorientation'.[18] Thus, even if they left some record of their *dérives*, it was simply meant to document a 'gathering of ambiences' (both physical and psychical) as experienced by a handful of explorers.[19]

Alÿs's approach is not a programme to forge a new type of urbanism. Instead, it is better understood as part of the plurality of what sociologist Michel de Certeau called 'urban practices', the manifold social activities that directly oppose the regimentation of the city 'founded by utopian and urbanistic discourse'. From the beginning, Alÿs walked to criticize and even disturb the homogeneous, synchronic, universal and classified notion of urban space, as projected by an ideal spectator who conceives urban planning from above. Instead, his horizontal narratives, his attempt to disrupt the social grid by introducing new urban parasites, correspond to what Certeau calls 'the Concept-city', which is 'simultaneously the machinery and the hero of modernity'. Alÿs's walks were conceived on the assumption that they would be read, thought, seen, imagined and retold by others, and that their agency would depend on their dissemination as stories. 'The invention of a language goes together with the invention of a city. Each of my interventions is another fragment of the story I am inventing, of the city that I am mapping. In my city everything is temporary.'[20] This is similar

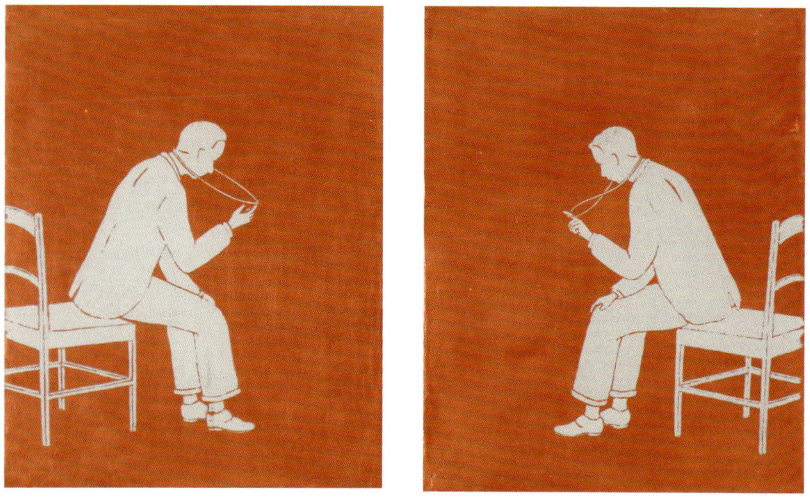

SET THEORY, 1996
DIPTYCH
OIL AND ENCAUSTIC ON CANVAS
EACH 28 X 22 CM

right,
UNTITLED, 1990
MEXICO CITY
SPOON, NAPKIN, AND MAGNET
16 X 11 CM

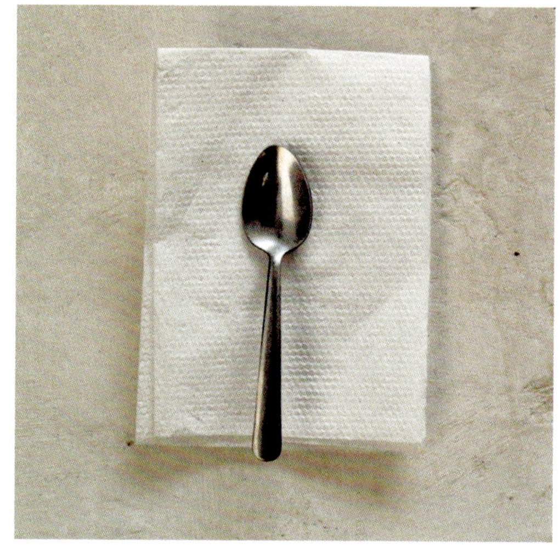

to what Certeau had envisioned when suggesting that 'Physical moving about has the itinerant function of yesterday's or today's "superstitions". Travel (like walking) is a substitute for the legends that used to open up space to something different.'[21]

The notion of travelling as an escape from an apparently locked situation can be epitomized by Alÿs's contribution to the San Diego and Tijuana public art festival InSite 97. At a time of a particularly stringent prosecution of 'illegal aliens' from Mexico living in the United States, Alÿs physically circumvented the border by systematically travelling south from Tijuana until he had circumnavigated the globe in twenty-nine days. *The Loop* (1997) showed the extent to which his narrative actions could work as a means of both social and artistic critique. A trip that began as 'a vain arty joke' (to the extent that the artist blew the production money on a vacation) eventually became 'a sentimental quest for redemption'.[22] However, this escapade was not an indulgent one. Confronted with the universality of anonymous airports, cheap hotels and banal Kodak beauty spots, unable to 'read the local codes', Alÿs found that his trip became a first-hand exposure to life pasteurized by the advance of globalization. Writing from Shanghai, Alÿs remarked, 'Hardly any dogs around. The few I saw are discreetly being walked late at night. Most have been killed during a cleansing of the city. They are the advance victims before a three year plan of "modernization" of the whole downtown area. After a methodical packing ceremony, the morning's next ritual is the quest for coffee.'[23] Alÿs took the self-sufficiency of the wish to travel (the essence of contemporary tourism) to a logical extreme in which (as critic Olivier Debroise has written) 'the trip has no other goal than the trip, a state of consciousness.'[24] It is due to this purity that the action embodies the notion of the artist as a social and cultural wanderer – in other words, the artist as the witness of a shrinking world.

Why Painting?

Painting and image-making have been complementary to the enactment of Alÿs's street fables. The works of artists from the Italian *trecento* and *quattrocento* such as Fra Angelico, the Bellinis and Ambrogio Lorenzetti, and particularly the small scenes featured on *predella* – the little paintings at the base of an altarpiece – helped develop his sensibility to the microscopic anecdotes of urban living. Christian imagery (and in particular paintings about holy miracles) shaped his understanding of the symbolic repertoire of the human body. Alÿs's interest in painting has little to do with questions of historical progression; in fact, it is mostly alien to modernist assumptions about the art of painting as a self-absorbed and autonomous practice. For Alÿs, the pictorial field is above all the surface for an apparition of images, bound to different forms of circulation and displacement, and involved in a number of social and economic relationships. The canvas is for him an everyday artefact (a portable inner space) that is constantly interacting with its surroundings.

Thus, beginning with his early exercises in the medium in the late 1980s, Alÿs has played with the objecthood of painting, refusing to conceive of it as pure form. With his images of intriguing situations involving animals and domestic spaces, he produced objects that were halfway between sculptures, installations and paintings – canvas bent or rolled to reveal the stretcher and the painted wall behind it, or veiled with bubble-wrap to add an evocative, tactile quality. Almost paintings and almost sculptures, their seductiveness relied to a great extent on the precariousness with which Alÿs approached the issues of the artistic medium – a simplicity at that time related to his lack of technical mastery, to be sure, but which already suggested a graceful scepticism regarding the medium that has remained a feature of his work for almost two decades. As curator Kitty Scott once

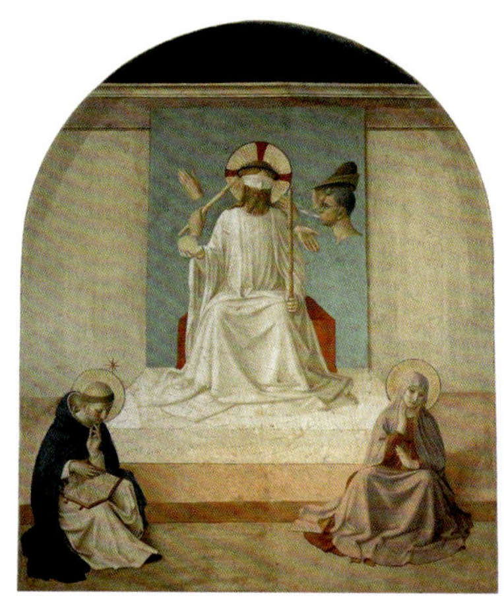

FRA ANGELICO
MOCKING OF CHRIST, C. 1442–50
FRESCO
CONVENT OF SAN MARCO, FLORENCE

SET THEORY, 1996
IN COLLABORATION WITH
EMILIO RIVERA
DIPTYCH
ENAMEL ON METAL SHEET
EACH 160 X 110 CM

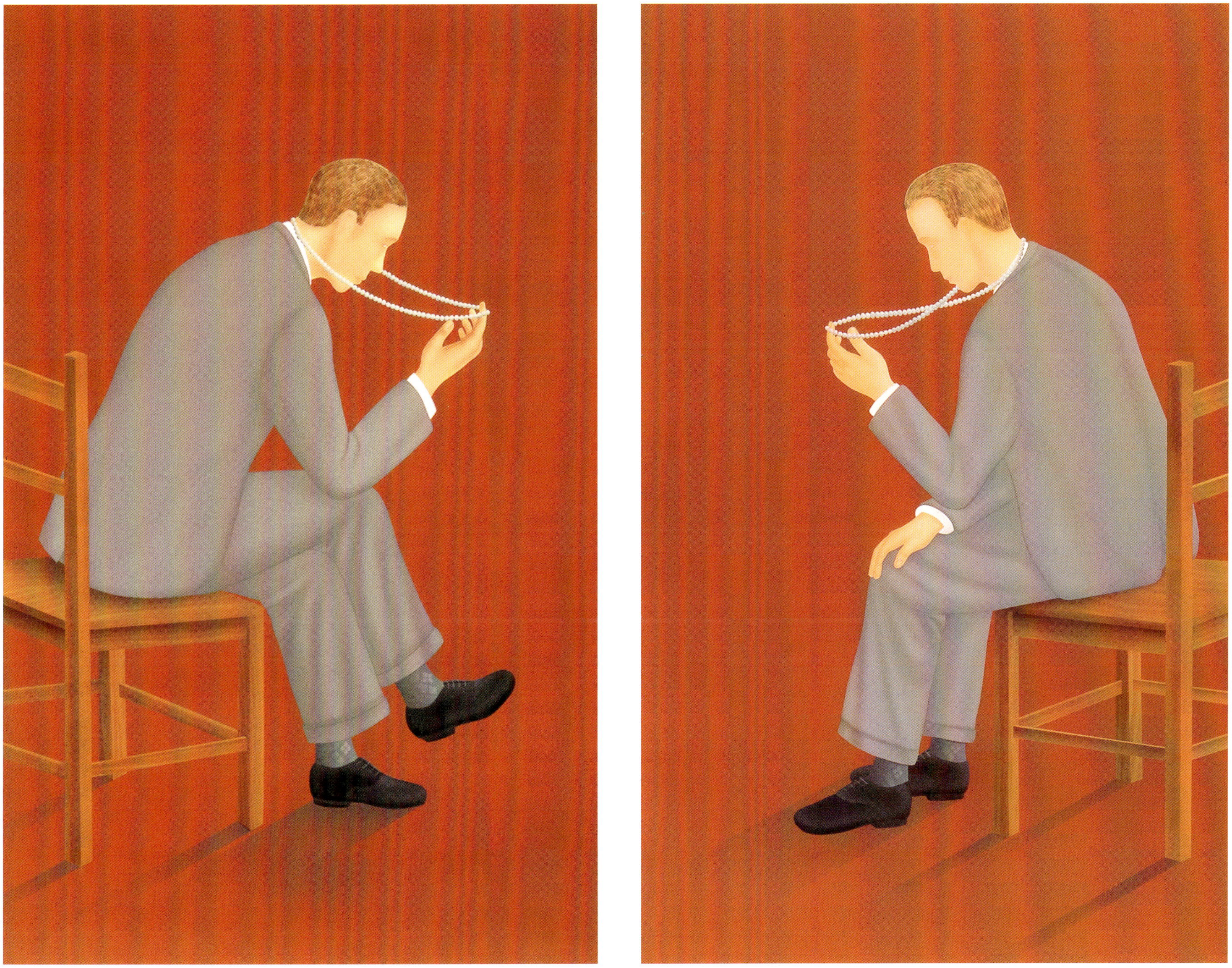

SET THEORY, 1996
IN COLLABORATION WITH
JUAN GARCIA
DIPTYCH
ENAMEL ON METAL SHEET
EACH 140 X 110 CM

JUAN GARCIA (right) IN A SIGN-PAINTING STUDIO, MEXICO CITY

In the spring of 1993 I tried to break down my working methods and sculptural obsessions with a string of figurative scenes illustrating my interventions on the streets of Mexico City. Moving from sketches on paper to small canvases, I would combine a man in a suit with a piece of furniture or some other object, subjecting his body to a range of physically feasible arrangements of weight, balance and so on. The style of these paintings – and their male protagonist – was directly borrowed

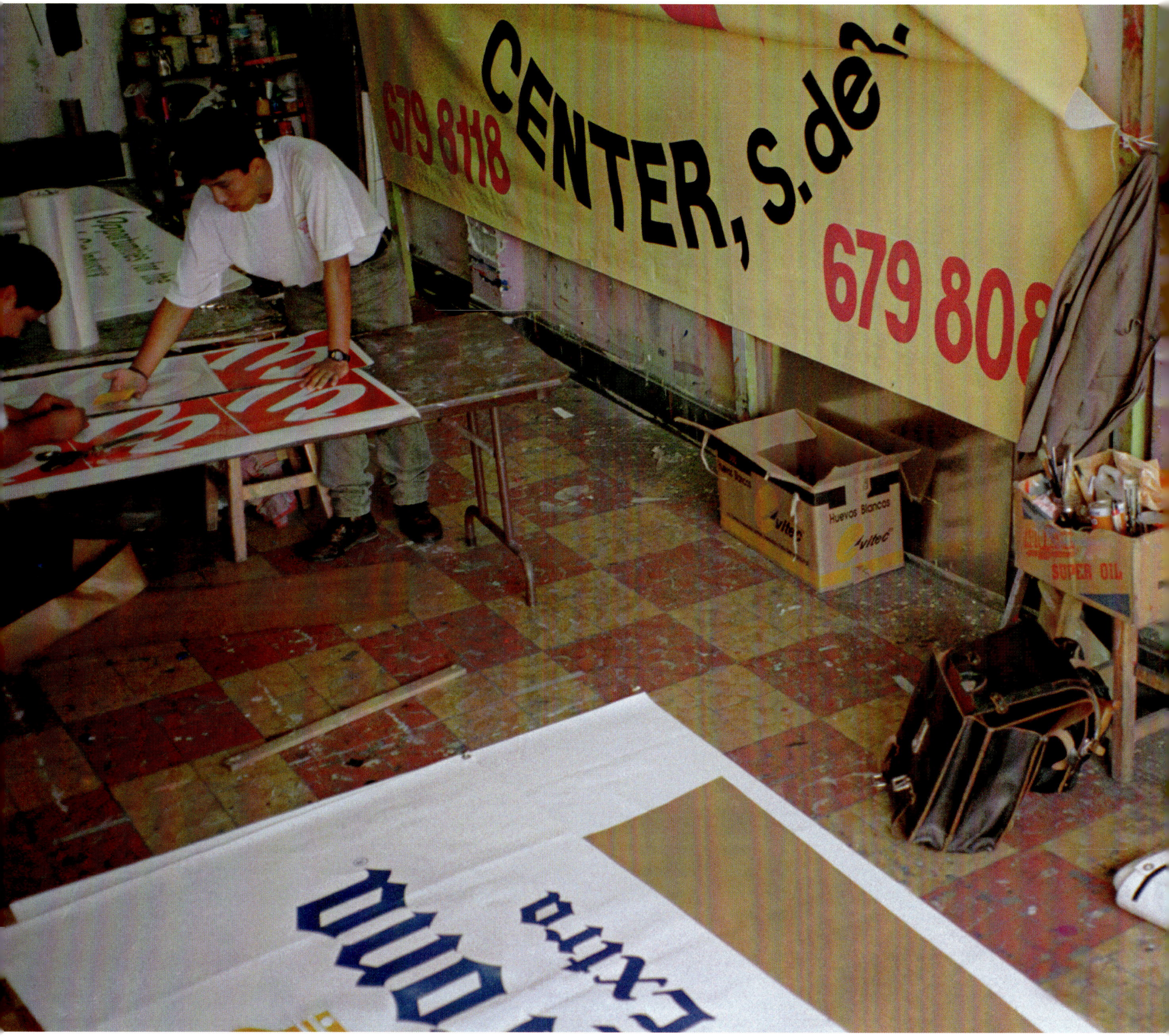

from the painted metal street advertisements I encountered in the Centro Histórico, which impressed me with the communicative power of their iconography.

By the summer of 1993 I had completed a first body of paintings, and the temptation grew to return the images to the people who had inspired them. I commissioned various sign painters to produce enlarged copies of my originals. Once several versions had been completed, I produced a new 'model' that incorporated the most significant elements of each painter's interpretation.

This compiled image was in turn used as the basis for a new generation of copies made by sign painters, and so on, ad infinitum, according to market demand. The underlying intention behind this collaborative process was to work against the idea of a painting as a unique object and to reduce its market value by producing an open edition of images while maintaining copyright on each of them. As time went on, the elaboration of the originals became increasingly influenced by the prospect of the upcoming collaboration, and as mutual dependency grew, considerations about authorship arose. Further blurring the line between the model, the copy and the copy of the copy, I began copying my own models under the influence of the subsequent versions.

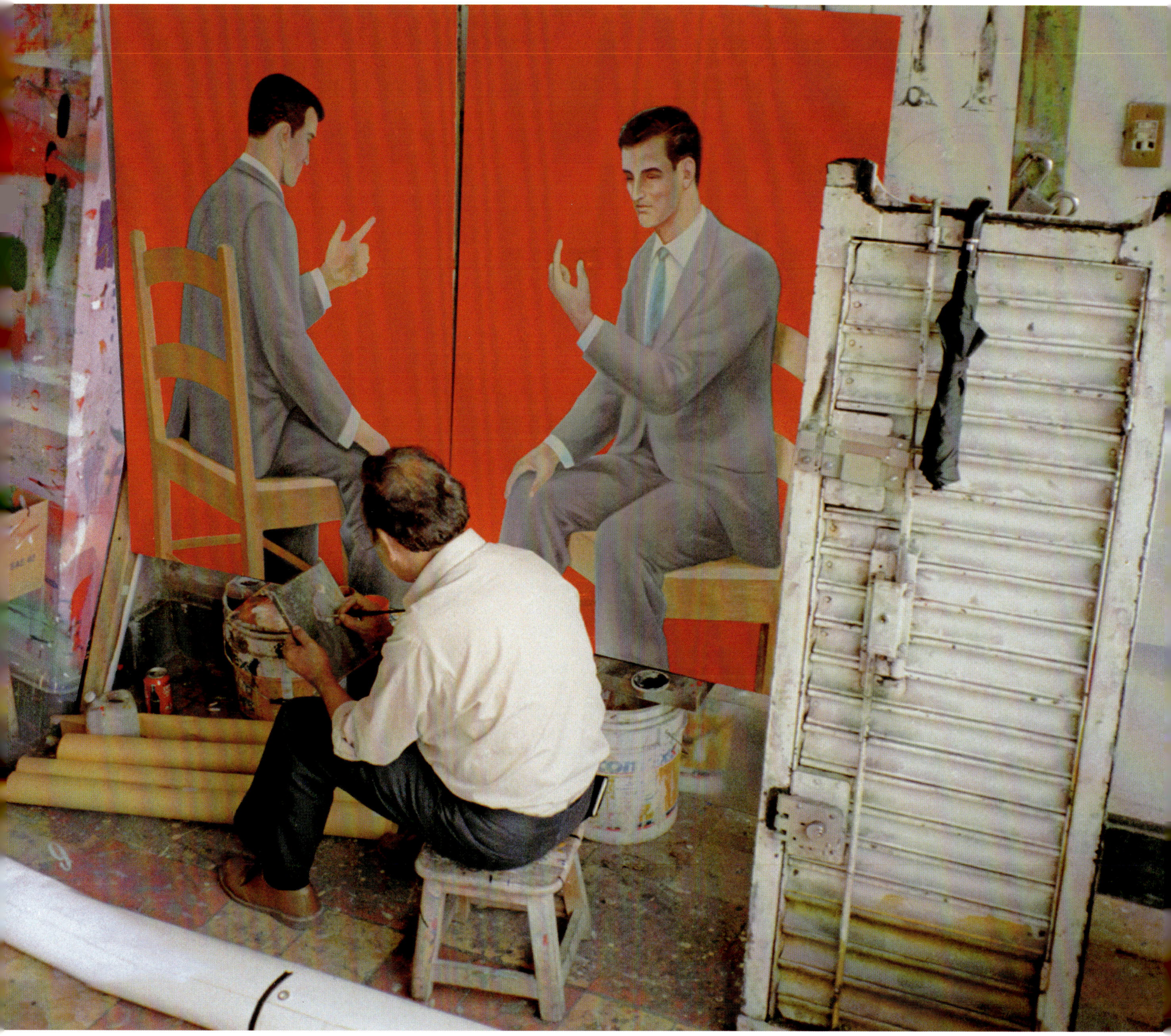

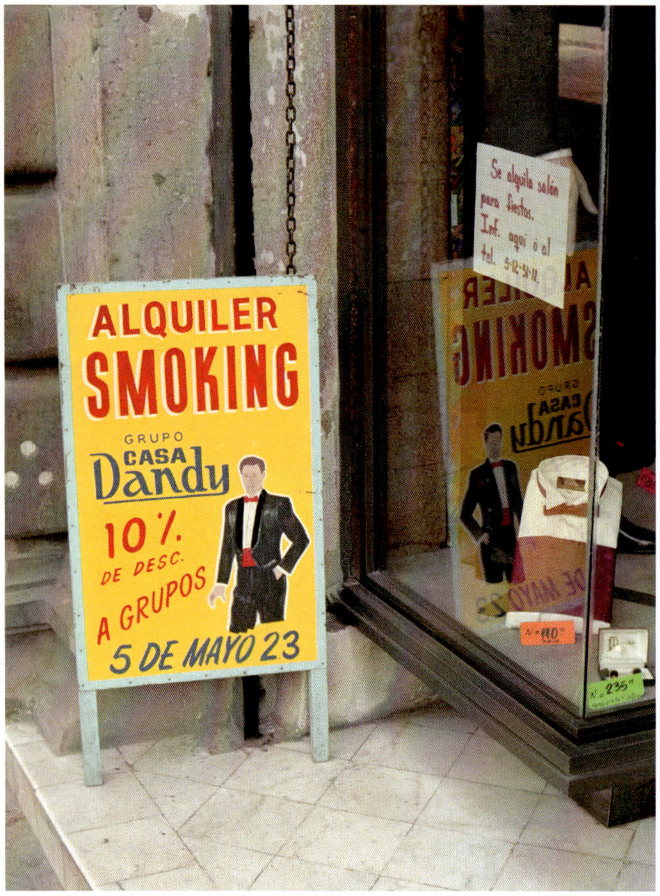

MEXICO CITY, 1994
COLOUR PHOTOGRAPH

THE LIAR/THE COPY OF THE LIAR, CAT 8.1, 1994
OIL ON CANVAS
22 X 17 CM

opposite, from left,
THE LIAR/THE COPY OF THE LIAR, CAT 8.3, 1994
IN COLLABORATION WITH JUAN GARCIA
ENAMEL ON METAL SHEET
132 X 100 CM

THE LIAR/THE COPY OF THE LIAR, CAT 8.2, 1994
IN COLLABORATION WITH JUAN GARCIA
ENAMEL ON METAL SHEET
90 X 70 CM

THE LIAR/THE COPY OF THE LIAR, CAT 8.4, 1994
IN COLLABORATION WITH ENRIQUE HUERTA
ENAMEL ON METAL SHEET
78 X 56 CM

INSTALLATION, SIGN-PAINTING STUDIO, MEXICO CITY

elegantly argued, 'Much of Alÿs's work eludes the medium it employs.'[25]

This avoidance of formalistic or disciplinary commitment was related not to a longing for a subcultural or raw authenticity but to a concern with the social location of art. Once he had started to work as a visual artist, Alÿs found himself concerned by a central paradox of contemporary art: the more art became enmeshed in everyday experience, refusing any attachment to specific media, the more esoteric it became for the majority of the audience. While the images and references of his art were in the street, his early installations and walks were unreadable except to the small circle of those 'in the know'. Once again, the street provided Alÿs with an answer to this conundrum. Wandering about downtown Mexico City in the early 1990s, he was struck by the widespread use of hand-painted signs to identify shops and workshops. Unlike in the industrial world, sign painters in Mexican society still had a significant role in the society, producing street advertisements, banners with political slogans and portraits of leaders and presidents that were prominently displayed at official rallies. Alÿs came to recognize that, in contrast to contemporary art, the language and media of the sign painter still constituted a social lingua franca equally able to transmit information, seduction, demagogy and illusion. In Mexico City, as in other parts of the Third World, painting was not only a fine art. It was still an essential means of social communication.

Early in 1993 Alÿs started to collaborate with the authors of those street paintings in developing a circuit of artistic production. Borrowing the smartly dressed characters depicted in the signs for tuxedo-rental establishments and tailor shops, along with their communicative style, Alÿs depicted his 'sculpture ideas' on small canvases that usually portrayed a lone man, an archetype of the modern subject, dressed in a suit and tie and involved in a number of sculptural fantasies. These were figurative translations of imaginary transitions between objects and the body, in which body parts and everyday things collided, fused and overlapped with the same unassuming magic of street situations. His character would sit at a table, for example, with a small installation of interconnected objects emanating from his elbows, or would play a ruler over his shoes. The iconography triggers obvious associations with René Magritte, who was originally a commercial artist and was thus conversant in the visual language of advertising. That Alÿs started to paint in a flat and somewhat anti-stylistic fashion emanated from the fact that for him painting was a means of visual communication and intellectual exploration rather than a form of optical enchantment.

It was in an attempt to return his images to those who had inspired them that in 1993 Alÿs decided to produce his paintings through a process of inter-subjective collaboration. He took his small canvases to a handful of commercial sign painters (*rotulistas*, as they are known in Mexico) who were masters of their craft. (One of

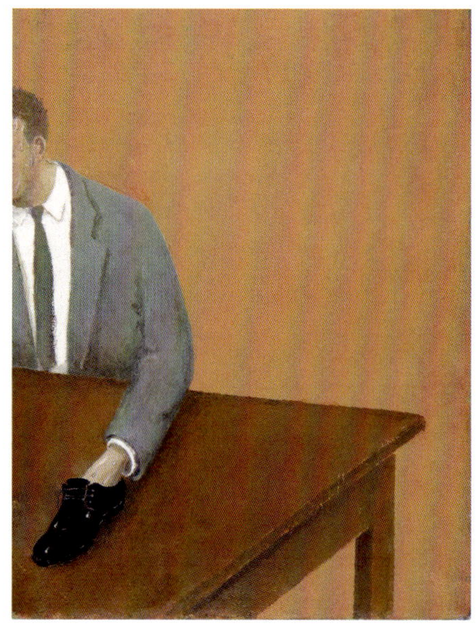

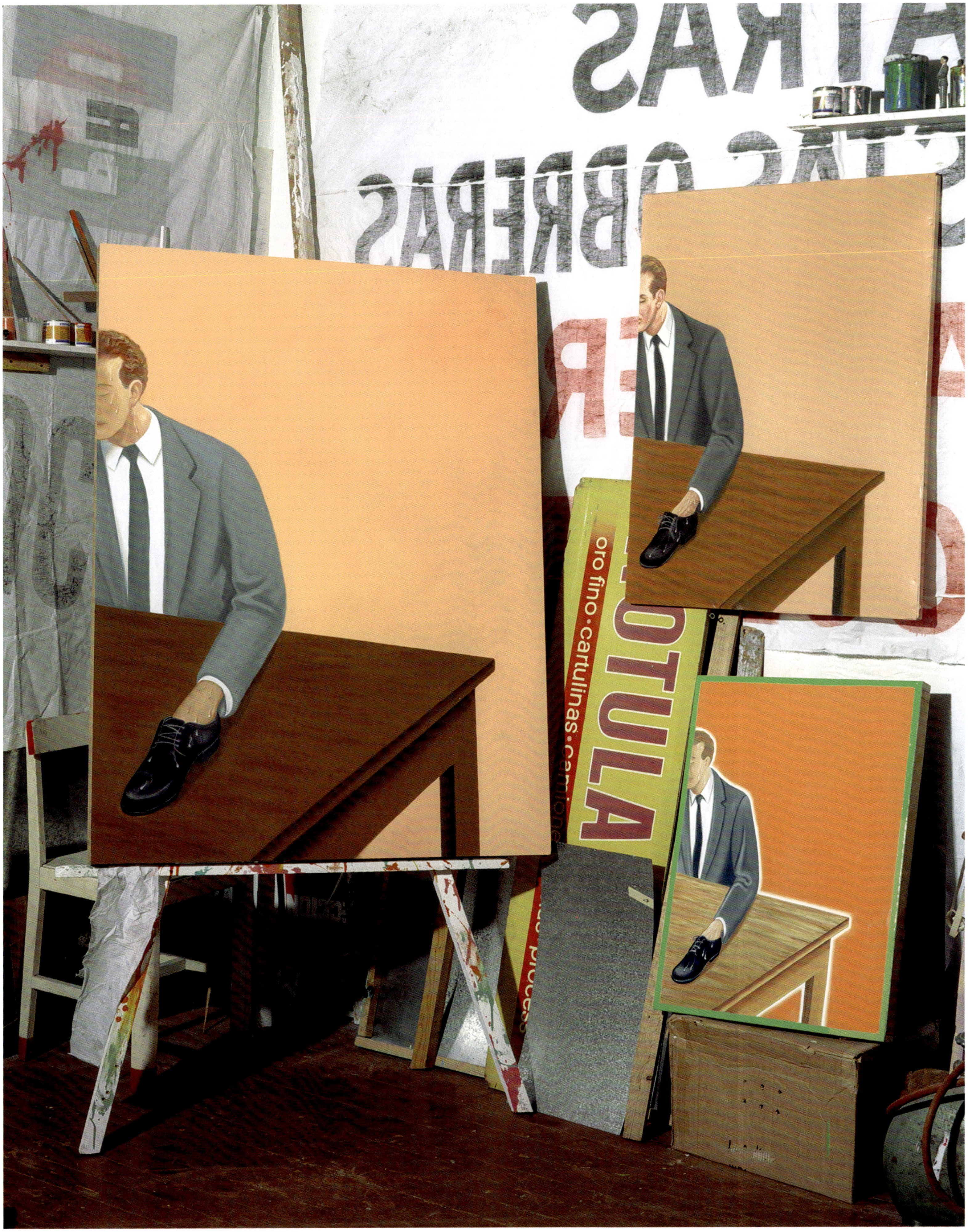
oro fino•cartulinas•
OTULA

STUDY FOR EL SOPLÓN, 1995
PENCIL, OIL AND COLLAGE ON TRACING PAPER
28 X 23 CM

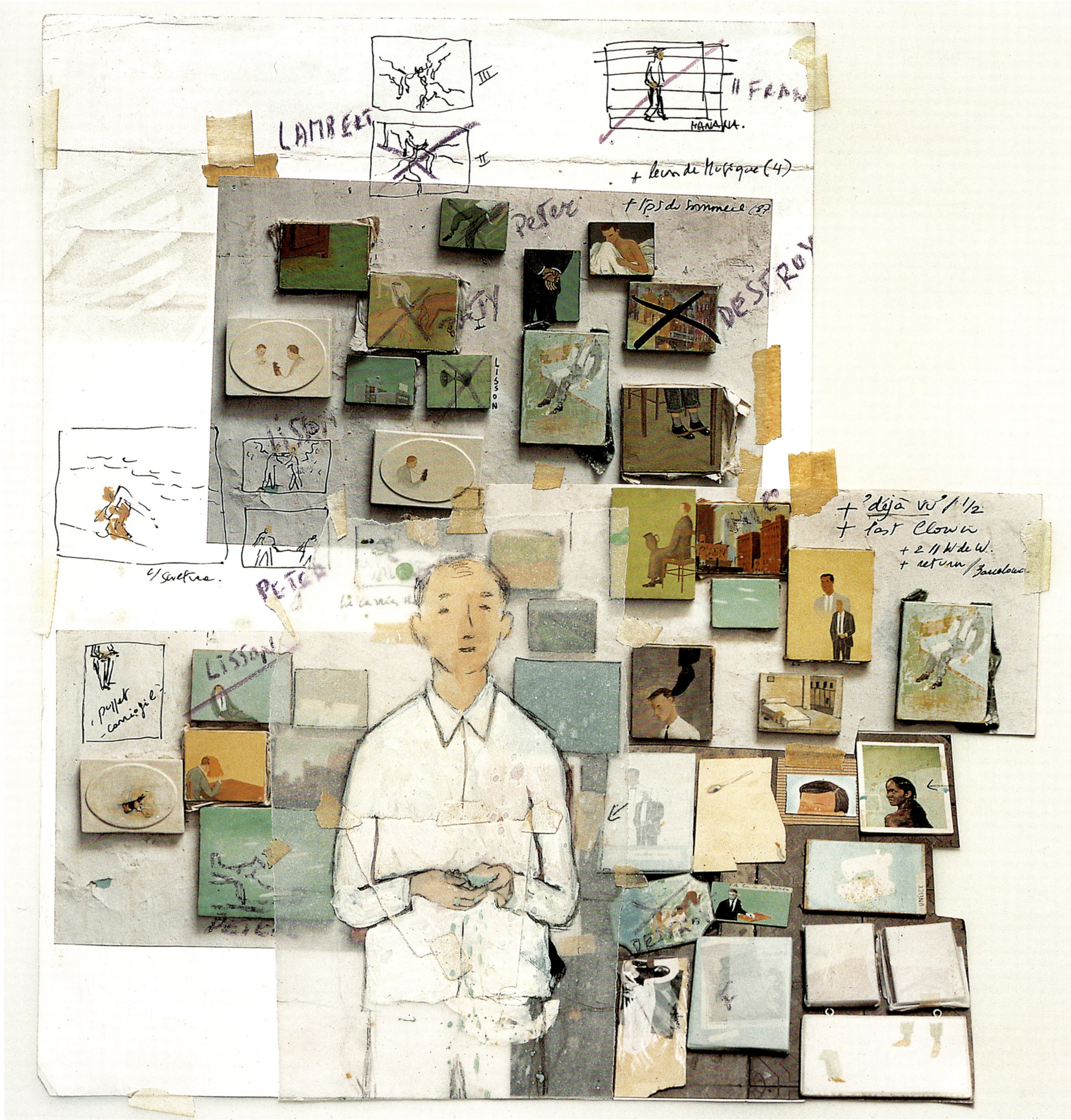

EMILIO RIVERA IN HIS STUDIO WITH
EL SOPLÓN, 1995
ENAMEL ON METAL SHEET
160 X 122 CM

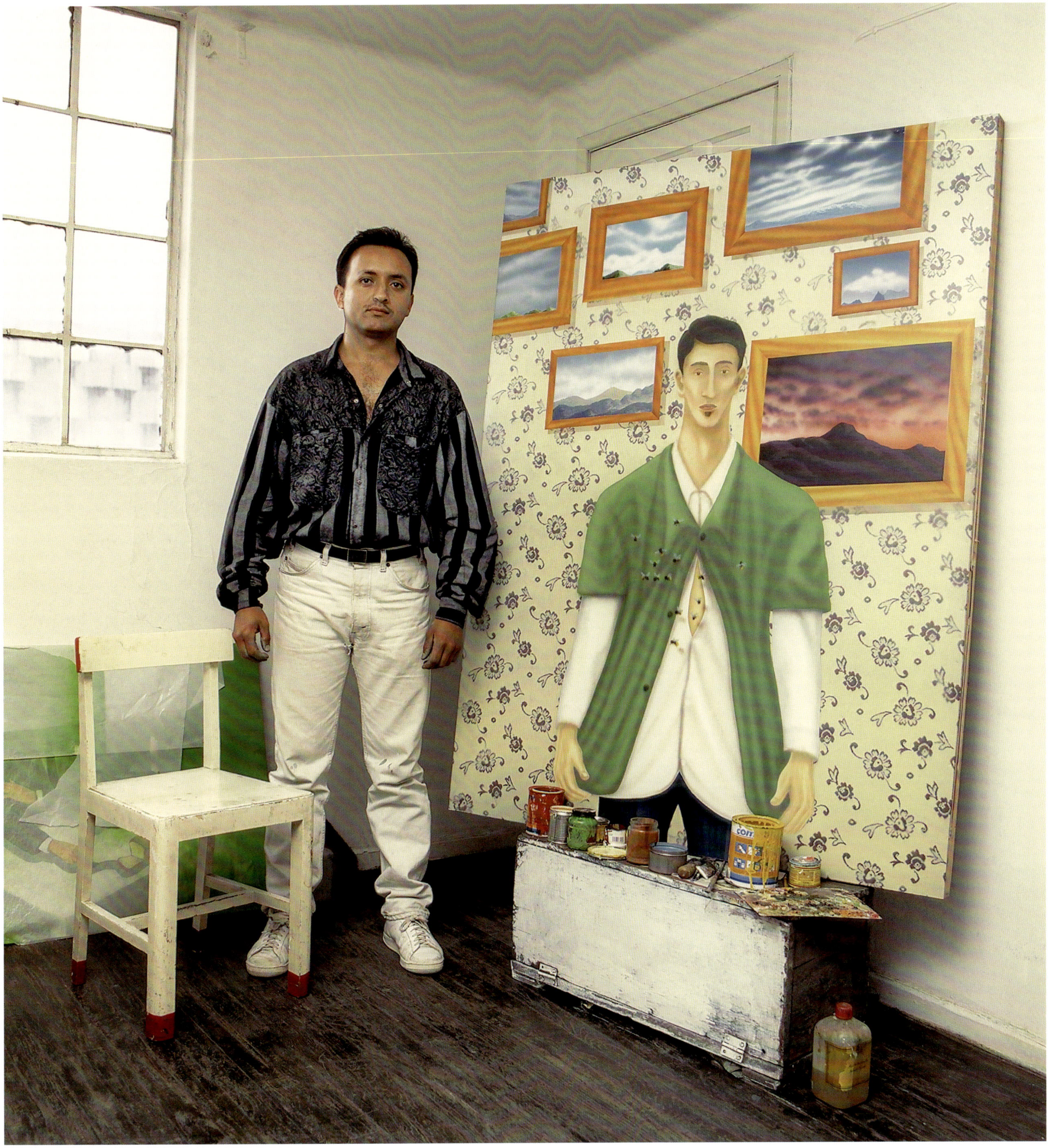

them, Juan Garcia, had been in charge of painting film billboards, until mechanically produced posters made him redundant.) The *rotulistas* were encouraged to amplify, simplify, reinterpret and improve upon Alÿs's 'originals'. Working on metal boards, they took his basic images (which they described, in the manner of Goya, as *caprichos*, or caprices) and introduced iconographic and formal variants, developing the original theme with the same hermeneutic freedom that copyists employed through the centuries when imitating the prototypes of classical imagery. Going full circle, Alÿs would then systematically re-copy the improved versions, giving rise to new ideas and variations. The works were classified according to a numerical system that described the different generations and families of the paintings, similar to the geneology of works produced by artists' workshops in Europe during the Middle Ages and the Renaissance. Alÿs saw the *rotulistas*' work as akin to that of an ancient *scuola*, sharing both a common iconography and a set of social relationships. Selling the paintings at a flat rate independent of their actual makers, he hoped that collectors would follow the progression of each series as a kind of narrative, keeping the production line moving forward. How an image would progress was solely determined by its market demand. In the context of this small circuit of borrowings and collaborations, painting was not only a medium; it became the site of a complex cultural negotiation on the basis of the progression of visual images and their reception by the market.[26] In other words, rather than practising painting as a visual religion, Alÿs turned to the medium as a pragmatic part of living: a means of exchange, communication and participation, a business of personal survival and a field of interpersonal association. Instead of novelty and uniqueness, the collaboration involved the concept that cultural significance lay in the distribution of images – in fact, in the need to reproduce them. This emphasis on the creative side of copying was conveyed in the title Alÿs gave the project: *The Liar/ The Copy of the Liar* (1994). It goes without saying that the project was aimed at calling into question authorship, expression and originality. Alÿs managed to keep this method of production operating for four years, and eventually one of the *rotulistas*, Emilio Rivera, became his assistant as well as a close friend and collaborator.

Paintings usually work for Alÿs as carriers of metaphors, cultural references and linguistic and visual associations. They are there to make the artist's symbolic baggage visible: the sexual and physical fantasies evoked by the contact between objects and beings, the political expectations projected on to social behaviours, the literary allusions behind a specific adventure. If his photographs dutifully record the referent of his actions, walks and constructions, painting is there to project them into a wider field of images. In turn, painting also becomes the laboratory in which he re-elaborates his basic repertoire of actions and symbols. In that sense, it is the oneiric field that both reveals the hidden meanings of many of his works and socializes their general condition as fictions.

There is no better example than the series *Le Temps du sommeil*, which Alÿs started producing in the summer of 1996 and continues to rework today. The series consists of approximately one hundred small canvases eleven by fifteen centimetres each, uniformly treated with a dark brown background, on which Alÿs records a number of sculptural scenes. To record their oneiric origin, Alÿs dates them dutifully with a rubber stamp.

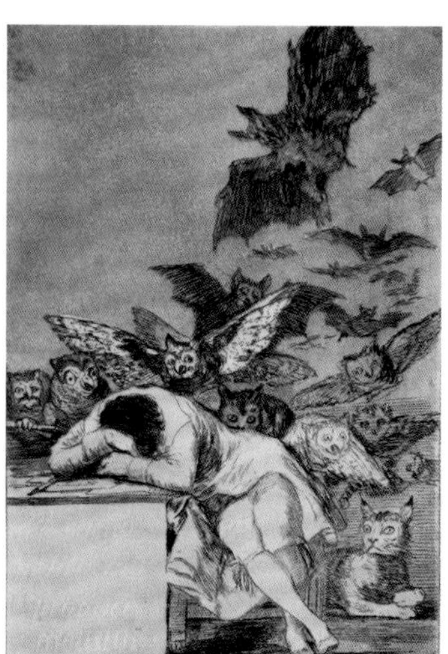

FRANCISCO GOYA
THE SLEEP OF REASON PRODUCES MONSTERS, C. 1798
FROM THE SERIES CAPRICHOS
ETCHING AND AQUATINT
22 X 15 CM

LE TEMPS DU SOMMEIL, 1996–PRESENT
OIL ON WOOD
12 OF 111 PANELS
EACH 12 X 16 CM

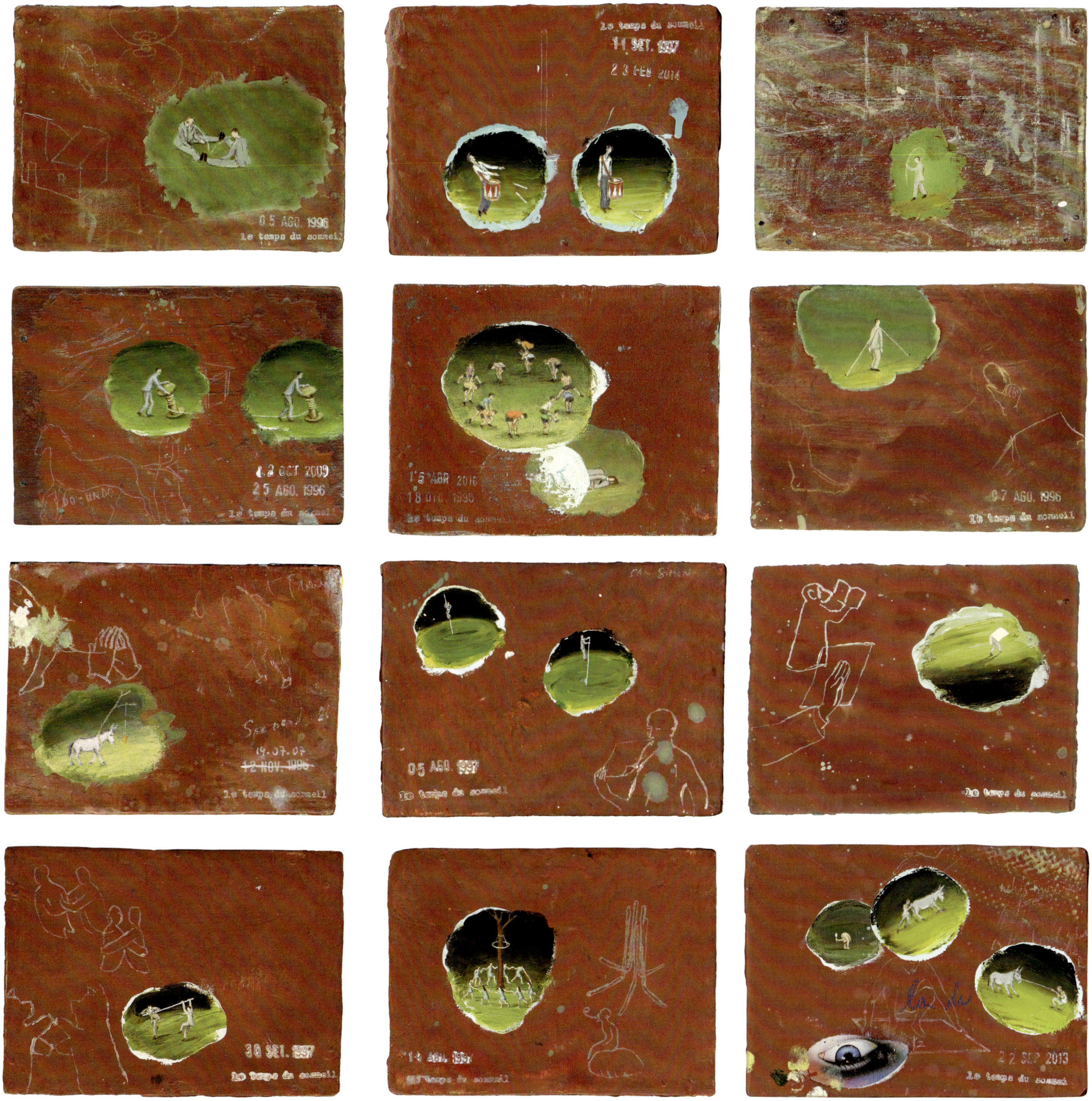

VIVIENDA PARA TODOS (HOUSING FOR ALL), 1994
PHOTO DOCUMENTATION OF AN ACTION, ZÓCALO, MEXICO CITY

On 21 August 1994, the day of presidential elections in Mexico, a shelter made of recycled political propaganda banners was taped together and placed on top of a subway grating, where the hot air coming out of the Zócalo metro station held it aloft.

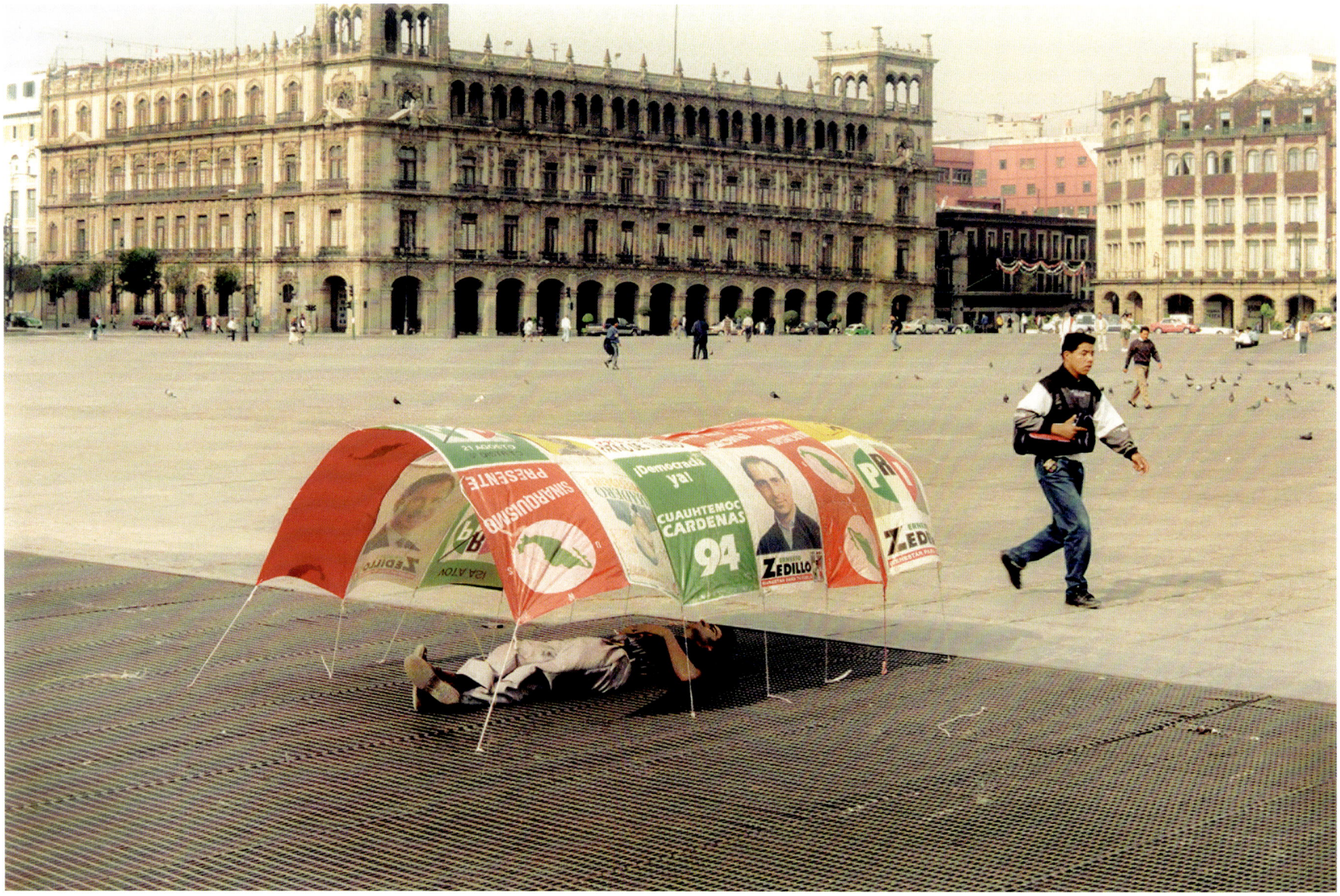

ZAPATISTA, 1995
COLOUR PENCIL ON PAPER
14 X 10 CM

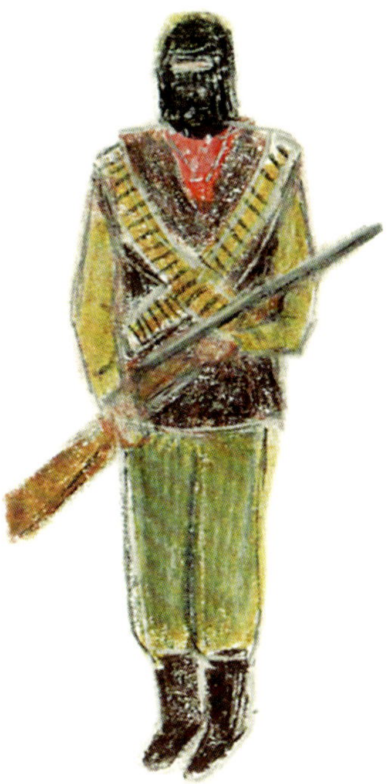

He then returns several times to the same canvas, adding not only new imagery but also new dates to indicate that it is a palimpsest. The images are a springboard for visual ideas: adventures, reflections and games based on his interaction with sticks, trees, stones, pipes, boxes and pieces of cloth. Reminiscent of the tortured characters of Bosch or the punished souls in the circles of hell, *Le temps du sommeil* reveals that Alÿs's actions and objects are an allegorical reflection on the human condition. Ultimately, they remind us that no position, action or posture is devoid of a certain moral significance.

The Tequila Effect

Initially upon his arrival in Mexico, Alÿs did not feel entitled to criticize the local conundrums without understanding the issues involved. Traditionally, Mexican politics have been shrouded in a veil of xenophobia. Inscribed in the constitutional law as well as in public attitudes is an explicit prohibition forbidding foreigners not only from participating in local politics but even from expressing their opinions about them.[27] A principle born from old memories of foreign intervention, this approach has, however, served to empower the censorship of criticism and, for a while, to brush aside international concerns on matters such as human rights.

Alÿs's first intervention in this field was a reaction to one of the worst crises in Mexico's history. On 1 January 1994, the very same day on which the North American Free Trade Agreement (NAFTA) came into effect, several municipalities of the southern state of Chiapas were taken by the Zapatista Army of National Liberation (EZLN). In the following months a series of assassinations dominated Mexican politics, including the killing of the presidential candidate of the official party, Luis Donaldo Colosio. The troubles continued with the ensuing administration. A dramatic financial crisis in December 1994 was followed by the ill-fated attempt of president Ernesto Zedillo to arrest Subcomandante Marcos and the Zapatista Army leadership in February 1995.

Alÿs, like his Mexican friends, passionately followed all these events, and on election day in August 1994, when Mexican citizens were concentrating on the results of the polling stations, Alÿs constructed a fitting allegory of the country's long wait for political reform. Using found plastic campaign banners, he built a temporary shelter in the centre of Mexico City's main square, known as the Zócalo. This vaulted structure was kept up merely by the force of the air blown from the ventilators of the metro, like Marilyn Monroe's skirt in *The Seven Year Itch*. The title of the installation, *Vivienda para Todos (Housing for All)* (1994), was a brutal satire on Mexican demagogy, being one of the many irresponsible slogans articulated by the Mexican presidential candidates in their campaign. Thus the work physically realized an empty phrase. Conflating both Alÿs's dissatisfaction with architectonics and professional politics as part of the same dream world of power, *Vivienda para Todos* offered an extraordinary combination of immanent critique, black humour and concrete utopianism.

This installation provided Alÿs with a way of translating forms of political resistance into poetic allegory, turning social conflicts into light-hearted political explorations. Soon the social crisis of 1994–95 diverted his attention to the question of the parallel economies that urban populations had developed to survive the mishaps of rising global capitalism. In December 1994 the Mexican peso collapsed to a third of its value. While thousands of millions of dollars flooded out of the country, Mexicans were plunged into a spectacular social crisis, with more than a million jobs lost in less than six months, the doubling of crime rates and one of the biggest increases in foreign debt in world history. Dubbed 'the Tequila Effect' because it soon affected most South American economies, the crisis was rightly perceived as a hangover of the ridiculous promises of global integration. As in 1976 and 1982, the crisis was a setback of historical proportions that once again caused Mexicans' hopes of an economic take-off to evaporate into thin air.

The brutal economic integration was accompanied by paradoxical local developments. Bartering, for instance, once again became an extensive practice, with people offering goods and services in street ads and even the newspapers to circumvent the lack of credit and cash. Following this trend, Alÿs entered the metro one morning to exchange his sunglasses for any other commodity the passengers felt able to part with. Throughout the day he performed dozens of exchanges, using a camera to document a chain of subterranean trade. *Trueque* (The Swap, 1996) replaced the mobility of Alÿs's walks with the imaginary routes of the objects he exchanged. This interest in the migration of objects through different social layers and across social borders became a central feature in the works he was to produce in the following years.

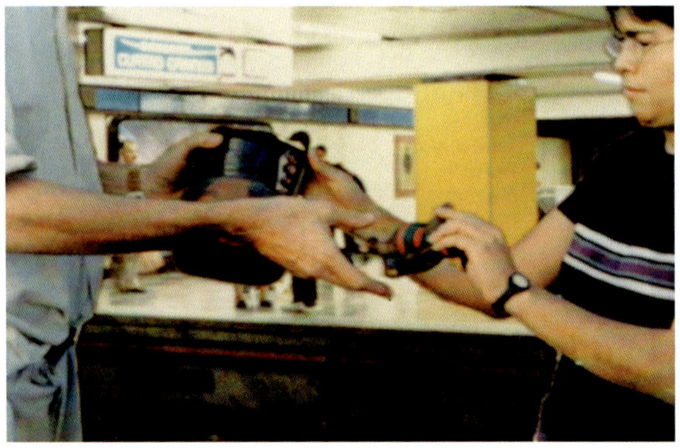

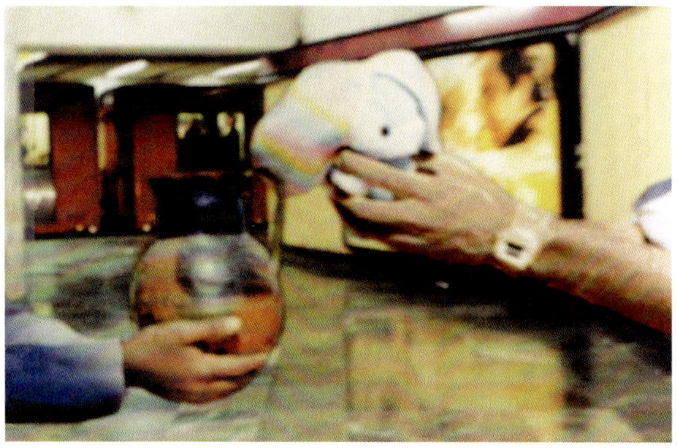

THE SWAP, 1995
PHOTO DOCUMENTATION OF AN ACTION, MEXICO CITY

In the beginning there is a given situation where many people cross paths. The protagonist enters the situation with an object. He swaps it for another. A succession of transactions follows in which each object is in turn exchanged for another, and so on until the end of his visit.
The protagonist leaves the last object.

opposite,
NARCOSALINAS, 1995
MEXICO CITY–NEW YORK
PHOTO DOCUMENTATION OF AN ACTION

Project of smuggling 6.35 grams of cocaine from Mexico City to New York City under the guise of a painted figurine of Mexican president Carlos Salinas de Gortari.

In Mexico City, an urban centre of twenty million people, the disposal of garbage is not industrialized as it is in the developed world. Trash is scavenged from outside people's homes or from municipal dumps. Alÿs decided to put this informal system of garbage processing to the test. For *The Seven Lives of Garbage* (1995) he placed seven bronze snails in rubbish bags he found in different sites around the city. In the following days and months, he searched for them in flea markets. To date, he has found two, of which he bought one to document the process. The action suggests the extent to which city life is interconnected by means of its informal circuits, symbolized by the slow progression of the snails along different social strata.

These experiences with the circulation of objects and symbols led Alÿs to one of his most daring actions. After the social catastrophe of the mid-1990s, Mexicans found respite in a form of symbolic reprisal. President Carlos Salinas, who governed Mexico during the period of the most rabid neo-liberal modernization (1988–94), was caricatured in hand-crafted objects that were sold in the streets of Mexico City. In 1995 Alÿs devised a project to smuggle six grams of cocaine from Mexico into the United States hidden in one of these small painted effigies. *Narcosalinas* (1995) reflected on the links between the illegal drugs trade and the globalization project by suggesting the complicity between local southern politics and the drug consumption in the north, both of them expressions of the thrill of power.

PRI, Mexico's ruling party for almost seventy years, was a paradoxical political regime: a post-revolutionary body that conducted the capitalist modernization of a Third-World country behind the ideological facade of populism and demagogy. Such 'dictatorship moderated by corruption' – as the vox populi defined it – had been plunged into a more or less permanent state of crisis ever since a massive pro-democracy student movement was violently suppressed by the army on 2 October 1968, a few days before the start of the Olympic Games. Three decades later, Alÿs evoked these events with *Cuentos Patrióticos (Patriotic Tales)* (1997). For this video he walked around the flagpole of the main square in Mexico City, leading a line of sheep that increased one by one until they formed a full circle. Here Alÿs made explicit reference to one of the defining moments of the 1968 crisis. In August a demonstration organized by the government to protest against the students' alleged desecration of the Mexican flag had backfired when the civil servants forced to attend started to bleat as a sign that they were not there of their own will. *Cuentos Patrióticos* not only pointed out the lasting significance of the 1968 rebellion but exemplified the way in which Alÿs was to approach the critique of politics through the enactment of living parables.

Economy Postponed

Very early on in his artistic practice, Alÿs came to understand that as much as he may have been an external and objective observer in the sites he explored, his works were to a great extent a product of the interference between reality and its record – in other words, art was never entirely 'about' or 'from' a place, but rather a product of an experience of friction and contamination. As his video *If you are a typical spectator, what you are really doing is waiting for the accident to happen* (1996) demonstrated, the mere presence of the camera can activate daily life, provoking people to kick a plastic bottle from one side of a square to the other, until the artist himself, who was merely filming the scene, is brought into the work by being hit by a car. Drawing an analogy to Werner Heisenberg's uncertainty principle, Alÿs came to realize that 'you can't observe a phenomenon without, after a while, interfering with the natural course of it.'[28]

UNTITLED, 1996
FROM THE SERIES DÉJÀ VU
OIL ON CANVAS
DIPTYCH (PART 2)
17 X 23 CM

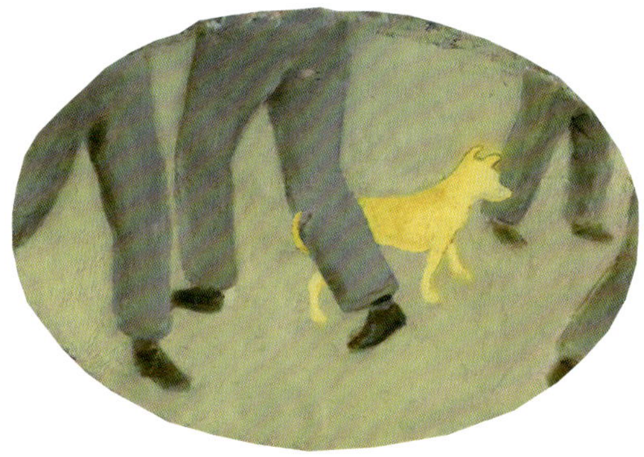

Given such interaction, Alÿs turned Mexico City into a living laboratory of the tensions between modernization and its resistance, the entropic forces operating in so-called 'developing societies'. Triggered by a request from the curatorial team of the twenty-fifth São Paulo Biennial to explore the way in which artists had historically been involved in cultural exchange and absorption, in 1996 and 1997 Alÿs produced several works aimed at describing his relation to the ways of living in downtown Mexico City. This time it was not a matter of recording the evidence of the population's silent

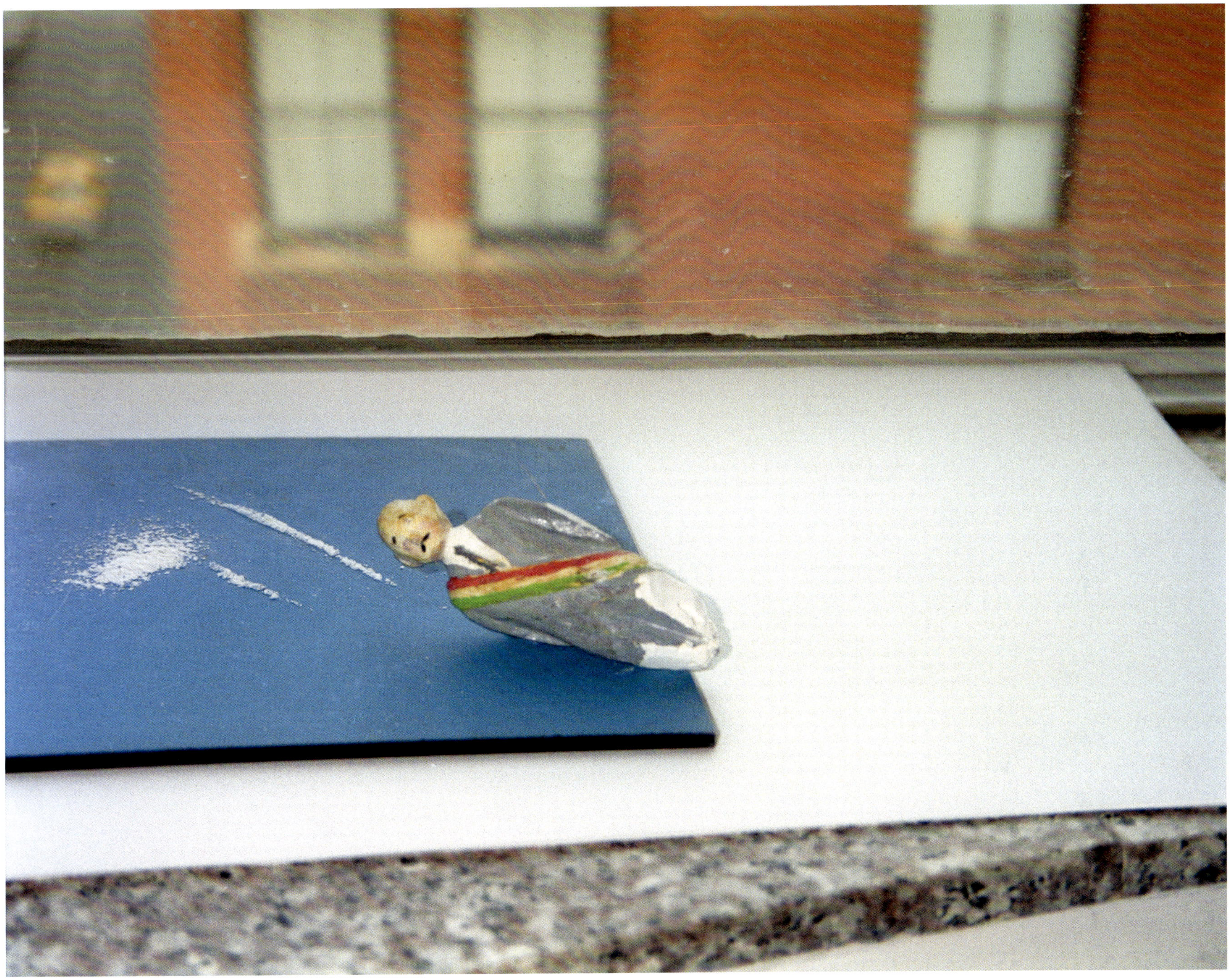

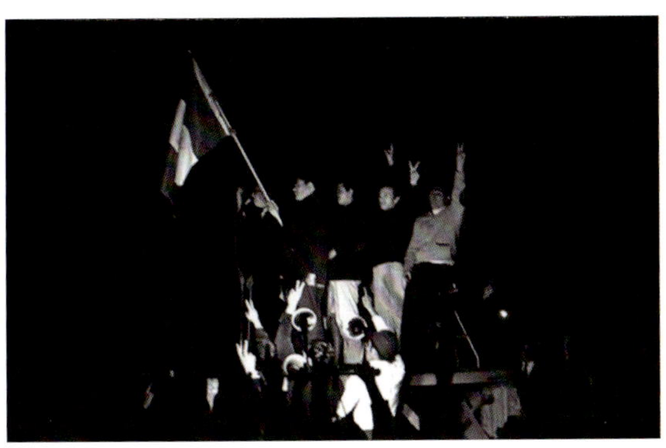

NEWS PHOTOGRAPH OF PRO-DEMOCRACY
PROTEST IN MEXICO CITY, 1968
FROM THE ARTIST'S ARCHIVE

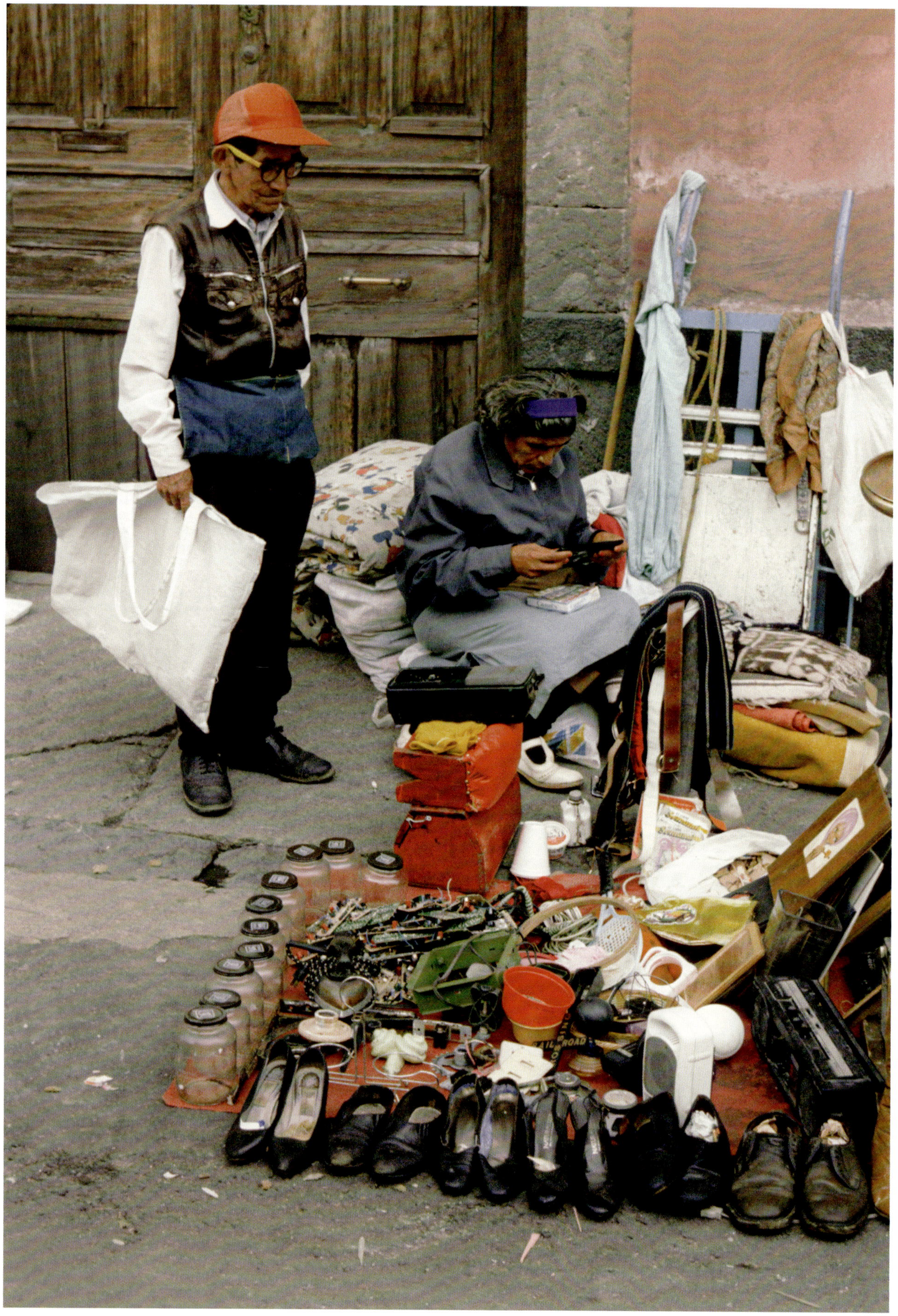

THE SEVEN LIVES OF GARBAGE, 1995
PHOTO DOCUMENTATION
OF AN ACTION, MEXICO CITY

It is said that all garbage in Mexico City goes through seven stages of sifting from the moment it is left on the street until its final destination at the garbage dump on the outskirts of the city.

On the night of 4 February 1994, I placed seven small bronze sculptures, painted seven distinct colours, in seven different garbage bags. I then dropped the bags in garbage piles in seven different districts of the city. In the following days, months, years, I have wandered the flea markets in the city looking for the sculptures to resurface. To date I have found two of the seven.

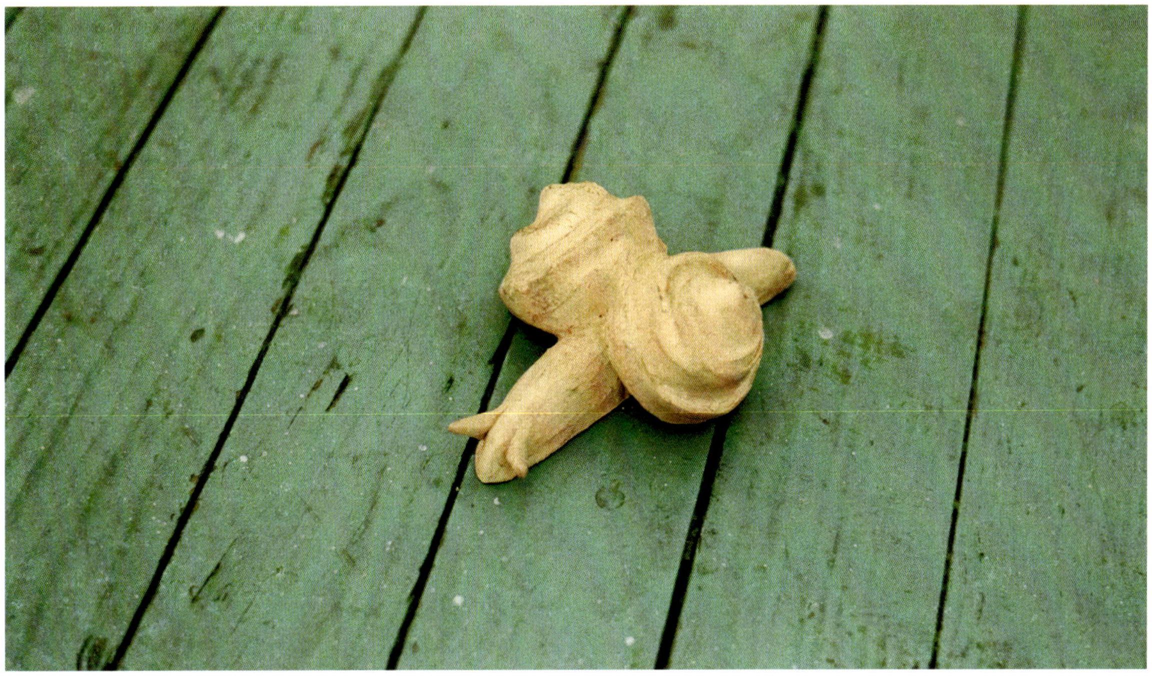

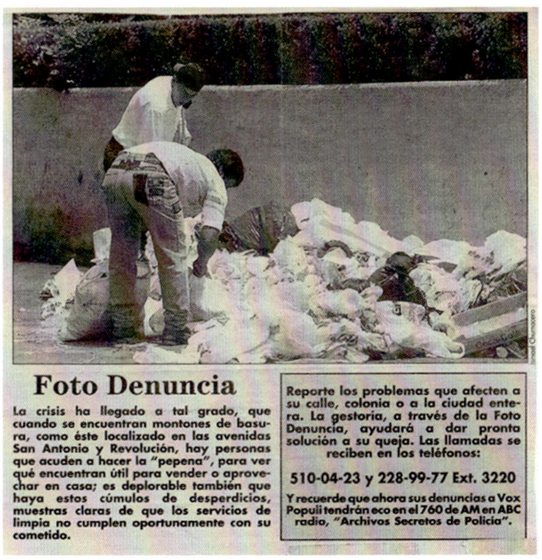

Foto Denuncia

La crisis ha llegado a tal grado, que cuando se encuentran montones de basura, como éste localizado en las avenidas San Antonio y Revolución, hay personas que acuden a hacer la "pepena", para ver qué encuentran útil para vender o aprovechar en casa; es deplorable también que haya estos cúmulos de desperdicios, muestras claras de que los servicios de limpia no cumplen oportunamente con su cometido.

Reporte los problemas que afecten a su calle, colonia o a la ciudad entera. La gestoría, a través de la Foto Denuncia, ayudará a dar pronta solución a su queja. Las llamadas se reciben en los teléfonos:

510-04-23 y 228-99-77 Ext. 3220

Y recuerde que ahora sus denuncias a Vox Populi tendrán eco en el 760 de AM en ABC radio, "Archivos Secretos de Policía".

NEWSPAPER CLIPPING ON GARBAGE SCAVENGERS IN MEXICO CITY, 1998
FROM THE ARTIST'S ARCHIVE

resistance, but of producing a general allegory of a life ruled by scarce productivity.

All the painful hilarity embedded in the notion of historical failure that Alÿs wanted to discuss is captured in the title of one of his most famous walks: *Paradox of Praxis 1* (1997), subtitled 'Sometimes making something leads to nothing'. In this action, the first of a two-part project that fittingly took the artist a decade to complete, Alÿs pushed a huge block of ice through the streets of Mexico City, from early in the morning to sunset, until the block completely melted. This act, which was documented on video by Alÿs's collaborator, the former sign painter Enrique Huerta, was meant to stand for the widespread personal and social experience of waste of effort in Latin America. At the same time, it critiqued the pervading Minimalist aesthetic of recent art. By strenuously pushing his block of ice through the streets of the megalopolis, Alÿs created a parable about the thaw of Minimalism: the physical and conceptual erosion of the inert, reductionist Minimalist aesthetic that living cities such as Mexico provoke. The work summarized Alÿs's dissident approach to the traditional concept of public art, and his adoption of an ephemeral sculptural vocabulary that, rather than presenting an object for contemplation, intervenes in the social space to turn sculpture into a means of social research. Streets such as those in Mexico City, with their intense social activity, demonstrate the obsolescence of traditional sculpture as a means to produce a social symbol. As a substitute, Alÿs's proposal consists of the creation of urban myths able to reflect aesthetically and politically on the contemporary conditions of living. With hindsight, *Paradox of Praxis 1* is also important in the sense that it helped Alÿs to explore an aesthetics based on failure.

Fuite en avant

Despite its apparent neutrality, few notions are as ideologically charged as that of national 'under-development'. It was Harry S. Truman who, during his inaugural presidential address of 1949, proposed the idea that the poverty and social turmoil of under-developed nations made them vulnerable to the influence of the Soviet Union, and that bringing progress and technology to the South was necessary to the security of the Western world. Springing from outmoded discourses around the *mission civilatrice* of Europe towards its colonies, the concept of under-development posited Western societies as the model for other nation states to pursue in their movement from 'tradition' to 'modernity'.

This value system, disguised under the technochratic consensus of international agencies and social critics, poses a linear concept of history that, as Frederic Jameson has pointed out, promotes the 'illusion that the West has something no one else possesses but which they ought to desire for themselves'.[29] Seen in retrospect, however, the twentieth-century project of development was caught up in an eternal paradox: no matter how hard they have tried, 'backward' societies have been unable to match the model of their forerunners.

In 2006, Alÿs translated this thought into images in a 16 mm film made in Patagonia. His initial intention was to chase *ñandús*, South American ostriches, through the plains, as the aboriginal inhabitants of Patagonia are said to have hunted them. The work evolved, however, into a pursuit of mirages. It was a search for 'a point amiss, beyond the horizon line, out where images occur'.[30] In collaboration with artists Rafael Ortega and Olivier

LOOKING UP, 2001
VIDEO DOCUMENTATION OF
AN ACTION, MEXICO CITY
VIDEO
4 MIN.

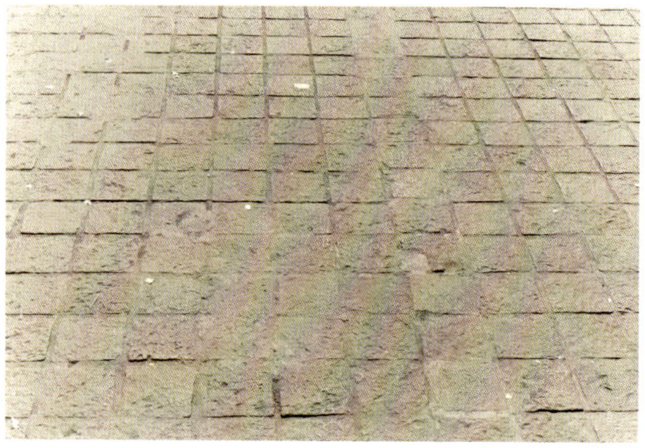
10:00 A.M.

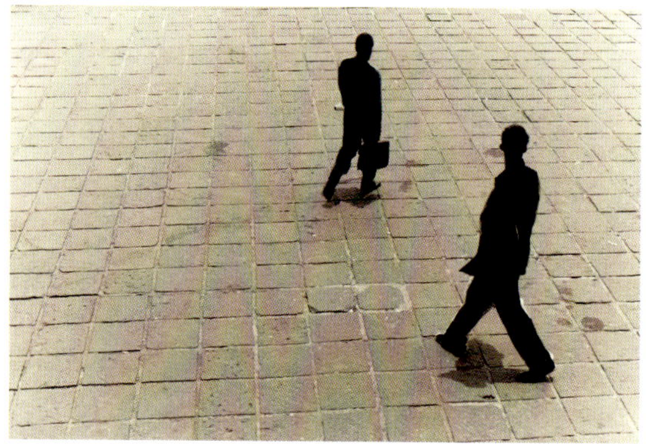
10:01 A.M.

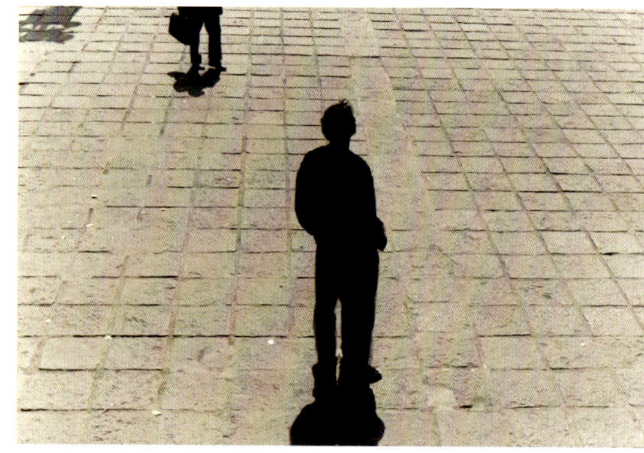
10:10 A.M.

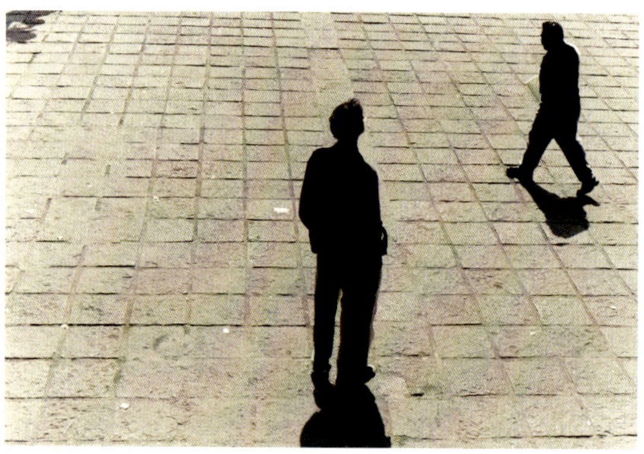
10:20 A.M.

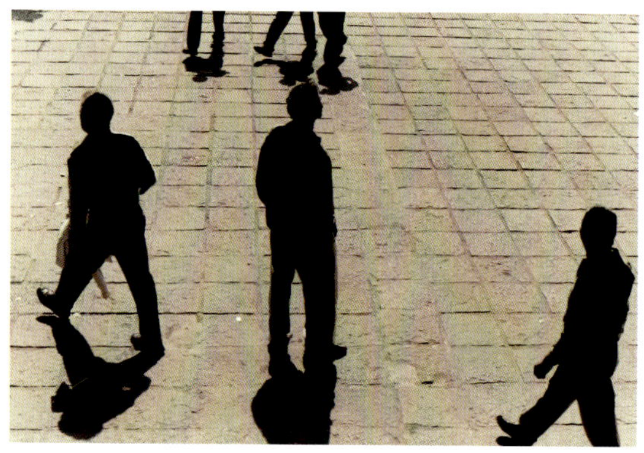
10:30 A.M.

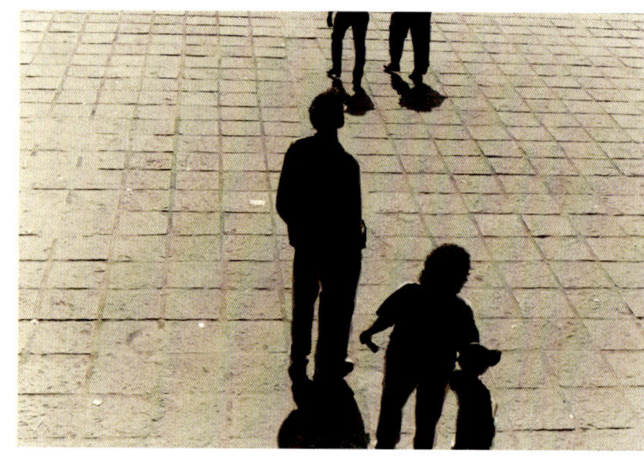
10:32 A.M.

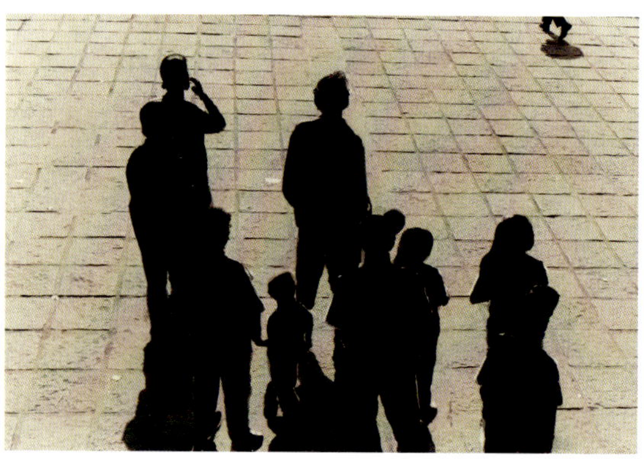
10:36 A.M.

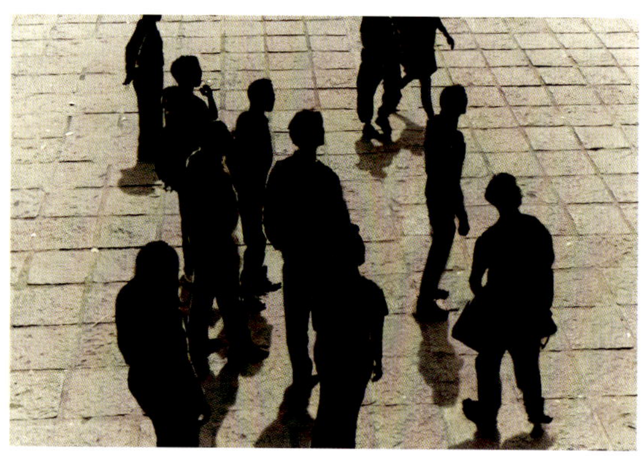
10:36 A.M.

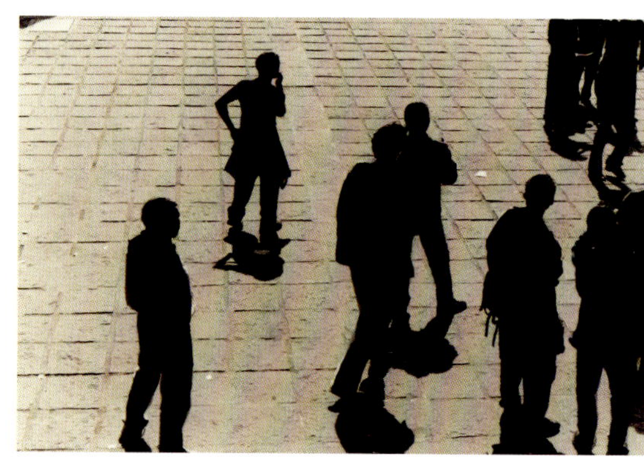
10:37 A.M.

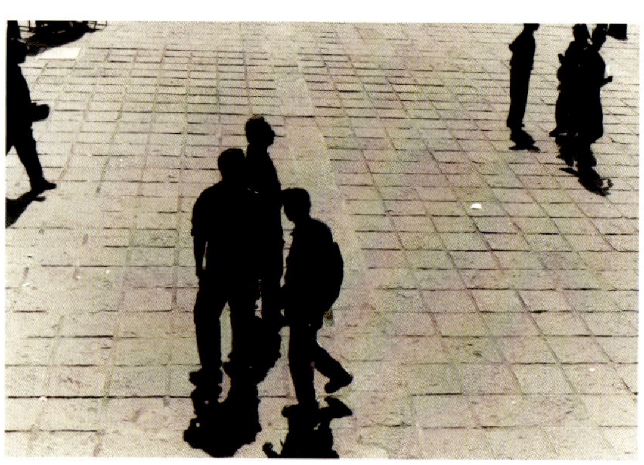
10:38 A.M.

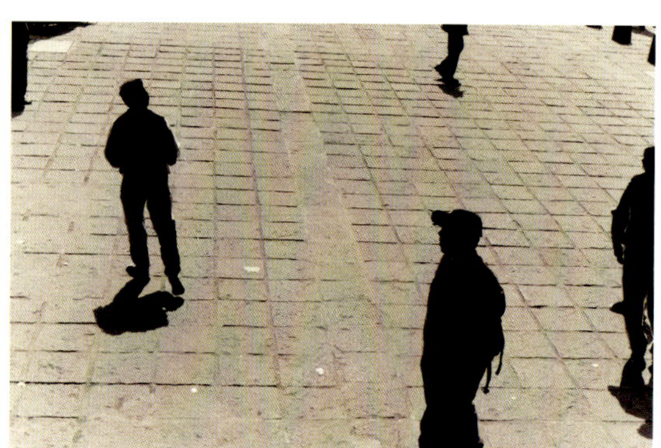
10:38 A.M.

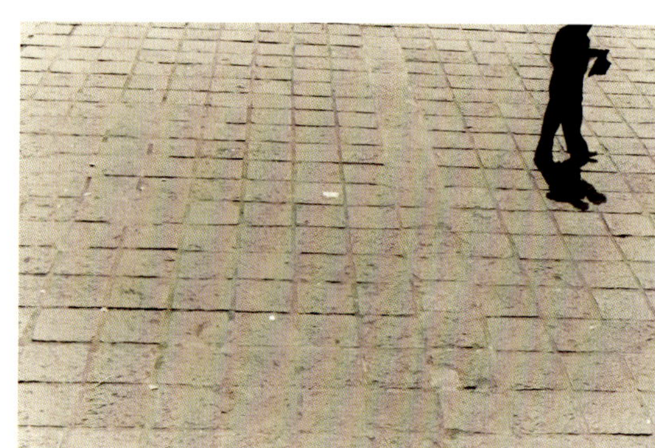
10:39 A.M.

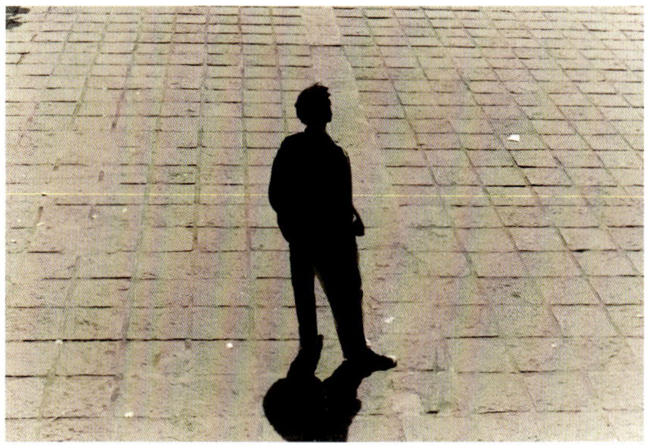

10:15 A.M.

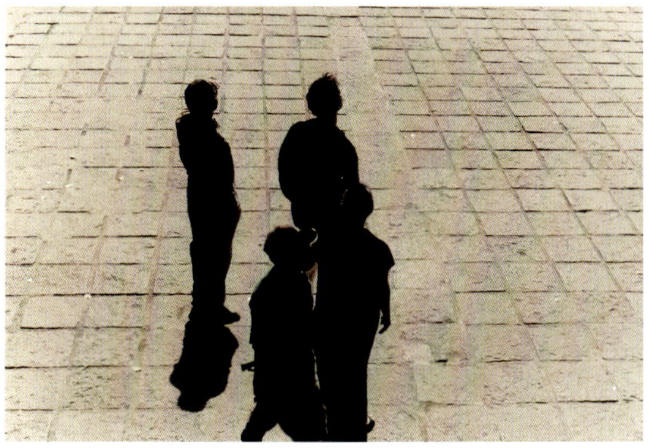

10:35 A.M.

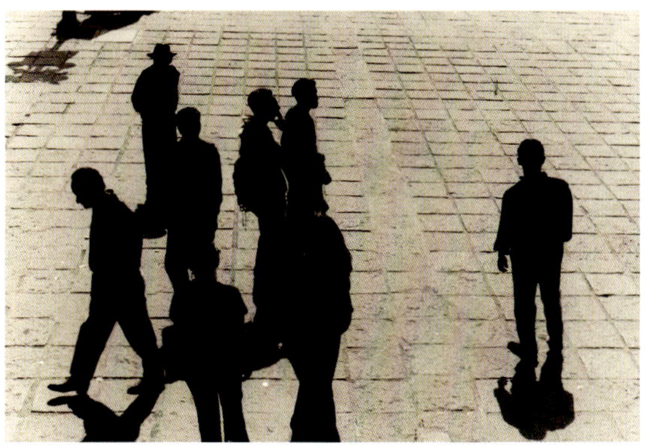

10:37 A.M.

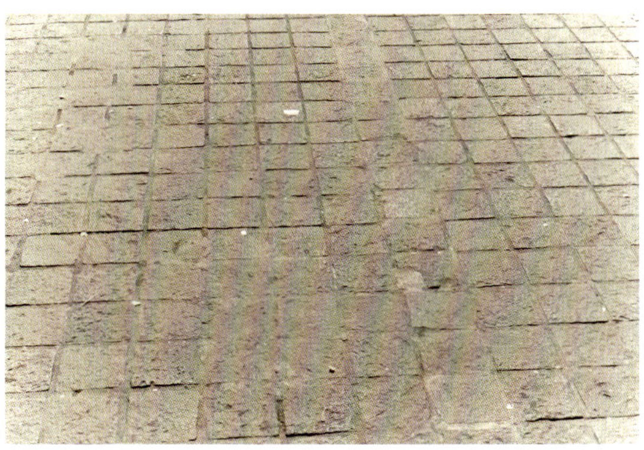

10:39 A.M.

Debroise, Alÿs filmed the emergence of the iridescent area at the vanishing point of the road. As the artist put it, this was 'the image of *fuite en avant*, of fleeing forward'.[31] The title of this project, *A Story of Deception*, summarizes his understanding of the seduction of development. If the pursuit of modernity is fatal, this work suggests, it is because it becomes a 'chasing after the vanishing point'.[32]

False Starts (Never Ending)

In a number of his recent works, Alÿs has articulated a catalogue of the different economic practices that derive from the shaky process of modernization in the South. These works highlight the transformation of the apparent linearity of development into a variety of modalities, from repetition, stagnation, oscillation and regression, to forms of action that make effort and energy vanish, or that imply a sudden 'irrational' gain. Underneath their humorous and lyrical presentation, Alÿs has encoded in them a view of time that differs greatly from the metaphysical ramblings that often accompany artiststs' allegedly philosophical approaches to the subject of duration. Alÿs's approach, as he once put it, is a meditation on 'the vicious circle of demand', and the emphasis is on the nature of the time of production, rather than on the status of the product. To borrow a distinction made by the political theorist Hannah Arendt, this is a meditation on the nature of labour as an endless task, marked by the relationship between our bodies and the social system rather than by the condition of the work as an activity that is materialized in its product: 'Unlike working, whose end has come when the object is finished, ready to be added to the common world of things, labouring always moves in the same circle, which is prescribed by the biological process of the living organism.'[33]

Alÿs's first approach to this issue was *Turista*, in which he presented his contemplation of the everyday work of others as a professional activity, thus conflating labour and leisure and questioning the notion of efficiency. In *The Swap* and *The Seven Lives of Garbage*, he recorded the chain of things passing from hand to hand, revealing a whole array of social possibilities encrypted in systems normally considered only in relation to poverty. *Paradox of Praxis 1*, while evoking the sense of an unstoppable waste of energy (and the apparent pointlessness of action) and enacting the disproportionate relationship between effort and effect as often experienced in Latin American economies, also gave rise to its opposite – for ten years, Alÿs, in collaboration with his friend the filmmaker Rafael Ortega, has been working on the

SONG FOR LUPITA, 1998
IN COLLABORATION WITH LOURDES VILLAGOMEZ AND ANTONIO HERNANDEZ ROS
45 RPM RECORD
4 MIN. 20 SEC.

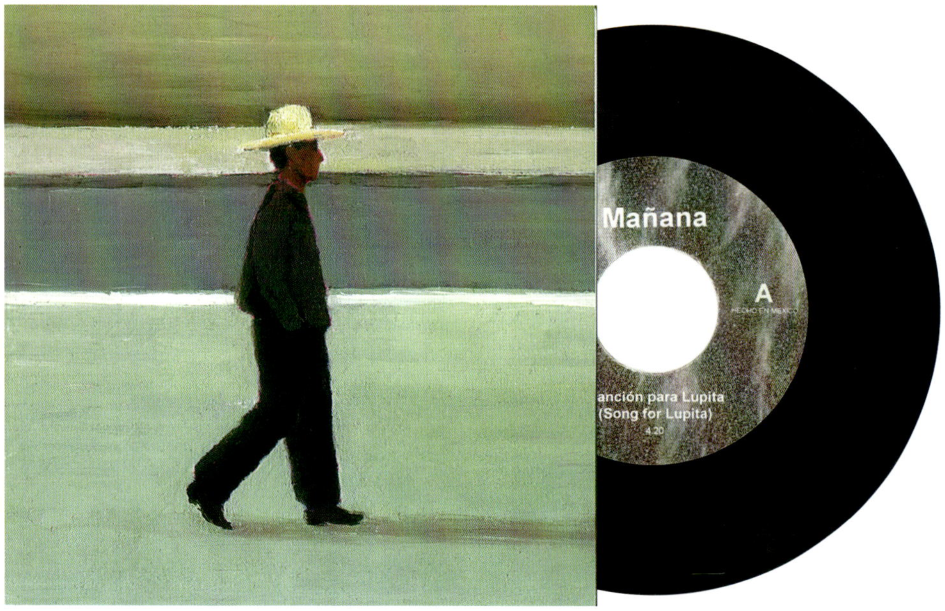

POLITICS OF REHEARSAL, 2005
IN COLLABORATION WITH RAFAEL ORTEGA, CUAUHTÉMOC MEDINA AND PERFORMA
PHOTO DOCUMENTATION OF A PUBLIC PERFORMANCE, NEW YORK
VIDEO
30 MIN.

Soundtrack:
Franz Shubert's 'Lied der Mignon'

Performers:
A striptease artist,
a soprano and
her pianist

Mechanics:
The stripper listens to
a rehearsal session of the
soprano with the pianist.

While the pianist plays
and the soprano sings,
the stripper undresses.

When the soprano or the
pianist loses track over
a musical phrase and stops,
the stripper holds her act.

While the soprano and the
pianist discuss the musical
phrase in question, the
stripper dresses up again.

The rehearsal session will
go on until the stripper
completes her act.

second part of this project: *Sometimes doing nothing leads to something*. One of the best works in the series so far is *Looking Up* (2001), which was inspired by a recent media craze for UFOs. Alÿs simply stood in a square, looking intensely up at the sky, until people started to gather around him and gaze up as well. At one point, he walked away, leaving the other spectators behind as if abandoning a residue. Both actions involve, through the enactment either of loss or of a creative excess, an argument against the dogma of efficiency.

The next step for Alÿs was to intervene in the timing of the work's narrative by introducing complex routines that break the obvious continuity of an action. The video installation *Cantos Patróticos (Patriotic Songs)* (1998–99) involves a constant negotiation of duration. The artist hired three musical performers – a street violinist and a two-man Mariachi band – to play a *corrido* (a traditional Mexican song) that Alÿs had written about a boatman who loses his sense of orientation while trying to take illegal immigrants across the river to the United States. 'Afloat between two waters' (like the artist himself) the boatman is unable to find out where 'the start, the finish is / Where the end is, the beginning'. This is, of course, a metaphor for the disorientation provoked by the dream of modernization, understood for societies in the South as 'heading North'. But perhaps more important is the way in which Alÿs challenges the taste for simplicity in much contemporary art with a work made up of layers of social and temporal variables. The music and images revolve around a filmed game of musical chairs, which goes backwards and forwards according to a rhythm defined by a complex edit of the footage of the musicians. The result is an expansion of the time 'in between', a temporality elongated by the intervals that open up when the flow of our expectations is interrupted. The feeling generated by these cycles and waves of expansion is something like the movement of a spiral.

In 1998, Alÿs once again reflected on the notion of development and circularity with a subtle line-drawing animation titled *Song for Lupita*. The work is deceptively simple: a young woman endlessly pours water from one glass to the other as if trapped in an eternal loop, which, according to the artist, follows the principle of 'doing without doing' or 'not doing but doing'. The film is accompanied by a song recorded on 45 rpm vinyl and entitled 'Mañana' (Tomorrow), a word that is redolent of a common tactic against the pressures of efficiency: as the lyrics say, 'Mañana, mañana is soon enough for me.' *Song for Lupita* is, in a way, a meditation on a form of procrastination that is based on the promise of the future.

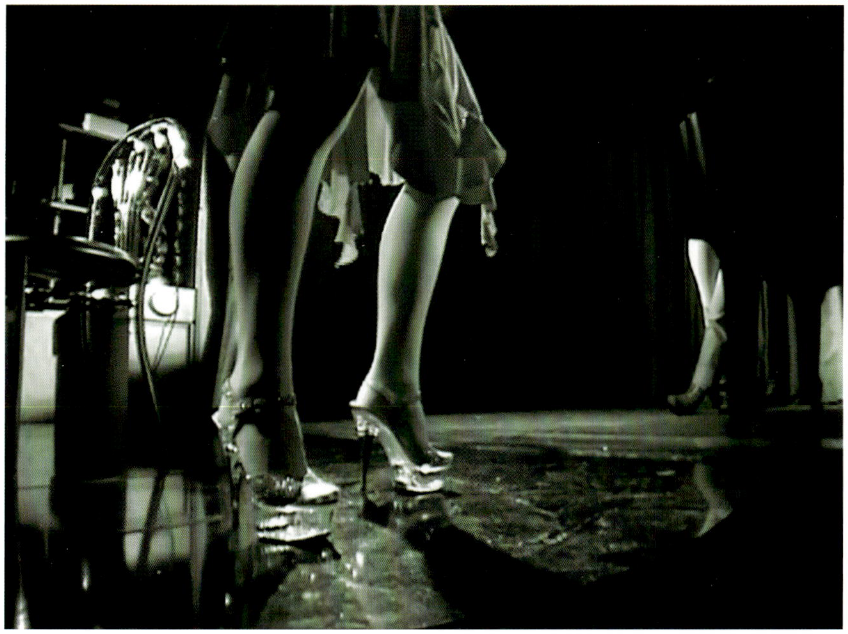

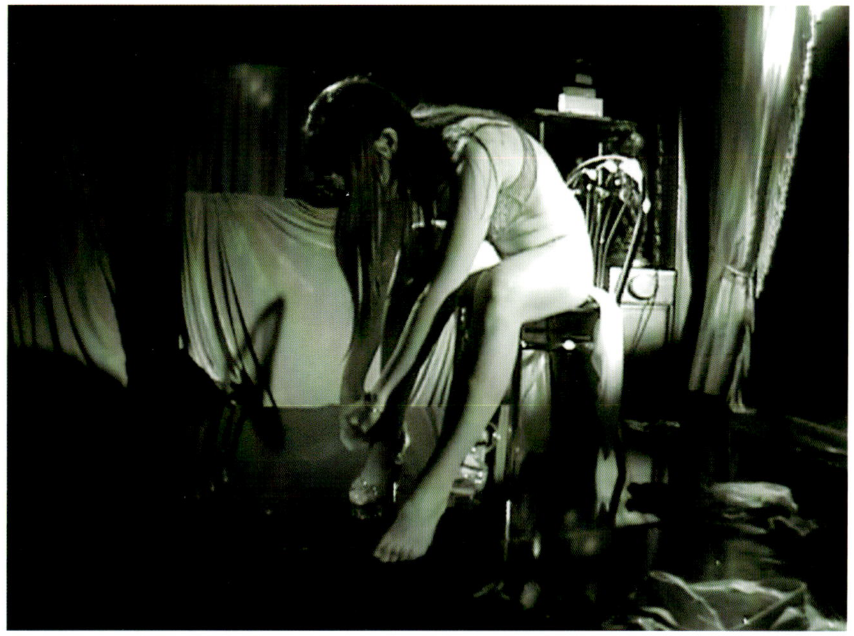

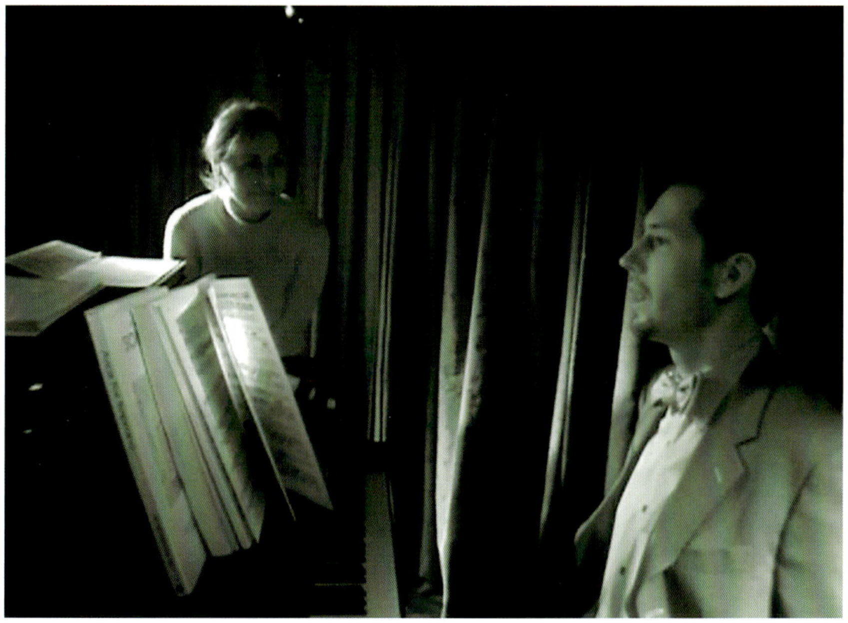

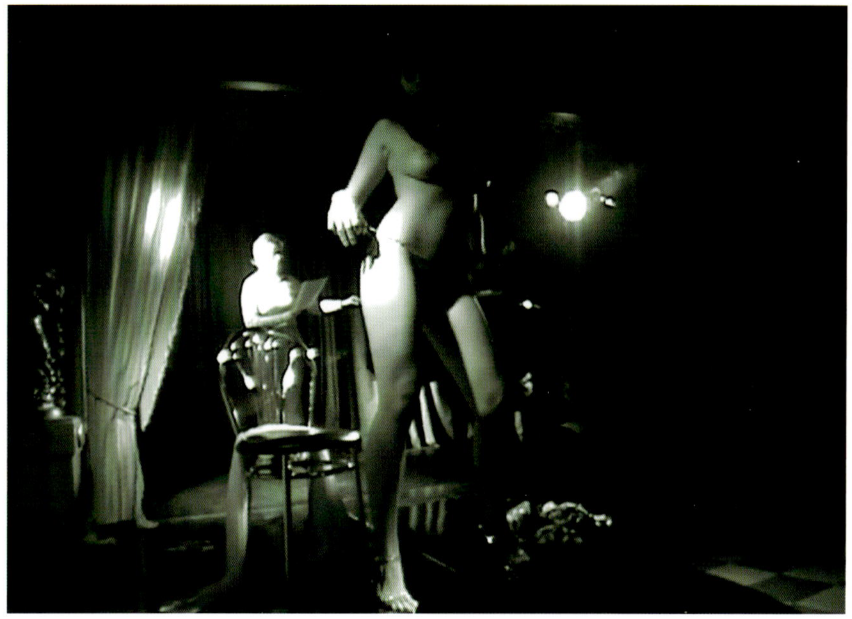

ZÓCALO, 22 MAY 1999, 1999
IN COLLABORATION WITH RAFAEL ORTEGA, MEXICO CITY
VIDEO
12 HOURS

The filming begins at dawn with the flag-raising ceremony and ends at dusk with the flag's descent. The camera follows the progression of the shadow of the flagpole over the course of the day.

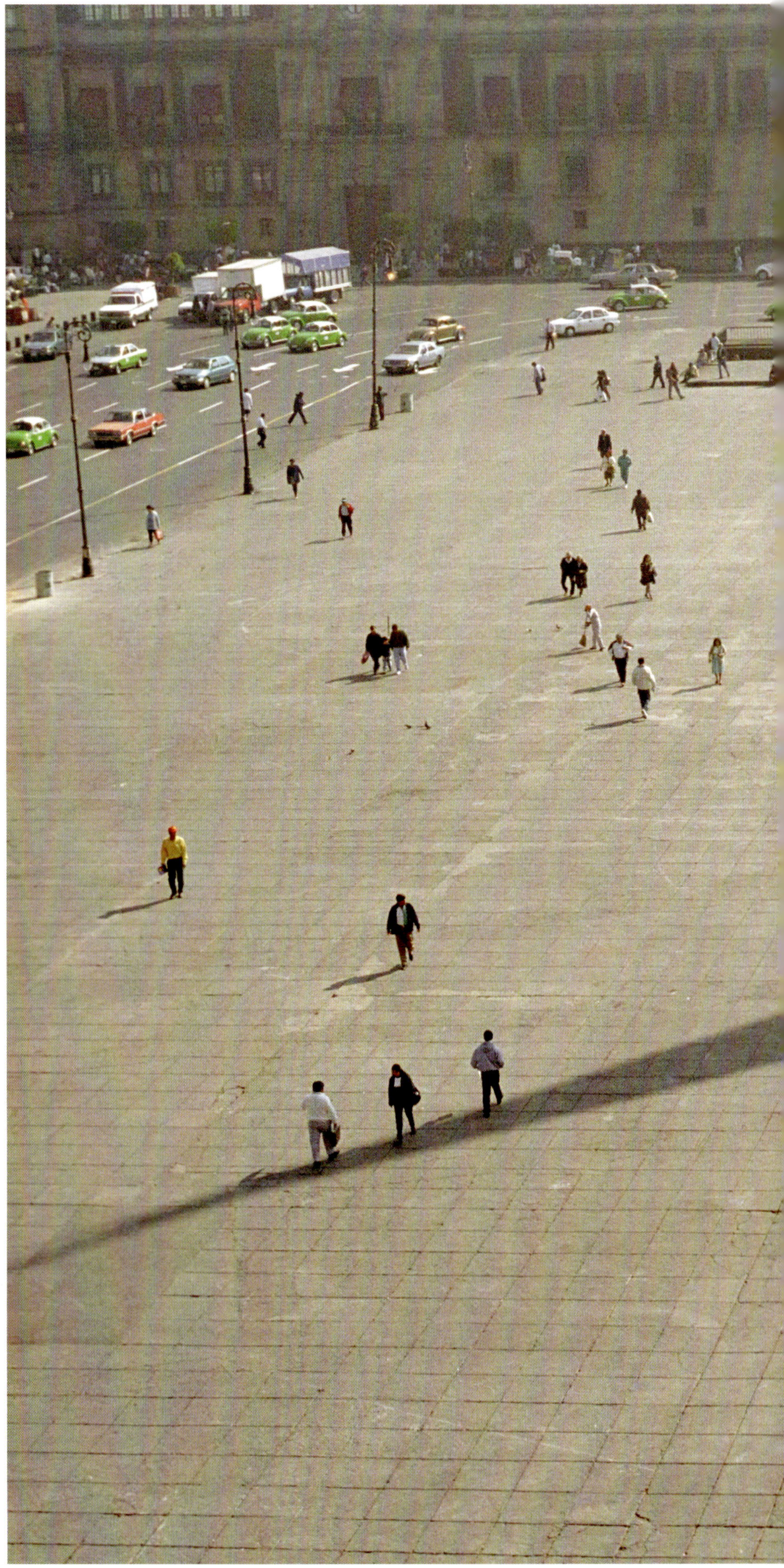

In all these works, the relationship between image and sound serves as a means to induce an experience of interruption and delay. In the relationship between music and movement, Alÿs was looking for metaphors to describe the tension between the violence of development and the frustration of its arrest, which in turn can be experienced as a form of progress. Those notions were to lead him directly to the idea of the musical and theatrical rehearsal, which involves the constant interruption of the flow of action, and the notion of 'failure' as an inevitable part of any experience of progress. For Alÿs, to use Mikhail Bakhtin's concept, the rehearsal is a 'chronotope',[34] a means of describing a specific articulation of time and space. In a way, the rehearsal has become Alÿs's symbol to describe the notion of a 'Mexican time'.

All the *Rehearsals* involve the intrusion of banality into the fabric of illusion, a mismatch between real experience and an ideal model. Some of these works are short videos in which Alÿs uses the rehearsal of a musical score to dictate the action, which is delayed each time the music is interrupted. In *Rehearsal 1* (1999–2001), an old Volkswagen Beetle that fails to climb over a steep hill is reminiscent of the economic crisis in the South. In a more erotic mode, *Rehearsal 2* (2001–06) pictures a stripper who undresses and dresses according to the rehearsal of a Schubert *lieder*, a fitting symbol of the ebb and flow of desire. A sound work like *Rehearsal 8* (2002) offers a recording of the efforts of a school band to learn a patriotic anthem as a symbol of the shaky process of national formation. And, in 2001, Alÿs reworked unused footage and sketches from Alejandro González Iñárritu's film *Amores Perros* (2000), trying to seize the borderline between social documentation and fiction. On the one hand, the *Rehearsal* works emphasize the unfinished, the wish to sidestep the false sense of unity generated by any kind of representation. On the other, they stand

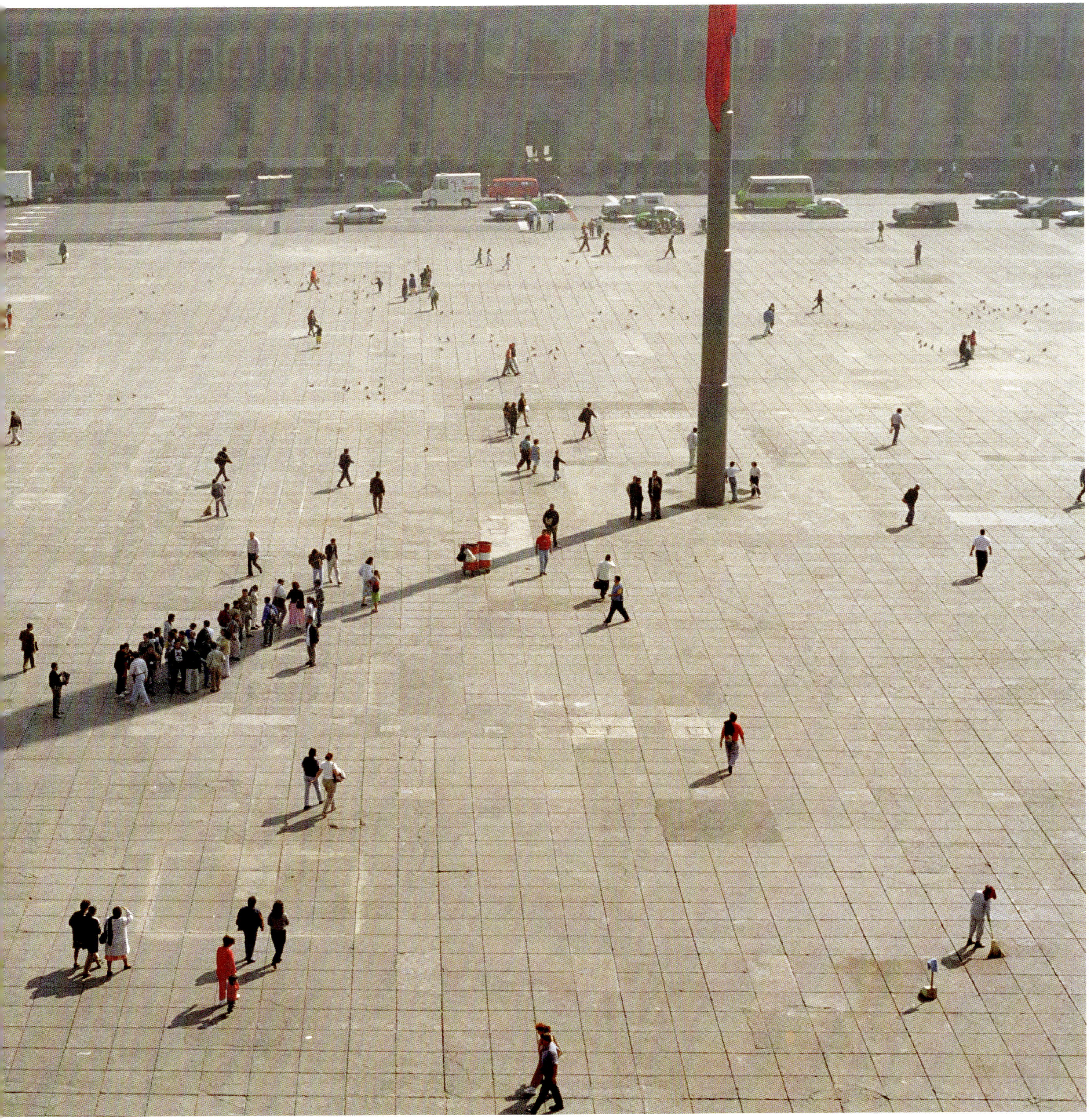

ZÓCALO, 4 FEBRUARY 1998, 1998
MEXICO CITY
12 OF 16 PHOTOGRAPHS

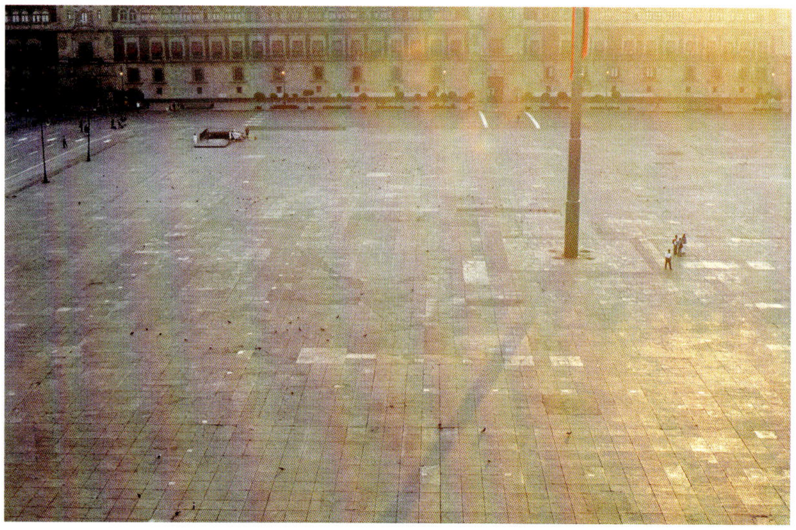
7:30 A.M.

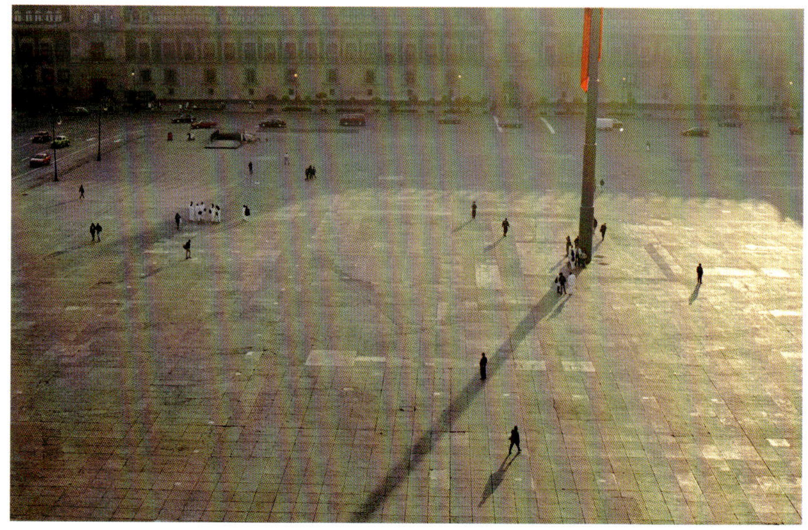
7:45 A.M.

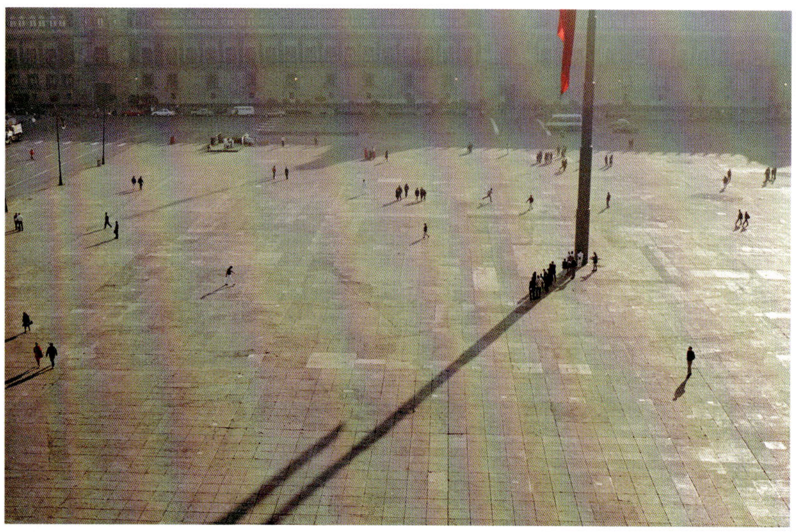
8:00 A.M.

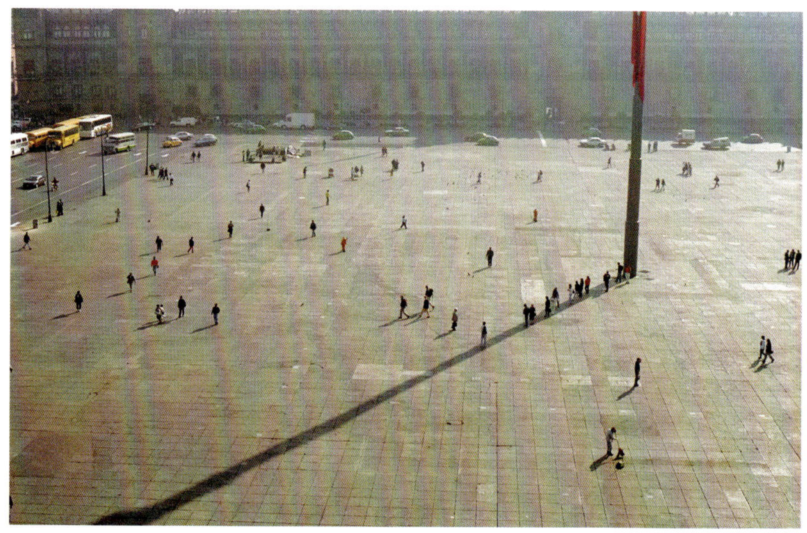
9:00 A.M.

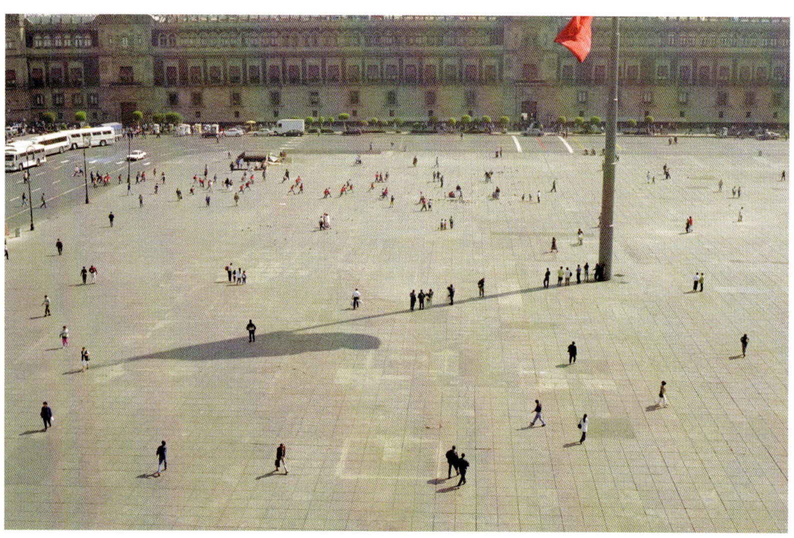
11:00 A.M.

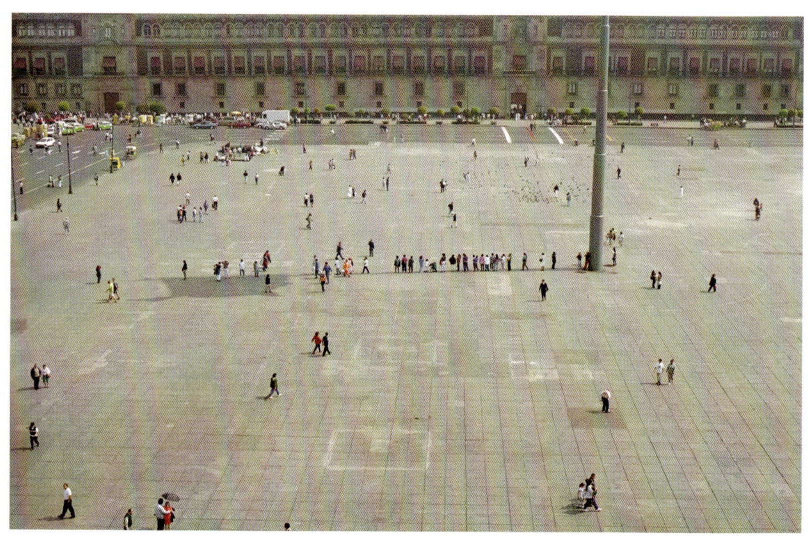
1:00 P.M.

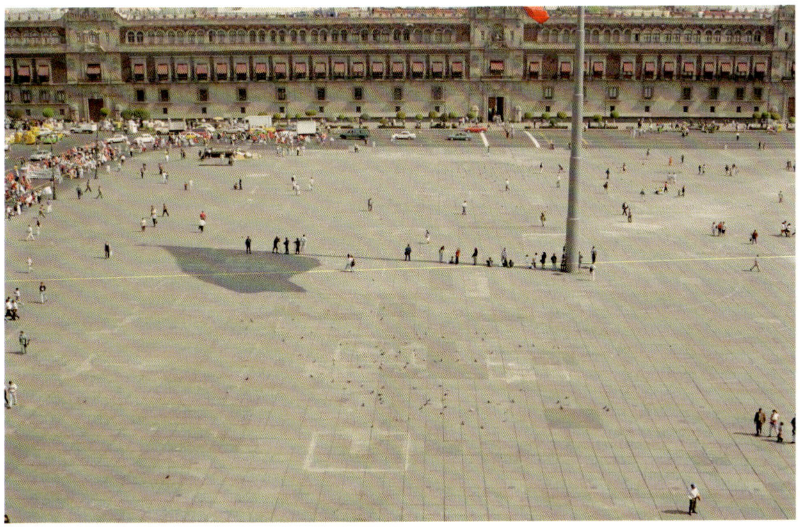

3:30 P.M.

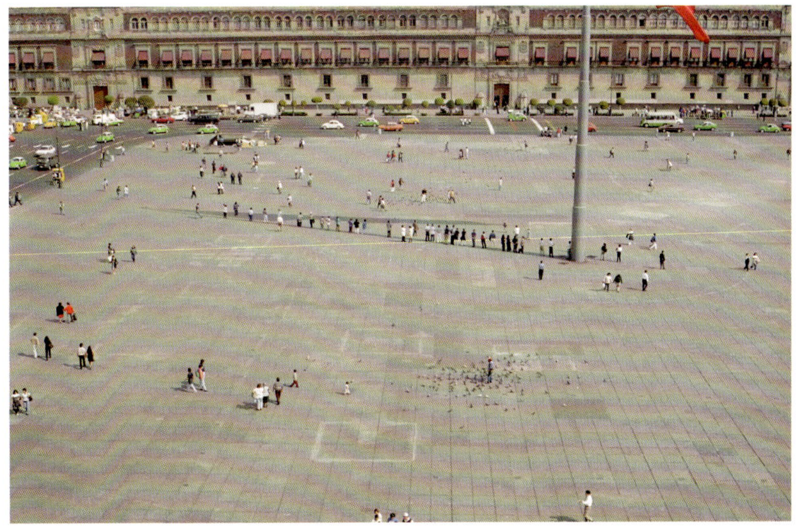

4:30 P.M.

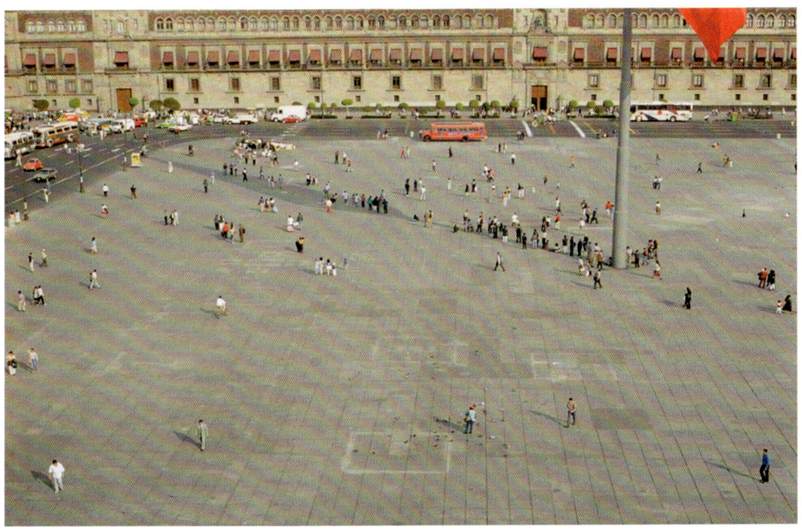

5:30 P.M.

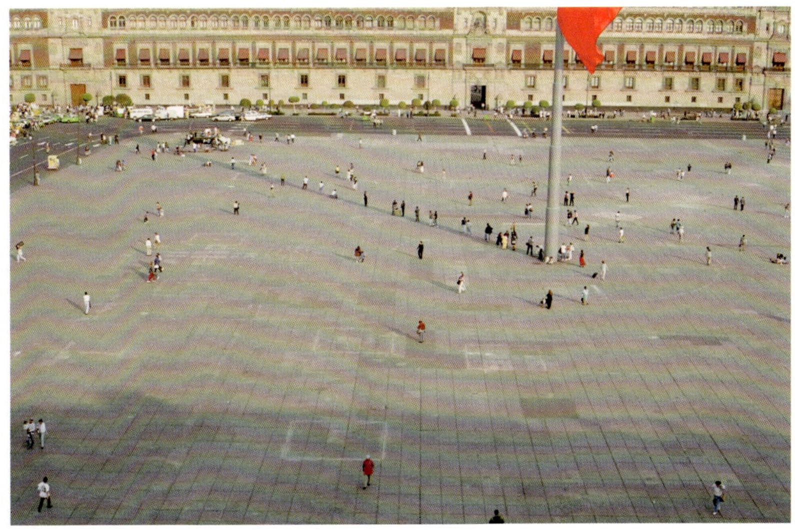

6:00 P.M.

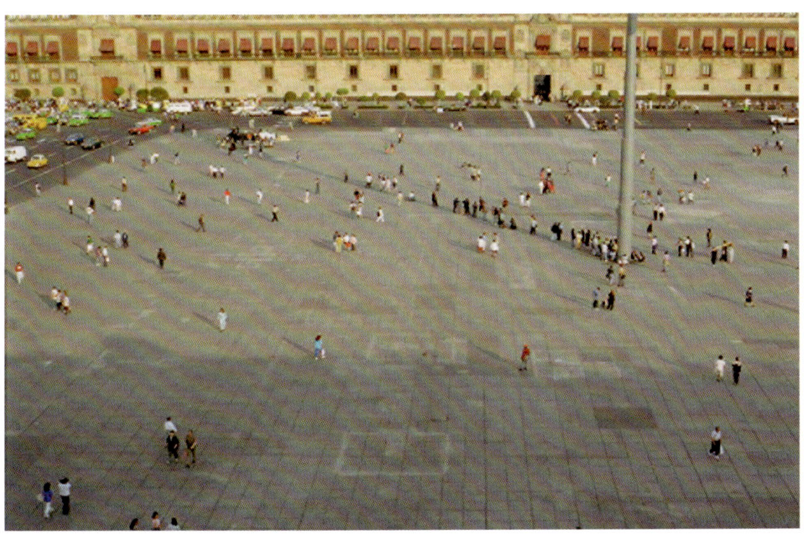

6:15 P.M.

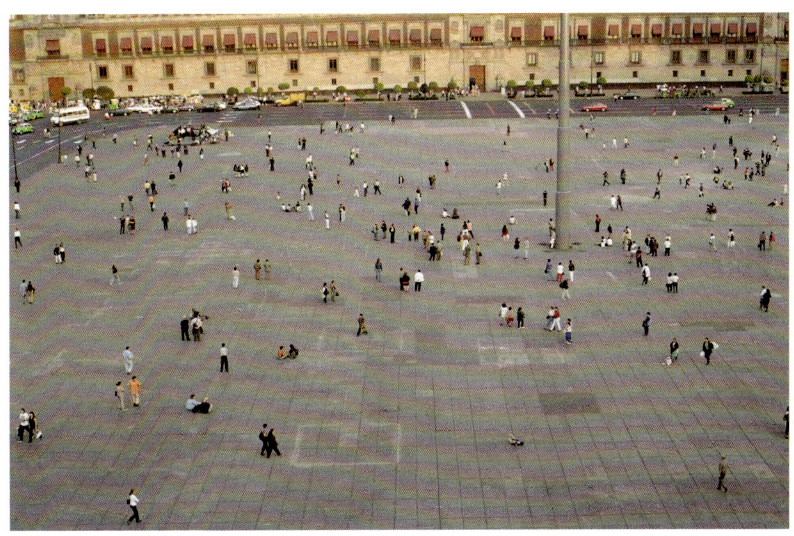

6:45 P.M.

as a means of economic critique that hints at the way in which the passage of time is, above all, dependent on the fulfilment of desire – or on its lack of fulfilment. In that sense, the *Rehearsals* evoke *l'étreinte qui ne peut s'achever, l'orgasme à jamais repoussé* (the embrace that cannot be achieved, the orgasm forever delayed), for only in relation to the longing for satisfaction can we understand the impulse of modernization. The rehearsal also stands as a means of social critique, in as much as it exists in an 'ambiguous affair with modernity, forever arousing, and yet always delaying the moment it will happen'.[35]

Tenuous Tenacity

It would be a mistake, however, to assume that Alÿs's works are only a matter of social critique or denunciation. Although they never fail to describe or indicate injustice, their drive is to explore alternative ways of living, practices that open up of the sphere of possibilities. This is the reason that Alÿs constantly fluctuates between production and documentation. On one level, he keeps an eye on the moments and occasions in which urban reality provides a moment of condensation. In 1999, for instance, for twelve hours he recorded the line of people who take refuge under the shade of the flagpole in the Zócalo, drawing attention to an unconscious daily ceremony (*Zócalo*, 1999). In showing how 'social encounters provoke sculptural situations', Alÿs resists the progressive disenchantment of urban space, evoking the function of the polis as place for the expression for collective desires and fears, the stage for mass events and political ceremonies, the site of shared dreams. But in parallel his task is to intervene in social situations to suggest a change in perspective, showing in particular that no matter how slight its effects, action is neither fruitless nor meaningless.

Several of Alÿs's recent works have involved collaboration or interaction with collectives, the members of which may appear either as the participants of an experience proposed by the artist or as characters in a staged anecdote that is used as a means to shake off political passivity. In many instances these works have aimed to introduce an allegorical action into the history of a specific location. In *When Faith Moves Mountains* (2002), for example, Alÿs summoned hundreds of participants to provoke the slight displacement of a sand dune north of Lima, Peru. *Modern Procession* (2002) was

RAFAEL ORTEGA AND FRANCIS ALŸS
1 MINUTE OF SILENCE, 2003
PHOTO DOCUMENTATION
OF AN EVENT, PANAMA CITY
FLYER ANNOUNCING THE EVENT
32 X 23 CM

On April 3, 2003, a group of forty-five volunteers attempted to silence a selection of crowded locations with the intention of materializing one minute of silence. No specific meaning was attributed to the said minute. The intervention took place in the National Lottery hall; a popular grand café in the old town; a street squatted by two soccer teams; a mall and during a live radio programme.

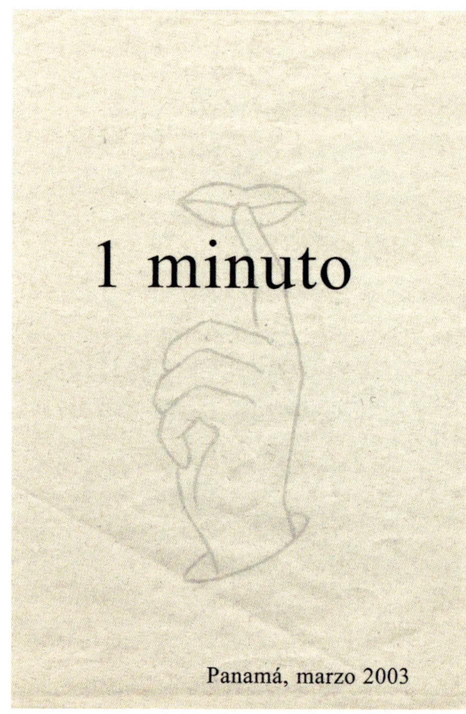

BRIDGE/PUENTE, 2006
IN COLLABORATION WITH TAIYANA PIMENTEL
AND CUAUHTÉMOC MEDINA
STUDIES ON PAPER FOR THE EVENT,
KEY WEST, FLORIDA, AND HAVANA

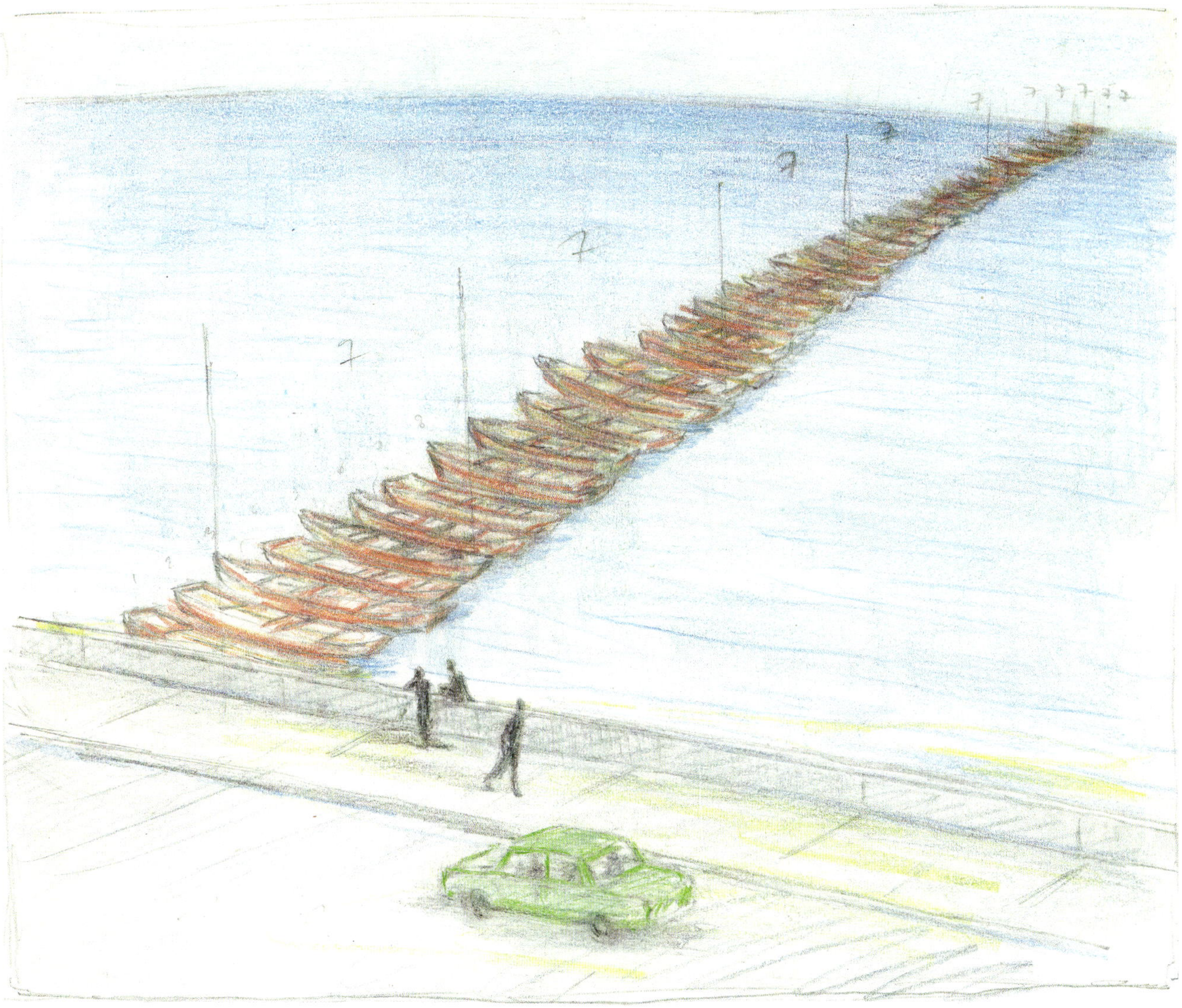

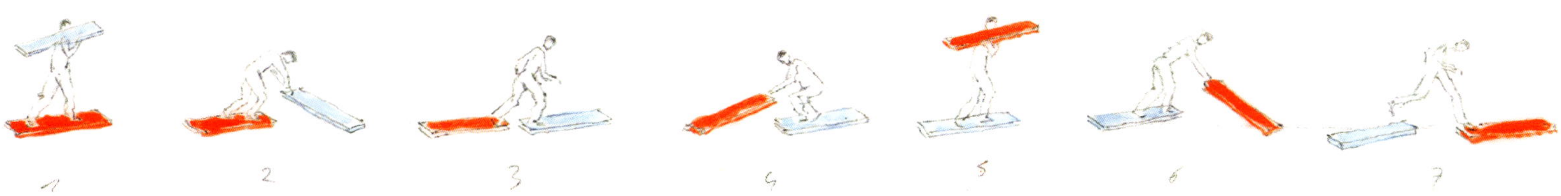

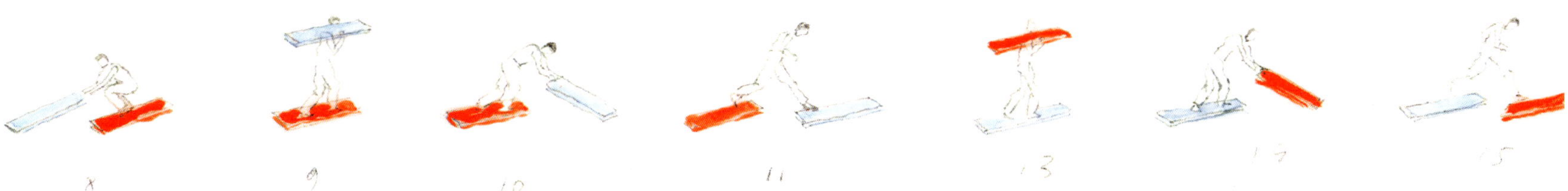

BRIDGE/PUENTE, 2006
IN COLLABORATION WITH TAIYANA PIMENTEL
AND CUAUHTÉMOC MEDINA
PHOTO DOCUMENTATION OF AN EVENT,
KEY WEST, FLORIDA, AND HAVANA

On 29 March 2006, 150 boats lined up from Key West, Florida, and from Santa Fe, Havana, to send out a floating bridge between the United States and Cuba. The two lines headed from opposite shores towards the same horizon to create the illusion of a bridge.

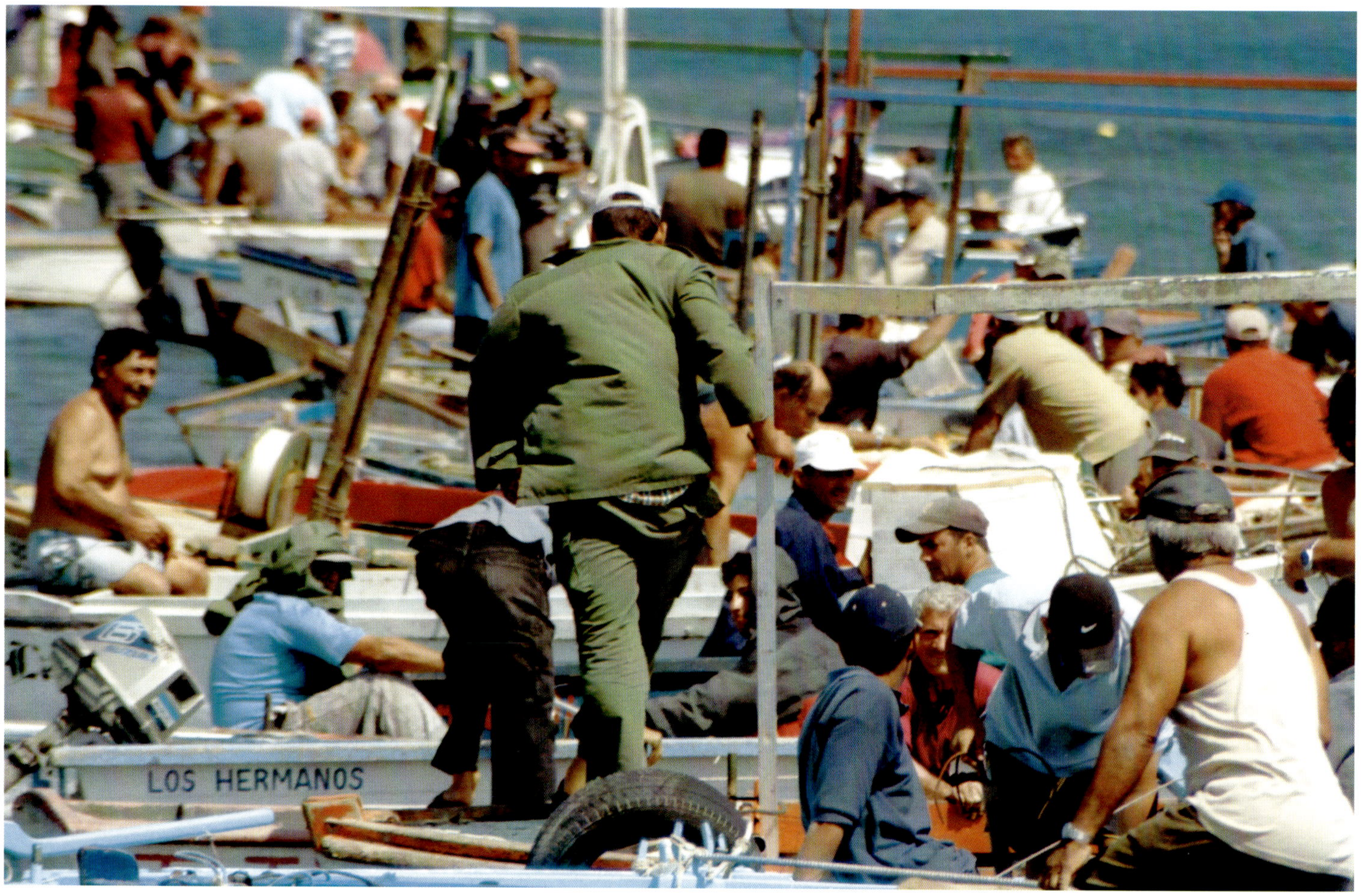

a procession to mark the transportation of modern icons from the Museum of Modern Art in Manhattan to its temporary site in Queens. *1 Minute of Silence* (2003) aimed to induce an unannounced minute of silence in the streets of Panama City, while in *Bridge/Puente* (2006), Alÿs suggested the feasibility of bridging two regions of conflict with a line of boats coming from two different shores. In all these works Alÿs upholds the emotional, ethical and strategic significance of the emergence of collective agency. After all, what is the purpose of the city if not to 'offer a remedy for the futility of action and speech' by allowing a space of social demonstration? Or as Arendt put it, 'The organization of the polis is a kind of organized remembrance. The polis, properly speaking, is not the city-state in its physical location; it is the organization of the people as it arises out of acting and speaking together, and its true space lies between people living together for this purpose, no matter where they happen to be.'[36] It is this space that Francis Alÿs locates, preserves and activates.

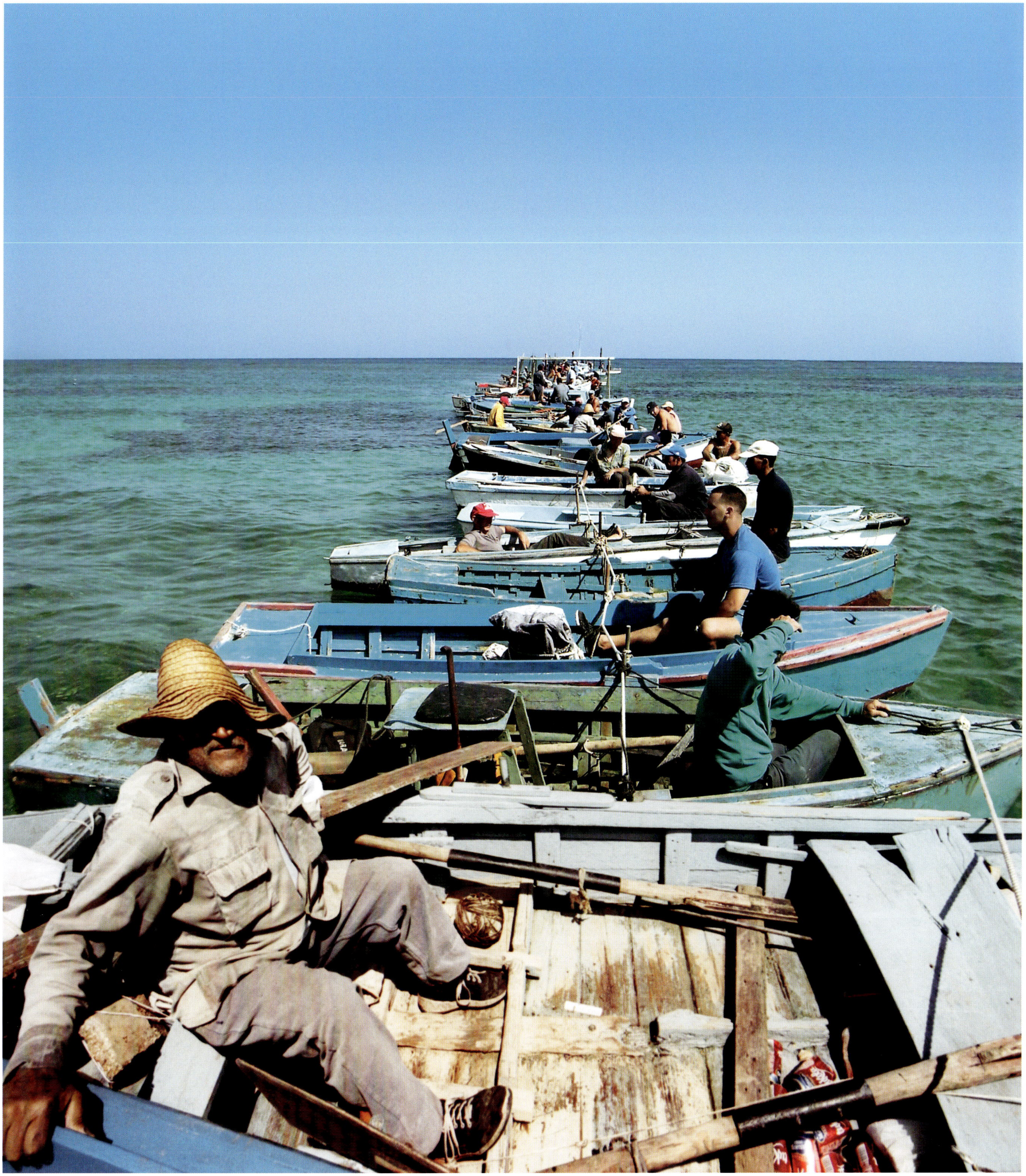

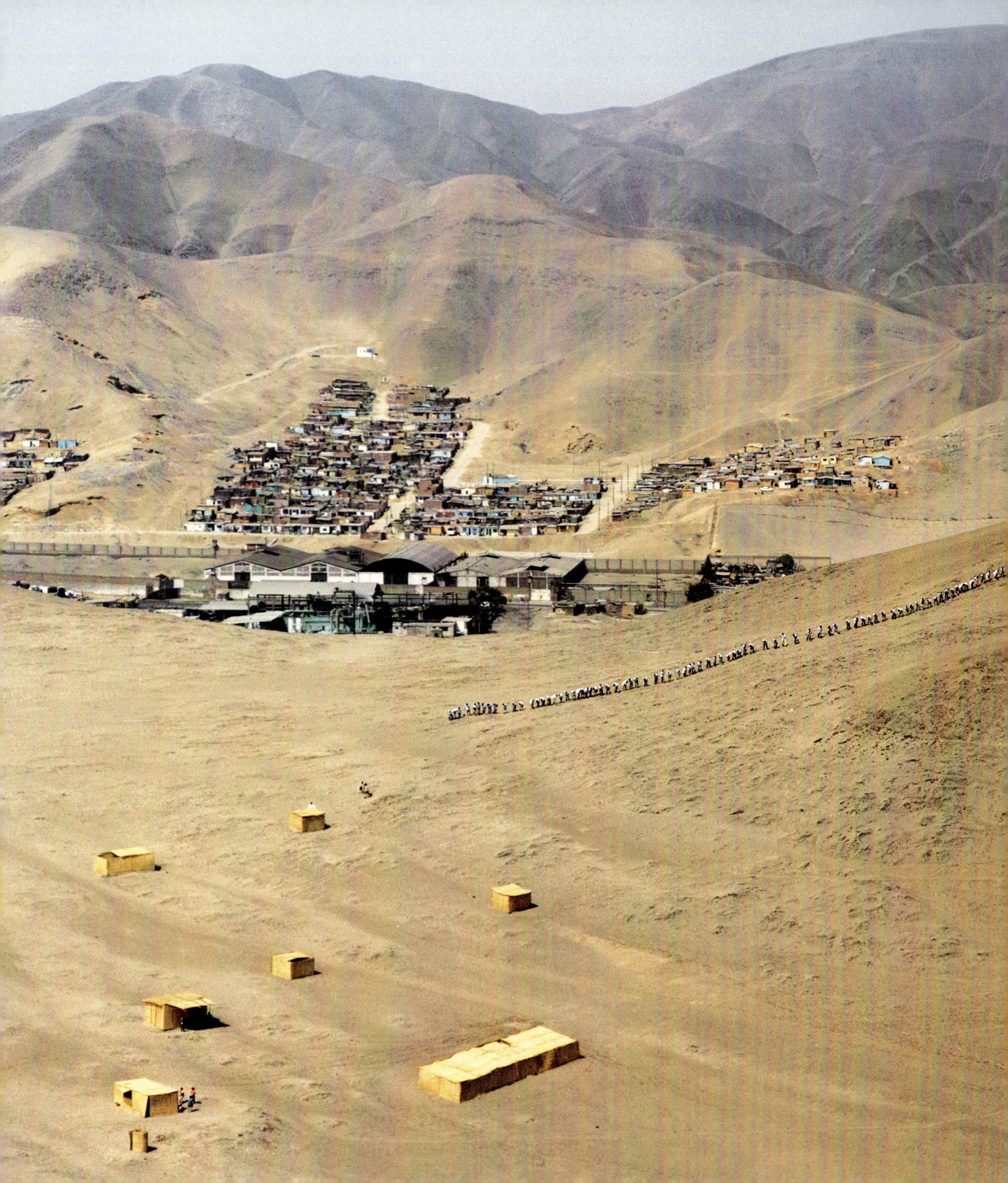

107 FOCUS

In the Spirit of Conviviality: When Faith Moves Mountains

Jean Fisher

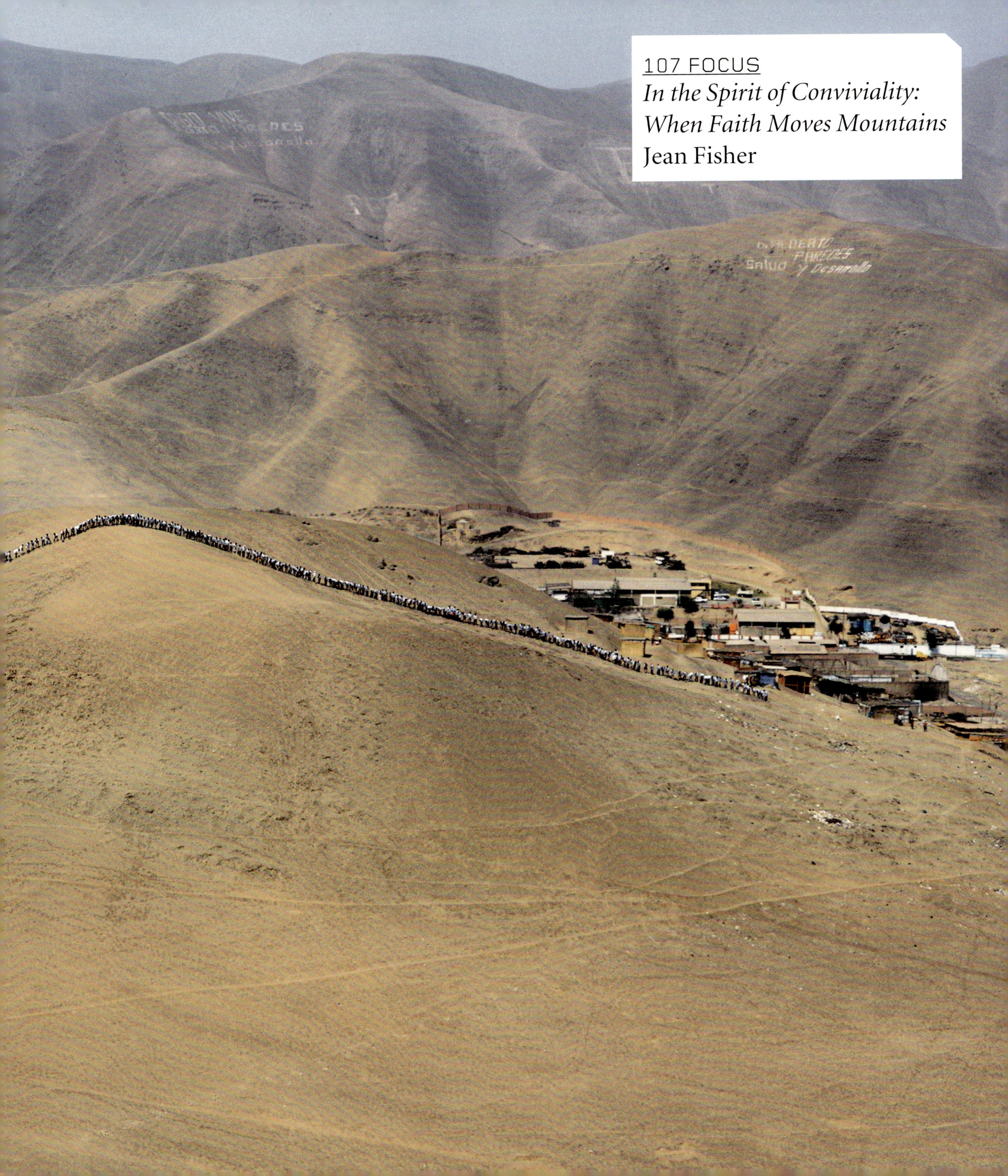

STUDY FOR WHEN FAITH MOVES MOUNTAINS, 2002
PENCIL ON PAPER
31 X 23 CM

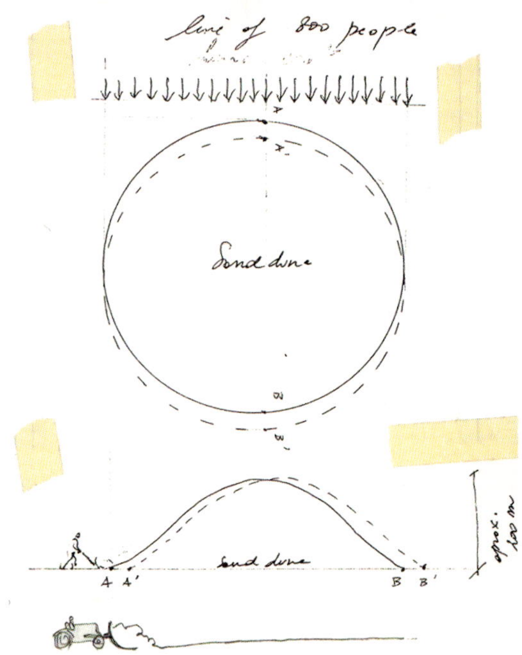

Few commentators would dispute that, on the face of it, When Faith Moves Mountains (2002) was a ludic, if not ludicrous, gesture. A huge deployment of voluntary human labour with nothing to show for it – on site, at least – except some tracks in the sand, sooner or later to be obscured by the forces of wind and gravity. And few artistic gestures have so lucidly laid bare the Sisyphean absurdity of the human condition, caught between utopian aspiration and frail endeavour in the larger space-time schema of the world. The very play of grounded and groundlessness, materiality and immateriality in the work conjures up that abyssal gap between the burden of everyday existence and the weightlessness of the imagination, in which the sheer gravity of the former in most regions of the world, including Peru, lends the latter at times an air of the frivolous. Kant himself may have appreciated the extent to which Alÿs's project colludes with his assessment of art as 'purposiveness without purpose', as may Hans-Georg Gadamer, for whom both art and play were 'movement as movement', setting their own rules in an 'autonomous temporality' – a time-out-of-time – and expressing an overabundance of life.[1] Art – like play, garbage and wastelands in general (notably, the outskirts of cities where most shanty towns of the world are sited) – is an 'excess' or 'unproductive' expenditure, a continuous production of 'otherness', neither reducible to commodification nor wholly subject to the disciplinary mechanisms of the system that engenders it. And, as such, it always presents a latent form of resistance to prevailing structures of power.

Máximo esfuerzo Mínimo resultado

We should not, then, underestimate the role of the gratuitous in Alÿs's project. It was a collaboration – a working together – between the artist, the critic, the filmmaker, the volunteers and the local people in a spirit of free will and conviviality, a sharing of a space of existence, if only momentarily, to perform a seemingly inconsequential act. But there is, of course, more to it than this. What grabs our attention here, and what cuts to the heart of what we may mean by art practice nowadays, is the very freedom to think and act upon such a thought. In what sense can praxis – in the classical sense, an act that is an end in itself and pertains to the labour of everyday existence – be at the same time poiesis – an act whose end is not in itself but in the 'pro-duction' (in the sense of a bringing-into-being) of a truth? What kind of truth is at stake in the work? And what can be the relevance of a poetic act in the context of sustained political crisis, such as that experienced in Peru itself, of which the displacement of people and the coming-into-being of Ventanilla, and other pueblos jóvenes like it, is but one of its consequences – a symptom, in fact, of a fundamental void of meaning in the structure of polity to which the work's entire play on displacement alludes? The argument I should like to advance is that the space of freedom opened up by When Faith Moves Mountains provides the conditions of possibility for

VIRTUES, 1992
OIL AND ENCAUSTIC ON CANVAS
24 X 34 CM

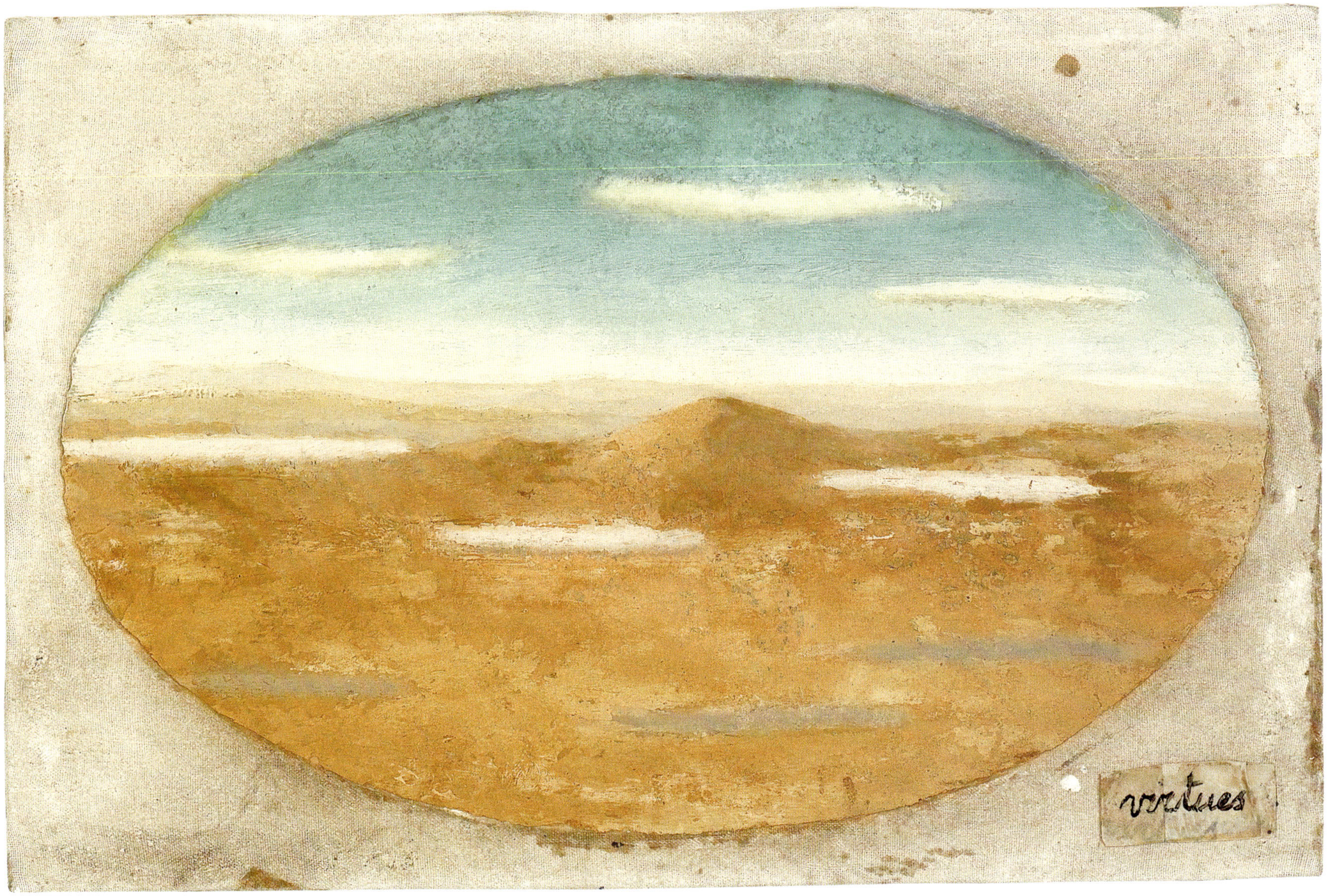

a new thought of the political, here understood not simply as the mechanism of political discourse or the structures of power and the state, but as 'conviviality', or the founding moment of community.

When Faith Moves Mountains was not, of course, without purpose or consequence. We know of it through its meticulous documentation: aerial footage of the overall topography showing the work in progress as a serpentine chain of workers battles up and down the dune in the heat of the noonday sun, and on-the-ground footage of the volunteers, their shovels scraping through the gritty surface and throwing up clouds of sand. We are given a sense of both its material and immaterial conditions. Based on its re-presentation through video, photography and written documentation, knowledge of the work has already been disseminated through art publications, gossip and various interpretative commentaries. This absence of any tangible art object, the displacement – from preparatory work to event to re-presentation (what Alÿs describes as the three successive and distinct lives of the project) – entangles us again in the dilemma of where, between concept and object, 'art' lies, an issue that has been unresolved since the 1960s. But the mythopoeic effect of dissemination is how we know the vast majority of the world's cultural productions, especially site-specific ones, from the Easter Island sculptures to Giotto's Arena Chapel frescoes to the Land Art projects of the late 1960s and 1970s.

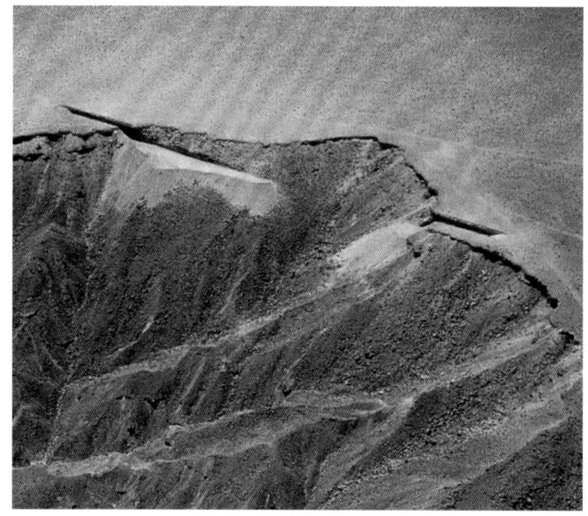

MICHAEL HEIZER
DOUBLE NEGATIVE, 1969-70
244,900 TONNE DISPLACEMENT
RHYOLITE, SANDSTONE
457 X 15 X 9 M
MORMON MESA, OVERTON, NEVADA

In some respects When Faith Moves Mountains invites comparison with these earlier Land Art and Conceptual practices. Just as they were born out of the politicized climate of the 1950s and 1960s, so the forces of globalism have confronted us again with the question of the nature and place of art practices and their relevance to the social and political networks in which we are all now irrevocably entangled. And yet, despite their ambitions to democratize art through its redefinition (as in the case of Joseph Kosuth) or through avoidance of its elitist institutions (as in the case of Land Art), these earlier practices nonetheless produced image-based objects still conventionally encoded as 'art' in exclusive, modernist terms. Typically, Land Art projects sought out remote and seemingly unpopulated landscapes; among the most infamous of these are Michael Heizer's Double Negative (a displacement of 244,900 tonnes of earth in the Nevada desert), Walter de Maria's The Lghtning Field (400 steel lightning conductors set in a grid over a square mile of the New Mexico desert), and Robert Smithson's Spiral Jetty (over 5,000 tonnes of earth and stone curling into Utah's Great Salt Lake). As with When Faith Moves Mountains, Spiral Jetty is known to us through the documentary film of its making. Similarly, Smithson's concern with entropy meant that it was not intended to survive the forces of nature.

WHEN FAITH MOVES MOUNTAINS, 2002
IN COLLABORATION WITH CUAUHTÉMOC MEDINA
AND RAFAEL ORTEGA
PHOTO DOCUMENTATION OF AN EVENT,
LIMA, PERU

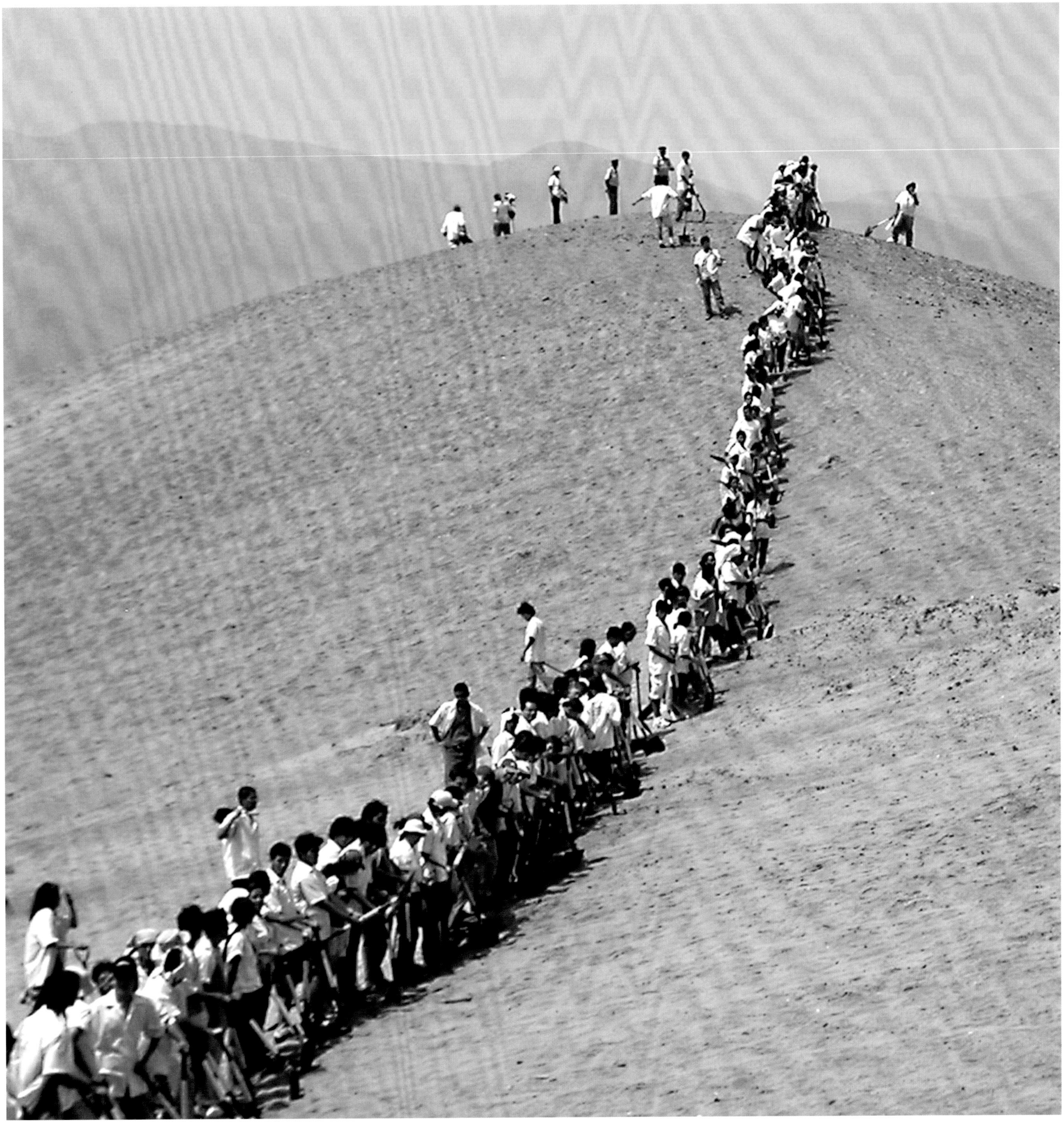

WHEN FAITH MOVES MOUNTAINS, 2002
IN COLLABORATION WITH CUAUHTÉMOC MEDINA AND RAFAEL ORTEGA
PHOTO DOCUMENTATION OF AN EVENT, LIMA, PERU

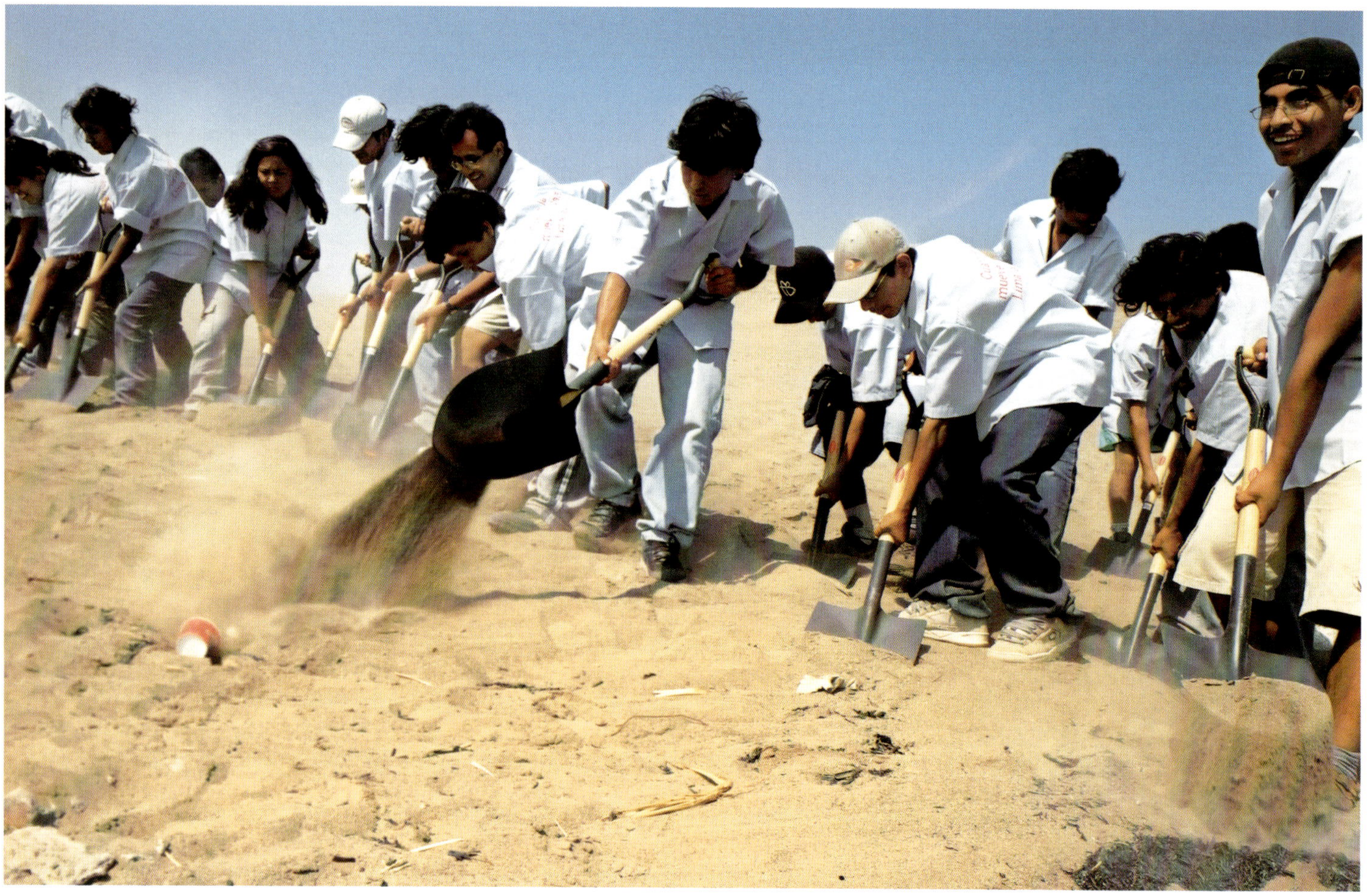

All of these earlier sculptural sites were realized through the use of backhoes and other heavy earthmoving machinery, in contrast to the shovel and manual labour of When Faith Moves Mountains. The difference, however, is more than the macho affluence of the United States versus the material poverty and labour-intensive necessity of Latin America. To understand the fuller significance we might think also of Richard Long, who, like his American counterparts, trekked around what he liked to call 'empty landscape'[12] but manually moved rocks or driftwood into configurations that nostalgically invoked a prehistoric or pre-industrial arcadia. Nonetheless, these practices retain a residue of the colonial mentality that assumes the right to make one's mark on or exploit the land as material for art no matter whose territory, 'empty' or not, it may be. By contrast, When Faith Moves Mountains was an act without possession. One crucial distinction, then, between these earlier practices and Alÿs's project is that the former are authorized, delimited reconfigurations of nature that draw the world into the orbit of the privileged subject rather than engage the self with the space and rhythm of the world. They remain consistent with what Giorgio Agamben describes as modernism's progressive displacement of poiesis by praxis, which gave rise to the notion of art as an expression of the artist's creative will and, in the

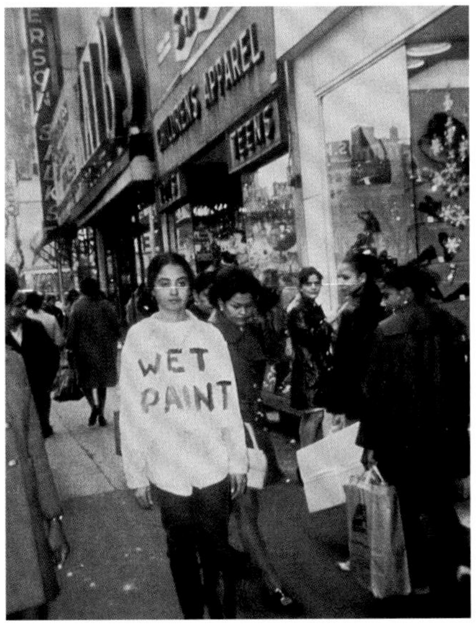

ADRIAN PIPER
CATALYSIS III, 1970-1
PERFORMANCE, NEW YORK

process, detached aesthetics from ethics. And yet, as Agamben continues, 'what the Greeks meant with the distinction between poiesis and praxis was precisely that the essence of poiesis has nothing to do with the expression of a will (with respect to which art is in no way necessary): this essence is found instead in the pro-duction of truth and in the subsequent opening of a world for man's existence and action.'[3]

When Faith Moves Mountains is consistent with Alÿs's tendency to withdraw as the artistic subject of the work. This does not at all mean that he also withdraws responsibility for it, but it does acknowledge that the significance of an artistic event lies in its potential to open a world 'for man's existence and action'. Alÿs shares this reticence with certain Conceptual practices of earlier decades. For instance, his 'paseos', although derived from a different set of parameters, recall Adrian Piper's 1970–71 Catalysis series of absurd street performances; intended to elicit surprised responses from the passers-by, these interventions were, as she has said, not 'art' in so far as she was not posing herself as the object, but 'propositions' about art. Or one might invoke Lawrence Weiner's text 'sculptures' about form or materials, and Luis Camnitzer's text-based work of the late 1960s; rather than impose an image or object, these works were intended to activate the individual imagination of the viewer, since anyone could visualize the work according to his or her own experience. This attentiveness to the way the viewer imaginatively negotiates the work, although still based in formal concerns, is already political in so far as it posits a concept of art as inherently dialogical and non-hierarchical. And yet Alÿs's projects (like Piper's and Camnitzer's subsequent work) extend this propositional dimension of art much further into the socio-political sphere, such that the very absence of tangible object in When Faith Moves Mountains brings the frame, or socio-political context in which the work was produced, into sharper relief. For this reason it also poses some rather difficult questions regarding the ethical responsibility of the artist, questions that also demand that we rethink the aesthetic and the political as not inherently irreconcilable categories of experience.

To make art more answerable to 'real life' has been a persistent drive of the politically conscious artist at least since the 1960s, but politically motivated art has always been caught in a dilemma between the desire for artistic freedom and the demands of political activism, a dilemma in which poiesis has too often ceded to praxis. And yet one has to ask whether this is not a false antinomy based on the old assumption that the aesthetic was necessarily detached from everyday life, which is tantamount to claiming that the creative act could have nothing to say about the truth of existence, a patent absurdity. Art may be an excess of life, but in our encounter with it it brings its world to ours in what Gadamer described as a 'fusion of

WHEN FAITH MOVES MOUNTAINS, 2002
16 MM FILM DOCUMENTATION OF AN
EVENT, LIMA, PERU
36 MIN.

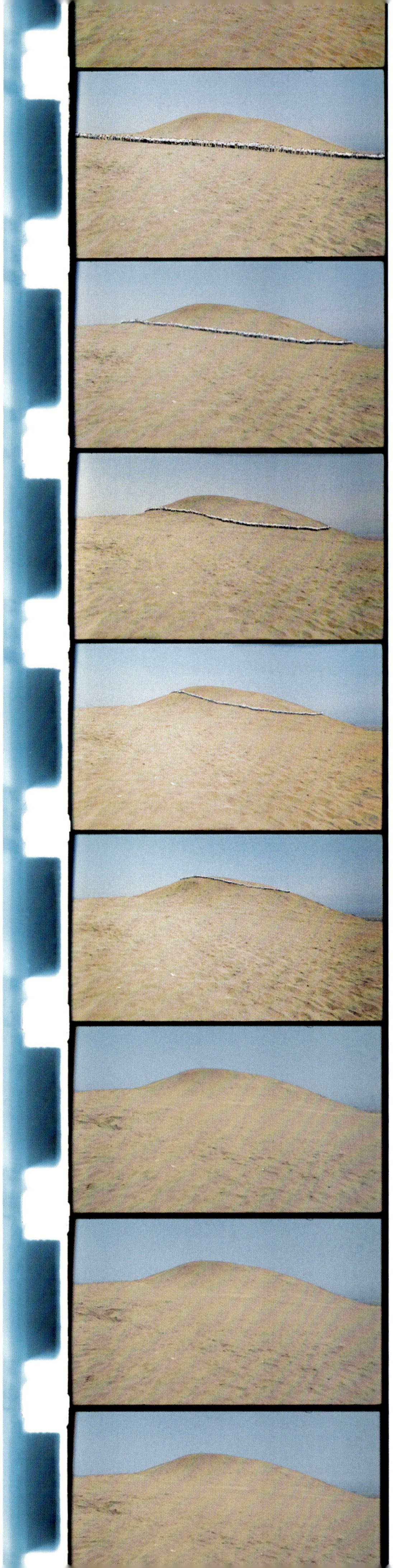

horizons'. It is a space of interpenetration between these two worlds in which, rather than one mimicking the other, they are both put into mutual crisis. The need of contemporary art to understand and test the limits of this horizon, which I take to be one of the drives behind When Faith Moves Mountains, was also manifest in Documenta 11 in 2002. The exhibition's curators deliberately set out to interrogate the relation of artistic practices to neo-colonial globalization; against the historical convention of such international events to showcase formally inventive work, they selected practitioners who sought ways by which to confront real social and political issues. The consequence, however, was a slippage between documentary and artistic practices that begged the question of their respective efficacy in producing new truths for understanding reality.

Among the primary goals of the documentary – and of activist art – is persuasion, which means that the language it uses must be unambiguous and already commonly understood; that is, there is an assumption that words and images are directly communicable. But if one reproduces the language of established, hegemonic discourses without challenging the ideological motives that underline both their structures of representation and forms of reception – in effect, their claims to truth – then one ends up conforming to the conservative politics one wants to oppose. Hence the rhetoric of politically motivated art has tended either to reconfirm authority – often by seeking to occupy its place – or to become appropriated and neutralized by it, a problem that dogged activist art of the 1960s and 1970s.

If, however, we take the view that the poetic and political efficacy of art lies not in the transmission of mere information but in insight – what Heidegger called the 'unconcealment' of truth – then its modus operandi must involve a suspension of signification. This may be experienced as liberatory joy or intense anguish, but in either case it mobilizes the feelings and imagination of the viewer, an affectivity that depends less on its status as a physical image per se than as an encounter with an event and a vector of a thought. By this route we come closer to appreciating the subtlety of Alÿs's work. Art, for Heidegger, 'institutes a world', meaning that art as poiesis produces a hitherto unthought configuration of reality. To do this, art needs to provide the conditions of an event, but for it to be an event it cannot, strictly speaking, present what is already known. Thus the radical event of art precipitates a crisis of meaning or, rather, it exposes the void of meaning at the core of a given social situation, which is its 'truth'. This truth is not something already there to be discovered – like the laws of gravity, or how many civilians were killed in the American bombing of Baghdad – but is created in response to a world and a self in a continuous state of

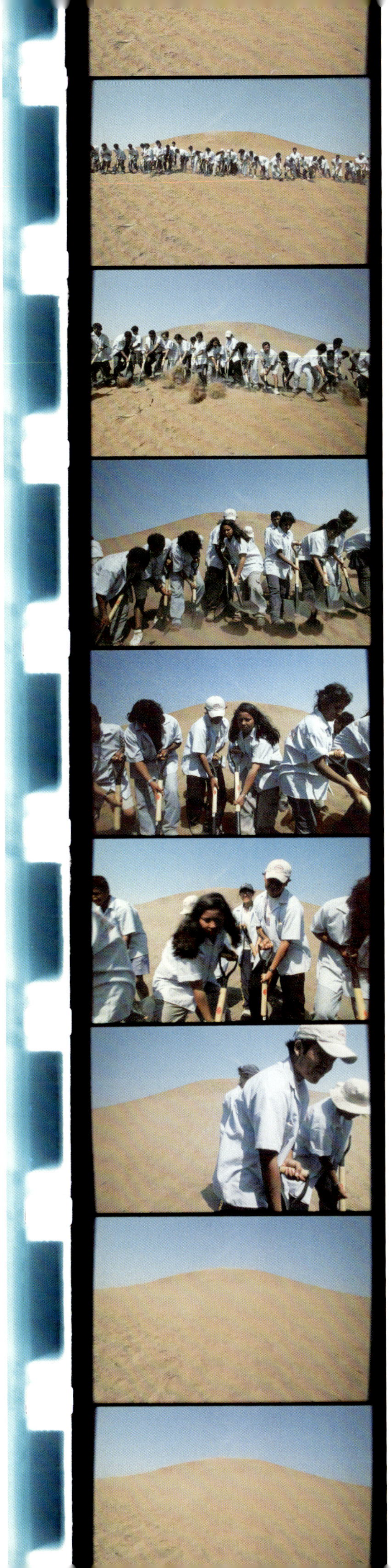

transformation. What this means, as Bakhtin recognized, is that each act performed in the world at each singular moment has its transformative consequences, however localized, and herein lies the ethical responsibility not only of the artist but of us all: that the ethical arises in our answerability to our own actions, not in any prior moral rules.

Typically, Alÿs's work does not attempt to fill this unconscious void with a plethora of images but to hollow it out, and this is the trait we see playfully excavated in, among other works, Magnetic Shoes (1994), The Loop (1997) and Paradox of Praxis 1 (1997). Deleuze maintained that, contrary to conventional opinion, the artist was not so much the patient suffering some form of psychosis in need of treatment, but the 'diagnostician' of civilization, capable of identifying the symptoms of a social pathology prior to any general awareness of it.[4] And it is precisely this moment of artistic insight, when our habitual structures of reality are shown to no longer make sense, that the potential arises for a collective demand for change.

What When Faith Moves Mountains shares with Alÿs's earlier 'demonstration', Cuentos Patrióticos (1997), is the articulation of a poetic metaphor with collective agency.[5] The question is, what is it that links a movement seemingly originating in individual sensibility to a collective response? What is it about When Faith Moves Mountains that enables an apparently absurd thought to gather to it a body of unpaid participants and then touch the imagination of an art world at a considerable distance from its site of execution? Agency is experienced in the decisions subjects and communities make in mapping and positioning themselves relative to sites of power. This is precisely the point of articulation of the ethical – not a given set of rules, which are by no means universal, but something produced in the encounter with an event for which one has no ready-to-hand explanations. This is the moment of the ethical that Bakhtin refers to and that Zygmunt Bauman describes as preceding the moral law.[6] Alain Badiou relates this moment to Lacan's notion of the Real, a realization of a truth – a void of meaning at the core of any situation, which is nonetheless its unacknowledged or hidden foundation.[7] The subject is seized by a realization that alters its existing perception of the world and sense of self within it, producing a 'becoming-other' than itself. The subject is what the intuition produces. Hence, if each act performed creates a new configuration of self and world, then it also animates a new ethical evaluation.[8] Badiou's famous example is Saint Paul's conversion on the road to Damascus, and we might add that both artistic insight and faith, referred to in Alÿs's title, are experiences of the human spirit that exist in excess of scientific proof or of instrumental reason in general. What this means is that art as insight does not render up a subject of knowledge, since it is precisely the privileged subject that is dissolved here, but access to what Jean-Luc Nancy calls the 'origin': neither the origin of the world nor of a psychological self, but of each moment in its singularity, where artist and viewer find common ground.

Central to all these accounts is the proposition that each singular moment is constitutive of shared existence. As Bakhtin insists, 'To live from within myself, from my unique place in Being, does not yet mean at all that I live only for my own sake; as I approach the other in its own singularity I acknowledge my answerability to that other and to myself as a responsible participant in the always becoming world-as-event.'[9] As Nancy argues, we must forge a different path from the post-Enlightenment privilege of Being, which conceals the fact that 'I' is mutually constituted with others. 'I' is always and already 'us', 'being-together': 'Being does not have meaning. There is no meaning if meaning is not shared.'[10] From this point of view, art's origin and destiny no longer move from and to an autonomous self, the assumption of modernism, but in 'being-together', an essential sharing of existence in which the Western notion of the privileged artistic subject is no longer sustainable.

This spirit of conviviality is, for me, the motivating force behind When Faith Moves Mountains, initiating and uniting community as a shared experience of a thought, from the group of mostly engineering students who participated in the event at the site, to the people of the pueblo jóven who took it upon themselves to protect the site from interference while the work was in progress, to the art world, which receives the idea through the chain of documentation and commentary – a movement connecting the local to the global. In other words, as several commentaries have pointed out, When Faith Moves Mountains initiates a storytelling function, and Alÿs himself has spoken of the work's potential to become a 'fable or urban myth', consistent with the intentions of his work in general.[11] Deleuze calls this 'fabulation', which he emphatically places in the domain of collective utterance.[12] Fabulation concerns neither psychological nor historical memory as such (although it may draw on this) but the event through which teller and listener, or image and viewer, enter into a mutual relation of transformation. For the author, it is the task of the artist to invent new uses of language through which the collective may see the possibility of reinventing itself. Every new community needs its myths and storytellers on which to found its cohesion, or right to exist against the forces of fragmentation, as Patrick Chamoiseau's epic novel Texaco, set in the post-slavery conditions of Africa's descendants in Martinique, perfectly describes.[13] As it happens, both Texaco – the jumble of 'hutches' on the outskirts of City (Fort-de-France) – and the pueblo jóven of Ventanilla on the dunes outside Lima are founded in the

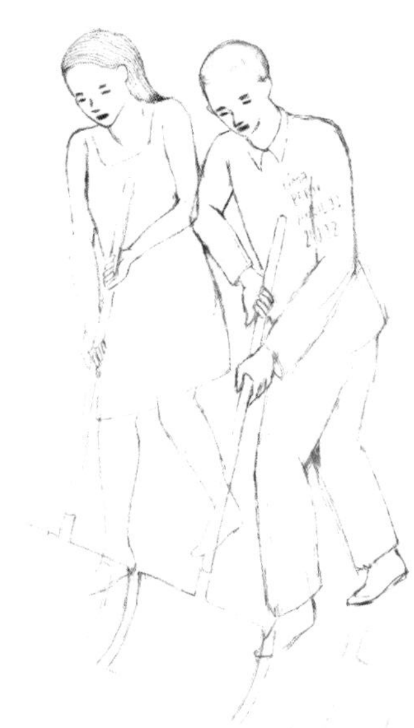

STUDY FOR WHEN FAITH MOVES MOUNTAINS, 2002
PENCIL ON TRACING PAPER
17 X 11 CM

WHEN FAITH MOVES MOUNTAINS, 2002
IN COLLABORATION WITH CUAUHTÉMOC MEDINA AND RAFAEL ORTEGA
PHOTO DOCUMENTATION OF AN EVENT, LIMA, PERU

unpromising shadow of an oil refinery. Sand, an organically inert material, provides little sustenance for life but is nonetheless an ingredient in the material for building foundations. Both When Faith Moves Mountains and Texaco invite us to consider that in repressive regimes the cruellest act is perhaps not to deprive a people of its body but of the ground and will to imagine new possibilities of life. Art, of course, does not produce grand revolutions, but as an event that opens up a new narrative about reality it provides the conditions of possibility for a nascent political consciousness, one born from conviviality, a being-together as a coming-into-being of community: the realization of shared existence.

When Faith Moves Mountains is a reminder that, faced with the ever-increasing instrumentalization of life under globalism, the responsibility of artistic practices is not to relinquish the right to imagine, but to invent new uses of language and new tactics of engagement with community – in other words, not the patronizing notion of 'bringing art to the masses', which still inscribes the attitudes of Western institutions and 'social' art practices, but a reconfiguration of practices capable of penetrating different social spaces and collective imaginaries. Or, as Camnitzer puts it, 'The discussion is not one about the ethics of art-making under dire circumstances, or the measurement of its direness, but about the possibility and duty of sustaining a useful militancy and, further, society's critical ability and sanity. That is, keeping alienation in check, everybody's alienation, no matter what.'[14] To keep alive the will to imagine is also to invent new ethical landscapes, new narratives and new agents of social change. It is utopian without promising Utopia.

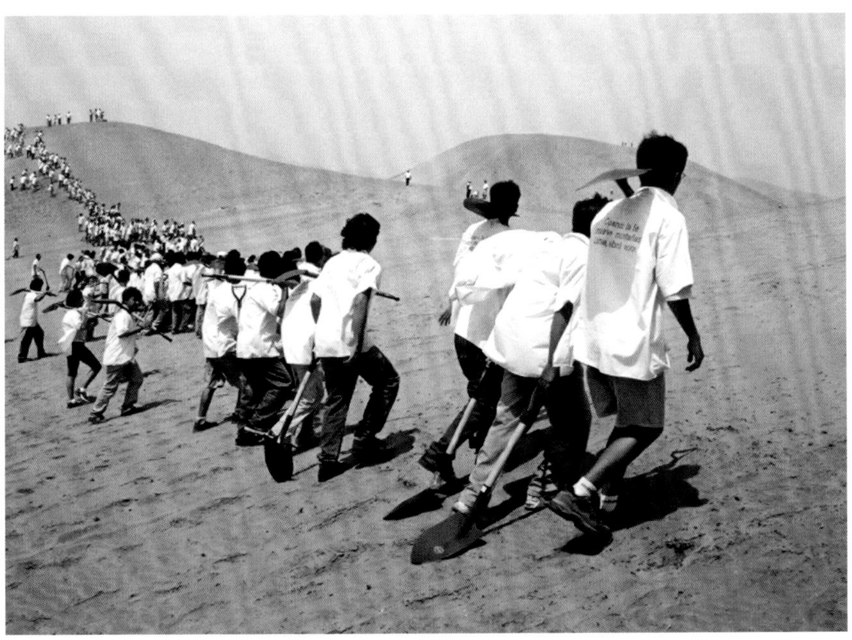

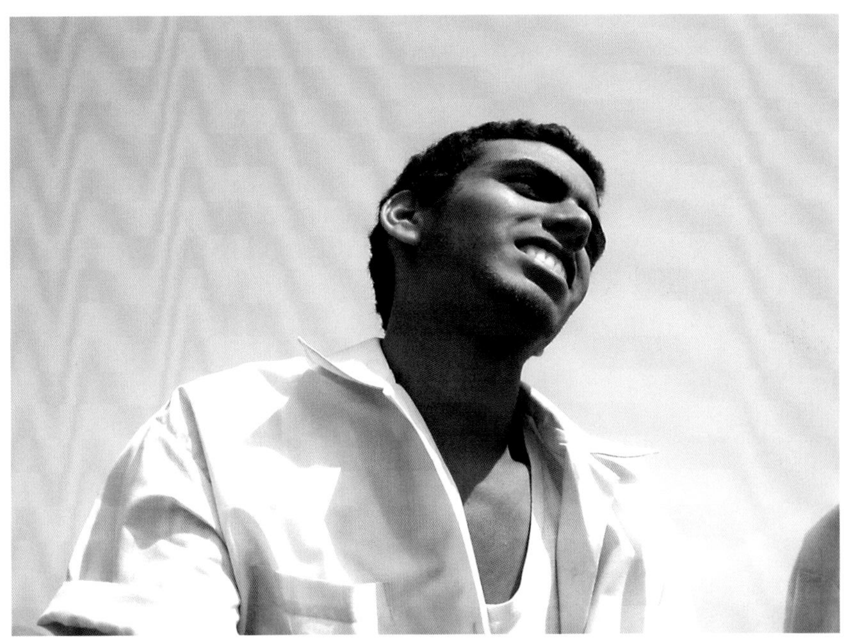

WHEN FAITH MOVES MOUNTAINS, 2002
IN COLLABORATION WITH CUAUHTÉMOC MEDINA AND RAFAEL ORTEGA
PHOTO DOCUMENTATION OF AN EVENT, LIMA, PERU

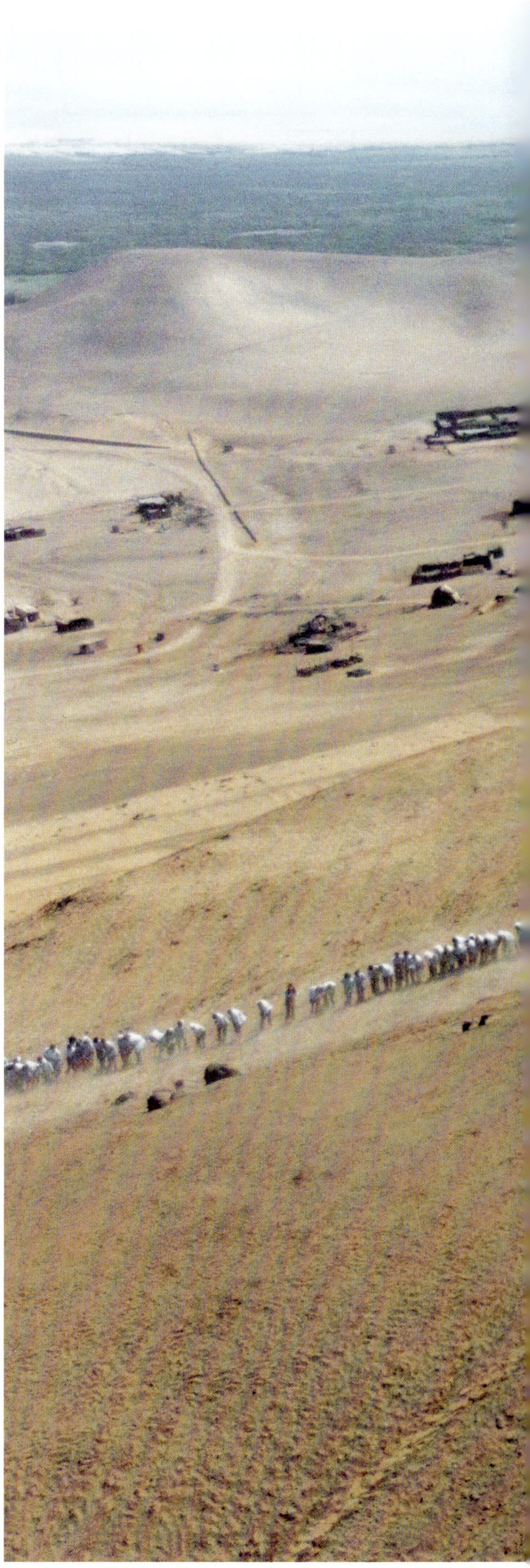

The Green Line (2004), Alÿs's 'paseo' through Jerusalem, revisits the question posed in When Faith Moves Mountains: what can be the relevance of a poetic act in the context of sustained political crisis?[15] As such, The Green Line functions as an extended and complementary exploration of the earlier work. The difference is that Jerusalem is a more militantly political context than Ventanilla, problematizing any notion of 'aesthetic neutrality'. To perform an act objectively in Jerusalem would be to succumb to the compromised liberal strategy favoured by Western media of reporting a 'balanced view' when the prevailing unequal relations of power demanded an ethical critique. Given that, as an outsider, the artist also could not be partisan, and so direct collaboration with local communities, as in When Faith Moves Mountains, was not an option, what position was available to him? Alÿs's solution was to retrace the map drawing made by Moshe Dayan in 1948, known as the 'green line', that inaugurated the partition of the city, but which topographically represented a contested sixty to eighty metre wide tract of land. Alÿs was filmed walking the 'green line' with a leaky tin of green paint, and the film then combined with recorded commentaries on Alÿs's action by both Palestinian and Israeli interviewees. By making a minimal intervention in a 'cartographic gap' no one can possess and hence from which no one can speak, the artist offered another position from the paradoxical ground of groundlessness.

In both When Faith Moves Mountains and The Green Line, meaning lies not in Alÿs's gesture but in what its absurdity discloses of the historical and sociopolitical framework that surrounds it. A poetic gesture intrinsically does not state a political position from which any determinate meaning can be derived; on the contrary, its value is its capacity to 'put meaning on trial' (as Adorno once said of Beckett's plays), to induce in its interlocutor a momentary loss of control over meaning from which a new insight and configuration of reality can emerge. Both When Faith Moves Mountains and The Green Line speak to questions of human belonging and dispossession, of the cartographies of colonialism. But this is not simply a territorial matter; it touches those relations that dehumanize feeling on both sides of a repressive divide. If the effect of conventional politics and its technologies is to disable human exchange and shrink existence to the limited world of 'interests', the effect of Alÿs's poetics is subversively political in its gift of the gesture as a potential catalyst for working through and reconfiguring reality, from senselessness to sense, impasse to passage, inhuman to human, towards a more expansive politic of solidarity and conviviality.

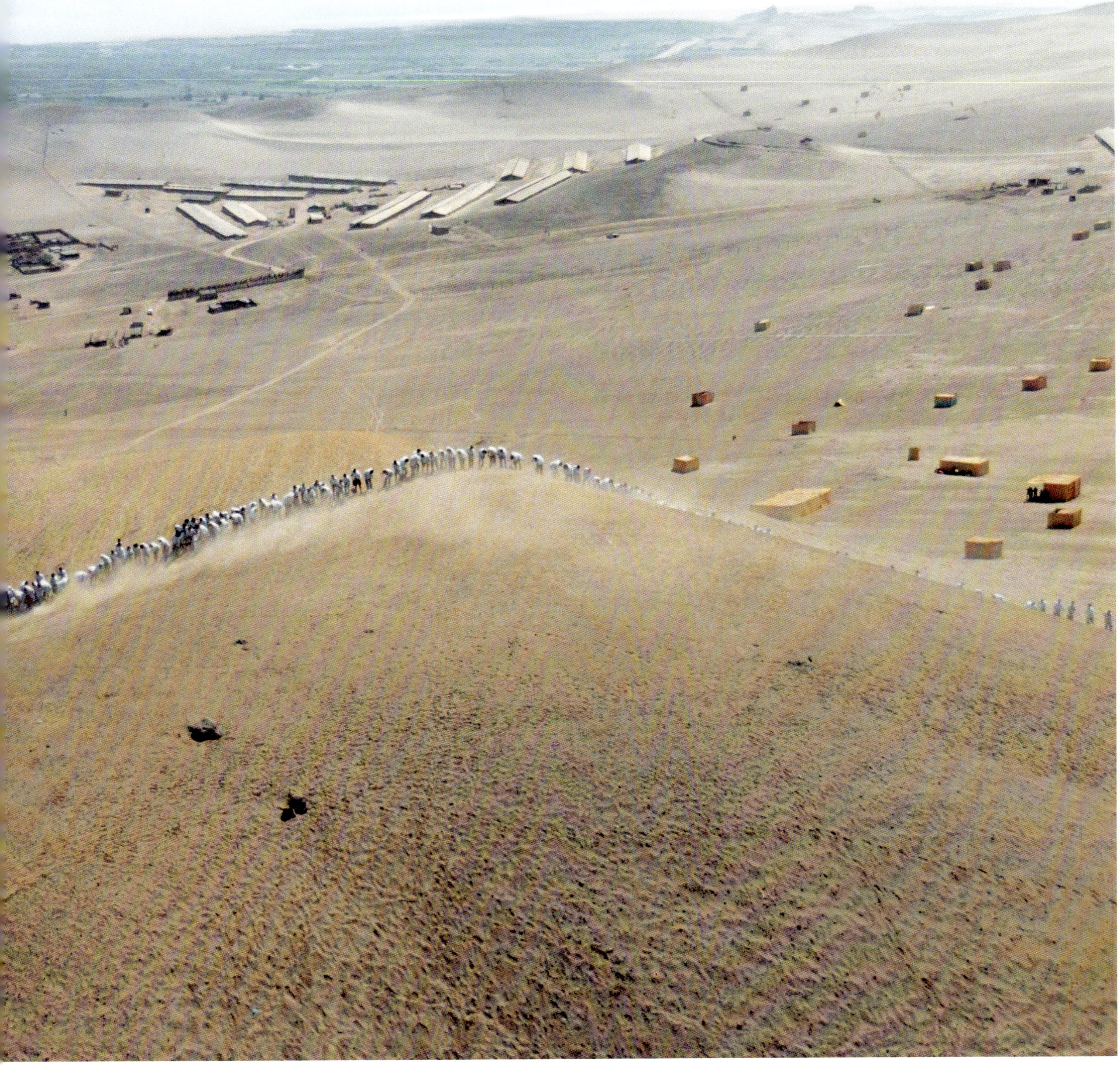

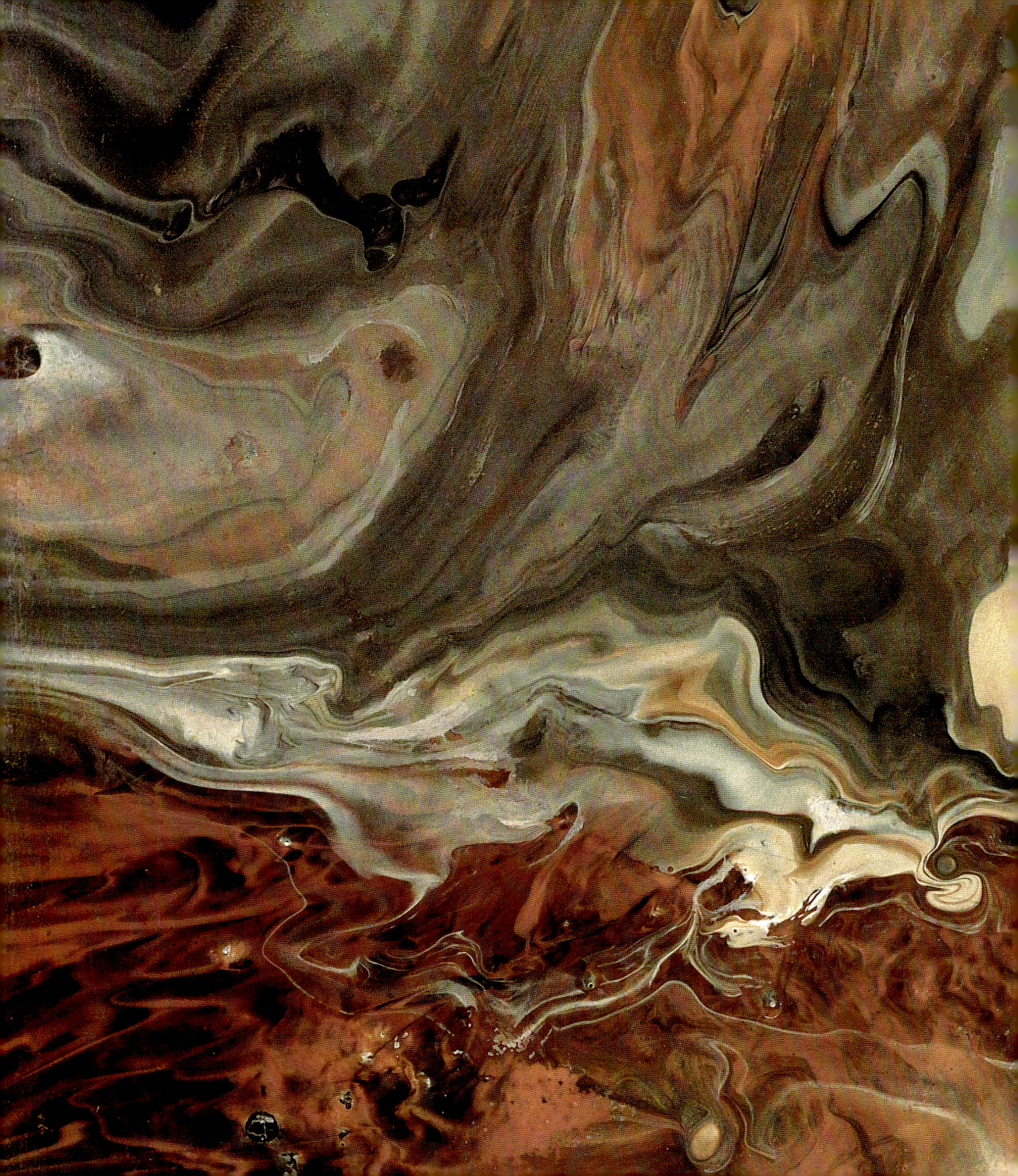

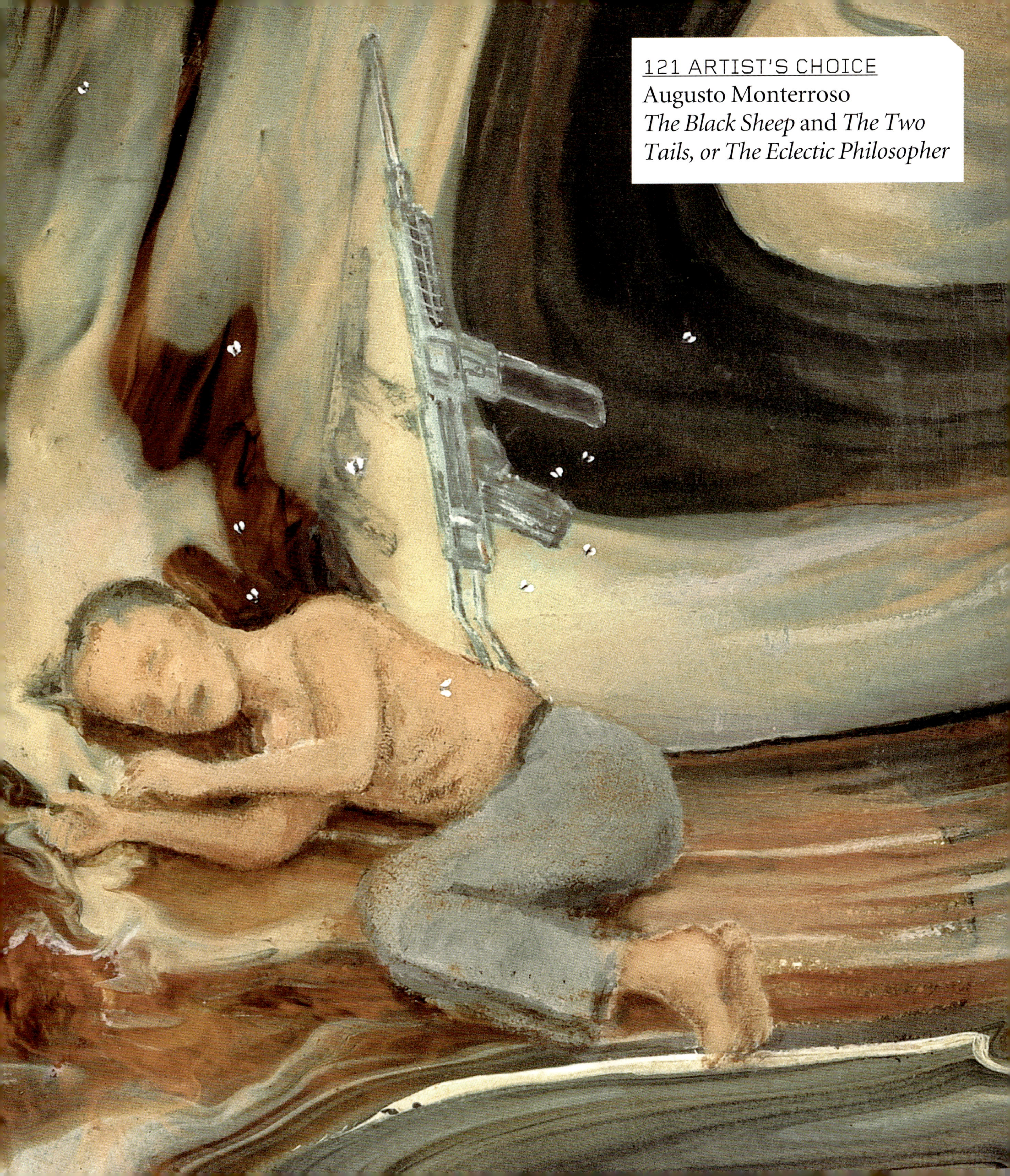

121 ARTIST'S CHOICE

Augusto Monterroso

The Black Sheep and *The Two Tails, or The Eclectic Philosopher*

Augusto Monterroso
The Black Sheep (La oveja negra)
1969

Many years ago in a faraway land there lived a Black Sheep.

It was shot.

A century later the sorry flock raised an equestrian statue to it, which looked very fine in the park.

So from then onward whenever a black sheep appeared it was quickly shot so that future generations of common sheep could also practise the art of sculpture.

TRANSLATED FROM SPANISH BY MARION IVERSON

En un lejano país existió hace muchos años una Oveja negra.

Fue fusilada.

Un siglo después, el rebaño arrepentido le levantó una estatua ecuestre que quedó muy bien en el parque.

Así, en lo sucesivo, cada vez que aparecían ovejas negras eran rápidamente pasadas por las armas para que las futuras generaciones de ovejas comunes y corrientes pudieran ejercitarse también en la escultura.

below, UNTITLED, 2006
PHOTO DOCUMENTATION
OF AN ACTION, MEXICO CITY

previous pages,
UNTITLED, 2002
OIL, ENAMEL AND ENCAUSTIC ON MASONITE
20 X 30 X 1 CM

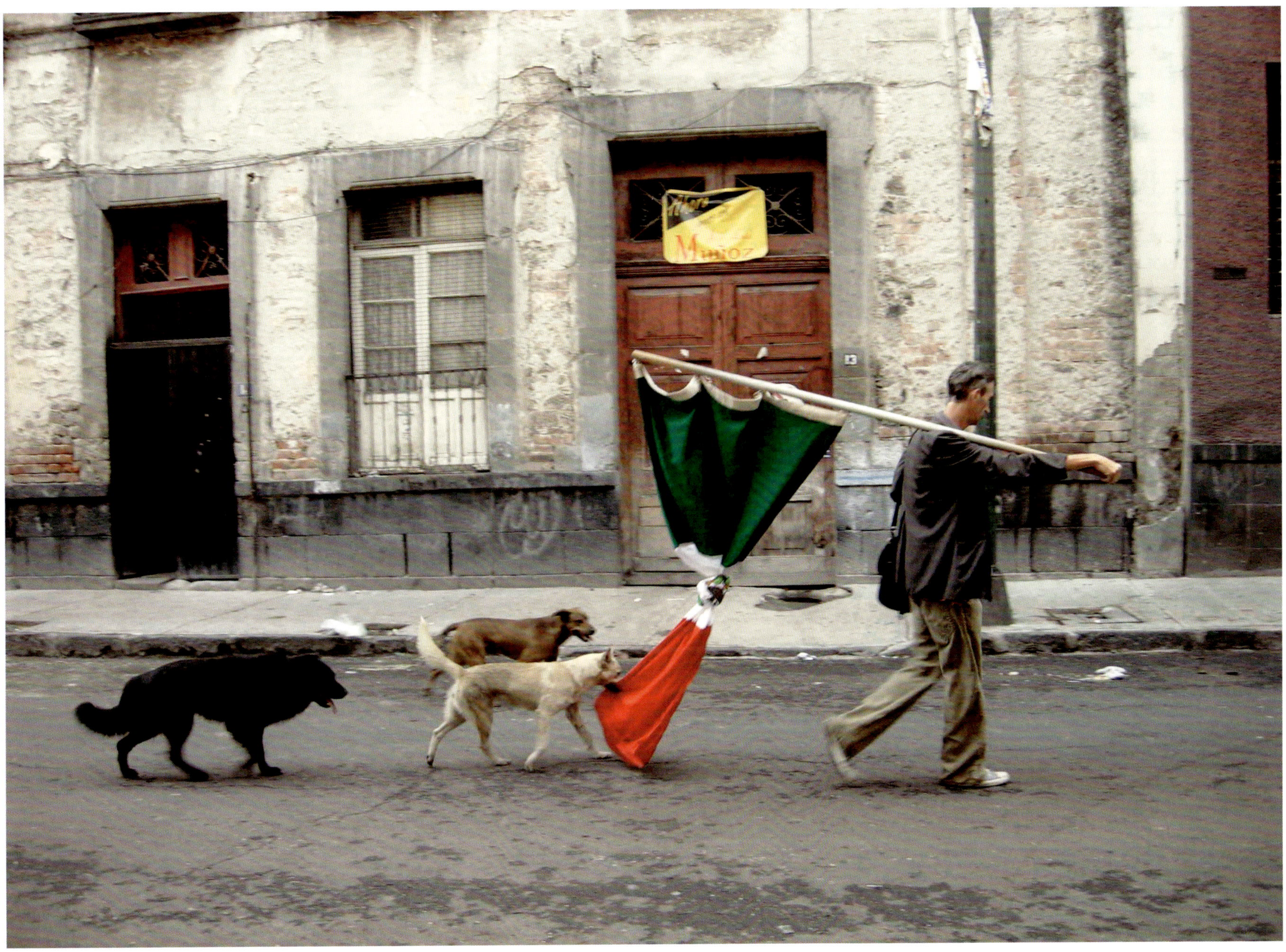

Augusto Monterroso

The Two Tails, or the Eclectic Philosopher
(Las dos colas, o el filósofo ecléctico)
1969

According to legend, every morning in the crowded market of an Ancient City there walked an eclectic philosopher, a renowned observer of Nature, whom many people approached with their most troubling conflicts and doubts.

One time, while a dog was chasing itself in circles and biting its own tail, to the laughter of the children who stood around it, several worried merchants asked the philosopher what all this commotion could mean, and if it might not be an unfortunate omen.

The philosopher explained that by biting its tail the dog was only trying to get rid of its fleas.

With this, the general curiosity was satisfied, and the people left in peace.

On another occasion, a snake charmer was displaying his basket of serpents, one of which was biting its own tail, eliciting seriousness in the children and laughter in the adults.

When the children asked the philosopher what might be the cause, he responded that the serpent that bites its tail represents the Infinite and the Eternal Return of people, facts and things, and this is what serpents mean when they bite their tails.

On this occasion, too, the people left satsified and equally peaceful.

TRANSLATED FROM SPANISH BY MARION IVERSON

Cuenta la leyenda que en el populoso Mercado de una Antigua ciudad se paseaba todas las mañanas un filósofo ecléctico, célebre observador de la Naturaleza, a quienes muchos se acercaban para exponerle los más peregrinos conflictos y dudas.

Cierta vez que un Perro daba vueltas sobre sí mismo mordiéndose la cola ante la risa de los niños que lo rodeaban, varios preocupados mercaderes preguntaron al filósofo a qué podía obedecer todo aquel movimiento, y que si no sería algún funesto presagio.

El filósofo les explicó que al morderse la cola el Perro trataba tan solo de quitarse las Pulgas.

Con esto, la curiosidad general quedó satisfecha y la gente se retiró tranquila. En otra ocasión, un domador de Serpientes exhibía varias en un canasto, entre las cuales una se mordía la cola, lo que provocaba la seriedad de los niños y las risas de los adultos.

Cuando los niños preguntaron al filósofo a qué podía deberse aquello, él les respondió que la Serpiente que se muerde la cola representa el Infinito y el Eterno Retorno de personas, hechos y cosas, y que esto quieren decir las Serientes cuando se muerden la cola.

También en esta oportunidad la gente se retiró satisfecha e igualmente tranquila.

L'IMPRÉVOYANCE DE LA NOSTALGIE, 1999
COLOUR PHOTOGRAPH

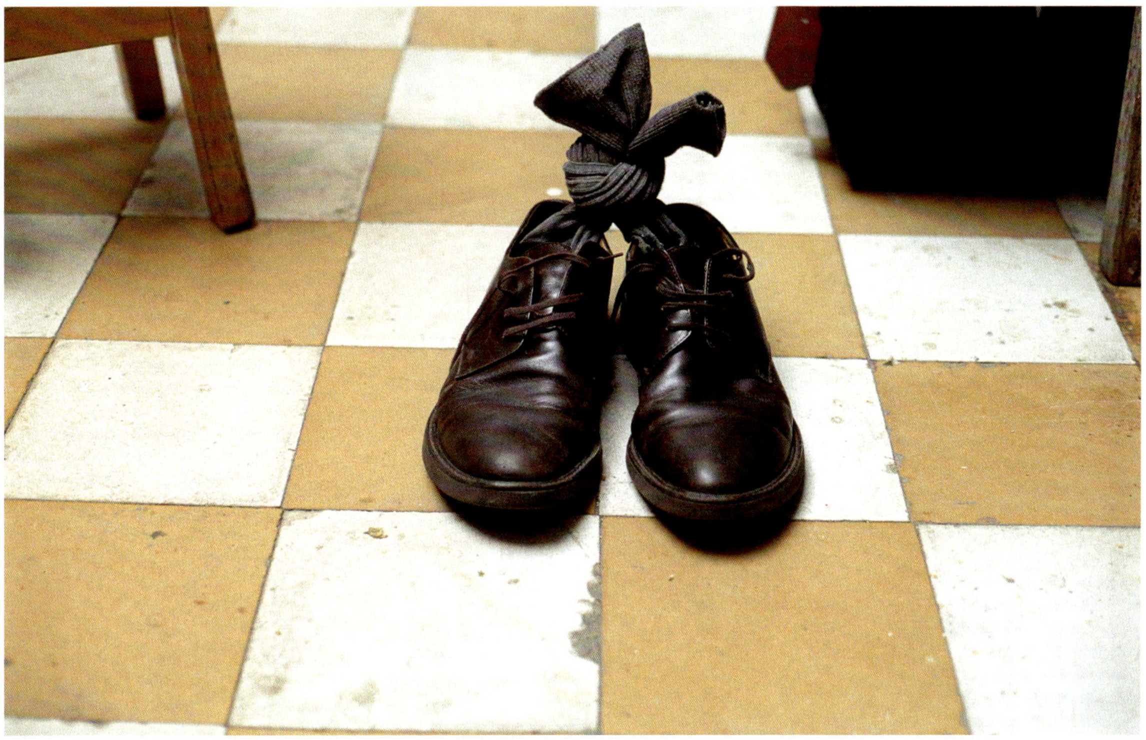

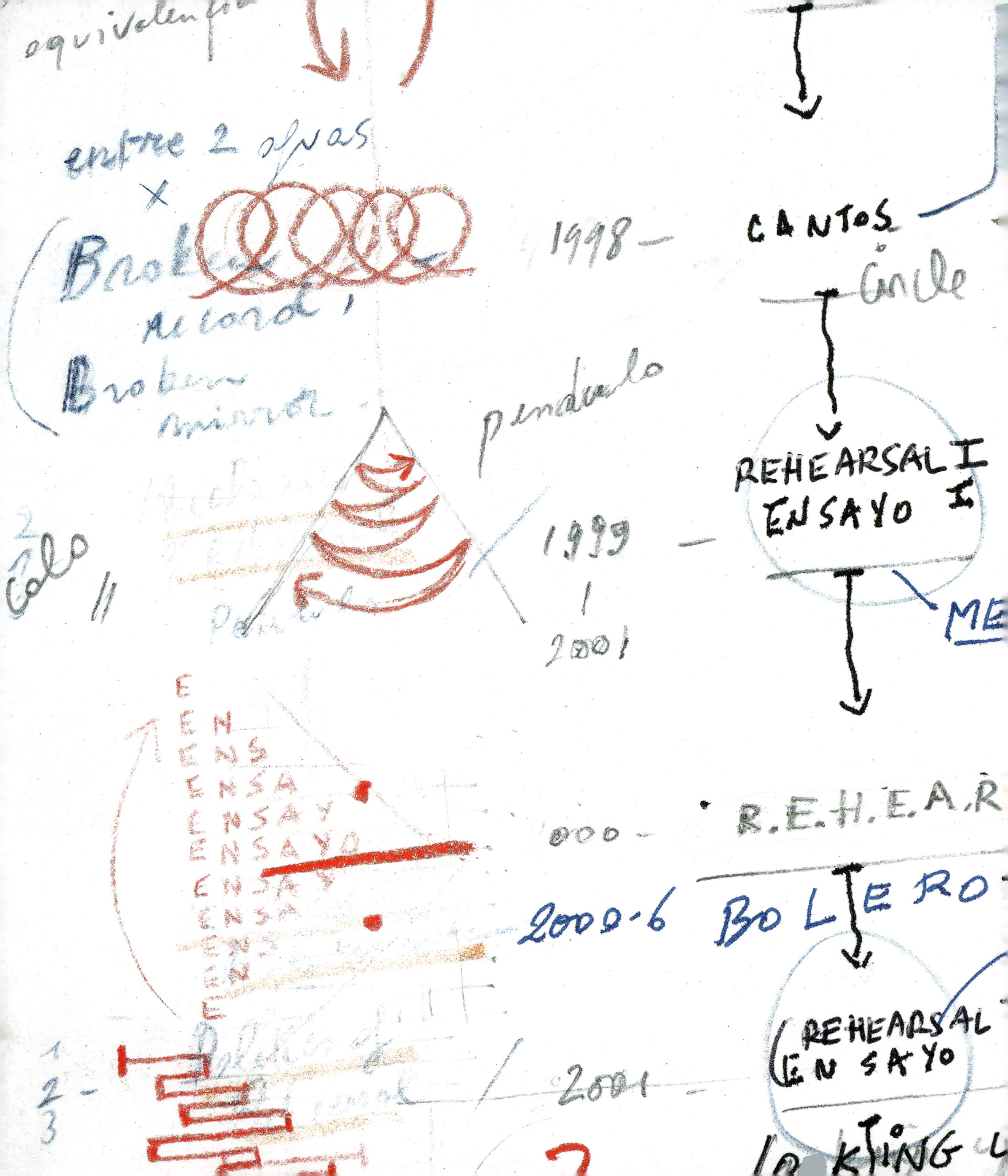

equivalen
entre 2 obras
Broken accord,
Broken mirror
pendulo
1998
CANTOS
Circle
REHEARSAL I
ENSAYO I
1999
2001
E
EN
ENS
ENSA
ENSAY
ENSAYO
ENSA
ENSA
EN
EN
E
R.E.H.E.A.R
2000-6
BOLERO
REHEARSAL
ENSAYO
2001

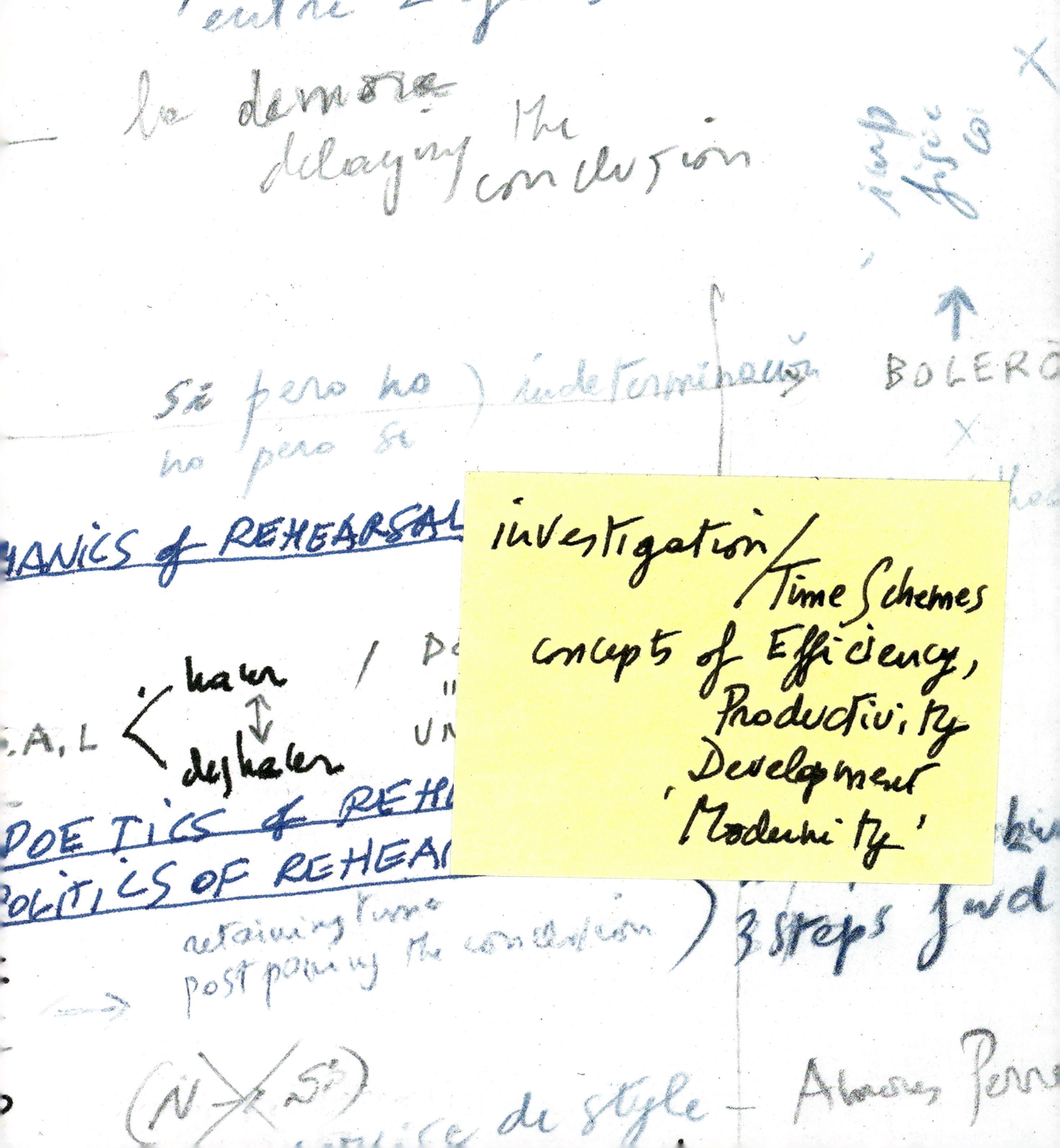
la demora
delaying the conclusion
Sí pero no
no pero sí
indeterminacy
BOLERO
HANICS of REHEARSAL
investigation/
Time Schemes
concepts of Efficiency,
Productivity
Development
'Modernity'
POETICS of REHE
POLITICS OF REHEAR
postponing the conclusion
3 steps fwd
de style

Feeling my hair / hair of the dog /
dog watching painter / painter in a bag /
bag in the river / river in frame /
framing the scene / seen through my eyes /
eyes to his mind / mind to my hand /
hand to his brush /
brush for a tail / tail to the nose /
knows as through skin / skin of my hands /
hands feel like gloves / ~~gloves tracing lines~~ /
~~lines drawing words~~ / words will ~~not~~ you do ? /
do-it-yourself .

gloves in between /
in between words /

1991

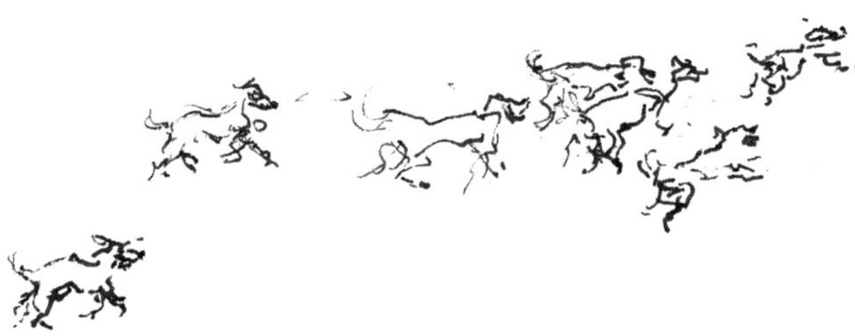

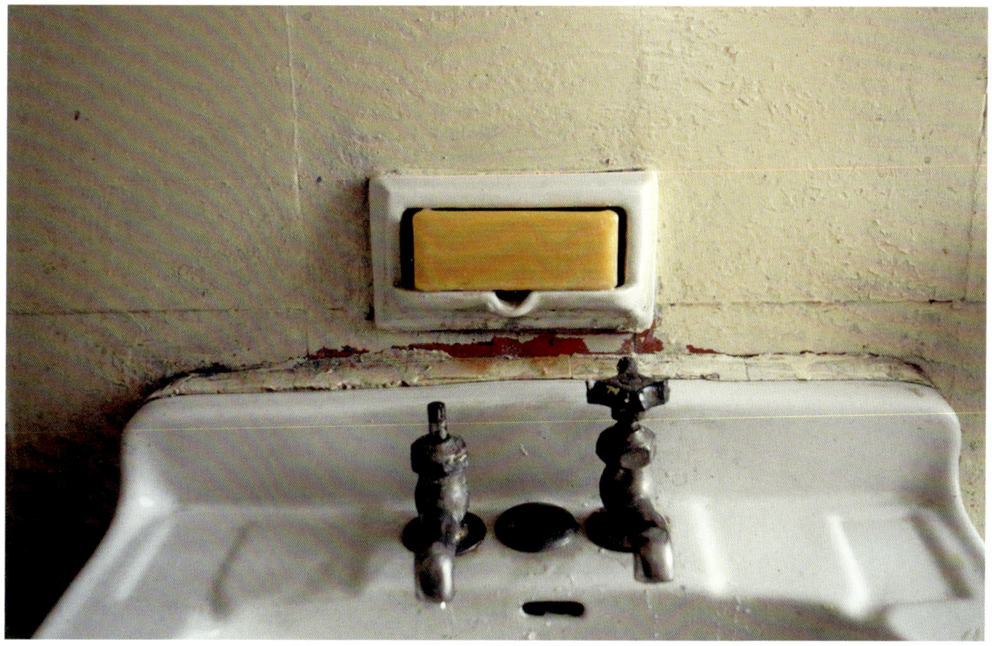

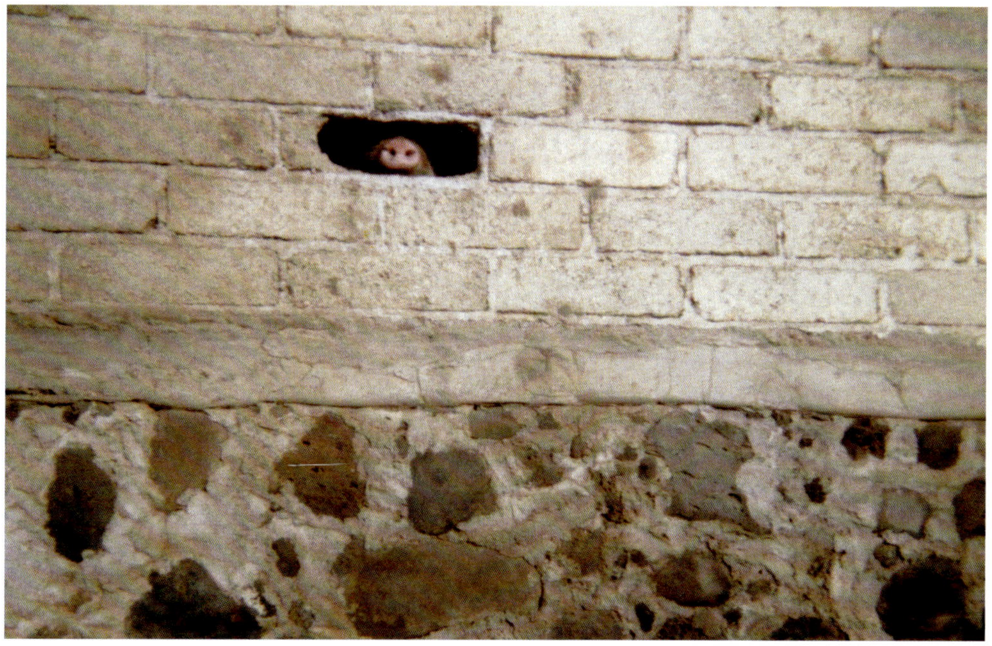

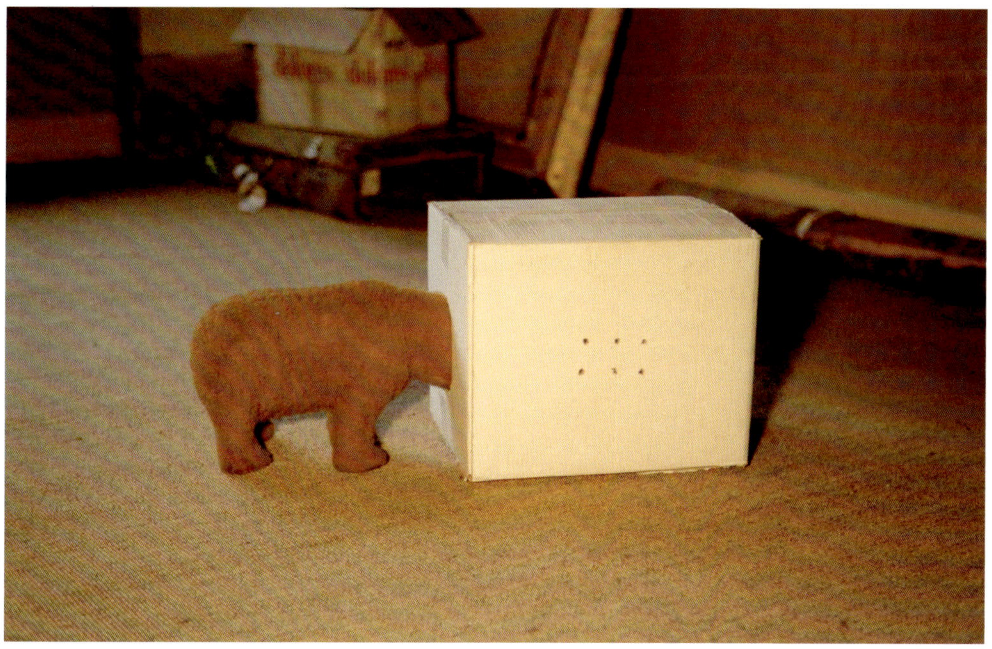

UNTITLED (MEXICO CITY), 1990
COLOUR PHOTOGRAPH

UNTITLED (TLAYACAPAN, MORELOS), 1992
COLOUR PHOTOGRAPH

UNTITLED, 1990
CARDBOARD BOX AND FOUND TOY
35 X 35 X 70 CM

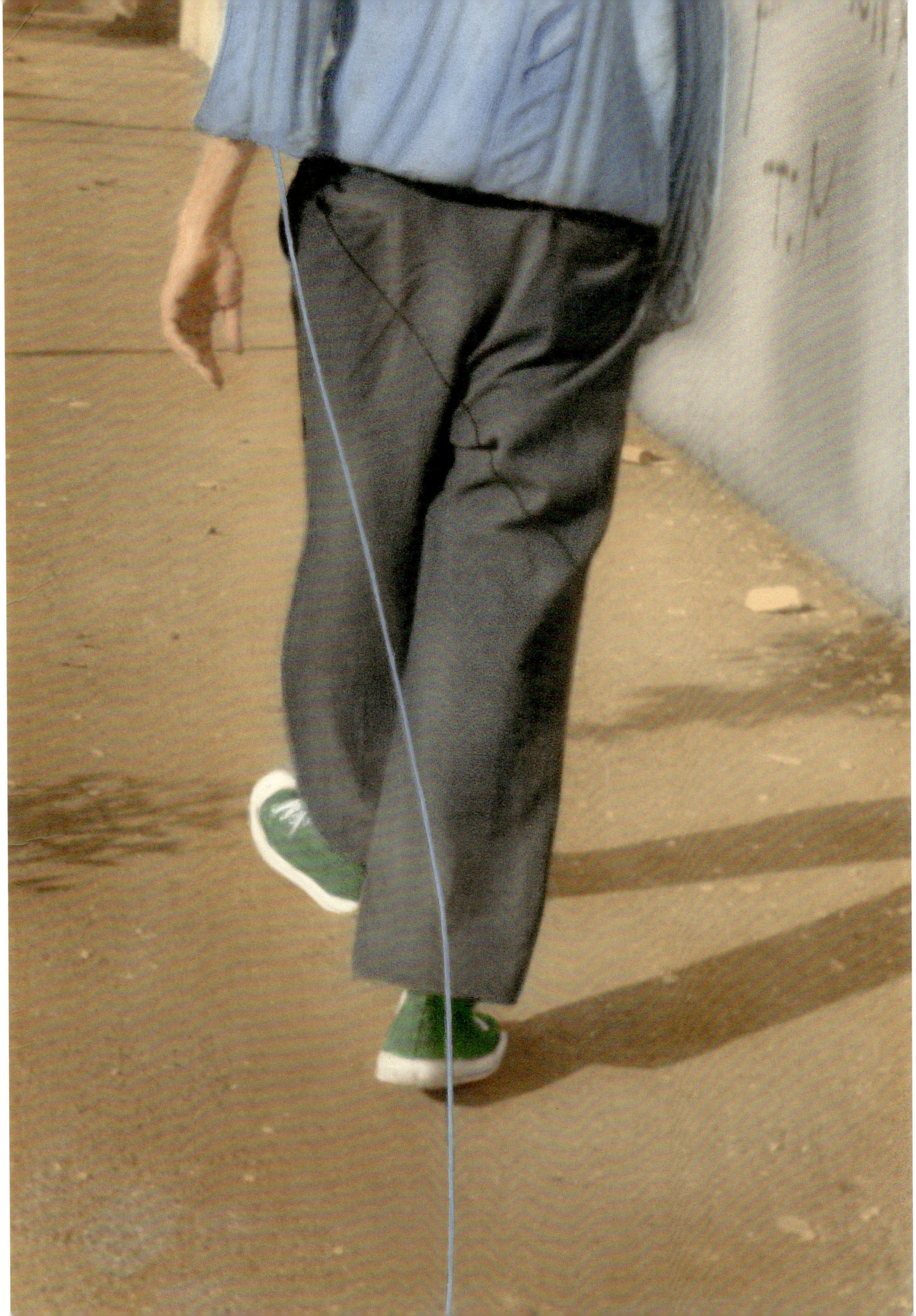

FAIRY TALES, 1995
PHOTO DOCUMENTATION OF AN
ACTION, MEXICO CITY

AS LONG AS I'M WALKING, I'M NOT CHOOSING
" " " " " , I'M NOT SMOKING
" " " " " , I'M NOT LOSING
" " " " " , I'M NOT MAKING
" " " " " , I'M NOT KNOWING
" " " " " , I'M NOT FALLING
" " " " " , I'M NOT PAINTING
" " " " " , I'M NOT HIDING
" " " " " , I'M NOT COUNTING
" " " " " , I'M NOT ADDING
" " " " " , I'M NOT CRYING
" " " " " , I'M NOT ASKING
" " " " " , I'M NOT BELIEVING
" " " " " , I'M NOT FUCKING
" " " " " , I'M NOT DRINKING
" " " " " , I'M NOT CLOSING
" " " " " , I'M NOT STEALING
" " " " " , I'M NOT MOCKING
" " " " " , I'M NOT FACING
" " " " " , I'M NOT CROSSING
" " " " " , I'M NOT CHANGING
" " " " " , I'M NOT CHEATING
" " " " " , I'M NOT TALKING
" " " " " , I'M NOT REACHING
" " " " " ,
" " " " " ,
" " " " " ,
" " " " " , I WILL NOT REPEAT
" " " " " , I WILL NOT REMEMBER

Every day

I would go out and walk

pacing the grid of Manhattan

there would be no expectations

or destinations

just the walking

and the counting

North to South and South to West

West to East and East to South

South to North and North to West

West to South and South to East

East to West and West to East.

NYC, sept to dic 200I

PACING, 2001
GRAPHIC DOCUMENTATION
OF AN ACTION, NEW YORK
PENCIL ON NOTEBOOK PAGES
EACH 16 X 22 CM

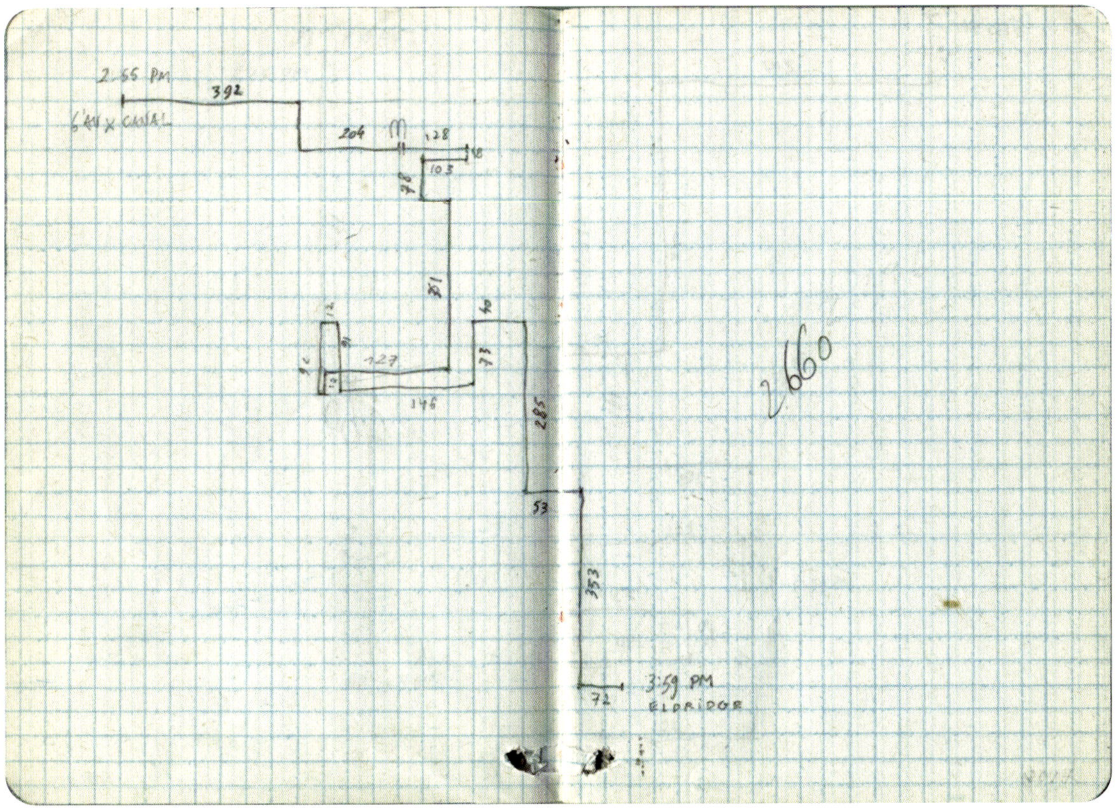

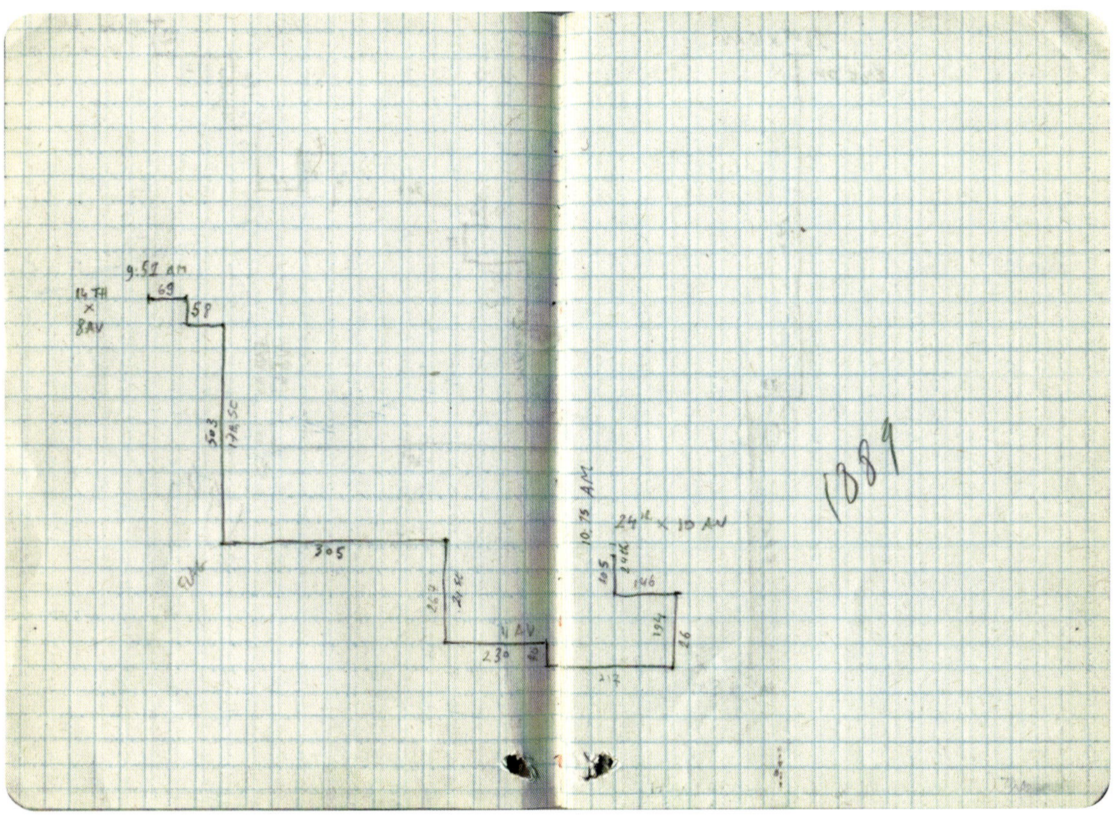

They say that the Tehuelches hunted the ñandu (Rhea americana)
by physically exhausting the animal
The entire tribe would walk for weeks
chasing the flock until the ñandu would give up or die of exhaustion.
We, of our time, must chase mirages.

THE LOGIC OF ÑANDU, 2005
PHOTO DOCUMENTATION OF AN
ACTION, PENINSULA VALDES

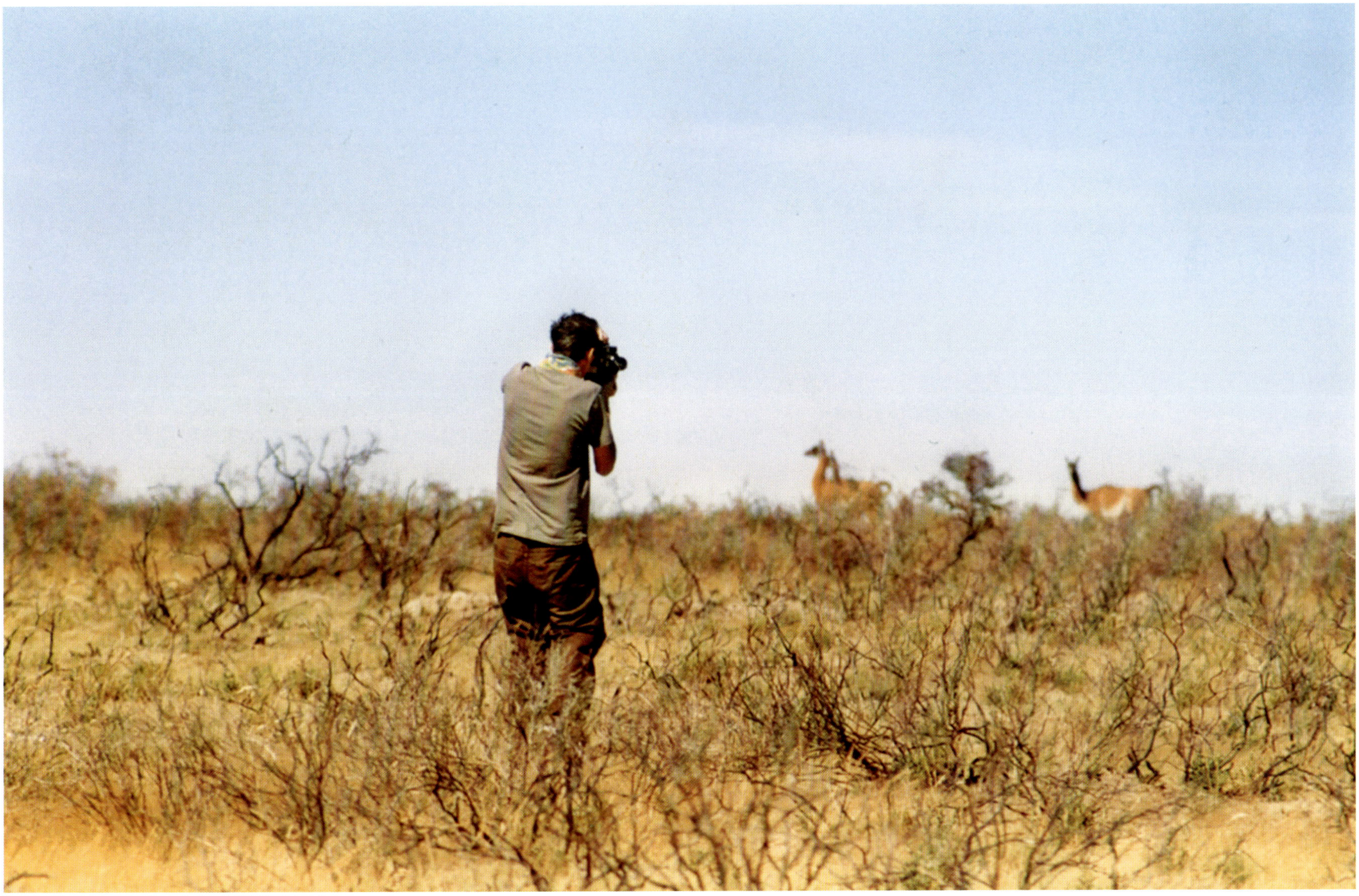

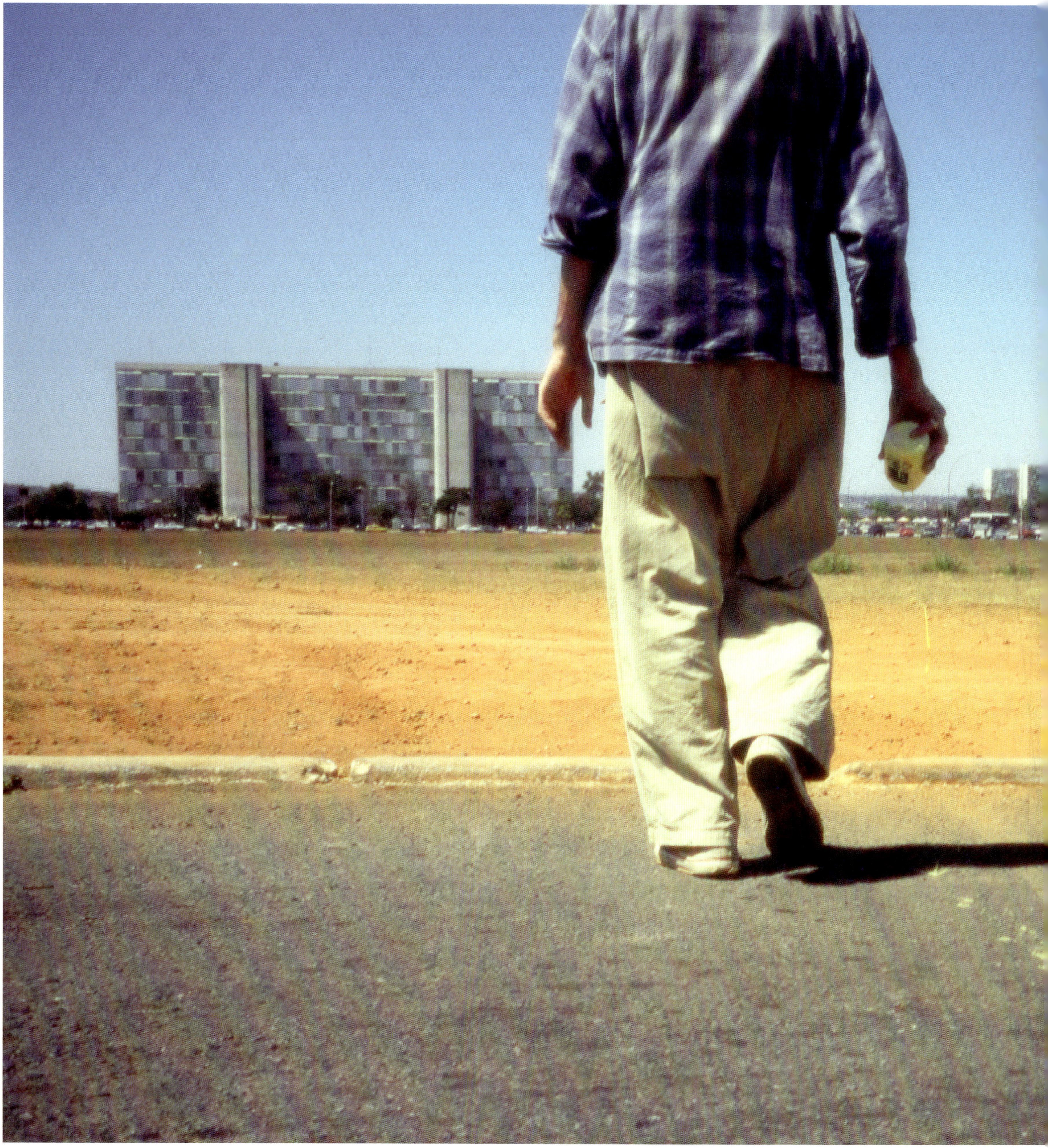

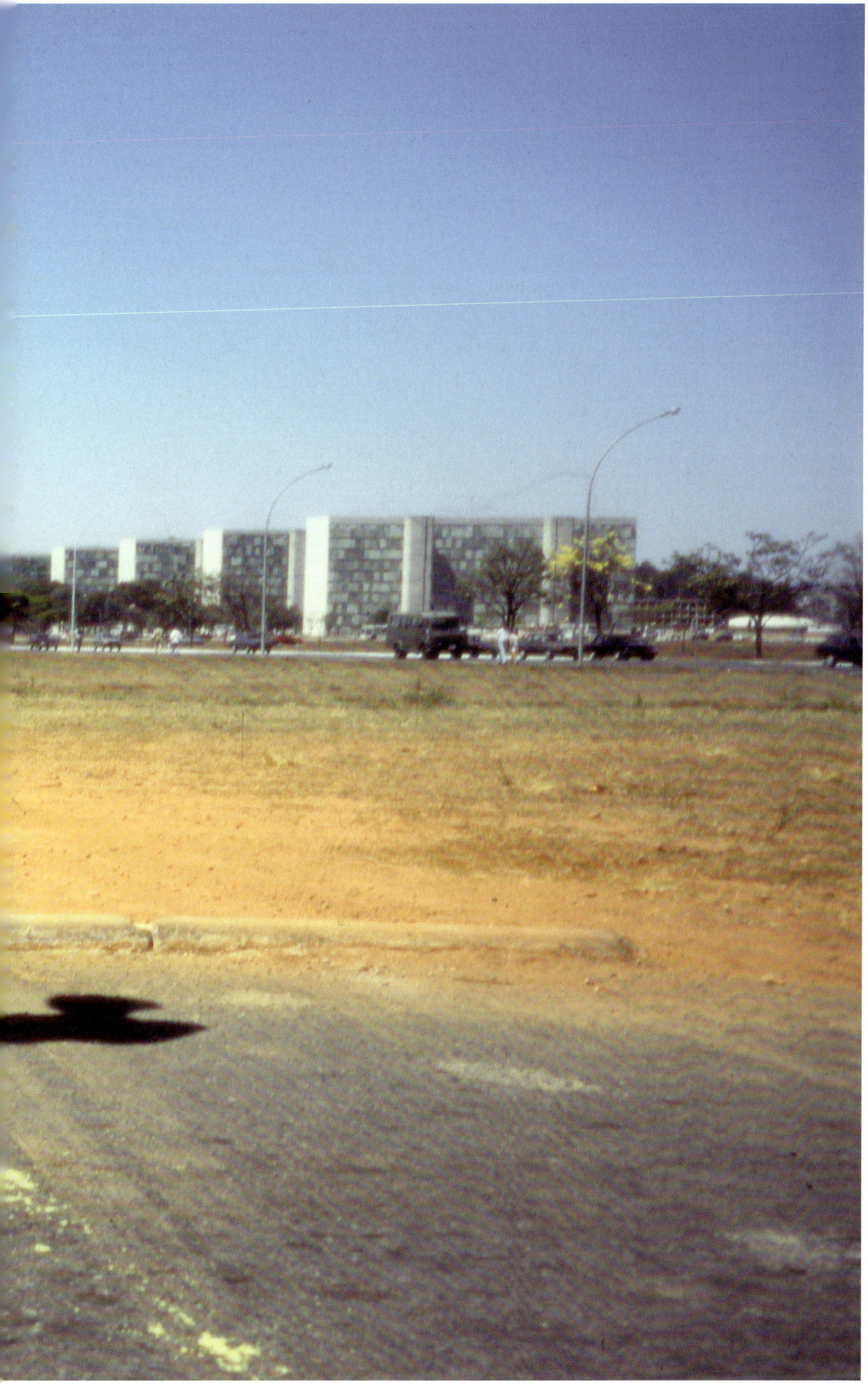

THE LEAK, 1995
PHOTO DOCUMENTATION OF AN ACTION
BRASÍLIA

1994
Turista, Mexico City: Offering my services as a tourist in the middle of a line of carpenters and plumbers. Oscillating between work and leisure, between observing and interfering. Standing on the fence.

1997
The Loop, Pacific Rim: Circumnavigation of the globe from Tijuana, Mexico to San Diego, California to avoid crossing the border between the U.S.A. and Mexico. Ridicule as a means to remain ambivalent towards a political stance.

2002
When Faith Moves Mountains, Lima, Peru: the mechanics of the displacement of a dune oscillate between the poetical and the political. Translating social tensions into narratives that could intervene in the imaginary landscape of a place. Walking on a tight rope between fiction and reality.

2004
The Green Line, Jerusalem: Carrying a leaking can of green paint along 'The Green Line' traced in 1948 during the cease-fire between Israeli forces and the Arab Legion. Questioning the relevance of a poetical act in a situation going through a state of political, military and confessional crisis/reaching a stage where it is no longer possible to hide behind poetic license.

2005
Projects don't come out of the blue. You don't wake up one morning thinking: 'tomorrow I will cross the city pushing a block of ice' or 'next week I'll invite hundreds of volunteers to move a sand dune of a few centimetres'…

The 'spark' for the *Bridge* projects was an article I read in *El País* in the fall of 2005. The piece was reporting on a legal dispute between Cuban migrants and the U.S. immigration authorities when a group of *balseros* – Cuban boatpeople – was intercepted by a U.S. Coast Guard Patrol while they were disembarking on the North American continent. As a large numbers of Cubans attempt to cross the Gulf of Mexico to migrate to the USA every month, the story per se would not have justified an article in a European newspaper. But in this case there was a twist: the migrants had disembarked on one of the many bridges that link the keys of Florida's Southern peninsula. The event has to be examined in the light of what's also known as 'La ley del pie seco y del pie mojado'. This 'wet feet-dry feet' policy refers to a 'deal' settled by Jimmy Carter's administration at the time of the Mariel boatlift episode in 1980, when over 100,000 Cubans mass-emigrated to the U.S. over the span of just a few months. 'Dry foot' applies when Cuban migrants get intercepted after having stepped on U.S. land = they are automatically granted legal right to remain in USA, whereas 'wet foot' applies when they are caught off shore and on the sea, i.e. they are immediately repatriated to Cuba. As the migrants of the article were caught on a bridge, the question was: should a bridge be considered 'land' or 'sea'? (FYI, after a long legal battle the *balseros* of the story were granted U.S. residency)

Around the same time, I visited a survey show of Robert Smithson at the Whitney Museum. Walking around the exhibition, I noticed that most of his projects were the results of his own initiative. With the present plethora of Biennale commissions and other site-specific invitations, it was healthy to be reminded that when something has to be exposed, there is no time to lose.

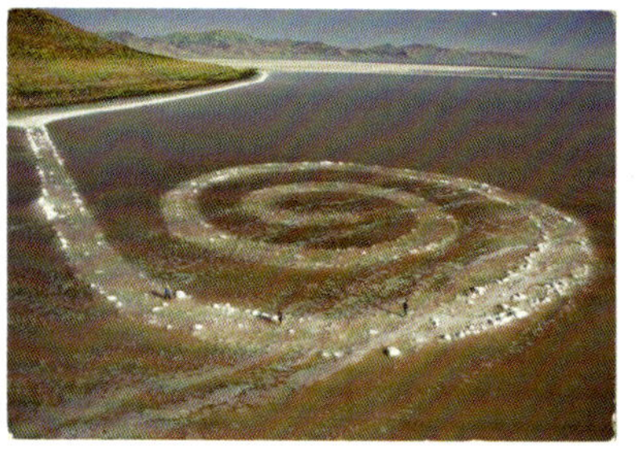

ROBERT SMITHSON
SPIRAL JETTY, 1970
BASALT ROCK, SALT CRYSTALS, EARTH, WATER
ROZEL POINT, GREAT SALT LAKE, UTAH

Soon after I had to be in Miami to install a video for a group show organized by Cuban-Mexican curator Taiyana Pimentel. As installing basically means spending lots of time waiting, it gave me the opportunity to discover the nearby *gusano* (Cuban expat) neighbourhood of Little Havana.

The convergence of those three episodes over a short period of time led to a conversation with Taiyana who was to become the co-conspirator for the *Bridge/Puente* project. Curator friend Cuauhtémoc Medina joined the discussion later. The plot I had in mind was very simple: to create the illusion of a floating bridge between Florida and Cuba with a chain of boats going from horizon to horizon across the Gulf of Mexico.

EPISODE 1
Bridge/Puente, Key West, Florida/Havana, Cuba, 29 March 2006

BEFORE THE EVENT

November 2005, Barra de Coyuca, Pacific, Mexico: trial (1) of floating bridge with boats from the local fishing community.

3 DECEMBER 2005
Key West: scouting the southern Keys of Florida.

CUAUHTÉMOC MEDINA: On the way from Miami to Key West we were faced with a revelatory image: several of the bridges connecting the different keys were actually cut, leading to nowhere. Key West itself was somewhat of a broken bridge itself: 'the end of the road' of America takes you to a community of trailer parks and military bases. The only suggestion of Cuba's proximity was the enormous amount of antennas and satellites scanning and interfering with the island's airwaves. Florida ends in a sort of constructivist nightmare of military detection equipment.

STUDY FOR BRIDGE/PUENTE, KEY WEST, FLORIDA, AND HAVANA, 2006
PENCIL AND OIL ON TRACING PAPER
36 X 30 CM

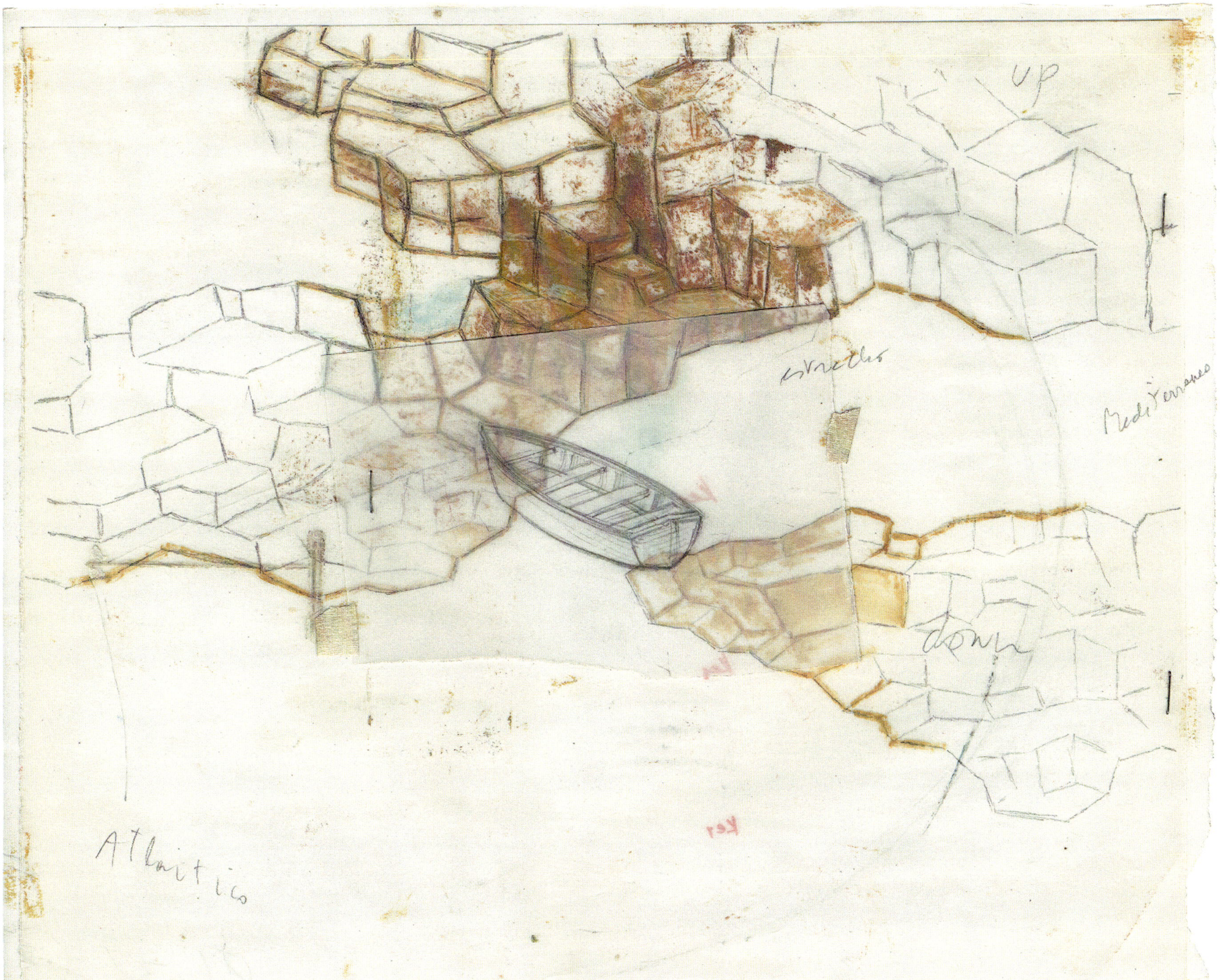

5 JANUARY 2006
Havana: first scouting trip to Cuba.

– TAIYANA PIMENTEL: A bridge allows you to move on but not to stay; it's about displacement rather than about permanence.

The ingredients are falling into place. We have:
– a plot: two lines of boats enter the sea and meet metaphorically on the horizon to create the illusion of a bridge.
– a location: Cuba and Florida facing one another across the Gulf of Mexico.
– the protagonists: the fishing communities of Havana and the private boat owners of Key West, Florida.
– an occasion: The opening week of the 9th Havana Biennale in April 2006. We wanted to produce the floating bridge event during the opening ceremonies of the Biennale because the local authorities show an exceptional permissiveness for public events staged during that special week.

16 FEBRUARY 2006
Havana: second visit to Cuba.

Chasing permits and meetings with the three main fishing communities of Havana: Jaimanitas, Santa Fe and Baracoa.

FRANCIS ALŸS: And what's life like around here?
OLD FISHERMAN: Like everywhere else, with complaints… with political problems… Like in any other part of the world. I've walked a lot. Here the sea is something wonderful, but if you take me to a mountain, I will love the mountains, and if you take me to a river, I'll fish in the river… One has to smile to life; don't look for problems – they come on their own…

15 MARCH 2006
Key West: second visit to Florida.

Landing on the project with Cuauhtémoc and Peter; meeting with coordinators Denise and Dave; selecting the event's location and soliciting local boat owners to participate.

CUAUHTÉMOC MEDINA: This is the beach of Key West. Exactly in that direction – to the south – is Cuba and our bridge will go directly from here, which is the southernmost point of the United States, towards the island which is on the other side; and Francis, who is on the other side, will come towards us and in a sort of search the two lines will want to meet each other on the horizon.

18 MARCH 2006
Havana: arrival of Taiyana.

19 MARCH 2006
Key West: arrival of Cuauhtémoc, Amy and Peter.

22 MARCH 2006
Havana: arrival of Francis.

PANCHITO: To mobilize one hundred boats in Cuba, it's the first time that it happens in the history of the Revolution.
ALDERETE: One hundred rafts with boat people, yes. But one hundred boats, no.
PANCHITO: Cubans watch the world from Miami. It's their border. They all have a cousin there.

24 MARCH 2006
Havana: meetings in Baracoa, Jaimanitas and Santa Fe.

TAIYANA PIMENTEL: Look, Francis Alÿs is the artist, the one who conceived what we are going to do. I am Cuban, I am a curator and I am working as the art curator of this project. The idea we want to develop is a choreography of boats forming geometric figures on the sea, with the fishing communities of Baracoa and Jaimanitas and Santa Fe.

25 MARCH 2006
Havana: trial with a dozen boats in the bay of the former Casino of Santa Fe.

TAIYANA PIMENTEL: It's not a sculpture, it's an event.
FRANCIS ALŸS: It's the portrait of a community.
MIGUELITO: There is a moment of walking on water.
RAMON: A rare feat.
MIGUELITO: Something unheard of…

26 MARCH 2006
Key West: arrival of Julien and the film crew.

CUAUHTÉMOC MEDINA: All the Cubans come here to long for their country. They look at the horizon, and they see the beard of Fidel. That's truly the southernmost point of the U.S. That's military. One of the last remnants of the Cold War.
DAVE: Even though the Wall fell…
CUAUHTÉMOC MEDINA: I know it's a bit tropical, but there is a cold war here…
DAVE: So the invasion of Pigs Bay in 1962 was launched from here, I guess?
CUAUHTÉMOC MEDINA: Yes… It's the perfect combination – warm weather with cold war… A perfect love story.

26 MARCH 2006
Havana: the 9th Havana Biennale opens while a frente frío (tropical storm) enters the city.

– MIGUEL: Del otro lado está el enemigo.

27 MARCH 2006
Havana: the frente frío perseveres and forces us to postpone the event on both sides.

Horizon to horizon.

When does a line of boats become a bridge?
How many boats does it take to create the illusion of a bridge?
– Enough boats to show the desire of each community for a bridge to happen.
– Enough boats to create the illusion that the line of boats is meeting the horizon.
The line has to be long enough so as to carry the imagination of the viewer all the way across the Gulf to the other coast. We figured that this would take around one hundred boats leaving from each opposite shore.

28 MARCH 2006
Havana: end of the frente frío.

EPHEMERA FOR BRIDGE/PUENTE, 2005
NEWSPAPER CLIPPING
FROM THE ARTIST'S ARCHIVE

Pateras de lujo en Cancún

Un centenar de balseros cubanos intenta cada semana alcanzar EEUU a través de la turística ciudad mexicana

JACOBO GARCÍA
Especial para EL MUNDO

MÉXICO.– Aunque el Estrecho de la Florida sigue siendo la ruta preferida por los balseros para alcanzar suelo estadounidense, desde hace años miles de cubanos miran también hacia México como primera parada en su camino a Miami. El tráfico ilegal de personas y embarcaciones a través del canal de Yucatán se incrementa día a día y ha colapsado las cárceles de Cancún.

En las calles del exclusivo complejo turístico es fácil escuchar el particular acento caribeño y ver cómo el puerto no descansa por la noche. A bordo de precarias embarcaciones o potentes lanchas, 14 personas llegan diariamente a Cancún, según las autoridades cubanas, usando para ello una ruta bastante más larga que la que los separa de Florida (EEUU), pero de aguas más tranquilas y menos vigiladas.

Además del arribo masivo, en la capital del turismo mexicano se han encendido las alarmas ante la ola delictiva ligada al tráfico de personas que se extiende por la zona y que ha dejado más de una decena de muertos en lo que va de año, el último caso, un cubano asesinado el lunes de un tiro en la cabeza en un *parking* de la zona hotelera.

En enero los servicios de Inteligencia mexicana ya alertaron sobre la existencia de varias redes asentadas en Cancún y dedicadas a mover a cubanos entre la isla y la península de Yucatán, distanciadas por 135 millas (217 kilómetros). Las investigaciones apuntaban siempre hacia Miami como el lugar desde el que se organizaban los viajes, a un precio de entre 8.000 y 10.000 dólares, y advertían de que el flujo de balseros entre ambos países se multiplicó por cuatro en los últimos tres años.

Disfrazados de turistas

El pasado jueves el *Granma*, diario oficial cubano y muy poco a dado a airear estos asuntos, publicó un reportaje titulado «100 cubanos desembarcan semanalmente en Cancún», en el que acusaba a Estados Unidos de provocar el éxodo.

Según el diario, los traficantes operan en el circuito turístico de Isla Mujeres, Cancún, Playa del Carmen y Mérida. Para ello disponen de lanchas rápidas –*cigarretas*– equipadas con motores fueraborda de 275 caballos, con las que alcanzan la costa cubana para llevarse hasta 40 pasajeros en cada viaje.

En alta mar los cubanos reciben guayaberas, camisas, gafas de sol o zapatos que los convierten en turistas. «Una vez en Isla Mujeres, los ilegales cubanos cruzan en *ferry* a Cancún. Luego remontan México hasta la frontera con EEUU», señalaba el periódico.

Y acusaba de provocador a Bush porque «a diferencia de los otros inmigrantes latinoamericanos, una vez en la frontera estadounidense se presentan a las autoridades y asunto terminado, como ocurrió con el terrorista Luis Posada Carriles, quien pasó por Isla Mujeres en su ingreso ilegal a Estados Unidos utilizando la red ilegal creada desde Miami», recogía un reportaje firmado desde Cancún.

El canal de Yucatán es desde hace muchos años una vía de escape para los cubanos. En 2004 fueron detenidos 500 balseros por intentar llegar de forma irregular a México, la mayoría interceptados en alta mar a bordo de rudimentarias embarcaciones, encallados en la playa o a la deriva. En los ochos primeros meses del año, hasta agosto, han sido 2.200 los cubanos detenidos. Lejos, sin embargo, de los 10.000 que lo han intentado vía Florida.

México devuelve habitualmente a la isla a los cubanos interceptados en el mar, pero si llegan a tierra son liberados con una multa de 10.000 pesos (650 euros) y el compromiso de salir del país antes de 30 días.

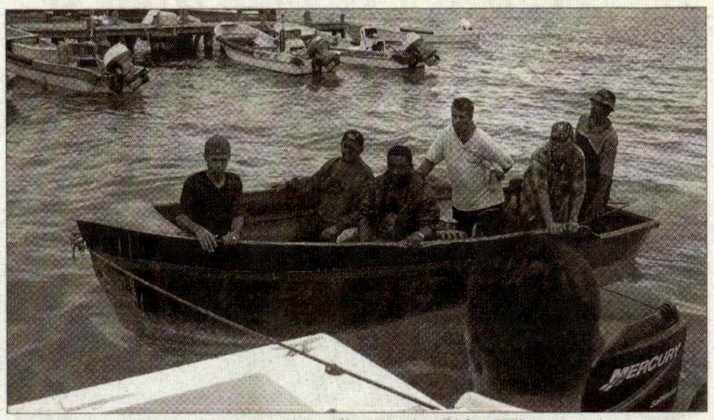

Bote con siete cubanos interceptados por las autoridades mexicanas cuando se dirigían a EEUU. / AP

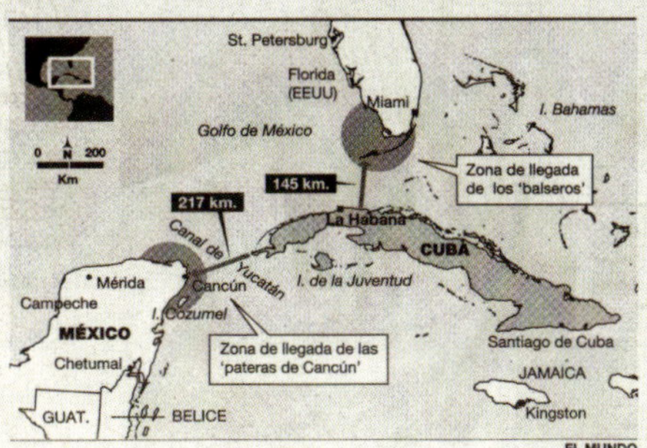

BRIDGE/PUENTE, 2006
IN COLLABORATION WITH
TAIYANA PIMENTEL AND
CUAUHTÉMOC MEDINA
PHOTO DOCUMENTATION OF AN
EVENT, KEY WEST, FLORIDA,
AND HAVANA

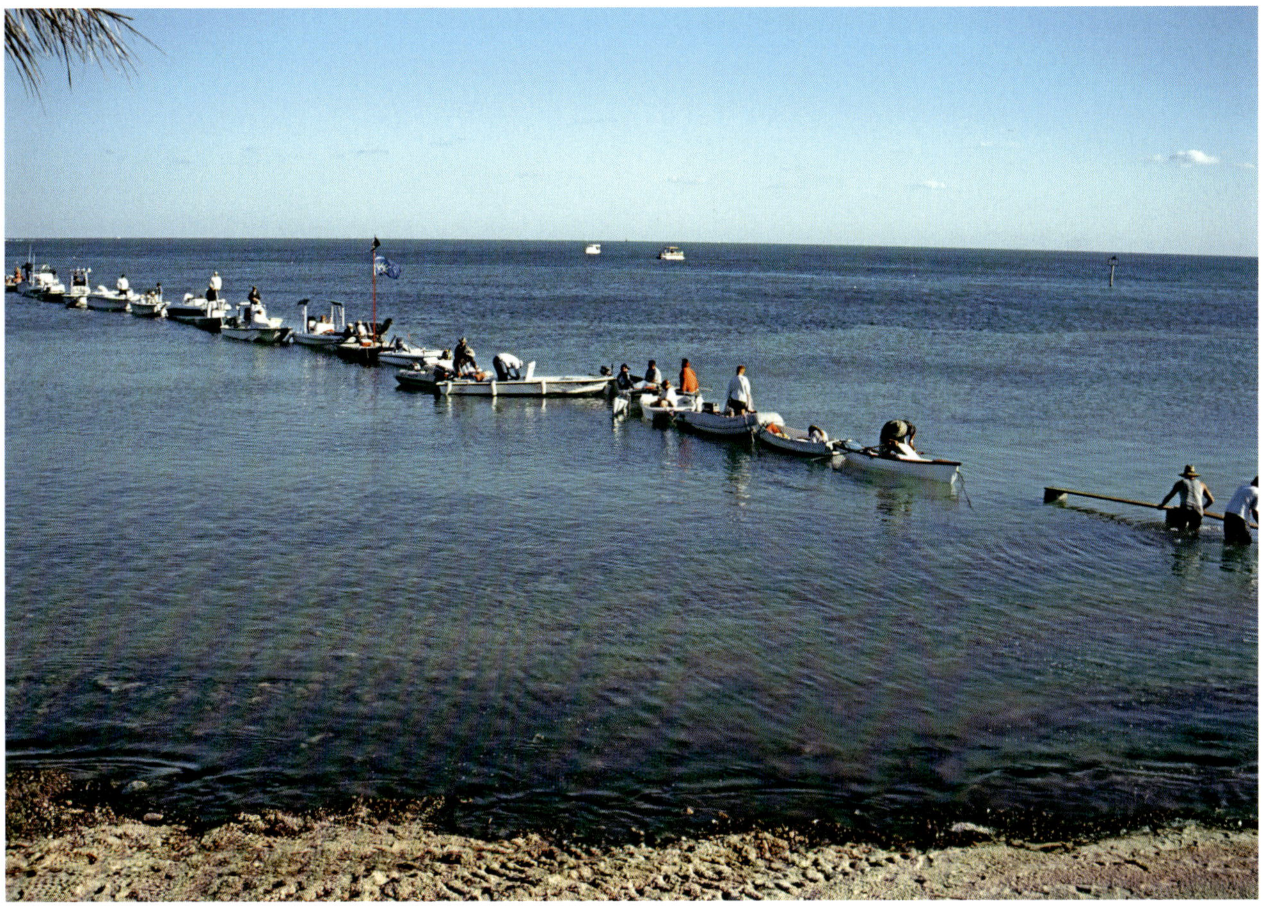

STUDY FOR *DON'T CROSS THE BRIDGE BEFORE YOU GET TO THE RIVER*, 2007
OIL PAINT AND PENCIL ON TRACING PAPER
29 X 35 CM

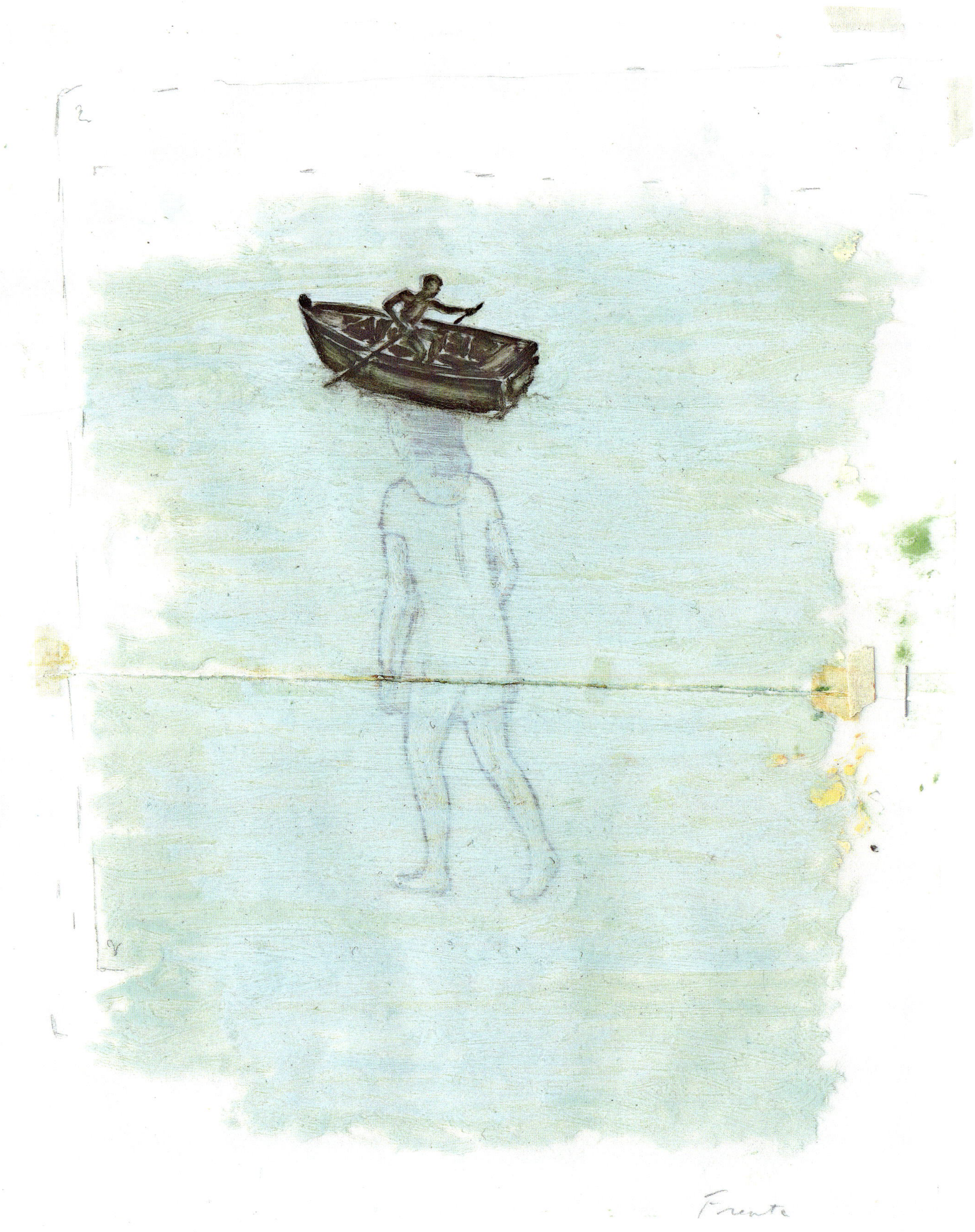

STUDY FOR <u>DON'T CROSS THE BRIDGE BEFORE YOU GET TO THE RIVER</u>, 2007
OIL AND ENCAUSTIC ON CANVAS
15 X 20 CM

STUDY FOR <u>DON'T CROSS THE BRIDGE BEFORE YOU GET TO THE RIVER</u>, 2007
OIL AND ENCAUSTIC ON CANVAS
AND PENCIL ON TRACING PAPER
35 X 29 CM

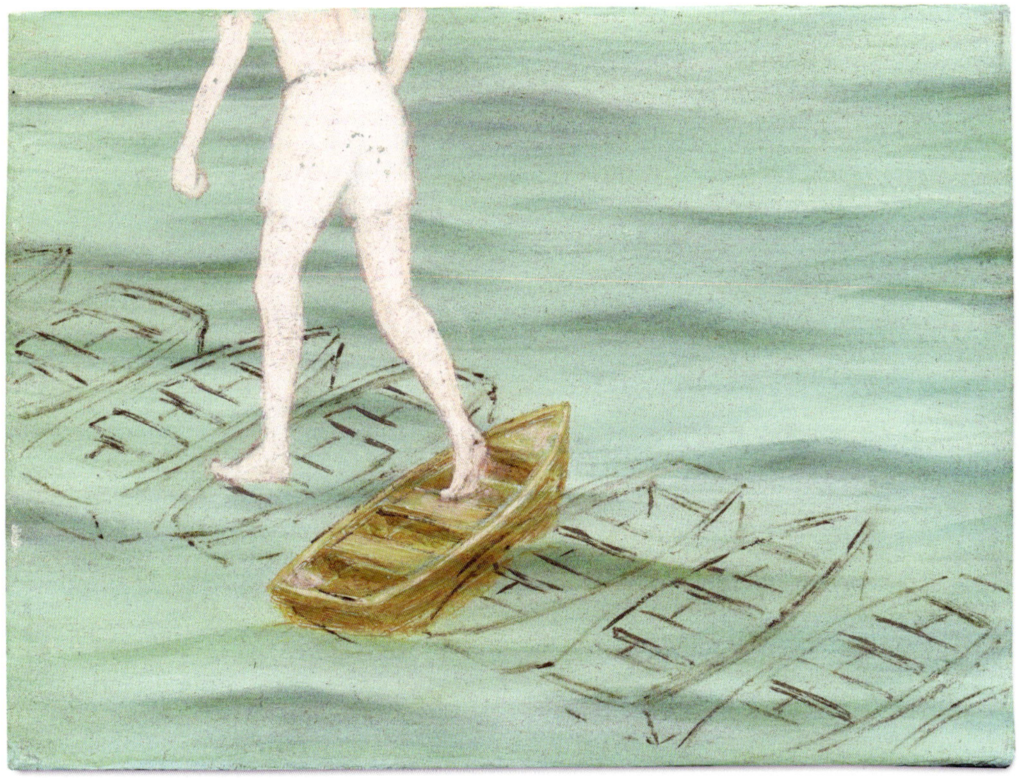

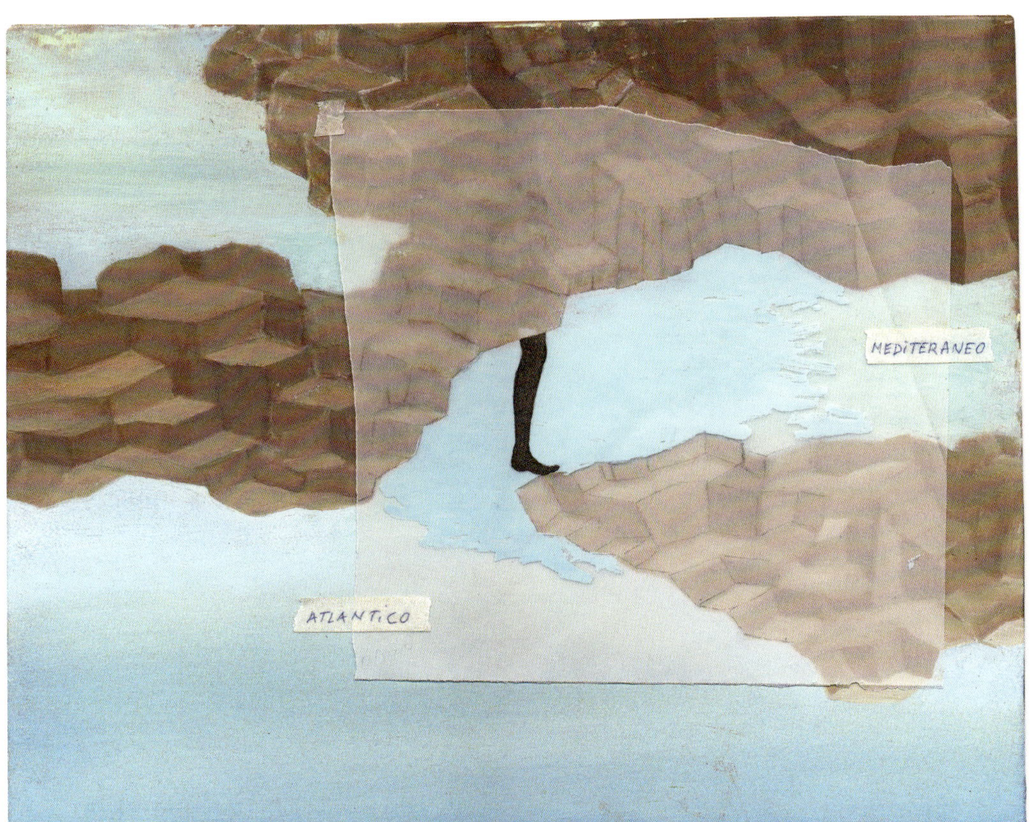

THE EVENT

29 March 2006, Havana/Key West

Bridge/Puente

On 29 March 2006, the fishing communities of Havana and Key West are invited to line up boats to send out a floating bridge between the United States and Cuba. The two lines will head from opposite shores towards the same horizon to create the illusion of a bridge.

- 6:25am: sunrise
- 6:30am: film crew arrives on location
- 7:00am: boats leave their respective bases to reach location (the call)
- 7:30am: opening scene with empty sea (the location)
- 8:00am: the boats arrive to location from left and right (the protagonists)
- 8:20 am: one after another the boats join in the line (the meeting)
- 9:20am: the line is formed (the bridge)
- 9:40am: participants walk from one boat to another (the crossing)
- 10:15am: the boats leave the line in all possible directions (the dispersion)

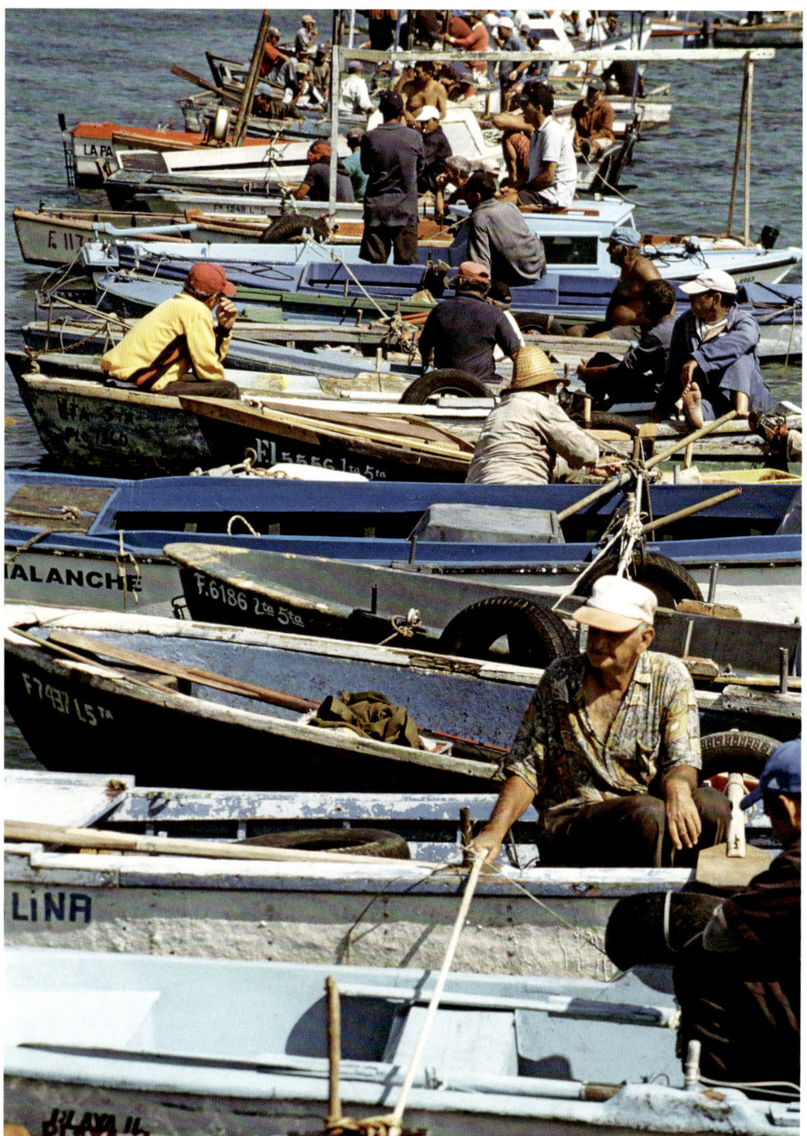

BRIDGE/PUENTE, 2006
IN COLLABORATION WITH TAIYANA PIMENTEL AND CUAUHTÉMOC MEDINA

PHOTO DOCUMENTATION OF AN ACTION, KEY WEST, FLORIDA, AND HAVANA

- 11:00am: closing scene with empty sea (the loop)
- 11:30am: film crew leaves location

FRANCIS ALŸS: Listo?
CUAUHTÉMOC MEDINA: Ready?
FRANCIS ALŸS: Van 49, 50, 51 barcos…
CUAUHTÉMOC MEDINA: We have 35.
FRANCIS ALŸS: We are counter light.
CUAUHTÉMOC MEDINA: We have the sun in the face.
FRANCIS ALŸS: The sky is clear. You?

(Phone exchange between Key West and Havana during the event)

AFTER THE EVENT

30 MARCH 2006
Havana

ALDERETE: We are two people. One gives the other a slap in the face and that's it, we broke the dialogue. That means that you and I won't be able to discuss anything, or process anything, nor will we agree on anything. There has to be a third person who speaks for the two of us. And who can makes us agree on deciding something. There has to be someone, and I believe it should be the artist, who can be that third person, who can create a dialogue, who can soften the political tensions between the two countries so there can be a dialogue afterwards.

Hay los que saben.
Hay los que no saben.
Hay los que no saben pero sospechan.
Hay los que sospechan pero no quieren saber.
Y está el que sabemos.

APRIL 2006
Mexico: The Deception.

From the beginning we knew that the tense geopolitics between the two regions would make it difficult for an event to take place on Cuban waters under Castro's regime. In order to improve the project's chances, we decided – not without debate – to hide our critical discourse under the guise of a formal exercise. We would make no mention of a floating bridge but instead we would talk of 'geometrical figures on the sea', of 'aquatic ballet' while making references to Land Art or Minimal Sculpture. And as we could not take any risk of a leak between the two communities, neither side was informed of the parallel attempt that would take place simultaneously on the other side of the Gulf.

As a result we had to maintain the overall project at a level of secrecy and trick the participants into the project to protect them from the consequences of their performance and of our discourse. So there we were in blatant self-contradiction: the floating bridge wanted to be an image of dialogue in between two communities subjected to governments that were (ab)using geopolitics to divert public attention from their respective internal problems. But to make the *Bridge/Puente* project happen we had to use a similar tactic: we had to lie and bluff. However, by then we could no longer stop the rolling inertia of what we had started: the expectations that the project had provoked were inexorably pushing things ahead.

GERARDO MOSQUERA: Every act of subversion has a necessary component of deception.

FRANCIS ALŸS: Of the others and of one self. *Es más fácil pedir perdón que pedir permiso*. It's easier to ask for pardon than for permission.
– Havana, February 2006

As we spent more time with the fishing communities, complicity grew. Sooner rather than later, we found ourselves all too busy resolving all sorts of logistical problems and rivalries between the different fishing communities to even notice that our original critical discourse was surreptitiously being replaced by a collective obsession to just make 'it' happen.

MAY 2006
Mexico: a bridge over troubled water.

When one becomes obsessive it's easy to lose sight of the bigger picture. Our primary assumption had been that the operation in Cuba would be more complex than in Florida. Consequently, as soon as the initial contacts had been made with the boat owners in Key West, we delegated the call of participants to two marine coordinators – Dave and Denise – and focused all our efforts on the Cuban front. Involved as we were in getting myriads of permits on the island, we lost track of the situation on the other side of the Gulf. Only a couple of days prior to the event did we realize that the level of commitment of the Florida participants was too weak and that they were not feeling truly concerned with the project. And there was another factor we underestimated: in Cuba we were dealing with fishermen unions, a fact that guaranteed us a collective commitment by the moment the union representatives were backing the project, whereas in Florida we were dealing with individual private boat owners who did not feel bound to a common will. In the event, the misbalance of our involvement with each community lead to a drastic disparity in their respective responses: whereas well over a hundred boats came to the rendez-vous in Cuba, only forty-two boats showed up in Key West.

Even when you go to the sea you should bring a bottle of water.

One can anticipate but not determine the outcome of a plot. Once the axiom is posed, once the actors are on location and the cameras are rolling, all we can do is watch. Whatever unfolds thereafter is the response to our invitation. Few boats showed up in Florida and too many in Cuba. However, the disparity of the participation was largely a consequence of our uneven involvement with each community and could not be read as an objective manifestation of each side's intention. Nevertheless, I was left with the feeling that the end result was misleading and what is more, only encouraging the cliché expectation that 'Cubans are eager to leave whereas North Americans aren't'.

'What made the project possible in Cuba was the power of conviction we carried and we transmitted, and you cannot delegate that. It's the necessary fuel to make those projects happen. What transcends from the documentation is a love story with the island, with the fishing communities'. And she added: '*Y el amor también es engaño*; to love is also to deceive'.
– Taiyana Pimentel, Havana, 30 March 2006

Lo bailado nadie te lo quita
Did the Cuban fishermen at any point realize what we were really trying to do? During the action, once the line of boats had been completed, didn't they see that each of their boats had become a dot in a line forming a bridge? When they started walking from one boat to another towards the horizon, didn't a sudden insight occur among the participants? Anyhow, this is the moment when it all came back to us: what turns a line of boats into a bridge is the flow of people passing from one boat to another.

CUBAN FISHERMAN: I don't understand what was the meaning of the line?

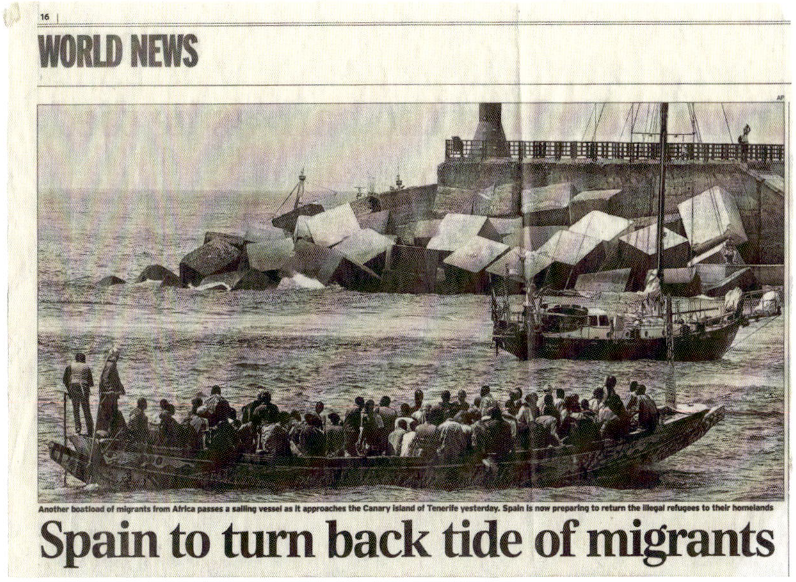
16 | WORLD NEWS

Another boatload of migrants from Africa passes a sailing vessel as it approaches the Canary island of Tenerife yesterday. Spain is now preparing to return the illegal refugees to their homelands

Spain to turn back tide of migrants

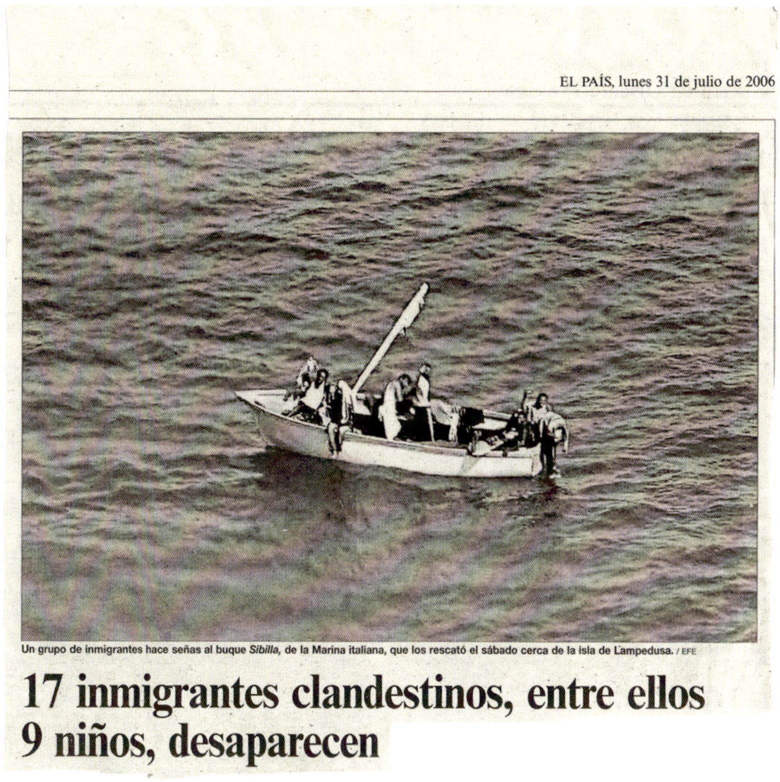
EL PAÍS, lunes 31 de julio de 2006

Un grupo de inmigrantes hace señas al buque *Sibilla*, de la Marina italiana, que los rescató el sábado cerca de la isla de Lampedusa. / EFE

17 inmigrantes clandestinos, entre ellos 9 niños, desaparecen

EPHEMERA FOR DON'T CROSS THE BRIDGE BEFORE YOU GET TO THE RIVER, 2006
NEWSPAPER CLIPPINGS
FROM THE ARTIST'S ARCHIVE

FRANCIS ALŸS: What did you think of it?
OTHER CUBAN FISHERMAN: Secret, it's a secret, it's an absolute secret which you cannot reveal.... it's a secret.
FIRST FISHERMAN: But it is the incognita for...
SECOND FISHERMAN: You cannot say it!
Discussion among Cuban fishermen on the evening after the event, Baracoa, Havana, 29 March 2006.

TAIYANA PIMENTEL: [Commenting on the Cuban revolution] Look, that's how our history began: partly real and partly fictional. So we, too, have the right to invent our own fiction, you understand? Each of us incorporates a personal imaginary to his or to her reality, but it's an imaginary built from a historical perspective (...) It has to

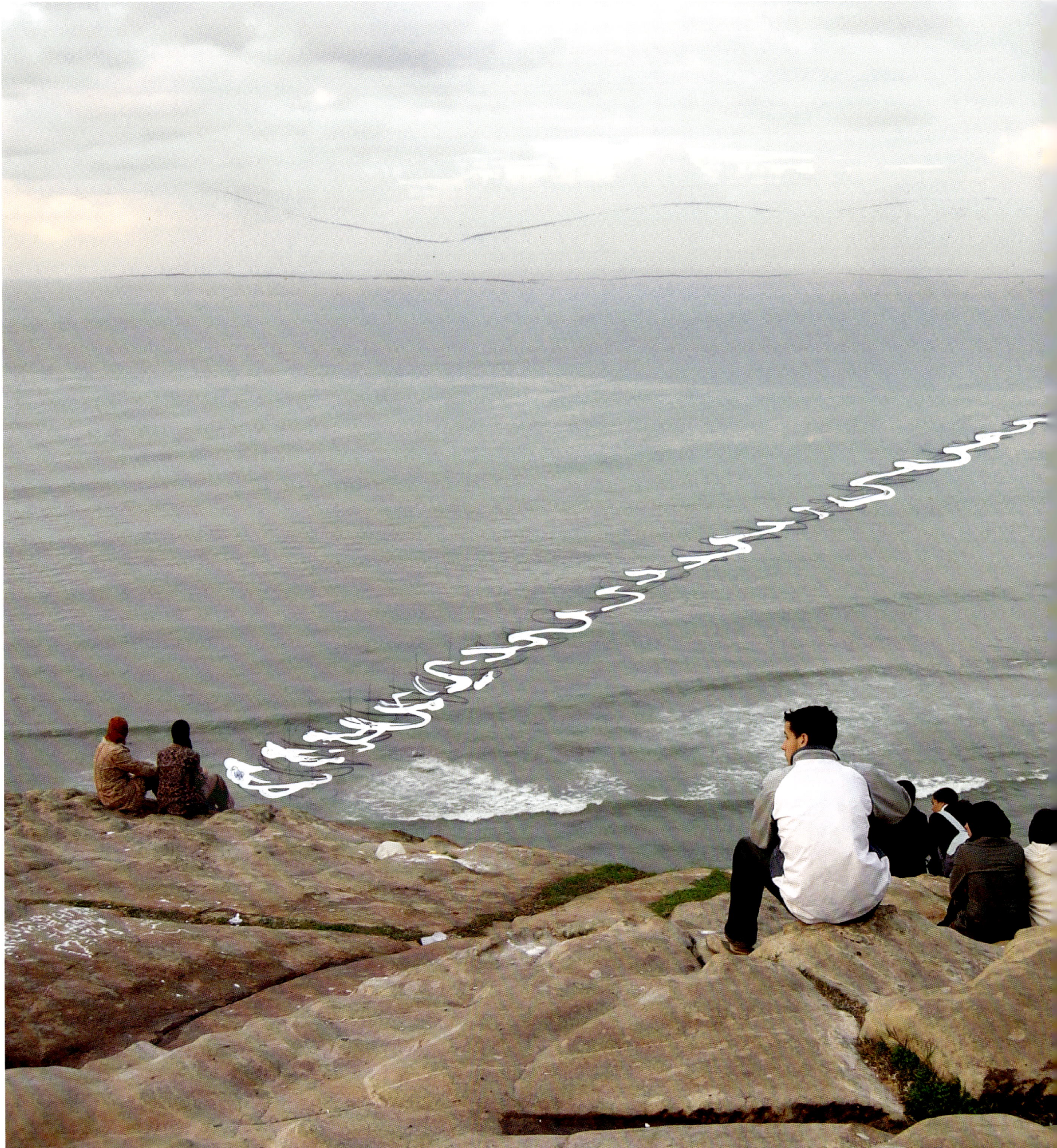

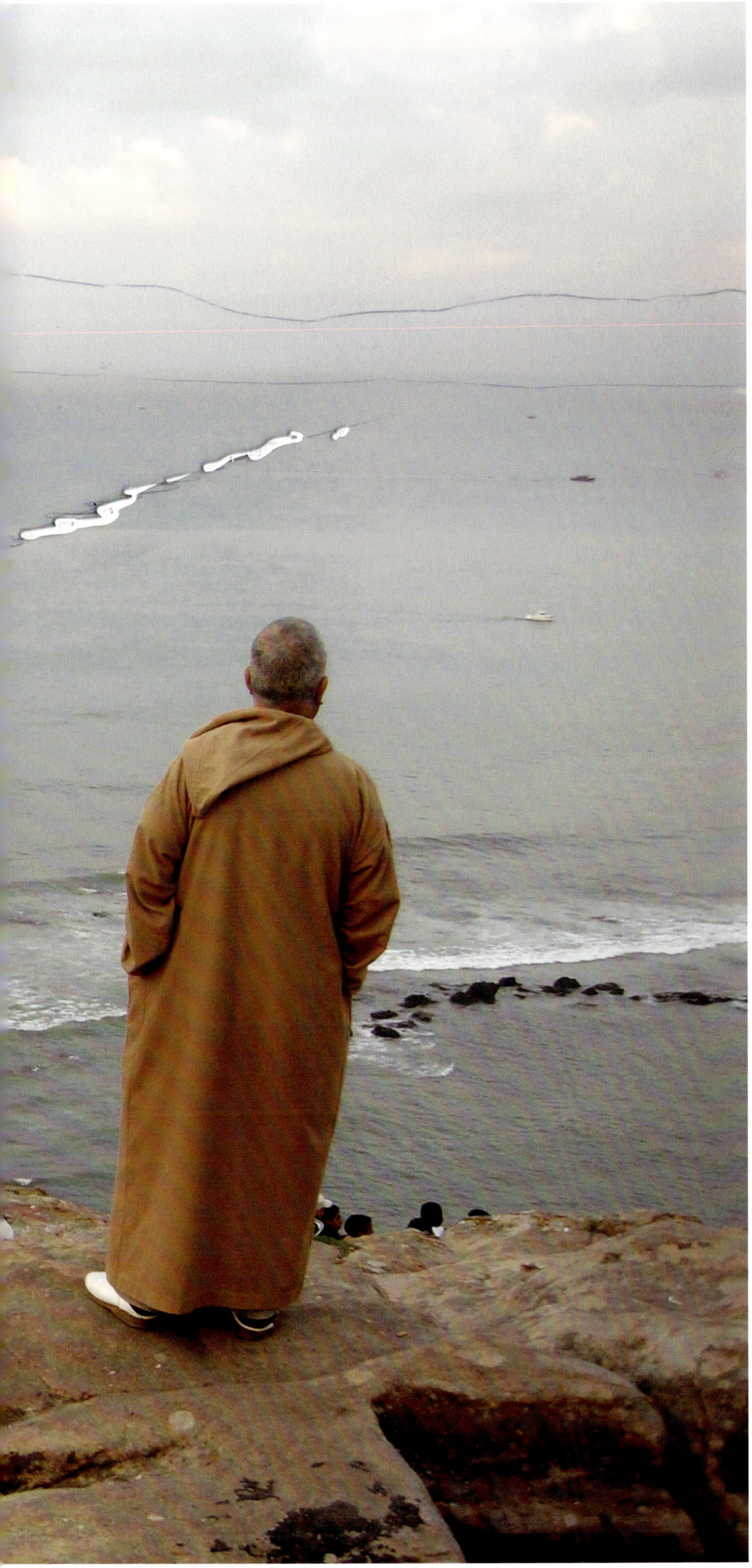

MIRADORES (MOROCCO LOOKING AT SPAIN), 2008
RETOUCHED PHOTOGRAPH
25 X 32 CM

do with how one imagines things should be and how somehow that fantasy became part of our life on the island.
– Havana, sometimes before the event.

EPISODE 2: DON'T CROSS THE BRIDGE BEFORE YOU GET TO THE RIVER

12 AUGUST 2008
Strait of Gibraltar, Spain/Morocco.

BEFORE THE EVENT

SUMMER 2006
England: back in Europe.

Temporary move to the Old Continent after twenty years of absence. Feeling in-between two waters, at once local and immigrant, everything around me looking familiar and foreign at once. Landing into the obsessive debate by local media and politicians on South/North migrations issues and the protectionist immigration policies promoted by most European governments.

SEPTEMBER 2006
London

As he was performing his Twelve Labours, Hercules had to cross the Mount Atlas on his way to the island of Erytheia. Rather than climbing to the summit, the Greek hero brandished his indestructible mace and split the mountain in half. To open the way, his legs pushed apart the two massive rocks while a river surged under his feet.

According to the myth, the Strait of Gibraltar is the place where Hercules separated Europe from Africa and opened the Mediterranean Sea to the Atlantic Ocean. The Strait seemed like the obvious place to illustrate this contradiction of our times: how can one promote global economy and at the same time limit the global flow of people across continents?

The image of a bridge...

Questions:

Can one imagine a similar scenario 10,000 km away in the waters running between Morocco and Spain?
Can one make a similar call to communities living under such different latitudes?

You never swim twice in the same water.

OCTOBER 2006
London: a different equation.

Whereas there are 170 km of sea between Key West and Havana, the shortest crossing of the Strait of Gibraltar from Morocco to Spain is only 14 km. On a clear night in Tangier you can see the lights of cars driving along the Spanish coast. It's so narrow that a chain of seventy-two cargo boats (or forty-three 'mega' cargo boats) touching another could physically join Africa and Europe. But even supposing I could get enough cargo boats to close the Strait and connect the two continents, wouldn't that turn the whole project into an engineering enterprise or a military operation, like with those bridges built overnight during floods or wars? The difference between a military operation and an artistic gesture lies in the missing fragment of the bridge: the gap that has to be filled by our imagination. That's what triggers the poetry and makes the artistic operation happen, that's what opens a moment of suspension. The context of the Strait is already so loaded that, if anything, one has to minimize the geopolitical component and enhance the poetic dimension:
– Let the images talk on many different levels as only poetry can.
– Leave space for doubt. If in Lima the question was: 'did the dune move?' here it should be: 'Did the two lines of boats meet?'
– Insist on the ephemeral nature of the action, turn the meeting of boats into a furtive rendez-vous.
– Stay away from the temptation of leaving a mark in the seascape.
– Insert a story into the history of the Strait.

'To draw a line is to unite and suspend two points in a state of tension'.
– Jean Fisher, commenting on *The Green Line* project, 2005

NOVEMBER 2006
Strait of Gibraltar: first visit to both sides.

Scouting coastal locations, making contacts with the fishermen communities of Tarifa and Tangier, promoting the project and courting both sides' local authorities for support and permits: in Morocco from the top (Wali-Viceroy of Tangier) to the base (fishermen unions) and in Spain from the base (fishermen unions) to the top (port authorities, mayor of Tarifa).

Communicating our desire to make the project happen.

DECEMBER 2006
Strait of Gibraltar: assessing the first complications.

– Discovering the existing rivalries between the Moroccan and Spanish fishing communities and their ageless war for territories.
– Encountering logistical problems with the strong currents present in the Strait.
– Looping around the large maritime zones under military control.
– Resisting to fall into the 'game of interests' of the local politicians who want to appropriate the project for the benefit of their own politics.

Cada barco es un pais,
cada pais tiene un rey,
cada rey piensa diferente.

FEBRUARY 2007
Strait of Gibraltar: preparations to produce the floating bridge of boats between Europe and Africa with the fishing communities of Tarifa and Tangier in April 2007.

Dogma:

1. It's not a line of boats. It's a chain of boats forming a line.

2. What turns a chain of boats into a floating bridge is the flow of people passing from one boat to another.

3. The boats must touch land.

4. The boats must touch one another.
5. Each line of boats will head towards its counterpart across the Strait of Gibraltar.

6. The actions must happen simultaneously on the two opposite shores.

7. Whatever happens on one side must happen on the other.

8. The boats join the line one after another, like a zipper.

9. The line of boats is completed when the viewer's (or camera's) eye registers the optical illusion of a line of boats touching the horizon.

10. When completed, the illusion of the bridge will last only a few minutes.

11. After that, the boats will disperse in all possible directions.

12. Each side will be easily identifiable by the typology of the boats and the language spoken by the participants.

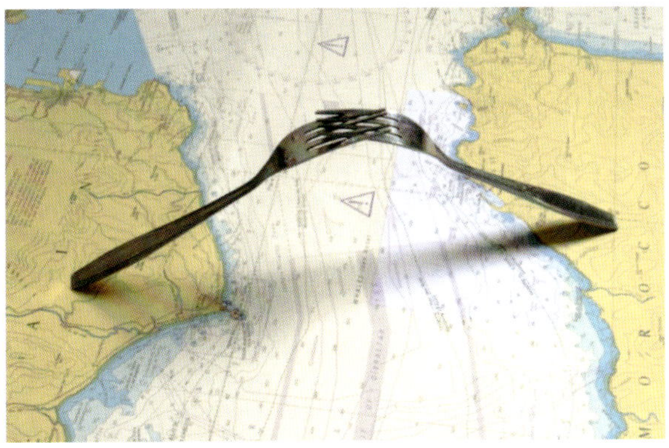

DON'T CROSS THE BRIDGE BEFORE YOU GET TO THE RIVER, 2008
INSTALLATION VIEW

MARCH 2007
London: false start.

A couple of weeks before the scheduled event I realize I lack the sufficient focus, conviction and personal commitment and I call the whole thing off.

MARCH 2007–APRIL 2008
London: la vie entre parenthèses.

Legal parenthesis that force me to put the project to sleep. Painting bridges, free flows and wandering Jews from my bedroom in London. Keeping in touch with the project. Keeping it alive, maintaining head above water.

APRIL 2008
London: back into action.

By the time I get back into the project, the rumour of 'a floating bridge of boats across the Strait of Gibraltar' has spread. Before anything actually took place, friends are asking: 'How was it? Is it true that the two lines met?'

1. How to beat the rumour?

How can one beat the mental image that was sparked just by hearing about the project's plot? Isn't that mental image going to beat anything that could reasonably happen on the sea? Should I let the *Bridge/Puente* project live as a rumour only?

2. What if it escalates?

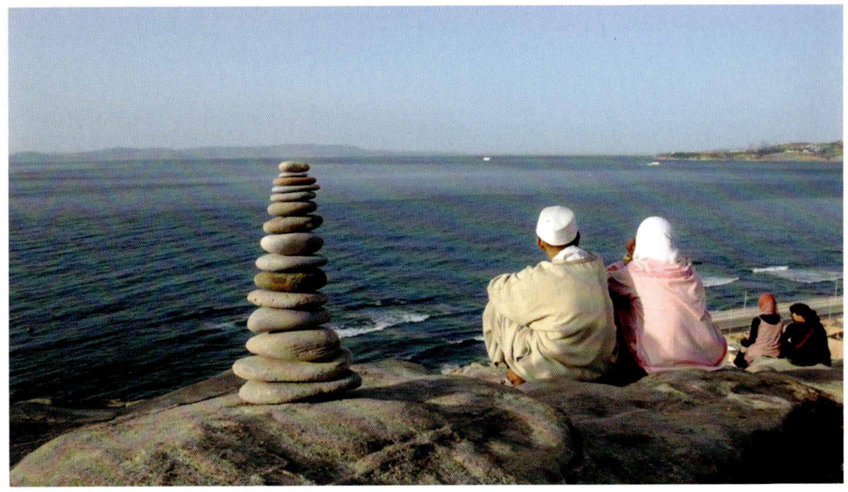

STRAIT OF GIBRALTAR, 2008
PHOTO DOCUMENTATION OF AN ACTION

Meanwhile, our contacts tactics are getting out of control. It turns out that the planned date for the bridge project coincides with the proximate opening of Tanger-Med: The Door Towards Europe, a new harbour project backed by Sa Majesté Le Roi Mohammed VI. As a result, we get an enthusiastic support from Sa Majesté for our walking bridge image but this comes with a collateral effect: Moroccan fishermen would not be entering the project out of conviction but out of fear of losing their jobs.

3. Who for?

The general lack of interest by the fishermen of both communities makes me wonder if I'm not barking at the wrong tree? Who really wants a bridge?

'Maybe what you are celebrating is the impossibility of a bridge'.
– Yto Barrada

'Isn't the bridge going in one direction only?'
– Cuauhtémoc Medina

4. Why?

Because of the need to turn a concept into an fact?
Because of the urge to anchor an idea in reality?
Because of the desire to provoke, in the heat of the action, this moment of complicity that could open up the possibility of change?
Because of the inertia of all the people involved which ineluctably pushes the project forward?

'The show must go on'.
– Simone, Tangier, April 2008.

4 MAY 2008
Mexico: deceive all expectations and move onto a mock project by:

1. FEEDING THE RUMOUR: through a massive mailing of postcards from Tangier and from Tarifa, propagate the rumour that a line of boats closed the Strait of Gibraltar and physically connected Europe to Africa for an hour.

2. TURNING THE EVENT INTO A CHILDREN'S GAME: Given that what matters

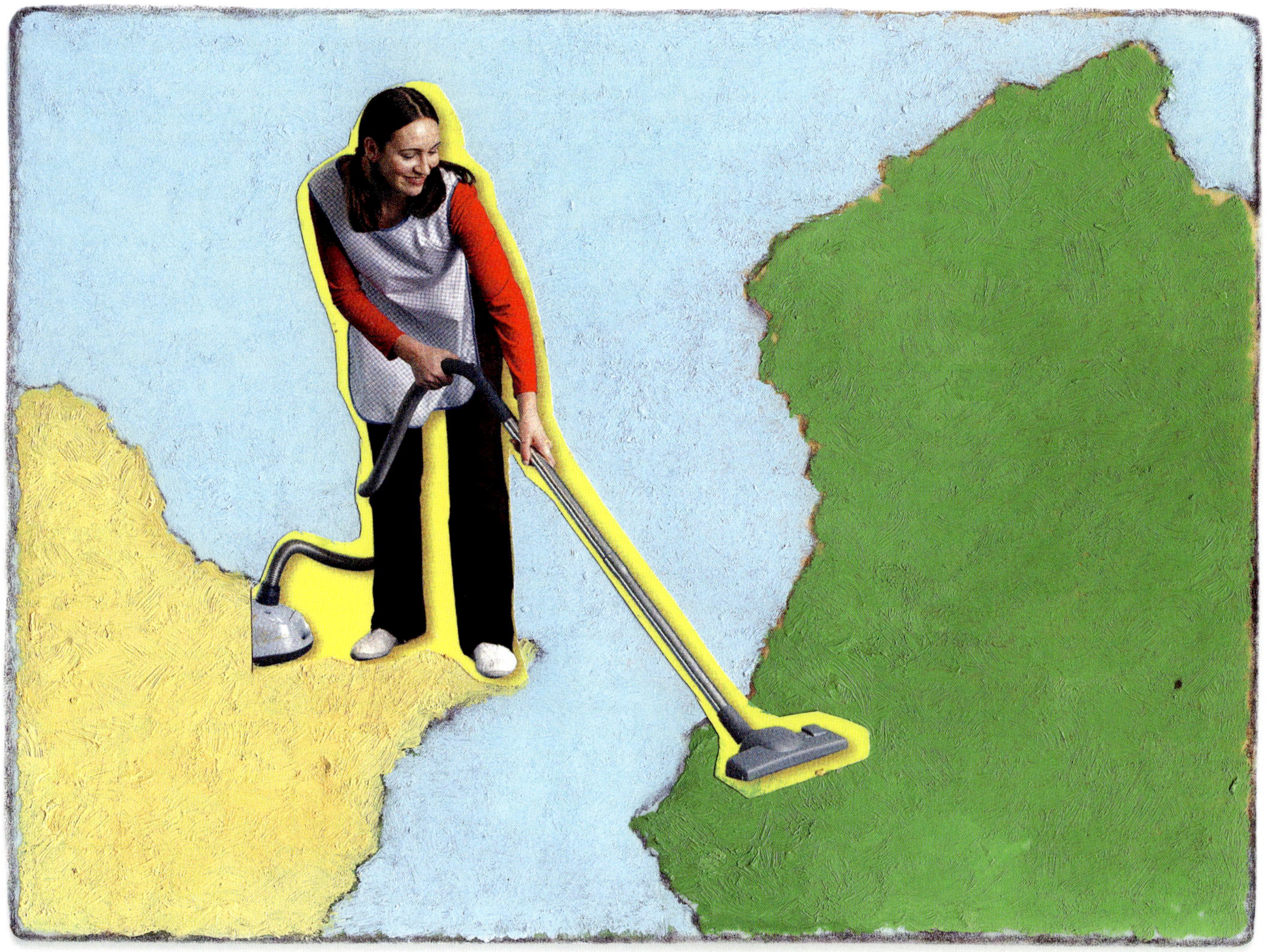

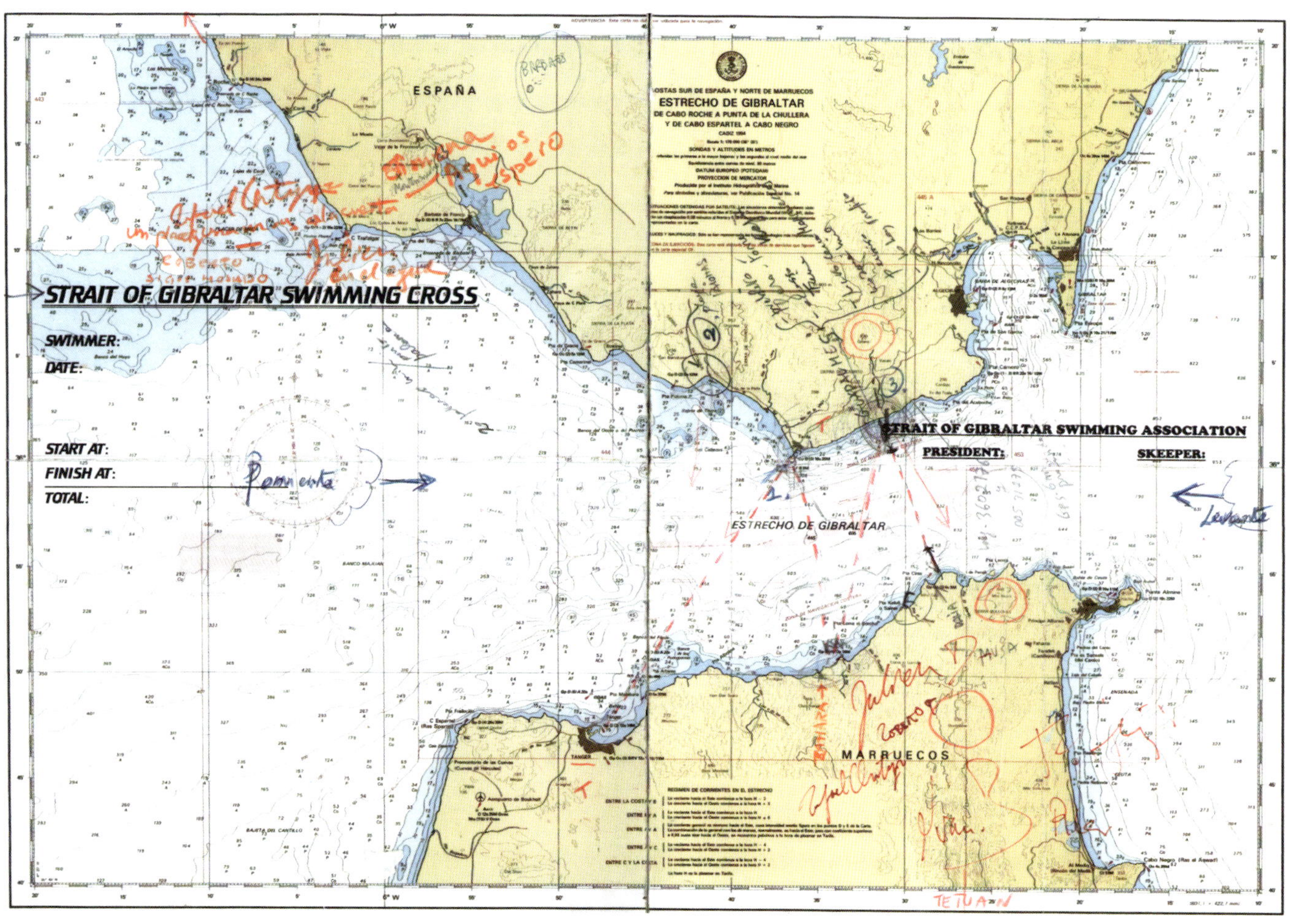

STUDY FOR DON'T CROSS THE BRIDGE BEFORE YOU GET TO THE RIVER, 2008
OIL AND COLLAGE ON CANVAS
11 X 15 CM

RETOUCHED MAP OF THE STRAIT FOR DON'T CROSS THE BRIDGE BEFORE YOU GET TO THE RIVER, 2008
45 X 31 CM

is that the event truly represents the mutual desire of each community to send out a floating bridge:

Change of scale by moving from the fishing boats to model boats made of babouches and flip-flops: the shoe-boats.
Change of protagonists by moving from adults to the only ones who seem to be genuinely interested in (or amused by) our project: the kids from both sides of the Strait.
Turn the whole operation into a celebration of free flow, a ritual of passage.
Return to guerilla tactics: minimum of permits/maximum of flexibility; do and run tactic. Pas vu, pas pris.

'What importance has my life? I only want it to remain faithful until the end to the child I was... the child I was and who is now like a grandfather to me.'
– Georges Bernanos, *Les Grands Cimetières sous la lune*, 1938

24 MAY 2008
Coyuca, Pacific coast, Mexico: return to the bay for a second trial of floating bridge, but this time with children and with prototypes of the shoe-boats made out of babouches and flip-flops.

As if they were real boats.
As if someone would walk from one boat to another.
As if you couldn't let a fish pass between the boats.
As if they were 'shoed boats'.
As if it was a bridge.
– Maestra Jenny, Barra de Coyuca

27 MAY 2008
Mexico: the story within the story.

To: Ivan Boccara, Los Animantes, Roberto Rubalcava
Rafael Ortega, Pilar Corrias, Jimena Blázquez, Julien Devaux
On 27 May 2008, at 10:07 AM, Francis Alÿs de Smedt wrote:

As a result of the recent change from collaborating with adults to children and from using real boats to model boats, there are now four moments in the story:

The filming starts by registering an action that is happening above the water.
(1. The Realm of Reality). Moment 1 finishes when the line of shoeboats is completed. Then one kid takes a deep breath and plunges; he dives further and further into deep waters until his silhouette completely disappears in a blue-green monochrome. (2. The Crossing of the Mirror). There, the film leaves The Realm of Reality to enter the world of a children's tale where the model boats become real boats, where the kids become giants, where there is no sound, no up or down, no here or there, no border. (3. The Fantasy). Finally, the diver suddenly whirls back up to the surface, springs out of the water like a cork
(4. The Awakening) and the film loops back to Moment 1.

'Documentary is what happens to the other guy, fiction is what happens to me'.
– Jean-Luc Godard

9 JULY 2008
Strait of Gibraltar: last scouting trip before event

– Filming Europe watching Africa at the Mirador del Estrecho, Tarifa, Spain.
– Filming Africa watching Europe at the Roman Baths, Tangier, Morocco.

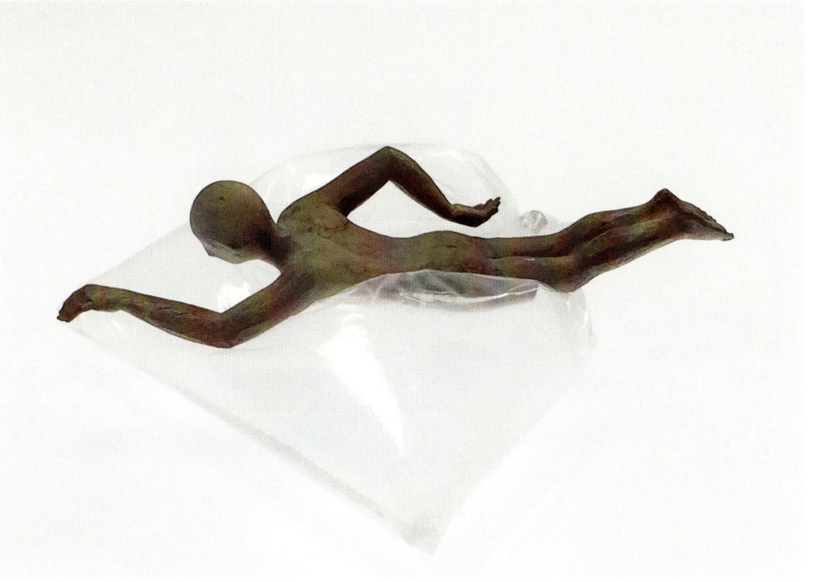

STUDY FOR DON'T CROSS THE BRIDGE BEFORE YOU GET TO THE RIVER, 2008
WOOD, AIR, PLASTIC BAG
18 X 30 X 23 CM

THE EVENT
12 AUGUST 2008
Strait of Gibraltar

Don't Cross the Bridge Before You Get to the River.

The Strait of Gibraltar is 7,7 nautical miles wide (14 km) and separates Africa from Europe.
If a line of kids leaves Europe towards Morocco, and a line of kids leaves Africa towards Spain, will the two lines meet in the chimera of the horizon?

AFTER THE EVENT
SEPTEMBER–DECEMBER 2008
Mexico: watching the rushes of the material filmed on 12 August 2008.

The early period of a project, the moment when you start playing with an idea, when you're imagining how to make it happen, that's the most exciting moment of the project, when everything is still possible.

When you land into the production, with all its financial and technical contingencies, you start feeling the limits of your idea.

When you are filming, you stick to the original idea as much as possible, but you start messing it up and compromising.

Next you find yourself in an editing studio trying to rescue the essence of the idea but you know that the film will never meet your original expectations.

The Gibraltar project is bizarre: a place was chosen, a plot was written, an event took place in real time with real people, yet cameras recorded an imaginary meeting. Only now am I getting to the heart of the problem:
– Who are my interlocutors?
– Where does it lead?

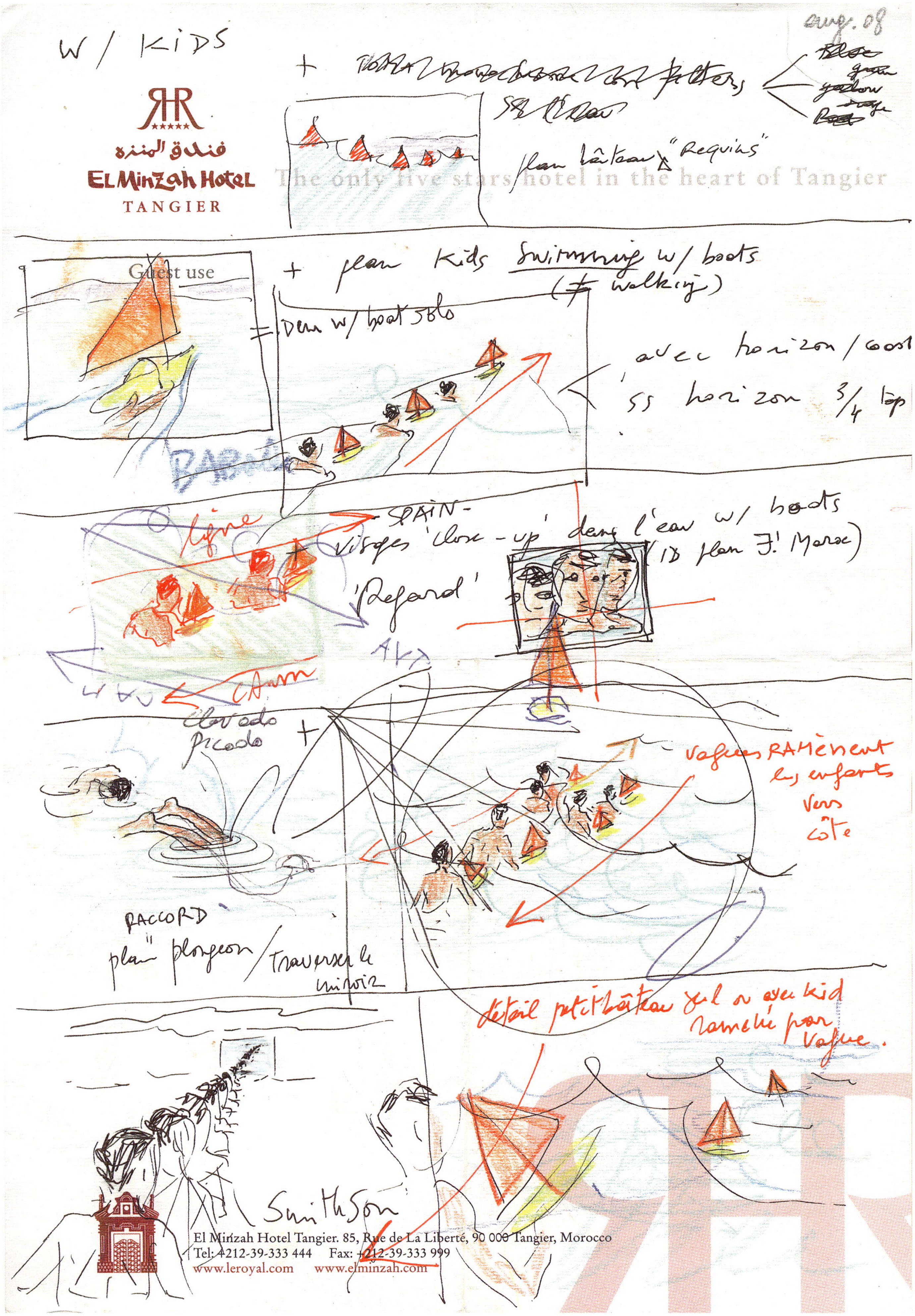

STUDY FOR DON'T CROSS THE BRIDGE BEFORE YOU GET TO THE RIVER, 2008
PENCIL AND COLOUR PENCIL ON PAPER
30 X 21 CM

opposite,
DON'T CROSS THE BRIDGE BEFORE YOU GET TO THE RIVER, 2008
PHOTO DOCUMENTATION OF AN ACTION
STRAIT OF GIBRALTAR, SPANISH SIDE

next spread,
DON'T CROSS THE BRIDGE BEFORE YOU GET TO THE RIVER, 2008
PHOTO DOCUMENTATION OF AN ACTION
STRAIT OF GIBRALTAR, MOROCCAN SIDE

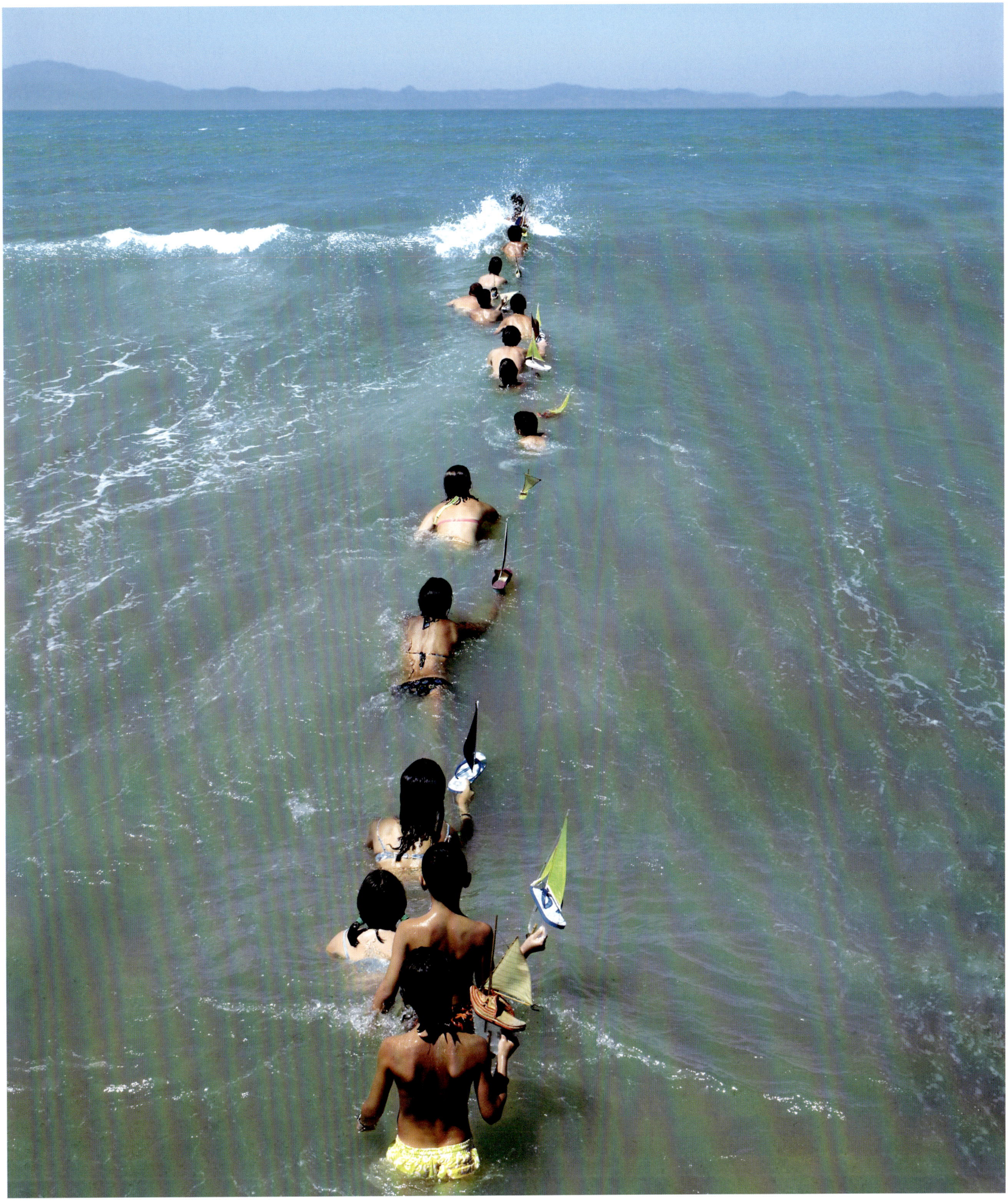

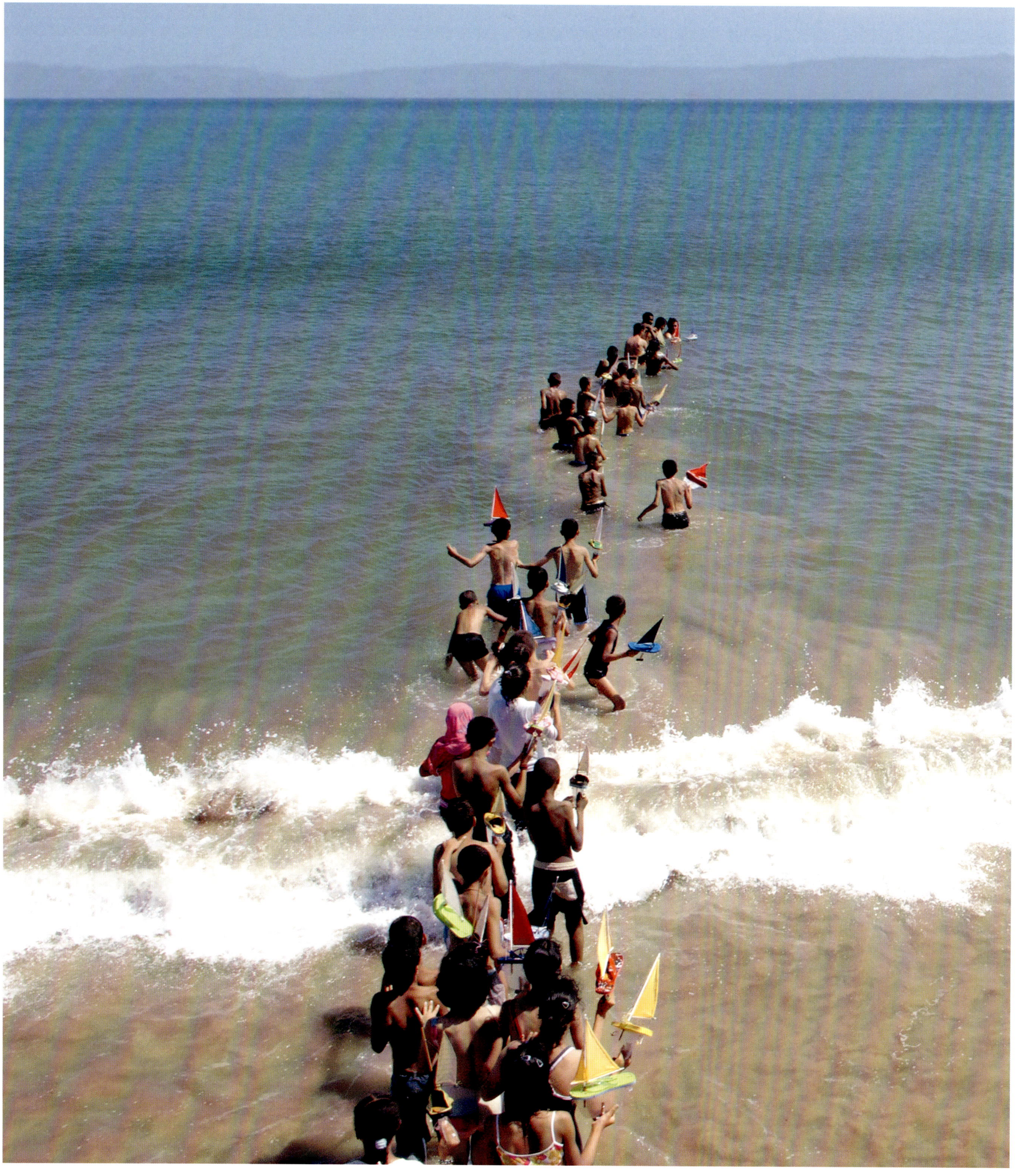

– How far can I push such utopian projections?
– Who really wants to believe in the possibility of change?
– Who wants a bridge?

There is a story, but no happy end.
All I have is a *mise-en-scène*.

'As soon as he crossed the bridge the phantoms came to meet him.'
– Serge Daney, *Postcards from the Cinema*, 2007

DECEMBER 2008
Mexico: damned allegories.

While editing with Julien the material filmed in August, I work with Lulu on an animation that could better illustrate Moment 2. The Crossing of the Mirror. However, we soon abandon that route as we feel that the drawings and paintings spontaneously produced along the making of the project are more suggestive than any animation we could create post-event.

'A myth remains a myth for as long as it is perceived as such.'
– Claude Lévi-Strauss, *Myth: A Symposium*, 1955

FEBRUARY 2009
Mexico: a story of negotiation

This chronicle is the account of an artistic process, with all its progresses and regresses, its doubts and convictions, its agendas and compromises: the usual negotiation between reality and artistic fantasy – *entre le geste et la parole*. Its first outline was drafted for a talk in Beirut in December 2008 while the project was still in process. But this logbook is also a fiction: it derives from my notes and sketches, our conversations and emails, the press and graphic material accumulated along the making of the two successive *Bridge* projects.

APRIL 2009
Mexico

Le problème n'est pas de raconter des histoires, de fabriquer des images ou de créer des fables; le problème c'est quand on commence à y croire.

The problem is not to tell stories, to make up images or to create fables; the problem is when you start believing them.

On peut traverser une histoire locale mais peut-on l'affecter? Peut-on changer sa perception interne ou externe? La ligne des gosses poussant leurs petits bateaux vers l'horizon ne va nulle part. Il n'y aura pas de rencontre, pas de 'happy end'. Tout ceci n'est qu'une illusion, la ligne part en queue de poisson.

You can pass through a local history but can you intervene it? 'All the boats on the water aren't going anywhere, all the boats on the water are going nowhere' goes the song. There will be no meeting, no happy end. Our line is fizzling out, our story is tailing off, it's all a trick of the mind.

Plutôt que s'enfoncer plus loin dans l'illusion, l'édition va tenter d'illustrer et de transcender notre impasse tout en rappellant que, pour vaine qu'elle puisse paraître, l'action reste nécessaire.

Rather than sinking further into an illusion, this last session of editing will try to illustrate and transcend a deadlock while reminding us that, for vane as it may seem, action is necessary.

Crossing one bridge at a time.

19 MAY 2009
Mexico: The Collapse of Poetics.

To: Ivan Boccara, Los Animantes, Abdellah Karroum, Félix Blume,
Rafael Ortega, Julien Devaux…
On 19 May 2009, at 11:11 AM, Francis Alÿs de Smedt wrote:

'Las olas siempre regresan'.
– Cuauhtémoc Medina

The last chapter of this chronicle begins here, when the lead is given back to the kids. Or is it that the lead is taken by the sea? In any scenario, it'll be the story dictated by the images we filmed on 12 August 2008 and our collective memory of that day.

In contrast to Lima or Key West/Havana, there is no narration. Instead of building a story, what we are doing is installing a situation, a dance of the kids with the waves. As a result, there is no introduction, no development, no climax: there is only movement. The sea is portrayed as the force always dragging the kids back to the shore, the kids are the heroes trying to cheat destiny, the ebb and flow of the waves dictate the kids' progress and regress.

13 AUGUST 2008
Tangier: the wave of Tarifa.

Walking on the beach the next morning, I watch ferries departing for Tarifa every hour. When the ferry leaves the bay, its propellers create a wave that keeps growing as it approaches the coast. When people on the beach see the wave getting close, they get up and run to the sea to jump it, roll with it, embrace it or throw their bodies to clash with it. For most, this will be as close as they'll ever get to make contact with Europe.

Epilogue

One tale is good till another is told.

DON'T CROSS THE BRIDGE BEFORE YOU GET TO THE RIVER, SEIGENSHA ART PUBLISHING, KYOTO, 2013

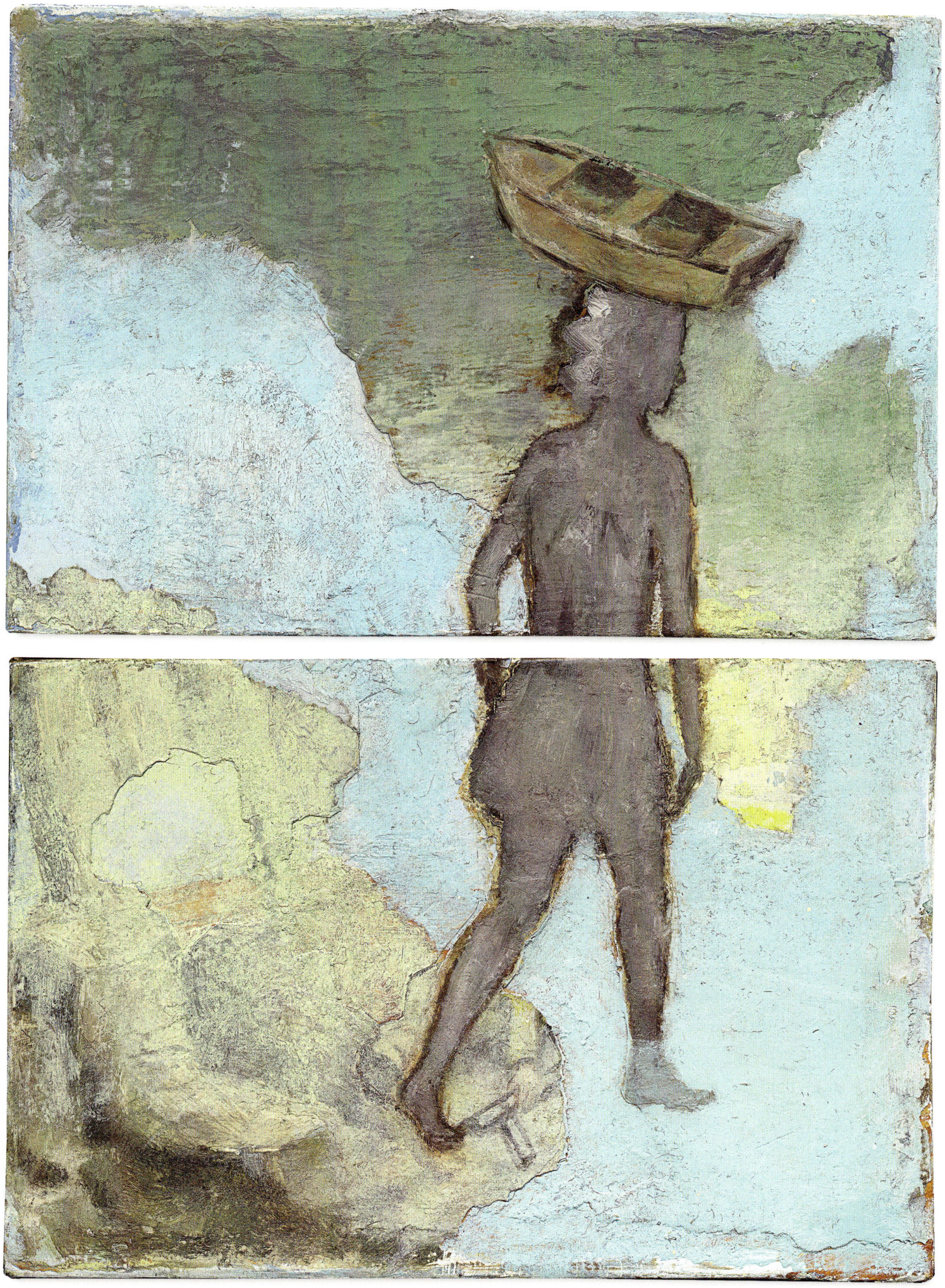

DON'T CROSS THE BRIDGE BEFORE YOU GET TO THE RIVER,
2008
DIPTYCH
OIL ON WOOD
EACH 14 X 20 CM

DON'T CROSS THE BRIDGE BEFORE YOU GET TO THE RIVER,
2008
PHOTO DOCUMENTATION OF AN ACTION
STRAIT OF GIBRALTAR

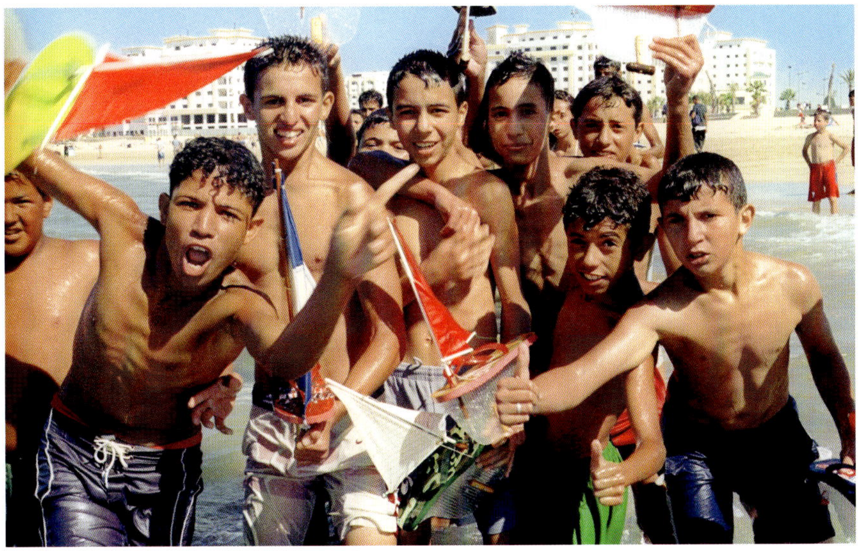

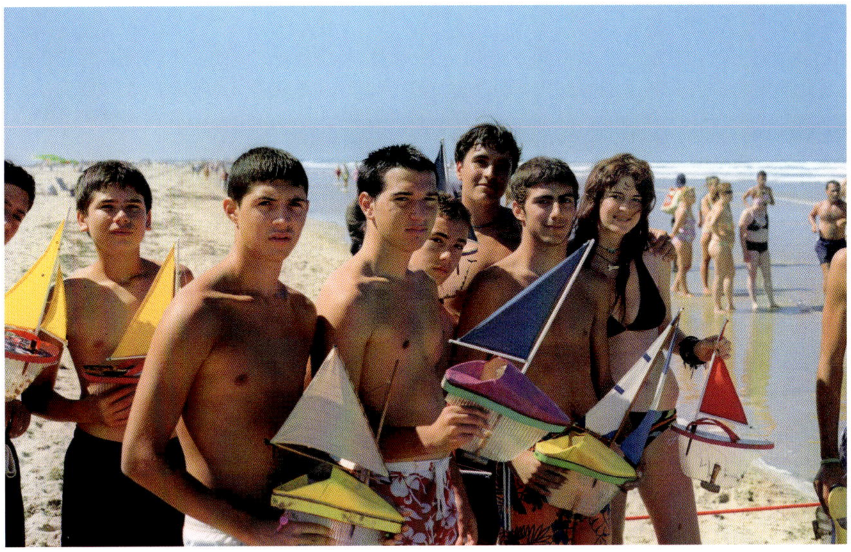

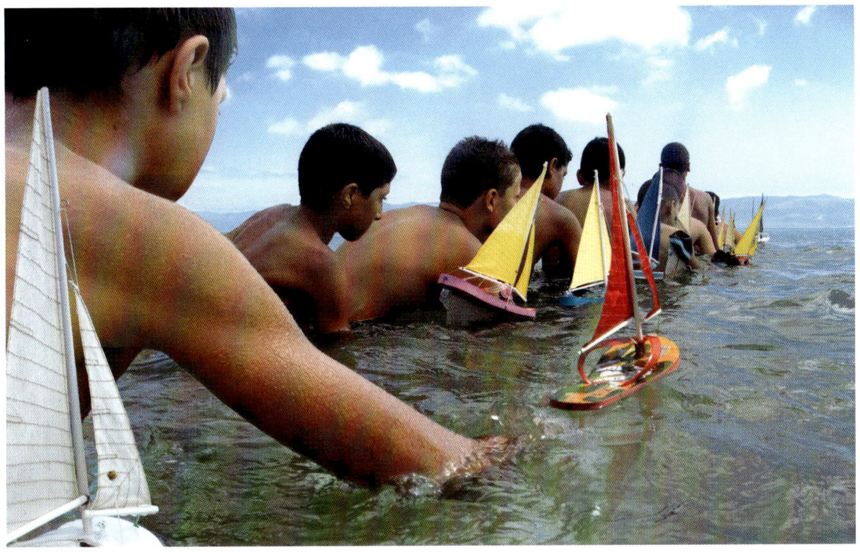

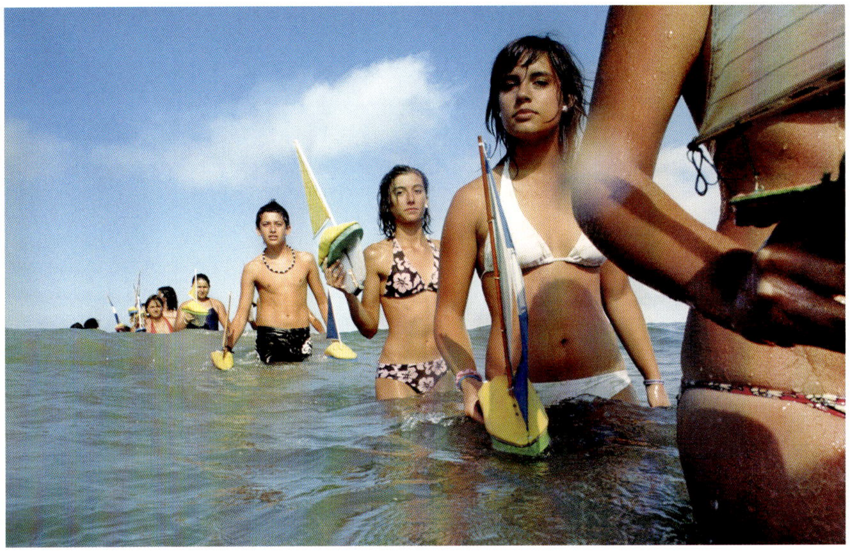

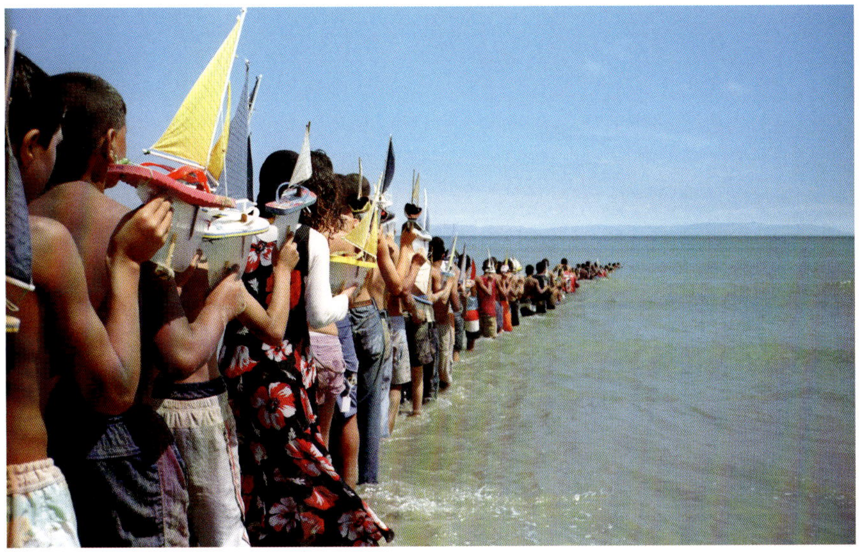

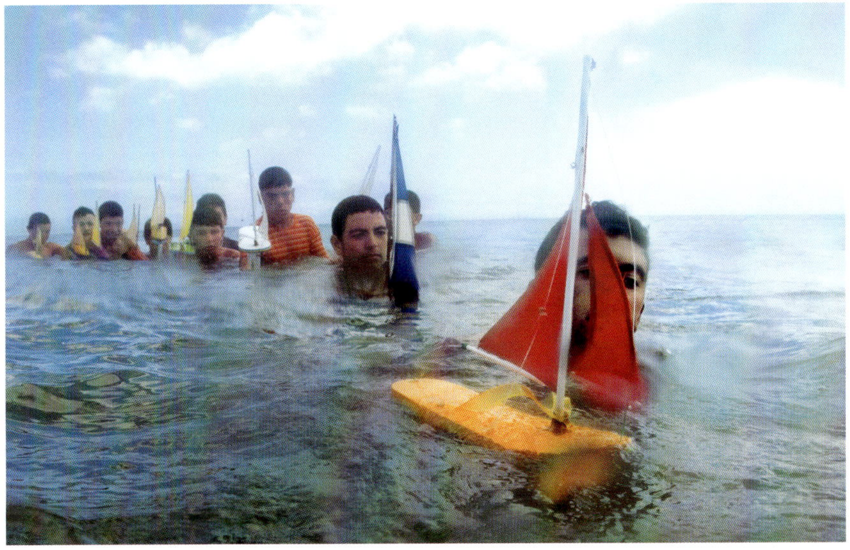

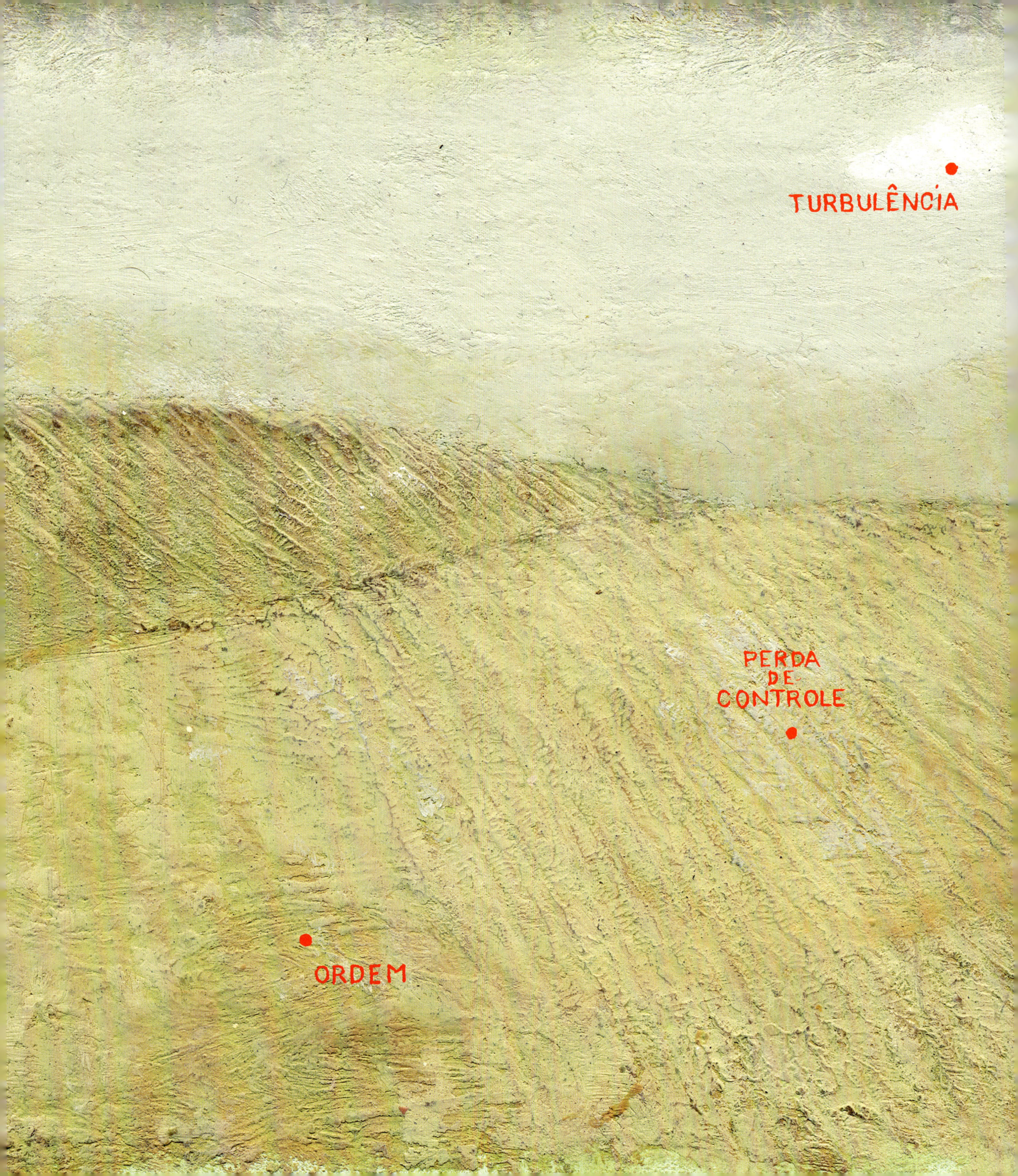
TURBULÊNCIA
PERDA
DE
CONTROLE
ORDEM

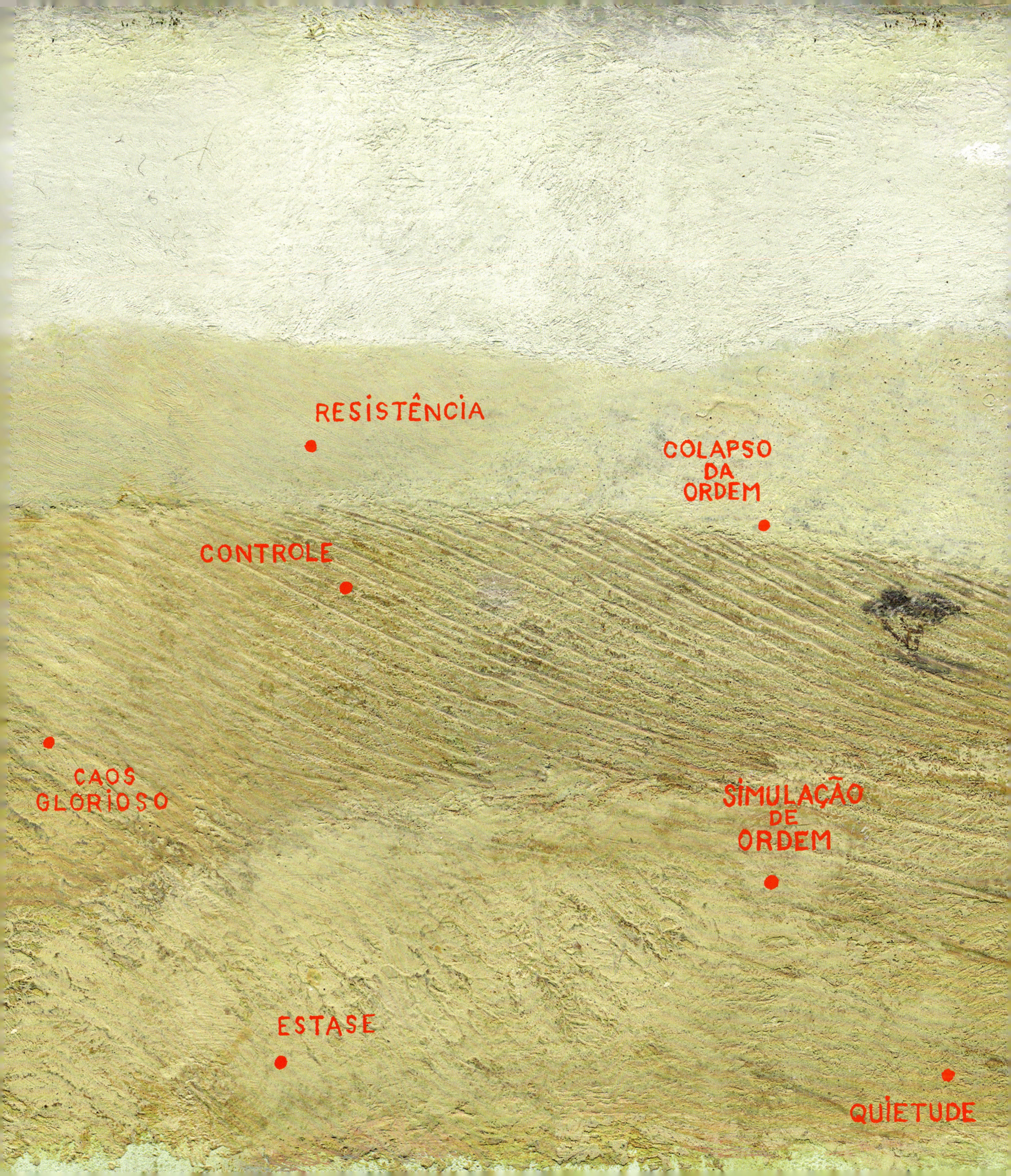
RESISTÊNCIA
COLAPSO DA ORDEM
CONTROLE
CAOS GLORIOSO
SIMULAÇÃO DE ORDEM
ESTASE
QUIETUDE

Sometimes doing right goes wrong, and sometimes doing wrong turns right, 2012–14

PUBLIC SCREENING OF REEL-UNREEL IN CINE BEHZAD, KABUL, AFGHANISTAN, 2012

previous pages,
STUDY FOR TORNADO (DETAIL), 2009
OIL AND PIGMENT ON WOOD
14 X 36 CM

In June 2010, I was invited by to take part in a dOCUMENTA (13) scouting trip to Afghanistan. Freshly arrived in Kabul, I was standing in the hotel lobby with my travel companions when we were told that there was a jirga – a tribal elders assembly – in town and that a curfew had been imposed for the next twenty-four hours. Reading my disappointment, a tall Afghan man stepped aside from the group and discreetly asked me if I wanted to meet him the next morning at dawn for a drive on the outskirts of Kabul. So we did, and while we were watching the sunrise over the city, we started a conversation that continues to the present day. This chance encounter with architect Ajmal Maiwandi just a few hours after my arrival determined the entire course of my relationship with Afghanistan. I acknowledge that I was at first sceptical about the role of international art enterprises such as dOCUMENTA (13)'s project in Afghanistan and in particular about the relevance of my personal participation: what could a Belgian artist based in Mexico say about the situation in Afghanistan? However, by the end of that visit I had found an entry point for my research and Ajmal's passion for his homeland had got me hooked to the place.

It took another two trips to Kabul and all around Afghanistan before I could get a grasp of how to operate – weeks of traveling, observing, sipping tea, watching, listening, smiling, communicating through drawings, and most of all, sharing meals in people's homes. Everywhere Ajmal and I went, sooner than later we would end up sitting cross-legged with our hosts around a shiny plastic tablecloth covered with dishes. I sometimes feel that, in the absence of a common language, the ritual of chewing replaced the function of talking. By November 2011 a project had taken shape, nearly without volition. Whereas the mechanics of the film I was envisioning (*Reel-Unreel*) had been inspired by local children's games, its subject was a reflection on the real-unreal image of Afghanistan that was conveyed by the media in the West. Once the basic parameters of the action were set – the rules of the game – the development and outcome of the film relied mostly on improvisation – starting with the casting of the film's protagonists that took place in the Old City of Kabul on our first day of shooting. For the following five days, we filmed from 10AM to 5PM, moving location every couple hours or so. We circumnavigated the checkpoints along the way and passers-by looked more amused than suspicious. We were aware of the limits imposed by the local cultural codes and acted consequently. In many ways I had felt more restrictions when we produced *The Modern Procession* in New York City in 2002: a myriad of permits required, an imposed routing, little space left to improvisation, etc… In Kabul we crossed the city from one hill to another without a determined route, zigzagging through the crowded markets and tracing a journey that two young boys spontaneously turned into a plot.

I am fully conscious that: (1) had I been a woman, my access to these places and people would have been immensely more complicated, if at all possible; (2) I had a privileged introduction and relationship to Afghanistan thanks to Ajmal; and (3) I am in a position where I can decide when to leave. But so it happened and that's my story. This may sound politically incorrect, but I loved and love every minute of my time in Afghanistan. Instead of the concrete-walled residential and embassy areas, we filmed in the popular adobe neighbourhoods of Kabul, infinitely more welcoming to our loose style of operation. Occasionally a NATO convoy would surge out of the dust; people-cars-bicycles-dogs-donkeys and our mini crew would pull to the sides of the road to give way to a queue of massive army engines and, once the alert passed, everyone would pull back in a matter of seconds and chaos would resume its reassuring course. To show this instead of that are personal choices. When confronted with such an overwhelming context you can't cheat and you can't force: you negotiate. As for my original scepticism, I grew convinced that to open up the possibility of a conversation between Western and Muslim worlds is one of today's most urgent tasks of culture. The question no longer is: why did we go? The question is: now that we opened a conversation, how can it continue?

FRANCIS ALŸS, KASSEL, 29 MAY 2012

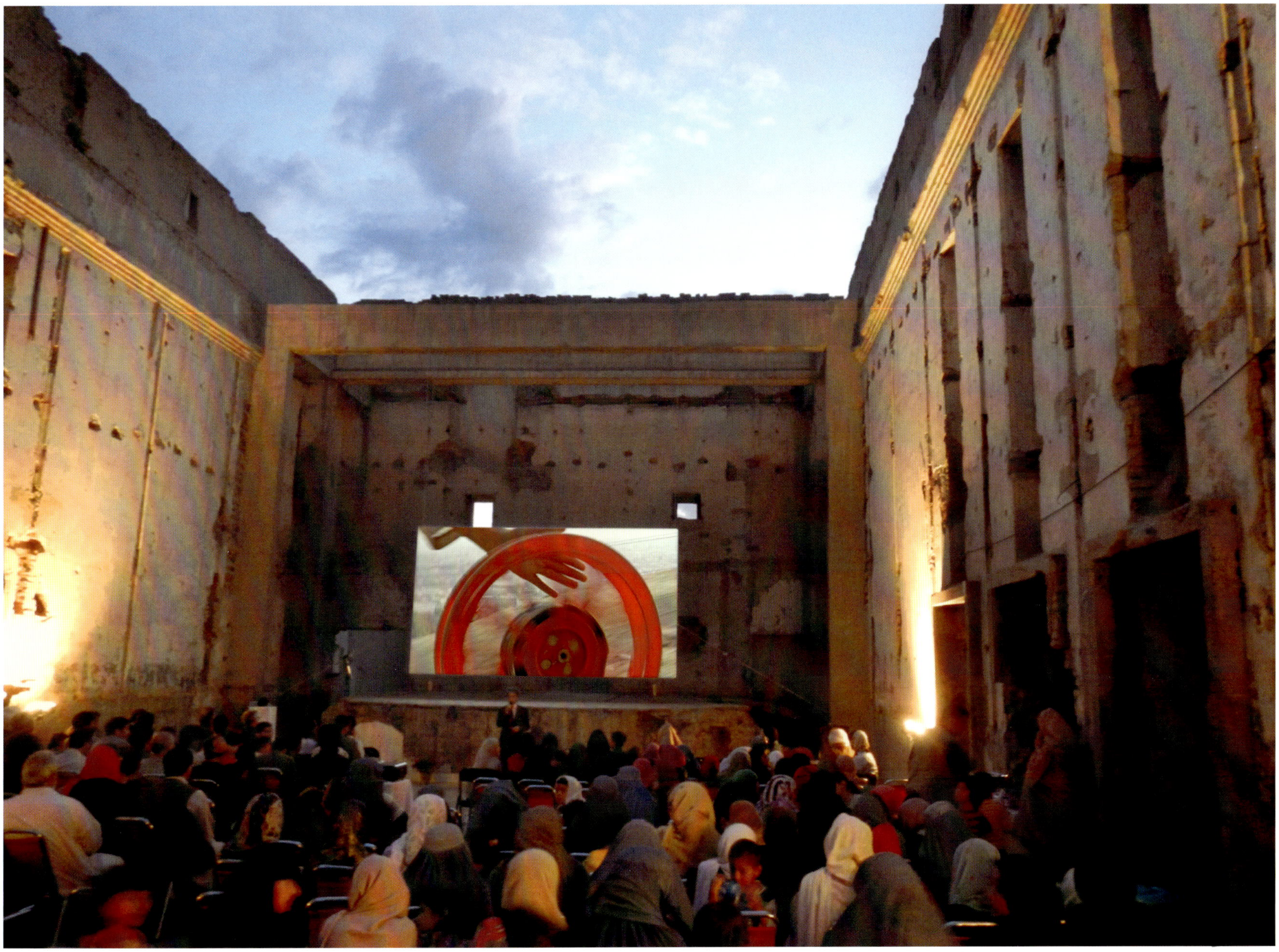

When I draw, I let my mind wander: my drawings don't bear any responsibility but my own. They help me processing the intentions behind a new project and explore its potential along its anarchic coming-to-life. But it can also be a way of making contact when I travel. During the embed with the British army in Helmand province, I drew compulsively. The activity of drawing created a situation opposite to that of filming: in the presence of the camera, the soldiers would shy away from me. But when I drew, they would furtively go around my back to look over my shoulders. And they'd start making comments on the scene I was depicting, especially if I was drawing one of their comrades. A conversation of sorts could be engaged.

What do I search for when I look at these images later on? Not so much the information the actual image gives me. What I search is the memory of how I was when I did them, what was I wearing, how was I feeling, how had my persona been perceived by the people of the scene depicted; where it is that I was at that very moment of my life? They may belong to the past but whenever I look at them they are totally in the present.

AFGHAN NOTEBOOKS, 2010–14

1943,
I think about Morandi painting on top of a hill surrounded by fascism,
I think about Marinetti returning sick from the Russian Front,
I think about Duchamp playing chess in his New York apartment,
I think about Ronald Searle POW in the Kwai jungle,
I think about Ensor playing harmonium during the bombardments of Ostend,
I think about Otto Dix watching his works being destroyed by the Nazis,
I think about Dali, Ernst and Breton re-united by their New York exile,
I think about Magritte painting Fantômas walking over Paris,
I think about Picabia finding inspiration in soft porn magazines on the Côte d'Azur,
I think about Derain much courted by the Nazis in Paris,
I think about Tatlin observing bird flights in his garden in Moscow,
I think about Beuys flying his Stuka dive-bomber over Crimea,
I think about Jacob Lawrence painting on a Coast Guard vessel,
I think about de Chirico hiding his self-falsifications under his bed,
I think about Matisse 'painting with scissors' on the French Riviera,
I think about Beckett joining the Resistance in occupied France,
I think about Soutine dying from an ulcer while escaping the Gestapo in Paris,
I think about Grosz repudiating his past from his new home in Long Island,
I think about Mondrian painting *Broadway Boogie-Woogie*,
I think about Lee Miller photographing English women driving tractors,
I think about Kandinsky in Paris ceasing to write,
I think about Paul Nash once again War Artist for the British Army,
I think about St Exupéry finalizing *Le Petit Prince* in New York,
I think about Leni Riefenstahl filming Tiefland with extras from concentration camps,
I think about Schlemmer forbidden to paint and dying in Baden-Baden,
I think about Picasso making a sculpture out of a bicycle in occupied Paris,
I think about Hannah Höch painting the Totentanz triptych in Nazi Germany,
I think about Camille Claudel dying forgotten in the asylum of Montdevergues,
I think about Siqueiros publishing *In War Art of War* from his Cuban exile,
I think about Emil Nolde painting 'unpainted pictures' in Seebüll,
I think about Schwitters in Norway learning that his *Merzbau* had been destroyed,
I think about Cartier-Bresson escaping from a German labour camp,
I think about Blinky Palermo born in the rubbles of Leipzig

UNTITLED (KABUL, AFGHANISTAN), 2010
OIL AND COLLAGE ON CANVAS
13 X 18 CM

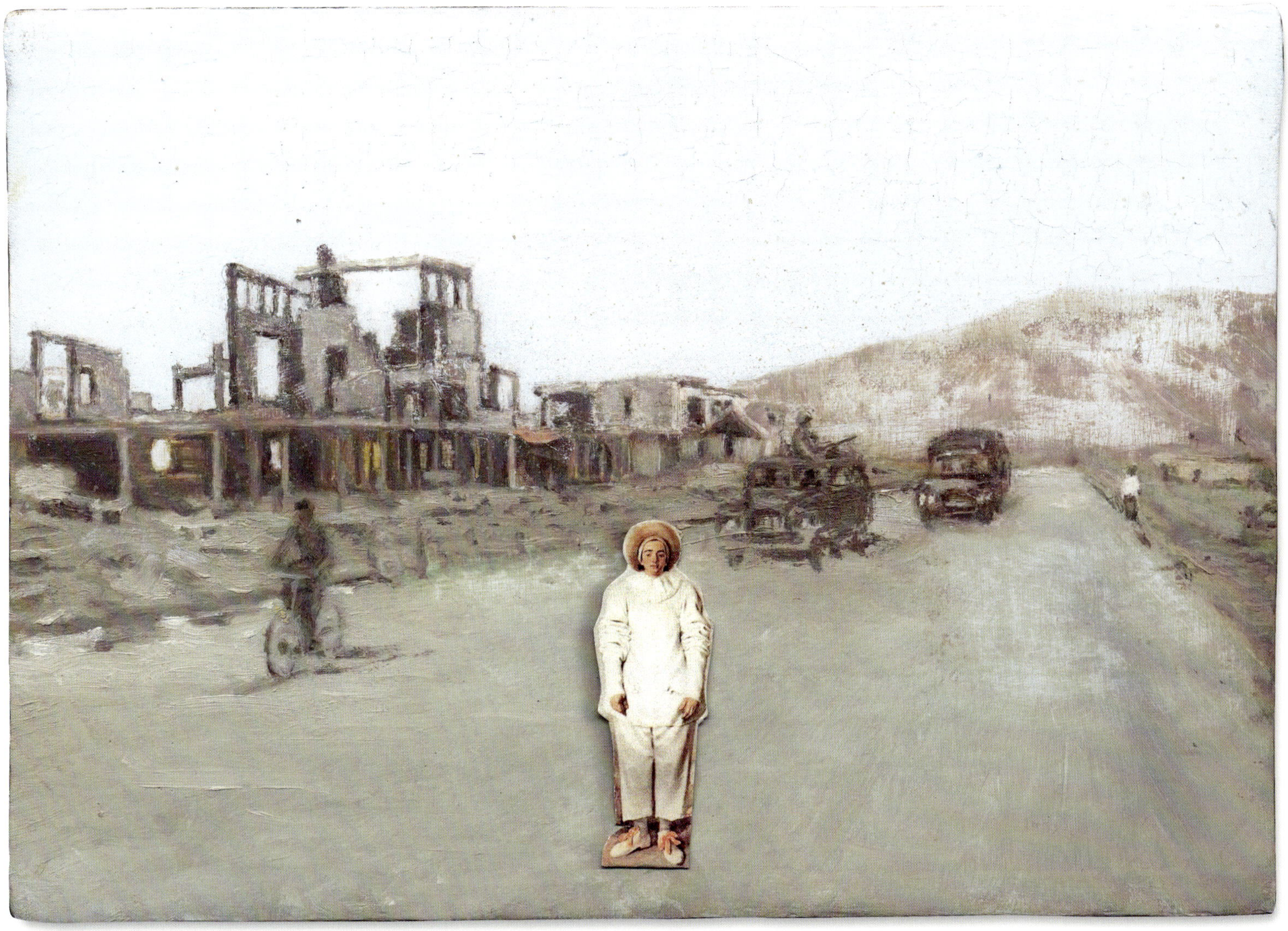

I arrived in Iraq on 28 October 2016. My intention was to document the displacements of population provoked by the Mosul offensive against ISIS. Yet, for a combination of circumstances, I instead found myself dropped somewhere along the fourteen-mile Iraqi Kurdistan military Peshmerga's front line on the eastern flank of Mosul, with a small bag and no plan of action. At first, the stupefying reality of combat and the smell of terror nearby numbed me and frustrated any coherent creative process. However, as I had to somehow make contact with my Peshmerga guardian angels, drawing turned out to be a providential way of communicating, plus it gave me the illusion of being part of the scene. Images started filling my notebook and words soon followed.

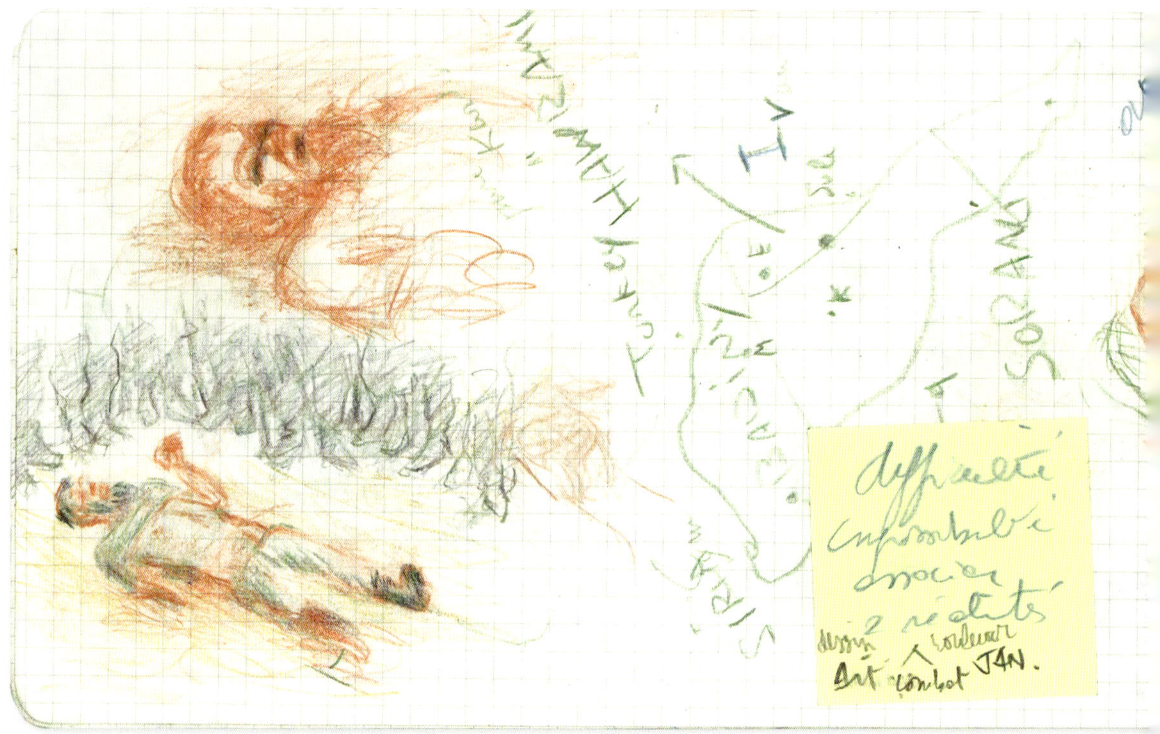

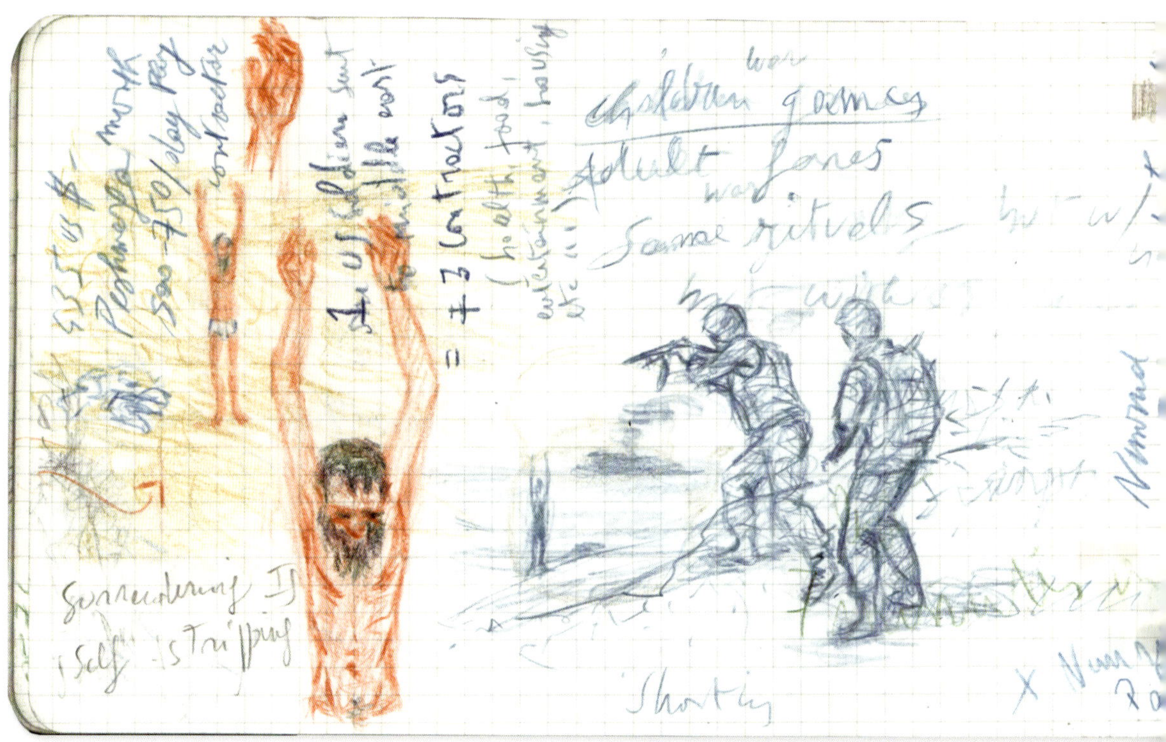

NOTEBOOK PESHMERGA EMBED, MOSUL, IRAQ, 2016
13 X 42 CM

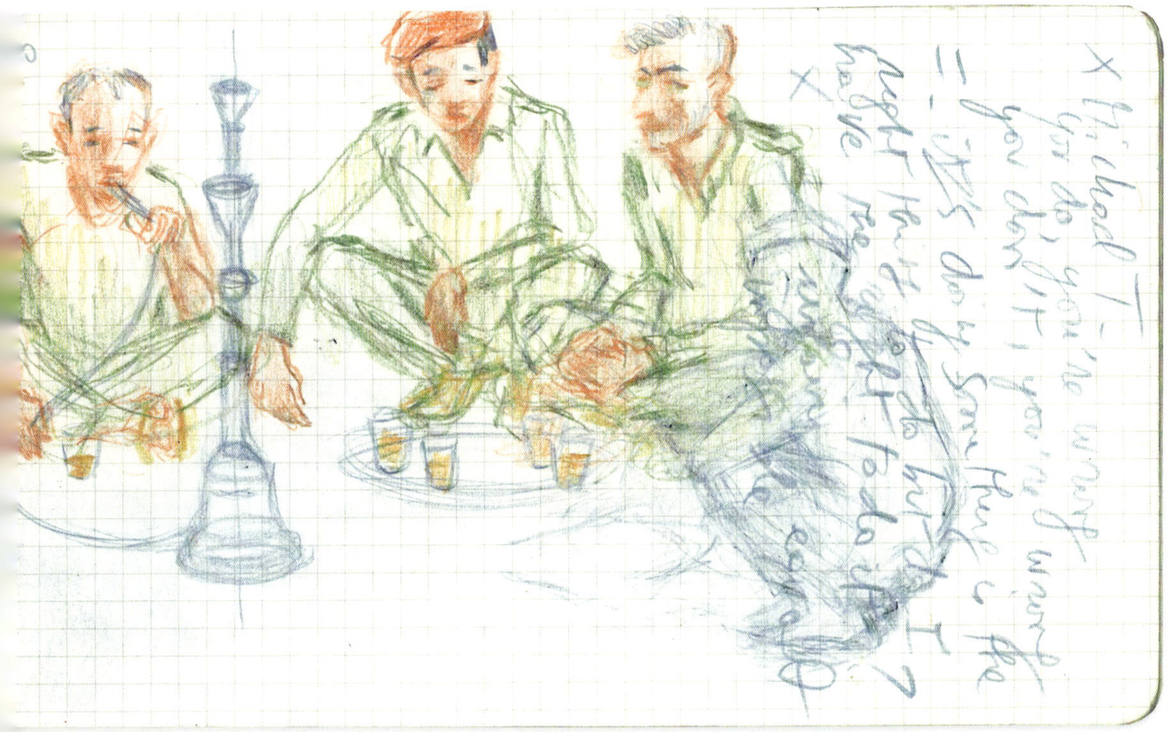

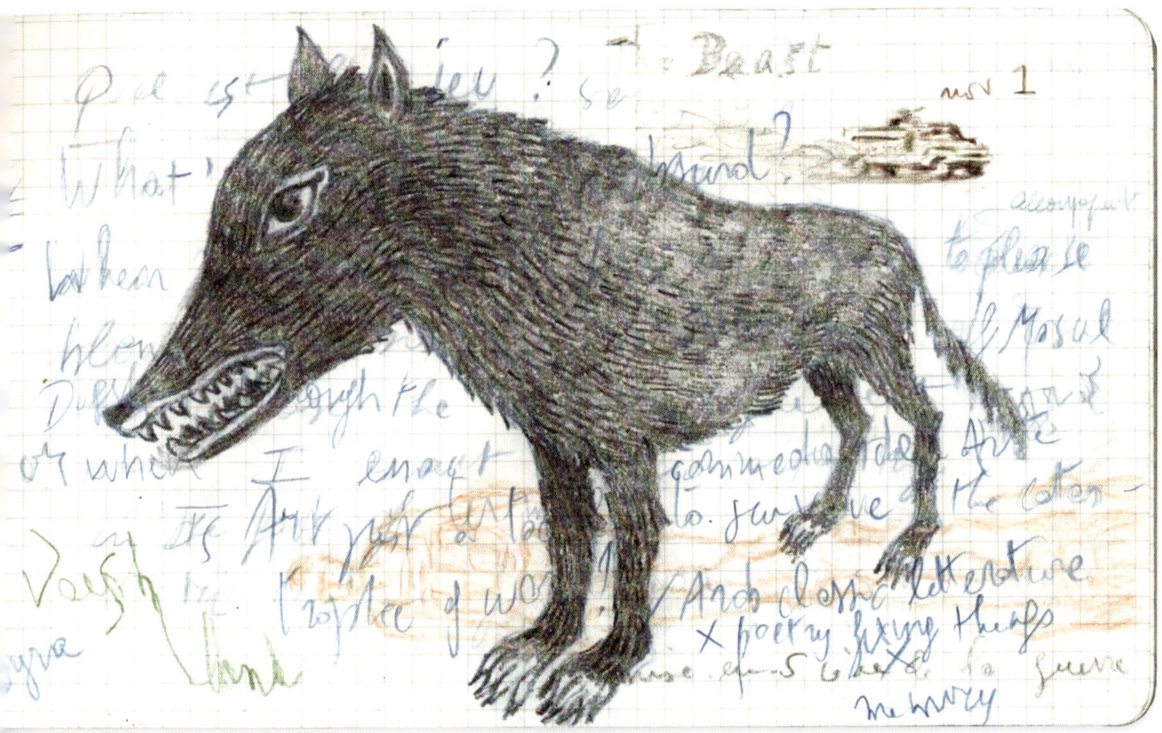

Saturday, 29 October 2016

Fighting the jetlag, breaking the ice, waiting for the subjects to forgive my presence. Early night/foreground soundtrack of mobile phones playing Arab rap with background music of the U.S.-led coalition bombardment.

Sunday, 30 October 2016

Earthworks. The Peshmerga offensive is a massive engineering enterprise, a monumental Land art operation. Behind each platoon there is a bulldozer waiting. Every hundred metres of gained territory results in hundreds of tons of dry earth pushed forward in order to move the front line ever closer to the suburbs of Mosul. Landscape is refashioned daily by the shelling, ISIS's tunnels are behind, under, and beyond our mobile front line; the dunes are scarred by the infinite lines of trenches while on the Syrian-Iraqi border ISIS's bulldozers breach a passage through a hill to erase the Sykes-Picot Agreement's fatal design. The desert is no longer an exotic escape. It's pure naked exposure. The closest to protection from the snipers is by running from one shadow to another.

4.00 PM – While we were driving from one FOB to another, a yellow sand storm passed over the narrow strip of land regained by the Peshmerga deep into ISIS territory. We couldn't see shit and weren't sure what side of the frontline we were driving on? As we passed the top of a sand dune the driver made a steep turn to avoid hitting a donkey that was standing in the middle of the road. It looked wounded and stared at us, haggard, as if it was trying to convey its utter incomprehension of this world. A thicker cloud of dust descended and we lost track of the earth path connecting the two bases. The two very young recruits accompanying me stopped talking but one look at their faces and I knew we were on the wrong side of the frontline. For the five long minutes it took us to eventually find our way back into Peshmerga territory, my sole reflex was to reach out my iPhone and film, focusing all my attention on the tiny screen, to fictionalize the moment, as if it was a movie.

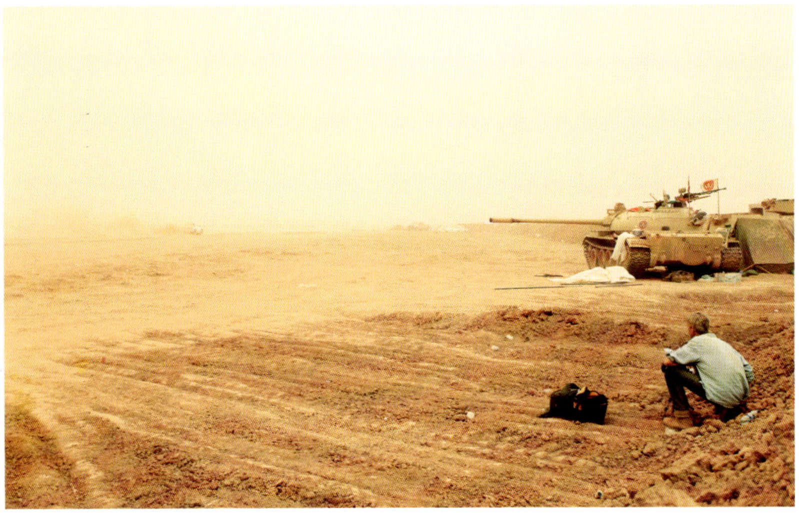

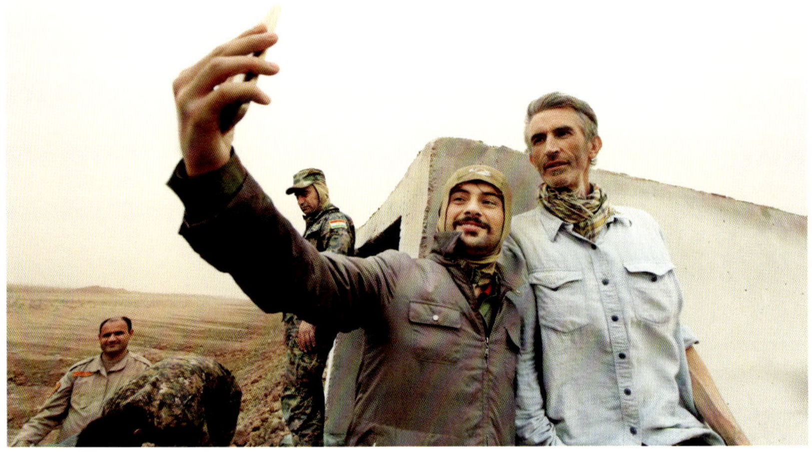

Tuesday, 1 November 2016

In an era when any insignificant event is instantly made public online – and governments are tapping millions of cell phones – how on earth is it possible that no intelligence whatsoever can tell us how many ISIS fighters are left in Mosul? There lies the power of terror.

Heard among the Peshmerga returning from a village they freed: 'This morning they were shooting at us; this afternoon they receive us with open arms, as if nothing had happened'.

Thinking of the Yazidi kids of the refugee camp near Dohuk I visited in February 2016. What can we tell to a child in the face of terror? In a child's imagination, what is the image of terror? How can one make sense of terror to a child? How can one integrate the unacceptable? Can a human tragedy be testified to by way of a fictional work?

Wednesday, 2 November 2016

In the midst of gunfire the rain caught us all by surprise. What could the ISIS fighters possibly make of the rain? Strangely it brought us closer, we shared that moment. Did I film the rain?

Thursday, 3 November 2016

Second day of trying to match on small canvases the colours of the scenes I'm witnessing in an attempt to coincide with the moment I am living – this is the abstraction of war within the spectacle of combat. Meanwhile, I watch a Peshmerga rushing to take a selfie on the background of an exploding rocket. The smiles of this war will be well kept in cell phones, in between photos of sweethearts and motorcycles. What happens in Mosul stays in Mosul.

UNTITLED (MOSUL, IRAQ), 2016
OIL ON LINEN
19 X 14 CM

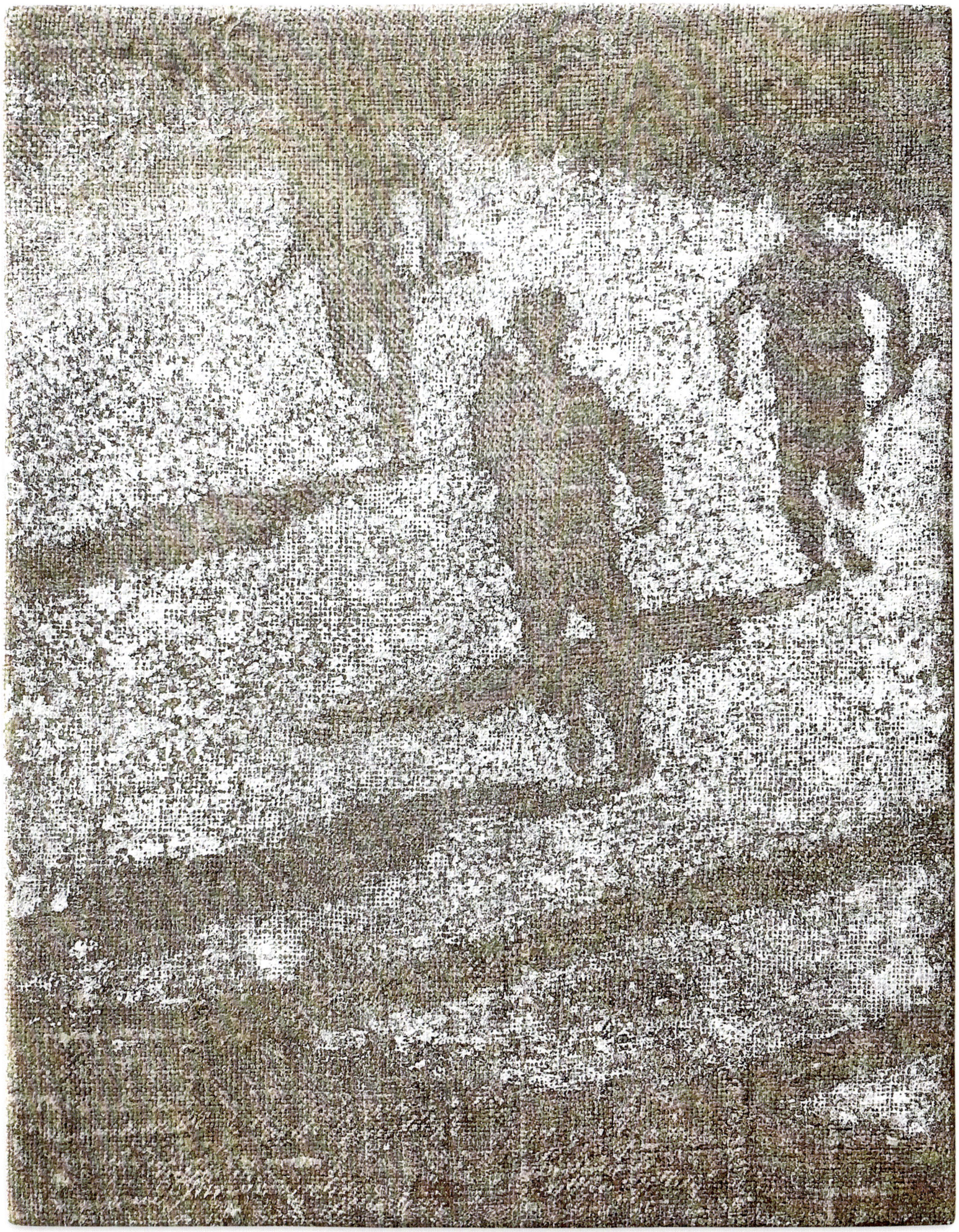

UNTITLED (MOSUL, IRAQ), 2016
OIL ON LINEN
19 X 14 CM

UNTITLED (MOSUL, IRAQ), 2016
OIL ON LINEN
14 X 19 CM

UNTITLED (MOSUL, IRAQ), 2016
OIL ON LINEN
14 X 19 CM

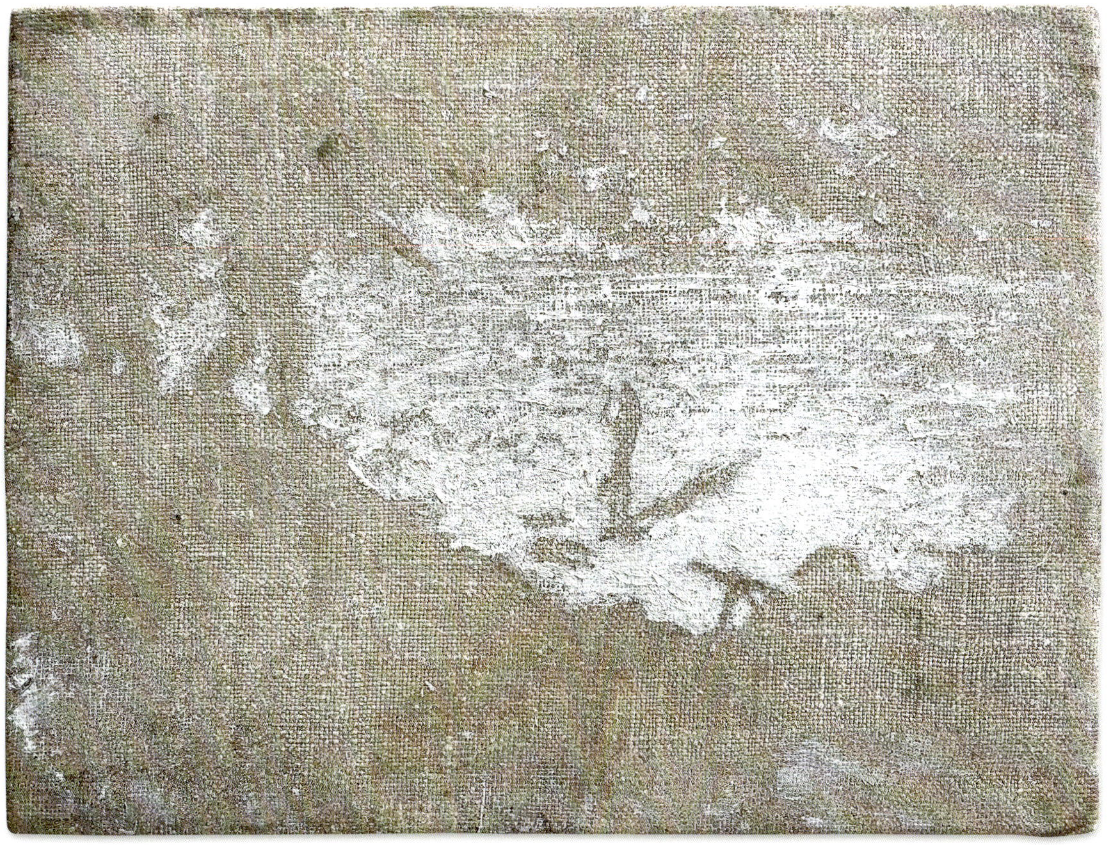

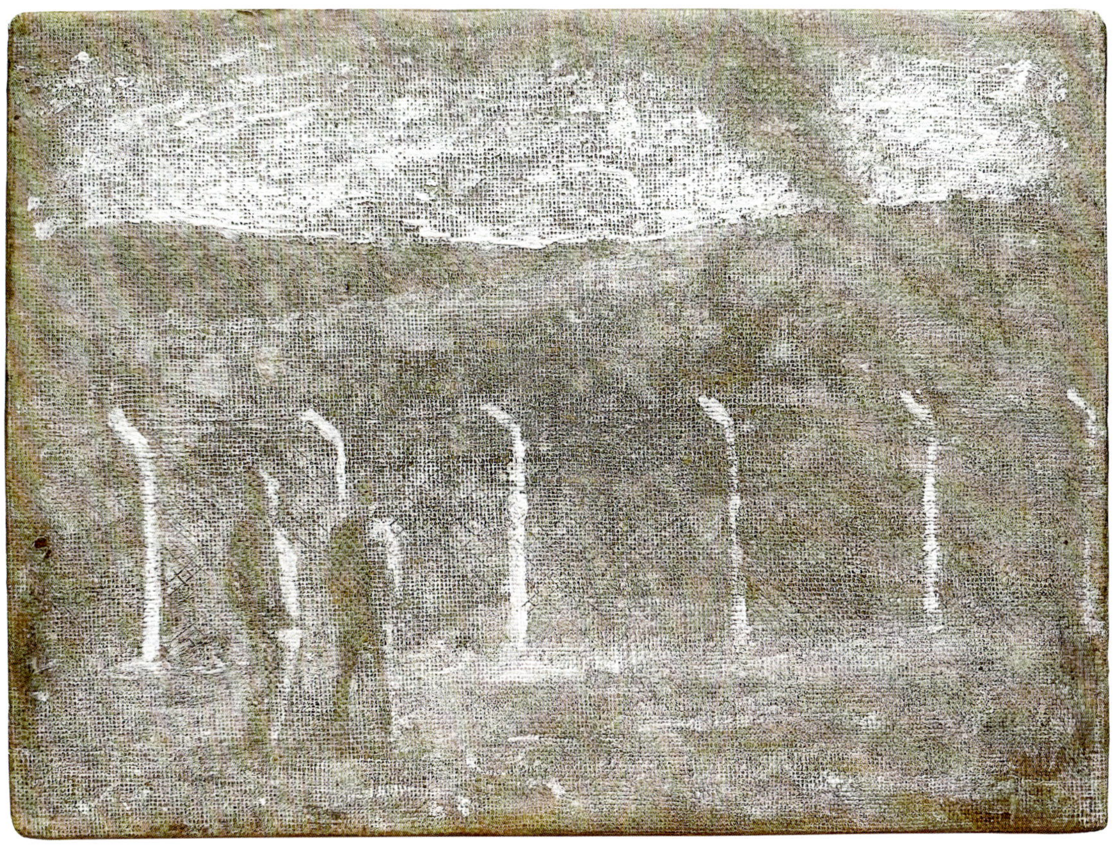

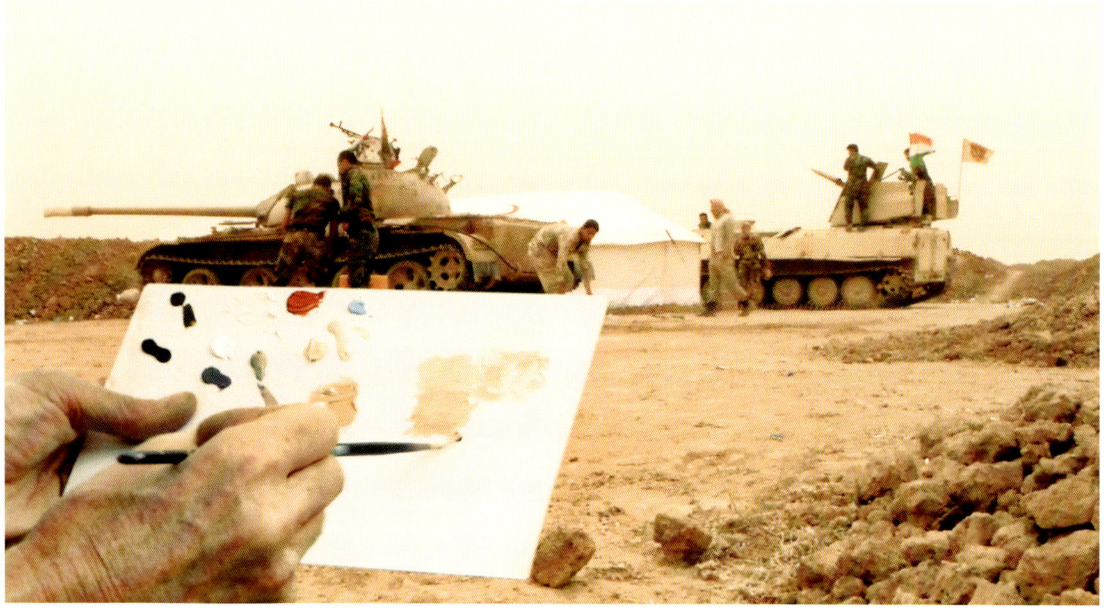

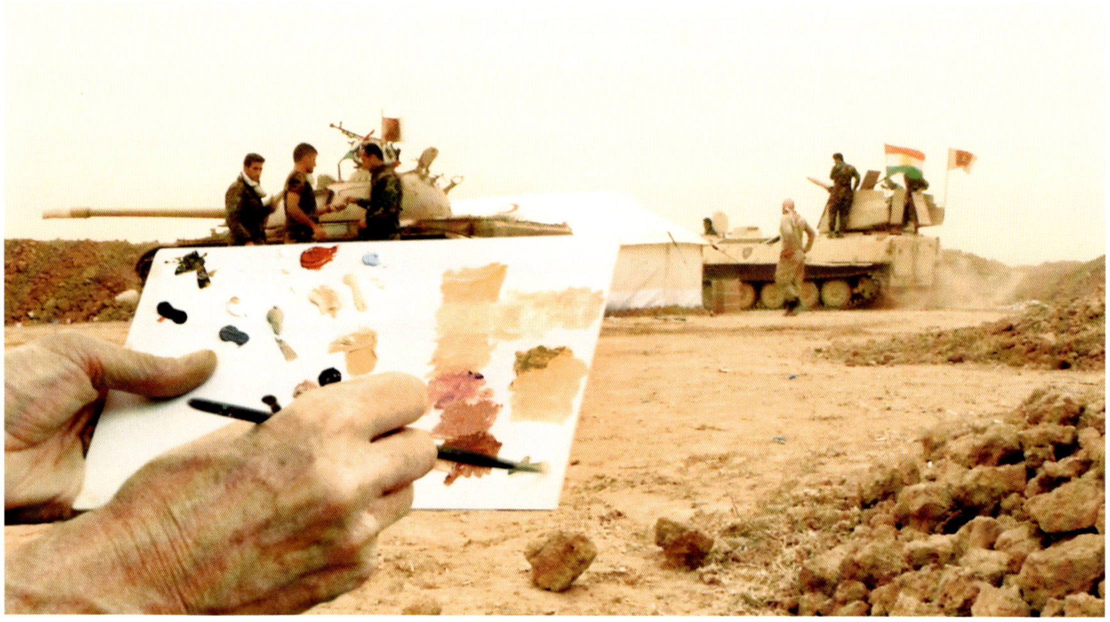

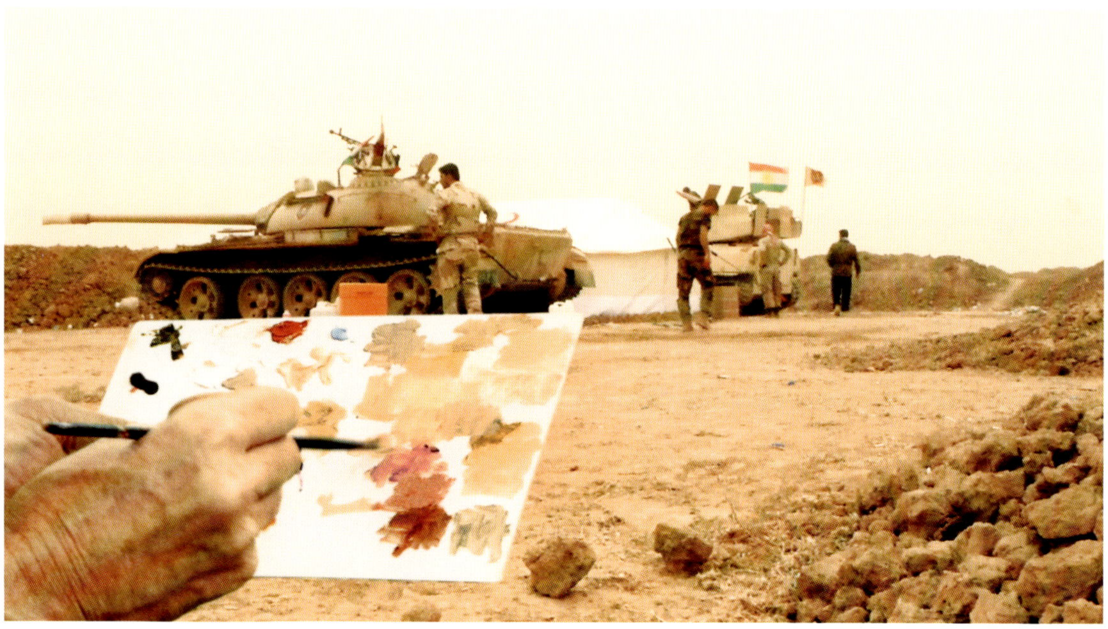

COLOR MATCHING, 2016
VIDEO DOCUMENTATION OF AN ACTION
MOSUL-IRAQ, OCTOBER
4 MIN. 56 SEC.

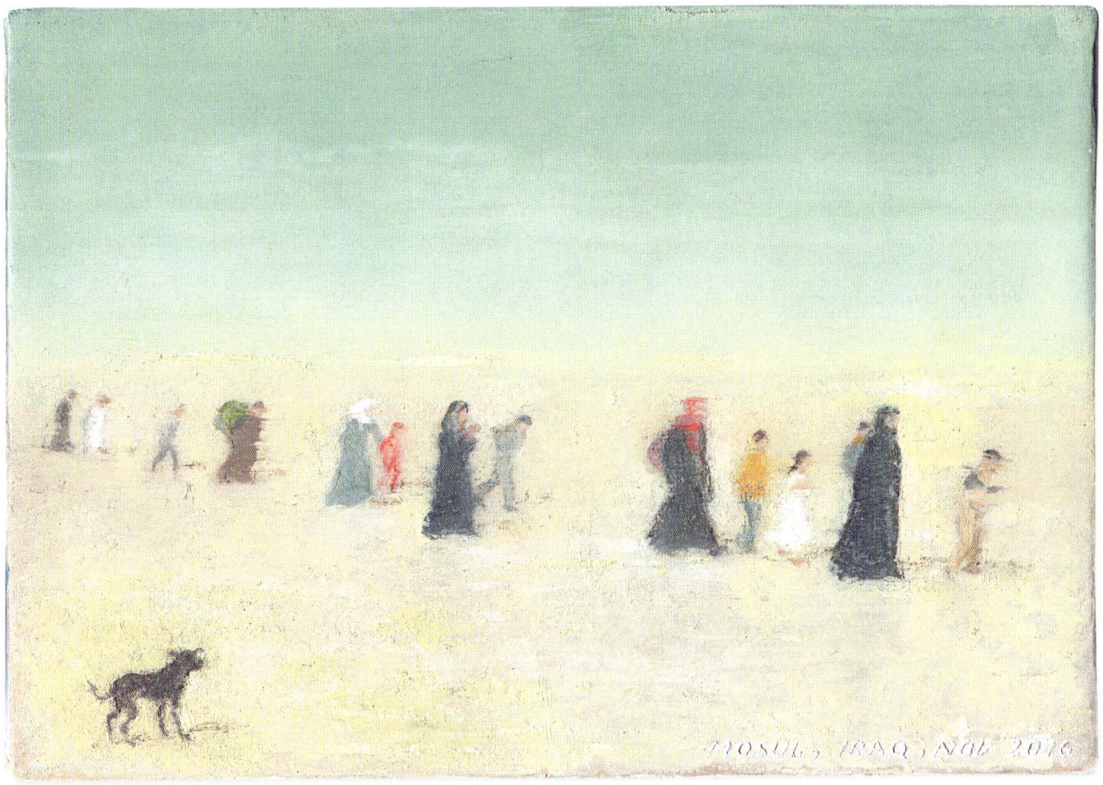

UNTITLED (MOSUL, IRAQ), 2016
OIL ON CANVAS
14 X 19 CM

The Mosul offensive is like the making of a movie: ninety percent waiting, ten percent action. With tea and Turkish biscuits served in the intermezzo.

The disturbing beauty of the white flags waved on the Mosul rooftops against the sky blacked out by the smoke of the bombings. …

…Beauty? A few months earlier, in the market of Baghdad, we came across an elegant man playing a cello. This was soon after a suicide bombing had destroyed a significant part of the market and Kalim Wasfi wanted to play a Bach sonata in the rubbles to 'oppose beauty to the nihilism of terror'. The issue of beauty was brought up again during a talk I gave the next day at the Ruya Foundation, several members of the assistance asking me – if I was to do a film in Iraq – to present also a 'beautiful image' of their country. Their desire was not coming from some banal national pride; it was the manifestation of a genuine desire to abstract oneself from the ambient horror, to oppose eternal values to the precariousness of daily life.

In the absence of language, I miss the way in which talking helps to materialize an idea.

Furat (Iraqi friend filmmaker), referring to European ISIS volunteers: 'The young Europeans did not live a war. All they know is through video games. They come here because they live war as a fiction.'

Figures

50,000 euros = classic bomb GBU-US
200,000 euros = missile AASM
600,000 euros = cruise missile SCALP
500 to 750 USD = daily pay of a private security contractor in Iraq
435 USD = monthly pay of a Peshmerga fighter

The disturbing beauty of counter-light explosions at dusk.

Friday, 4 November 2016

Quel est l'enjeu? What's more absurd? When the Big Friendly General fires his cannon towards the suburbs of Mosul to entertain the press, or when I play my *Commedia dell'arte* in the face of terror? What does it mean to make art while Nimrud and Palmyra are being destroyed? If ISIS's logic is 'destroy to exist', does it mean we ought to create in order to survive? Is art just a means of survival through the catastrophe of war? Do we live because we narrate? In classic Arab literature, poetry fixes things and fractures parts of the past from the present. Within a situation of continuous conflict, does memory allow us to reinvent/reset ourselves and escape the vicious circle in which violence calls for more violence? 'It's not about turning your back, it's about how you turn your back'. (Elias Khoury, Beirut, November 2015)

I against my brothers,
I and my brothers against my cousins,
I and my brothers and my cousins against the stranger.
(Arab saying)

Saturday, 5 November 2016

Symptomatology of Embedment: Intellectual and neurological arousal, all senses on alert / urge to register the moment no matter how / hyperactive mental space where the most disparate elements can be connected / acute 360 degrees perception / state of total submission to the events, I absorb them like a sponge / sleeping like a log in spite of the bombings.

Sunday, 6 November 2016

Lately I have found myself working more in locations going through a state of conflict. It's not a case of 'war journalism' but a chronicle of the tactics of survival when the system is no longer operative, when everything is uncertain. In such situations there is a moment of aperture, there is a call for creativity – a need for alternative proposals. It's more about adaptation than invention, some sort of intuitive initiative at the most. A bit like with tornadoes, where there is some form of order emerging out of chaos.

In his writings covering wars in Iraq, Afghanistan or Bosnia, Chris Hedges describes his encounters with roughly four types of 'witnesses':

- The anthropo-novelists in search of a situation where one can observe the 'human beast' naked, to witness first-hand the dark side of our nature.
- The adventurers in quest of self-exploration, self-escapism, thrill and wanderlust.
- The journalists in pursuit of a 'good story' whose meaning will transcend conflicts of religion, nationality and culture as it embraces all of them.
- And, last but not least, the group of war junkies getting off the adrenaline flying around?

Which category do I belong to? It probably comes down to the question: 'What is it that I'm best at at this point of my life?'

There is something peculiar about the times we live in, and with them, a different expectation of the artist's role. When the structure of a society collapses, when politicians and media have lost credit and terror invades daily life, society turns towards culture in pursuit of answers. The painter is expected to look at his or her reality without any filters; the writer is asked to produce stories that will help make sense of the madness going on; the musician is urged to transcend the present; the poet is invited to translate social tensions into verses. Even Hollywood actors are meant to have a cause! Yet, is the artist able to assume these roles from a moral, intellectual and emotional point of view? Artists have their own agendas and their own subjective view of facts. When does witnessing become denouncing? When does denouncing become accusing?

Is the artist's role to reveal the hidden reality of things without naming them, like Akram once told me? Or is our job just to open up a different perspective – rather than change the world, to challenge it?

Paradoxically, it sometimes takes the absurdity of the artistic operation to introduce a measure of meaning in a situation that seems to have stopped making any sense.

Reading over my notes… Is all the above relevant? Is it sincere? What am I doing writing if I chose to be a visual artist? Is it because in some situations taking notes is quicker than drawing? What's the part of self-exhibitionism and opportunism involved in this embed?

Back in Afghanistan, a friend told me: 'If you do, you're wrong; and if you don't do, you're wrong'. Otherwise said: Doing something is the right thing to do, but do I have the right to do it?

UNTITLED (MOSUL, IRAQ), 2016
DIPTYCH
PENCIL AND OIL ON CANVAS
EACH 15 X 19 CM

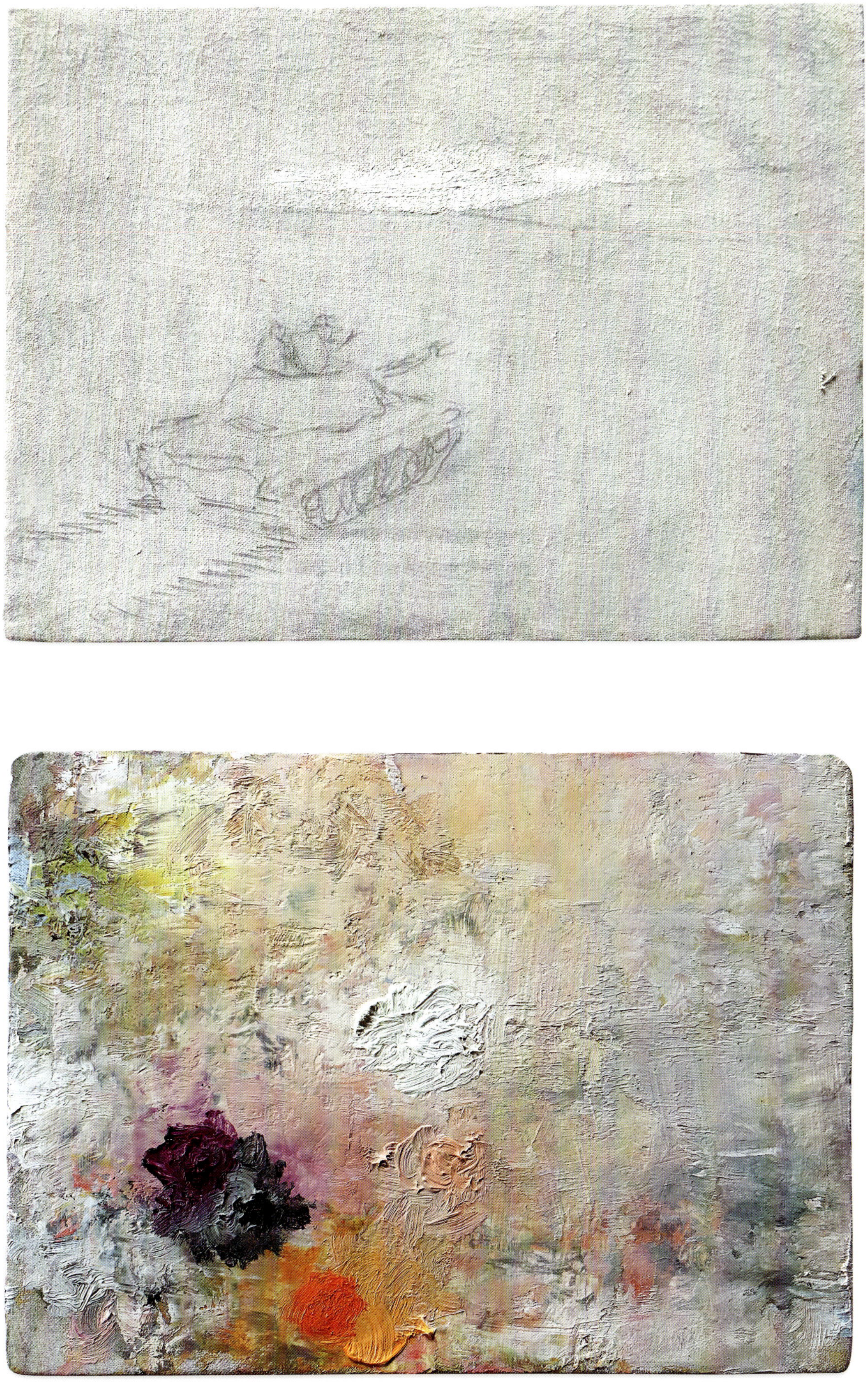

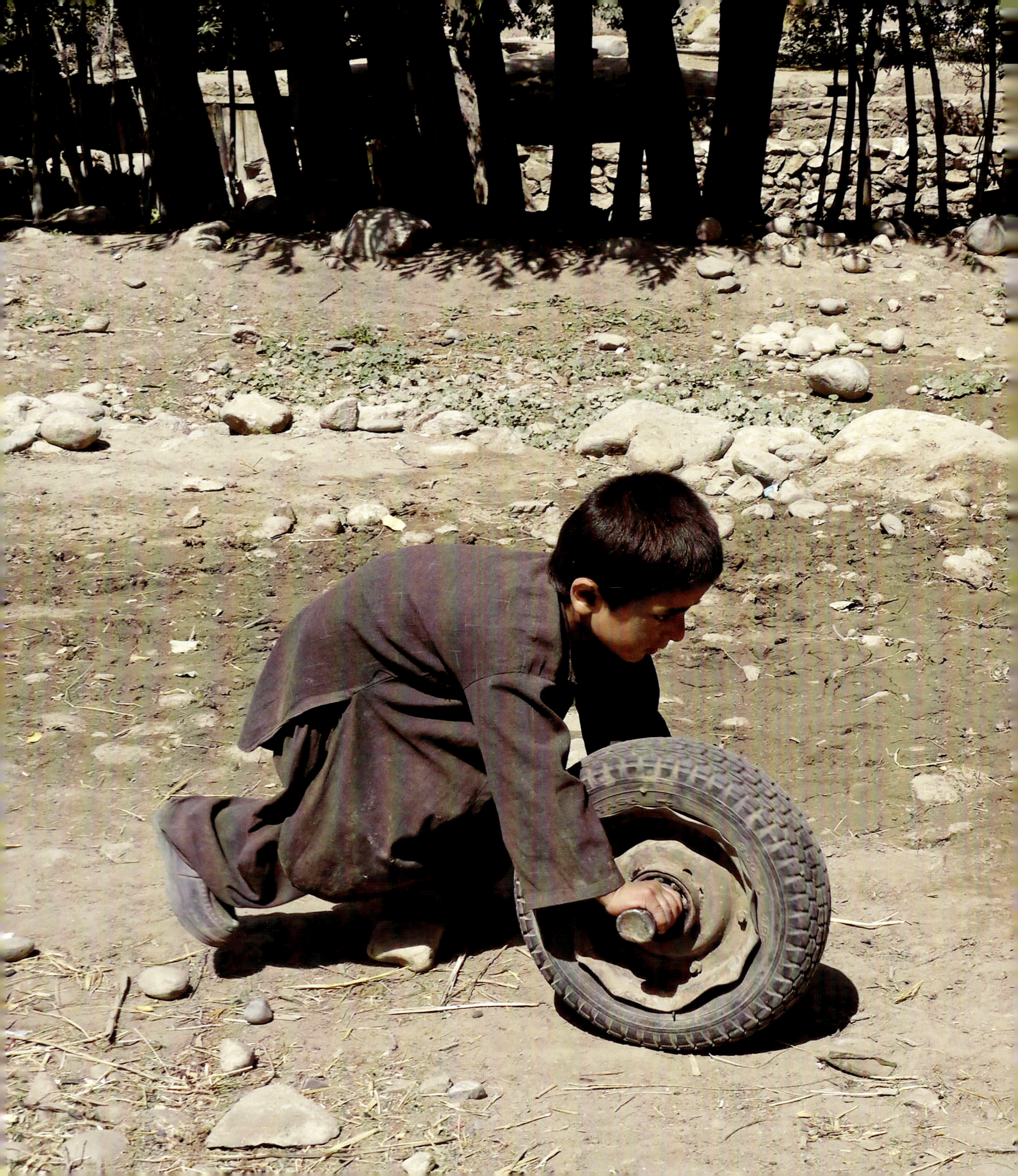

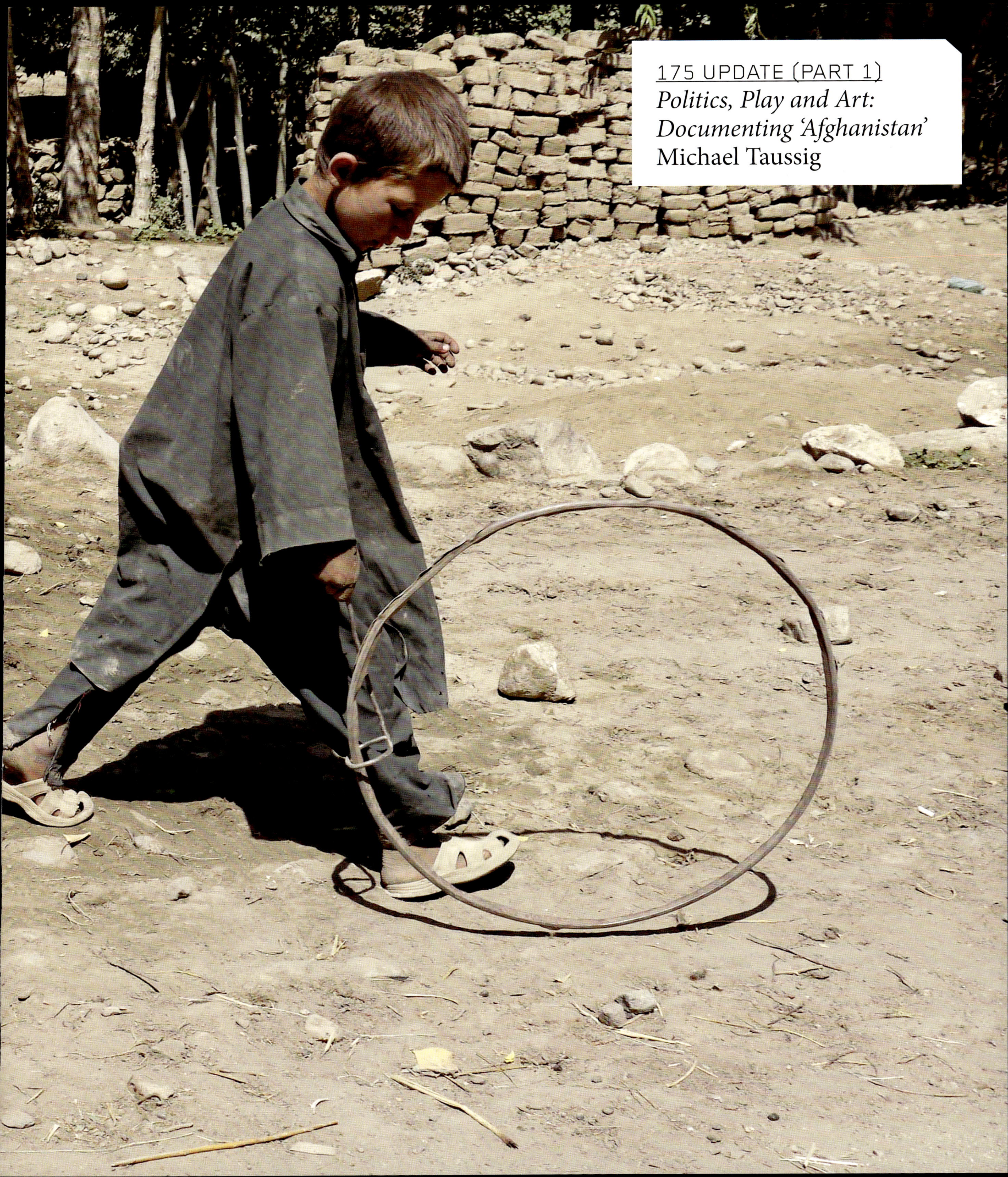

175 UPDATE (PART 1)

Politics, Play and Art: Documenting 'Afghanistan'

Michael Taussig

In Kabul with Francis Alÿs during early June 2010, I slept in a luxury hotel behind massive concrete bunkers and every time I entered it, I had to suffer five pat-downs by security guards. They looked at me as a potential suicide bomber and I looked at them the same way. They could act mean and they could act efficient better than professional actors. It was a game we played, many times a day, just to get in and get out, never knowing whom to trust.

I played a game of badminton out on the lawn there with young Tom Francis, but after a few tries was mystified and frightened to learn that I could not coordinate my body. Every time I threw the shuttlecock in the air to serve, I missed it, and with that I realized that I was missing an awful lot of other things as well, not so much about Afghanistan and the wars there as how to come to grips with that, meaning in the first instance how to frame it and talk about it, how to 'serve' it.

'Very disorganized', pouted the German ambassador after his fourth attempt to get a cup of iced mint tea in our bunkered luxury hotel. He might have been referring to the Western presence in Afghanistan. Was he also referring to what he perceived as our foolish mission 'making art' in Afghanistan?

After all, anyone with the slightest acumen knew that there was no way out of the hopelessly routinized way the West talked to itself about Afghanistan, moving the pieces around the same old chess board that had been used for Iraq and many countries before that. In his novel *Kim* (1901), Rudyard Kipling referred to this stretch of territory as subject to the Great Game between super powers, and you really had to wonder if we were not inside a variant of that same game, with three men slugging it out – Bin Laden, Bush and Cheney – collapsing world-historical forces into a grotesque puppetry of good and evil, where billions of dollars were at stake, especially for Cheney's old outfit Haliburton. Everyone sensed this, but in the chaos of mixed motives, secrecy, deceit, short-term necessities and games concealing other games, the more you tried to figure it out, the more it slipped through your fingers. Truth was a grey mist of rumour, guerrilla tactics and entangled bureaucracy, made mistier still by the 'certainties' propounded daily by the experts. Truth was make-believe. All 'very disorganized', that's for sure, something that Alÿs, with that great calm he exudes, must have felt during his eight trips to Afghanistan since 2010 to make art.

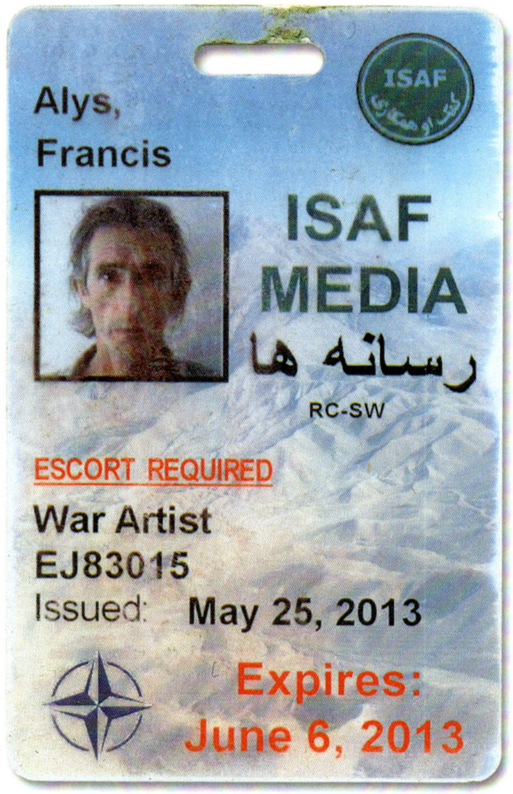

ADRENALINOTOURISM, 2013
HELMAND PROVINCE, AFGHANISTAN

Adrenaline is arguably the oldest psychedelic drug known to mankind.

During the Spring of 2013 I was embedded in Afghanistan as war artist with UK Task Force Helmand. By intentionally engaging in a hazardous situation I wanted to investigate if exposure to danger would alter my senses and produce a different response in the field of representation.

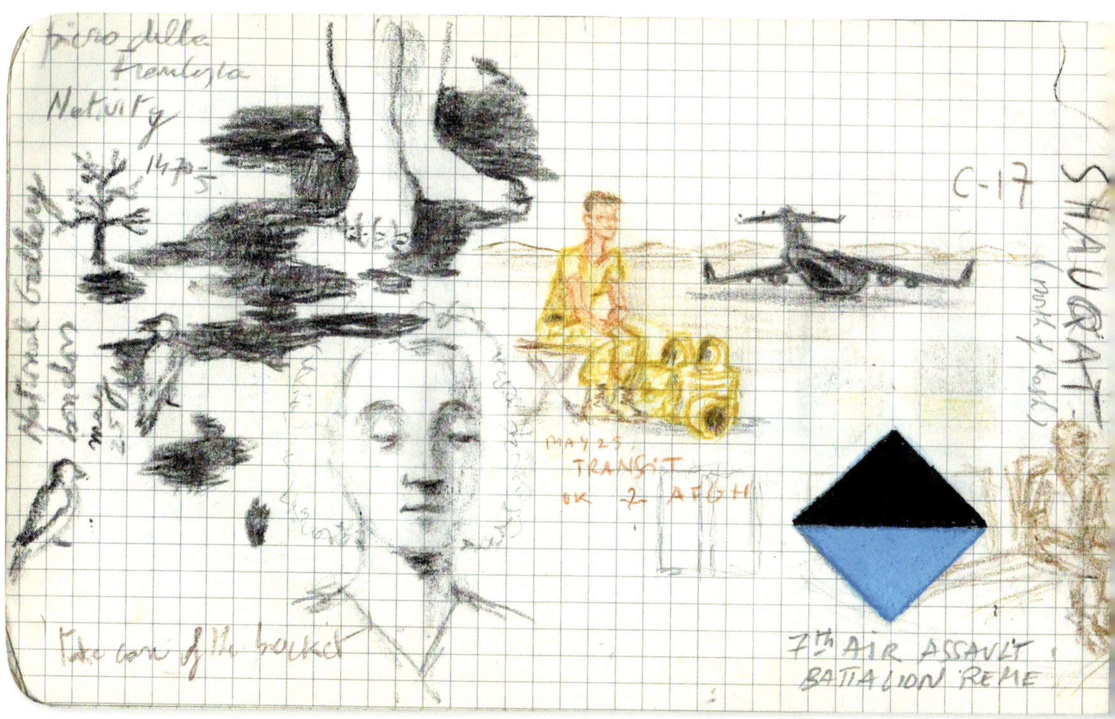

NOTEBOOK EMBEDDED TASK FORCE HELMAND, AFGHANISTAN, 2013
13 X 42 CM

opposite,
STUDY FOR REEL-UNREEL, AFGHANISTAN, 2011–12
OIL AND COLLAGE ON CANVAS
13 X 18 CM

previous pages,
YAMGUN, AFGHANISTAN, 2011

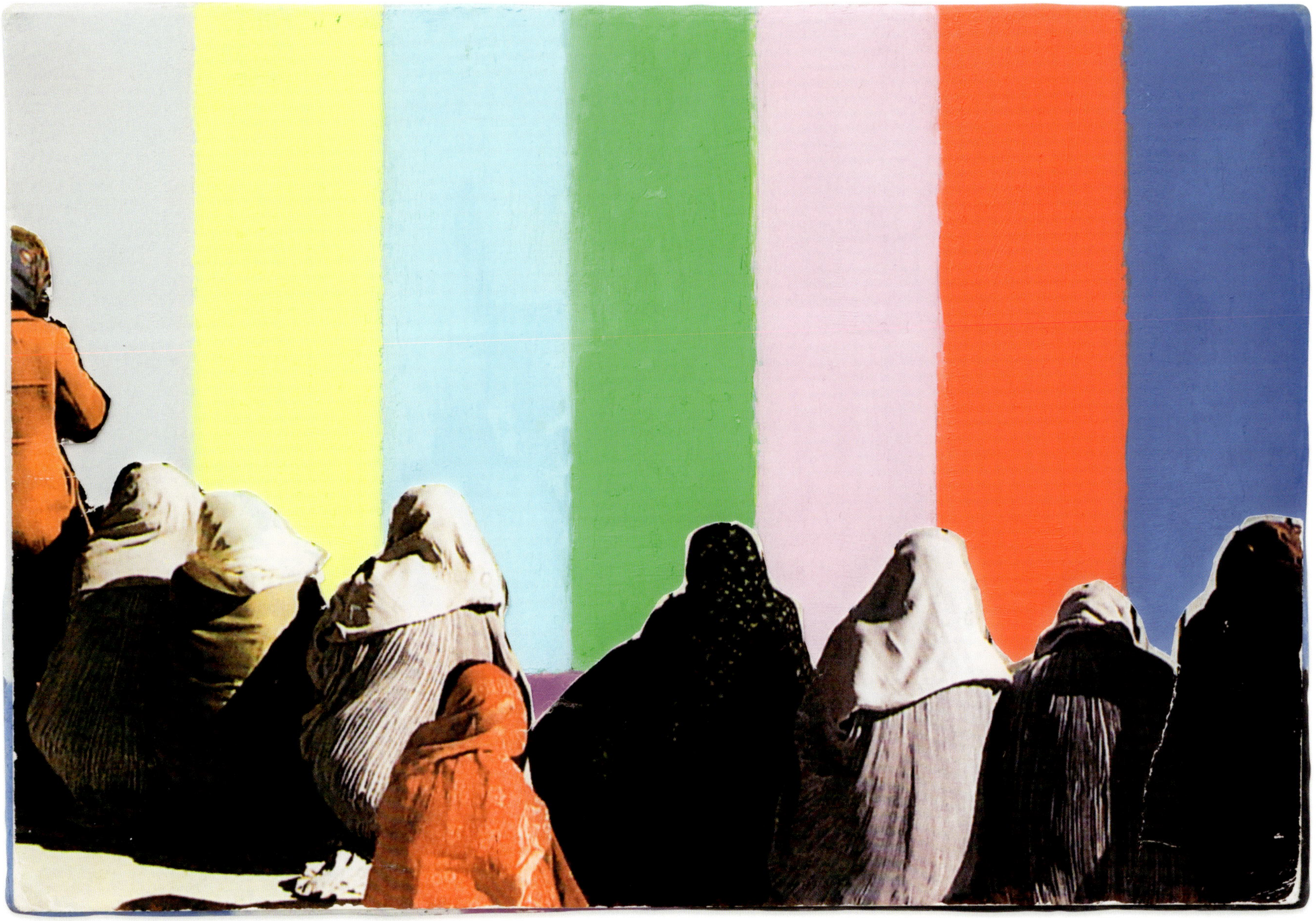

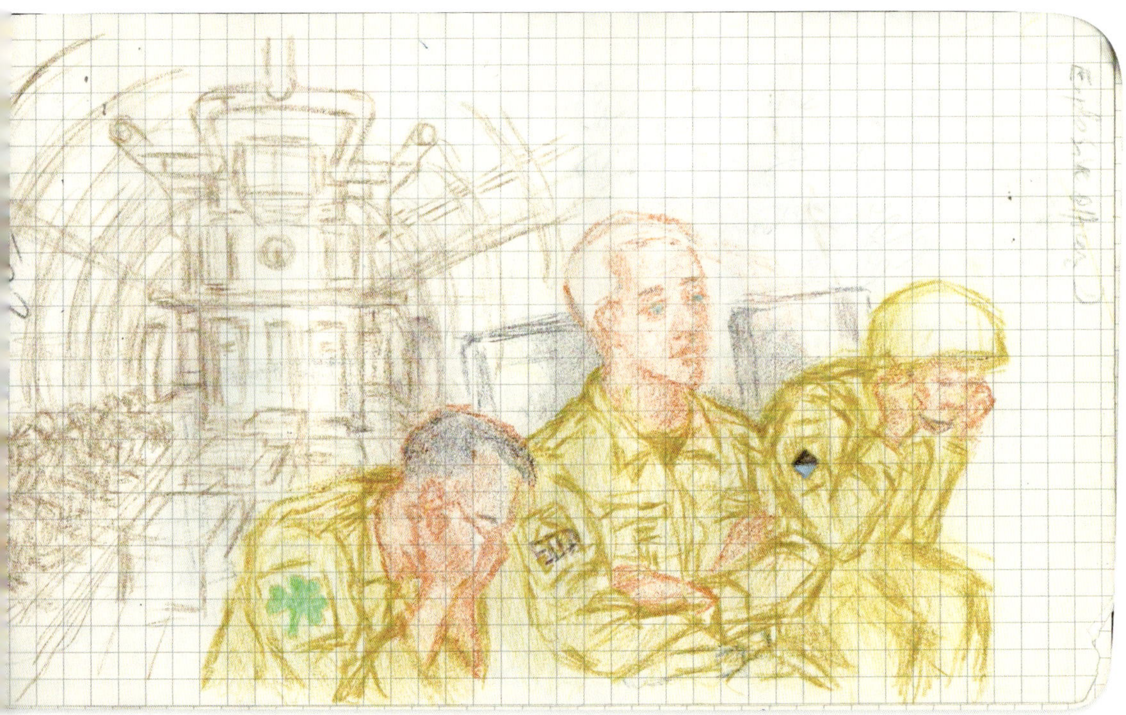

UNTITLED (FOB SPARTA, AFGHANISTAN), 2013
OIL AND COLLAGE ON CANVAS
13 X 18 CM

UNTITLED (PANJSHIR, AFGHANISTAN), 2012
OIL ON CANVAS
13 X 18 CM

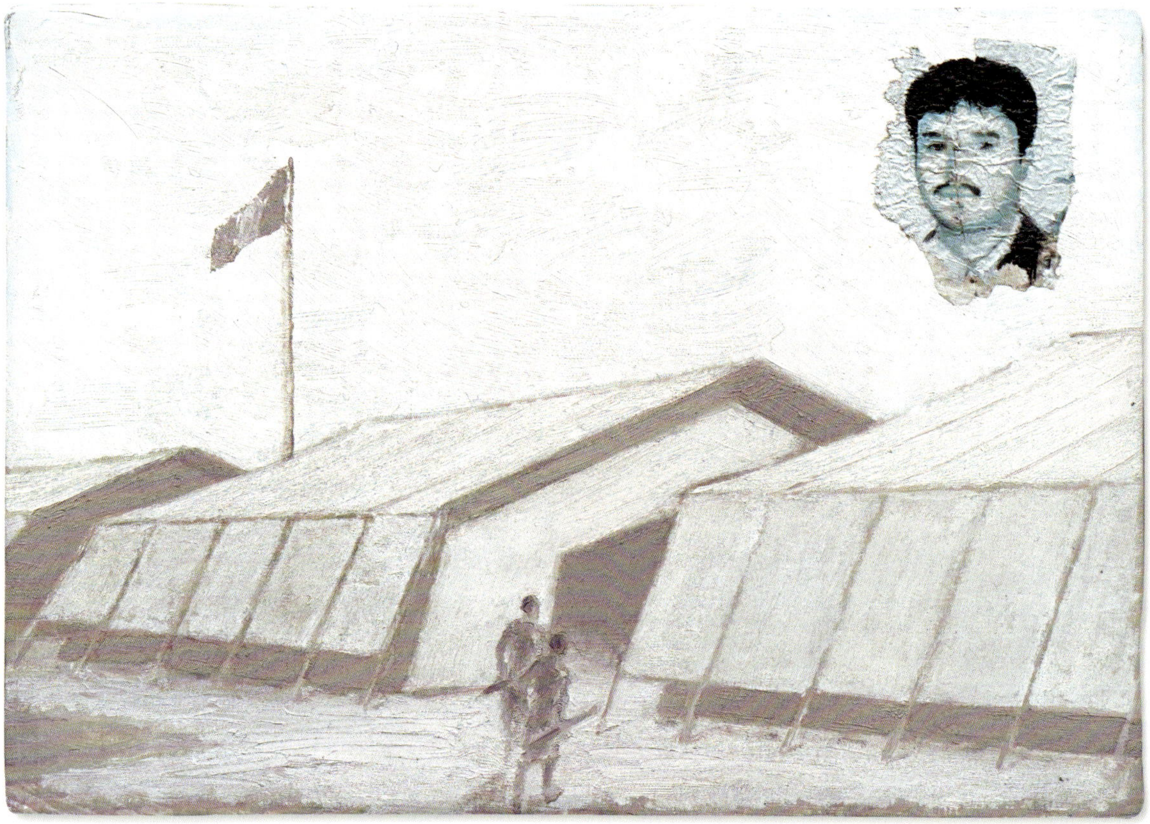

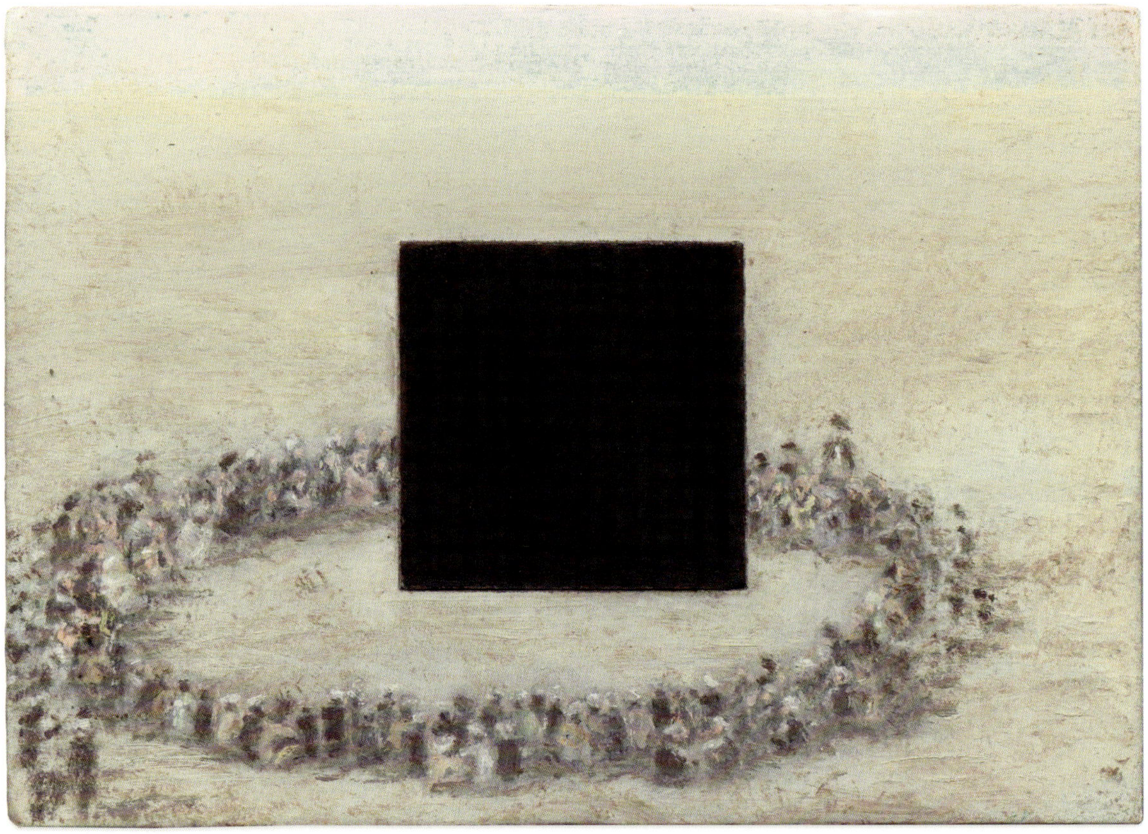

UNTITLED (4TH BATTALION PARACHUTE REGIMENT TACTICAL RECOGNITION FLASH), AFGHANISTAN, 2014
ENCAUSTIC AND OIL ON CANVAS
23 X 23 CM

In this situation, 'making art', such as his *Reel-Unreel* and *Color Bars,* suggests a way out of the game. Both of these works are about games, too, if not games themselves. The first is about two kids racing through the streets of Kabul using film reels as hoops; the other is about the game armies love to play with stripes of colour, as with medals, and in this case, with the blazons that troops wear on their upper sleeve, ostensibly for identification but also, surely, to ward off evil spirits.

But first, to gain a sense of what's required to get in close enough to make such art, think of how foreign journalists work in this situation of danger and fluid boundaries. They need a 'fixer', someone who speaks English as well as a couple of Afghani languages and has, as they say, 'connections'. In 2010, I was told a good fixer cost 150–250 USD a day, 1,000 for an interview with a Talib. A somewhat unsettling term, 'fixer' hovers between a cluster of words like translator, prostitute, pimp, sleuth and anthropologist. It is a highly risky occupation. But then, so is being a foreign journalist and photographer. The journalists I met were usually young, under twenty-five, stunningly smart, not yet jaded, still overcome by the enormity of it all, and great risk-takers. So I could never understand why the material published by their editors back in London or New York always sounded the same, no matter who wrote it or what it was about, a regular sausage machine with a dash of 'human interest', like death and torture, thrown in.

There was a pale, slender woman wearing a blue chador down to her ankles, her face largely uncovered, waiting on the tarmac at Herat on the Iranian border for the flight to Kabul. She was a Dutch journalist on her way to cover the assembly of (all male) tribal elders on 3 June, the rumour being that Kabul was going to be attacked by some Taliban-instigated suicide bombers. 'Boring', she said, referring to these assemblies. She wore the face of a saint, the grace, too. Her eyes were tired. She had been on the beat for years: Cambodia, East Timor, Iraq and now Afghanistan. 'Iraq fatigue', she explained, was what was preventing the translation of her book on Baghdad into English. This trip started three months ago. In her chador she looked at home here. In Herat she was researching the suicide in 2003 of a woman writer. She worked for the Dutch weeklies, she told me, describing her work as 'slow journalism', which I guess evaded the worst of the sausage machine, as Michael Herr had been able to do, writing on the war in Vietnam at his own pace for *Esquire* magazine in the 1960s. His book *Dispatches* is generally considered one of the finest, if not the best, book on that war from the viewpoint of the American soldier. Fredric Jameson wrote that it changed our very language. It is hard to imagine that happening today. The soul has been sucked out of representation. Not even irony and cynicism can get a toehold.

Which brings us to art – or 'Art', as James Agee, that untamed genius of *Let Us Now Praise Famous Men*, would have put it – 'Art' being something he abhorred in the writing and photography of the poor when he accepted a commission to report on the condition of white share-croppers in Alabama in the 1930s. On one of his eight trips, Alÿs was 'embedded' for fifteen days

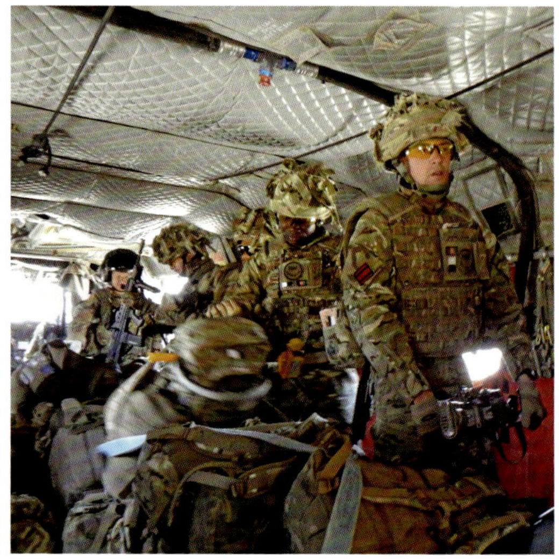

EMBEDDED HELMAND PROVINCE, 2013

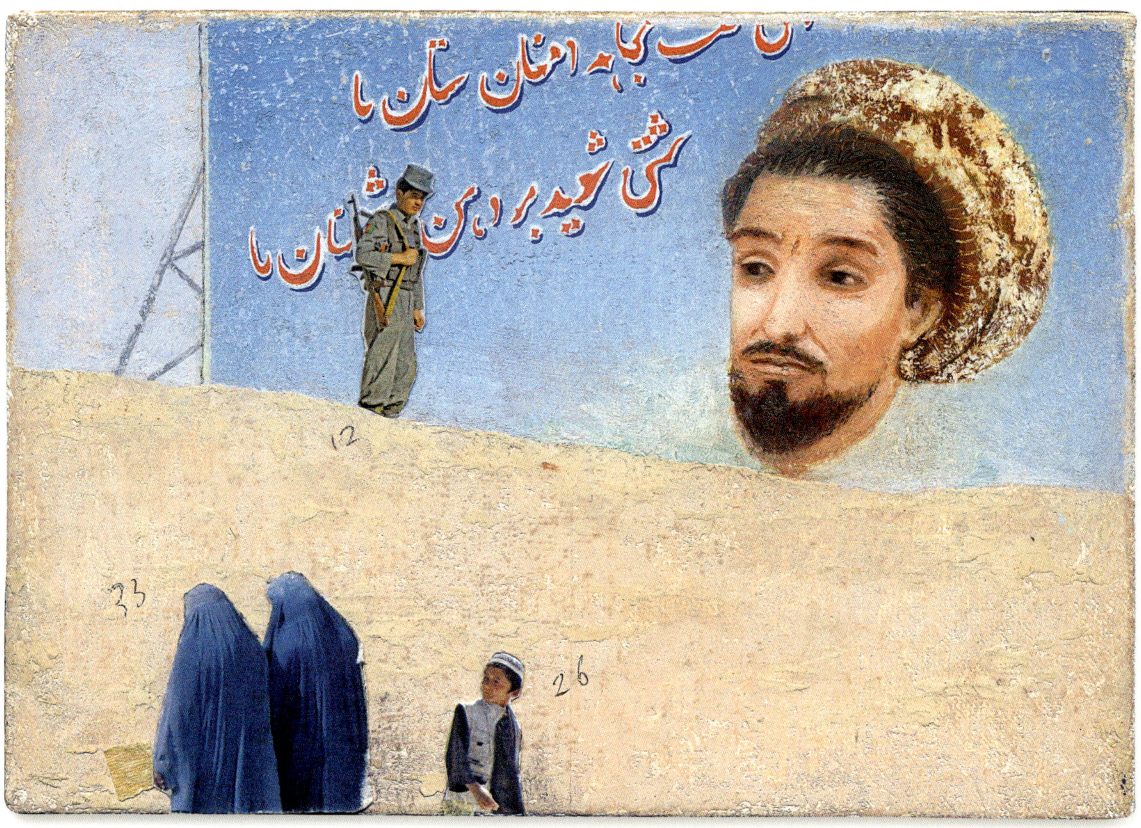

UNTITLED (COMMANDER MASSOUD), 2010
OIL AND COLLAGE ON CANVAS
13 X 18 CM

UNTITLED (ROYAL ENGINEERS TACTICAL RECOGNITION FLASH) AFGHANISTAN, 2013
ENCAUSTIC AND OIL ON CANVAS
20 X 23 CM

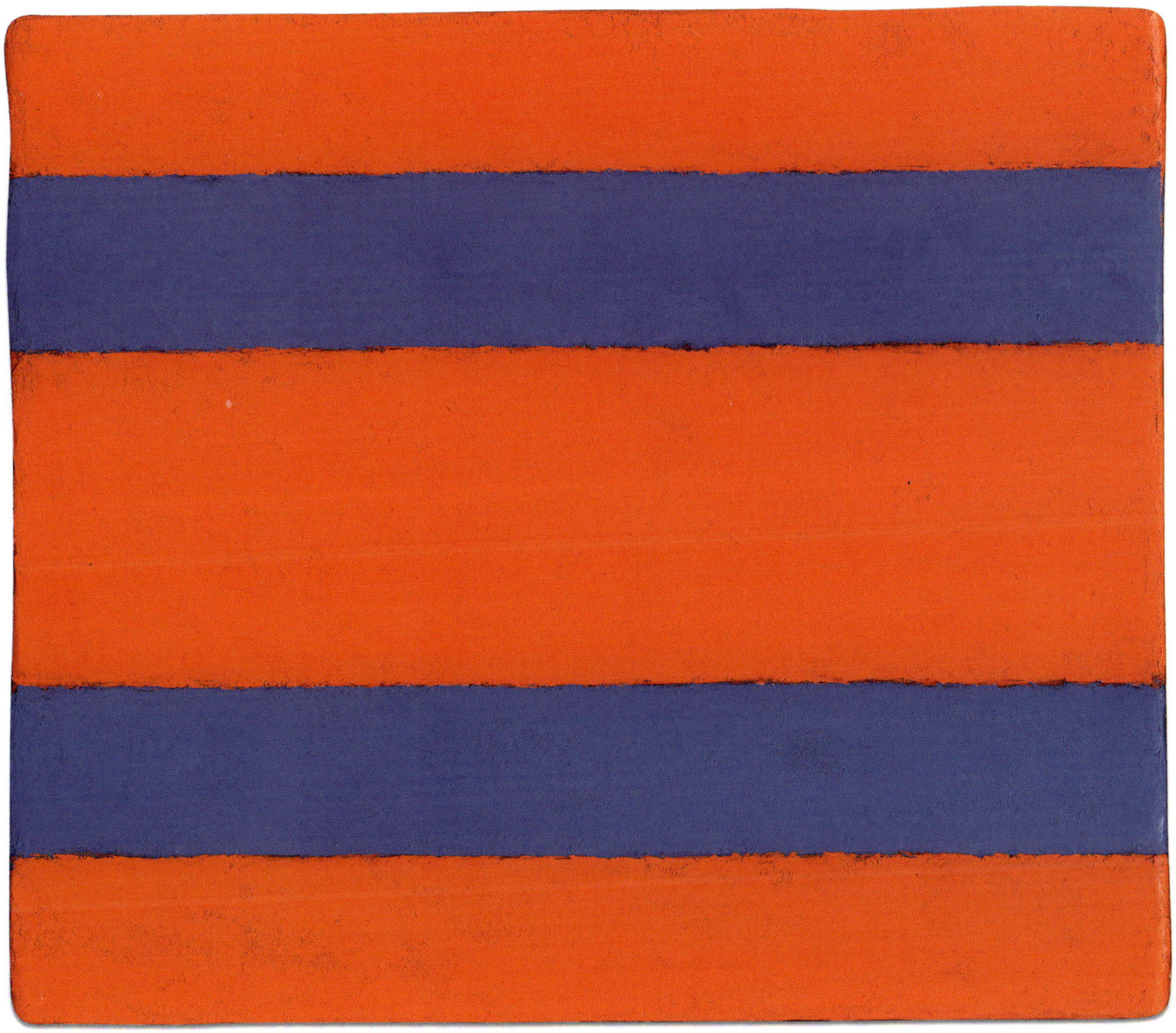

UNTITLED (HERAT
AFGHANISTAN), 2012
OIL ON CANVAS
13 X 18 CM

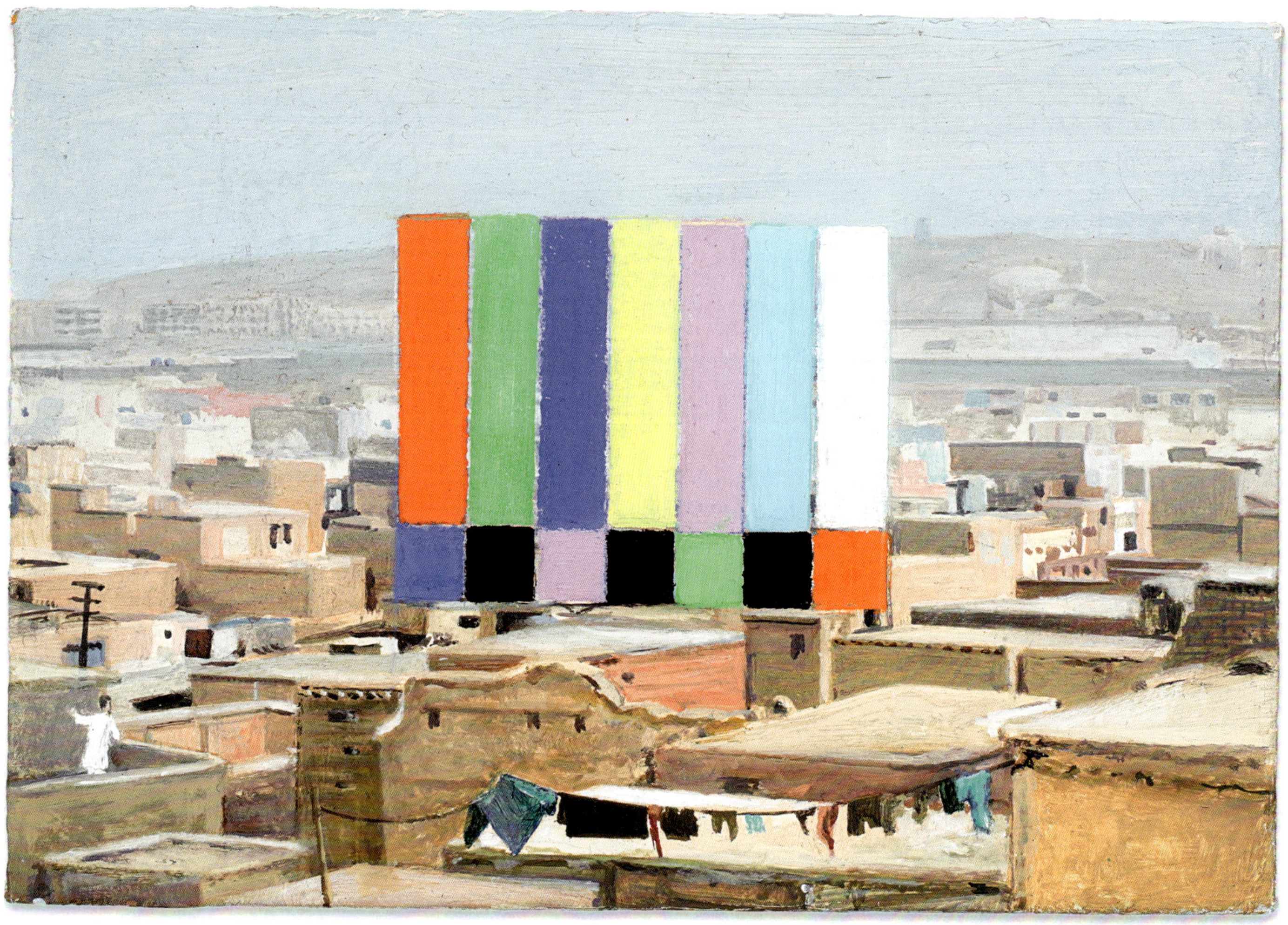

UNTITLED (ROYAL ENGINEERS TACTICAL RECOGNITION FLASH) AFGHANISTAN, 2013
ENCAUSTIC AND OIL ON CANVAS
20 X 23 CM

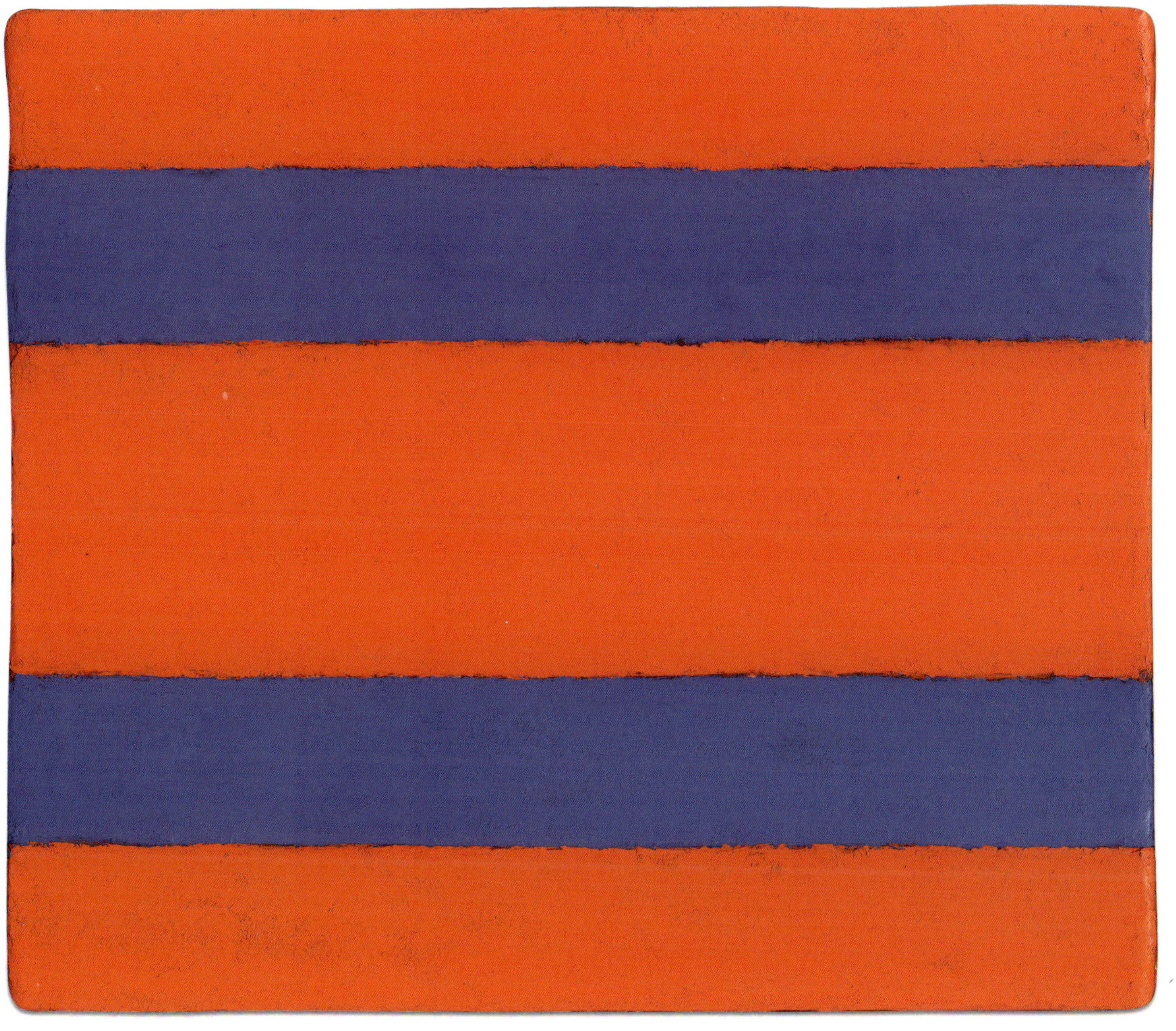

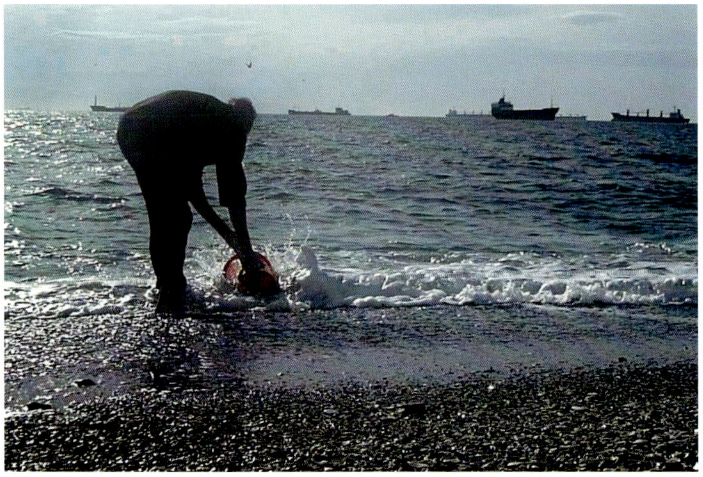

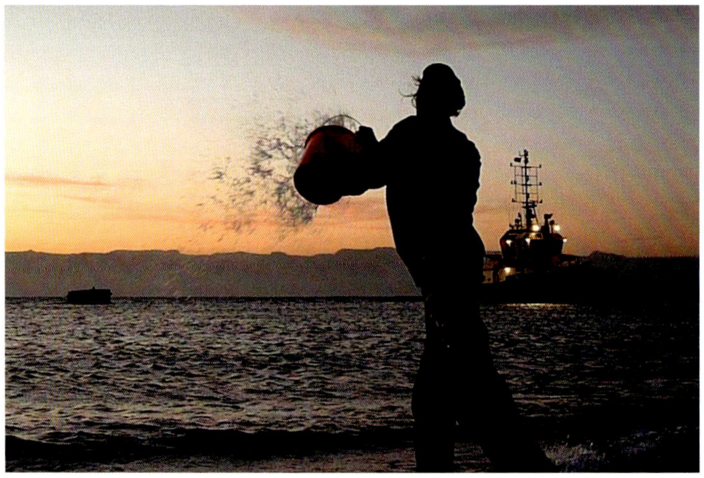

WATERCOLOR, 2010
TRABZON, TURKEY – AQABA, JORDAN
VIDEO DOCUMENTATION OF AN ACTION,
1 MIN. 19 SEC.

Mixing water from the Red Sea with water from the Black Sea

as an artist in five 'forward operating bases' with UK forces (the U.S. would not accept him) in Helmand province. It was then that he got the idea for his *Color Bar* drawings of the 'tactical recognition flashes' that these British soldiers wore on their upper-left sleeve. Why make 'Art' out of these flashes, and why are they called 'flashes'? Listening to the artist I get the idea that the basic simplicity of the flashes – these little patches of coloured stripes – is a catharsis from the bewildering overload of conflicting information that 'Afghanistan' generates. Yet doesn't such simplicity succeed through combining with an abstraction that is not simple at all? It is a catharsis because the simplicity is too simple. It is a mystery. In other words, despite the staid, ever-reliable stolidity of the flashes, they are actually just that: 'flashes' of this and that like fireflies in the night-land that is Afghanistan.

From the moment I met him, Alÿs struck me as an odd bird. A flash, you might say. A firefly, for sure. Blessed with an ever-surprising imagination, he was searingly practical as well. If Charles Fourier needed an engineer to construct his utopias, well, here he was! Francis took in detail like a sponge and, more than that, saw connections and patterns in the eye of the hurricane dissolving all patterns. Meticulous and cerebral as his work is, it owes much to children's games. 'They are a major source of inspiration in my work', he once told me, adding that he had to date made at least fifteen videos of kids' games (which you can see as the first item on his website).

Does this mean his work is generally 'childish'? Well, yes. And no. Is Magritte childish? Or Duchamp? It is childish in its studied innocence and self-absorption, cut off from the busy world of the adults, the pesky mothers and the demanding fathers. Like a children's game, it sails off into uncharted seas. And by children's games I mean the games children have played *with each other* for a long, long, time, not the ones invented by adults such as video games, generally isolating the child from other children and from their own bodies.

Actually, I first met not Alÿs but his shadow or empty space, because he had disappeared, causing our chaperone all manner of anxiety. Like a naughty child, he had played hooky to wander around threatening Kabul with his newly found architect Afghani friend, thereby manifesting yet again his ceaseless curiosity as to the ways of the world. You could see that curiosity in the marvellous photographs he would email me of our travels together, shots that I would carefully archive as much for their aesthetic power as for what they were about. You could see it in the extra mile he would go to get some other view, that extra question, that extra immersion that comes to fill a notebook.

Much, if not most, of Alÿs' artwork involves games in which exchange and circulation recur, invoking the idea of the gift in the circuitry of the social. 'Work' as in 'artwork' is somewhat of a misnomer for this art. 'Art-game' would be a more appropriate term for what are so often jokes about overworked jokes. In *Watercolor,*

UNTITLED (KABUL), AFGHANISTAN, 2011
OIL ON CANVAS
18 X 13 CM

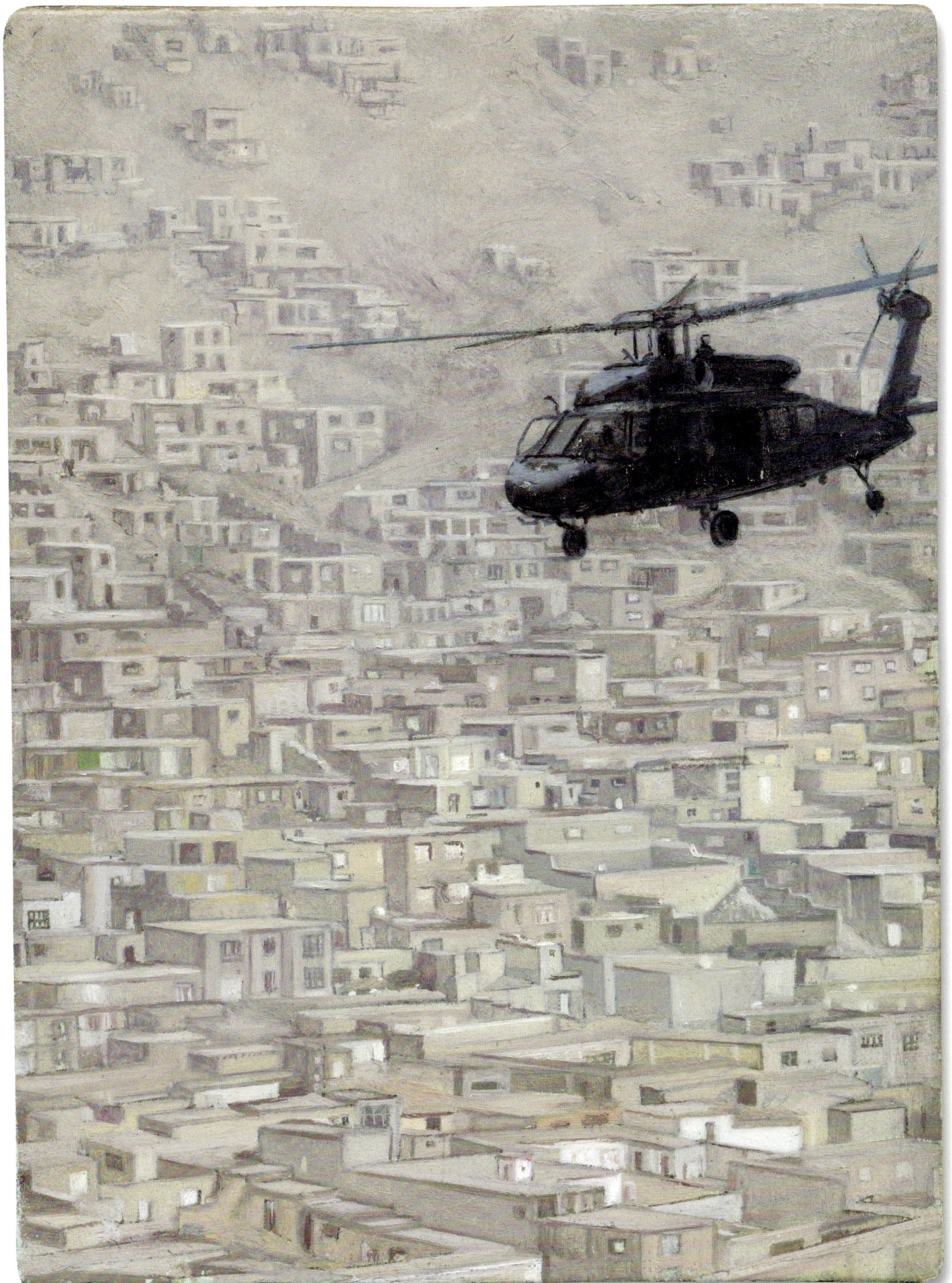

UNTITLED (HERAT AFGHANISTAN), 2012
OIL ON CANVAS
13 X 18 CM

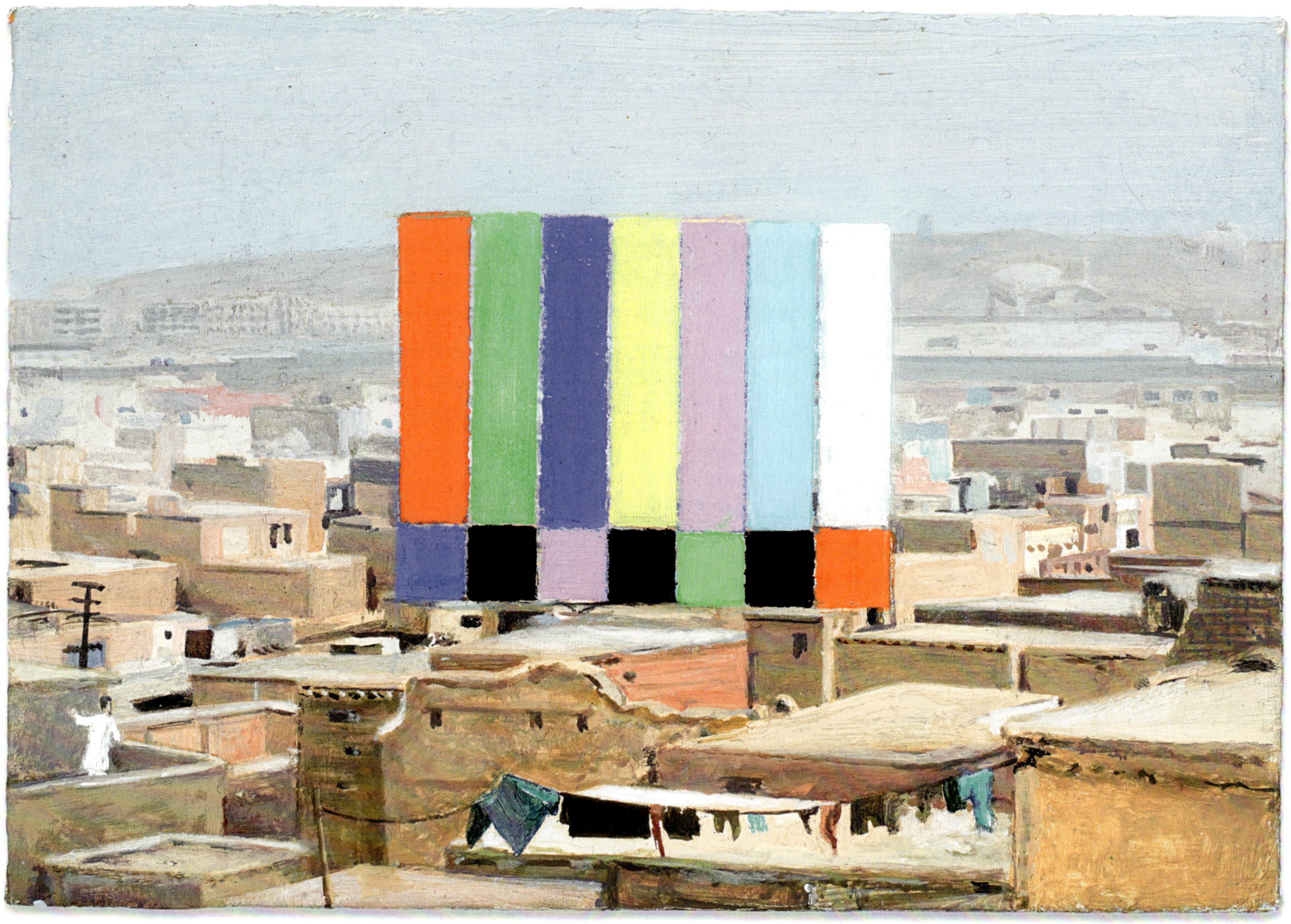

UNTITLED (AFGHANISTAN),
2011–12
OIL AND ENCAUSTIC
ON CANVAS
24 X 31 CM

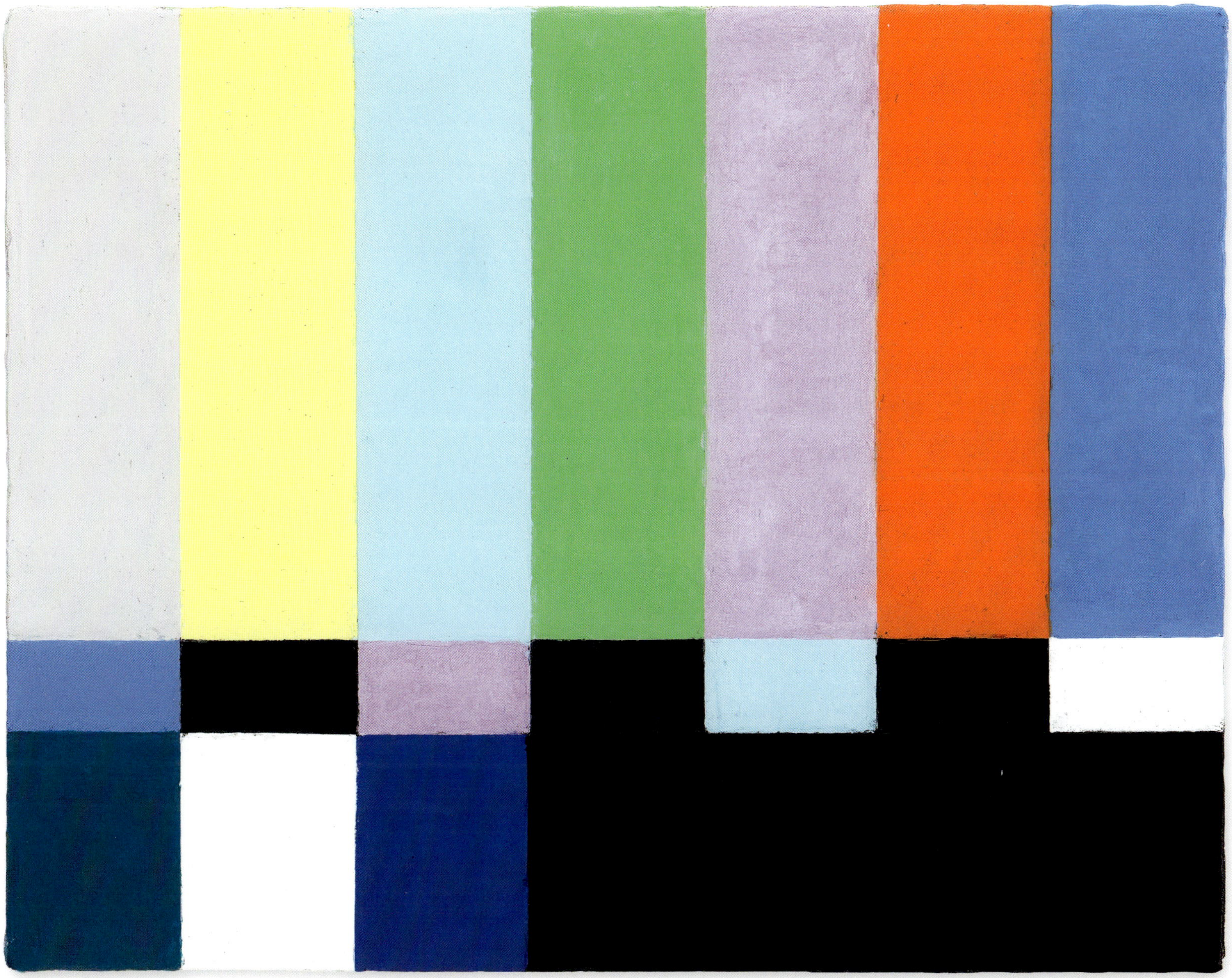

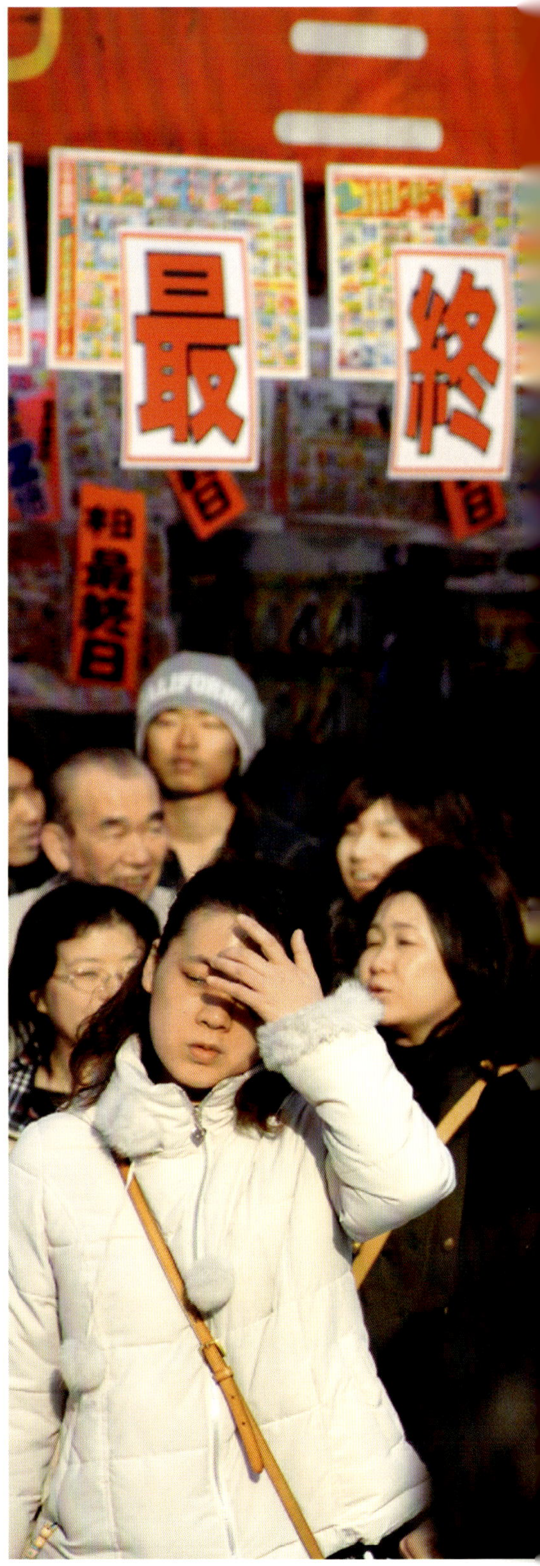

BONJOUR MR ALYS, 2009
PHOTO DOCUMENTATION
OF AN ACTION
TOKYO, 2009

`I will wander in the streets of Tokyo until someone calls my name.`

for example, a video 1:19 minutes in length, a plastic pail of water is dipped into the Black Sea in Turkey and emptied into the Red Sea in Jordan. That's it – 1:19 minutes! But how long did it take to travel from The Black Sea to the Red?

This humour – uncovering exchange circuits that were not obvious before the artwork – is immediately apparent in *le temps du sommeil* (the time of sleep), 111 little paintings (roughly seven by five inches) created between 1996 and 2009, exhibited in the Irish Museum of Modern Art and published as a small book in 2010. The exchanges depicted may be between objects, such as pouring the contents of one glass into another, back and forth, or they may involve uncanny dimensions of the social world, as evident in the very last item in the book, 'I will wander in the streets of Tokyo until someone calls my name'.

The most significant gift involving exchange and circulation, however, occurs at the meta-level, where the painting on one page is juxtaposed with a short text of one or two lines on the page facing it, the connection being a gift exchange between image and text – barely a connection, a 'flash', we could say, yet in its tenuous fragility just right, meaning more than right, making you stare at the painting and then back again to the statement, your mind never still, oscillating, like playing badminton.

There is another 'childish' aspect to this, and it lies with the very character of the drawings – deceptively simple, petite, sketchy, impish and wistful. As for the gift in this back and forth, it kick-starts the process of exchange and circulation where one side – the image, for instance – offers itself as a gift to the other – the text, for instance. And then there is the return gift, the fruit or reward of the interchange, creating a surplus that perforce becomes metamorphic of the text-image mix. Bataille's notion of *depense* or *unproductive expenditure* comes to mind, *depense* itself being indispensable to gaming. Are children's games dying out, like a threatened species? Are the streets the world over ever-more empty of kids playing – except for in the poor parts of town and poor parts of the world, like Afghanistan? Have our cityscapes become ever more denuded and less sonorous, with the cries of children replaced by cars and trucks? I look back at my own childhood in Sydney and certainly see this evolution, which sets me to wonder about the history of children's games and toys.

In his *Centuries of Childhood*, Philippe Aries argues that childhood in western Europe is an invention of the late seventeenth century and that before then children were little adults, as testified by Velásquez's *Las Meñinas*. But what does that imply for our understanding of toys and play? 'Little adults' were surely not averse to play, even if the 'cult' of childhood had not yet been invented.

Benjamin, for example, whose work – like that of Alÿs – can be seen as one big toy, a toy of theory, was entranced by children's toys, which he saw as in continuous negotiation with the world of adults, including adults' notion of play and of childhood. Above all, he insisted that the locus of joy and fascination with toys lay in the child's love of mimesis and the body more than in the toy itself: 'a child wants to pull something, and so he becomes a horse; he wants to play with sand, and so he turns into a baker; he wants to hide, and so he turns into a robber or a policeman.'[1]

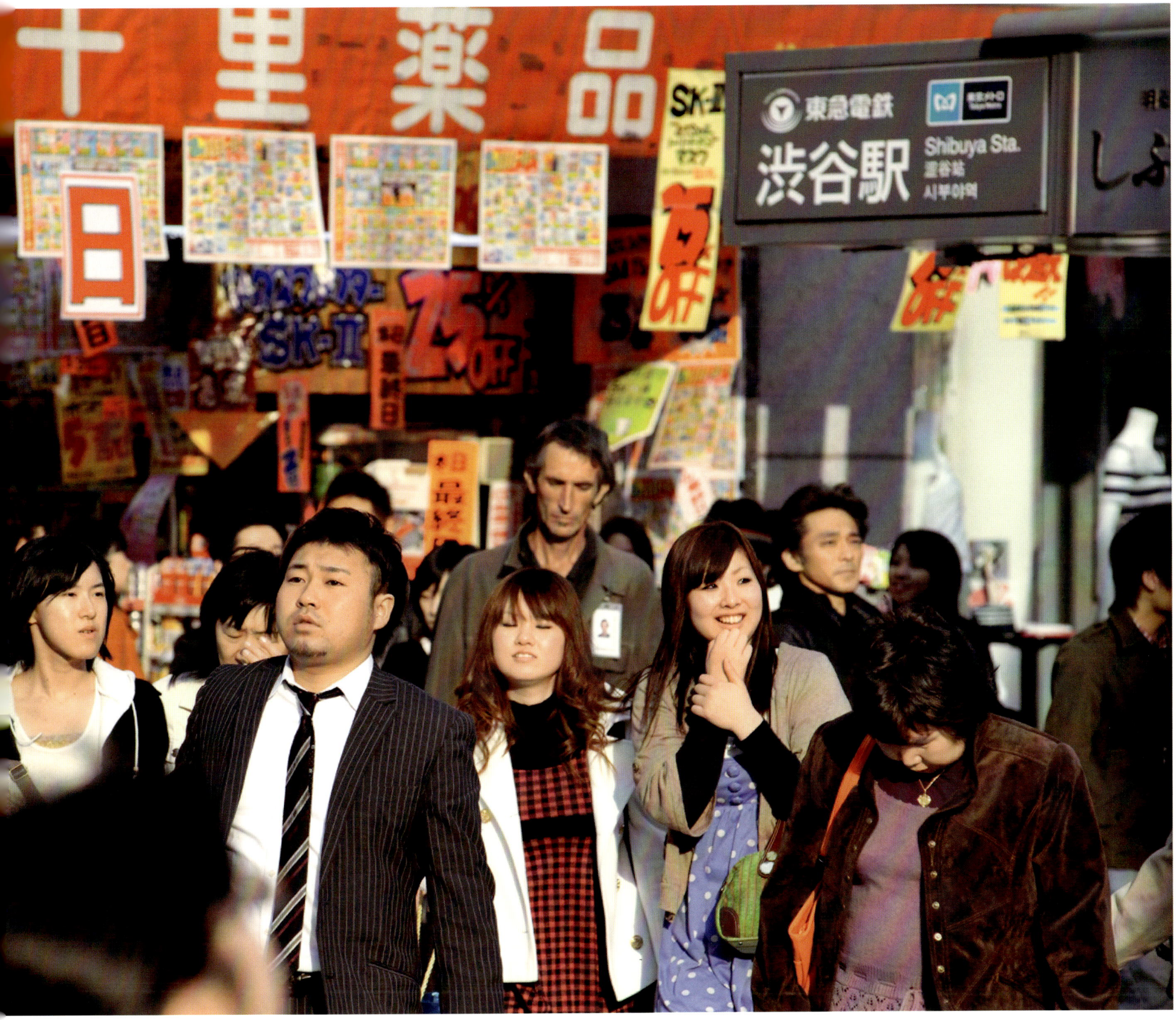
東急電鉄
渋谷駅
Shibuya Sta.
澀谷站
시부야역
SK-II

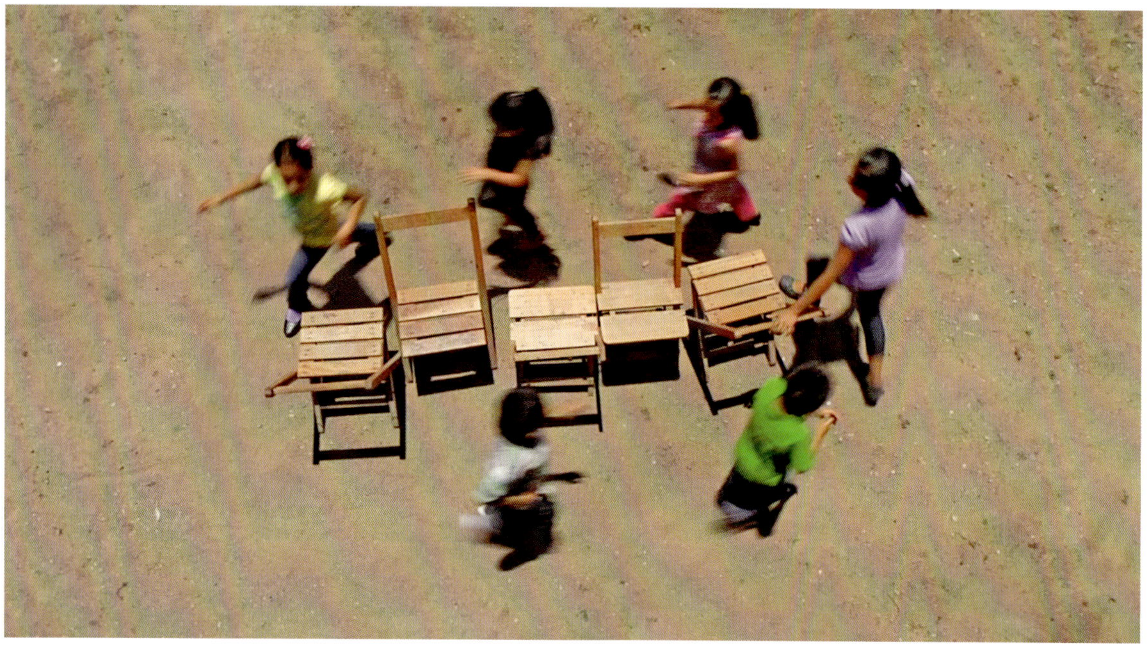

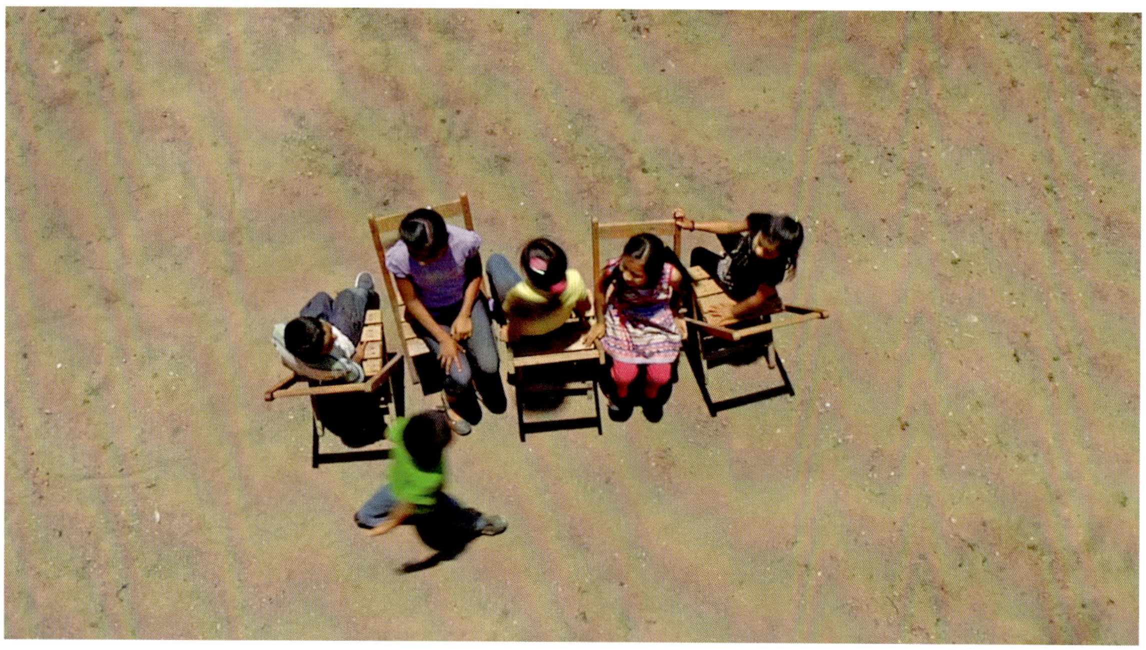

CHILDREN'S GAME #12: SILLAS MUSICALES, 2012
OAXACA, MEXICO
VIDEO DOCUMENTATION OF AN ACTION
8 MIN. 17 SEC.

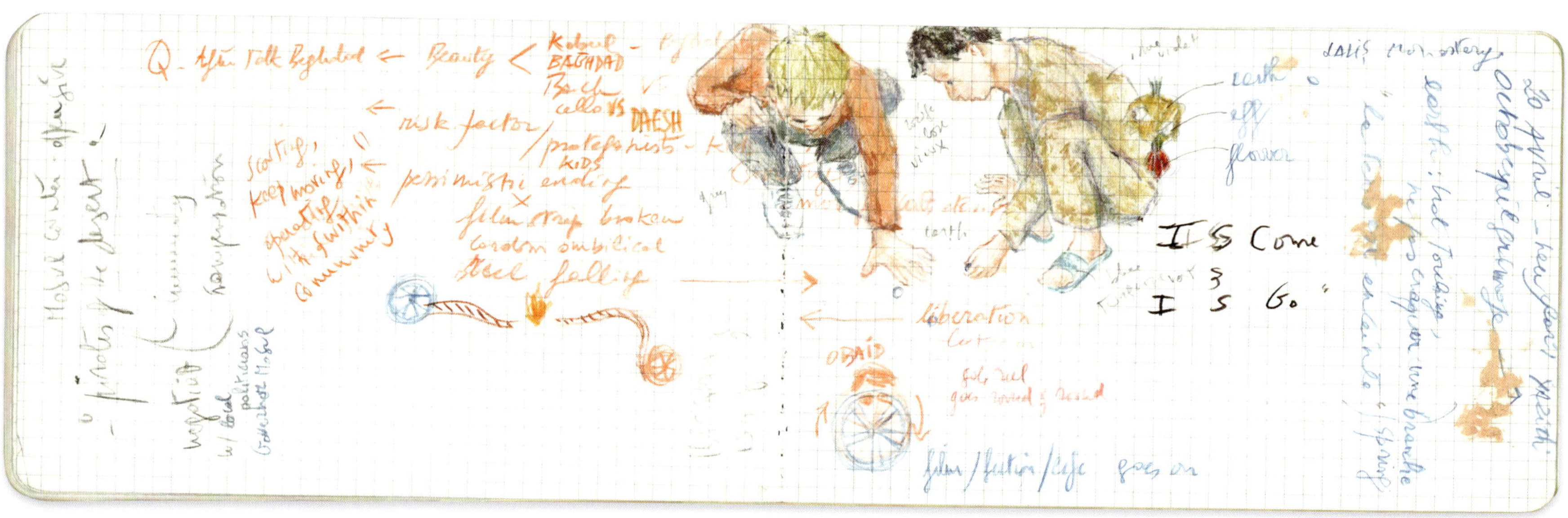

NOTEBOOK, IRAQ, 2016
13 X 42 CM

UNTITLED (BAMIYAN, AFGHANISTAN) (DETAIL), 2010
OIL ON CANVAS

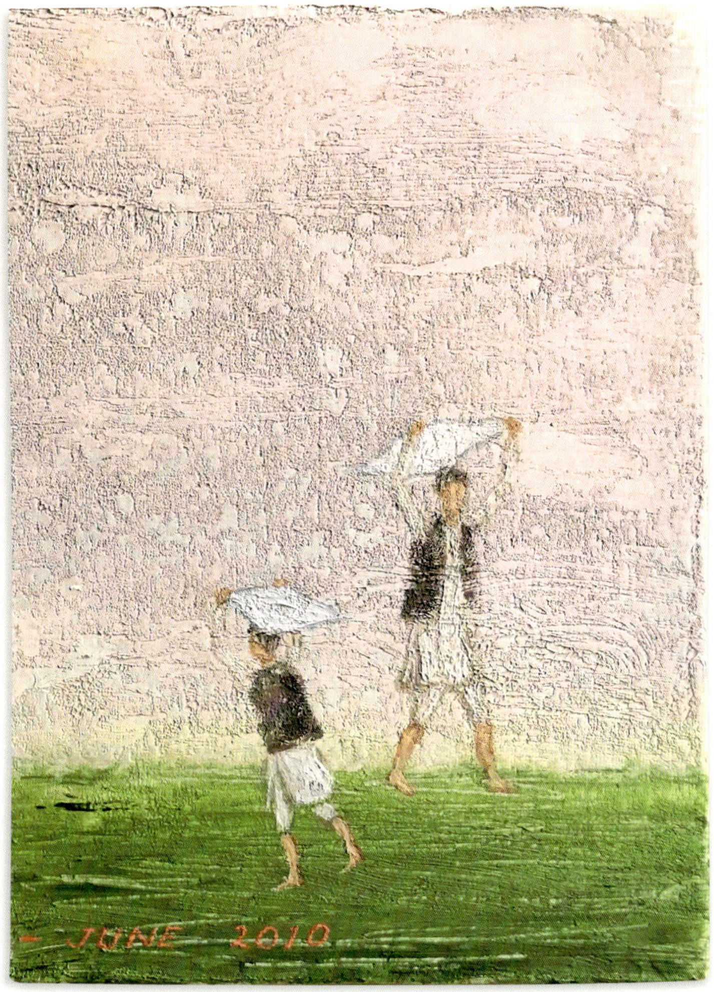

I cannot but think of Alÿs s pushing his block of ice through Mexico City.

And as regards the age and origins of toys, Benjamin suggests that the baby rattle has its source in the need to ward off evil spirits and that hoops, kites, balls and spinning tops were once what he calls 'cult objects'. The spinning top is the main 'character' in José Maria Arguedas' novel, Los ríos profundos, set in the highlands of Peru in the mid-twentieth century. The spinning top with which the children play not only becomes animated, but it becomes human-like and, more than that, a spirit that coordinates the narrative and unfolding events. In his book on play, Roger Caillois states that hopscotch, commonly performed in the street or in the schoolyard, derives from the labyrinth in which one pushed a stone – meaning one's soul – towards the exit. With Christianity, the labyrinth took the form of the basilica and the exit was heaven.[2]

So where does that put Alÿs' ice-block, pushed into nothingness through the labyrinth of the third-world city? What does this latest manifestation of the labyrinth say about our long-forgotten connections to ancient mythology and to forgetting?

To invoke history and pre-history is to ask if Alÿs' work is inspired not so much by children's games as by their world historical loss. I myself think this is so. As Benjamin says in relation to the art of the storyteller, it would be fatuous to see this merely as a symptom of decay and of modernization. Instead, this loss is a symptom of the secular forces of economic production combined with the loss of narrative from the realm of living speech, 'making it possible to see a new beauty in what is vanishing'.[3] Is it therefore all that surprising that our architect-artist from western Europe who has chosen to live in Mexico City would be sensitive to this 'new beauty in what is vanishing'.

But what about screens? What about kids glued to video games and computers the world over? Is this not a sign that gaming is alive and well, at least electronically? In which case, what do you make of the elimination of the body from such games and that the majority of such games are not only about war but U.S. led war in the Middle East?

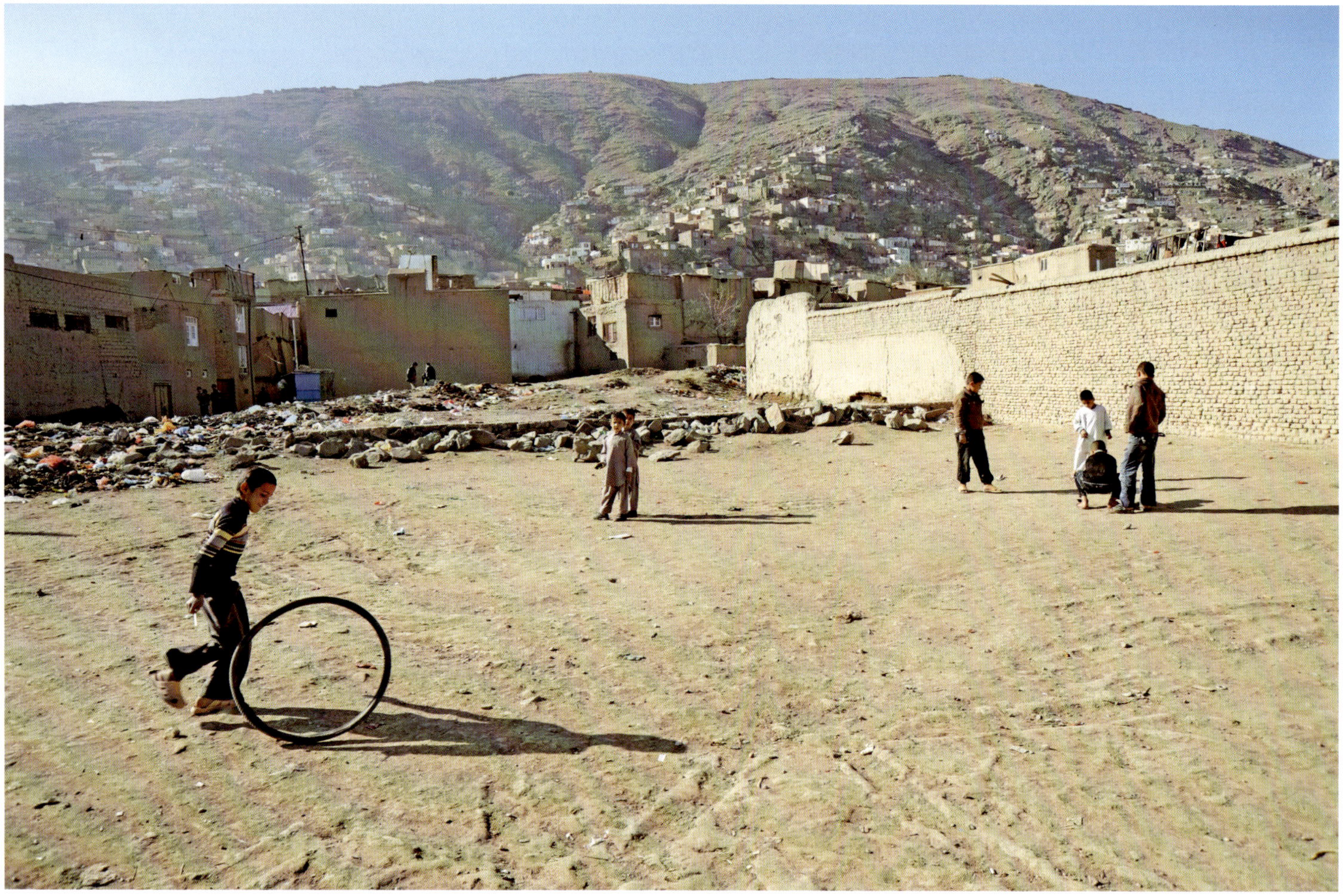

KABUL, AFGHANISTAN, 2010

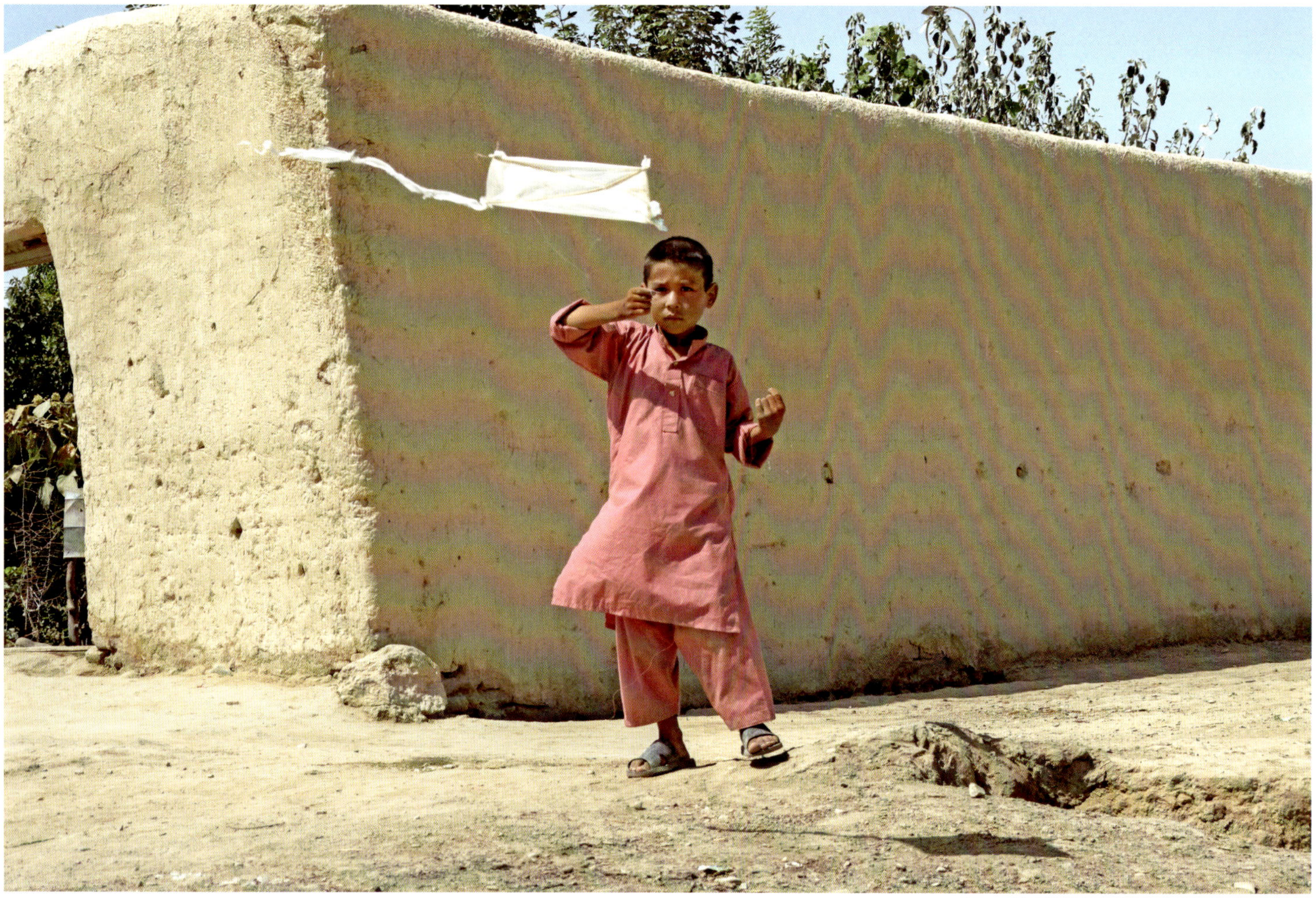

CHILDREN'S GAME #10: PAPALOTE, 2011
BALKH, AFGHANISTAN
VIDEO DOCUMENTATION OF AN ACTION
4 MIN. 13 SEC.

CHILDREN'S GAME #14:
PIEDRA, PAPEL Y TIJERAS,
2013
MEXICO CITY
VIDEO DOCUMENTATION OF
AN ACTION
2 MIN. 51 SEC.

Bodily involvement is starkly obvious in all Alÿs' movies of children's games, especially and gut wrenchingly so in *Papalote* (4:10 minutes) set in Balkh, Afghanistan, featuring a ten-year-old boy flying a kite. The involvement of the body is overwhelming yet as finely wrought as a mirage. Against a dun-coloured adobe wall, standing under a powder blue sky, the boy wears a pinkish trouser suit. He is emitting a frenzied gesture language, seemingly conversing in stops and starts with the heavens, or at least with the gusting wind, because you do not immediately see the kite and because the string is so fine you can't see that either. All you observe is the body in action with unknown forces, pulling to the left, pulling to the right, up, down, quick, over to the left again, and so on and on. The body is all the more obvious because it is connected like this to the coursing wind by an invisible string. This is not only the body of the boy but the body of the world in a deft mimesis of each other, amounting to what I call 'the mastery of non-mastery', which after all is the greatest game of all, a guide, a goal, a strategy – all in one – for dealing with man's domination of nature (including human nature).

An analogous trick – or should we call it a game? – makes mesmerizing magic out of the game 'Rock, Paper, Scissors' (*Piedra, papel y tijeras*, 2:51 minutes). Here we see not the hands themselves, but their shadows on a whitish background as the two antagonists play with that tremendous skill that only kids can muster in what seems impossibly fast motion: the clenched fist of 'rock', the two open fingers of 'scissors' and the flat hand of 'paper' – 'Conceptual art', you say, the kind you could watch for hours, the hands as synecdoche not of the body but of the two bodies in a controlled frenzy of elegant interaction and dissolution.

I wonder what the Taliban's attitudes are towards children's games like this, let alone towards videos thereof? But as we quickly learned once we got to Afghanistan in 2010, there is more than one 'Taliban' and the ban on images is hardly uniform or coherent. But then, what is an 'image'?

The Director of the National Museum in Kabul, elegant in a fawn linen suit and golden tie, told me how in 1996 he had personally painted flowers and trees in watercolours over paintings featuring human and animal figures in the museum to protect them before the Taliban came and smashed all the figurative art. The Taliban also forbade all photography and Xeroxing – except for those documents indispensable for state control, IDs and passports. Someone else explained to me that the ban on image-making meant that you couldn't image *animate* beings, and suggested breathing as the criterion of such animatedness.

In the longest and most ambitious of the Afghan videos, *Reel-Unreel*, the notion of *animate* is really put to the

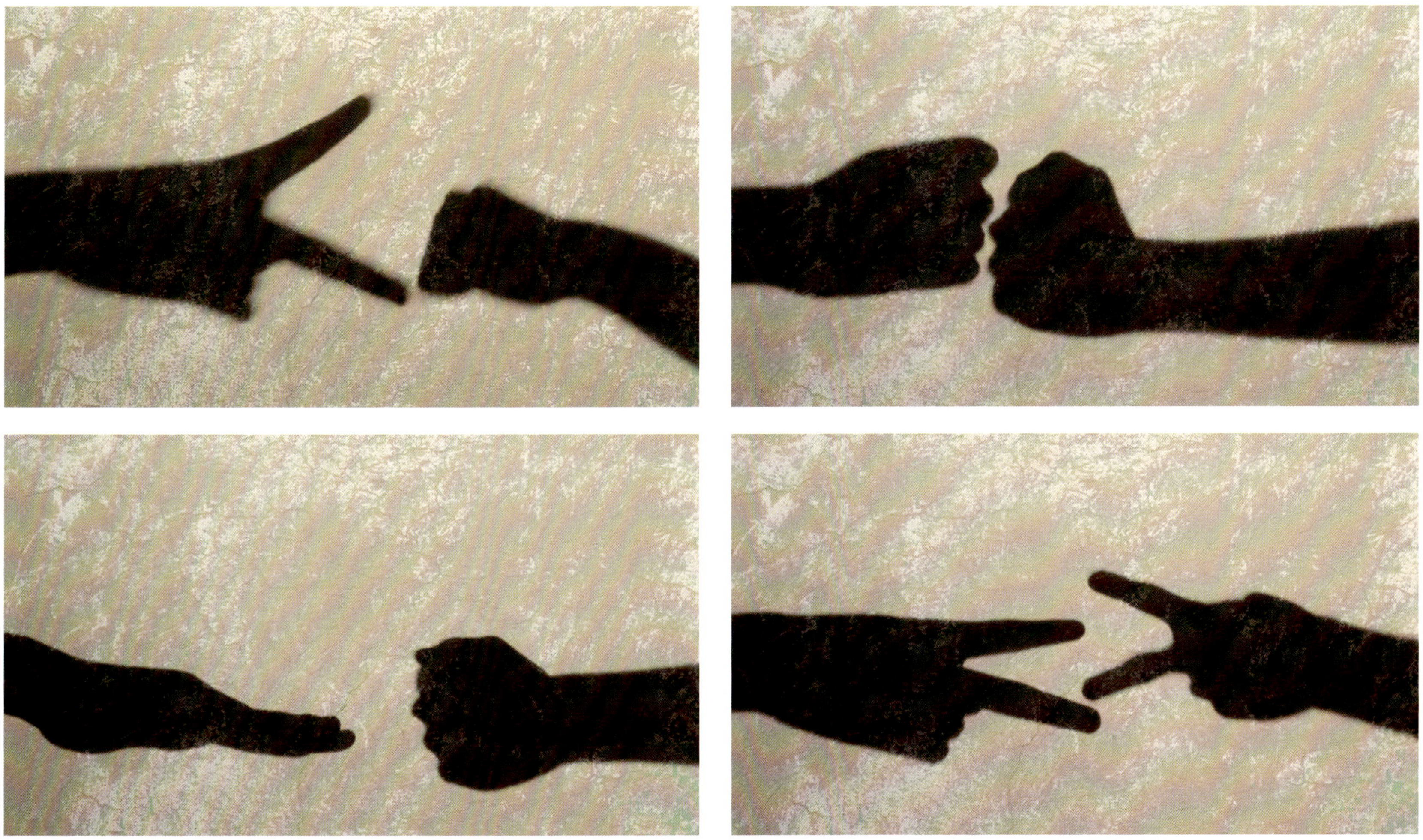

Taliban test, as well as testing, in ways delightful and exploratory, western notions of what *animate* might encompass. Thanks to the skill and derring-do of two boys spinning film reels like hoops as fast as they can, the pixilated multitude that is Kabul springs to life as the camera follows the boys' will-o'-the-wisp chase – completely aimless except for the mad intensity with which the boy behind races to keep up with the boy some twenty feet in front, and the boy in front races to keep ahead of the one twenty feet behind. The two boys and their reels are bound together. The boy in front has his reel unwinding its load of celluloid while the one behind winds it onto his reel at pretty much the same frenzied pace. Could this be an allegory for that which is today called 'Afghanistan' – the continuous state constituting that Great Game in which the more you know, the less you know? Blind Man's Buff also comes to mind. One is tempted to invoke the 'cult objects' idea of hoops and kites, let alone rattles.

Like Alÿs' earlier works, such as the magnetic shoes and the magnetic 'horse' that he set perambulating the streets of Havana and Mexico City, the spools in *Reel-Unreel* attract all manner of debris. This is film that has been developed and has frames with pictures, as we see when a boy holds up a segment to the light to look at the images. Much is made in this work of the destruction of the film and its picking up scratches and dirt as it slithers, snake-like, along the rough ground. This is above all a sonic phenomenon, with scratching, screeching matter-in-torment, at once playful and sinister, at other times a whiplash. You ask yourself, 'Is this playing with Taliban prohibition of film? Is it another way of filmmaking and un-filmmaking?'

Certainly *Reel-Unreel* offers an unusual perspective on reality, for not only does it animate the landscapes through which the reels pass, but it often does this at knee-height, the height of the boys and the height of the reels bouncing their ways precariously through thick and thin. This is political filmmaking in a new key, the perspective from the ground up with wheels in motion. It is up to you, the viewer, to decide whether this is the wheels of Nietzche's Eternal Return, Marx's locomotive of history, a Deleuzian post-Nietzchean 'becoming intense, becoming animal', or something you make up yourself.

In *The Accursed Share*, Bataille makes a big point about war in the twentieth century being the privileged instance of *depense* – of spending the surplus in orgies of waste that displace by far Roman carnival with its bread and circuses, and Aztec sacrifice with its thousands of victims offered to the gods. Now entering its fourteenth year, that gargantuan spending spree of life and *treasure* (not money but 'treasure', as they say repeatedly in the U.S. Senate) the U.S.-led war in Afghanistan surely qualifies as The Great Depense as much as the Great Game.

Kipling narrated this Great Game through a young boy, Kimball O'Hara, just as Alÿs has the two boys chasing each other over the mountains and choked streets of Kabul, but the boys' game auto-cannibalises narration. It is – as Bataille would have it in his essay on Van Gogh and the sacred dimension of auto-mutilation – the self-sacrifice of narration and of the very idea of a purpose – which is, after all, what you need to make sense. A sense of purpose, that is. There is no beginning and no end to *Reel-Unreel*, just this mad breathless chase to no purpose other than itself. The very title cleverly expresses just this. One would also like to say that the tension is not only intense but continuous. Yet like the state of exception/emergency, it is not so much continuous, not so much like a river flowing, as it is staggered and chaotic, with each 'moment' a world on its own and unpredictable from what came before. Yes, there is an end, when the leading reel plunges to its destruction over a cliff. But this end is totally unexpected, more a nervous system collapse than an ending. Game Over.

REEL-UNREEL, 2011
IN COLLABORATION WITH JULIEN DEVAUX AND AJMAL MAIWANDI
PHOTO DOCUMENTATION OF AN ACTION, KABUL
VIDEO
19 MIN. 32 SEC.

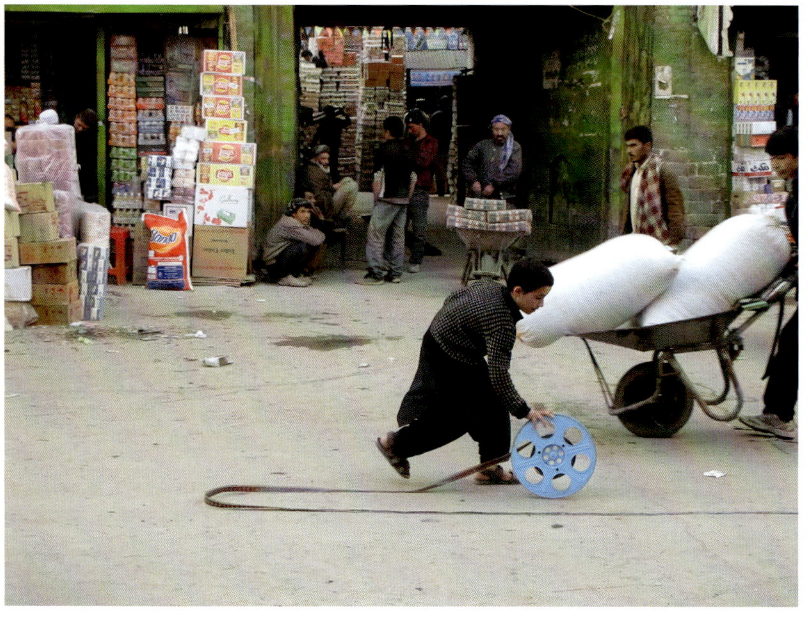

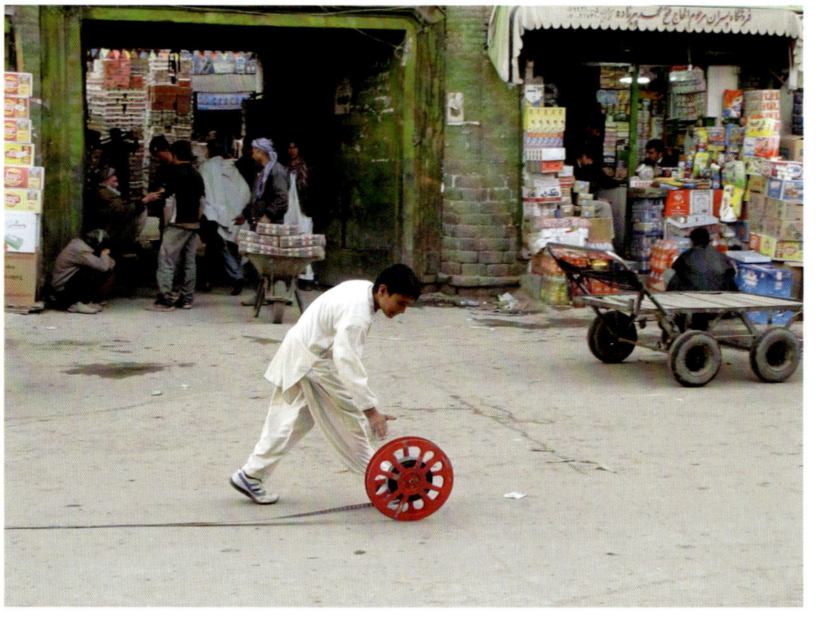

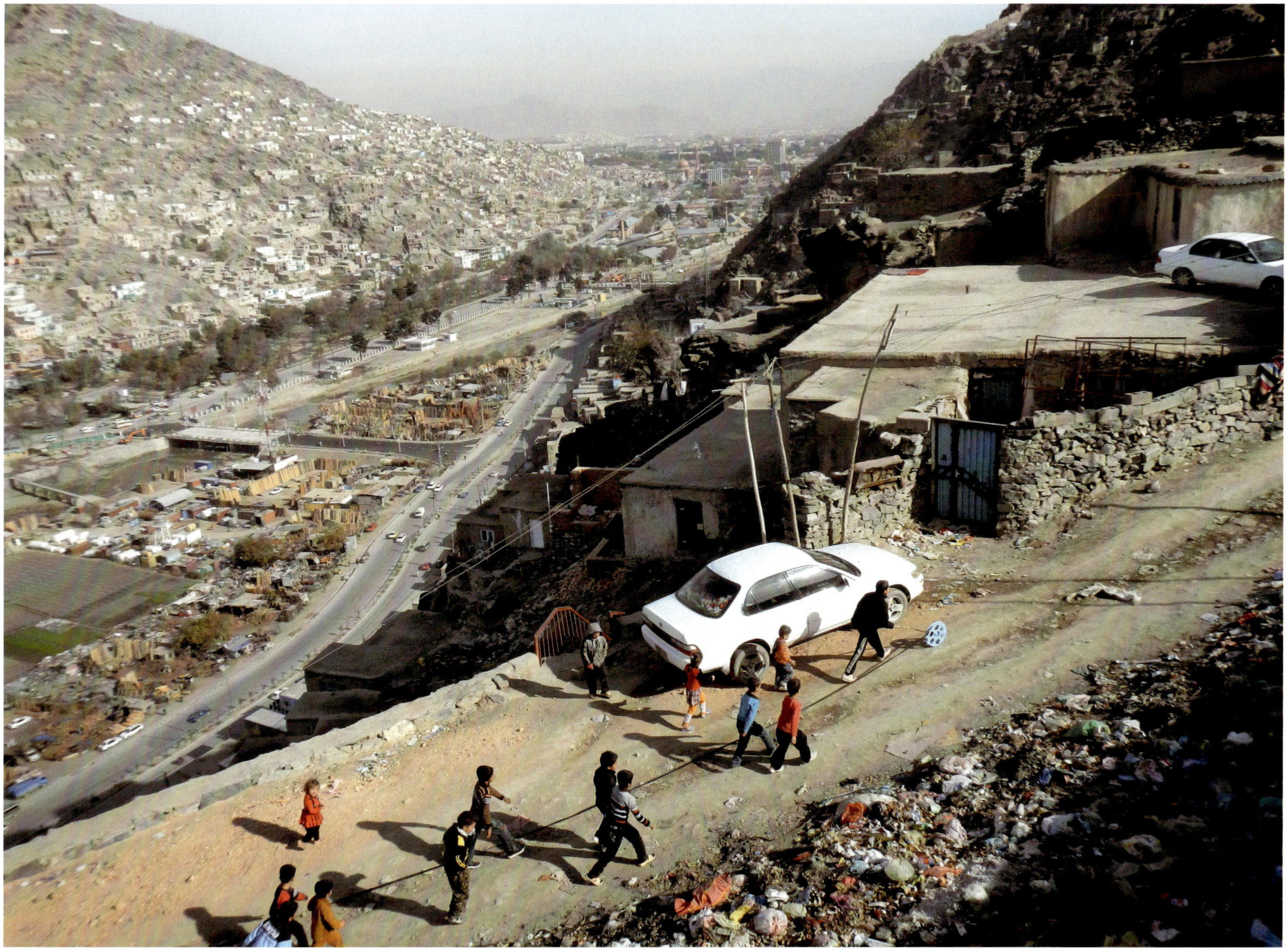

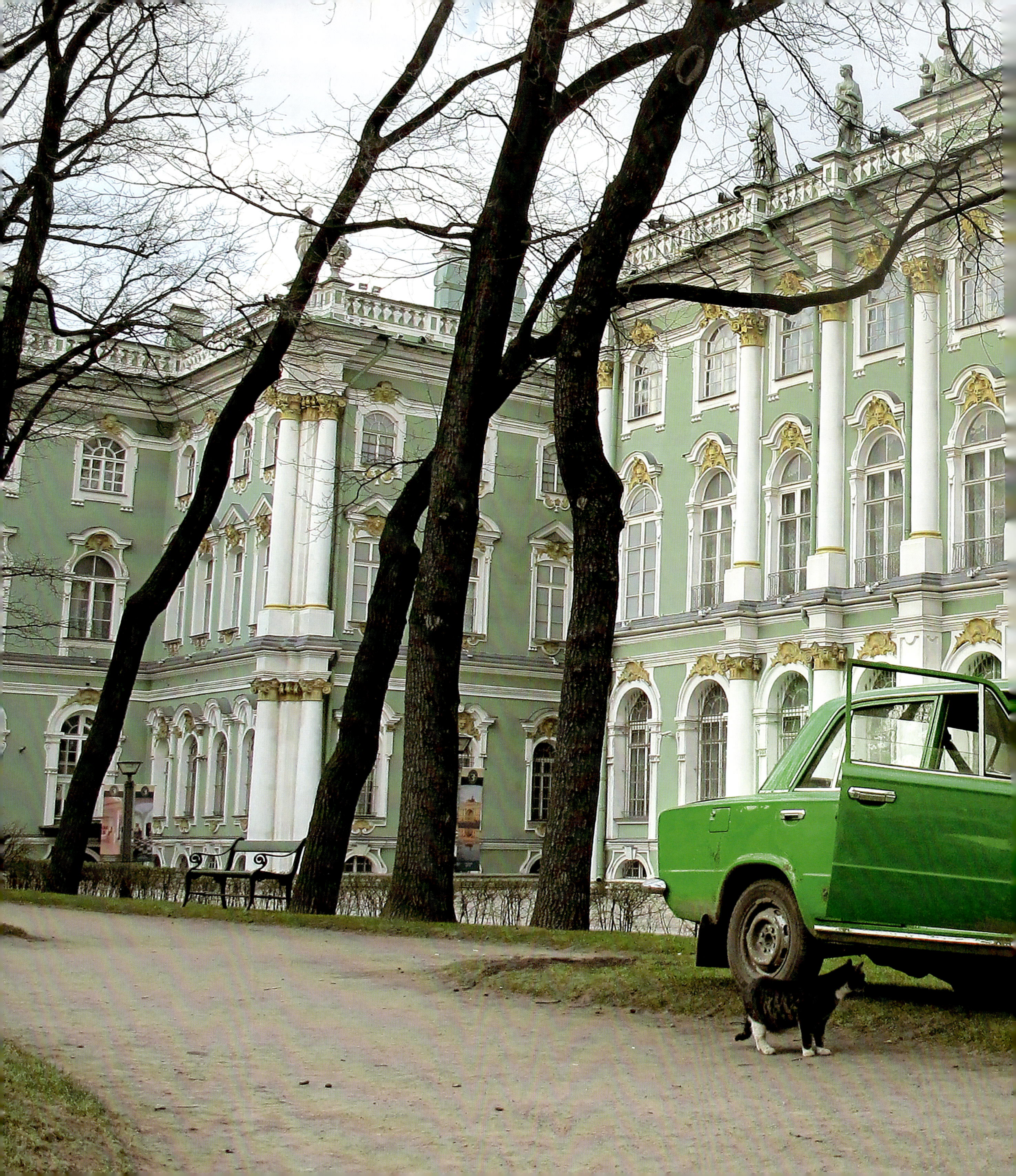

195 UPDATE (PART 2)

Francis Alÿs: Colporteur

Michael Taussig

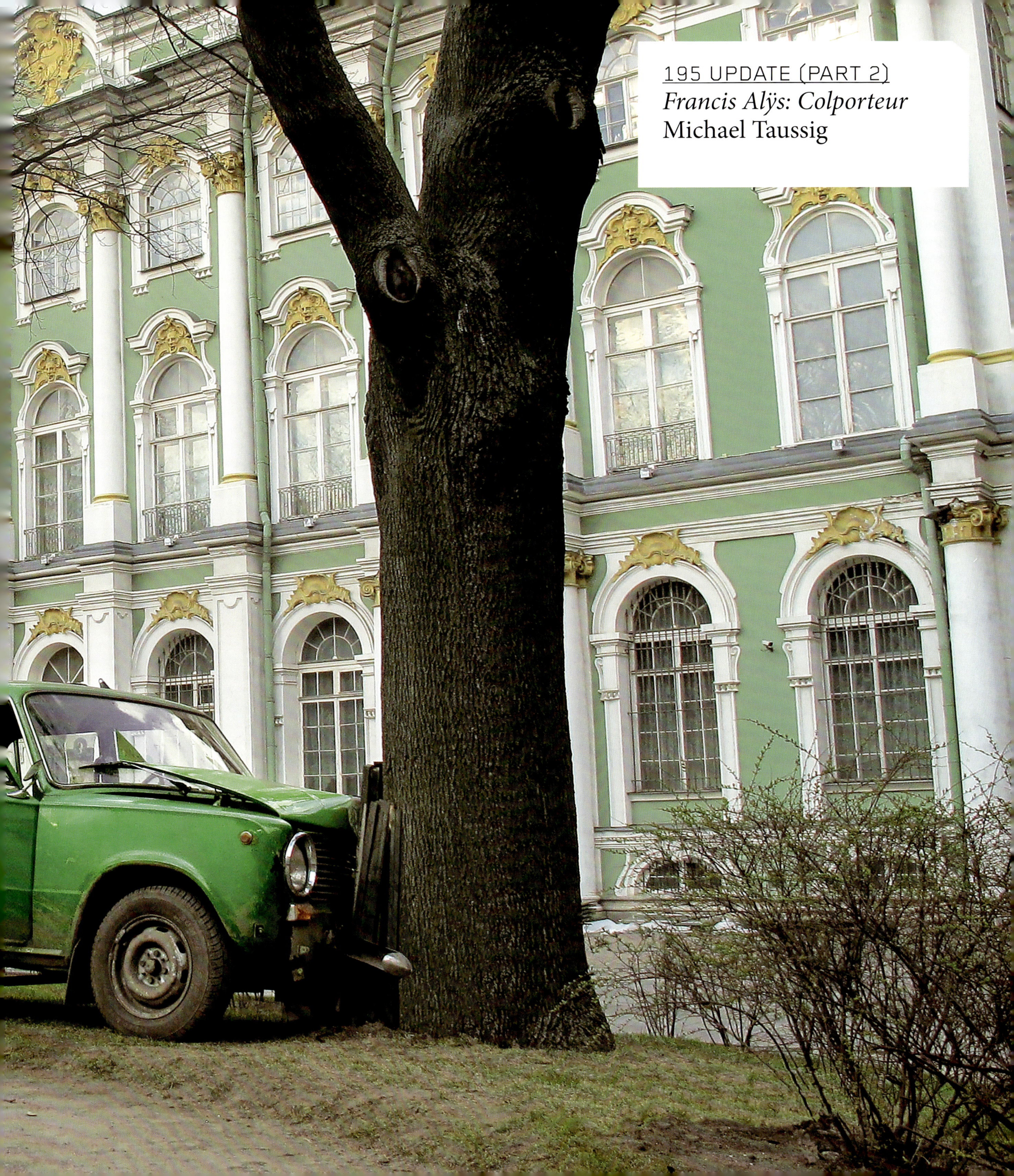

There's no doubt about it – Francis Alÿs is a walker. What else could he be with that angular frame, those endlessly long legs, scuffed-up tennis shoes and a dangling video camera that seems fascinated by the world it captures from the knee down? This creates a 'diffident aesthetic', as befits Alÿs' character, and invites the unexpected, especially at midnight in ill-lit parts of the city. Police sirens and the wail of a goods train evoke the mythic forces of prehistory as the artist stubbornly kicks a flaming soccer ball along the deserted streets of Ciudad Juárez, a border town devastated by violent drug cartels with a special taste for femicide. 'Sometimes doing something poetic can become political', the artist says about another work, *The Green Line*, where he walked the boundary made between Israel and a vastly shrunken Palestine after the 1967 war, 'and sometimes something political can become poetic'. An Israeli border guard looks on uncomprehendingly at this Chaplinesque figure in oversized clothing, calmly making his linear way while dribbling green paint onto the Holy Land. Like that guard, we also stare, if not uncomprehendingly then in wonder. This lanky fellow is definitely out of place, a disrupter of categories and borders. But he does it so easily, like a puff of wind across the still waters of a lake. 'Philosophise not with a hammer but with a tuning fork', says Nietzsche. The hammer smashes, while the tuning fork trembles, emits sonorous tones and sets the standard to which others must adapt. To drip green paint on the Green Line is not only to literalize and perform the fictions by which nation-states live, but to satirize them.

This ambulatory artist walks in the shoes of the *colporteurs* brought to our attention by Walter Benjamin – the itinerant book peddlers from whose necks (col) were suspended a tray of wares, often including religious tracts, pulp novels and sheet music, from which they earned a meager living selling door-to-door. Alÿs

STUDY FOR LADA KOPEIKA PROJECT, SAINT PETERSBURG, 2014
COLLAGE WITH GOLD LEAF
12 X 13 CM

previous pages,
LADA KOPEIKA PROJECT, 2014,
IN COLLABORATION WITH
WITH FRÉDÉRIC DE SMEDT, CONSTANTIN FELKER, AND JULIEN DEVAUX
PHOTO DOCUMENTATION OF AN ACTION, SAINT PETERSBURG

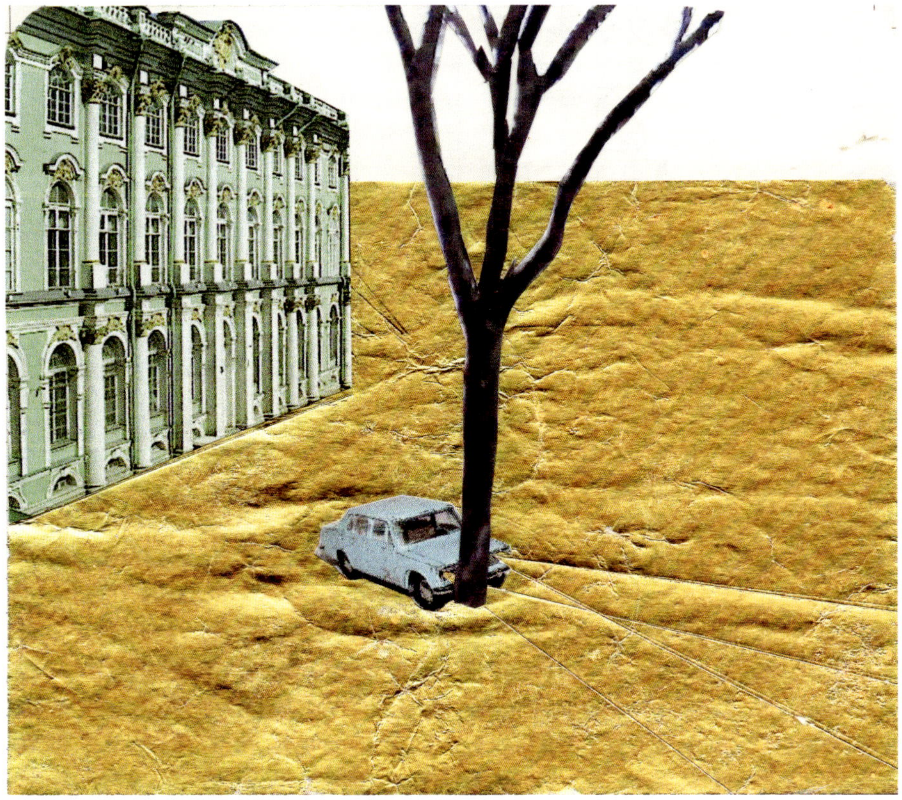

STUDY FOR LADA KOPEIKA PROJECT, SAINT PETERSBURG, 2014
RETOUCHED PHOTOGRAPHS
20 X 45 CM

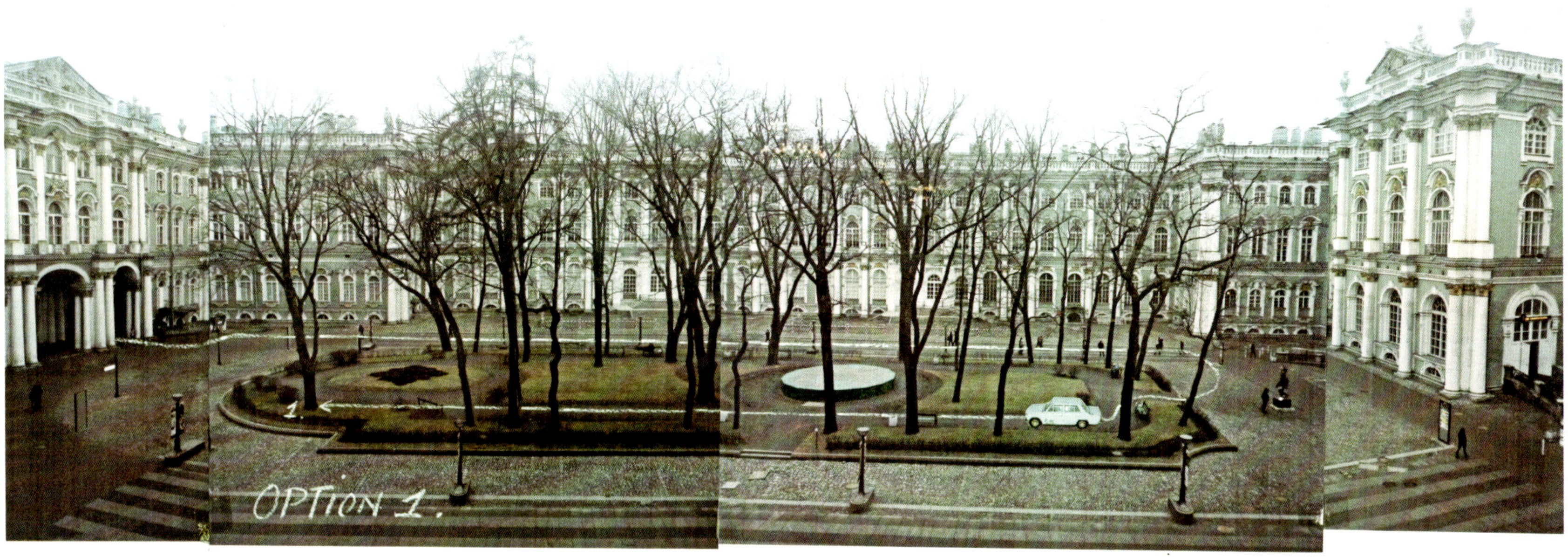

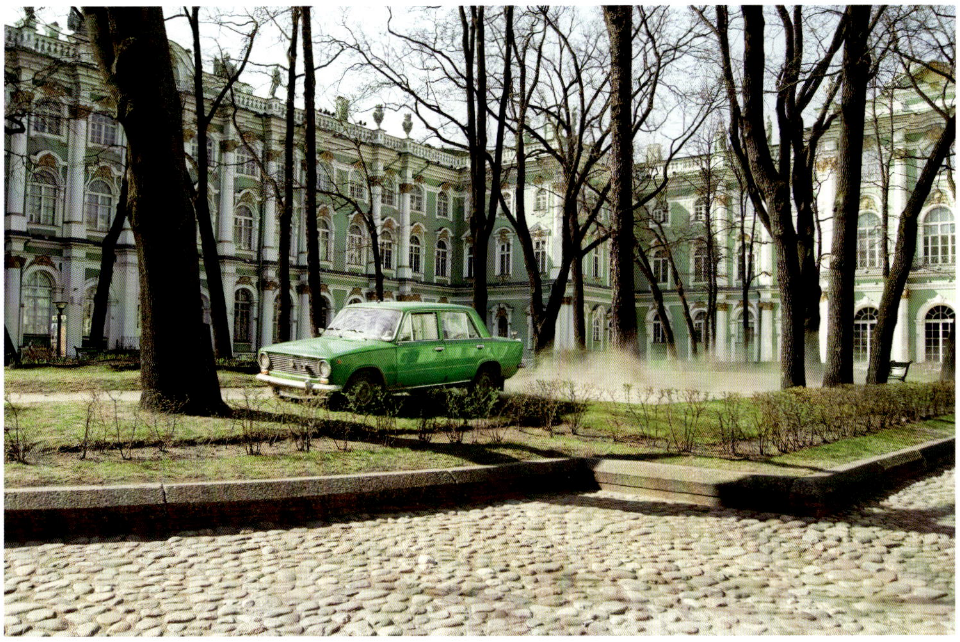

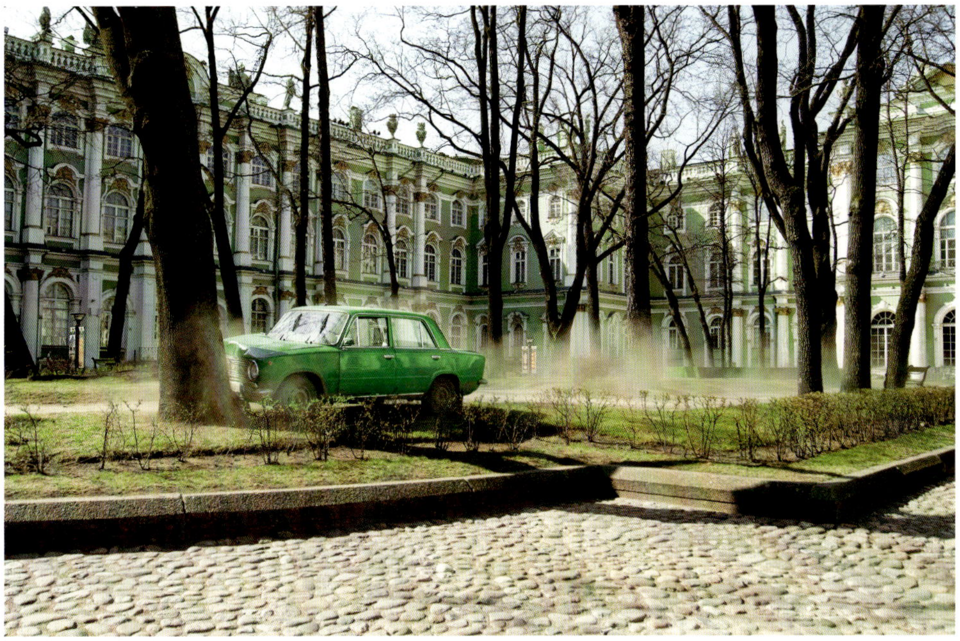

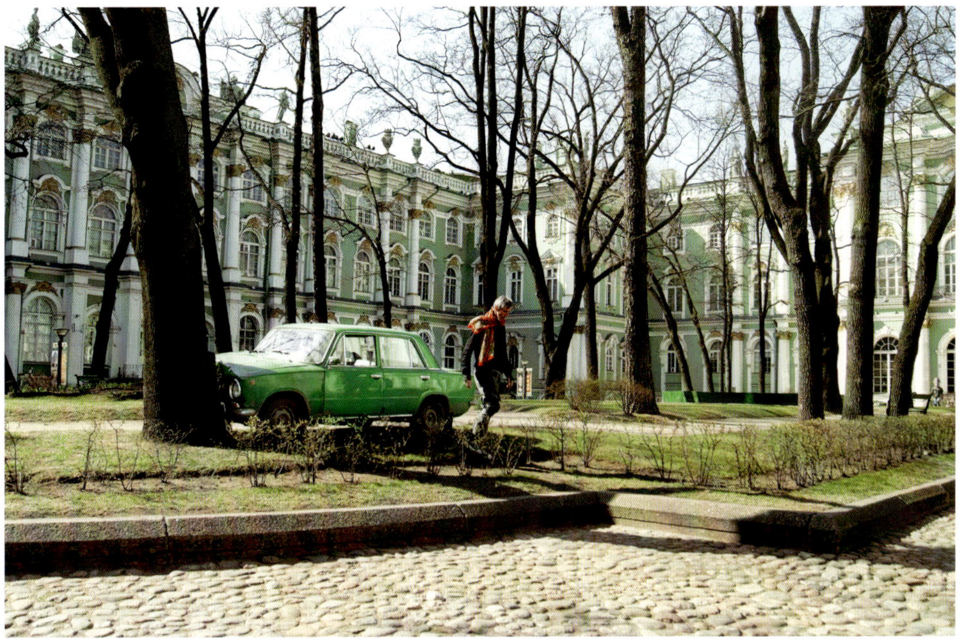

LADA KOPEIKA PROJECT, 2014
IN COLLABORATION WITH
WITH FRÉDÉRIC DE SMEDT,
CONSTANTIN FELKER, AND
JULIEN DEVAUX
PHOTO DOCUMENTATION OF AN
ACTION, SAINT PETERSBURG

When we were young, my brother and I decided to escape our bourgeois Belgian society and drive to Leningrad in our 1981 Lada. But the car broke down and soon after our lives parted. 30 years later I invited my brother to drive from Belgium to Saint Petersburg in a 1977 Lada. Upon arrival we crashed the car into a tree of the courtyard of the Winter Palace, together with the illusions of our youth. Without an ending there is no beginning.

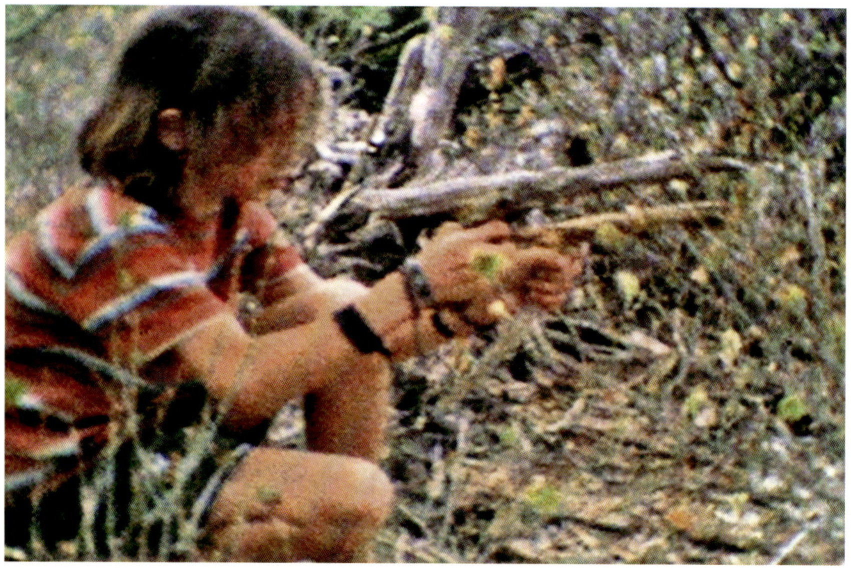

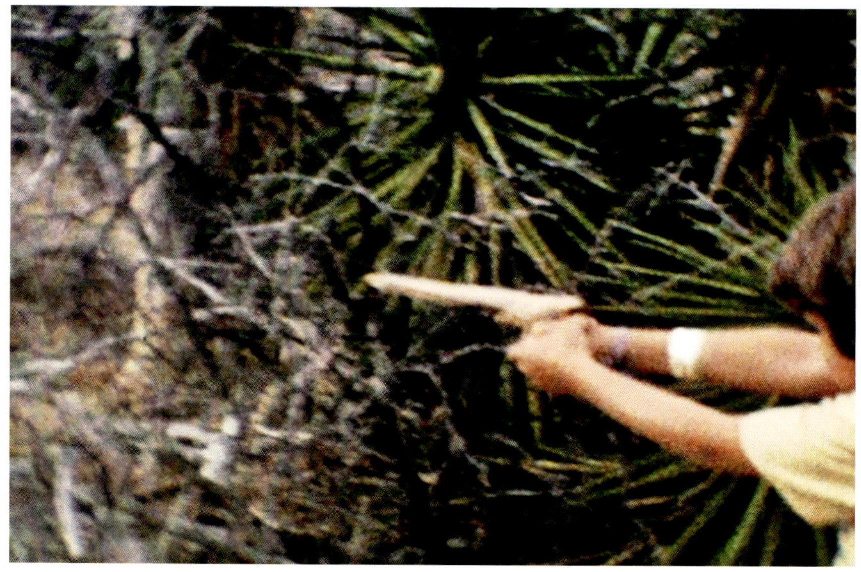

belongs to this tribe. He has nothing to sell, but the prehistory of the commodity saturates his art.

Walking, a word suggestive of narration, has been much in vogue recently: walking as a way of thinking, walking as a way of both interrogating and integrating oneself into one's surroundings, getting close only to keep on moving on. Nietzsche was a great walker-thinker, every day, rain or shine, with his short, myopic, steps. In her book *Wanderlust*, Rebecca Solnit takes us walking as a way of getting to know both ourselves and social history in and around San Francisco. Anke Gleber's publication, *The Art of Taking a Walk*, subtitled, 'Flanerie, Literature, and Film in Weimar Culture,' is a study motivated by Walter Benjamin and his friend Franz Hessel walking Paris and Berlin. The French artist Jean Selz tells us how Benjamin frequently walked in Ibiza in the summer of 1932, constantly stopping with the exclamation, Tiens!, as he collected his thoughts.

Benjamin claimed that the best way to get to know a city is to get lost in it and *colportage* became for him an amalgam of walking the city as an explorer interested not in the great 'sights' but in the unexpected, similar to the experience of being absorbed in watching a film, or ingesting hashish.

Alÿs goes one better. He is the subject of film, or rather its 'agent', whose walking activates the subliminal side of the urban everyday through a process that Benjamin in his 1928 essay on Surrealism called a 'profane illumination'. Resembling an epiphany, it is profane yet perplexing and enigmatic, verging on the mystical, like the title of one of Alÿs' early pieces, *Paradox of Praxis 1* (1997) in which he pushes a block of ice through Mexico City until it melts to nothing.

It is not the city of Paris – that most favoured of all surreal objects for André Breton and his friends – but Mexico City that unfurls through Alÿs' art when, for instance, he spends all day bent over, body straining, pushing a knee-high block of ice through the crowded downtown streets until it melts. What happens, as with the flaming soccer ball being kicked through Ciudad Juárez, is that the surroundings come alive and leap to the forefront. The block of ice or the flaming ball are like a conjuror's misdirection, used to trick the audience into relaxing their gaze so that the real miracle can occur, in this case the miracle of the everyday, the abundant life in the crowded streets of Mexico City or the ominous shadows and depths of Ciudad Juárez at night. To use Brecht's terminology, estrangement sets in as the invisible becomes visible, which with Alÿs' videos owes much to sound.

The trick here is to allow the mundane to have its say and express its hidden dimensions through a common object and though an unusual, but simple, activity. The flaming soccer ball kicked along the deserted streets of Ciudad Juárez is certainly a wondrous sight. Perhaps it is symbolic as well. But how much more wondrous and creepy are the shadows it illuminates – recalling the 'negative sacred' of Bataille and Michel Leiris – the legs of a prostitute, the solitary bus that heaves rattling into sight and disappears, the tired wheezing of an accordion, all emerging from the shadows of consciousness thanks to the disconsolate, obsessive, kicking of the ball, at once aggressive, playful and pointless. Perhaps there is a rhythm to this walking and kicking. The first kick is the more aggressive one. It says 'How can this be, this crazy violence?' The second kick is more meditative. It asks, 'How is it that we get used to it so quickly?'

CAMGUNS, 2005–06
WOOD, METAL, PLASTIC AND FILM REELS

Evoking the simulated weapons used by the Zapatista Army when they appeared on the Mexican scene in 1994, this work explicity connects the 'shooting' of images to that of the bullets.

previous page,
CHILDREN'S GAME #5: REVOLVER, 2009
BAJA CALIFORNIA, MEXICO
8MM FILM DOCUMENTATION OF AN ACTION
2 MIN. 49 SEC.

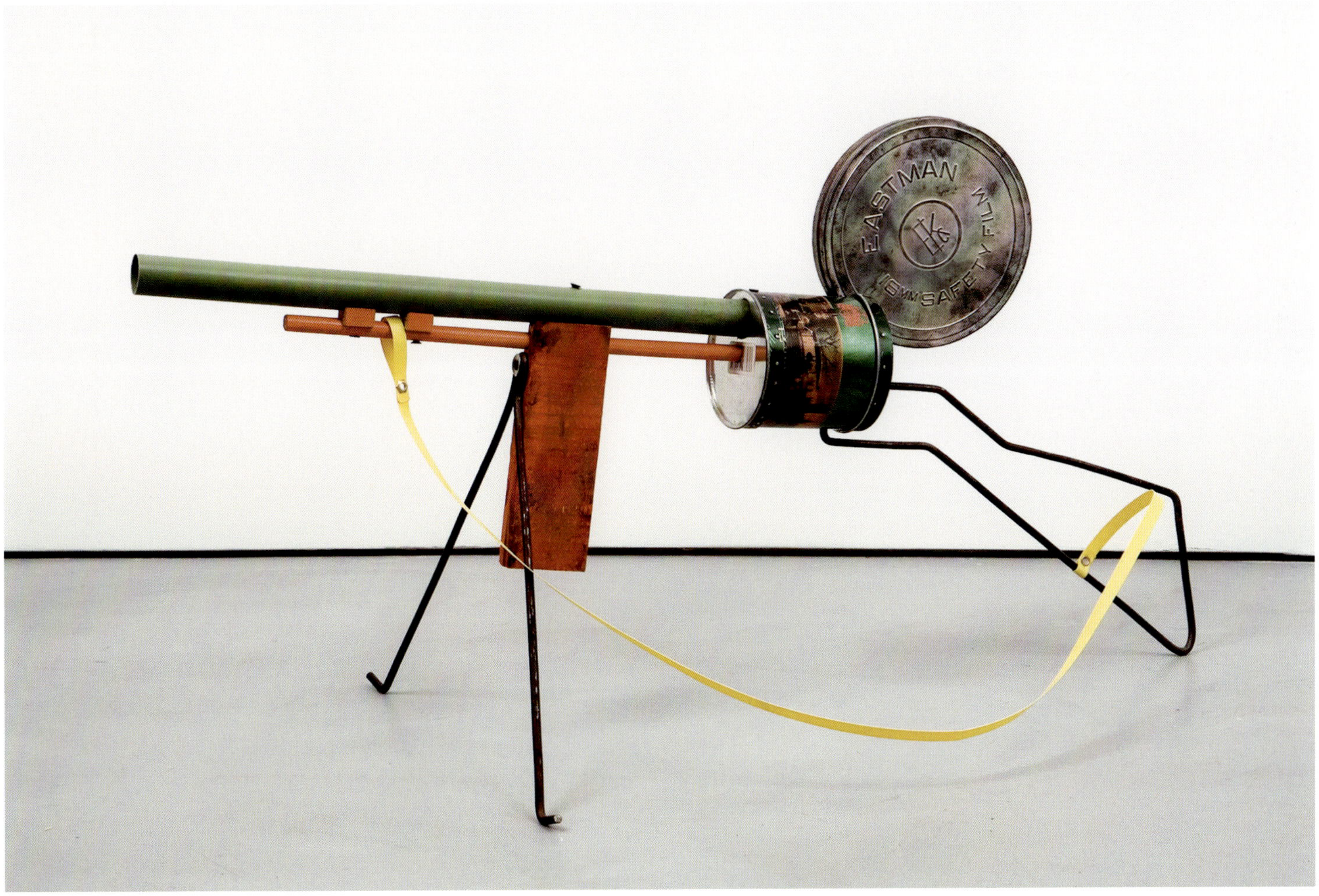

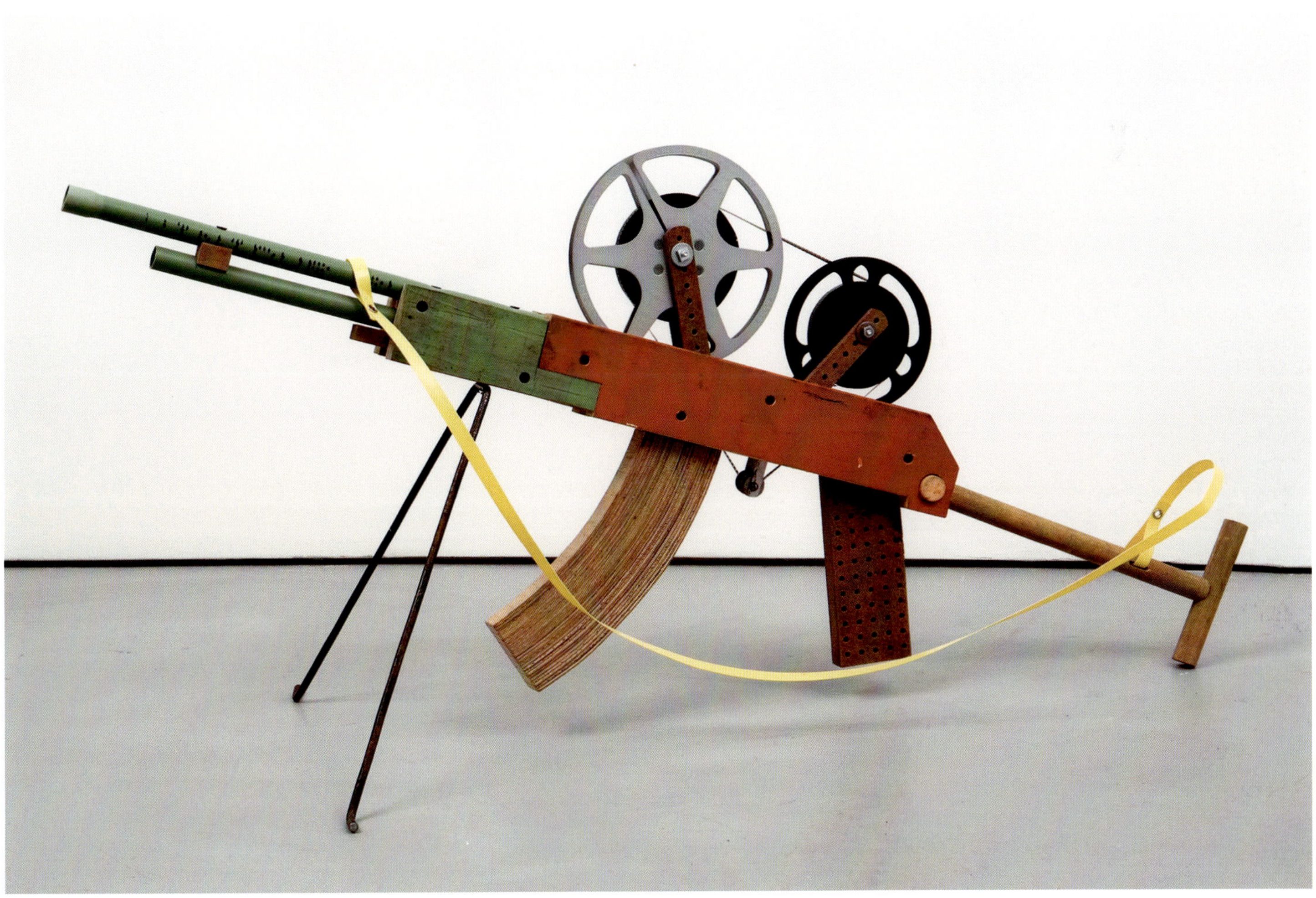

This is of a piece with Alÿs' enthusiasm for paradox (and its rhythm), as evidenced in the enigmatic titles of many of his works, which bear the looping of action and reversal: *Sometimes Doing is Undoing and Sometimes Undoing is Doing; Reel-Unreel; Don't Cross the Bridge Before You Get to the River; Sometimes Reality Meets Fiction and Sometimes Fiction Meets Reality.* To see only cynicism in such paradox would be to miss the point, to miss the whimsy that is the gift-wrapping around what I call the mastery of non-mastery, a formula at once political and philosophical. Hegel dug deeply into the mastery of non-mastery in his infamously difficult 'Lordship and Bondage' chapter in *The Phenomenology of Spirit.* Derrida extended this in a sparkling essay on Bataille, 'From Restricted to General Economy; An Hegelianism Without Reserve'. Alÿs' artworks present another twist to this mastery of non-mastery, that of the trickster.

BEIRUT, LEBANON, 2016

Sometimes reality meets fiction and sometimes fiction meets reality.

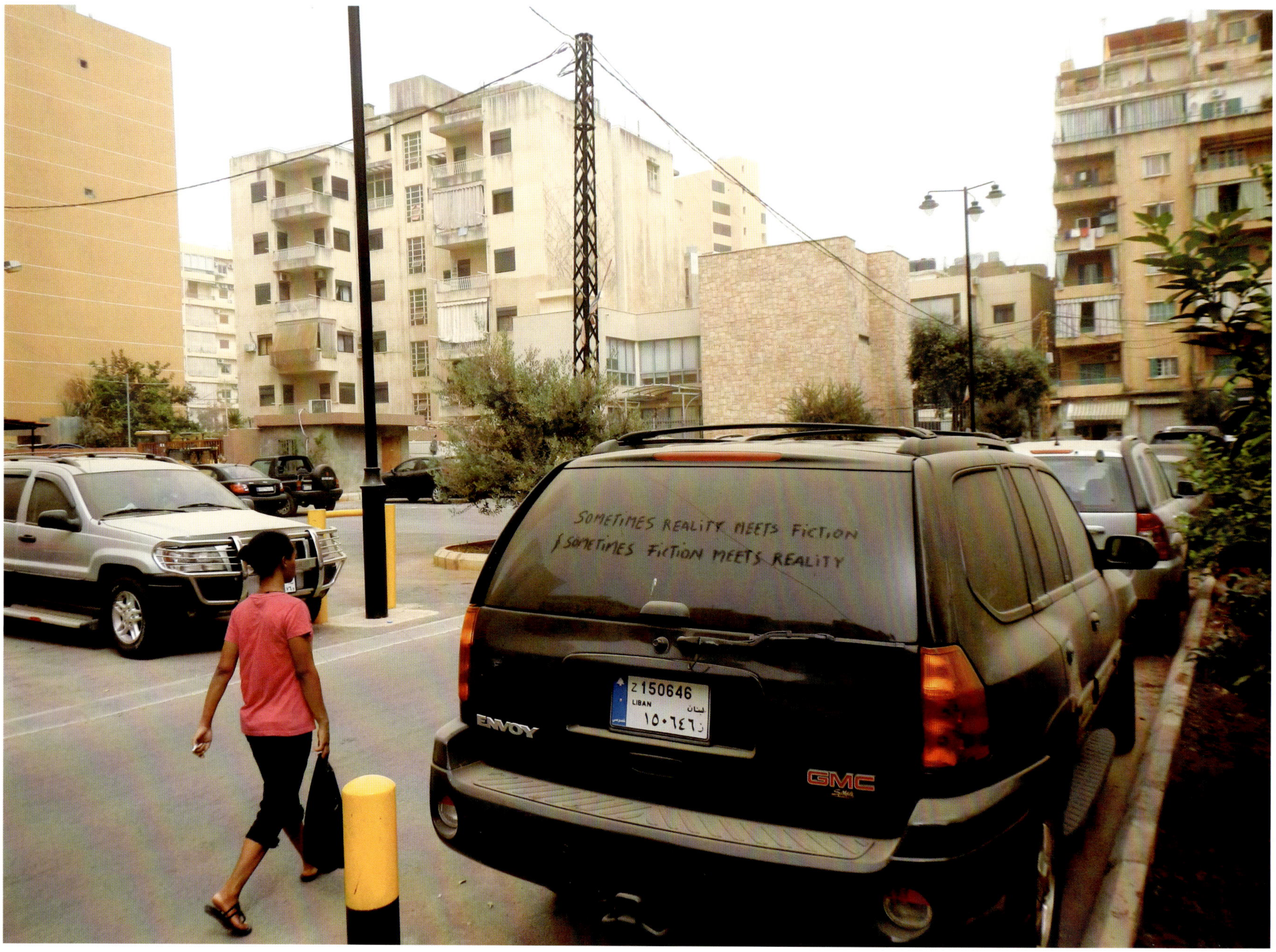

BEIRUT, LEBANON, 2016

Sometimes losing is winning and sometimes winning is losing.

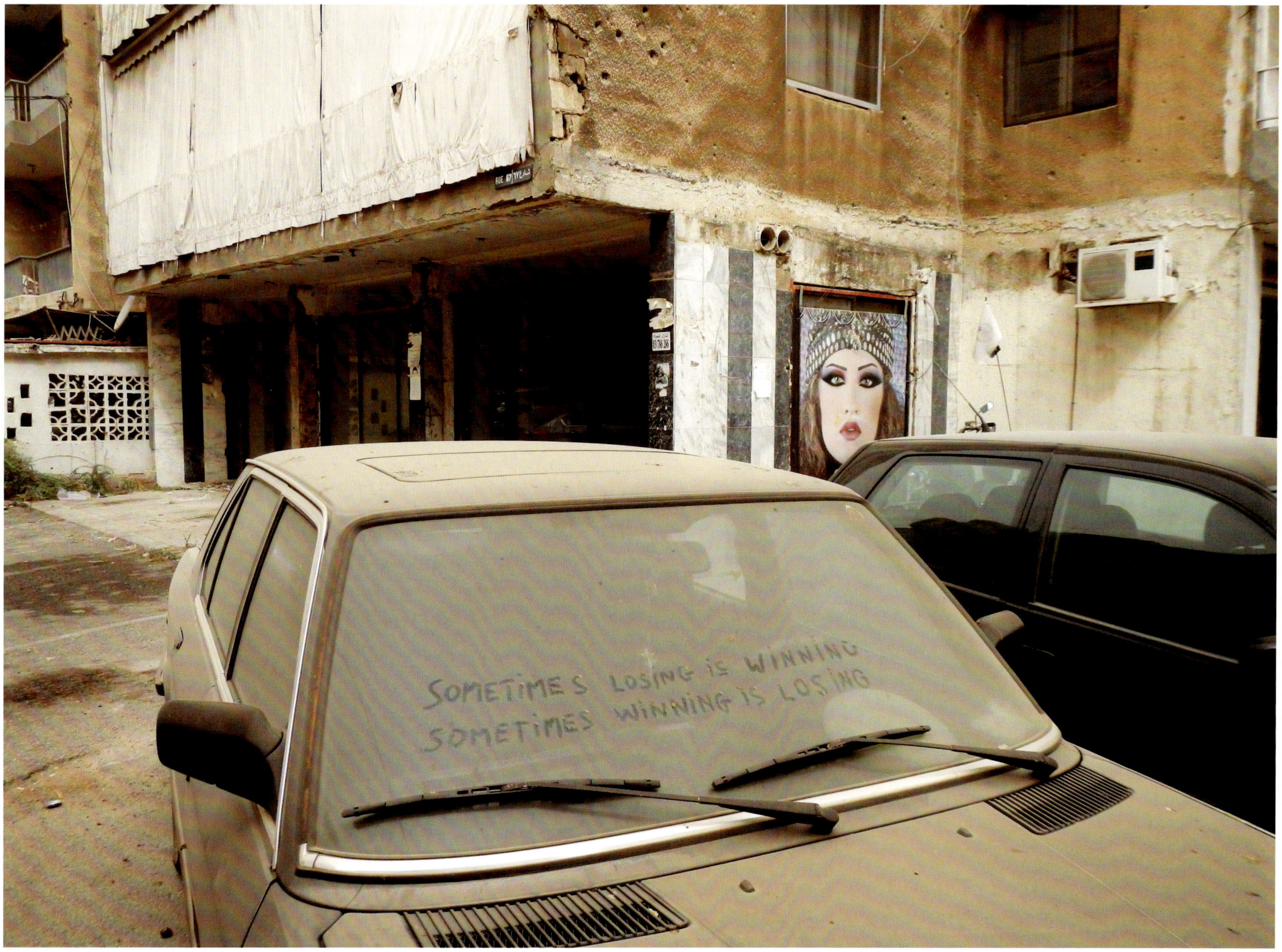

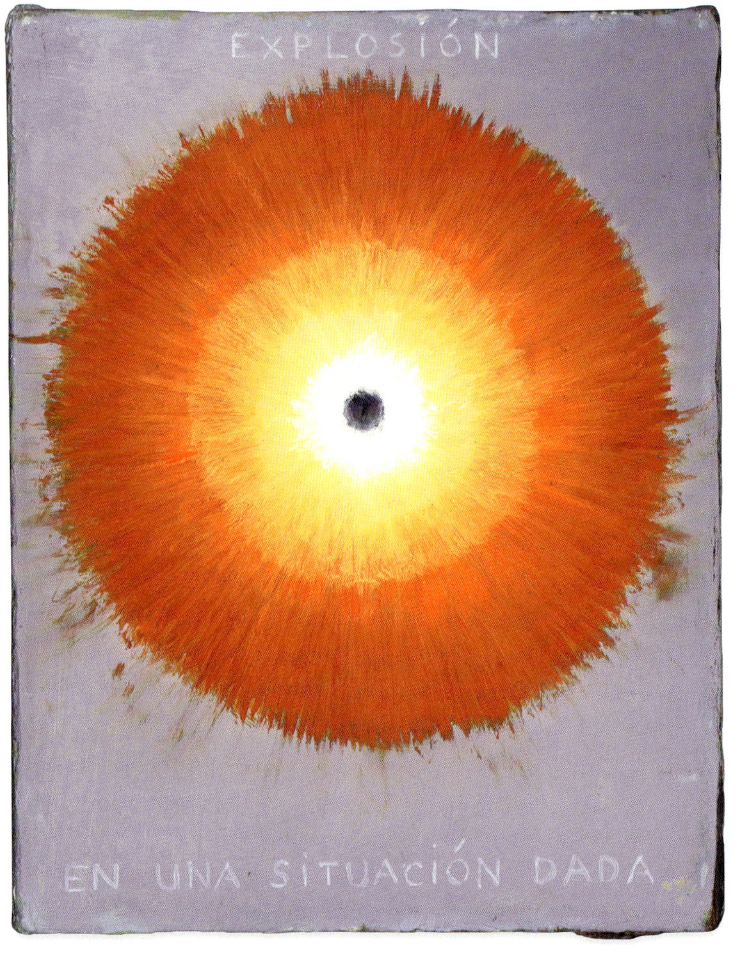

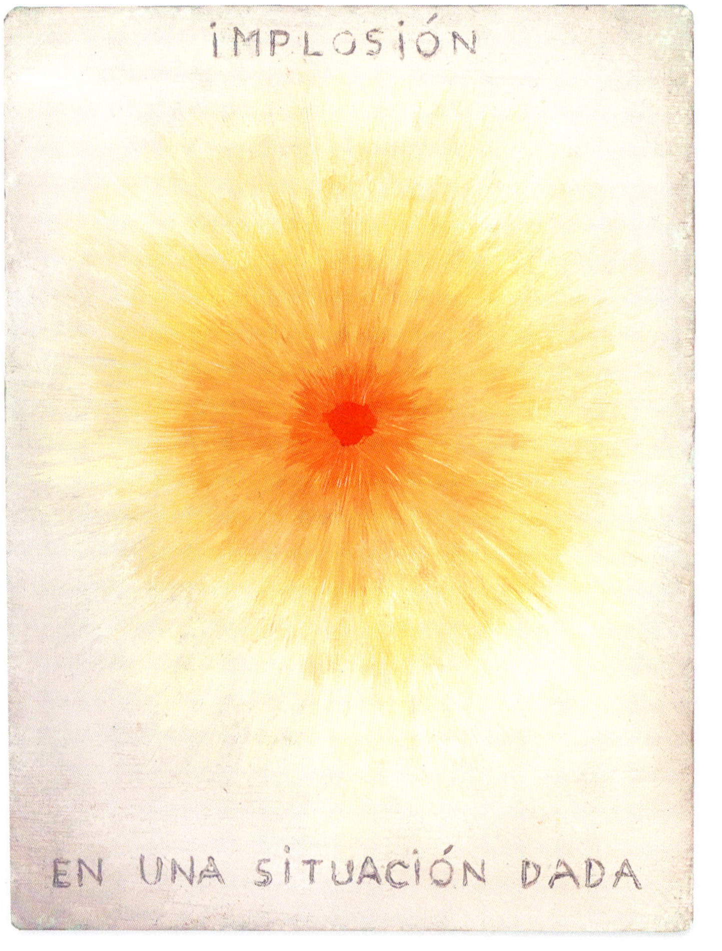

Lest there should be any misconception that the trickster avoids or makes light of eviscerating trauma and the cruelty weighing on us in today's world, take the pamphlet accompanying the 2013 'Ciudad Juárez Project's. Diminutive in size, its twelve colour pages on cheap paper contain some of the artist's notes to himself, along with newspaper cuttings of the faces of abducted women, yellow-press images of women's corpses ('killed for conducting conversations with other women'), and a centrefold in blasting fire colour of the artist's legs kicking the ball. Here and there are drawings that evoke other realities and other perspectives: tiny child-like figures playing with fire, a drawing of a woman washing her hair in a blood-red pool with a close up sketch of her hands squeezing her hair, maps of the city, and several frenetic diagrams attempting to get to grips with the ungraspable, as expressed in the following terms: 'How can such evil take place?' 'Collapse of the ethic of evil?', 'What is the relation between resilience and resistance?'

There is to my mind here also a concern with dreamwork. You feel this in the aura generated by the fragility of the drawn images, as well as in the implicit question about the cruelty and wealth animating the drug cartels. It is even in the title: *Paradox of Praxis 5: Sometimes We Dream as We Live and Sometimes We Live as We Dream.*

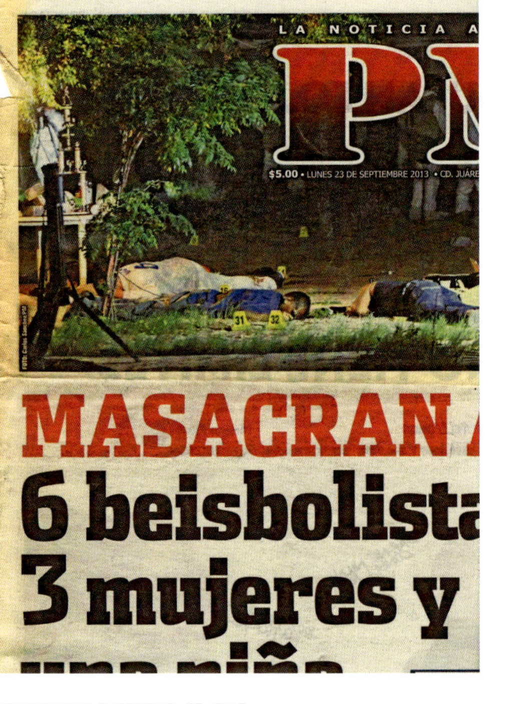

NEWSPAPER CLIPPING, CIUDAD JUÁREZ, MEXICO, 2013
FROM THE ARTIST'S ARCHIVE

previous page,
IMPLOSION/EXPLOSION, 2009
DIPTYCH
OIL ON CANVAS
EACH 20 X 14 CM

PARADOX OF PRAXIS 5, 2013
IN COLLABORATION WITH RAFAEL ORTEGA, JULIEN DEVAUX, ALEJANDRO MORALES AND FÉLIX BLUME, CIUDAD JUÁREZ, MEXICO
VIDEO DOCUMENTATION OF AN ACTION, 7 MIN. 49 SEC.

Sometimes we dream as we live
Sometimes we live as we dream

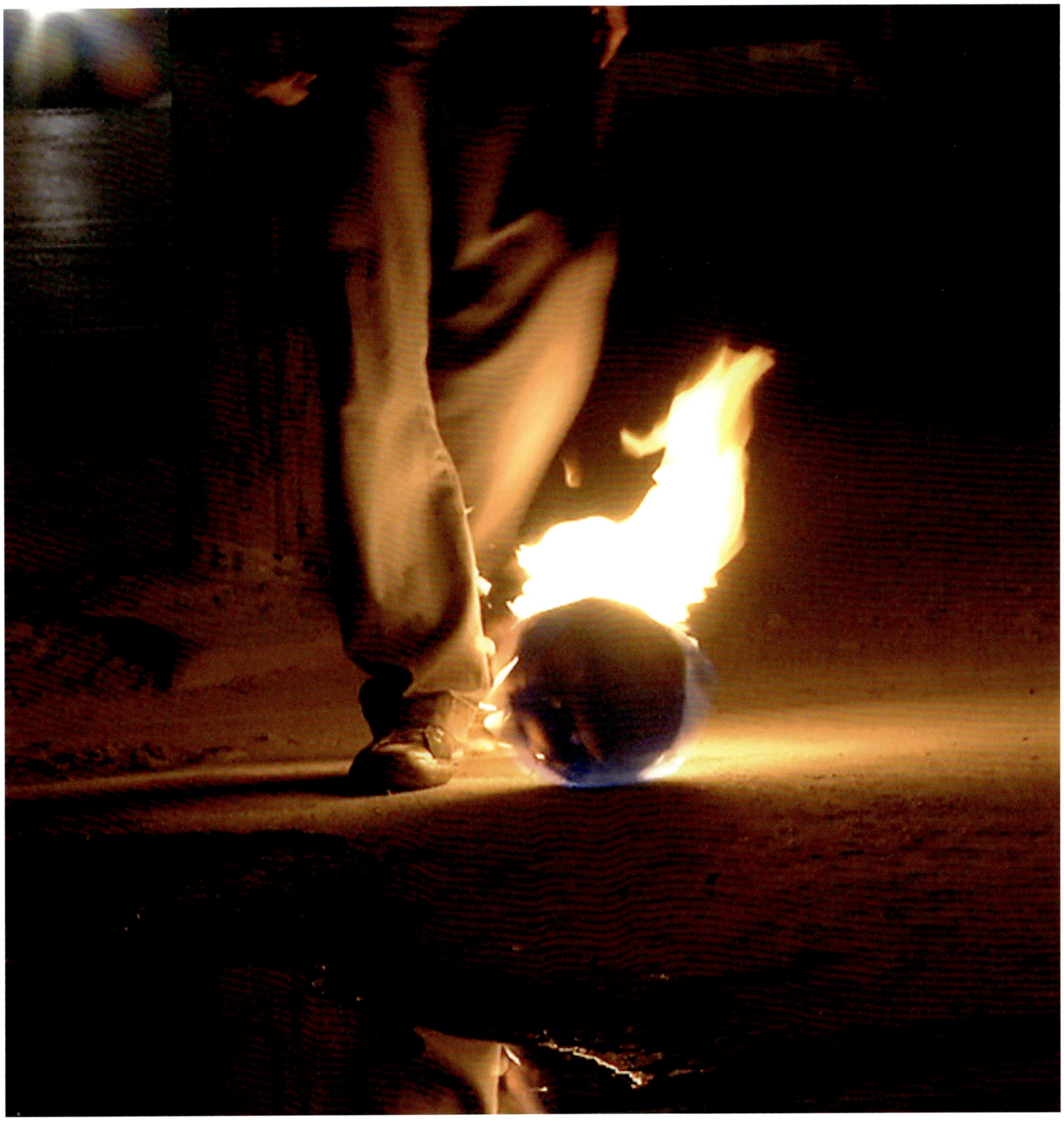

LYNCHINGS, 2005
OIL AND COLLAGE ON CANVAS
ON WOOD
18 X 12 CM

In the first decade of the twenty-first century, due to the growing rate of criminality and the loss of confidence in the justice system, Mexico witnessed a series of public lynchings where purported criminals were attacked by mobs convinced that this was the only way justice would be done.

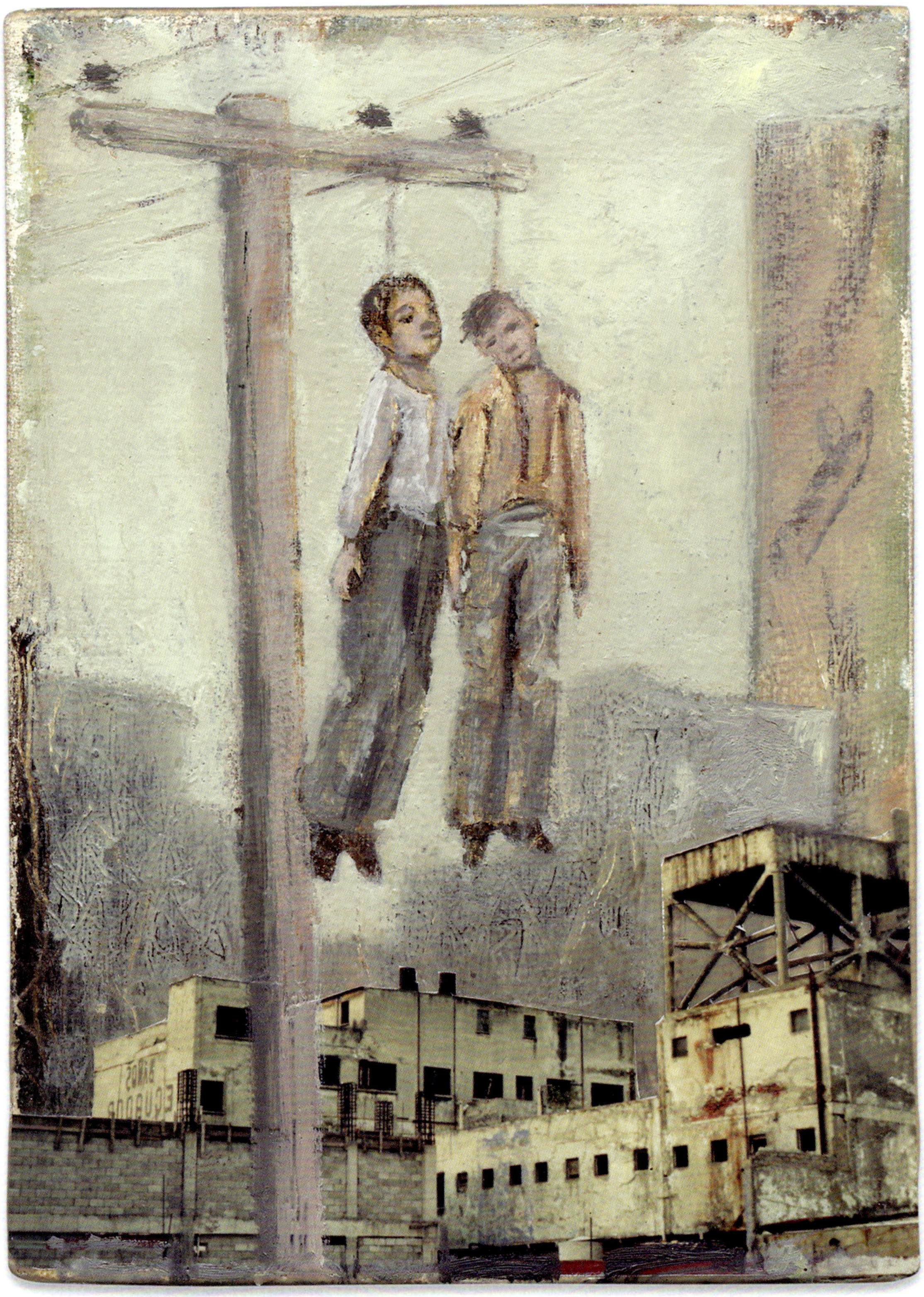

STUDY FOR LYNCHINGS, 2005
OIL AND PENCIL ON TRACING PAPER
20 X 20 CM

LYNCHINGS, 2010
OIL ON CANVAS
12 X 17 CM

next pages,
UNTITLED (FOB SHAWQAT, AFGHANISTAN), 2013
OIL ON CANVAS
13 X 18 CM

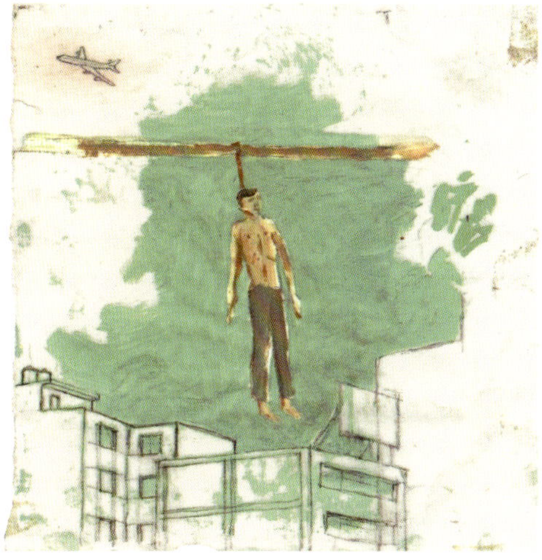

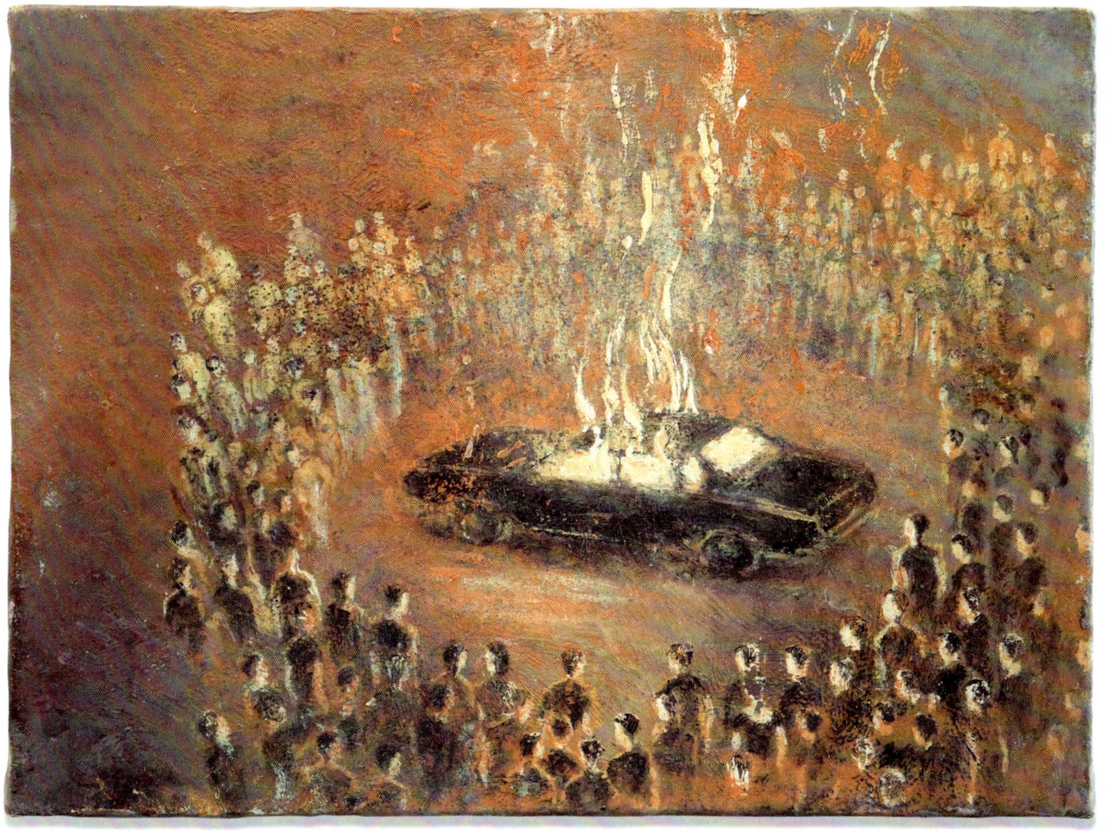

It is like whimpering while asleep, this little pamphlet. Everything is provisional and 'on hold', till the next time. This is the Alÿs leitmotif. Hence his frequent recourse to rehearsal. With its material lifted from notebooks, you can think of the pamphlet as yet another notebook – another rehearsal – and hence as a background to the video, which we see as the finished work. But isn't the idea of a finished work a convenient fiction? Couldn't the notebook be just as much a work of art? Isn't the notebook in some ways the more real and more daring version?

The flaming ball finds another counterpoint in *Espejos* (Mirrors, 2013), one of Alÿs' many short videos of children's games. Here a bunch of boys 'shoot' each other in Ciudad Juárez with beams of sunlight reflected in jagged shards of mirror. It must be difficult, sneaking through the newly built houses, now deserted on account of the violence, angling the sun so as to get a bead on your 'enemy' and not be seen. The boys run and dodge at great speed. The sullen desert, with its wispy growth, encroaches on the windowless, doorless structures that once were homes. Desert meets the deserted. The harsh light under the bluest of skies hides the secrets of the cartels. The boys secrete themselves as only kids can. The sudden glare of the sun in one of the mirrors catches you off balance. At the end of the video, which lasts for four minutes, each boy's face is reflected in a mirror-piece along with his first name: Benjamin, Isaac, Sergio. Something miraculous happens at that moment. Nietzsche's tuning-fork effect, perhaps? The breaking of the spell? Or its thickening? Stepping outside the game? Or realizing there is no outside?

Let's not forget the forbidding parallel between 'shooting' with sunrays and the violence of the cartels. The children in *Saltamontes* (Grasshopper, 2015), a video that Alÿs filmed in Venezuela, pull the legs off grasshoppers then fling the insects into the air with shrieks of joy, delighting in the insects' aerial gymnastics. And, guess what? When they land they can't jump away. They have no legs. You can be sure of that because of the popping sound you hear as they are removed. Yes children can be cruel, too, and it would be a grievous mistake to think of Alÿs' consuming interest in children's games as a delight in the innocence of childhood in a nasty world.
Even though one sort of game is kids pretending and the other sort, the adult sort, is for real, do they not share something? This is best expressed in the shadows of childrens' hands playing Rock, Scissors, Paper at incredible speed in the video *Piedra, papel y tijeras* (Rock, Paper and Scissors, 2013). We see no actual hands, only their moving shadows. It could be a quaint

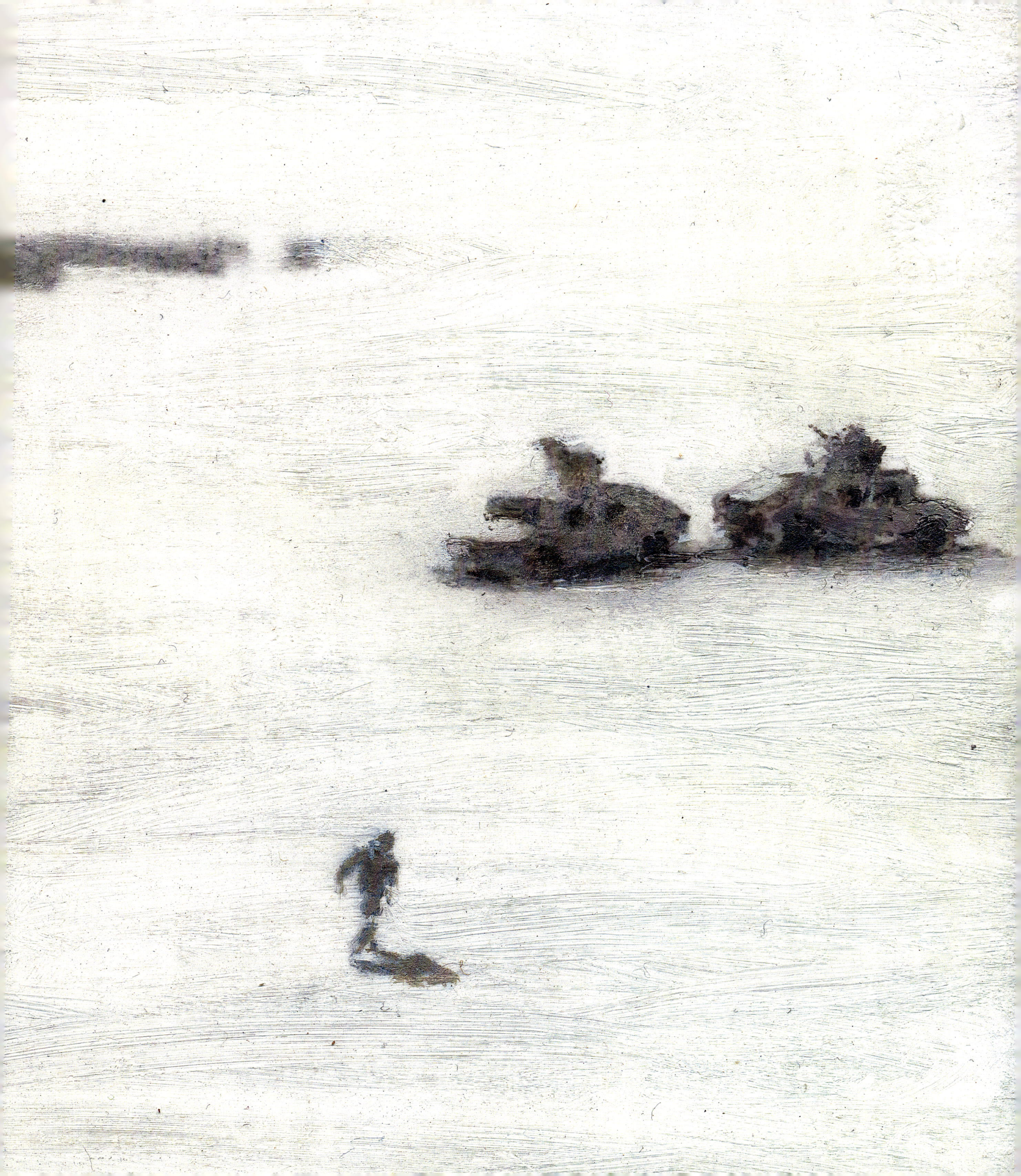

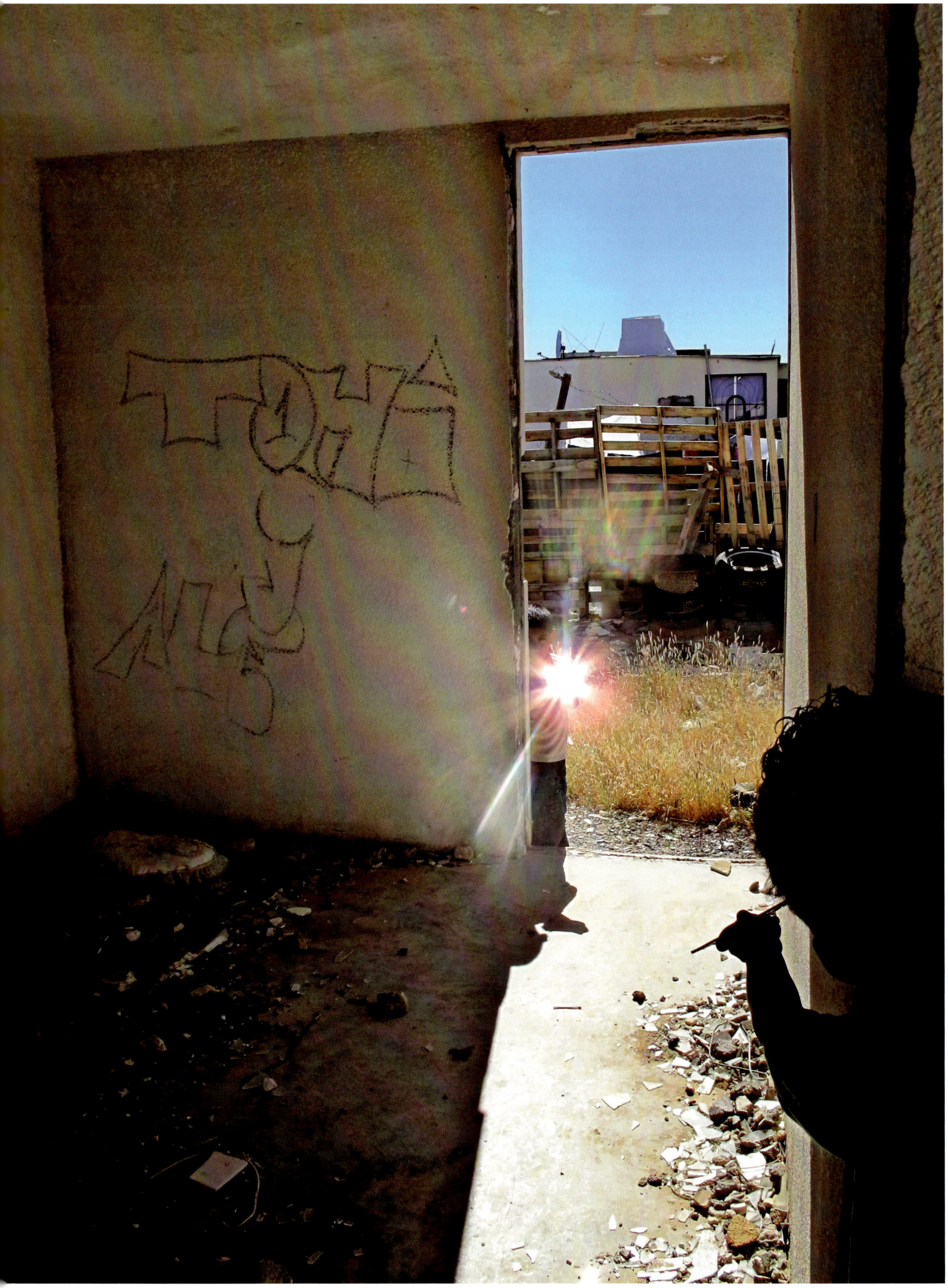

CHILDREN'S GAME #15: ESPEJOS, 2013
CIUDAD JUÁREZ, MEXICO
VIDEO DOCUMENTATION OF AN ACTION
4 MIN. 53 SEC.

opposite,
CHILDREN'S GAME #19: HARAM FOOTBALL, 2017
MOSUL, IRAQ
PHOTO DOCUMENTATION OF AN ACTION

CHILDREN'S GAME #9: SALTAMONTES, 2011
IN COLLABORATION WITH FÉLIX BLUME, SALTO ACHA, VENEZUELA
VIDEO DOCUMENTATION OF AN ACTION
6 MIN. 10 SEC.

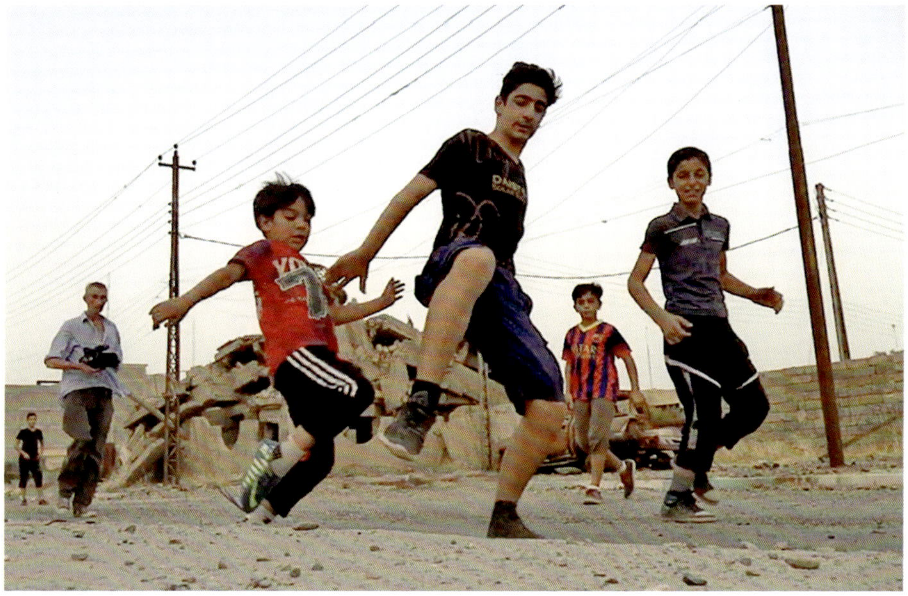

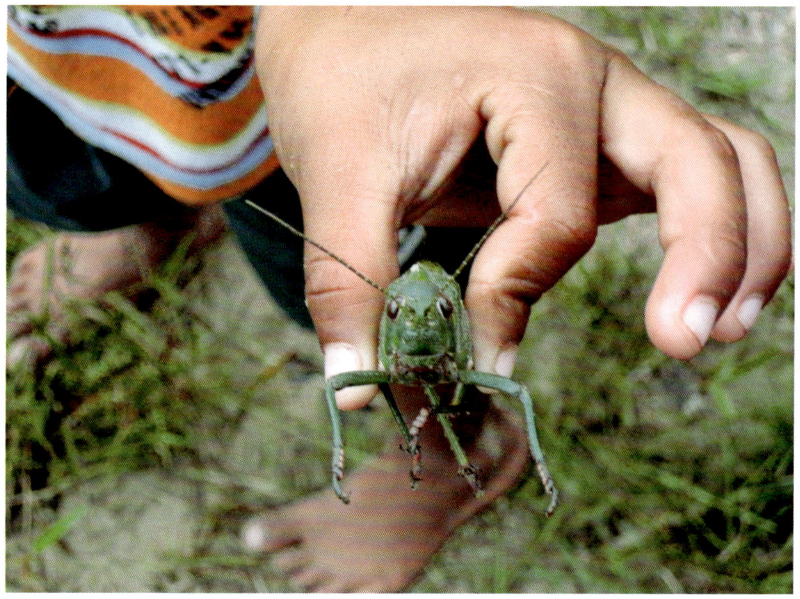

sign-language known only to coyotes and school kids who share the dark secrets of the violence of the border. All that is Alÿs.

Your mind reels trying to take in these unexpected contingencies and connections whereby insides become outsides and vice versa as mirrors shoot sunrays and the vibration of the tuning fork resonates with shamanic conjuring insinuating into the unsayable. Surely this is what Alÿs' work is increasingly about, this stepping outside of the ways in which war and violence are commonly represented?

In his October 2016 work created at the front line on the outskirts of Mosul (first presented in the Iraq Pavilion at the Venice Biennale of 2017), his representation of war terminates in violence of another sort, a white screen, a blank nothing. Well, not quite. In the video *Color Matching* we see Alÿs's hands, apparently painting a scene of two heavily armoured Peshmerga vehicles in a sandbag enclosure, their Kurdish crew milling around. His colours fall like animal droppings onto the canvas. Yellow. Blue. Red. No form is discernible here, other than a swirly swirl. The artist's brush becomes a blur of nervous trepidation. Yes, another war here: the war of getting the damn thing right, here in the state of emergency in Mosul. What is Mosul? A name. A place on TV. He abruptly, violently, wipes the swirly swirl off with a rag. At first, the canvas glows orange and yellow like the sand of the desert. Then all is white, a dirty white, its scum the record of failure and something more than failure, namely the strain and stain of history as process, history as a loop, by which I mean telling a story that collapses in on itself as essential to that very self. It seems significant that we never see the artist. We never see Francis Alÿs. What we see is a pair of frenetic hands, the canvas and the Peshmerga vehicles. Things talking to things. Or trying to.

This is a history lesson, beginning with a blank slate on which to sketch men and weapons of war on vast deserts where even the grains of sand seem like playthings of madmen lusting for oil, God and the destruction of 'the enemy'. Always an enemy. Hence the frenzy of the painter's brush trying this, then that, followed by a last-gasp strategic nothingness that for all the world seems like the blind power of a desert storm. This is by no means the same as saying that war and violence cannot or should not be represented. The question is how? Let's have another shot.

As we swivel to survey the side of the room opposite to where this video is playing, we see eight unframed postcard-sized canvases. The grey grain of the canvas competes with the imagery, which is itself grey and barely discernible; just a smudge of the real, you might say. With some coaching and an eagle eye, you might just see, depending on the light and your angle of vision, that one of these depicts in shadowy form a member of ISIS decapitating someone, which is what these Peshmerga fighters repeatedly watch on their cell phones. In these miniature, unobtrusive, paintings, in which forms disappear in shadowy greys, the violence performs its own disappearing act, its own 'decapitation'. As with the attempted painting in the video, it seems crucially important that the effort was made, and failed, and made again, and failed again, such that we are left with a dirty white canvas.

Oh! And one other thing: the wind ripping across the desert in a vibrating whine.

The sound is as important as the absent presence of the visual imagery. Is this the trick, combining the visible and the invisible?

This repeated performance of representational failing is central to the Alÿs oeuvre, most boldly in *Rehearsal I* (1999–2001), *Rehearsal II* (2001) and *The Politics of Rehearsal* (2005). Here, as in all of Alÿs' work, the point is not only the concept, but the brio with which the concept is set into play. These small narratives of repeated effort and failing awaken a terrible fear and longing, performing the repetition of which Freud spoke as the effort to overcome trauma in *Beyond the Pleasure Principle.*

In the case of *Rehearsal I* (El Ensayo) it is the strident music of a *mariachi* band winding up a red VW beetle to ascend a steep hill, almost making it, then sliding back down, again and again. Filmed in the border town of Tijuana it could be an allegory of border crossings that don't succeed, but it also performs a contradiction, namely the impossibility of representing unrepresentability. As the VW ascends and rolls back, the music swells with hope, only to die away, pause in silence, then begin again full of hope and inspiration as the car has another go at the hill. How you cross such a border turns out to be the same question as how can you represent the unrepresentable. Politics and philosophy merge in performing attempts at border crossings.

In *Rehearsal II* a woman slowly strips, seductive and graceful, to the soundtrack of a singer accompanied by a piano. The voice is beautiful, taking you to unknown places, but this is a rehearsal. 'Let's try it this way!', then 'Let's try it another way!', is what seems to be going on between the female singer and a male voice advising or directing her. Each time they stop, the stripper replaces her garments again. *The Politics of Rehearsal* also begins with a singer performing vocal exercises, before switching to footage of President Harry Truman at the beginning of the Cold War and a voiceover by the brilliant art historian Cuauhtémoc Medina, which make it clear that all this stopping and starting is an allegory of so-called 'development' as a US-inspired strategy to head off the commies gaining traction in the 'undeveloped' world. Like waiting for the Messiah or for Godot, 'development' rarely comes and if it does come it is likely to be a mixed blessing.

Here is the inside story, for is not Alÿs 'undeveloped' too, forever doubled in his experience of growing up (should I say 'developing') in Western Europe on the one hand, and living, mouth agape, in the centre of Mexico City since 1986, feeling the categories of experience grate and churn? Imagine a Duchamp or a Magritte becoming an urban ethnographer with an intimate but estranged and estranging relationship to 'undeveloped' city life. Imagine the view of Europe from the global south. Along with its muted ache of despair and satire, Alÿs' work is pixilated by these reciprocating perspectives.

In light of this, I cannot but refer to the politics and ethics of his choice to freely share his film work with us all by means of the internet. In contrast to those artists who make films with high production values for one or two collectors at Goldman Sachs' prices, and whose precious work is rarely if ever seen by the unwashed public, Alÿs is able to freely distribute his projects because he funds them through selling his small paintings. He also makes postcards, which are given away free where his work is shown. (In 2010, Tate Modern, London, and MoMA, New York, produced a postcard-sized booklet displaying much of his oeuvre in the form of thirty postcards that fold out like an accordion. The captions are funny and thought-provoking. At once an artisanal, self-help, sustainable solution, this economy is an artful contribution to building community and fair play. In other words, Alÿs' artwork is mirrored by his economic practice, which is an artwork in its own right.

Alÿs attributes several functions to these small paintings other than their economic contribution. They are like pages from an artist's notebook, for instance, in which he tries ideas out as he develops a theme. This strikes me as significant. What is on sale is a record of the artist's travails and inspiration, not finished works. We are being taught to respect the processes of exploration, to ponder praxis. This is the sign of an artisanal attitude, in which subject and object, artist and materials, swim in a flux of adjustment and readjustment.

By his own admission, Alÿs felt unconfident and disappointed with his drawing in Europe, where he worked as an architect with an interest in urban design. It was only when he moved to Mexico in 1986 and became aware of a type of sign-painting that he found his style. From his first Mexican paintings (*Set Theory*, 1997, for example) to the present, you cannot but be struck by this sign-painting aesthetic: a flatness of figuration, along with a frozen immobility that is uncanny, unsettling, and charming.

In Colombia in the 1970s and 1980s, especially in small country towns, I recall seeing murals in bars and cheap restaurants with this same sign-painting aesthetic, depicting human dilemmas, such as a man desperately clinging to a branch that he has almost sawn off, with bees attacking him while a crocodile awaits, teeth glistening, in the swamp below. Alÿs' paintings in his many books share in this fanciful element that shines through the sign-painting aesthetic.

For all its commercial function, sign-painting bears a striking resemblance to the icon, to the tiny glass-covered pictures of the saints and religiously inspired themes that you can buy throughout Latin America, including Mexico. The caricature-quality and the flatness, together with the uncanniness, is the same. This tying together of religion and commerce links to the aesthetics of the commodity that lay at the heart of

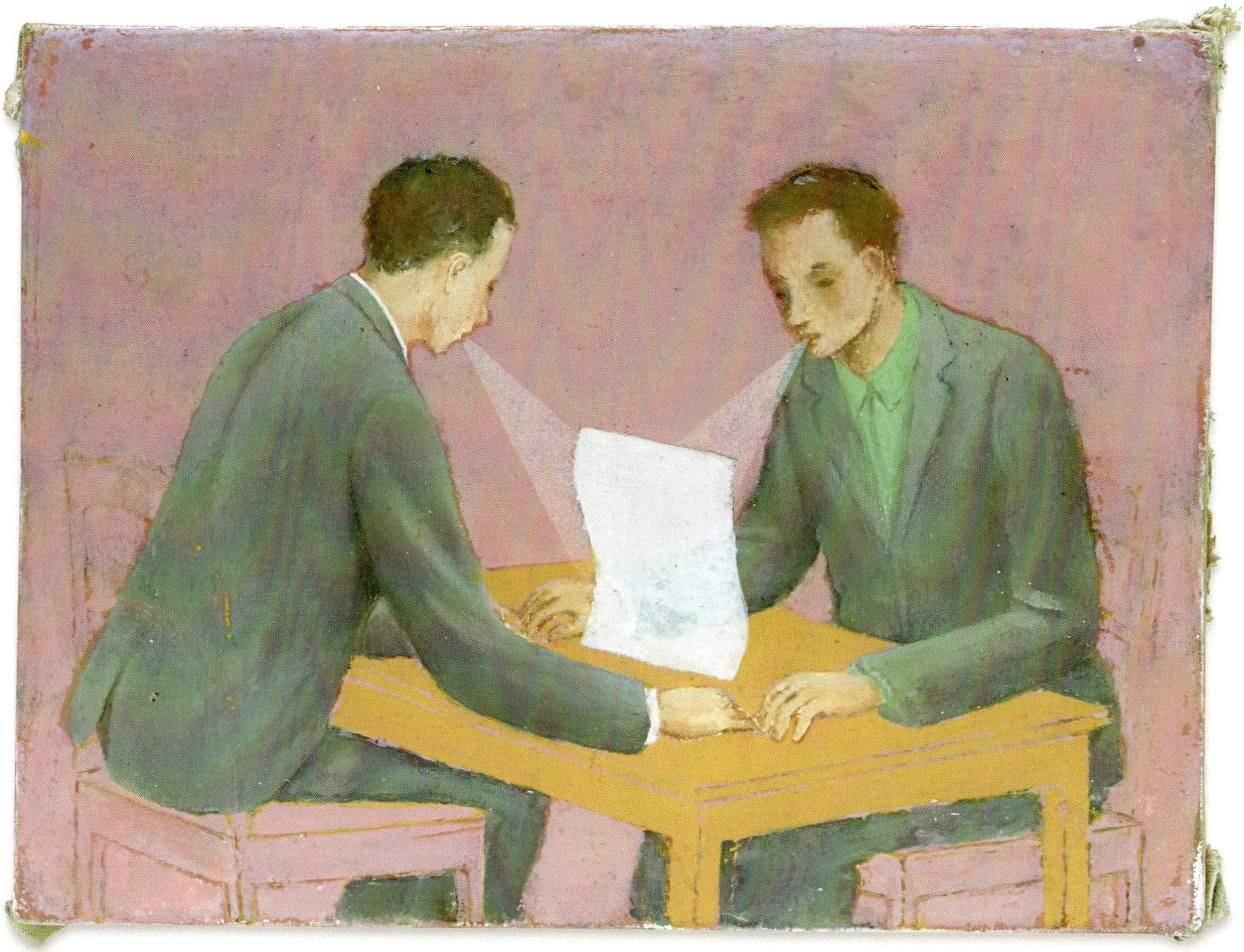

LA LEÇON DE MUSIQUE, 2000
OIL AND ENCAUSTIC
ON CANVAS
30 X 40 CM

Benjamin's later work such as *The Paris Arcades* inspired by the concept of commodity fetishism. It also brings us back to the *colporteur,* the street-walker with a tray of commodities, including religious tracts, and I'm sure if we looked hard we might even find icons in that tray too, as with the itinerant Indians from the Upper Amazon who station themselves in the markets in western Colombia selling amulets for babies, healing potions, herbs, sulphur, iron filings, pamphlets on magic and images of saints.

The *colporteur* entrances his audience with wit and storytelling. With his distinctive haircut and striped cloak, the Indian ensures that magic veils his commerce – the magic of his hallucinatory herbs, the magic of the traveller and, of course, the magic of the 'primitive'. The Mexico City signs, unsettling, frozen, charming and uncanny, are like this too, and all of these – *colporteur*, Indian and commercial street-sign – each in its own way forms what I earlier referred to as a pre-history of the commodity.

Wit and magic, along with the commercial art of street signs can be seen as corollaries and instantiations of the fetishisation of commodities, the secret of which, according to Karl Marx, was the looping back and forth between what he called use-value and exchange value, such that mere things brim over with life, as do Alÿs' flaming football and ice. Fetishization for Marx meant the animation granted things by the market, making us all the more sensitive to Alÿs' frequent allusions to the story of deception which we can take to also mean the way that truth and appearance are rendered suspect by the rumour driven culture of violence tearing Mexico apart. For me Alÿs' work (or should I say games) are in this regard a balm, granting a moment of peace from the turmoil while engaging with it. And this is an extraordinary accomplishment.

Is size critical here, too? I am thinking of the knee-down diminution of perspective, just as I am thinking of an aesthetic of diffidence, the little postcards, the 'littleness' of even his larger paintings in his several books with their flat people and things in understated pastel colours, and also of the small creatures that accompany his walks.

Just as Kafka's writing is scattered with animals and strange assistants, Alÿs has his creatures: the boys in the *Espejos* video, the magnetic shoes that pick up metal off the streets of Habana, his magnetic 'dog' to which stuff adheres in the streets of Mexico city at night; the guard dog that grips his trousers and lunges at his camera (*El Gringo*, 2003); the block of ice that he pushes through the heat of Mexico City. Here we see the process of something becoming smaller and smaller until ultimately the hour of diffidence has struck and there is nothing – that is, nothing but the memories of the voyage. Then there's the lone fox with a bushy tail slinking like quicksilver through the National Portrait Gallery (*The Nightwatch*, 2004). Caught by surveillance cameras, this low-to-the-ground fellow, scurrying along the gallery floor, steals the limelight from the portraits on the wall and, with that, estranges painting itself. The portraits will never look the same and painting achieves a strange afterlife, now subject to an eye that includes animal life as well as human. And why not? For too long painting, no less than art in general, has been monopolized by a single species.

Finally, to arbitrarily bring this list of animals to an end, consider the twenty-one sheep in the film *Cuentos Patrióticos* (1997), walking in a circle around what must be the tallest flagpole in the world in the Zocalo, the ceremonial political centre of Mexico. Back in 1968, the government marshalled thousands of civil servants to prevent students from raising the red and black flag of anarchy on this same flagpole. But instead, the civil servants turned their backs and bleated like sheep. Thirty years later, Alÿs resurrects the sheep, this time literally (just as he does with the Green Line, literalizing the symbolic). Round and round they go, these dutiful sheep, in what must be the cruellest depiction of patriotism ever conceived. Is it cruel because it is so funny? A terrible narrative is at work here. Alÿs leads one sheep around the pole on a halter. Then a second sheep runs in with that pitifully comic gait that running sheep have, closely following the first as if drawn by a magnetic force. Then a third is introduced, and so on. Except for the first sheep, all the rest follow this circuit voluntarily without a leash, one behind the other. Roughly halfway though this twenty-five minute video, Alÿs slips the halter off the first sheep (just where the sharp shadow of the pole crosses the ground; Alÿs is always precise). The first sheep leaves, and you find yourself tensing up, wondering if another will follow, but all the rest continue walking the circuit, one close behind the other, until, having reached that same shadow, a second sheep leaves, then another, and so forth, as now Alÿs instead of leading is in the rear of the circuit (how did that happen?) until one by one all have left and we suddenly recall the very beginning of the film: the massive cathedral, the crowd milling in this huge square, and a strange image of a 'back to front' sheep – the buttocks of one sheep side by intimate side with the face of a second sheep. It could be a mythological monster in a medieval bestiary. Bataille's synthesis of the human face with the ape's anus comes to mind. But Alÿs works in a different register, more the tuning fork than Bataille's hearty hammer, but the humour and ridicule are as sharp.

Take that skinny fellow in *Turista* (Tourist, 1994) standing by the railings only a hundred yards away from where he filmed the sheep. He is waiting to sell his wares as a colporteur with the sign 'Turista' at his feet. Despite his dark glasses, we recognize our friend Francis Alÿs lining-up alongside people looking for work, a man with a sign saying 'Plumber' and another saying 'Painting and Plastering'. Yet they are not so much looking for work as exhibiting what they have to sell, namely their skilled labour and in this they are *colporteurs,* too. Why is this funny? And cruel? It seems that vital categories have got jumbled up. Can a tourist be thus aligned with a plumber? Can a painter of art be aligned with a house painter? And what service does a tourist provide? Would someone actually hire him? So it goes, this Alÿs game, suspending the rules, and we sheep realize (at least partially; after all, we are only sheep) that we too can be thus objectified with a sign – 'art critic' or 'writer' or 'anthropologist'. This *turista* with his little sign is the sand that gets into the gearbox of categories.

Ideas are one thing, the postures of bodies another. Alÿs is so languid, propped up against the cage-like railing, the plumber and the painter by his side tense and curious, as are we when gazing at this image. Can there be a concept, as in Conceptual art, without a body? What is an idea, after all? Can an idea exist alone in the empyrean or do all ideas require a real plumber, a real painter, and a dubiously real tourist?

The performance of the mastery of non-mastery at work in *Turista* is endless because its paradoxical character ensures continuous unwinding. Whatever position you take in this unwinding back and forth between mastery and non-mastery, that position entails movement. Here, all positioning is ephemeral and temporary. (Can a tourist be thus aligned with a plumber, a painter with a house painter, etc?)

Alÿs' art suggests to me that political struggle involves *art versus art* – the art of resistance, for instance, versus the artfulness, the rhetoric and cunning of those who would ban Muslims, destroy state-funded health care, corrupt the law, and abduct the women of Ciudad Juárez and elsewhere. There is art – considerable art – not

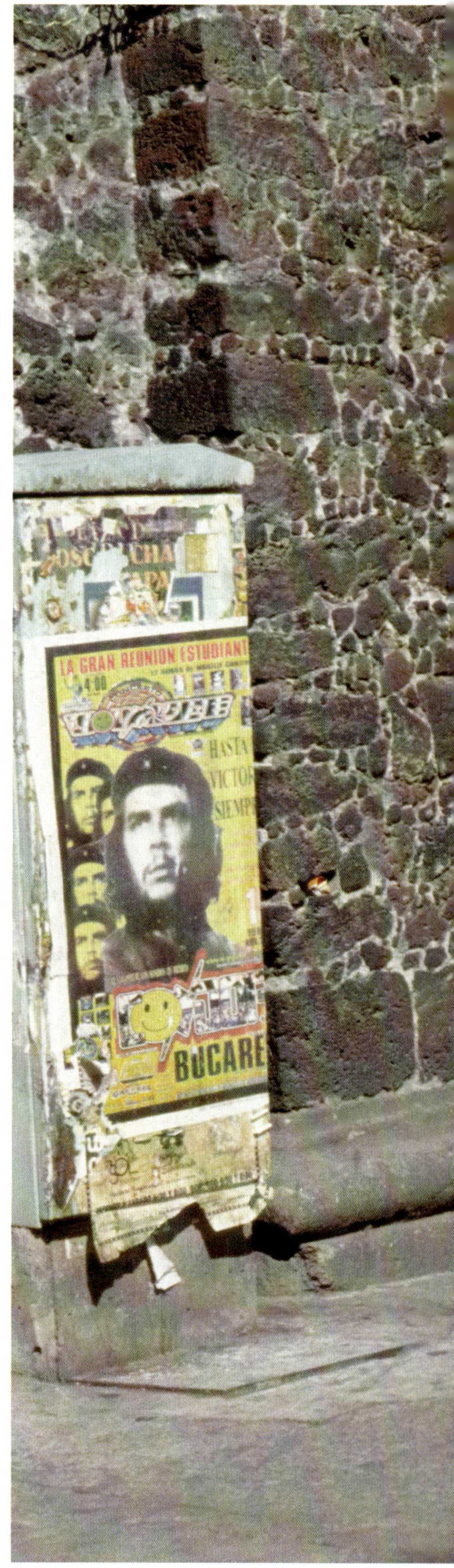

RE-ENACTMENTS, 2000
IN COLLABORATION WITH
RAFAEL ORTEGA
VIDEO DOCUMENTATION OF
AN ACTION
MEXICO CITY
5 MIN. 20 SEC.

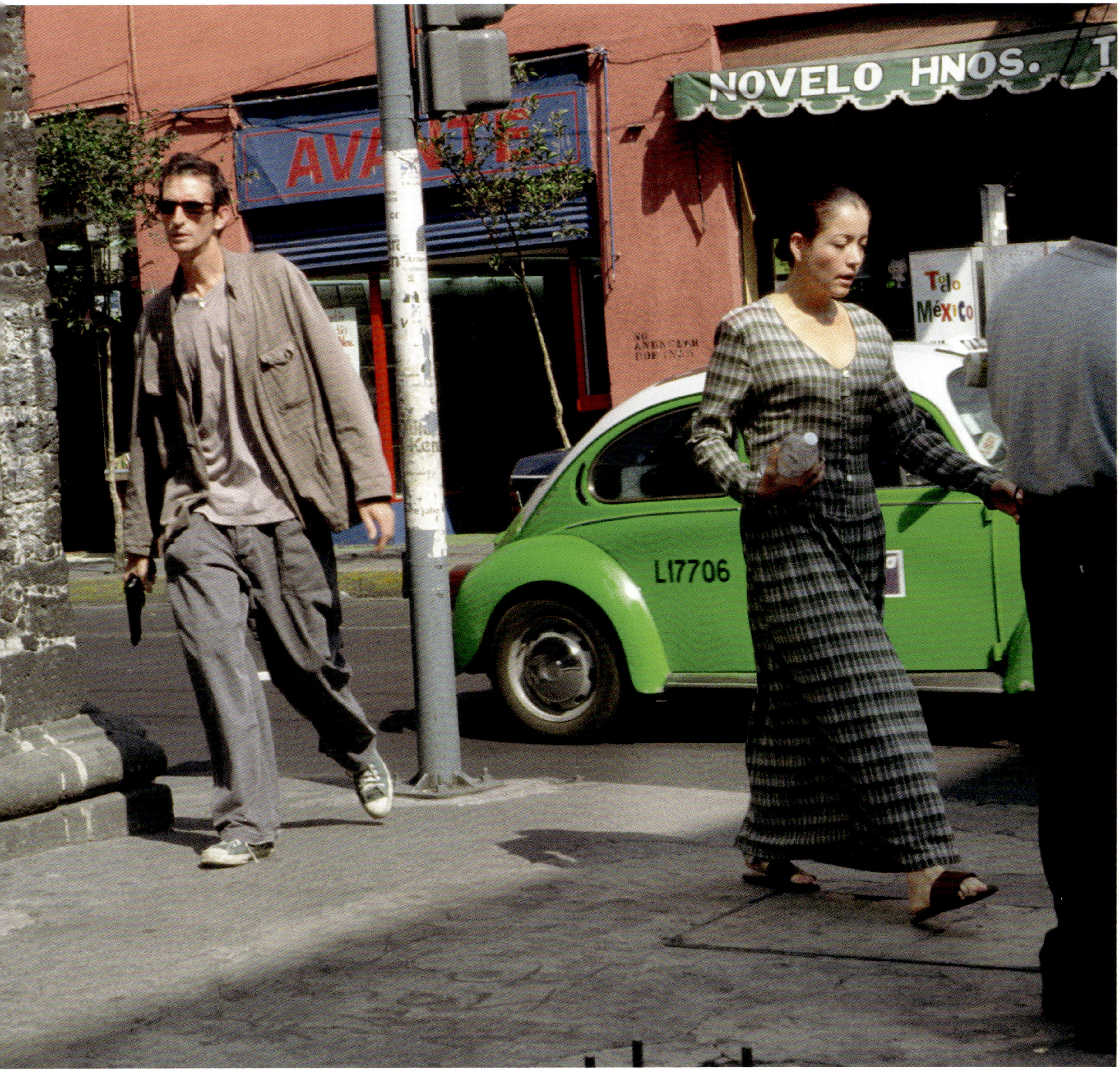
NOVELO HNOS.
Todo México
L17706

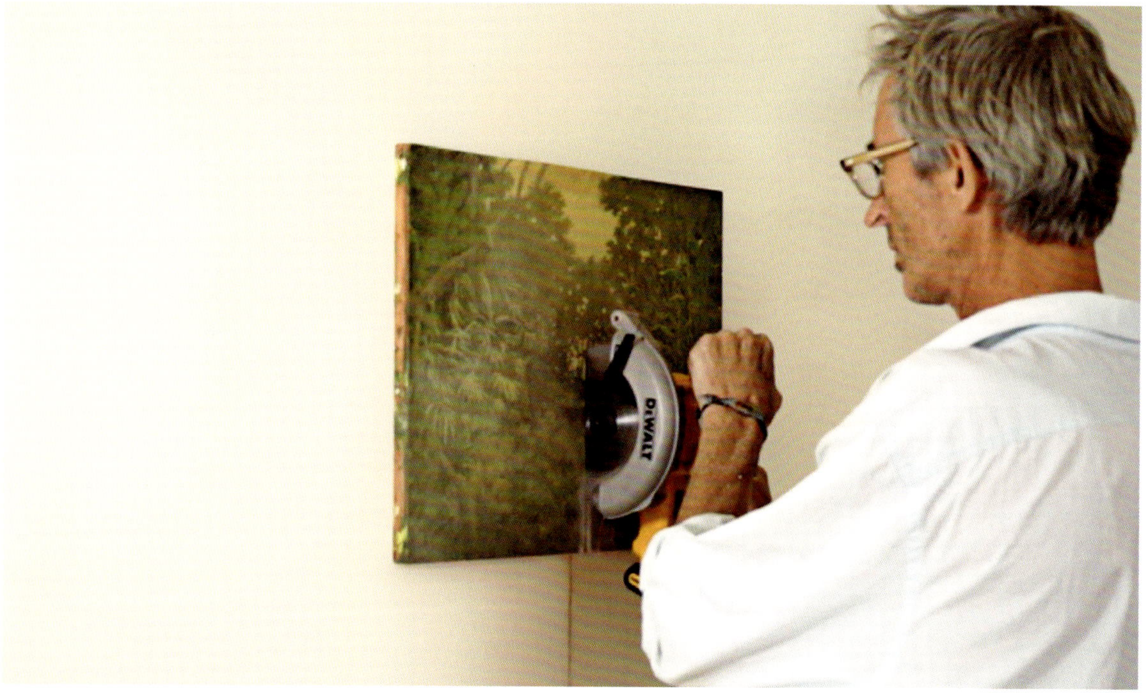

CUT, 1992–2015
IN COLLABORATION WITH JULIEN DEVAUX AND RAFAEL ORTEGA
VIDEO DOCUMENTATION OF AN ACTION
1 MIN. 3 SEC.

only in governance but in terror too and since all power produces resistance, this sort of art produces an art of resistance, such as we see with Alÿs.

When I say that Alÿs suspends the rules, we should also note his insistence that games are interesting because they combine rules with chance. A walk through Mexico City with a revolver in one's hand (*Reenactments,* 2000) or pushing ice through the streets is in fact a game – a game with chance. What will happen? It is also a game with sociology. How will the people of the city respond to this strangeness in their midst?

Hegel is famous for his idea of suspension of rules. His notion is that in negating something (such as breaking a rule), the thing negated continues to exist as a sort of shadow, after-life, or ghost within the new form. Alÿs' works allow us to consider the presence of this ghost, as in the last drop of water that was the massive ice-block, or the last kick of the fiery soccer ball, or the final flicker of flame in Ciudad Juárez, along with a mournful train whistle. Games of chance open up and play in this space of suspension, an atmosphere that holds out the possibility of new rules and other ways.

Yet Hegel would consider the unwinding of the paradoxes that lie at the heart of so much of Alÿs' works as dialectical. He would be perplexed by their lack of closure. For in Alÿs' rendering, the dialectic never comes to rest. It is continuously surging, as in the night that is Ciudad Juárez, as in rehearsing Harry Truman's Cold War fear-inspired 'development', as in the Green Line containing the uncontainable, and as with the ice-pushing artwork and its title, *Paradox of Praxis 1.*

What is this last gasp, this final drop, this last kick, the final piece of clothing not removed by the stripper, the last run of the red VW up the hill? Is it nothing or the last tremulous step before the nothing? With Alÿs, as in Beckett's *Waiting for Godot,* nothing never comes.

Famously, however, for all his desire for closure, Hegel made a good deal out of this nothingness, as with his often-quoted remarks about the death-space that playing with negation produces. To take thinking seriously is to negate, and to negate is to dwell in such a space and allow one's self to be torn apart and be dismembered (reminding us once again that there is no concept without a body or without a something). Yet this too can be considered a game: the game of tarrying with the negative. But then Hegel insists on somehow getting through this space of death once we have been torn to shreds.

Which brings us to *The Cut* (2015). This, more than any of Alÿs' other works, flagrantly highlights transgression. The video of the performance in the Museo Tamayo in Mexico City shows the artist with a power saw cutting in half one of his paintings of the Lacandon forest, Chiapas, Mexico, from bottom to top. The painting is secured to a white wall. The cut begins well below the painting and extends in a neat vertical line upwards, to end well above the painting. As we have learnt to expect from Alÿs' works, sound is crucial, in this case the sickening screech of the power saw, along with the smoke it creates. There is certainly no sense of failure or rehearsal here. The entire action takes a mere forty-five seconds and is efficient and complete, brutal in its surgical precision. This is not an aesthetic of diffidence.

The portrayal of the artist in the video is disturbing, too. All we see is his back from the waist up in a dazzlingly white long-sleeved shirt as he determinedly guides the saw. With a victory flourish, he pulls the saw back from the wall when done. All in a blink of an eye.

STUDY FOR <u>THE SILENCE OF ANI</u> (DETAIL), 2015
PENCIL ON PAPER

below,
STUDY FOR <u>THE SILENCE OF ANI</u>, 2015
RETOUCHED PHOTOGRAPH
21 X 28 CM

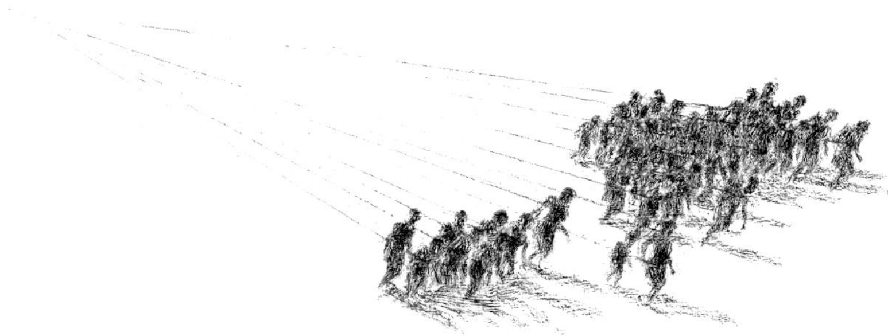

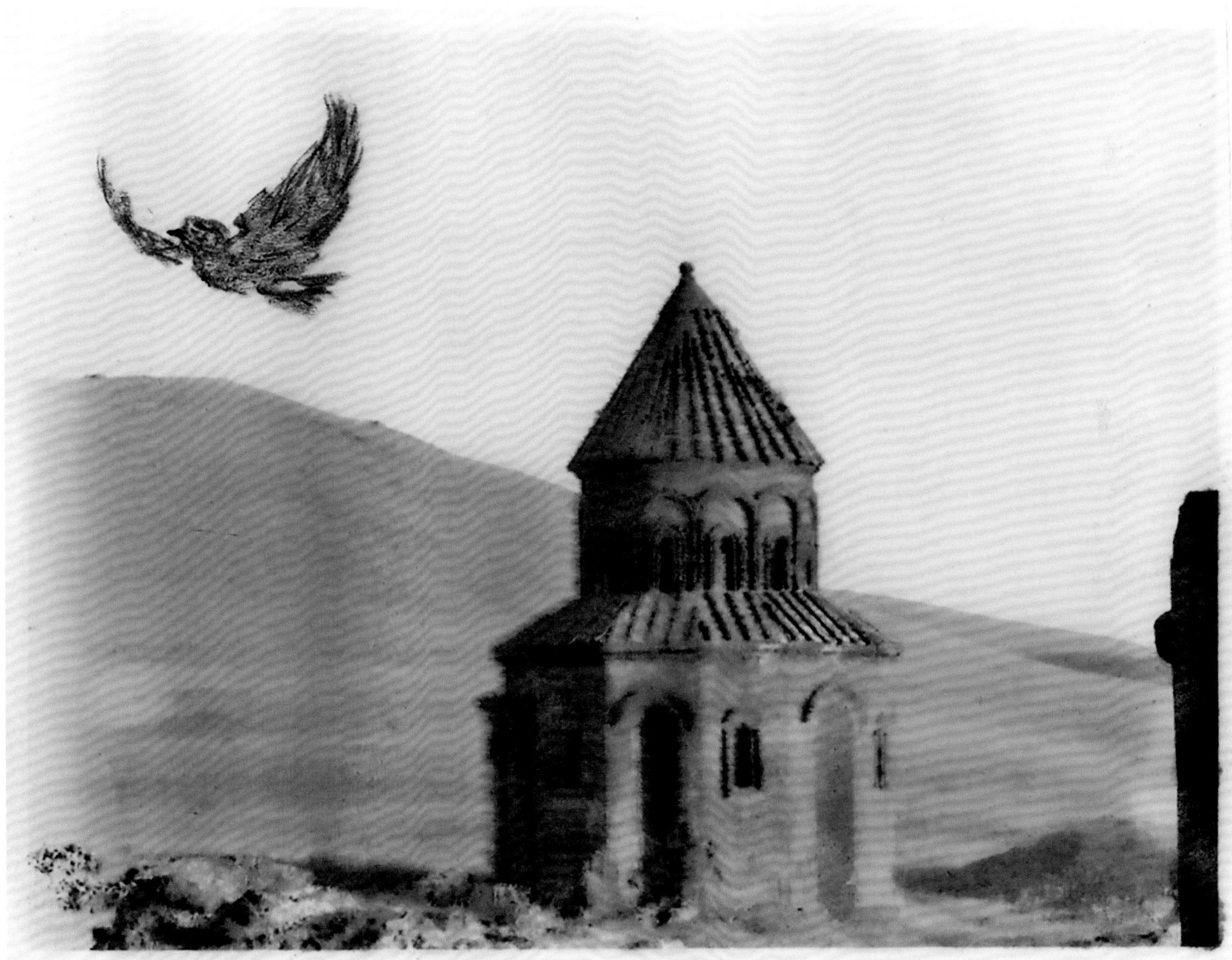

THE SILENCE OF ANI, 2015
IN COLLABORATION WITH
ANTONIO FERNÁNDEZ ROS,
JULIEN DEVAUX, FÉLIX BLUME
AND THE TEENS OF KARS
VIDEO DOCUMENTATION
OF AN ACTION
13 MIN. 20 SEC

In the former Armenian city of Ani, a group of teens is given instruments designed to imitate birds. They play hide and seek in the ruins and call the birds 'until a chorus of birdcalls echo across the valley, all the way to Armenia, until the birds return to Ani and life comes back to the forgotten city.'

opposite,
THE SILENCE OF ANI, 2015
IN COLLABORATION WITH
ANTONIO FERNÁNDEZ ROS,
JULIEN DEVAUX, FÉLIX BLUME
AND THE TEENS OF KARS
VIDEO DOCUMENTATION
OF AN ACTION
13 MIN. 20 SEC.

How does this compare with the representation of unrepresentability, as with the red VW with its mariachi music or the Peshmerga video and its associated paintings?

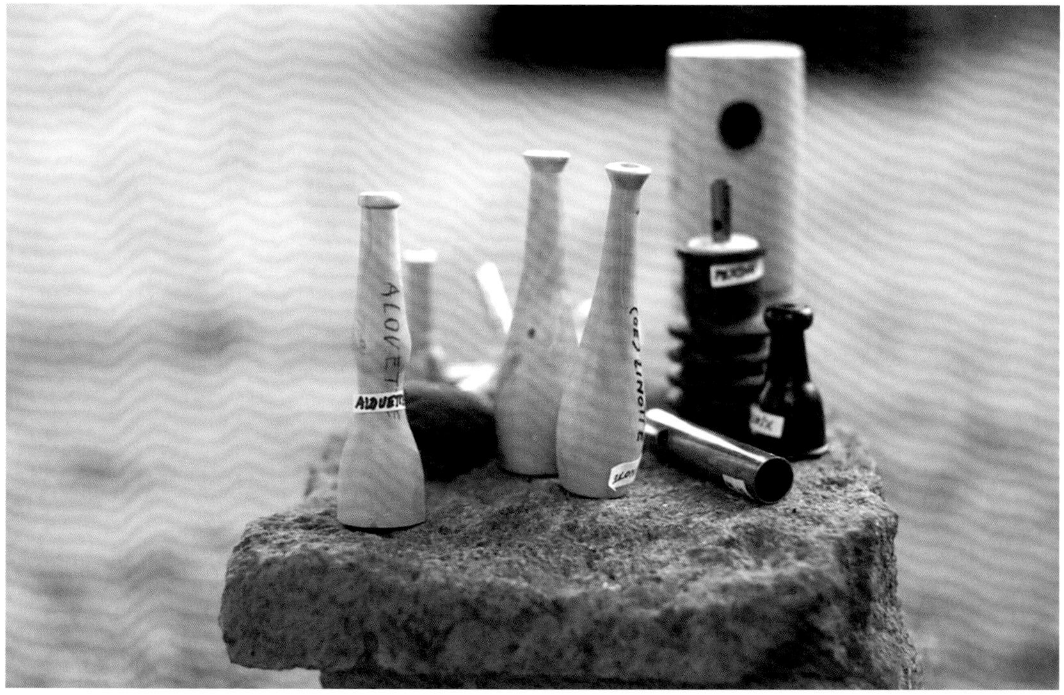

First of all the obvious: the destruction of the painting. Second, a step away from this, a reversal, which is that the brutality and speed of the piece signify light-heartedness, a sort of bluff and satire. 'Look at Alÿs, the rough tough artist flexing muscle. Let's appreciate the long heroic genealogy of avant-gardism. Didn't Duchamp paint a moustache on the Mona Lisa and give this a funny trick name?'

More to the point, perhaps, is the way in which the video shows several close-ups of the saw blade spinning, screeching and smoking, such that – and this is the trick – the representation that is the painting of the Lacandon forest being cut through fuses in its destruction with what it represents. Paradoxically, the cutting unites, not the two sides sundered forever, but the representation with the represented; and the leaves of the trees now come alive, fluttering and shaking, it seems, at least for the split-second duration of the actual cutting. Yes, representation succeeds; it succeeds when it destroys and it succeeds to such a degree that it actually, concretely, becomes what it was at first merely about.

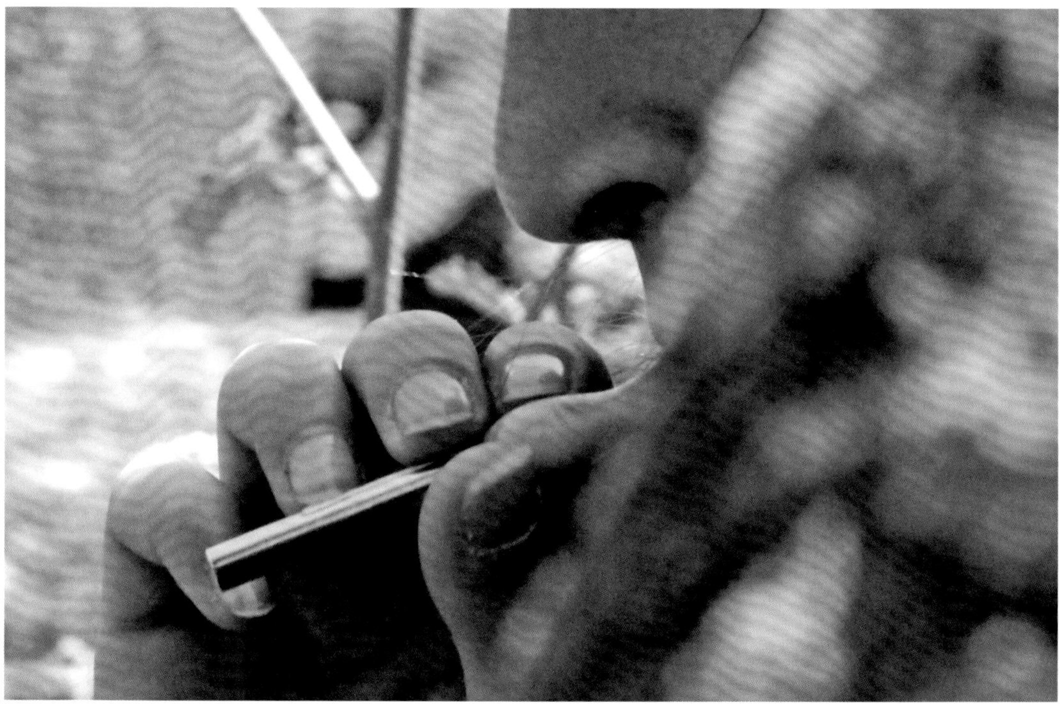

The ghosts in the death-space also come alive in ways that resist dialectic closure in *The Silence of Ani* (2015) and *Albert's Way* (2014). In the former work, exhibited at the Istanbul Biennale of 2015, the ghosts of the Turkish holocaust of Armenians in 1915 are recalled one hundred years later. Still today, despite clear evidence, the Turkish state refuses to admit its role in this slaughter. It is hard to understand the motives for this denial. After all, the Turkish state has made no bones since then about its discriminatory policies and has been practising widespread ethnic cleansing against the large Kurdish minority in Turkey and, to the extent that it can, against the Kurds in northern Syria and Iraq. It seems that one half of the Turkish population approves this, if the recent national elections are a guide. Hence there is

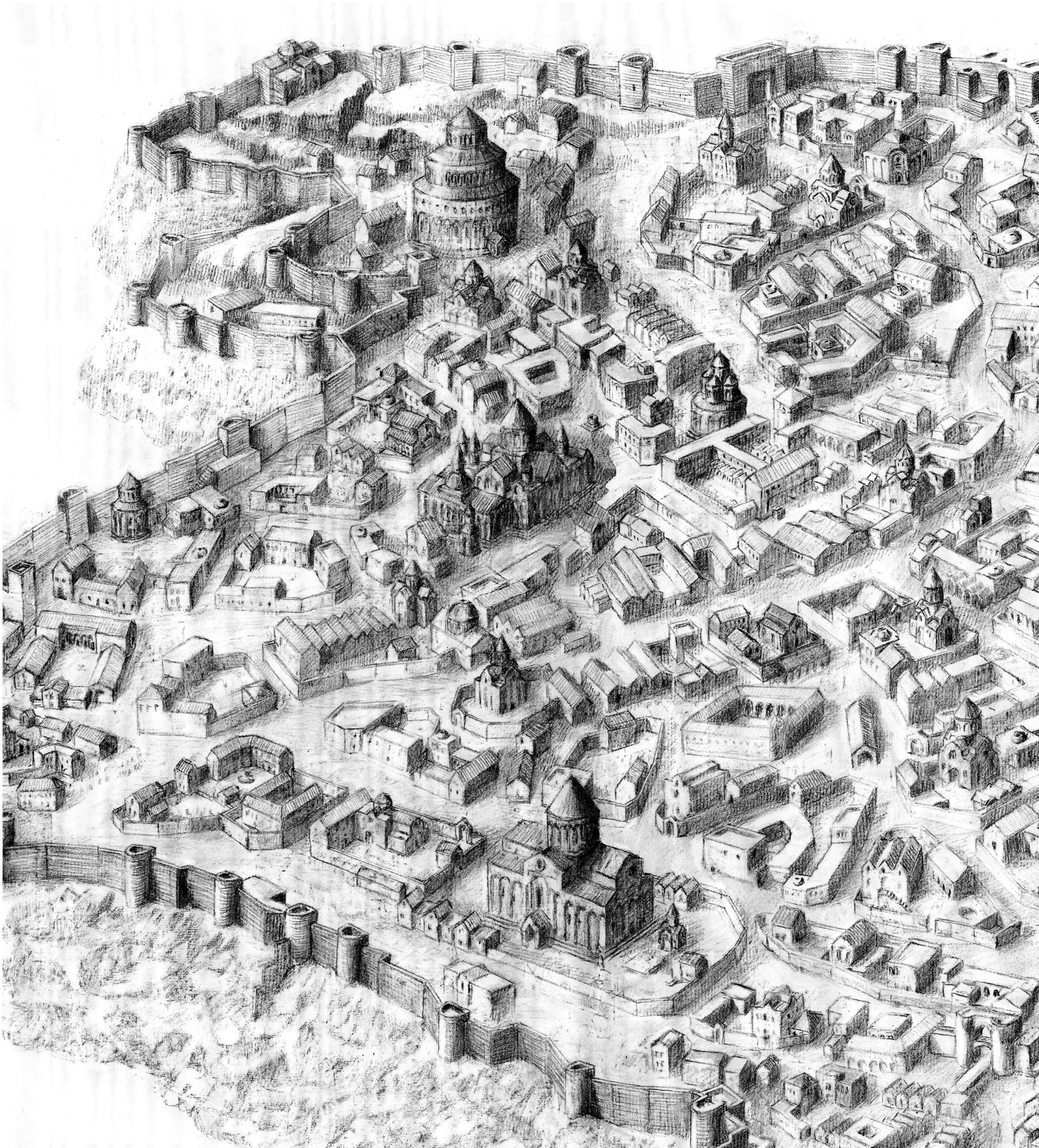

ALBERT'S WAY, 2014
IN COLLABORATION WITH
JULIEN DEVAUX AND
FÉLIX BLUME
VIDEO DOCUMENTATION OF
AN ACTION, ARTIST'S STUDIO,
MEXICO CITY
4 MIN. 48 SEC.

For 7 days from 9:00 AM to 7:00 PM I will walk in my studio a distance equivalent to that of the Camino Ingles, the 118km route walked by the pilgrims from the port of El Ferrol on the Atlantic to the holy city of Santiago de Compostela.

considerable pressure on an artist who enters into this battlefield of representation and deception.

Here, indeed, politics as a matter of 'art versus art' coupled with the mastery of non-mastery seems relevant. Try not the hammer, but Nietzsche's tuning fork, especially because the key element regarding the Armenian holocaust concerns memory, notoriously fickle and nowhere more so than when subject over a century to state propaganda and the invention of Turkish identity crafted around the notion of repellent, threatening others, Kurds as well as Armenians. What Alÿs chose to do was to make a thirteen-minute black and white video that winds its way through this minefield by focusing on the scant ruins of the ancient city of Ani on the border of Armenia and Turkey, a city that has more in common with fairy tales than chronologically oriented history. The scene is set by a gaping crevasse in the mountains separating these countries. The silence is deafening. Gradually, soft bird cries can be heard, piping, curious, querulous. The tall grasses move in the wind. You discern rather than see the movement of an animal – or is it a child? – running through the grass and through the ruins, the curious shapes of which suggest all manner of beings. The bird sounds become louder. They seem to be urgently calling. Even crying. Mysterious two-legged creatures – are they people? – leap and hide, blowing different notes on their bird whistles. Some – stone-men and women from ancient times, perhaps – are immersed in cracks in the ruins. Are they ascending or descending? We don't know. The mountainous landscape framing the situation lies deathly still, heaving slightly with our breath. The camera backs off. The ruins appear as a whole and then, wonder of wonders, and quite out of keeping with the aesthetic of the video, for the briefest of moments, a crudely drawn dove flutters out of the sky to alight on the ruins. At which point, everything changes.

Now appears a truly fairy-tale image, exquisitely drawn in pencil, of a city sloping on a hill surrounded by a wall, full of little houses and streets. The camera keeps coming close, then retreats as a voiceover in Turkish with English subtitles explains that Ani was once a great world city like Constantinople and Jerusalem, only to decline following the Turkish-Seljuk invasion of 1064. 'This happened a long time ago', purrs the speaker, 'but can't we do better than silence?'

The camera keeps moving over and into the city, meaning over and into this fairy-tale drawing of the city of Ani. It is so out of time, this city, being a drawing and because of its being drawn this particular way. It is a mirage, a toy, that draws you into timeless time, walking those very streets, which is when, unexpectedly, this forgotten past connects in a flash, as in montage, with the silence of the state of emergency that is the present. You hear the birds being called, no less than ghosts fluttering their wings.

Something of this past surfacing in the present with hallucinatory vigour occurs when Alÿs walks 118 km in his studio seven days in succession, recapitulating the walks that Hitler's architect, Albert Speer, took in an exercise yard in Spandau prison. Rumour has it that Speer would imagine he was walking between places that he had previously visited on his travels. Another rumour is that he walked the distance from Berlin to Guadalajara in Mexico. (Could he walk on water?) Alÿs' video is disturbing. Is the studio also a prison in which an artist not only wanders but resolutely travels from A to B?

As if in a delirium, the video displays six views simultaneously of the confined site in which he is walking. The perspective on each view is convex and giddying. One of these views is of Alÿs' legs from the knee down, walking. His footsteps are loud and repetitive. Looking at this you are likely to feel trapped, even nauseous, and the saccharine colours more than match this sensation. If ever there was a comment on the strangeness of the imagination of walking – of colportage blending hashish, film, and walking the city – this is it. Walking not in the city, but in a prison. Walking and walking and still more walking, all in circles. Is this the 'story of deception' writ large? Do we today walk in prisons thinking we are free while a fellow pushing ice along city streets for no good reason shows us there is no way out until we start to hum like Nietzsche's tuning fork?

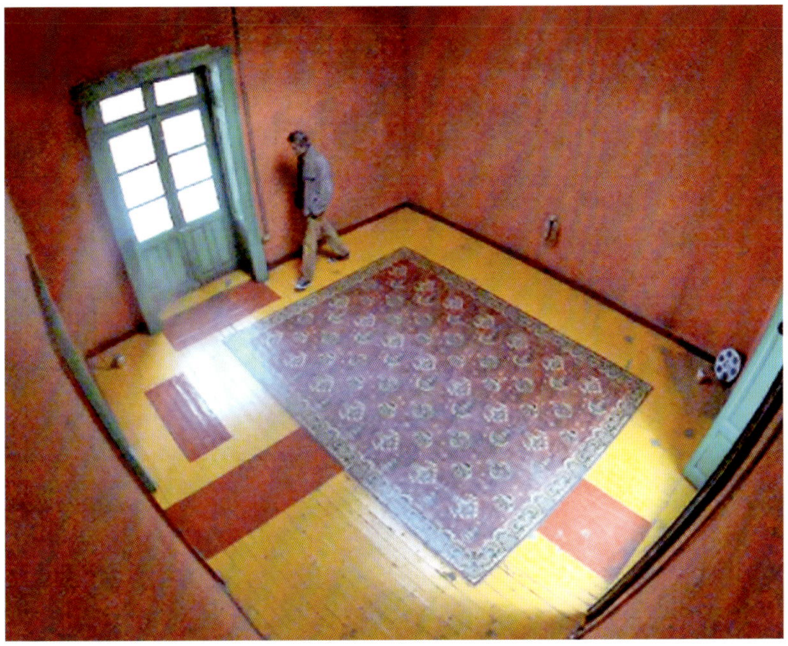
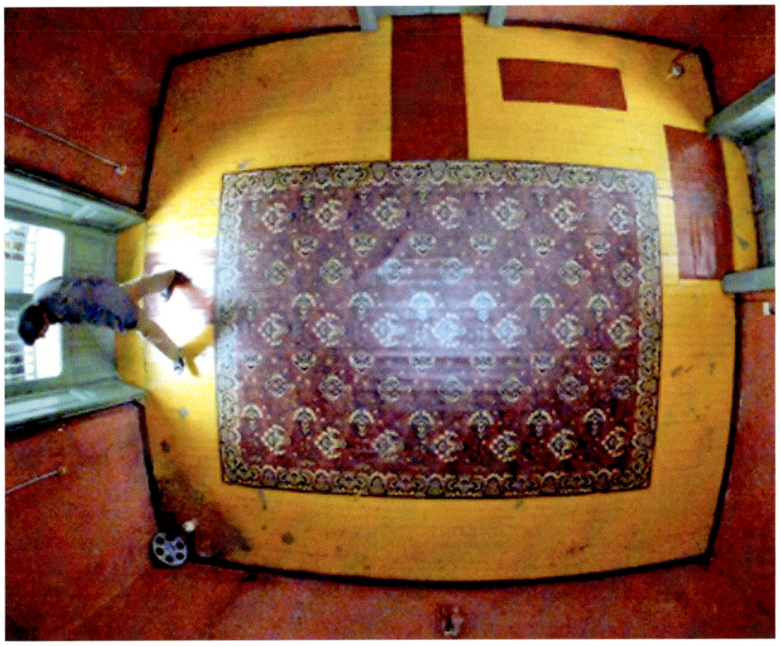
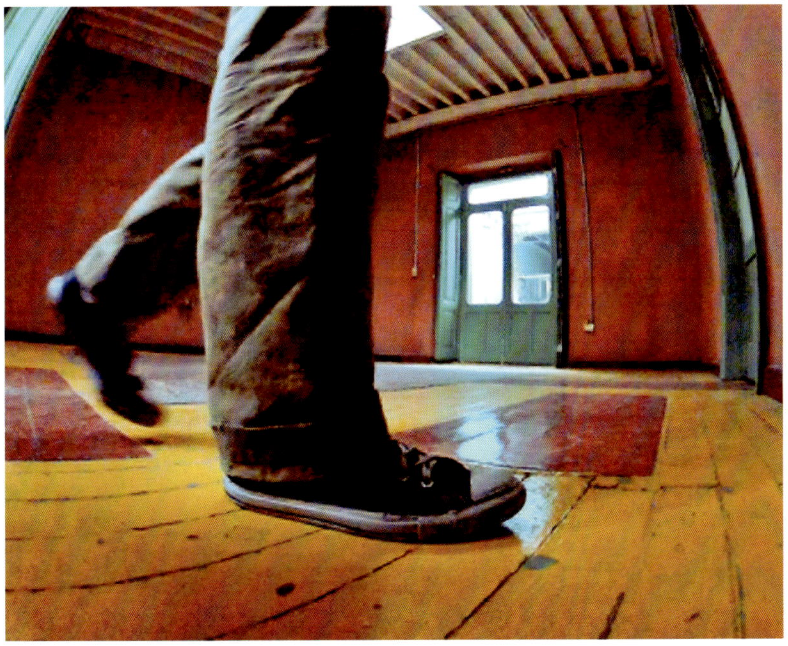
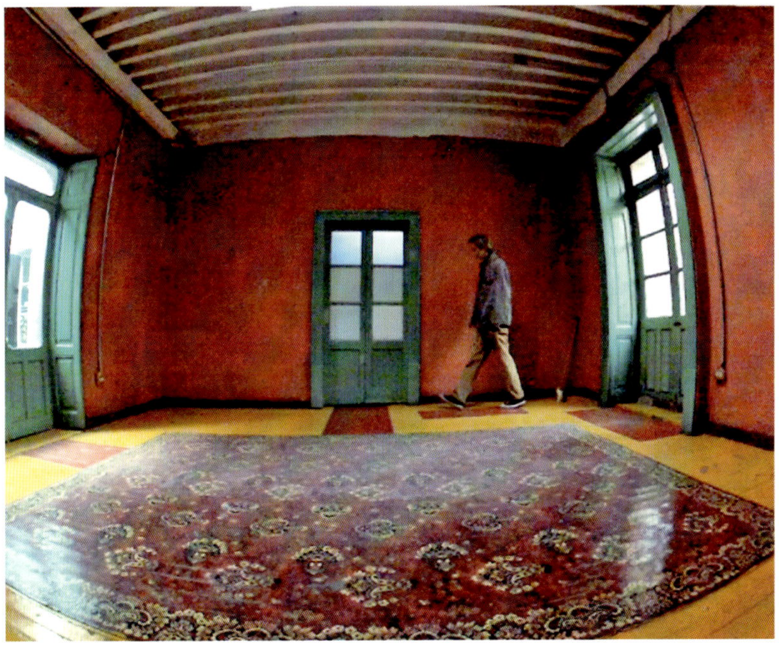
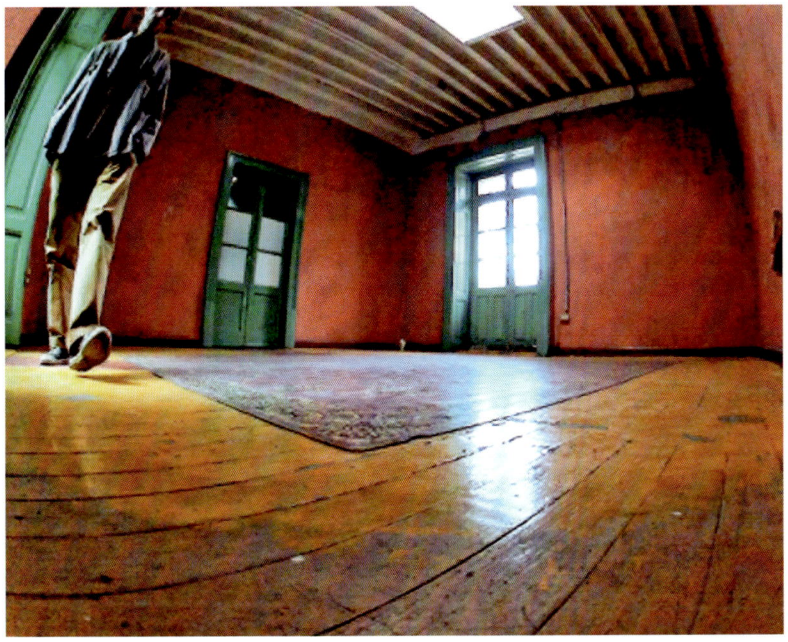
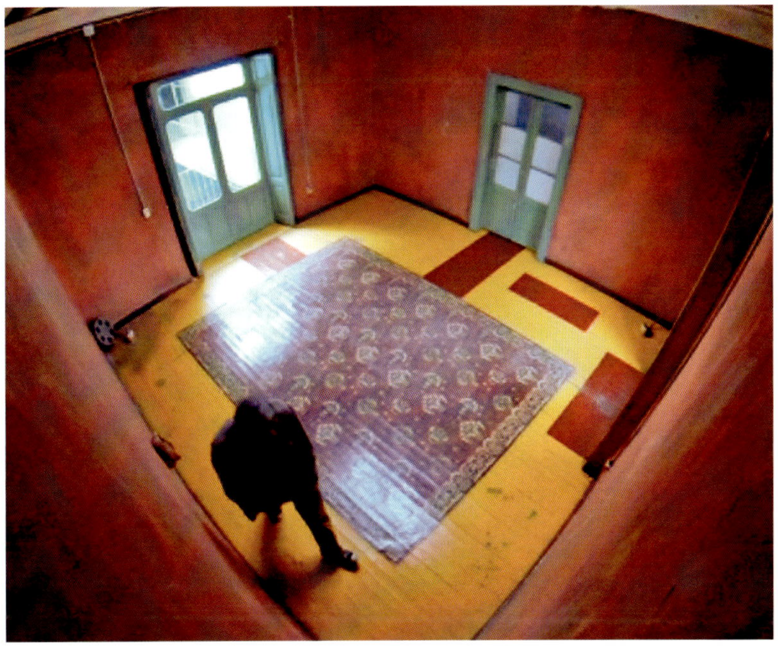

RETOQUE/PAINTING, 2008
EX-US PANAMA CANAL ZONE
VIDEO DOCUMENTATION
OF AN ACTION
8 MIN. 31 SEC.

Action of repainting 60 median strips erased by the passage of time in the former Panama Canal Zone.

next pages,
TORNADO, 2000–10
IN COLLABORATION WITH
JULIEN DEVAUX, RAFAEL
ORTEGA AND FELIX BLUME
VIDEO DOCUMENTATION
OF AN ACTION
30 MIN.

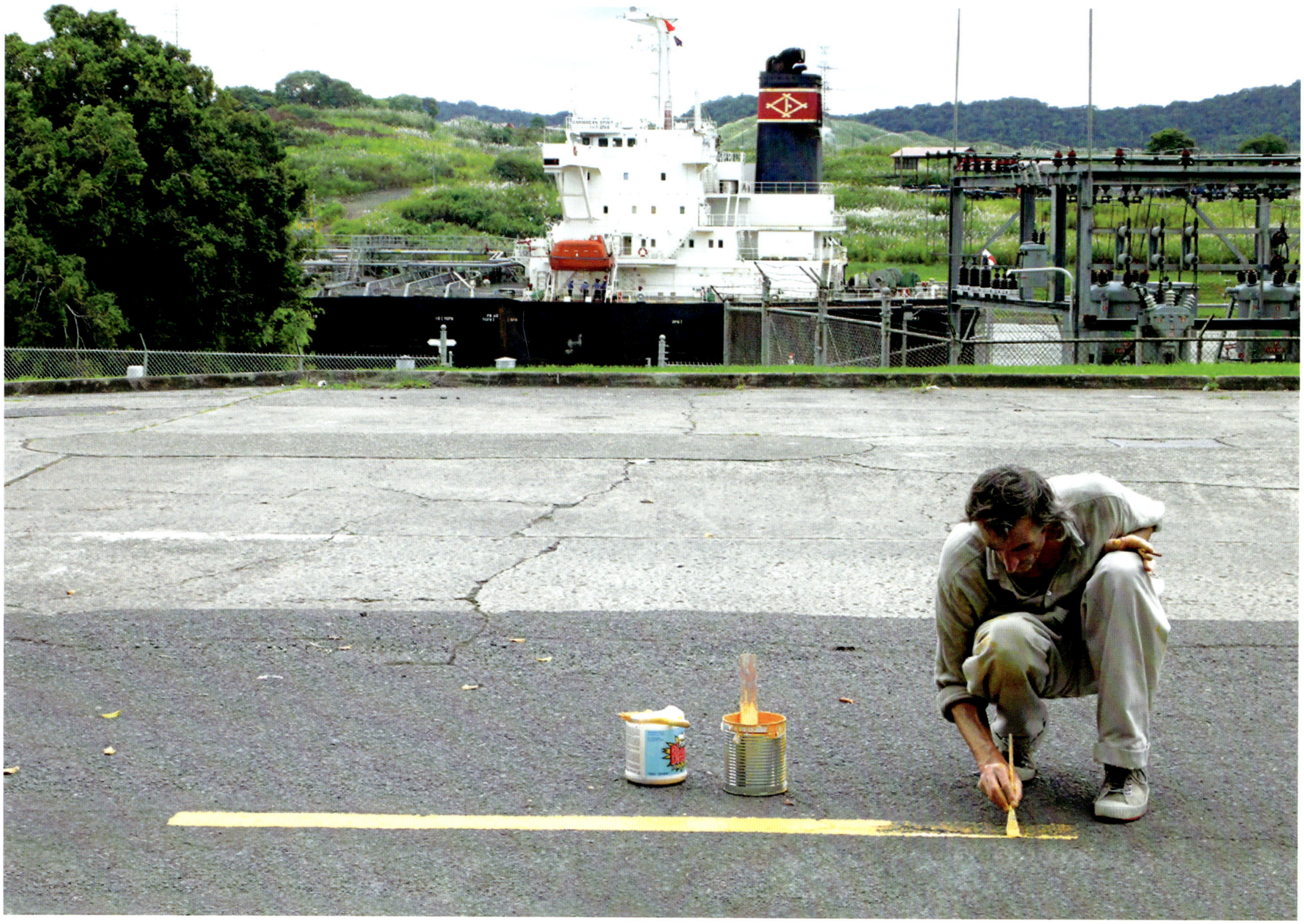

NOTES

SURVEY: PAGES 057–105

1 Francis Alÿs, notes on *Remolinos*, c. 2004.
2 Miguel de Cervantes Saavedra, *Don Quixote, Part 1* (1605), in *The Harvard Classics Chapter VIII*, Harvard University Press, Cambridge, Massachusetts, 1909–14.
3 Francis Alÿs, handwritten note, c. 1990
4 Although he has lost this dissertation, Alÿs has consistently referred to it as the origin of his way of thinking in many areas.
5 Francis Alÿs, handwritten note, c. 1990.
6 Francis Alÿs, subtitle of the artwork *Fairy Tales*, 1995.
7 Francis Alÿs, 'Statement', Mexico City, 1993, in *Walks/Paseos*, Travesías, Mexico City, 1997, p. 15.
8 Francis Alÿs, from an outline of a talk, c. 1992.
9 Francis Alÿs, draft notes, c. 2002.
10 I am quoting both from Francis Alÿs's 'Blueprint for The Collector', which includes the drafts of his statements around this piece and a record of its fabrication, and the texts by Kurt Hollander and Cuauhtémoc Medina in the catalogue of the first exhibition of the object in one of his earliest gallery shows: *Francys Alÿs*, Galería Arte Contemporáneo, Mexico City, 1992.
11 This object, and the documentation of its production, was finally exhibited in the spring of 1992 in Alÿs's solo show at the Galería Arte Contemporáneo in Mexico City, curated by Maria Guerra.
12 Charles Baudelaire, 'El pintor de la vida moderna', in Balzac et al., *El Dandismo*, Prol. Salvador Clotas, Anagrama, Barcelona, 1974, p. 88 (author's translation).
13 Walter Benjamin, 'The Paris of the Second Empire in Baudelaire', in *Walter Benjamin: Selected Writings, Vol. 4, 1938–1940*, Belknap/Harvard University Press, Cambridge, Massachusetts, p. 19.
14 Walter Benjamin, 'On Some Motifs in Baudelaire', in *Walter Benjamin: Selected Writings, Vol. 4, 1938–1940*, p. 329.
15 Attila Kotányi and Raoul Vaneigem, 'Elementary program of the bureau of Unitary Urbanism' (1961), in Ken Knabb (ed.), *Situationist International Anthology*, Bureau of Public Secrets, Berkeley, California, 1981, pp. 65–7. See also, Guy Debord, *The Society of the Spectacle* (trans. Donald Nicholson-Smith), Zone Books, New York, 1994, pp. 119–27.
16 Guy Debord, 'Theory of the dérive', in Libero Andreotti and Xavier Costa (ed.), *Theory of the Dérive and Other Situationist Writings on the City*, Museo d'Art Contemporani de Barcelona-Actar, Barcelona, 1996, pp. 22–7.
17 See 'Unitary Urbanism at the End of the 1950s' (unsigned), in *Situationist International Anthology* (op. cit.), pp. 83–8.
18 Gilles Ivan, 'Formulary for a New Urbanism' (1958), in *Theory of the Dérive and Other Situationist Writings on the City*, op. cit., p. 17.
19 See Guy Debord, 'Two Accounts of the Dérive' (1956), in ibid., p. 31.
20 Francis Alÿs, 'Statement' (1993), in *Walks/Paseos*, op. cit., p. 15.
21 Ibid., pp. 106–7.
22 E-mail from Francis Alÿs, Rangoon, 21 June 1997, to Olivier Debroise.
23 E-mail from Francis Alÿs, Shanghai, 23 June 1997, to Olivier Debroise. See in this volume, p. 52.
24 Olivier Debroise, 'Diario de una deriva VI', 1995, unpublished.
25 Kitty Scott, 'Permutations of a failed idea', in *Francis Alÿs: Le Temps du Sommeil*, Contemporary Art Gallery, Vancouver, 1998, p. 39.
26 'In 1993 I commissioned various sign painters to produce enlarged copies of my smaller original images. Once they had completed several versions, I produced a new 'model', compiled from the most significant elements of each sign painter's interpretation. This second 'original' was in turn used as a model for a new generation of copies by sign painters, and so on, ad infinitum, according to market demand.' Francis Alÿs, in Barry Schwabsky, et. al., *Vitamin P: New Perspectives in Painting*, Phaidon, London & New York, 2002, p. 35.
27 Article 33 of the Constitution of Mexico states that foreigners 'may not, in any manner, involve themselves in the political affairs of the country' and that they can be expelled from the country 'immediately and without the necessity of previous legal action' by the govermnment.
28 Francis Alÿs, 'Statement on Heisenberg's uncertainty principle', c. 1998.
29 Frederic Jameson, *A Singular Modernity: Essay on the Ontology of the Present*, Verso, London, 2002, p. 8.
30 Letter from the artist to curator Olivier Debroise, 15 February 2006, quoted in Olivier Debroise, 'White Spot', in *Francis Alÿs: A Story of Deception/ Historia de un desengaño*, Museo de Arte Latinoamericano de Buenos Aires, 2006, p. 74.
31 Francis Alÿs, 'Fragments of a conversation', in ibid., p. 81.
32 Note on the project in Patagonia, repoduced in ibid., p. 33.
33 Hannah Arendt, *The Human Condition*, University of Chicago, Chicago, 1958, p. 98.
34 Mikhail Bakhtin, 'Forms of Time and of the Chronotope in the Novel: Notes toward a Historical Poetics', in Michael Holquist (ed.), *The Dialogic Imagination*, trans. Caryl Emerson and Michael Holquist, University of Texas Press, Austin, 1981, pp. 84–5.
35 Francis Alÿs, 'Statement on the Politics of Rehearsals', c. 2003.
36 Hannah Arendt, op. cit.

FOCUS: PAGES 107–119

1 Hans-Georg Gadamer, *The Relevance of the Beautiful and Other Essays*, trans. Nicholas Walker, Cambridge University Press, Cambridge, England, 1986, p. 22–23.
2 Richard Long interviewed by Colin Fitzpatrick in *Transcript*, vol. 2, no. 2, 1996: 'There is some comment on the lack of people in my work, but it is just a question of choice, the subject of my work is walking, or making sculpture in empty landscape. Most of the world's surface is still open landscapes. I feel I'm a realist working in the real spaces of the world.'
3 Giorgio Agamben, *The Man Without Content*, trans. Georgia Albert, Stanford University Press, Palo Alto, California, 1999, p. 72.
4 Gilles Deleuze, *The Logic of Sense*, trans. Mark Lester with Charles Stivale, Columbia University Press, New York, 1990, pp. 237–238.
5 For a full analysis of this work see Cuauhtémoc Medina, 'Action/ Fiction', in *Francis Alÿs*, Musée Picasso, Antibes, 2001, pp 16–20.
6 Zygmunt Bauman, *Postmodern Ethics*, Blackwell, Oxford, England, 1993, pp. 47–61.
7 Alain Badiou, *Ethics: An Essay on the Understanding of Evil*, trans. Peter Hallward, Verso, London & New York, 2001, pp. 47–52.
8 A crude illustration of this is the moment in the film Matrix when the hero Neo (Keanu Reeves) becomes aware that his reality has been a fantastic construction of the computer, and henceforth he must reinvent himself and destroy the machine.
9 M. M. Bakhtin, *Toward a Philosophy of the Act*, trans. Vadim Liapunov, University of Texas, Austin, 1993, p. 48. Bakhtin's reading of the ethical as mutual answerability derives from his attempt to reconcile the seemingly insurmountable gap between lived experience and its cultural representation, which is also the trajectory traced through the three 'lives' of *When Faith Moves Mountains*.
10 Jean-Luc Nancy, *Being Singular Plural*, trans. Robert D. Richardson and Anne E. O'Byrne, Stanford University Press, Palo Alto, California, 2000, p. 2.
11 Francis Alÿs, 'A Thousand Words', *Artforum*, Summer 2002, p. 147.
12 Gilles Deleuze, *Cinema 2: The Time-Image*, trans. Hugh Tomlinson and Robert Galeta, The Athlone Press, London, 1989, pp. 215–224. In speaking of the critique of disabling myths in Brazilian Glauber Rocha's cinema, Deleuze says, 'the agitprop is no longer the result of a becoming conscious, but consists of putting everything into a trance, the people and its masters, and the camera itself, pushing everything into a state of aberration.' This echoes Alÿs's desire for the event of *When Faith Moves Mountains* to provoke a 'collective hallucination'.
13 Patrick Chamoiseau, *Texaco*, trans. Rose-Myriam Réjoulis and Val Vinokurov, Vintage International, New York, 1997.
14 Luis Camnitzer, 'Conflict', *ArtNexus*, no. 47, March 2003.
15 *The Green Line* was designed to test the axioms, 'sometimes doing something poetic can become political' and 'sometimes doing something political can become poetic'.

UPDATE: PAGES 175–221

1 Walter Benjamin, 'The Cultural History of Toys,', in Michael W. Jennings, Howard Eiland and Gary Smith (eds), *Walter Benjamin: Selected Writings, Vol. 2*,. p. 115. See also Jeffrey Mehlman, *Walter Benjamin for Children*, University of Chicago Press, 1993.
2 Roger Caillois, *Man, Play, and Games*, University of Illinois Press, Urbana and Chicago, 2001 (originally published in 1958).
3 Walter Benjamin, 'The Storyteller', in *Illuminations*, Schocken, New York, 1968, p. 87.

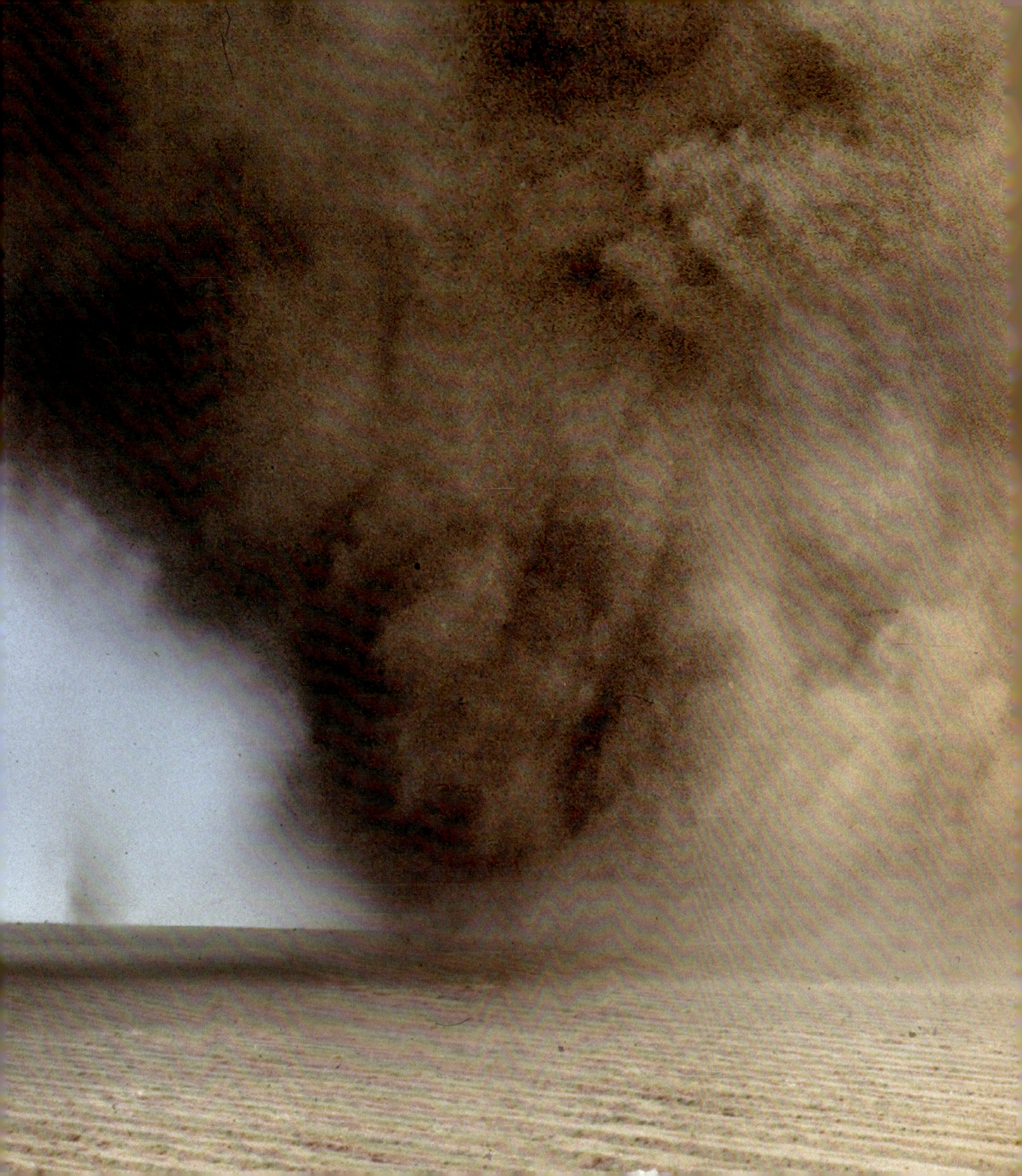

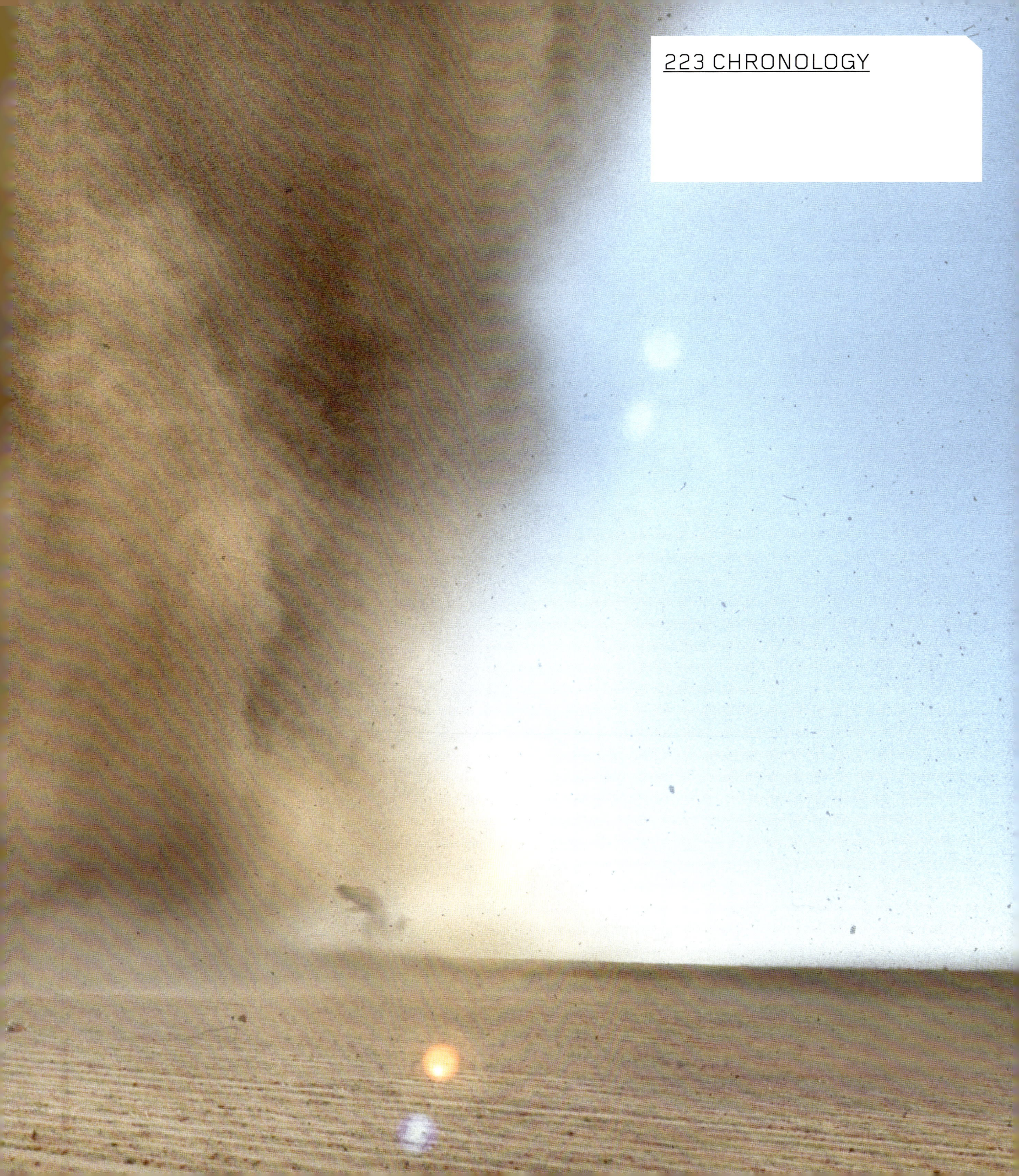

223 CHRONOLOGY

CHRONOLOGY: Francis Alÿs, born 1959 in Antwerp, lives and works in Mexico City.

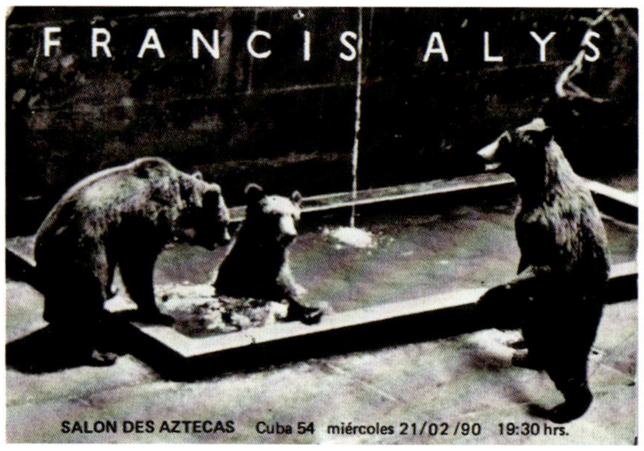

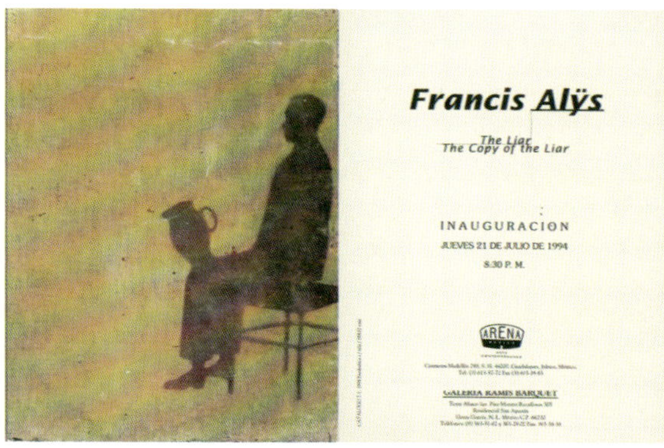

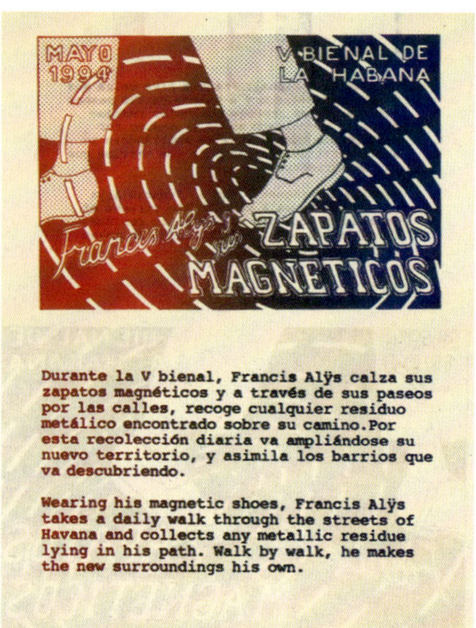

SELECTED EXHIBITIONS AND PROJECTS
1978–1996

SELECTED ARTICLES AND INTERVIEWS
1978–1996

1978–1983
Attends the Institut d'Architecture de Tournai, Belgium

1983–1986
Attends the Istituto Universitario di Architettura di Venezia, Venice

1986
Moves to Mexico City

1990
SALÓN DES AZTECAS, Mexico City (solo)

1991
GALERIA ARTE CONTEMPORÁNEO, Mexico City (group)

BLUE STAR ART SPACE, San Antonio, Texas (group)

LATITUDE 53 GALLERY, Edmonton, Canada (group)

1992
'Francis Alÿs & Melanie Smith',
ESPACE L'ESCAUT, Brussels (solo)

GALERIA ARTE CONTEMPORÁNEO, Mexico City (solo)

'México hoy',
CASA DE LAS AMERICAS, Madrid (group)

1992
Medina, Cuauhtémoc, 'Painter in a Bag', Poliester, no. 2, Summer

Springer, José Manuel, 'Garbage and Art in Mexico', Poliester, no. 3, Fall

1993
'Rueda como Naturaleza',
MUSEO DE ARTE MODERNO, Mexico City, toured to INSTITUTO CULTURAL CABAÑAS, Guadalajara (group)

1994
'The Liar/The Copy of the Liar',
GALERIA RAMIS BARQUET, Monterrey, toured to ARENA MÉXICO ARTE CONTEMPORÁNEO, Guadalajara (solo)

FOODHOUSE, Santa Monica (group)

5th HAVANA BIENNIAL (group)

1994
Hollander, Kurt, 'Francis Alÿs', Flash Art, no. 179, November–December

1995
OPUS OPERANDI, Ghent, Belgium (solo)

'El Soplón',
GALERIA CAMARGO VILAÇA, São Paulo (solo)

JACK TILTON GALLERY, New York (solo)

'Longing and Belonging: From the Faraway Nearby',
SITE SANTA FE, New Mexico (group)

ESPACE 251 NORD, Liège, Belgium (group)

1995
Jusidman, Yishai, 'Francis Alÿs at Galeria Ramis Barquet', Artforum, January

Rubinstein, Raphael, 'Francis Alÿs at Jack Tilton', Art in America, November

Lerner, Jesse, 'The Work of Others', Poliester, no. 11, Winter

1996
ACME, Santa Monica (solo)

'The Counterfeit Subject' (with Yishai Judisman),
MUSEO DE ARTE CONTEMPORÁNEO DE OAXACA, Mexico (solo)

'NoWhere',
LOUISIANA MUSEUM, Copenhagen (group)

CASTELLO DI RIVARA, Italy (group)

1996
Ferguson, Bruce, 'Francis Alÿs', Flash Art, no. 188, May–June

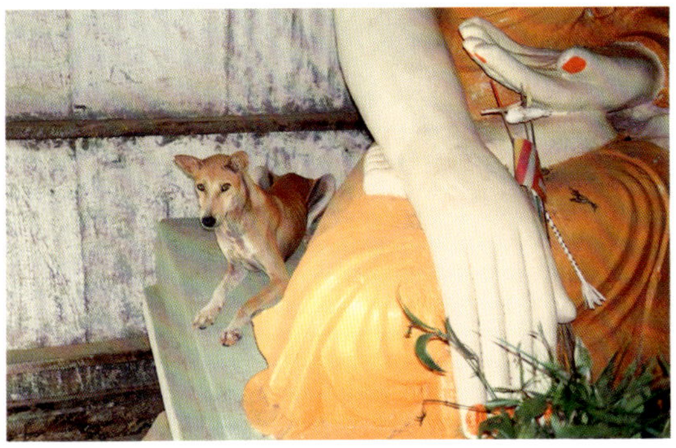

THE LOOP, 1997
PHOTO DOCUMENTATION OF AN ACTION, BURMA, 1997

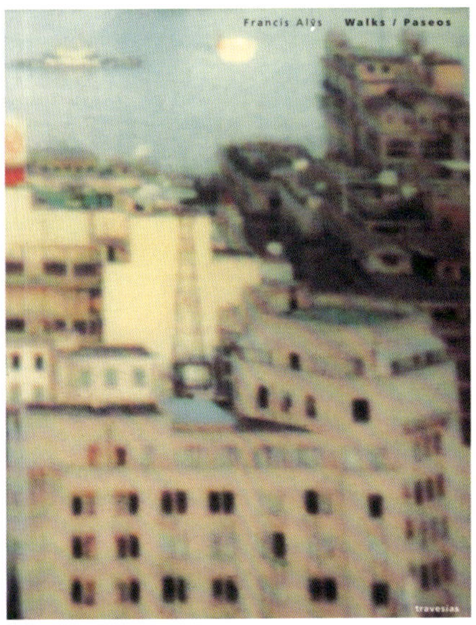

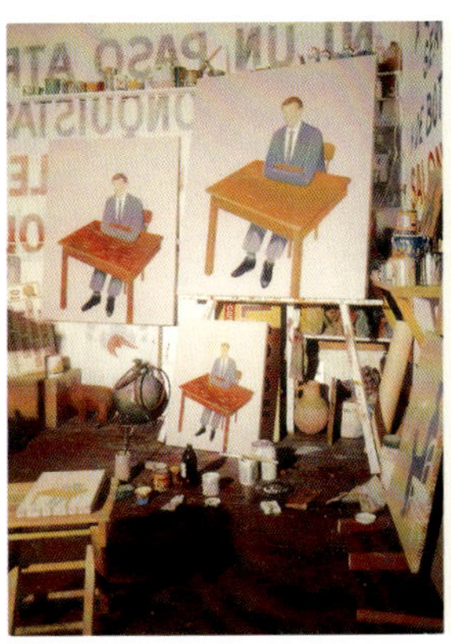

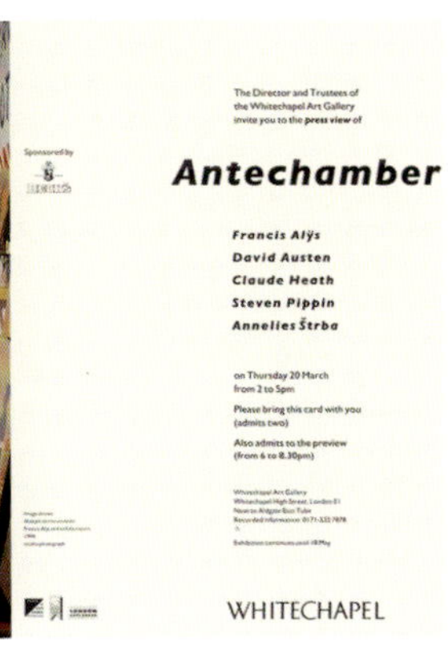

SELECTED EXHIBITIONS AND PROJECTS
1997–1999

1997
'Francis Alÿs: Walks/Paseos',
MUSEO DE ARTE MODERNO, Mexico City (solo)

JACK TILTON GALLERY, New York (solo)

'inSITE 1997'
CENTRO CULTURAL, Tijuana, and SAN DIEGO MUSEUM OF ART (group)

'Antechamber',
WHITECHAPEL GALLERY, London (group)

'Addenda',
MUSEUM DHONDT-DHAENENS, Machelen, Belgium (group)

1st BIENAL DE ARTE TRIDIMENSIONAL, Mexico City (group)

2nd BIENNIAL OF SAAREMA, Estonia (group)

'Asi està la cosa',
CENTRO CULTURAL ARTE CONTEMPORÁNEO, Mexico City (group)

1998
'Le Temps du Sommeil',
CONTEMPORARY ART GALLERY, Vancouver (solo)

PORTLAND INSTITUTE FOR CONTEMPORARY ART, Oregon (solo)

24th SÃO PAULO BIENNIAL (group)

'Insertions',
ARKIPELAG, Stockholm (group)

'Loose Threads',
SERPENTINE GALLERY, London (group)

'1er Salón Internacional de Pintura',
MUSEO DE LA CIUDAD, Mexico City (group)

'Longitude de Onda',
MAO, Caracas (group)

3rd BIENAL BARRO DE AMÉRICA, Caracas (group)

'Imaginarios Mexicanos',
MUSEO DE LA CIVILISACIÓN, Quebec (group)

'Mexcellente',
YERBA BUENA CENTER FOR THE ARTS, San Francisco (group)

'Cinco Continentes y una Ciudad',
MUSEO DE LA CIUDAD, Mexico City (group)

1999
'Standby',
LISSON GALLERY, London (solo)

GALERIE PETER KILCHMANN, Zurich (solo)

MARIO FLECHA GALERIA, Girona, Spain (solo)

'Reality and Desire',
FUNDACIÓN JOAN MIRÓ, Barcelona (group)

48th VENICE BIENNALE (group)

1st MELBOURNE BIENNIAL (group)

'Thinking Aloud',
HAYWARD GALLERY, London (group)

SELECTED ARTICLES AND INTERVIEWS
1997–1999

1997
Darling, Michael, 'Francis Alÿs and the Return to Normality', Frieze, no. 33, March–April

Guilbaut, Serge, 'Rodney Graham and Francis Alÿs', Parachute, no. 87, Spring

Medina, Cuauhtémoc, 'Francis Alÿs: Tu subrealismo', Third Text, no. 38, Spring

Hollander, Kurt, 'Francis Alÿs', Poliester, no. 18, Spring

Rondi, Joëlle, 'Various Places', Art Press, June

Phillips, Andrea, 'A Path is Always Between Two Points', Performance Research, no. 3, September

Hollander, Kurt, 'Under the Influence', Poliester, no. 20, Fall

Rubinstein, Raphael, 'Francis Alÿs at Jack Tilton', Art in America, November

1998
Gallo, Rubén, 'Francis Alÿs at Jack Tilton', Flash Art, no. 198, January–February

Gallo, Rubén, 'Francis Alÿs', ArtNexus, no. 27, March

Arriola, Magali, 'Francis Alÿs: The Liar and the Copy of the Liar', ArtNexus, no. 28, June

Alÿs, Francis, 'The Loop', Untitled, no. 16, Summer

Laurence, Robin, 'Geometries of Conjecture', Border Crossings, no. 4, October

Levin, Kim, 'Voice Choices', The Village Voice, 22–28 October

1999
Basualdo, Carlos, 'Head to Toes: Francis Alÿs's Paths of Resistance', Artforum, April

Green, Charles, 'Signs of Life', Artforum, September

Kurjakovic, Daniel, 'Finten des Geistes', Die Weltwoche, no. 37, 16 September

Aranda Marquez, Carlos, 'Frequent Stops: Carrillo Gil Museum, Mexico City', Flash Art, no. 208, October

Romano, Gianni, 'Why Not Painting?', Flash Art Italia, no. 218, October–November

Yard, S., 'Space on the Run: Life on the Loose: Recent Projects Along the San Diego-Tijuana Frontier', Architectural Design, no. 7–8

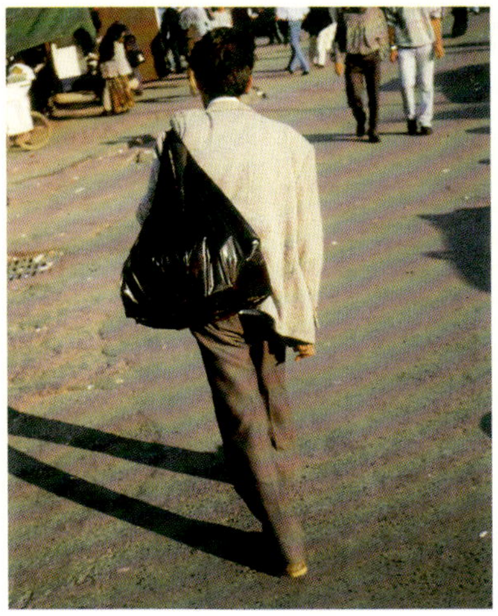

When arriving in Istanbul (new city), wander, looking for someone who could be you. If the meeting happens, walk beside your doppelgänger until your pace adjusts to his/hers. If not repeat the quest in .London.(next city).

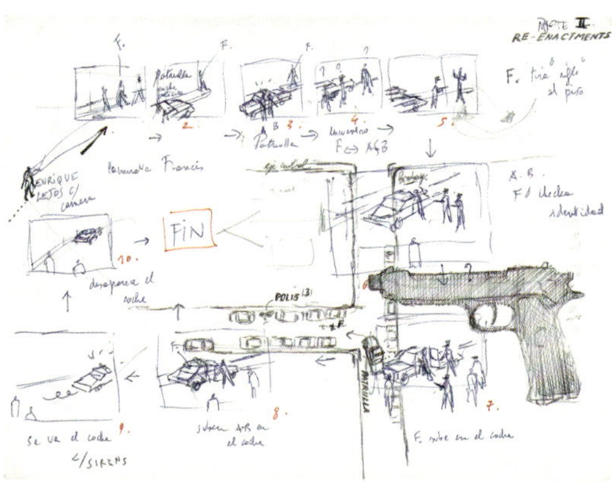

STUDY FOR RE-ENACTMENTS, 2000
PENCIL AND INK ON PAPER

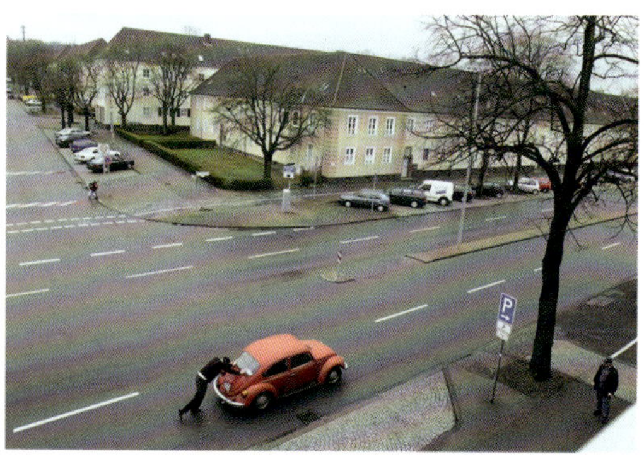

SELECTED EXHIBITIONS AND PROJECTS
1999–2000

1999 (cont.)
'Stimuli',
WITTE DE WITH, Rotterdam (group)

6th ISTANBUL BIENNIAL (group)

'Mirror's Edge',
BILDMUSEET, Umeå, Sweden, toured to VANCOUVER ART GALLERY; CASTELLO DI RIVOLI, Turin; TRAMWAY, Glasgow; CARRILLO GIL MUSEUM, Mexico City (group)

'The Thief',
DIA CENTER FOR THE ARTS, New York (online project)

2000
'Francis Alÿs: The Last Clown',
FUNDACIÓ LA CAIXA, Barcelona: toured to McGILL UNIVERSITY GALLERY, Montreal; PLUG IN, Winnipeg, Canada (solo)

'Mixing Memory and Desire/Wunsch und Erinnerung',
KUNSTMUSEUM LUZERN, Lucerne (group)

'Making Time',
INSTITUTE OF CONTEMPORARY ART, Palm Beach, toured to UCLA HAMMER MUSEUM, Los Angeles (group)

'Age of Influence: Reflections in the mirror of American culture',
MUSEUM OF CONTEMPORARY ART, Chicago (group)

'Dream Machines',
DUNDEE CONTEMPORARY ARTS, toured to MAPPIN ART GALLERY, Sheffield; CAMDEN ARTS CENTRE, London (group)

'Out of Space',
KÖLNISCHER KUNSTVEREIN, Cologne (group)

'Europe: Different Perspectives in Painting'
MUSEO MICHETTI, Francavilla al Mare, Italy (group)

FUORI USO 2000: THE BRIDGES, Pescara, Italy (group)

'Versiones del Sur: Latin America',
MUSEO NACIONAL REINA SOFÍA, Madrid (group)

'Residue',
KUNSTHALLE EXNERGASSE, Vienna (group)

7th HAVANA BIENNIAL, Havana (group)

29th UPPSALA INTERNATIONAL CONTEMPORARY ART BIENNIAL, Sweden (group)

2nd MONTREAL BIENNIAL (group)

SELECTED ARTICLES AND INTERVIEWS
1999–2000

1999 (cont.)
Williams, Gilda, '6th Istanbul Biennial', Art Monthly, no. 232, December–January

2000
Romano, Gianni, 'Webscape', and 'Francis Alÿs: The Thief'; Cuauhtémoc Medina, 'Mexican Strategies: Rarefied Painting'; Flash Art, no. 210, January–February

Herbert, Martin, 'Francis Alÿs', Time Out London, 19–26 January

Withers, Rachel, 'Francis Alÿs at Lisson Gallery', Artforum, March

Shier, Reid, 'Pause and Reflect', Vancouver, March

Romano, Gianni, 'Streets and Gallery Walls: Interview with Francis Alÿs'; Helena Kontova, 'Mirror's Edge'; Flash Art, no. 211, March–April

Moreau, Patric, 'Mirror's Edge', Camera Austria, no. 70

Craddock, Sacha, 'In and Out of the Sun', Untitled, no. 21, Spring

Phillips, Christopher, 'Report from Istanbul: Band of Outsiders', Art in America, April

Glover, Michael, 'Francis Alÿs', ArtNews, April

Benitez Dueñas, Issa Maria, 'Francis Alÿs: Hypotheses for a Walk', ArtNexus, no. 35, April–September

'International Shorts Preview: Athlete's Foot', Artforum, May

Mitchell, Charles Dee, 'Francis Alÿs at Lisson', Art in America, May

Packer, William, 'Screening Time', Financial Times Weekend, 6–7 May

Kent, Sarah, 'Watch this Space', Time Out London, 17 May

Kuoni, Carin, 'Gerüchte, Fährten und Trophäen: auf Spurensuche mit Francis Alÿs', Kunst Bulletin, June

Herbert, Martin, 'Francis Alÿs', Time Out London, 13–20 June

Jeffett, William, 'A Note on Francis Alÿs', NY Arts Magazine, July–August

Buchloh, Benjamin, 'Control, By Design', Artforum, September

Moreno, Gean, 'Polis as Playground: Contemporary Artists in Urban Space', Art Papers, no. 5, September–October

'Video Work', Frieze, no. 54, September–October

Medina, Cuauhtémoc, 'Formas políticas recientes: búsquedas radicales en México: Santiago Sierra, Francis Alÿs, Minerva Cuevas', Trans>arts, no. 8

Phillips, Andrea, 'A Dog's Life', Performance Research, no. 2

Marí, Bartomeu, 'Francis Alÿs: Lotgevallen van een grootstedelijk slaapvandelaar', Metropolis M, December

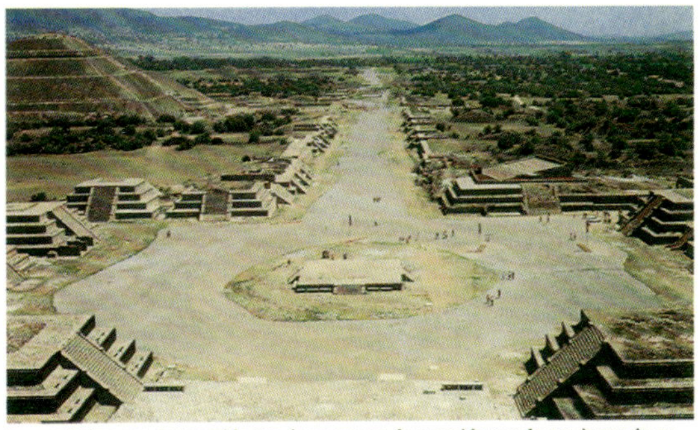

Ean wandeling van de pyramide van de maan naar de pyramide van de zon bezorgde me drie kiezelstenen in mijn linkerschoen en twee kiezeistenen in mijn rechterschoen.
A walk from the Pyramid of the Moon to the Pyramid of the Sun resulted in 3 pebbles in my left shoe and 2 pebbles in my right shoe.

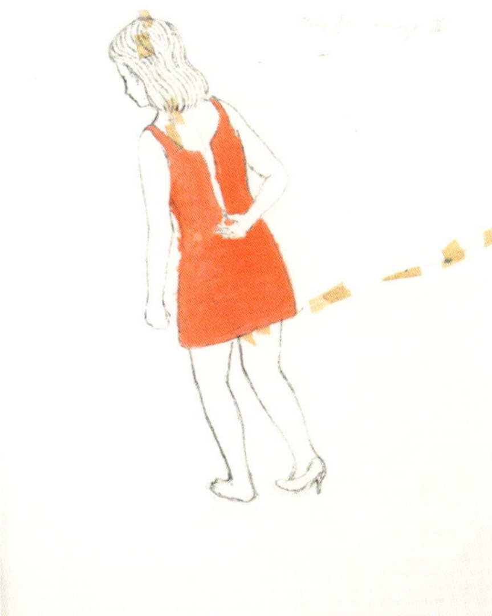

STUDY FOR REHEARSAL II, 2001
OIL AND PENCIL ON TRACING PAPER
38 X 28 CM

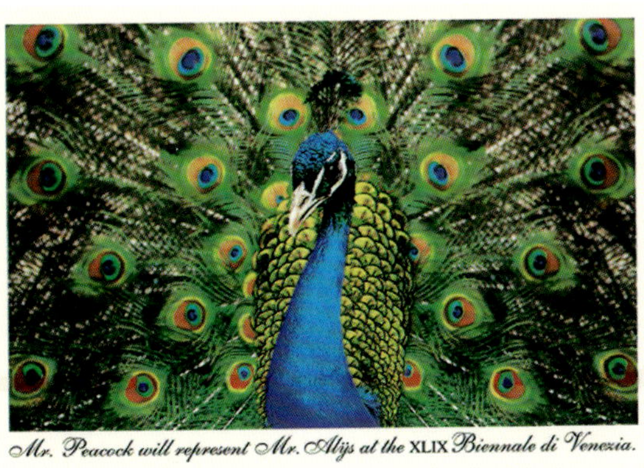

SELECTED EXHIBITIONS AND PROJECTS
2001–2002

2001
MUSÉE PICASSO ANTIBES, France (solo)

'1-866-Free-Matrix',
WADSWORTH ATHENEUM, Hartford, Connecticut (solo)

'L'Attente',
GALERIE PETER KILCHMANN, Zurich (solo)

'Amores Perros vs Camera' (with Alejandro Gonzales Iñarritu),
KUNST-WERKE, Berlin (solo)

'Douglas Gordon & Francis Alÿs',
LISSSON GALLERY, London (solo)

'Videoserie in der Black Box: 6 Künstler – 6 Positionen',
SAMMLUNG GOETZ, Munich (group)

'A Walk to the End of the World',
THE FOKSAL GALLERY FOUNDATION, Warsaw (group)

'Loop',
HYPO KUNSTHALLE, Munich, toured to P.S.1 CONTEMPORARY ART CENTER, New York (group)

'The Big Show',
NEW INTERNATIONAL CULTURAL CENTER, Antwerp (group)

7th ISTANBUL BIENNIAL (group)

'God is in the Details: Films et vidéos d'animation',
CENTRE D'ART CONTEMPORAIN GENÉVE, Geneva (group)

'Looking at You: Kunst Provokation Unterhaltug Video',
KUNSTHALLE FRIDERICIANUM, Kassel, Germany (group)

'Francis Alÿs/Rafael Ortega, Pierre Huyghe, Beat Streuli & Gillian Wearing',
IKON GALLERY, Birmingham, England (group)

'Squatters',
MUSEU SERRALVES, Porto, toured to WITTE DE WITH, Rotterdam (group)

49th VENICE BIENNALE (group)

'Da Aversida de Vivemos: Lateinamerikanische Künstler',
MUSÉE D'ART MODERNE DE LA VILLE DE PARIS (group)

'Painting at the Edge of the World',
WALKER ART CENTER, Minneapolis (group)

'Exploding Cinema: Cinema without Walls',
MUSEUM BOIJMANS VAN BEUNINGEN, Rotterdam (group)

'In Aktion: Performance heute',
KUNSTVEREIN HAMBURG, (group)

2002
'Projects 76: The Modern Procession',
MUSEUM OF MODERN ART, New York (solo)

'Matrix.2',
CASTELLO DI RIVOLI, Turin (solo)

'Walking a Painting',
THE PROJECT, Los Angeles (solo)

'Cuando la fe mueve montañas/When Faith Moves Mountains',
3rd BIENAL IBEROAMERICANA DE LIMA (solo)

'Coartadas',
INSTITUT DU MEXIQUE Á PARIS (group)

SELECTED ARTICLES AND INTERVIEWS
2001–2002

2001
Medina, Cuauhtémoc, 'Entre dos aguas: conversación entre Francis Alÿs', Curare, no. 17, January–June

'Francis Alÿs: Döppelganger', Tate Magazine, Spring

DeVuono, Frances, 'Tout le Temps/Every Time: La Biennale de Montréal', New Art Examiner, April

Mahoney, Elizabeth, 'Mirror's Edge', Art Monthly, April

Torres, David, 'Francis Alÿs: Simple passant just walking the dog', Art Press, April

Bishop, Claire, 'Kept in the Dark', Evening Standard, 22 May

Jetzer, Gianni, 'Protest! Respect!', Saiten, June

Alberge, Dalya, 'Portrait of the Artist as a Young Pearock', The Times, 6 June

Fallon, Michael, 'Minneapolis', Art Papers, no. 4, July–August

Cooke, Lynne, 'Venice Biennale', The Burlington Magazine, no. 1182, September

Lefkowitz, David, 'Edgy Painting at the Edge of the World'; 'This Just In: Painting is Back', New Art Examiner, September-October

Medina, Cuauhtémoc, 'Zones of Tolerance: Teresa Margolles, SEMEFO and Beyond', Parachute, no. 104, October–December

Dorn, Anja, 'Out of Space', Frieze, no. 55, November–December

2002
Kantor, Jordan, 'Loop', Artforum, April

Pohlenz, Ricardo, 'Leisure at Jumex', Flash Art, no. 224, May–June

Anton, Saul, 'A Thousand Words: Francis Alÿs talks about When Faith Moves Mountains', Artforum, Summer

Bohlen, Celestine, 'Making a Spectacle of MoMA's Big Move', International Herald Tribune, 29 June

Biesenbach, Klaus, 'Hunting Men Hunting Dogs: Fear and Loathing in Mexico City'; Priya Bhatnagar, Samuele Menin and Michele Robecchi, 'Focus Mexico', Flash Art, no. 225, July–September

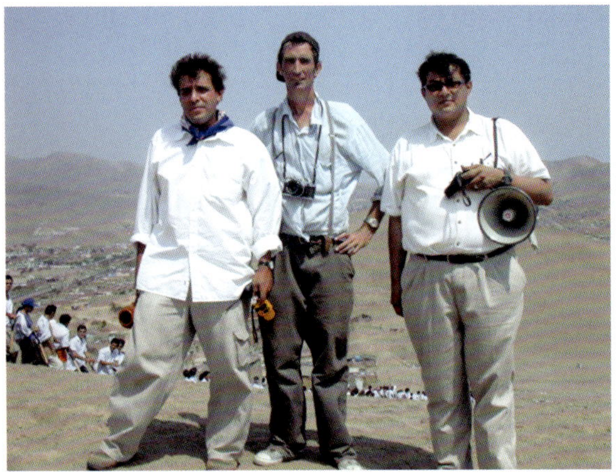

RAFAEL ORTEGA, THE ARTIST AND CUAUHTÉMOC MEDINA ON LOCATION OF <u>WHEN FAITH MOVES MOUNTAINS</u>, LIMA, 2002

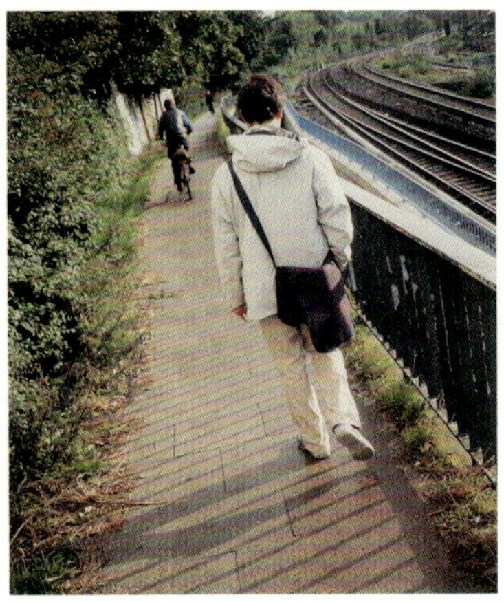

On your way to work everyday,
every morning, every Monday,
sow Marijuana seeds along the way.
Every morning, every Tuesday,
on your way to work...

Montags auf dem Arbeitsweg,
jeden Morgen, jeden Tag,
Marihuana Samen-leg,
jeden Abend, jeden Tag.
Dienstags auf dem Arbeitsweg...

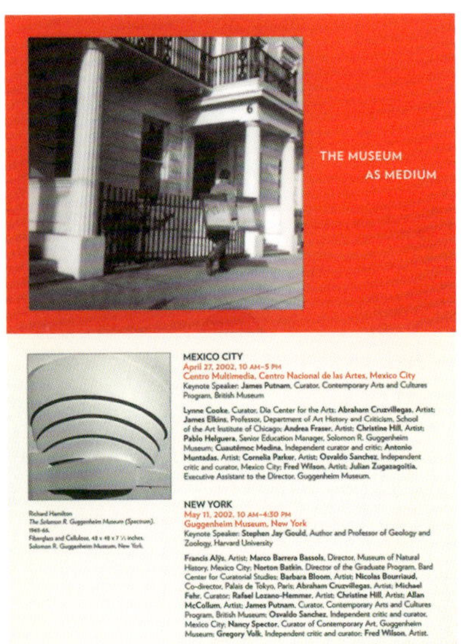

<u>SELECTED EXHIBITIONS AND PROJECTS</u>
2001–2003

2002 (cont.)
'En Route',
SERPENTINE GALLERY, London (group)

'Axis Mexico: Common Objects and Cosmopolitan Actions',
SAN DIEGO MUSEUM OF ART (group)

8th BALTIC TRIENNIAL OF INTERNATIONAL ART, Vilnius (group)

'Mexico: Sensitive Negotiations',
CONSULADO DE MEXICO EN MIAMI (group)

4th SHANGHAI BIENNIAL (group)

'Structures of Difference',
WADSWORTH ATHENEUM MUSEUM OF ART, Hartford, Connecticut (group)

'20 Million Mexicans Can't Be Wrong',
SOUTH LONDON GALLERY, London, toured to JOHN HANSARD GALLERY, Southhampton, England (group)

'Mexico City: An Exhibition about the Exchange Rates of Bodies and Values',
P.S.1 CONTEMPORARY ART CENTER, New York, toured to KUNST-WERKE BERLIN (group)

'The Museum as Medium',
GUGGENHEIM MUSEUM, New York, and CENTRO NACIONAL DE LAS ARTES, Mexico City (symposium)

Nominated for the Hugo Boss Prize, Solomon R. Guggenheim Museum, New York

2003
'The Leak',
MUSÉE D'ART MODERNE DE LA VILLE DE PARIS (solo)

'The Prophet and The Fly',
CENTRO NAZIONALE PER LE ARTI CONTEMPORANEE, Rome, toured to KUNSTHAUS ZÜRICH; MUSEO NACIONAL REINA SOFÍA, Madrid; COLLECTION LAMBERT EN AVIGNON (solo)

OUTLOOK, multiple venues, Athens (group)

'Somewhere Better Than This Place: Alternative Social Experience',
CONTEMPORARY ARTS CENTER, Cincinnati (group)

'Stretch: Artists from Canada, USA, Mexico, Cuba, Guatemala, Colombia and Brazil',
THE POWER PLANT, Toronto (group)

4th BIENAL DEL MERCOSUR, Porto Alegre, Brazil (group)

'Szenenwechsel',
MUSEUM FÜR MODERNE KUNST, Frankfurt (group)

'The Labyrinthine Effect',
AUSTRALIAN CENTER FOR CONTEMPORARY ART, Southbank, Victoria (group)

MULTIPLECITY, multiple venues, Panama City (group)

'Edén',
LA COLECCIÓN JUMEX in the ANTIGUO COLEGIO DE SAN ILDEFONSO, Mexico City, toured to BIBLIOTECA LUIS ANGEL ARANGO, Bogotá (group)

'El aire es azul/The Air is Blue',
CASA MUSEO LUIS BARRAGÁN, Mexico City (group)

1st JAFRE BIENNIAL, Spain (group)

<u>SELECTED ARTICLES AND INTERVIEWS</u>
2001–2003

2002 (cont.)
Edwards, C., 'Muralists, No!', <u>Art Review</u>, September

Gronlund, Melissa, 'Mexico City: An Exhibition About the Exchange Rates of Bodies and Values', <u>Contemporary</u>, no. 43

Heiser, Jörg, 'Walk on the Wild Side', <u>Frieze</u>, no. 69, September

Wilson, Michael, 'International Preview: Life on the Streets', <u>The Royal Academy Magazine</u>, no. 76, Autumn

Güner, Fisun, 'Everyday Drive-by Shooting', <u>Metro Life</u>, 23 September

Cowan, Amber, 'Move Any Mountain', <u>Sleazenation</u>, October

Dailey, Meghan, 'Mexico City: An Exhibition About the Exchange Rates of Bodies and Values', <u>Artforum</u>, November

Lavrador, Judicaël, 'Francis Alÿs', <u>Beaux Arts</u>

'Francis Alÿs: The Modern Procession', <u>In>process</u>, no. 3

Helguera, Pablo, 'Mexico City', <u>Tema Celeste</u>, no. 94 , November–December

'Mexico City: An Exhibition About the Exchange Rates of Bodies and Values', <u>ArtNexus</u>, no. 46, December

'Postcards from the Edge', <u>The Royal Academy Magazine</u>, no. 77, Winter

2003
Anton, Saul, 'One More Step'; Kitty Scott, 'Francis Alÿs: A Portrait'; Robert Storr, 'Strange Attractor', <u>Parkett</u>, no. 69

Herzog, Samuel, 'Im Wunderland', <u>Neue Zürcher Zeitung</u>, March

Ryser, Emmanuelle, 'Le Belge de Mexico', <u>Accrochage</u>, no. 46, April

Schindler, Anna, 'Der Wert des Lebens', <u>Kunstzeitung</u>, no. 81, May

Jolles, Claudia, 'Brütende Leere', <u>Kunst Bulletin</u>, May

Crowley, Tom, 'Mexico City on the Move', <u>Tema Celeste</u>, no. 97, May–June

Garrett, Craig, 'MultipleCity: Revolution in Panama', <u>Flash Art</u>, no. 230, May–June

Beil, Ralf, 'Kurze Geschichte eines langen Schlafes', <u>Kunst Bulletin</u>, May

Benitez Dueñas, Issa Maria, 'Francis Alÿs: Museo Nacional Centro de Arte Reina Sofia'; Craig Garrett, 'MultipleCity', <u>ArtNexus</u>, no. 50, July–September

'Silly Walks, Serious Concerns: Francis Alÿs', <u>The Economist</u>, 7 August

Lorés, Maite, 'The Prophet and the Fly', <u>Contemporary</u>, no. 53–54

Von Twickel, Felicitas, 'Spots, Aspekte', <u>ZDF</u>, October

Trainor, James, 'Walking the Walk: the Artist as Flâneur', <u>Border Crossings</u>, no. 4, November

Kreis, Elfi, 'Ein Preis, der Massstäbe setzt', <u>Kunstzeitung</u>, no. 87, November

Green, Charles, 'The Labyrinthine Effect', <u>Artforum</u>, December

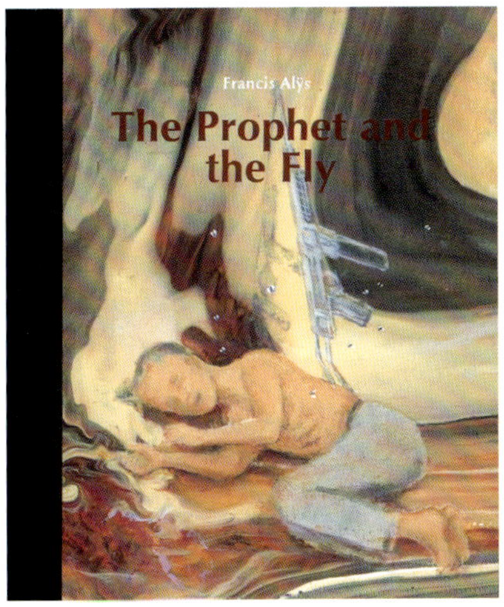

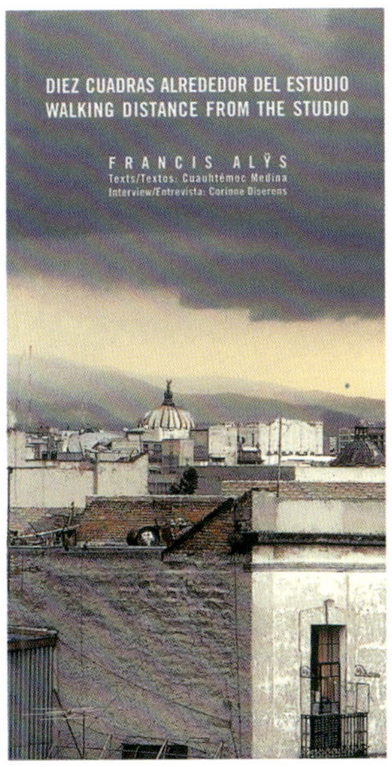

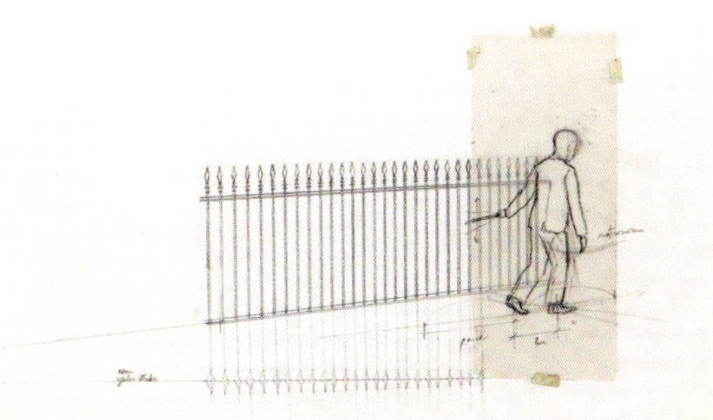

STUDY FOR RAILINGS, 2004
PENCIL ON TRACING PAPER
45 X 55 CM

SELECTED EXHIBITIONS AND PROJECTS
2003–2004

2003 (cont.)
'Animation',
KUNST-WERKE BERLIN (group)

'Imágenes en movimiento/Moving Pictures'
GUGGENHEIM BILBAO (group)

'Fast forward: Media Art – Sammlung Goetz',
ZENTRUM FÜR KUNST UND MEDIENTECHNOLOGIE (ZKM), Karlsruhe, Germany, toured to CENTRO CULTURAL CONDE DUQUE and MUSEO MUNICIPAL DE ARTE CONTEMPORÁNEO, Madrid (group)

2004
'Blue Orange 2004: Francis Alÿs',
MARTIN-GROPIUS-BAU, Berlin, Germany (solo)

'Walking Distance from the Studio',
KUNSTMUSEUM WOLFSBURG, Germany, toured to MUSÉE DES BEAUX-ARTS, Nantes; MUSEO D'ART CONTEMPORANI DE BARCELONA (MACBA); MUSEO DE SAN ILDEFONSO, Mexico City (solo)

'Time Zones: Recent Film and Video',
TATE MODERN, London (group)

'Dedicated to a Proposition',
EXTRA CITY, Antwerp (group)

2004 CARNEGIE INTERNATIONAL, Pittsburgh (group)

'Who if not we should at least try to imagine the future of all this?',
BASIS VOOR ACTUELE KUNST (BAK), Utrecht, Netherlands (group)

14th BIENNALE OF SYDNEY (group)

'20/20 Vision',
STEDELIJK MUSEUM, Amsterdam (group)

'Densité ± 0',
FRI-ART CENTRE D'ART CONTEMPORAIN, Fribourg, Switzerland, toured to ÉCOLE NATIONALE SUPÉRIEURE DES BEAUX-ARTS, Paris (group)

'Point of View: An Anthology of the Moving Image',
NEW MUSEUM OF CONTEMPORARY ART, New York, toured to HAMMER MUSEUM, Los Angeles (group)

'Made in Mexico',
INSTITUTE OF CONTEMPORARY ART, Boston, toured to HAMMER MUSEUM, Los Angeles (group)

'Artist's Choice: Mona Hatoum, Here is Elsewhere',
THE MUSEUM OF MODERN ART, New York (group)

'Cordially Invited',
CENTRAAL MUSEUM, Utrecht, Netherlands (group)

'O zero',
OFFICINAL PARA PROYECTOS DE ARTE, Guadalajara (group)

TRIENNALE POLIGRÁFICA, San Juan, Puerto Rico (group)

26th SÃO PAULO BIENNIAL (group)

'Revolving Doors',
FUNDACIÓN TELEFONICA, Madrid (group)

'Ailleurs, ici',
MUSÉE D'ART MODERNE DE LA VILLE DE PARIS (group)

SELECTED ARTICLES AND INTERVIEWS
2003–2004

2003 (cont.)
Gallo, Rubén, Arriola Magali and Issa Maria Benítez Dueñas, 'Flashback: Francis Alÿs', ArtNexus, no. 51, December–February

2004
Wetterwald, Elisabeth, 'Francis Alÿs: Collection Lambert', Art Press, January

Lafuente, Pablo, 'Francis Alÿs', Frieze, no. 80, January–February

Klaas, Heiko, 'Francis Alÿs', Artist Kunstmagazin, no. 4

Jiménez, Carlos, 'Alÿs, un exilado curioso', El País, 5 February

Stefanowski, Michael, 'Francis Alÿs: BlueOrange Prize', ZDF, 27 February

Loers, Veit, 'Auf Marlenes Spuren', Kunstzeitung, March

Manchester, Clare, 'Ailleurs, ici', Flash Art, no. 235, March–April

Colombo, Paolo, 'A Silent Presence', Tema Celeste, no. 102, March–April

Schindler, Anna, 'Die Arbeit des Künstlers ist das Reisen', Die Welt, 6 March

Lamm, April, 'I Feel Therefore I Am', Modern Painters, Spring

Bijutsu Shuppan-Sha, 'Very New Art 2004', Tokyo, vol. 56, April

Stoeber, Michael, 'Soziale Kreaturen: Wie Körper Kunst wird', Kunstforum, May–June

Smith, Trevor, 'Francis Alÿs: Spending Time and Travelling Free', Art & Australia, June–August

Knight, Christopher, 'Mexico Joins Global Club', Geo Topics, 23 June

Manchester, Clare, 'Densité ± 0', Flash Art, no. 237, July–September

Storr, Robert, 'Francis Alÿs', Villeurbane Semaine, no. 12, July

Wetterwald, Elisabeth, 'La rivoluzione non siamo noi: Pierre Joseph et Francis Alÿs', Parachute, no. 115, July–September

Mendelssohn, Joanna, 'The Biennale of Sydney', Tema Celeste, no. 105, September–October

Tappeiner, Maria, 'Francis Alÿs', Kulturzeit, 2 September

Pinto, Roberto, 'Subjectivity, Passion and Excess in Everyday Life', Work in Progress, no. 10, Autumn

Becker, Christoph, 'Veränderungen in der Sammlung: Schwestern treffen Brüder', Kunsthaus Zürich Magasin, no. 4 October

Gardener, Belinda Grace, 'Wolfsburg/Berlin: Francis Alÿs', Kunstzeitung, no. 98, October

Lafuente, Pablo, 'Art on Parade', Art Monthly, no. 280, October

Gioni, Massimiliano, 'Ojos bien cerrados', Matador, no. 9

SELECTED EXHIBITIONS AND PROJECTS
2004–2005

2004 (cont.)
'Faces in the Crowd: Images of Modern Life from Manet to Today', WHITECHAPEL GALLERY, London, toured to CASTELLO DI RIVOLI, Turin (group)

Recipient of the Kunstpreis BlueOrange, Bundesverband der Deutschen Volksbanken und Raiffeisenbanken, Berlin

2005
'Francis Alÿs: (to be continued) 1992–',
ARTSPACE, Auckland (solo)

'Sometimes doing something poetic can become political and sometimes doing something political can become poetic',
THE ISRAEL MUSEUM, Jerusalem (solo)

'Seven Walks',
ARTANGEL and NATIONAL PORTRAIT GALLERY, London (solo)

'Monopolis: Antwerp',
WITTE DE WITH, Rotterdam (group)

'The Hours: Visual Arts of Contemporary Latin America',
IRISH MUSEUM OF MODERN ART, Dublin (group)

'Eindhoven-Istanbul',
VAN ABBEMUSEUM, Eindhoven, Netherlands (group)

'Ecstasy: In and About Altered States',
MUSEUM OF CONTEMPORARY ART, Los Angeles, (group)

'Crowd of the Person',
CONTEMPORARY MUSEUM, Baltimore (group)

'Here Comes the Sun',
MAGASIN 3, Stockholm (group)

'inSITE 2005',
CENTRO CULTURAL, Tijuana, and SAN DIEGO MUSEUM OF ART (group)

'General Ideas: Rethinking Conceptual Art 1987–2005',
CCA WATTIS INSTITUTE OF CONTEMPORARY ARTS, San Francisco (group)

'Roaming Memories',
LUDWIG FORUM FÜR INTERNATIONALE KUNST, Aachen, Germany (group)

GLASGOW INTERNATIONAL (group)

'Irreducible: Contemporary Short Form Video',
MIAMI ART CENTRAL (group)

'Odd Lots: Revisiting Gordon Matta-Clark's Fake Estates',
WHITE COLUMNS and QUEENS MUSEUM OF ART, New York (group)

'Police',
LANDES GALERIE AM OBERÖSTERREICHISCHEN LANDESMUSEUM, Linz, Austria (group)

'Point of View: A Contemporary Anthology of the Moving Image',
HERBERT F. JOHNSON MUSEUM OF ART at CORNELL UNIVERSITY, Ithaca, New York (group)

'What's New Pussycat?'
MUSEUM FÜR MODERNE KUNST, Frankfurt (group)

PERFORMA 05, New York (group)

SELECTED ARTICLES AND INTERVIEWS
2004–2005

2004 (cont.)
Krepler, Ute, 'Francis Alÿs', Kunst und Markt, no. 2

Cooke, Lynne, 'Best of 2004'; Bettina Funcke, 'Francis Alÿs: Martin-Gropius-Bau and Kunstmuseum Wolfsburg', Artforum, December

Diez, Renato, 'Hugo Boss Prize', Arte, no. 376, December

2005
Siegel, Katy, '2004 Carnegie International', Artforum, January

Lasnier, Jean-François 'Francis Alÿs: Marcher, Créer', Beaux Arts, no. 248, February

Volk, Gregory, 'Report From Pittsburgh: Let's Get Metaphysical', Art in America, March

Boase, Gair, 'Faces in the Crowd at Whitechapel Art Gallery', Flash Art, no. 241, March–April

McCormack, Chris, 'Francis Alÿs at MACBA', Contemporary, no. 73

Bonami, Francesco, 'The Legacy of a Myth Maker', Tate Etc., Spring

Arriola, Magali, 'Francis Alÿs', Spike Kunstmagazin, Summer

'Francis Alÿs & Stanley Brown', Tema Celeste, no. 110, July–August

Laddaga, Reinaldo, 'Almost Brothers', Flash Art, no. 243, July–September

Debroise, Olivier, 'The Loop: Diary of a Drifting', Exit, no. 19, August–October

Pignatti, Lorenza, 'Francis Alÿs at MACBA Barcelona', Tema Celeste, no. 111, September–October

Scott, Andrea K., 'High Interest Rate', Time Out New York, 8–15 September

Irving, Mark, 'A Walk on the Wild Side', The Times, London, 24 September

Balcells, María José, 'Francis Alÿs at MACBA', Flash Art, no. 244, October

Buck, Louisa, 'Soldiers as Social Allegory: Interview with Francis Alÿs', Art Newspaper, no. 14, October

Arriola, Magali, 'Beaux Gestes', Art Review, October–November

Robecchi, Michele, 'The Celebrated Walking Blues: A Conversation with Francis Alÿs', Contemporary, no. 78

Huberman, Anthony, 'Missing in Action', Art Review, November

O'Reilly, Sally, 'Odd Lots: Revisiting Gordon Matta-Clark's Fake Estates', Modern Painters, November

Lafuente, Pablo, 'Francis Alÿs', Art Monthly, no. 291, November

Comer, Stuart, 'London'; Chrissie Iles, 'Best of 2005', Artforum, December

Sepúlveda, Luz, 'Group Shows: Only the Characters Change', ArtNexus, no. 55

Kennedy, Katie, 'Shooting Gallery: An introduction to guns in contemporary art', Small Arms Survey 2005: Weapons at War, Graduate Institute of International Studies, Geneva

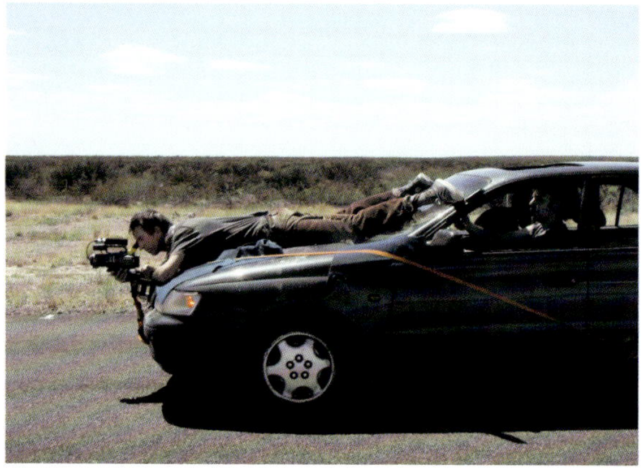

THE ARTIST FILMING A STORY OF DECEPTION IN PATAGONIA, 2005

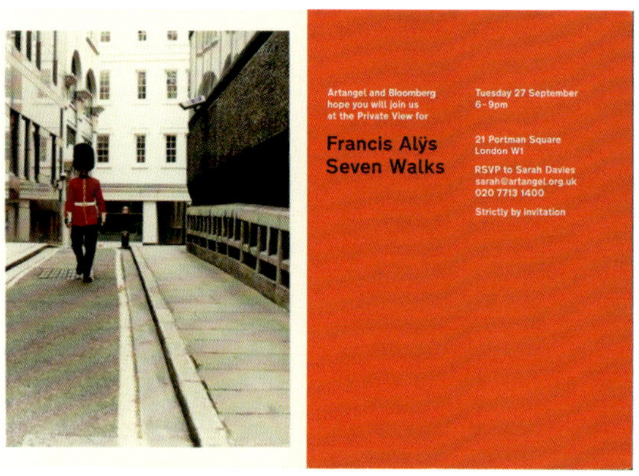

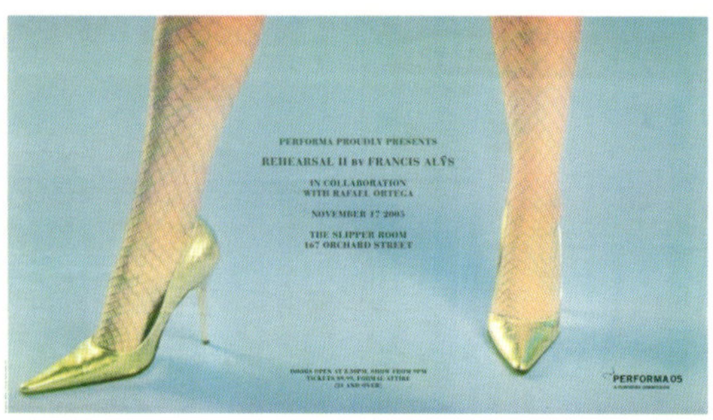

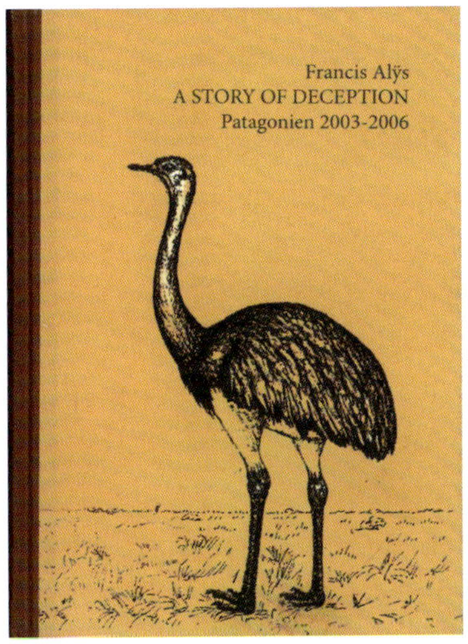

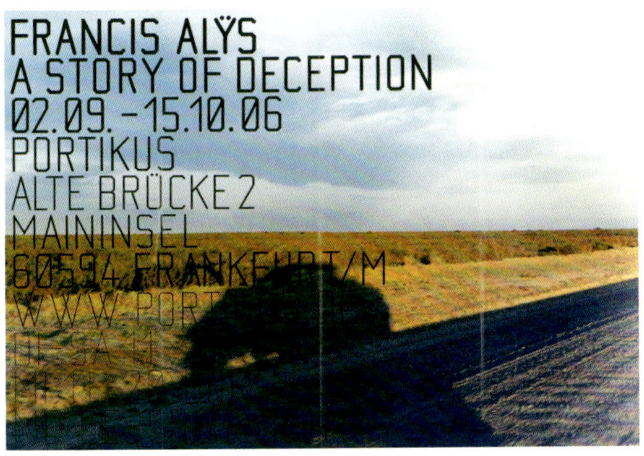

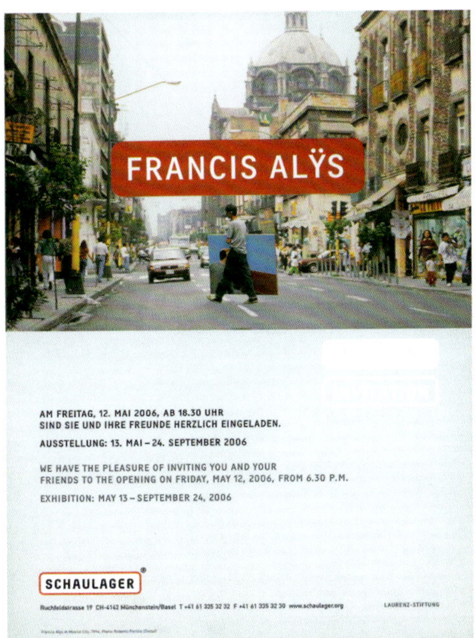

SELECTED EXHIBITIONS AND PROJECTS
2006–2007

2006

'A Story of Deception: Patagonia 2003–2006', PORTIKUS, Frankfurt, toured to MUSEO DE ARTE LATINO AMERICANO DE BUENOS AIRES (MALBA) (solo)

'Diez cuadras alrededor del estudio' ANTIGUO COLEGIO DE SAN ILDEFONSO, Mexico City (solo)

'The Sign Painting Project (1993–1997): A Revision', SCHAULAGER, Basel (solo)

'Black Box: Francis Alÿs', HIRSHHORN MUSEUM AND SCULPTURE GARDEN, Washington DC (solo)

'Mapping the City', STEDELIJK MUSEUM VOOR ACTUELE KUNST (SMAK), Ghent, toured to STEDELIJK MUSEUM, Amsterdam (group)

IDEAL CITY/INVISIBLE CITIES, multiple venues, Zamosc, Poland, and Potsdam, Germany (group)

'SNAFU: Medien, Mythen, Mind Control', KUNSTHALLE HAMBURG (group)

'Satellite of Love', WITTE DE WITH and TENT, Rotterdam (group)

'Die 90er', NEUES MUSEUM WESERBURG, Bremen, Germany (group)

'Version Animée', CENTRE POUR L'IMAGE CONTEMPORAINE, Geneva (group)

PRINTEMPS DE SEPTEMBRE 2006, Toulouse, France (group)

2007

'Politics of Rehearsal', HAMMER MUSEUM, Los Angeles (solo)

'Francis Alÿs: Works from Private Collections', VILLA GRISEBACH GALLERY, Berlin (solo)

'Sometimes doing something poetic can become political and sometimes doing something political can become poetic', DAVID ZWIRNER, New York (solo)

MUSEO DE ARTE DE LIMA (solo)

'Fabiolas' (organized by the DIA FOUNDATION), THE HISPANIC SOCIETY OF AMERICA, New York, toured to LOS ANGELES COUNTY MUSEUM OF ART; NATIONAL PORTRAIT GALLERY, London; MONASTERIO DE SANTO DOMINGO DE SILOS, Burgos, Spain; HAUS ZUM KIRSCHGARTEN, Basel; MUSEO DE ARTE DE LIMA; MUSEO AMPARO, Puebla, Mexico; PINACOTECA DO ESTADO DE SÃO PAULO; MUSEO DE ARTE ZAPOPAN, Guadalajara, Mexico; THE MENIL COLLECTION, Houston, Texas (solo)

52nd VENICE BIENNALE (group)

'Expats/Clandestines', WIELS CENTRE D'ART CONTEMPORAIN, Brussels (group)

'Idylle', DOMUS ARTIUM 2002 (DA2), Salamanca, Spain, toured to NATIONAL GALLERY, Prague (group)

'La Era de las Discrepancias', UNIVERSIDAD NACIONAL AUTÓNOMA DE MÉXICO, Mexico City (group)

6th MERCOSUL BIENNIAL (group)

SELECTED ARTICLES AND INTERVIEWS
2006–2007

2006

Cerio, Gregory, 'Contemporary Art: The New Blue Chips', Home & Garden, January

Gleadell, Colin, 'Contemporary Sales Set All-Time Records', ArtNews, January

Robecchi, Michele, 'Francis Alÿs: Seven Walks', Rodeo Magazine, no. 12, January–February

Marrón, Lorena, 'Francis Alÿs: Soy como un perro callejero', La Tempestad, no. 47, March-April

Escalante, Gabriel, 'Diez cuadras alrededor del estudio: Francis Alÿs en el Colegio de San Ildefonso', Rim Magazine, no. 8, Spring

Charpenel, Patrick, and María Minera, '5 piezas fundamentales del arte contemporáneo en México según Patrick Charpenel', DF por Travesías, no. 48, April

Calera-Grobet, Antonio, 'Todo lo que entendí o malentendí alrededor de la obra de Francis Alÿs', Arte al Día, no. 27, April–May

Godfrey, Mark, 'Walking the Line: The Art of Francis Alÿs', Artforum, May

Chaplin, Julia, 'Art on the Edge in Mexico City', The New York Times, 25 June

Scharrer, Eva, 'Francis Alÿs und Tacita Dean im Schaulager', Kunst Bulletin, July–August

Gopnik, Blake, 'Here & Now', Washington Post, 23 July

Goldberg, RoseLee, 'Be Here Now', Contemporary, no. 89

2007

Chilver, John, 'Displacements of Shadow', Art Papers, January–February

Herbert, Martin, 'The Distance Between: The Political Peregrinations of Francis Alÿs', Modern Painters, March

Hollander, Kurt, 'Thoughtful Wandering of a Man with a Can', The New York Times, 13 March

Mack, Joshua, 'Francis Alÿs', Time Out New York, 8–14 March

Cotter, Holland, 'Thoughtful Wanderings Of a Man With a Can', The New York Times, 13 March

Godfrey, Mark, 'The Artist as Historian', October, Spring

Smaldone, Andrew J., 'Francis Alÿs', ArtSEENJournal, Spring

Cruickshank-Hagenbuckle, Geoffrey, 'Francis Alÿs', The Brooklyn Rail, April

Rivera, Claudia, 'Francis Alÿs: A Story of Deception', Código, no. 06140, April–May

Lawn, Andrzej, 'Francis Alÿs', Flash Art, no. 254, May–June

Patrick, Martin, 'Snapshots from an Indefinite Vacation: Francis Alÿs and Photography', Afterimage, May–June

Villasmil, Alejandra, 'Francis Alÿs', Arte Aldia, May–June

Yumi, Yamaguchi, 'Francis Alÿs', Mac Power, July

Schambelan, Elizabeth, 'Francis Alÿs: Hammer Museum'; Katy Siegel, 'Venice: The Buck Stops Here'; Jessica Morgan, 'Categorical Imperatives', Artforum, September

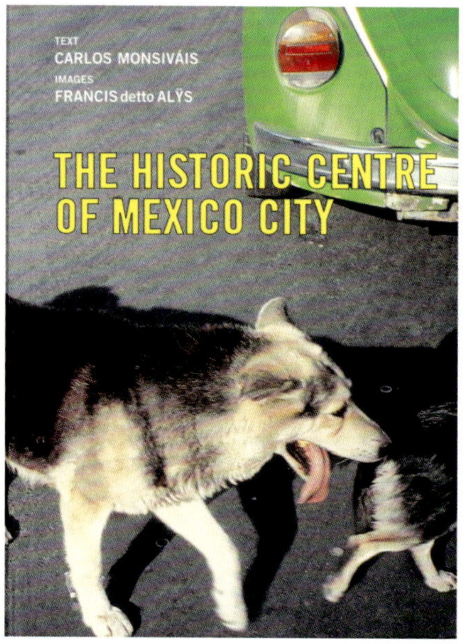

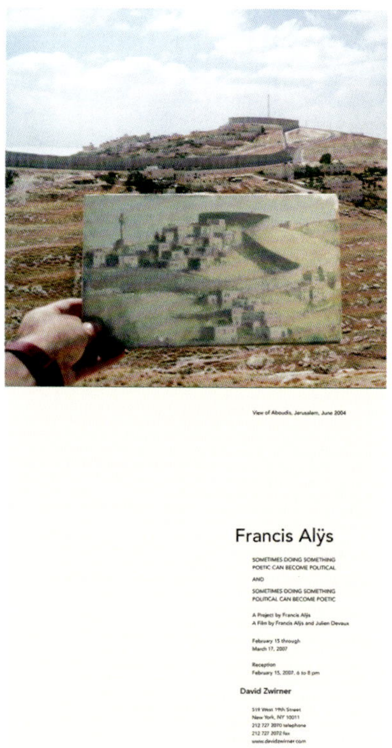

SELECTED EXHIBITIONS AND PROJECTS
2007–08

2007 (cont.)
'Come, Come, Come into my World',
ELLIPSE FOUNDATION CONTEMPORARY ART COLLECTION, Cascais, Portugal (group)

'Global Cities',
TATE MODERN, London (group)

'Multiplex: Directions in Art 1970 to Now',
MUSEUM OF MODERN ART, New York (group)

'No. 1: Destroy, She Said',
JULIA STOSCHEK COLLECTION, Düsseldorf (group)

'Poetics Country',
FERENBALM-GURBRÜ STATION, Karlsruhe, Germany (group)

'Prima Verra',
LA BF15, Lyon (group)

'Principio de Intertidumbre',
CENTRO DE LAS ARTES, Monterrey (group)

2008
SAMMLUNG GOETZ, Munich (solo)

'Francis Alÿs: Bolero (Shoe Shine Blues) and Politics of Rehearsal',
THE RENAISSANCE SOCIETY at the UNIVERSITY OF CHICAGO (solo)

8th BIENAL DE ARTE PANAMA (group)

16th BIENNALE OF SYDNEY (group)

'The Art of Participation: 1950 to Now',
SAN FRANCISCO MUSEUM OF MODERN ART (group)

'Arte ≠ Vida: Actions by Artists of the Americas 1960–2000',
EL MUSEO DEL BARRIO, New York, toured to MUSEO DE ARTE CARRILLO GIL, Mexico City; MUSEO AMPARO, Puebla, Mexico; BLAFFER GALLERY, Houston, Texas; INSTITUTO TOMIE OHTAKE, São Paulo (group)

7th GWANGJU BIENNALE, South Korea (group)

'Lost Paradise: Der Blick des Engels',
ZENTRUM PAUL KLEE, Bern (group)

'Notations: The Closing Decade',
PHILADELPHIA MUSEUM OF ART (group)

'The Object Quality of the Problem: Israel/Palestine',
HENRY MOORE INSTITUTE, Leeds (group)

SONSBEEK 2008, Arnhem, The Netherlands (group)

'Street & Studio: An Urban History of Photography',
TATE MODERN, London, toured to MUSEUM FOLKWANG, Essen, Germany (group)

'Street Art, Street Life',
BRONX MUSEUM OF THE ARTS, New York (group)

'TRANSactions: Contemporary Latin American and Latino Art',
HIGH MUSEUM OF ART, Atlanta (group)

'Try Again, Fail Again, Fail Better',
MŰCSARNOK KUNSTHALLE, Budapest (group)

'An Unruly History of the Readymade',
COLECCIÓN JUMEX, Mexico City (group)

Receives the The Vincent Award, Amsterdam

SELECTED ARTICLES AND INTERVIEWS
2007–08

2007 (cont.)
Wehr, Anne, 'Francis Alÿs, 'Fabiola', Time Out New York, 4–10 October

Knight, Christopher, 'Artist rolls out his Sisyphus Side', Los Angeles Times, 6 October

Root, Deborah, 'Stray Dogs and Urban Ghosts: Walking with Francis Alÿs', Prefix Photo, November

Gopnik, Blake, 'In New York, 286 Saint Fabiolas = One Epiphany', The Washington Post, 11 November

Berardini, Andrew, 'Francis Alÿs: Politics of Rehearsal', Art Review, December

Turner, Jonathan, 'Francis Alÿs: Hispanic Society of America', ARTnews, December

Bedford, Christopher, 'Francis Alÿs: Los Angeles', The Burlington Magazine, December

2008
Burton, Johanna, 'Francis Alÿs: DIA at the Hispanic Society of America', Artforum, January

Gardner, James, 'Instant Replay', The New York Sun, 3 January

Smith, Roberta, 'On Postcards and Even in Rice, Portraits of a Beloved Saint', The New York Times, 5 January

Mizota, Sharon, 'Francis Alÿs: The Politics of Rehearsal', Art on Paper, January–February

Emerling, Susan, 'Francis Alÿs', Border Crossings, February

Kwon, Miwon, 'Francis Alÿs', Artforum, February

Liew, Fredrik, 'Fotnot', Pequod, February

Volk, Gregory, 'Walkabout', Art in America, February

Montgomery, Harper, 'Francis Alÿs at Dia Art Foundation', ArtNexus, March–May

Auslander, Philip, 'On Procession', Artforum, May

Dillon, Brian, 'Street & Studio', Art Review, May

'Francis Alÿs: Re-enactments, 2000', Monopol, June

Leddy, Annette, 'Francis Alÿs: Politics of Rehearsal', X-TRA 10, no. 4, Summer

Warburton, Nigel, 'Appearances', Pluk no. 36, Summer

Golden, Thelma, 'Elsewhere: Art Beyond the Studio Museum, Completely Biased, Entirely Opinionated Hot Picks', Studio, Fall–Winter

Aletti, Vince, 'Critic's Notebook: Street Wise', The New Yorker, 6 October

Govan, Michael, 'The Esquire Museum of Contemporary Art', Esquire, October

Ruyters, Domeniek, 'Modellen voor consensus', Metropolis M, October–November

Gordon, Margery, 'Miami Madness', Art + Auction, December

Téllez, Javier, 'The Artists' Artists', Artforum, December

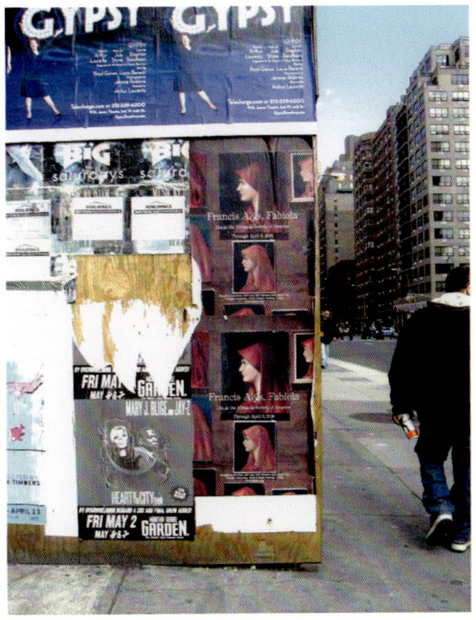

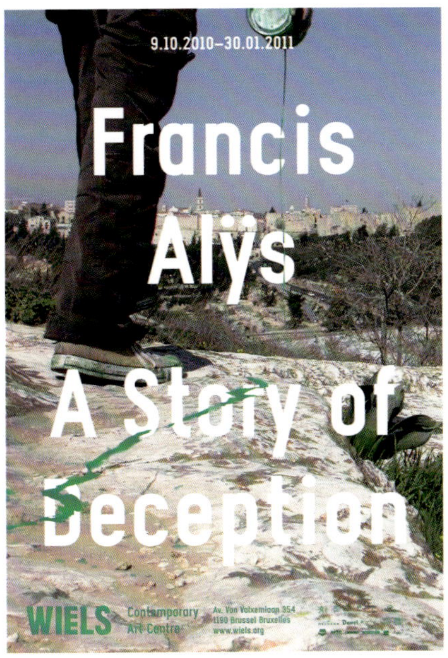

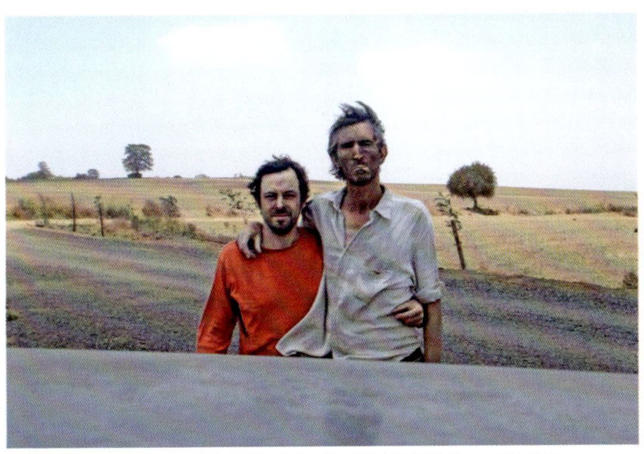

JULIEN DEVAUX AND THE ARTIST, DURING THE MAKING OF TORNADO, MEXICO, 2009

SELECTED EXHIBITIONS AND PROJECTS
2009–10

2009

'Francis Alÿs: Nightwatch', 0
BASS MUSEUM OF ART, Miami (solo)

3rd MARRAKECH BIENNALE, Morocco (group)

'Cézanne and Beyond',
PHILADELPHIA MUSEUM OF ART (group)

'Incidental Affairs: Contemporary Art of Transient States',
SUNTORY MUSEUM, Osaka (group)

1st CHILE TRIENNIAL, Valparaiso (group)

'Petit Mal',
MUSEO UNIVERSITARIO DE ARTE CONTEMPORÁNEO, Mexico City (group)

'The Quick and the Dead', WALKER ART CENTER, Minneapolis (group)

'Shift: Field of Fluctuation',
21ST CENTURY MUSEUM OF CONTEMPORARY ART, Kanazawa, Japan (group)

'Silent',
HIROSHIMA CITY MUSEUM OF CONTEMPORARY ART (group)

4th TIRANA BIENNALE (group)

'Voyage Sentimental 5',
MUSÉE DE VALENCE, France (group)

SELECTED ARTICLES AND INTERVIEWS
2009–10

2009

Dezeuze, Anne, 'Francis Alÿs', Art Monthly, no. 323, February

Rosenberg, Karen, 'Maverick, you cast a giant shadow', The New York Times, 6 March

Cumming, Laura, 'A Gem of a One-Woman Show', The Guardian, 3 May

Carey-Kent, Paul, 'Francis Alÿs: In search of a saint', Art World, June-July

Harris, Gareth, 'Art Unlimited: A decade of showing off', The Art Newspaper, 9 June

King, Sarah, 'The Earth Sublime', Art in America, June–July

Kester, Grant, 'Lessons in Futility: Francis Alÿs and the Legacy of May '68', Third Text, no. 99, July

Galvez, Paul, 'Cézanne and Beyond', Artforum, Summer

Fraser, Marie, 'Let the Festivities Begin', Esse, Fall

Andrews, Max, 'Una estaca en el lodo, un hoyo en la cinta', Art & Co., Winter

Rubini, Constance, 'Du Design Dans l'art', Azimuts, no. 33

Groys, Boris, 'Comrades of Time', Manifesta Journal, no. 9

2010 (Exhibitions and projects)

'Francis Alÿs: Le temps du sommeil',
IRISH MUSEUM OF MODERN ART, Dublin (solo)

'Francis Alÿs: A Story of Deception',
TATE MODERN, London, toured to WIELS CENTRE D'ART CONTEMPORAIN, Brussels; MUSEUM OF MODERN ART, New York and P.S.1 CONTEMPORARY ART CENTER, Long Island City, New York (solo)

'Fokus: Francis Alÿs',
MUSEUM FÜR GEGENWARTSKUNST, Basel (solo)

'Francis Alÿs: Dominó Caníbal',
SALAS VERÓNICAS, Murcia, Spain (solo)

'BACA Laureate 2010: Francis Alÿs',
BONNEFANTENMUSEUM, Maastricht, The Netherlands (solo)

17th BIENAL DE ARTE PAIZ, Guatemala (group)

29th SÃO PAULO BIENNALE (group)

7th SAINT ÉTIENNE INTERNATIONAL DESIGN BIENNALE (group)

'Adaptation: Between Spaces',
THE POWER PLANT, Toronto (group)

'Hareng Saur: Ensor and Contemporary Art',
STEDELIJK MUSEUM VOOR ACTUELE KUNST (S.M.A.K.), Ghent (group)

'Parallels and Patrons',
PETWORTH HOUSE AND PARK, England (group)

'Project Europa: Imagining the (Im)Possible',
HARN MUSEUM OF ART, Gainesville, Florida (group)

1st RIO DE JANEIRO BIENNALE (group)

2010 (Articles and interviews)

Hixson, Kathryn, 'The Quick and The Dead', Art Papers, January–February

Kastner, Jeffrey, 'Francis Alÿs at Tate Modern', Artforum, May

Milliard, Coline, 'Francis Alÿs: Walks of Life', Art Monthly, June

Searle, Adrian, 'Francis Alÿs treads the Thin Green Line', The Guardian, 15 June

Cumming, Laura, 'Francis Alÿs: A Story of Deception', The Observer, 20 June

Heingartner, Douglas, 'I'm Not Here: An Exhibition Without Francis Alÿs', Frieze, no. 132, June–August

McLean-Ferris, Laura, 'Francis Alÿs: A Story of Deception at Tate Modern', The Independent, 2 July

Platt, Edward, 'Telling Stories with a Life of their Own', Tate Etc., n. 19

Ebbert, Edward, 'Francis Alÿs: Tate Modern', Modern Painters, Summer

Smart, Alastair, 'Francis Alÿs at Tate Modern', The Sunday Telegraph, 15 August

Boaden, James, 'Francis Alÿs: London', The Burlington Magazine, no. 1290, September

Dillon, Brian, 'Francis Alÿs at Tate Modern', Frieze, no. 133, September

Meyer, James, 'Francis Alÿs at Tate Modern, London', Artforum, November

Ruby, Sterling, 'Best of 2010: The Artists' Artists', Artforum, December

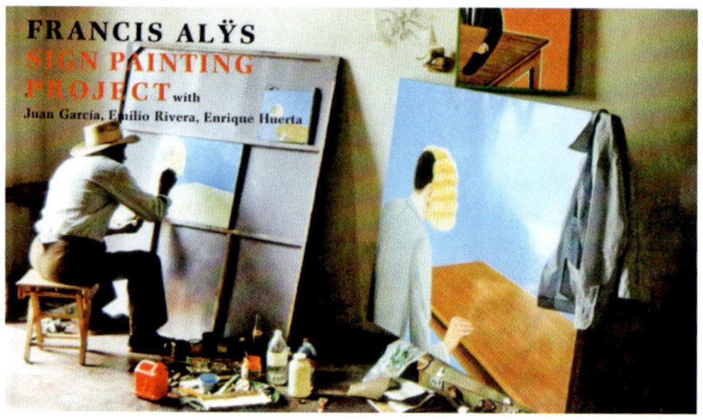

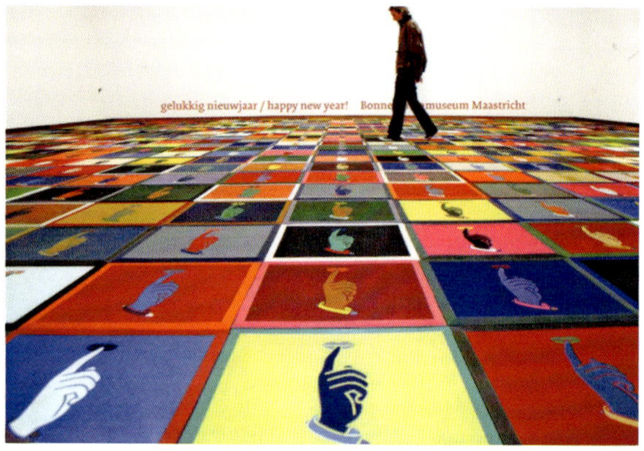

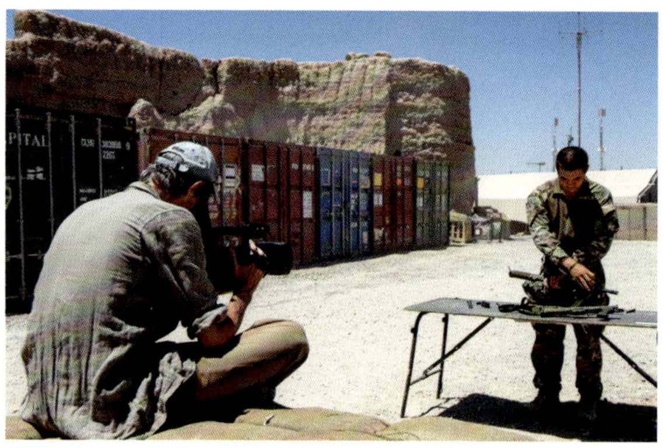

THE ARTIST DURING THE MAKING OF SOMETIMES DOING IS UNDOING AND SOMETIMES UNDOING IS DOING, HELMAND PROVINCE, AFGHANISTAN, 2013

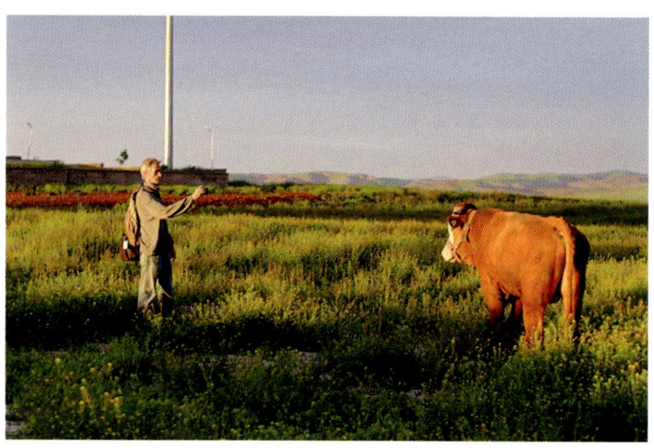

THE ARTIST DURING THE MAKING OF THE SILENCE OF ANI, TURKISH/ARMENIAN BORDER, 2015

SELECTED EXHIBITIONS AND PROJECTS 2011–12

2011

'Francis Alÿs: Untitled (Before the Prophet)',
MEESSEN DE CLERCQ, Brussels (solo)

'Francis Alÿs: The Moment Where Sculpture Happens',
DAVIS MUSEUM AND CULTURAL CENTER, Wellesley, Massachusetts (solo)

GALERIE PETER KILCHMANN, Zurich (solo)

3rd THESSALONIKI BIENNALE, Greece (group)

8th MERCOSUL BIENNIAL (group)

'The Dialectic City: Document–Context',
LABORATORIO DE ARTES BINARIOS, San Juan, Puerto Rico (group)

'I Promise to Love You',
KUNSTHAL ROTTERDAM (group)

'A Line Made Walking',
HAIFA MUSEUM OF ART, Israel (group)

'Living as Form',
ESSEX STREET MARKET, New York (group)

'Paradise Lost',
ISTANBUL MUSEUM OF MODERN ART (group)

'Wander: Labyrinthine Variations',
CENTRE POMPIDOU-METZ, France (group)

'We Have Woven the Motherlands with Nets of Iron',
APEXART FRANCHISE, Amman (group)

2012

'Francis Alÿs: Guards',
UNIVERSITY OF MICHIGAN MUSEUM OF ART, Ann Arbor (solo)

9th SHANGHAI BIENNALE (group)

2nd ADELAIDE INTERNATIONAL (group)

1st BIENNALE OF PAINTING, Deurle, Belgium (group)

'Desire Lines',
AUSTRALIAN CENTRE FOR CONTEMPORARY ART, Melbourne (group)

'Dimensions variables',
INSTITUT D'ART CONTEMPORAIN VILLEURBANNE/RHÔNE-ALPES, France (group)

DOCUMENTA 13, Kassel, Germany, and Kabul (group)

'Explosion! Painting as Action',
MODERNA MUSEET, Stockholm, toured to FUNDACIÓ JOAN MIRÓ, Barcelona (group)

'Migrations',
TATE BRITAIN, London (group)

'Posada to Alÿs: Mexican art from 1900 to the present',
KUNSTHAUS ZÜRICH (group)

'Skyscraper: Art and Architecture against Gravity',
MUSEUM OF CONTEMPORARY ART CHICAGO (group)

'Unfinished Journeys',
THE NATIONAL MUSEUM OF NORWAY, Oslo (group)

SELECTED ARTICLES AND INTERVIEWS 2011–12

2011

Desaive, Yves-Pierre, 'Francis Alÿs: A Story of Deception', Flash Art, no. 277, March–April

Conley, Kevin, 'A Dangerous Mind', Vogue, May

Loos, Ted, 'Shifting Sands of Societies and Politics', The New York Times, 1 May

Smith, Roberta, 'Ephemeral Events, Annotated', The New York Times, 6 May

Schjeldahl, Peter, 'For Laughs: Things that Francis Alÿs Does', The New Yorker, 23 May

Gopnik, Blake, 'The 10 Most Important Artists of Today', Newsweek, 13–20 June

Halle, Howard, 'Francis Alÿs: A Story of Deception', Time Out New York, 9–15 June

Rooney, Kara L., 'Francis Alÿs: A Story of Deception', The Brookyn Rail, July–August

Van der Lint, Roos, 'International Agenda: July–August', Kunstbeeld, July–August

Dorfman, John, 'A Walker in the City', Art & Antiques, Summer

Faesler, Carla, 'Francis Alÿs', Bomb, no. 116, Summer

Burstein, Amanda, 'When Faith Moves Mountains: Ethics and Relational Art', Esse, September

Thompson, M.J., 'Francis Alÿs', Border Crossings no. 120, December

2012

Levit, Karin, 'Beyond Borders', Haaretz, 12 January

Wullschlager, Jackie, 'Vertiginous Doubt', Financial Times, 19–20 May

Alÿs, Francis, Ajmal Maiwandi and Andrea Viliani, 'From Collapse to Recovery', Mousse, no. 34, Summer

Robecchi, Michele, 'Documenta 13: No Stone Unturned', Flash Art, no. 285, July–September

Birnbaum, Daniel, 'Documenta 13', Artforum, October

Sansom, Anna, 'Walking the Line: The Adventures of Francis Alÿs', Damn, October–November

Horyn, Cathy, 'Freedom of Choices', The New York Times, 30 December

Rabottini, Alessandro, 'Francis Alÿs: Exercises in Style', Inventario, no. 4

Burstein, Amanda, 'When Faith Moves Mountains: Ethics and Relational Art', Esse, no. 11, Autumn

SELECTED EXHIBITIONS AND PROJECTS
2013–14

SELECTED ARTICLES AND INTERVIEWS
2013–14

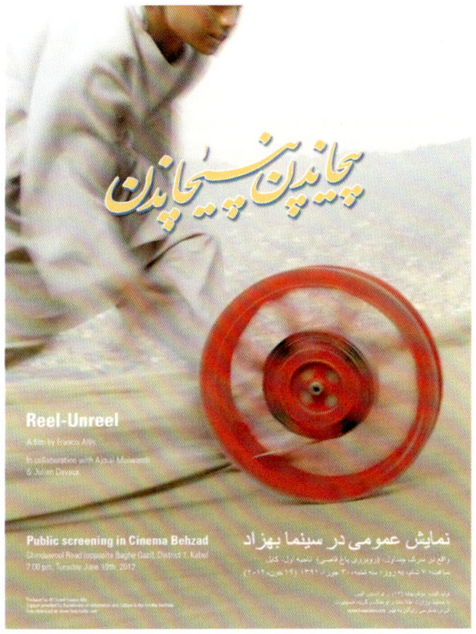

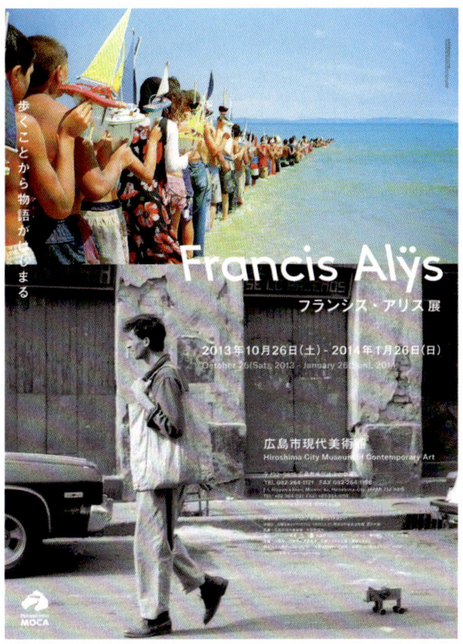

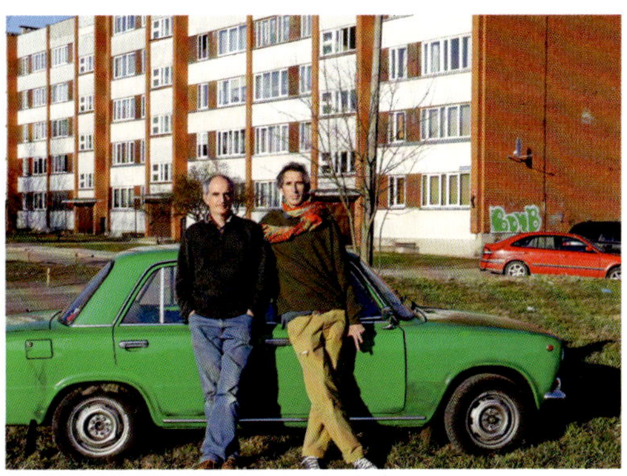

THE ARTIST AND HIS BROTHER FRÉDÉRIC DURING THE MAKING OF LADA KOPEIKA PROJECT, ST. PETERSBURG, 2014

2013
'Francis Alÿs: Seven Walks',
ART EXCHANGE at UNIVERSITY OF ESSEX, Colchester, England (solo)

'Francis Alÿs: Reel-Unreel',
DAVID ZWIRNER, New York (solo)

'Francis Alÿs: Reel-Unreel',
BÒLIT CENTRE D'ART CONTEMPORANI, Girona, Spain (solo)

'Francis Alÿs. Part I: Mexico Survey and Part II: Gibraltar Focus',
MUSEUM OF CONTEMPORARY ART, Tokyo, toured to HIROSHIMA CITY MUSEUM OF CONTEMPORARY ART (solo)

11th SHARJAH BIENNIAL (group)

'América Latina 1960–2013: Fotos + Textos',
FONDATION CARTIER POUR L'ART CONTEMPORAIN, Paris, toured to MUSEO AMPARO, Puebla, Mexico (group)

'Le Pont',
MUSÉE D'ART CONTEMPORAIN DE MARSEILLE, France (group)

'Through a Glass Darkly: Faces Past and Present',
ERNST MUSEUM, Budapest (group)

'Walk On: 40 Years of Art Walking from Richard Long to Janet Cardiff',
PITZHANGER MANOR HOUSE & GALLERY WALPOLE PARK, London, toured to NORTHERN GALLERY FOR CONTEMPORARY ART, Sunderland, England; MIDLANDS ART CENTRE (MAC) Birmingham, England; THE ATKINSON, Southport, England; PLYMOUTH CITY MUSEUM AND ART GALLERY, England (group)

2013
'Francis Alÿs, New York, David Zwirner', Art + Auction, January

Belcove, Julie, 'Walkabout', The New Yorker, 7 January

Russeth, Andrew, 'Francis Alÿs: Reel-Unreel', New York Observer, 21 January

Smith, Roberta, 'Francis Alÿs: Reel-Unreel', The New York Times, 8 February

Brisick, Jamie, 'Chasing Mirages: The Strange and Poetic Art of Francis Alÿs', Malibu, February–March

2013 (cont.)
Apisdorf Soto, Ximena, 'In and Out: A brief history of the Mexican Art Scene'; Patricia Martín, 'Ten Years after Turmoil', Flash Art, no. 289, March–April

Chang, Chris, 'Vision: Reeling Francis Alÿs Reports from Afghanistan', Filmcomment, March–April

Angeline, John, 'Francis Alÿs: David Zwirner', ArtNexus 12, no. 88, April

Markkus, David, 'Francis Alÿs', Art in America, April

Walsh, Brienne, 'Francis Alÿs', Modern Painters, April

Lin, Aimee, 'Sharjah Biennial 11: Re:emerge: Towards a New Cultural Cartography', Art Review, no. 69, Summer

MacAdam, Barbara, 'Architect of the Absurd', ARTnews, Summer

2014
'Francis Alÿs: Reel-Unreel',
MUSEO D'ARTE CONTEMPORANEA DONNA REGINA, Naples, toured to CENTRE FOR CONTEMPORARY ART UJAZDOWSKI CASTLE, Warsaw (solo)

'Francis Alÿs: La acción reveladora o poética de los intentos',
ESPACIO DE ARTE CONTEMPORÁNEO, Montevideo (solo)

'Argos Panoptes',
MUSEO DE ARTE CARRILLO GIL, Mexico City (group)

'Art as a Verb',
MONASH UNIVERSITY MUSEUM OF ART (MUMA), Melbourne, toured to ARTSPACE, Sydney (group)

'Beating around the Bush Episode #1',
BONNEFANTENMUSEUM, Maastricht, The Netherlands (group)

'Destinations Improbables',
LE MUSÉE LANCHELEVICI, La Louvière, Belgium (group)

'¡Ejemplos a seguir! Expediciones en estética y sostenibilidad',
MUSEO METROPOLITANO DE LIMA (group)

'Estudio Abierto #4: Máquina del Tiempo',
MUSEO DE ARTE ZAPOPAN, Guadalajara, Mexico (group)

'A Guest Without a Host is a Ghost',
BEIRUT AND TOWNHOUSE, Cairo (group)

'Manifest Intention: Drawing in All Its Forms',
CASTELLO DI RIVOLI, Turin (group)

MANIFESTA 10, St. Petersburg (group)

'Under the Same Sun: Art from Latin America Today',
SOLOMON R. GUGGENHEIM MUSEUM, New York (group)

2014
Vogel, Carol, 'The Philadelphia Museum Lands a Major Gift', The New York Times, 10 January

'Francis Alÿs: Tours et Détours Object Collector', L'Officiel Art, March

Keenan, Sandy, 'Break It and No Allowance', The New York Times, 6 March

Fajardo-Hill, Cecilia, 'Meaningful Abstractions', ArtNexus, March–May

Ross, Christine, 'Le temps spatialisé–Spatialized Time', Esse, Spring

Borcherdt, Gesine, 'Manifesta 10', Art Review, September

Robecchi, Michele, 'A Conversation with Kaspar König', RES, no. 11, October

Tikhonova, Yulia, 'Manifesta 10', Flash Art, no. 298, October

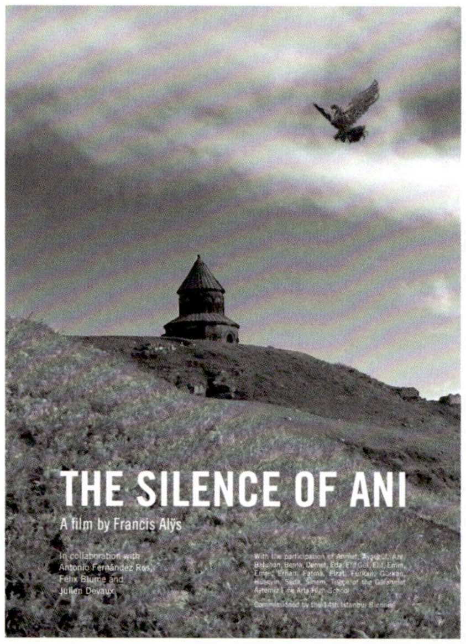

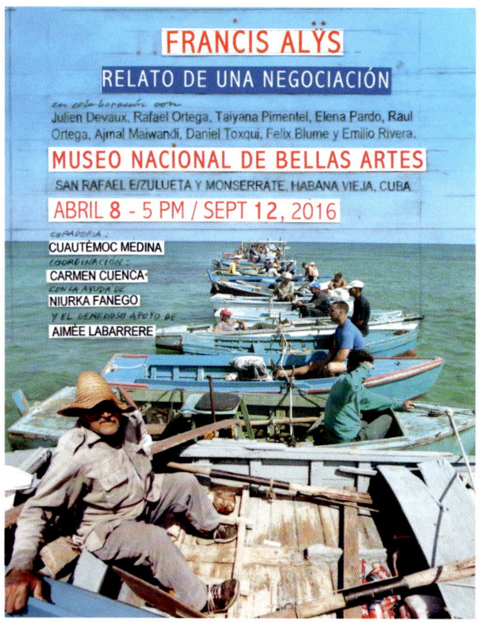

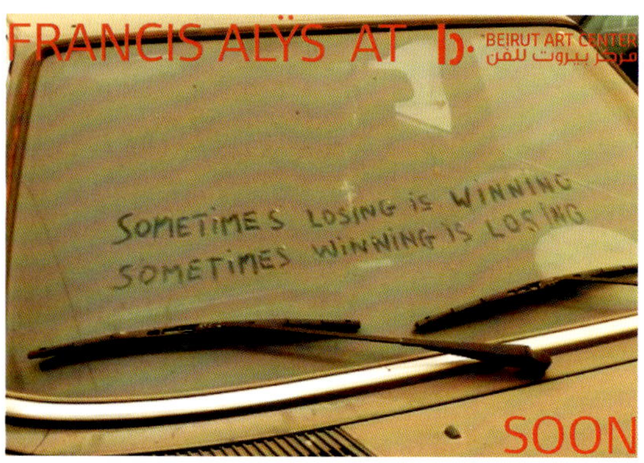

SELECTED EXHIBITIONS AND PROJECTS
2015–19

2015

'Francis Alÿs: A Story of Negotiation: An Investigation into the Parallel Activities of Painting and Performance', MUSEO TAMAYO ARTE CONTEMPORÁNEO, Mexico City, toured to MUSEO DE ARTE LATINOAMERICANO DE BUENOS AIRES (MALBA) and FUNDACIÓN COSTANTINI, Buenos Aires; MUSEO NACIONAL DE BELLAS ARTES, Havana; ART GALLERY OF ONTARIO, Toronto (solo)

'Francis Alÿs: Hotel Juárez, Proyecto Siqueiros', SALA DE ARTE PÚBLICO SIQUEIROS LA TALLERA, Mexico City (solo)

14th ISTANBUL BIENNIAL (group)

2016

'Le temps du sommeil', SECESSION, Vienna (solo)

'Francis Alÿs: Ciudad Juárez Projects', DAVID ZWIRNER, London (solo)

'The Lasting: Interval and Duration', GALLERIA NAZIONALE D'ARTE MODERNA E CONTEMPORANEA, Rome (group)

2017

'Francis Alÿs: Knot 'n' Dust, BEIRUT ART CENTER, Lebanon, toured to IKON GALLERY, Birmingham, England (solo)

'Francis Alÿs: Without an Ending There is no Beginning', JAN MOT, Brussels (solo)

1st BIENAL INTERNACIONAL DE ARTE CONTEMPORÁNEO DE AMERICA DEL SUR, Cucutá, Colombia (group)

3rd KATHMANDU TRIENNALE (group)

2nd ART ENCOUNTERS BIENNIAL, Timişoara, Romania (group)

'Archaic: National Pavilion of Iraq' (selected by Francis Alÿs, Tamara Chalabi and Paolo Colombo), 57th VENICE BIENNALE (group)

2018

'The Fabiola Project', MENIL COLLECTION, Houston (solo)

'Francis Alÿs, Silence of Ani', CORNUBIAN ARTS & SCIENCE TRUST, Helston, England (solo)

INSTITUTE OF CONTEMPORARY ART, Miami (solo)

'Francis Alÿs: Knots 'n' Dust', BEIRUT ART CENTER, Lebanon, toured to IKON GALLERY, Birmingham, England (solo)

12th GWANGJU BIENNALE (group)

3th TRIENNIAL DUFFEL, Belgium (group)

12th SHANGHAI BIENNALE (group)

Recipient of the 2018 EYE Art & Film Prize, Amsterdam

2019

TAI KWUN CENTER FOR HERITAGE & ART, Hong Kong (solo)

SELECTED ARTICLES AND INTERVIEWS
2015–19

2015

Ruiz, Isaura, 'Francis Alÿs at Museo Tamayo', ArtNexus, no. 97, June-August

Cahill, James, 'Mind The Gap', Elephant, Autumn

Searle, Adrian, 'Istanbul's 14th biennial depicts flood of despair', The Guardian, 8 September

Bell, Kristy, '14th Istanbul Biennial', Frieze, no. 175, November–December

Charlesworth, J.J., 'The Gap: Selected Abstract Art from Belgium', Art Review, December

2016

Córdova, Kim, 'Francis Alÿs', Art Review, Summer

Lange, Christie, 'Francis Alÿs: Re-Enactments', Frieze, no. 181, September

Arriola, Magalí, 'Best of 2015: Francis Alÿs at Museo Tamayo, Mexico City'; Kevin McGarry, '14th Istanbul Biennial', Artforum, December

Pes, Javier, 'Francis Alÿs to work with refugees in Iraq and meet victims of Isil', The Art Newspaper, 3 December

2017

Murphy, Jack, 'Francis Alÿs and the Politics of the Street', LOKÉ no. 1, January

Corbett, Rachel, 'On the Front Lines', Modern Painters, May

Phillips-Amos, Georgia, 'Spinning Fables', Border Crossings, no. 141, March

Corbett, Rachel, 'On the Front Lines', Modern Painters, May

2018

Wilson-Goldie, Kaelen, 'Francis Alÿs: Knot 'n' Dust', Artforum, January

BIBLIOGRAPHY

MONOGRAPHS AND ARTIST'S BOOKS

Alÿs, Francis, Kurt Hollander and Cuauhtémoc Medina, Francis Alÿs, Galeria Arte Contemporáneo, Mexico City, 1992

Alÿs, Francis, and Cuauhtémoc Medina, Fabiola: Una investigación de Francis Alÿs en colaboración con Curare Espacio Crítico para las Artes, Curare, Mexico City, 1994

Alÿs, Francis, and Thomas McEvilley, Francis Alÿs: The Liar, The Copy of the Liar, Arena Mexico Arte Contemporáneo, Guadalajara, and Galeria Ramis Barquet, Mexico City, 1994

Alÿs, Francis, Bruce W. Ferguson, Serge Guibault, Kurt Hollander, Cuauhtémoc Medina, Ivo Mesquita, Kitty Scott, Laureana Toledo and Pablo Vargas Lugo, Walks/Paseos, Museo de Arte Moderno, Mexico City, 1997

Alÿs, Francis, and Kitty Scott, Francis Alÿs: Le Temps du Sommeil, Contemporary Art Gallery, Vancouver, 1998

Alÿs, Francis, Cuauhtémoc Medina, Thierry Davila and Carlos Basualdo, Francis Alÿs, Musée Picasso, Antibes, France, 2001

Alÿs, Francis, and Catherine Lampert, Francis Alÿs, The Prophet and the Fly, Turner, Madrid, 2003

Alÿs, Francis, and Annelie Lutgens, Francis Alÿs: Walking Distance from the Studio, Hatje Cantz, Ostfildern-Ruit, 2004

Alÿs, Francis, and Andreas Bee, Time is a Trick of the Mind, Museum für Moderne Kunst and Revolver, Frankfurt, 2004

Alÿs, Francis, Lynne Cooke, Alejandro Diaz, Tom Eccles, Susan K. Freedman, Dario Gamboni, RoseLee Goldberg, Laurence Kardish, Harper Montgomery, Francesco Pellizzi and Robert Storr, Francis Alÿs: The Modern Procession, Public Art Fund, New York, 2004

Alÿs, Francis, Cuauhtémoc Medina, Susan Buck-Morss, Gustavo Buntinx, Lynne Cooke, Corinne Diserens and Gerardo Mosquera, When Faith Moves Mountains, Turner, Madrid, 2005

Alÿs, Francis, Robert Harbison, James Lingwood and David Toop, Seven Walks, Artangel and National Portrait Gallery, London, 2005

Alÿs, Francis, Corinne Diserens and Cuauhtémoc Medina, Diez Cuadras Alrededor del Estudio, Antiguo Colegio de San Ildefonso, Mexico City, 2006

Alÿs, Francis, Olivier Debroise, Eduardo F. Costantini and Marcelo E. Pacheco, A Story of Deception: Historia de un desengaño, Patagonia 2003–2006, Colección Costantini, MALBA, Buenos Aires, 2006

Alÿs, Francis, Nikola Dietrich and Olivier Debroise, A Story of Deception: Patagonien 2003–2006, Portikus and Revolver, Frankfurt, 2006

Alÿs, Francis, and Carlos Monsiváis, Centro Histórico de la Ciudad de México, Turner, Madrid, 2006

Alÿs, Francis, et al., Sometimes doing something poetic can become political and sometimes doing something political can become poetic, David Zwirner Gallery, New York, 2007

Alÿs, Francis, Russell Ferguson, Cuauhtémoc Medina and Jean Fisher, Francis Alÿs, Phaidon, London, 2007

Alÿs, Francis, Russell Ferguson and Ann Philbin, Francis Alÿs: The Politics of Rehearsal, Steidl, Göttingen, Germany, and Hammer Museum, Los Angeles, 2008

Alÿs, Francis, Stephen Bann, David Morgan, Lynne Cooke, Martha Buskirk and Susan Laningham, Francis Alÿs: Fabiola: An Investigation, Dia Foundation, New York, 2008

Alÿs, Francis, and Enrique Juncosa, Francis Alÿs: Le Temps du Sommeil, Irish Museum of Modern Art, Dublin, and Charta Art Books, Milan, 2010

Alÿs, Francis, Klaus Biesenbach, Francesco Careri, Carla Faesler, Mark Godfrey, Boris Groys, Miwon Kwon, Tom McDonough, Cuauhtémoc Medina, Laymert dos Santos, Eyal Weizman and Eduardo Abaroa, Francis Alÿs: A Story of Deception, Museum of Modern Art, New York, 2010

Alÿs, Francis, and Theodora Vischer, The Sign Painting Project 1993-97: A Revision, A Catalogue, Steidl, Göttingen, Germany, and Schaulager, Basel, 2010

Alÿs, Francis, and Mark Godfrey, Francis Alÿs: Postcards, Tate, London, 2010

Alÿs, Francis, Cuauhtémoc Medina, Alfonso Reyes and Ton Marar, Francis Alÿs: In a Given Situation, Cosac Naify, São Paulo, 2011

Alÿs, Francis, Kazuhiko Yoshizaki and Yukie Kamiya, Don't Cross The Bridge Before You Get To The River, Museum of Contemporary Art, Tokyo, Hiroshima City Museum of Contemporary Art, and Seigensha, Kyoto, 2013

Alÿs, Francis, and Cuauhtémoc Medina, Francis Alÿs: Relato de una negociación/A Story of Negotiation, Museo Tamayo, Mexico City, 2013

Alÿs, Francis, and Cuauhtémoc Medina, Pacing, Ivory Press, Madrid, 2014

Alÿs, Francis, Andrea Viliani, Fabio Cavallucci, Ajmal Maiwandi, Robert Slifkin et al, Francis Alÿs: Reel–Unreel, Museo d'Arte Donna Regina, Naples, Centre for Contemporary Art Ujazdowski Castle, Warsaw, and Electa Mondadori, Milan, 2014

Alÿs, Francis, Ciudad Juárez Projects, David Zwirner, London, 2016

Alÿs, Francis, Marente Bloemheuvel, Jaap Guldemond, David MacDougall and Cuauhtémoc Medina, Francis Alÿs: Children's Game, nai010, Rotterdam, 2020

Alÿs, Francis, Russell Ferguson, Cuauhtémoc Medina, Jean Fisher and Michael Taussig, Francis Alÿs, Phaidon, London, 2022

PUBLIC COLLECTIONS

21st CENTURY MUSEUM OF CONTEMPORARY ART, Kanazawa, Japan

THE ART INSTITUTE OF CHICAGO

CARNEGIE MUSEUM OF ART, Pittsburgh

CENTRE POMPIDOU, Paris

CENTRO DE ARTE VISUALES FUNDACIÓN HELGA DE ALVEAR, Cáceres, Spain

CENTRO NAZIONALE PER LE ARTI CONTEMPORANEE, Rome

COLECCIÓN JUMEX, Mexico City

COLLECTION LAMBERT EN AVIGNON, France

COLLEZIONE LA GAIA, Busca, Italy

DES MOINES ART CENTER, Iowa

DEUTSCHE BANK, Frankfurt

THE ELLA FONTANALS-CISNEROS COLLECTION, Miami

FONDACIÓN TELEFÓNICA, Madrid

FONDS NATIONAL D'ART CONTEMPORAIN, France

FONDS RÉGIONAL D'ART CONTEMPORAIN BOURGOGNE (FRAC), Dijon, France

FONDS RÉGIONAL D'ART CONTEMPORAIN HAUTE-NORMANDIE, Sotteville-Lès-Rouen, France

FONDS REGIONAL D'ART CONTEMPORAIN (FRAC) RHÔNE-ALPES, Villeurbanne, France

FUNDACIÓ LA CAIXA, Barcelona

HAMMER MUSEUM, Los Angeles

HUDSON VALLEY CENTER FOR CONTEMPORARY ART, Peekskill, New York

KUNSTHAUS ZÜRICH

JULIA STOSCHEK COLLECTION, Düsseldorf

THE ISRAEL MUSEUM, Jerusalem

LOS ANGELES COUNTY MUSEUM OF ART

LOUISIANA MUSEUM FOR MODERNE KUNST, Humlebæk, Denmark

MIDDLESBOROUGH ART GALLERY, England

MUSÉE D'ART MODERNE DE LA VILLE DE PARIS

MUSÉE D'ART MODERNE GRAND-DUC JEAN, Luxembourg

MUSÉE DES ARTS CONTEMPORAINS, Grand Hornu, Belgium

MUSÉE DES BEAUX-ARTS DE NANTES, France

MUSEION, Bozen, Italy

MUSEO AMPARO, Puebla, Mexico

MUSEO DE ARTE LATINOAMERICANO DE BUENOS AIRES FUNDACIÓN COSTANTINI, Buenos Aires

MUSEO NACIONAL CENTRO DE ARTE REINA SOFÍA, Madrid

MUSEO TAMAYO ARTE CONTEMPORÁNEO, Mexico City

MUSEU D'ART CONTEMPORANI DE BARCELONA

MUSEUM FÜR MODERNER KUNST, Frankfurt

MUSEUM OF CONTEMPORARY ART, Los Angeles

MUSEUM OF CONTEMPORARY ART, North Miami

MUSEUM OF FINE ARTS, Boston

THE MUSEUM OF MODERN ART, New York

THE MUSEUM OF MODERN ART IN WARSAW

MUSEUM VOORLINDEN, Wassenaar, The Netherlands

NATIONAL GALLERY OF CANADA, Ottawa

ORANGE COUNTY MUSEUM OF ART, Newport, California

PHILADELPHIA MUSEUM OF ART

PINAKOTHEK DER MODERNE KUNST, Munich

RUBELL FAMILY COLLECTION, Miami

SAMMLUNG GOETZ, Munich

SOLOMON R. GUGGENHEIM MUSEUM, New York

STEDELIJK MUSEUM, Amsterdam

TATE, London

VAN ABBEMUSEUM, Eindhoven, Netherlands

THE VERBUND COLLECTION, Vienna

WADSWORTH ATHENEUM, Hartford, Connecticut

WALKER ART CENTER, Minneapolis

ZURICH INSURANCE COMPANY, Frankfurt

ILLUSTRATED WORKS

COMPARATIVE IMAGES

PHAIDON PRESS LTD.
2 COOPERAGE YARD
LONDON E15 2QR

PHAIDON PRESS INC.
65 BLEECKER STREET
NEW YORK, NY 10012

PHAIDON.COM

First published 2007
Second edition, revised and expanded, 2022

ISBN:
978-0-7148-7500-2

A CIP catalogue record of this book is available from the British Library and the Library of Congress.

Commissioning Editor
Michele Robecchi

Production Controller
Sarah Kramer

Design
Melanie Mues, Mues Design, London

Printed in China

PUBLISHER'S ACKNOWLEDGEMENTS

Special thanks to Elizabeth Calzado Michel and Maco Sanchez Blanco at Francis Alÿs Studio, Mexico City; Bellatrix Hubert, Doro Globus, Rebecca Holmberg, Jaime Schwartz, Molly Stein and Lucas Zwirner at David Zwirner Gallery, New York and London; Abby Draycott, Melissa Larner, Lesley Malkin, Rosie Minney, Tracey Smith, Elaine Ward.

We would also like to thank David Zwirner Gallery, New York and London; International Editors Co., Barcelona, for its kind permission to reprint texts; and The Ruya Foundation, Baghdad.

Untitled (4th Battalion Parachute Regiment Tactical Recognition Flash), Afghanistan, 2014 (p. 179); Untitled (Royal Engineers Tactical Recognition Flash), Afghanistan, 2013 (p. 181); and Untitled (Royal Engineers), 2014 (p. 183) are courtesy of Her Majesty The Queen.

Photographers: Francis Alÿs, Thierry Bal, Michel Blancsubé, Félix Blume, Peter M. Cook, Dennis Cowley, Pip Day, Olivier Debroise, Frédéric de Smedt, Julien Devaux, Ian Dryden, Constantin Felker, Mario Flecha, Andrés Garay Nieto, Wolfgang Günzel, Akam Shex Hadi, Enrique Huerta, Kurt Hollander, Rachel Leah Jones, Ajmal Maiwandi, Captain Tom McShane, Cuauhtémoc Medina, Alejandro Morales, Victoria Muniz Barreto, Rafael Ortega, Raúl Ortega Ayala, Emilio Rivera, Roberto Rubalcava, Akam Shex Hadi, Melanie Smith, Laureana Toledo, Jesus Sánchez Uribe, Eric Weiss, Lourdes Villagómez.

ARTIST'S ACKNOWLEDGEMENTS

I would like to thank the following: Cuauhtémoc Medina, Russell Ferguson, Jean Fisher, Michael Taussig, Michele Robecchi, Craig Garrett, Gilda Williams, Melanie Mues, Bella Hubert, Jaime Schwartz, David Zwirner Gallery, Susan Sherrick, Jorge Golem, Louise de Smedt, Rafael Ortega, Julien Devaux, Taiyana Pimentel, Lourdes Villagomez, Antonio Hernández Rios, Juan Garcia, Felipe Sanabria, Olivier Debroise, Honoré d'O, Kitty Scott, Alejandro Aguinaco, Emilio Rivera, Enrique Huerta, Alejandro Morales, Félix Blume, Antonio Fernándo Ros, Ajmal Maiwandi, Frédéric De Smedt, Costantin Felker.

CONTEMPORARY ARTISTS

Contemporary Artists is a series of authoritative and extensively illustrated studies of today's most important artists. Each title offers a comprehensive survey of an individual artist's work and a range of art writing contributed by an international spectrum of authors, all leading figures in their fields, from art history and criticism to philosophy, cultural theory and fiction. Each study provides incisive anis and multiple perspectives on contemporary art and its inspiration. These are essential source books for everyone concerned with art today.

MARINA ABRAMOVIĆ KLAUS BIESENBACH, KRISTINE STILES, CHRISSIE ILES / VITO ACCONCI FRAZER WARD, MARK C. TAYLOR, JENNIFER BLOOMER / AI WEIWEI HANS ULRICH OBRIST, KAREN SMITH, BERNARD FIBICHER / DOUG AITKEN DANIEL BIRNBAUM, AMANDA SHARP, JÖRG HEISER / PAWEŁ ALTHAMER ADAM SZYMCZYK, ROMAN KURZMEYER, SUZANNE COTTER / FRANCIS ALŸS CUAUHTÉMOC MEDINA, RUSSELL FERGUSON, JEAN FISHER, MICHAEL TAUSSIG / UTA BARTH PAMELA M. LEE, MATTHEW HIGGS, JEREMY GILBERT-ROLFE / CHRISTIAN BOLTANSKI DIDIER SEMIN, TAMAR GARB, DONALD KUSPIT / MONICA BONVICINI ALEXANDER ALBERRO, JANET KRAYNAK, JULIANE REBENTISCH / LOUISE BOURGEOIS PAULO HERKENHOFF (WITH THYRZA GOODEVE), ROBERT STORR, ALLAN SCHWARTZMAN / MARK BRADFORD ANITA HILL, SEBASTIAN SMEE, CONNIE BUTLER / CECILY BROWN COURTNEY J. MARTIN, JASON ROSENFELD, FRANCINE PROSE / CAI GUO-QIANG DANA FRIIS-HANSEN, OCTAVIO ZAYA, TAKASHI SERIZAWA / MAURIZIO CATTELAN NANCY SPECTOR, FRANCESCO BONAMI, BARBARA VANDERLINDEN, MASSIMILIANO GIONI / VIJA CELMINS ROBERT GOBER, LANE RELYEA, BRIONY FER / NIGEL COOKE DARIAN LEADER, TONY GODFREY, MARIE DARRIEUSSECQ / RICHARD DEACON PIER LUIGI TAZZI, JON THOMPSON, PETER SCHJELDAHL, PENELOPE CURTIS / TACITA DEAN JEAN-CHRISTOPHE ROYOUX, MARINA WARNER, GERMAINE GREER / MARK DION LISA GRAZIOSE CORRIN, MIWON KWON, NORMAN BRYSON / PETER DOIG ADRIAN SEARLE, KITTY SCOTT, CATHERINE GRENIER / STAN DOUGLAS SCOTT WATSON, DIANA THATER, CAROL J. CLOVER / MARLENE DUMAS DOMINIC VAN DEN BOOGERD, BARBARA BLOOM, MARIUCCIA CASADIO, ILARIA BONACOSSA / JIMMIE DURHAM LAURA MULVEY, DIRK SNAUWAERT, MARK ALICE DURANT, KATE NESISN / OLAFUR ELIASSON MADELEINE GRYNSZTEJN, DANIEL BIRNBAUM, MICHAEL SPEAKS / ELMGREEN & DRAGSET LINDA YABLONSKY, MARTIN HERBERT, CONNIE BUTLER / PETER FISCHLI AND DAVID WEISS ROBERT FLECK, BEATE SÖNTGEN, ARTHUR C. DANTO / TOM FRIEDMAN DENNIS COOPER, BRUCE HAINLEY, ADRIAN SEARLE / THEASTER GATES CAROL BECKER, LISA YUN LEE, ACHIM BORCHARDT-HUME / ISA GENZKEN ALEX FARQUHARSON, DIEDRICH DIEDERICHSEN, SABINE BREITWIESER / ANTONY GORMLEY ERNST GOMBRICH, JOHN HUTCHINSON, LELA B. NJATIN, W. J. T. MITCHELL / DAN GRAHAM BIRGIT PELZER, MARK FRANCIS, BEATRIZ COLOMINA / PAUL GRAHAM ANDREW WILSON, GILLIAN WEARING, CAROL SQUIERS / HANS HAACKE WALTER GRASSKAMP, MOLLY NESBIT, JON BIRD / MONA HATOUM GUY BRETT, MICHAEL ARCHER, CATHERINE DE ZEGHER, NANCY SPECTOR / SHARON HAYES JULIA BRYAN-WILSON, JEANNINE TANG, LANKA TATTERSALL / THOMAS HIRSCHHORN BENJAMIN H. D. BUCHLOH, ALISON M. GINGERAS, CARLOS BASUALDO / JIM HODGES JANE M SAKS, ROBERT HOBBS, JULIE AULT, TIM HAILAND /JENNY HOLZER DAVID JOSELIT, JOAN SIMON, RENATA SALECL / RONI HORN LOUISE NERI, LYNNE COOKE, THIERRY DE DUVE / CHRIS JOHANSON CORRINA PEIPON, BOB NICKAS, JULIE DEAMER / ILYA KABAKOV BORIS GROYS, DAVID A. ROSS, IWONA BLAZWICK / ALEX KATZ ROBERT STORR, CARTER RATCLIFF, IWONA BLAZWICK, BARRY SCHWABSKY / ON KAWARA 'TRIBUTE', JONATHAN WATKINS, RENÉ DENIZOT / MIKE KELLEY ISABELLE GRAW, JOHN C. WELCHMAN, ANTHONY VIDLER / MARY KELLY MARGARET IVERSEN, DOUGLAS CRIMP, HOMI K. BHABHA / WILLIAM KENTRIDGE CAROLYN CHRISTOV-BAKARGIEV, DAN CAMERON, J. M. COETZEE / JANNIS KOUNELLIS 'TRIBUTE', PHILIP LARRATT-SMITH, RUDI FUCHS / YAYOI KUSAMA AKIRA TATEHATA, LAURA HOPTMAN, UDO KULTERMANN, CHATERINE TAFT / CHRISTIAN MARCLAY JENNIFER GONZALEZ, KIM GORDON, MATTHEW HIGGS / KERRY JAMES MARSHALL CHARLES GAINES, GREG TATE, LAURENCE RASSEL / PAUL McCARTHY KRISTINE STILES, RALPH RUGOFF, MASSIMILIANO GIONI, ROBERT STORR / CILDO MEIRELES PAULO HERKENHOFF, GERARDO MOSQUERA, DAN CAMERON / WANGECHI MUTU ADRIENNE EDAWRDS, COURTNEY J. MARTIN, KELLIE JONES, SALAH HASSAN / LUCY ORTA ROBERTO PINTO, NICOLAS BOURRIAUD, MAIA DAMIANOVIC / JEAN-MICHEL OTHONIEL GAY GASSMANN, CATHERINE GRENIER, ROBERT STORR / TREVOR PAGLEN LAUREN CORNELL, JULIA BRYAN-WILSON, OMAR KHOLEIF / JORGE PARDO CHRISTINE VÉGH, LANE RELYEA, CHRIS KRAUS / NICOLAS PARTY STÉPHANE AQUIN, STEFAN BANZ, ALI SUBOTNICK, MELISSA HYDE / ADAM PENDLETON ALEC MAPES-FRANCES, ADRIENNE EDWARDS, ANDRÉA PICARD / RAYMOND PETTIBON DENNIS COOPER, ROBERT STORR, ULRICH LOOCK / RICHARD PRINCE ROSETTA BROOKS, JEFF RIAN, LUC SANTE / LILI REYNAUD-DEWAR ÉLISABETH LEBOVICI, DIEDRICH DIEDERICHSEN, MONIKA SZEWCZYK / PIPILOTTI RIST HANS ULRICH OBRIST, PEGGY PHELAN, ELIZABETH BRONFEN / UGO RONDINONE LAURA HOPTMAN, ERIK VERHAGEN, NICHOLAS BAUME, JASON SCHMIDT / DAAN ROOSEGAARDE NICO DASWANI, FUMIO NANJO, CAROL BECKER / STERLING RUBY KATE FOWLE, FRANKLIN SIRMANS, JESSICA MORGAN / ANRI SALA HANS ULRICH OBRIST, MARK GODFREY, LIAM GILLICK / DORIS SALCEDO NANCY PRINCENTHAL, CARLOS BASUALDO, ANDREAS HUYSSEN / WILHELM SASNAL ANDRZEJ PRZYWARA, DOMINIC EICHLER, JÖRG HEISER / THOMAS SCHÜTTE JULIAN HEYNEN, JAMES LINGWOOD, ANGELA VETTESE / STEPHEN SHORE MICHAEL FRIED, CHRISTY LANGE, JOEL STERNFELD / ROMAN SIGNER PAULA VAN DEN BOSCH, GERHARD MACK, JEREMY MILLAR / LORNA SIMPSON KELLIE JONES, THELMA GOLDEN, CHRISSIE ILES, NAOMI BECKWITH / NANCY SPERO JON BIRD, JO ANNA ISAAK, SYLVÈRE LOTRINGER / SIMON STARLING FRANCESCO MANACORDA, DIETER ROELSTRAETE, JANET HARBORD / FRANK STELLA ANDRIANNA CAMPBELL, KATE NESIN, LUCAS BLALOCK, TERRY RICHARDSON / JESSICA STOCKHOLDER BARRY SCHWABSKY, LYNNE TILLMAN, LYNNE COOKE, GERMANO CELANT / SARAH SZE OKWUI ENWEZOR, BENJAMIN H. D. BUCHLOH, LAURA HOPTMAN / WOLFGANG TILLMANS PETER HALLEY, JAN VERWOERT, MIDORI MATSUI, JOHANNA BURTON / LUC TUYMANS ULRICH LOOCK, JUAN VICENTE ALIAGA, NANCY SPECTOR, HANS RUDOLF REUST / BERNAR VENET FLORENCE DERIEUX, BARRY SCHWABSKY, CLAIRE LILLEY / ADRIÁN VILLAR-ROJAS HANS ULRICH OBRIST, CAROLYN CHRISTOV-BAKARGIEV, EUNGIE JOO / JEFF WALL THIERRY DE DUVE, ARIELLE PÉLENC, BORIS GROYS, JEAN-FRANÇOIS CHEVRIER, MARK LEWIS / GILLIAN WEARING RUSSELL FERGUSON, DONNA DE SALVO, JOHN SLYCE / LAWRENCE WEINER BENJAMIN H. D. BUCHLOH, ALEXANDER ALBERRO AND ALICE ZIMMERMAN, DAVID BATCHELOR / FRANZ WEST ROBERT FLECK, BICE CURIGER, NEAL BENEZRA / JONAS WOOD MARK GROTJAHN, HELEN MOLESWORTH, IAN ALTEVEER / YIN XIUZHEN HOU HANRU, WU HUNG, STEPHANIE ROSENTHAL / ZHANG HUAN ROSELEE GOLDBERG, YILMAZ DZIEWOR, ROBERT STORR